Angelo Kinicki • Mel Fugate • Victoria Digby

Arizona State University   Southern Methodist University   Fanshawe College

Fourth Canadian Edition

Key Concepts, Skills, and Best Practices

McGraw-Hill Ryerson

Connect. Learn. Succeed.

OB: Key Concepts, Skills and Best Practices
Fourth Canadian Edition

ISBN-13: 978-0-07-105140-8
ISBN-10: 0-07-105140-6

1 2 3 4 5 6 7 8 9 0 QG 1 9 8 7 6 5 4 3

Printed and bound in the United States of America

Editorial Director: *Rhondda McNabb*
Publisher: *Kim Brewster*
Marketing Manager: *Cathie Lefebvre*
Developmental Editor: *Chris Cullen*
Supervising Editor: *Cathy Biribauer*
Photo/Permissions Researcher: *Tracy Leonard*
Senior Editorial Associate: *Christine Lomas*
Copy Editor: *Janice Dyer*
Production Coordinator: *Sheryl MacAdam*
Cover and Interior Design: *Laserwords/Jodie Bernard (Lightbox Visuals)*
Composition: *Laserwords Private Limited*
Cover Photo: *©Miguel Navarro/Getty Images*
Printer: *Quad/Graphics*

Cover images: Top row, left to right: *Design Pics/Don Hammond; Ingram Publishing; Ariel Skelley/Blend Images LLC;* © Corbis; © JGI/Tom Grill/Blend Images LLC; Middle row, left to right: *Pixtal/AGE Fotostock; Stockbyte/Getty Images; Purestock/SuperStock; DreamPictures/Blend Images LLC;* Bottom row, left to right: © Andersen Ross/Blend Images LLC; © Ereproductions LTD/Blend Images LLC; BananaStock/PictureQuest; © Andersen Ross/Blend Images LLC; © Mark Edward Atkinson/Blend Images LLC

Library and Archives Canada Cataloguing in Publication Data

Kinicki, Angelo
    OB : key concepts, skills, and best practices/Angelo Kinicki, Mel Fugate, Victoria Digby.—4th Canadian ed.

Third Canadian ed. by Robert Kreitner . . . et al.
Includes bibliographical references and index.
ISBN 978-0-07-105140-8

    1. Organizational behavior—Textbooks. I. Fugate, Mel II. Digby, Victoria III. Title.

HD58.7.K49 2013   658   C2012-905300-7

ABOUT THE AUTHORS

Victoria Digby, BA MA, has been a full-time business professor in the Ontario college system for over 23 years. She has been teaching at the Lawrence Kinlin School of Business at Fanshawe College in London, Ontario since 1995, focusing primarily on management and organizational behaviour. As well, Victoria has been a part-time lecturer at the Aubrey Dan Program in Management and Organizational Studies at Western University (formerly called the University of Western Ontario)—London since 2008.

Victoria owns her own consulting firm and has been designing corporate training and leadership development initiatives for over 23 years. Clients include the Corporation of the City of London, City of North York, RCMP O-Division, London Health Sciences Centre—Western University, Department of Veterans Affairs, National Defence, and the Canadian Forces.

Victoria's teaching awards include a 2008–09 and 2009–10 Nominee for the Undergraduate Teaching Award at Western University; the 2007 recipient of the ACCC Teaching Excellence Award in Ottawa; and the 2006 recipient of the President's Distinguished Teacher Award at Fanshawe College.

Before stepping into academics, Victoria worked as a contributing editor for the International Council of Shopping Centers in New York City, account services supervisor at Vickers & Benson Advertising in Toronto, and account executive at Campbell-Ewald Advertising in Detroit.

Victoria is currently a member of HRPAO London and District Chapter. Originally from Ferndale, Michigan, Victoria now lives in London, Ontario with her husband, Paul, of 32 years and two children, MJ and Drew.

Angelo Kinicki, pictured on the right, is a professor, author, and consultant. He is a professor of management and is the recipient of the Weatherup/Overby Chair in Leadership. He also is a Dean's Council of 100 Distinguished Scholar at the W. P. Carey School of Business. He joined the faculty in 1982, the year he received his doctorate in business administration from Kent State University. His primary research interests include leadership, organizational culture, organizational change, and multilevel issues associated with predicting organizational effectiveness. Angelo has published more than 90 articles in a variety of academic journals and is co-author of seven textbooks (25 including revisions) that are used by hundreds of universities around the world. Several of his books have been translated into multiple languages.

Angelo is an award-winning researcher and teacher. He has received several awards, including a best research paper award from the Organizational Behavior (OB) division of the Academy of Management, the All Time Best Reviewer Award (1996–99) and the Excellent Reviewer Award (1997–98) from the Academy of Management Journal, and six teaching awards from Arizona State University (Outstanding Teaching Award—MBA and Master's Program, John W. Teets Outstanding Graduate Teacher Award (twice), Outstanding Undergraduate Teaching Excellence Award, Outstanding Graduate Teaching Excellence Award, and Outstanding Executive Development Teaching Excellence Award). Angelo also has served on the editorial review boards for the *Academy of Management Journal, Personnel Psychology, the Journal of Management, and the Journal of Vocational Behavior.* Angelo has been

an active member of the Academy of Management, including service as a representative-at-large for the Organizational Behavior division, member of the Best Paper Award committee for both the OB and Human Resources (HR) divisions, chair of the committee to select the best publication in the *Academy of Management Journal,* and program committee reviewer for the OB and HR divisions.

Angelo is a busy international consultant and is a principal at Kinicki and Associates Inc., a management consulting firm that works with top management teams to create organizational change aimed at increasing organizational effectiveness and profitability. He has worked with many Fortune 500 firms as well as numerous entrepreneurial organizations in diverse industries. His expertise includes facilitating strategic/operational planning sessions, diagnosing the causes of organizational and work-unit problems, conducting organizational culture interventions, implementing performance management systems, designing and implementing performance appraisal systems, developing and administering surveys to assess employee attitudes, and leading management/executive education programs. He developed a 360-degree leadership feedback instrument called the Performance Management Leadership Survey (PMLS) that is used by companies throughout the United States and Europe. The survey is used to assess an individual's leadership style and to coach individuals interested in developing their leadership skills.

Angelo and his wife, Joyce, have enjoyed living in the beautiful Arizona desert for 30 years and are natives of Cleveland, Ohio. They enjoy travelling, golfing, hiking, spoiling Nala, their golden retriever, and spending time in the White Mountains.

Mel Fugate is a professor and consultant. He is an associate professor of Management and Organizations and Dunlevy Fellow in the Cox School of Business at Southern Methodist University. He teaches executive, MBA, and undergraduate courses. Prior to the Cox School, he was a visiting assistant professor of Organizational Behavior at Tulane University's A.B. Freeman College of Business. He also has international teaching experience (e.g., International MBA) at EMLYON Graduate School of Management in Lyon, France. Prior to earning his Ph.D. in Business Administration and Management from Arizona State University, Mel performed consulting services in marketing and business development and was a sales representative and manager in the pharmaceutical industry. He also has a BS in engineering and business administration from Michigan State University.

Mel's primary research interests involve employee reactions to organizational change and transitions at work. This includes but is not limited to downsizings, mergers and acquisitions, restructurings, and plant closings. He investigates employees' change-related cognitive appraisals, emotions, coping efforts, and withdrawal. Another research stream involves the development of a dispositional perspective of employability and its implications for employee careers and behaviour. Current interests also include the influence of leadership and organizational culture on performance and the influence of emotions on behaviour at work. He has published in and reviewed for a number of premier management and applied psychology journals, such as the *Academy of Management Journal, Academy of Management Review, Journal of Applied Psychology, Journal of Occupational and Organizational Psychology, Journal of Vocational Behavior,* and *Personnel Psychology.* He also served on the editorial boards of *Personnel Psychology* and the *Journal of Leadership and Organizational Studies.* Mel's research and comments have been featured in numerous media outlets: *The Wall Street Journal, The New York Times, Financial Times,* Dallas Morning News, CNN, Fox, ABC, and NBC.

His consulting work aims to enhance individual and organizational performance by utilizing a variety of practical, research-based tools related to leadership and management development, performance management, motivation, strategic talent management, organizational culture, compensation, and exceptional client service. Mel's consulting and research covers many industries (e.g., legal, energy, healthcare, information technology, and financial services). His research and consulting often overlap in the area of change management, where he assists managers in developing, implementing, and evaluating change initiatives designed to enhance employee performance and organizational competitiveness, including the integration and realignment of organizational cultures.

Mel and his wife, Donna, are both very active and enjoy fitness, travelling, live music, and catering to their sweet, savage Jack Russell "Terror," Scout Dog.

A MESSAGE TO PROFESSORS FROM THE CANADIAN AUTHOR:

Congratulations for selecting a contemporary Canadian OB text for your students. *Organizational Behaviour* 4th Canadian edition by Kinicki, Fugate, and Digby, was more like a merger rather than an adaptation of a highly successful US textbook. As this new edition was unfolding, our reviewers wanted the book to go beyond Canadian applications, examples, and cases of theoretical models originating from a host text. They also wanted to include new concepts that weren't mentioned in earlier editions or in currently existing US editions. They wanted more graphics, additional illustrations, and contemporary charts. So we had to do our homework: we conducted our own secondary OB research in several instances, as well as created our own unique tables and figures.

Years back, when the finishing touches were placed on the last edition, I personally wondered how the new features and upgrades would be received by the market. Evidence by virtue of this new 4th Canadian edition certainly places any concern I might have had to rest. We've continued to incorporate the successful items and features educators preferred from our past edition, while adding new teaching tools for faculty and learning tools for students.

From the start, I wanted to create an OB textbook that would speak to the changing student and evolving learning environment. In the end, what we have created in this new edition is a textbook that supports a contemporary just-in-time multimedia learning culture that serves the needs of any type of student with any kind of learning style. So, if (for example) you are teaching mature students in an industry or second career type of program, this text and much of its ancillary material will broaden their understanding of what happened in their last job to make sense of their previous experiences.

Many new international students studying in our Canadian classrooms today may have a large knowledge gap in terms of working in a western culture, or may have a language gap in not being able to pronounce or define an OB word. This textbook can help shed light on topics to help them assimilate into the Canadian workplace with more speed and success. In addition to the many graphics, illustrations, and tables included throughout the chapters, ESL student understanding and language skills can be enhanced using the audio Key Terms feature on the Connect site.

If you are teaching an online class, numerous e-book and online features through the publisher's enhanced Connect learning site can enrich online chat-room discussions, facilitate virtual group activities, and successfully bridge the virtual classroom experience. In fact, at the request of reviewers, some items like the Presentation Assistant and the OB Ethical Dilemma were moved from the hardcopy text onto the Connect site—which further enriches the online learning experience.

For the alternative hybrid or traditional face-to-face classroom, new experiential group exercises, new integrated chapter questions, more self-assessment exercises, and a variety of new case studies are included to fill hours of in-class time, discussions, and/or presentations. So, this 4th edition is not just theory in a textbook—it goes beyond theory to bring the concepts to life by providing a variety of learning tools.

As well, I wanted to provide a holistic context from which to learn rigorous theoretical principles. To do this, we have continued to include the well-received feature boxes from our past edition: Diversity, International OB, Skills & Best Practices, and Law and Ethics are incorporated into every chapter. In addition, the new chapter opening Facing an OB Challenge scenario presents a question to get the reader thinking about the soon to be discussed topic. Teachers often find themselves having to explain the relevancy of the material being taught. To address this issue, broad workplace applications are provided vis-a-vis hundreds of recently added Canadian business examples in chapter scenarios, new small and large case studies, built-in chapter examples, all new online ethical dilemma situations, and new or enhanced Google Searches. And finally, the new end-of-chapter feature titled Integration of OB Concepts: Discussion Questions is meant to bring earlier lessons into current discussions and topics. As you can see, the upgrades are numerous and make this new edition truly new and improved.

OB faculty are often asked the question, "Is OB truly a social science? Isn't it just common sense?" As OB professors, it is critical to dispel myths or misconceptions around OB. Our latest edition incorporates the findings from the latest rigorous research studies, provides classic behavioural models for understanding, describes contemporary system-based structures, and discusses recently released statistics around Canadian business examples. These and other items included in this 4th edition have been studied by experts for many years and are further supported by empirical research, not to be confused with arbitrary anecdotes. In addition, we have an obligation to provide such content using the language from our Canadian and/or North American culture.

While some professors need only a few ancillary materials, others need more. With this in mind, we have created an Instructors Manual for this text filled with SmartBoard suggestions, in-class activities, and current resources. The volume and quality of materials included on the Connect site is something that will make the 4th edition a valuable teaching tool for years to come.

A NOTE TO STUDENTS FROM THE CANADIAN AUTHOR:

This latest edition of *Organizational Behaviour*, 4th Canadian edition has been redesigned and enhanced with you in mind. It builds upon the modifications that transformed the 3rd Canadian edition into a strong learning tool for students, especially for those who have never taken a social science course before. We know that students want and deserve the most up-to-date information when they are studying at the post-secondary level. For this reason, many upgrades have been incorporated into this new edition: numerous up-to-date Canadian business examples, a new section of integrated chapter questions at the end of each chapter to help broaden understanding, several new self-assessments to act as diagnostic indicators for personal development, all new case studies at the end of each chapter and at the back of the book—all are meant to help in terms of theory application. You are encouraged to review the entire text and all of the learning materials that have been provided for you throughout the entire text package.

Students always ask me, "Can I use the old edition that my roommate has given me or do I have to buy the new text?" The quick answer: I strongly urge students to make the shift today by moving away from a hardcopy textbook and instead securing the current e-book format for learning as it will give access to the Connect learning site, which is the publisher's site for the online learning materials associated with this textbook. You will get all of the hardcopy content PLUS all of the online learning material for a fraction of the price of a hardcopy book. Many upgrades to material will only appear online for cost and efficiency purposes—what will you use if, for example, your professor assigns readings, an assignment, or an exercise that only appears on Connect? It makes no sense to disadvantage yourself and with the help of McGraw's competitive marketing strategy, you will quickly learn that the e-book price is incredibly affordable and worth the educational investment. The last point I'd like to make refers to assessment and evaluation learning tools. Since the chapter material has been rearranged and changed so much, the old test bank and page references will no longer apply. For example, suppose you are taking an online weekly quiz comprised of new test bank multiple-choice questions, and let's say you get questions #5, 10, and 28 wrong. The new test bank your professor used to design the test will refer back to current chapter pages only—not old ones. You'll be wasting precious studying time trying to transcribe pages from old to new rather than focusing on what is important—the correct answer.

Now, referring back to the online learning Connect site, this raises the question of computer use for students: Is it necessary? I cannot imagine a classroom today that doesn't integrate technology, so the answer is yes, and let me tell you why. Students need to stay current on business and world affairs because OB is in the news daily. People's behaviour in the world of work is changing so rapidly that it is hard to predict what will happen next! Canadian students need to know the impact these changes are having, especially on the Canadian business environment. I believe that students learning in Canada truly deserve a Canadian text as evidenced by the examples, case studies, feature box content, and language used throughout all associated material. The Google Searches found at the end of each chapter have been enhanced and expanded to allow just-in-time learning, making the material that much more relevant for you. In addition, the Connect site includes recent business examples in terms of OB Ethical Dilemmas case studies, videos, group assignments, and exercises.

One of the new features of this edition starts off each chapter. Facing an OB Challenge provides actual questions from people that have appeared in various media and publications. These questions are included at the beginning of each chapter to bring some relevance to what you are about to learn in classroom discussions. We trust it will grab your interest and get you thinking about the chapter topic.

OB does not exist in a vacuum. The theoretical concepts that are taught must exist and apply to the world of work. For this reason, we have continued to include feature boxes within the chapters to help you understand the legal/ethical considerations, international applications, on-going controversies related to diversity in the workplace, and the context of real-world application through skills and best practices. These feature boxes will help you understand the big picture by providing a context for learning OB.

Students must become familiar with business language, and for this reason we have continued to use challenging language in this textbook—but no worry, synonyms have been incorporated next to relevant words to assist with understanding. Although you may need to read some passages twice, don't panic. Just read it again—we've all had to do it as students. It doesn't mean you are a poor student. It means you are reading new material and stretching your mind. I urge you not to shy away from learning new business language and OB terminology. Instead, learn it, understand it, and embrace it, because future employers will expect it. Who knows, it may become your competitive advantage when applying for a job!

Although I am a lecturer who uses class discussion to teach large supersized classes, I am well aware of the strength behind student presentations. Whether online or in a face-to-face classroom learning environment, if you are asked to do a group presentation on an OB topic this semester, know that you don't have to start from scratch. On the Connect site, you will find The Presentation Assistant, which provides suggested topics on various subject matters related to a particular chapter. Within each topic are various YouTube sites, recommended readings, icebreaker exercises, and current multimedia resources to use and refer to when designing your presentations. The feedback from faculty who have encouraged students to use this learning tool in their classrooms has been positive, and if teachers like it, then students will want to consider using it.

In conclusion, I want to welcome you to the world of OB and the benefits it can provide to prepare you for the world of work. Although you may be a few years away yet, it will get you thinking. For those mature students who have already been out in the world working but have returned to the classroom, you'll have a chance to reflect on what may have gone wrong but also what went right in the past . . . and that is helpful for personal development. This text is only one learning tool in your toolkit; you are encouraged to read contemporary business literature and trade publications, talk to industry professionals, and share your insights with others as you journey through the world of OB. If at any time you need to see the big picture of what you have studied, the interconnectedness of material, or where a certain topic fits into the course, you can just refer to the opening inside front cover to review the OB At A Glance diagram or refer to the back of any chapter to review the Integration of OB Concepts: Discussion Questions. This textbook is designed to serve you and your learning needs. Highlight passages and create your own study guide and integrated chapter notes with all the Connect learning resources so that you'll be better prepared for class. I wish you all the best and future success in your course.

Victoria Digby

Brief Table of Contents

TABLE OF CONTENTS

04 UNIT 4 ▶ MANAGING SYSTEMS THAT AFFECT BEHAVIOUR

CHAPTER 11

CHAPTER 12

05 UNIT 5 ▶ MANAGING CHANGE AND CHANGE AGENTS THAT AFFECT BEHAVIOUR

PREFACE

Less is more! That famous adage is what we kept in mind for the latest edition of *Organizational Behaviour: Key Concepts, Skills, and Best Practices*. We have kept the same great information that will guide students through the dynamic world of organizational behaviour, but have also created new ways for busy students to engage with the material.

CONTINUED EXCELLENCE

Organizational Behaviour: Key Concepts, Skills, and Best Practices (4th Canadian edition), by Kinicki, Fugate, and Digby, builds upon the solid foundation laid in previous editions. The mantra of creating "a short, up-to-date, practical, user-friendly, interesting, and engaging introduction to the field of organization behaviour" has guided this revision. The authors have continued to use compelling pedagogical features and up-to-date cases and examples to provide rich coverage of a variety of important topics in organizational behaviour. In addition, the authors have updated OB examples and theories with the most recent research and studies. Most noticeably, the design of the book has also been changed to encompass the authors' philosophy.

STUDENT FOCUSED

At the beginning of each chapter, students will note a set of learning outcomes pedagogically aligned with Bloom's Taxonomy, which means the book is structured and entrenched with learning in mind. Further, each chapter uses business language that is commonly used in the field. Students will strengthen their language skills by first being exposed to this terminology within an OB context, but with the assistance of common synonyms alongside each unique word to help students learn terminology.

CONCISE AND FLEXIBLE STRUCTURE

The new design of the fourth Canadian edition has maintained the adaptability of the text to a traditional 12- or 13-week academic term, summer and inter-sessions, management development seminars, and distance learning programs via the Internet. The flow of the text guides students and instructors through OB from individual to groups and teams, through to organizations, starting out small and ending with how all of these smaller elements comprise the metaphorical big picture. We encourage you to mix and match chapters in various combinations to get the most out of your OB learning/teaching experience.

NEW FEATURES AND BENEFITS OF THE 4TH EDITION

The 4th edition demonstrates continued excellence when it comes to designing a current and relevant Canadian OB textbook. This is clearly more than an adapted US text, given the hundreds of new research sources, Canadian business examples, and references.

The new edition builds upon the benefits of the 3rd edition's features and styling: strong eye appeal; easy to read and quick sourcing of information; feature boxes that highlight global, ethical, legal, diverse, and best practice applications that bring the concepts to life; and experiential exercises and end-of-chapter assignments that make learning more relevant and enjoyable.

The upgraded Connect site means ease of use and greater access to multi-media applications of material. This will facilitate active and interactive learning for traditional, hybrid, or online instruction. Those looking for ancillary materials beyond the textbook will find Connect helpful in addressing the various learning styles of students, as well as the variety of teaching resources available to faculty.

New items in the 4th edition include the following:

- More graphics and new illustrations mean a fresh approach to keep students engaged in material.
- Fourteen new opening chapter situations presented in a question-like format, titled *Facing an OB Challenge,* replace old-style vignettes make the chapter material more personal and relevant to students as they begin each chapter of study.
- New and additional *Self-Assessment Exercise(s)* throughout the text facilitate ongoing personal development for students.
- New *Integration of OB Questions* at the end of each chapter help to link theory from previous chapter topics for greater holistic understanding and learning.
- New and more *Google Searches* keep lessons up-to-date and students engaged in a real time manner.
- New and improved *Experiential Exercises* at the end of each chapter apply theoretical principles in a creative way.
- Fifteen new *OB in Action Case Study* situations at the end of each chapter give students a chance to apply what they have learned to a case-based situation.
- Five new *Appendix—Unit Case Studies* located at the end of the text allow for more integration of concepts using the case-based method of instruction.
- The enhanced *Presentation Assistant* feature on Connect for team presentations gives students some ideas to consider beyond the textbook.
- All new *Ethical OB Dilemmas* on Connect continue to emphasize ethics across the curriculum.
- All new *Videos* on Connect provide an alternative to case-based study and are active learning tools for classroom and online learning.
- The all new *Management Asset Gallery* on Connect has been organized using the 4th edition chapter material. The integration of topics between text and online sources helps faculty and/or students who are looking for alternative resources to suit a variety of learning styles.

ACTIVE LEARNING

The authors have developed this text to provide efficient coverage of topics such as diversity in organizations, ethics, and globalization, which are recommended by AACSB International—the Association to Advance Collegiate Schools of Business. Up-to-date chapter-opening situations, learning outcomes, a wealth of skill building experiential end-of-chapter materials, four-colour presentation, a lively writing style, and real-world, in-text examples are all used to enhance this overall educational package.

The author team has collectively designed your text to facilitate active learning by relying on the following pedagogical features:

CHAPTER PEDAGOGY

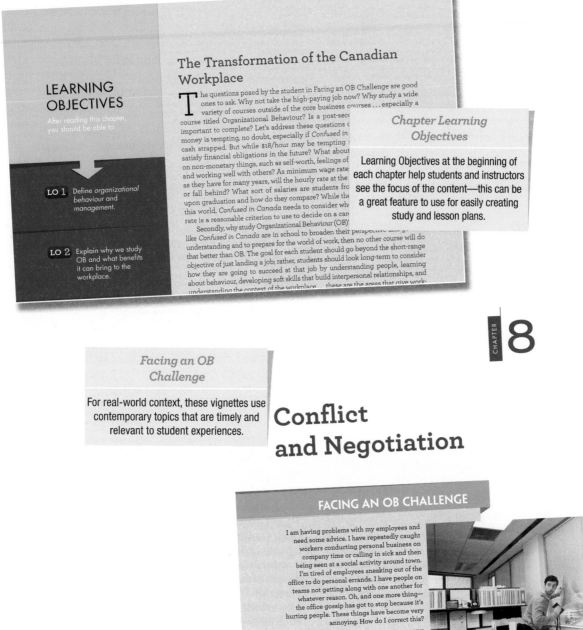

LEARNING OBJECTIVES

After reading this chapter, you should be able to:

LO 1 Define organizational behaviour and management.

LO 2 Explain why we study OB and what benefits it can bring to the workplace.

The Transformation of the Canadian Workplace

The questions posed by the student in Facing an OB Challenge are good ones to ask. Why not take the high-paying job now? Why study a wide variety of courses outside of the core business courses . . . especially a course titled Organizational Behaviour? Is a post-sec important to complete? Let's address these questions c money is tempting, no doubt, especially if Confused in cash strapped. But while $18/hour may be tempting satisfy financial obligations in the future? What about on non-monetary things, such as self-worth, feelings of and working well with others? As minimum wage rate as they have for many years, will the hourly rate at the or fall behind? What sort of salaries are students fro upon graduation and how do they compare? While th this world, Confused in Canada needs to consider wh rate is a reasonable criterion to use to decide on a car

Secondly, why study Organizational Behaviour (OB) like Confused in Canada are in school to broaden their perspective understanding and to prepare for the world of work, then no other course will do that better than OB. The goal for each student should go beyond the short-range objective of just landing a job; rather, students should look long-term to consider how they are going to succeed at that job by understanding people, learning about behaviour, developing soft skills that build interpersonal relationships, and understanding the context of the workplace . . . these are the areas that give work-

Chapter Learning Objectives

Learning Objectives at the beginning of each chapter help students and instructors see the focus of the content—this can be a great feature to use for easily creating study and lesson plans.

CHAPTER 8

Facing an OB Challenge

For real-world context, these vignettes use contemporary topics that are timely and relevant to student experiences.

Conflict and Negotiation

FACING AN OB CHALLENGE

I am having problems with my employees and need some advice. I have repeatedly caught workers conducting personal business on company time or calling in sick and then being seen at a social activity around town. I'm tired of employees sneaking out of the office to do personal errands. I have people on teams not getting along with one another for whatever reason. Oh, and one more thing— the office gossip has got to stop because it's hurting people. These things have become very annoying. How do I correct this?

—CONFLICTED AND CONCERNED

EMPLOYERS NEED TO FIND WAYS TO BUILD EMPLOYEE SELF-EFFICACY

Imagine you are a manager and you've just read a recent Gallup poll stating that employees acknowledge that they waste an average of about one hour a day at work. This has you concerned. Are your employees wasting hours at work each week or are they being productive? You decide to ask a colleague his opinion on how to monitor such activity in the workplace. He suggests installing NetVizor, the latest software that lets employers secretly monitor all computer and Internet activities of every employee on their _____. But is it legal? ___ communications,

makes it clear that Canadian companies have to justify surveillance and have written policies regarding Internet and phone use or face a possible civil lawsuit before the federal court.

Several decisions from the Canadian federal privacy commissioner clearly identify that employers must act in compliance with the purposes and limited collection provisions of PIPEDA that allow individuals the right to privacy so as to, in essence, monitor their own behaviour without coercive means from management.

SOURCES: A. Gahtan, "Big Brother or Good Business?," *WebWorld,* _____ p. 24; J. Allinson, "Companies Will Have To Justify _____ December 27, 2003; J. Allinson, _____ London Free _____ Tip-

Skills & Best Practices

Understanding Perceptual Process Can Assist Business Model Design

Organizations that are aware of the perceptual process and its outcomes enjoy a competitive edge. Take, for example Mark Wafer, a Toronto-based Tim Horton's franchise owner who, 17 years ago, hired an employee with an intellectual disability. Over the years, Wafer has hired more than 50 people with intellectual disabilities, and his stores experience a 45 percent lower turnover rate compared to industry averages.

"This is not because I am a better operator, it is simply because we have created an inclusive workplace where people with disabilities are treated as equals," said Wafer, who is partly deaf.

Wafer, who owns seven franchise stores, has become an advocate, encouraging other companies to hire people with disabilities as part of _____

Wafer believes that too often business owners, hiring managers, and human resource managers buy into the myths and misconception that people with disabilities will work slower, be sick more often, show up late, work in a less safe manner, or that accommodations will cost too much. "They are just that—myths! Telling owners to hire a person with a disability, that it is the right thing to do, simply doesn't work," said Wafer. "We have to show them how they will benefit and how their company will be stronger, be more profitable, (and) have higher staff morale."

SOURCES: "Workers with Disabilities – Tim Horton's Franchisor Serves Jobs," *Canadian HR Reporter,* June 6, 2011, p 1; "Workplace Bias Towards Hiring Canadians With Disabilities," *The National Post,* Authority, November 7, 2011, www.dia _____ workplace _____

APPLICANT TRACKING SYSTEMS CAN BIAS SELECTION PROCESS

During the recruitment stage of the hiring process, organizations complete a series of steps to find the best candidate. These steps can include sourcing candidates, screening potential candidates, managing and then tracking resumés, and so on. To help make the process more efficient and accurate, Canadian HR specialists have turned to technology. Applicant tracking systems, or ATS, have become popular among large organizations with thousands of employees, as well as with smaller _____ that may only have one or two HR profession- _____ ATS tend to screen out

of Diversity, Equity, and Inclusion at KPMG. Bach believes Aboriginal Canadians and people in remote and northern towns, who have limited access to computers and the Internet, are also disadvantaged by ATS.

An employer that relies only on its ATS may miss an applicant who has great job skills, but who doesn't know how modern recruiting and screening systems are based on keyword searches. Bach believes that people in a position to hire others should not depend only on computerized systems to find employees. He also suggests going beyond _____ traditional career fairs, open houses, and cam- _____ stead, organizations should _____ nderrepresented groups to _____ king with local community _____ can show applicants how to _____ d resumés that the ATS will

_____ Rely On Software To Find The Perfect _____ l, January 2012, p. 36.

CROSS-CULTURAL DIFFERENCES FOR SELF-ESTEEM

What are the cross-cultural implications for self-esteem? Self-esteem is a concept that has been called uniquely Western. In a survey of 13,118 students from 31 countries worldwide, a moderately positive correlation was found between self-esteem and life satisfaction. But the relationship was stronger in individualistic cultures (e.g., Canada, New Zealand, Netherlands, and the United States) than in collectivist cultures (e.g., Korea, Kenya, and Japan). The researchers concluded that individualistic cultures socialize people to focus more on

themselves, while people in collectivist cultures "are socialized to fit into the community and to do their duty. Thus, how a collectivist feels about him- or herself is less relevant to . . . life satisfaction."[20] Global managers and employees working in multi-cultural work environments, whether in Canada or abroad, need to remember to de-emphasize self-esteem when doing business in collectivist ("we") cultures, as opposed to emphasizing it in individualistic ("me") cultures.[21] Chapter 14 discusses cultural differences in greater detail.

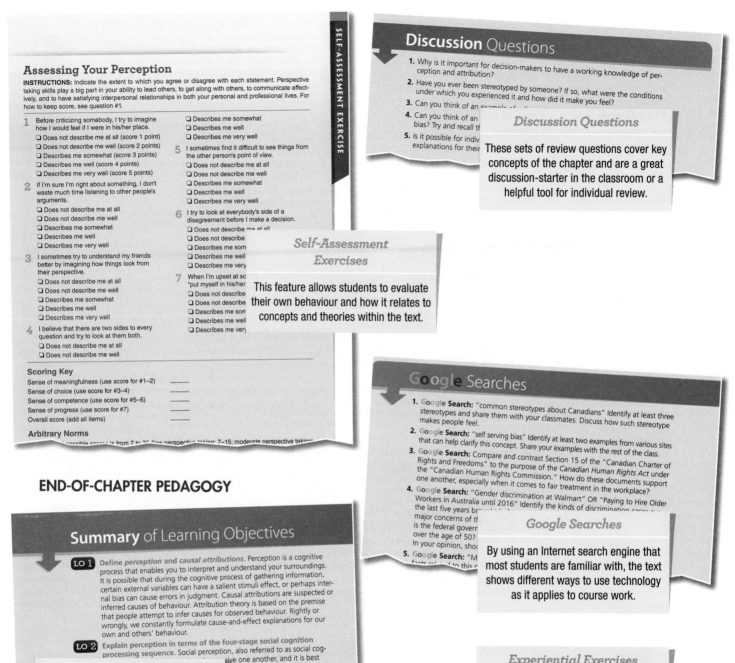

Assessing Your Perception

INSTRUCTIONS: Indicate the extent to which you agree or disagree with each statement. Perspective taking skills play a big part in your ability to lead others, to get along with others, to communicate effectively, and to have satisfying interpersonal relationships in both your personal and professional lives. For how to keep score, see question #1.

1 Before criticizing somebody, I try to imagine how I would feel if I were in his/her place.
❑ Does not describe me at all (score 1 point)
❑ Does not describe me well (score 2 points)
❑ Describes me somewhat (score 3 points)
❑ Describes me well (score 4 points)
❑ Describes me very well (score 5 points)

2 If I'm sure I'm right about something, I don't waste much time listening to other people's arguments.
❑ Does not describe me at all
❑ Does not describe me well
❑ Describes me somewhat
❑ Describes me well
❑ Describes me very well

3 I sometimes try to understand my friends better by imagining how things look from their perspective.
❑ Does not describe me at all
❑ Does not describe me well
❑ Describes me somewhat
❑ Describes me well
❑ Describes me very well

4 I believe that there are two sides to every question and try to look at them both.
❑ Does not describe me at all
❑ Does not describe me well

❑ Describes me somewhat
❑ Describes me well
❑ Describes me very well

5 I sometimes find it difficult to see things from the other person's point of view.
❑ Does not describe me at all
❑ Does not describe me well
❑ Describes me somewhat
❑ Describes me well
❑ Describes me very well

6 I try to look at everybody's side of a disagreement before I make a decision.
❑ Does not describe me at all
❑ Does not describe
❑ Describes me som
❑ Describes me well
❑ Describes me very

7 When I'm upset at so "put myself in his/her
❑ Does not describe
❑ Does not describe
❑ Describes me som
❑ Describes me well
❑ Describes me very

Scoring Key

Sense of meaningfulness (use score for #1–2) ____
Sense of choice (use score for #3–4) ____
Sense of competence (use score for #5–6) ____
Sense of progress (use score for #7) ____
Overall score (add all items) ____

Arbitrary Norms

possible score is 7 to 35 (low perspective taking: 7–15; moderate perspective taking:

Self-Assessment Exercises

This feature allows students to evaluate their own behaviour and how it relates to concepts and theories within the text.

Discussion Questions

1. Why is it important for decision-makers to have a working knowledge of perception and attribution?
2. Have you ever been stereotyped by someone? If so, what were the conditions under which you experienced it and how did it make you feel?
3. Can you think of an example of ...
4. Can you think of an ... bias? Try and recall th...
5. Is it possible for indiv... explanations for their ...

Discussion Questions

These sets of review questions cover key concepts of the chapter and are a great discussion-starter in the classroom or a helpful tool for individual review.

Google Searches

1. **Google Search:** "common stereotypes about Canadians" Identify at least three stereotypes and share them with your classmates. Discuss how such stereotype makes people feel.
2. **Google Search:** "self serving bias" Identify at least two examples from various sites that can help clarify this concept. Share your examples with the rest of the class.
3. **Google Search:** Compare and contrast Section 15 of the "Canadian Charter of Rights and Freedoms" to the purpose of the *Canadian Human Rights Act* under the "Canadian Human Rights Commission." How do these documents support one another, especially when it comes to fair treatment in the workplace?
4. **Google Search:** "Gender discrimination at Walmart" OR "Paying to Hire Older Workers in Australia until 2016" Identify the kinds of discrimination cases the last five years br... major concerns of th... is the federal govern... over the age of 50? In your opinion, sho...
5. **Google Search:** "M... facts related to this ...

Google Searches

By using an Internet search engine that most students are familiar with, the text shows different ways to use technology as it applies to course work.

END-OF-CHAPTER PEDAGOGY

Summary of Learning Objectives

LO 1 Define *perception* and *causal attributions*. Perception is a cognitive process that enables you to interpret and understand your surroundings. It is possible that during the cognitive process of gathering information, certain external variables can have a salient stimuli effect, or perhaps internal bias can cause errors in judgment. Causal attributions are suspected or inferred causes of behaviour. Attribution theory is based on the premise that people attempt to infer causes for observed behaviour. Rightly or wrongly, we constantly formulate cause-and-effect explanations for our own and others' behaviour.

LO 2 Explain perception in terms of the four-stage social cognition processing sequence. Social perception, also referred to as social cog... ... ive one another, and it is best ... e four stages are selective attention/ ... ation, storage and retention, and ... ognition, salient stimuli are assigned ... ng-term memory.

Summary of Key Concepts

A handy review tool for all users, the summary of key concepts includes responses to learning objectives in each chapter.

Experiential Exercises

These exercises are designed to sharpen students' skills by either recommending how to apply a concept, theory, or model, or giving an exemplary corporate application. Students will benefit from the applied experience and direct skill-building opportunities.

Experiential Exercise

Perception Group Exercise

PURPOSE This exercise is meant to help familiarize you with the OB concept of social perception. Approx. Timing: 20 minutes.

ACTIVITY ASSIGNMENT:

Work in teams of three or four members each. Each person should have his or her own sheet of paper to write responses.

■ Step #1: Without speaking or discussing with anyone, silently recall the first day of organizational behaviour class. Write as much as you can remember about that first day. What occurred? Who said what? Who sat where? What topics did people speak about? Who spoke the most? The least? Focus on as many

makes people feel.

2. **Google Search:** "self serving bias" Identify at least two examples from various sites that can help clarify this concept. Share your examples with the rest of the class.

3. **Google Search:** Compare and contrast Section 15 of the "Canadian Charter of Rights and Freedoms" to the purpose of the *Canadian Human Rights Act* under the "Canadian Human Rights Commission." How do these documents support one another, especially when it comes to fair treatment in the workplace?

4. **Google Search:** "Gender discrimination at Walmart" OR "Paying to Hire Older Workers In Australia until 2016" Identify the kinds of discriminati the last five years brought before the courts involving Walmart. V major concerns of the complainants and are they still happening? is the federal government in Australia paying for organizations to over the age of 50? Do you agree with public funds being used in In your opinion, should Canada institute the same policy?

5. **Google Search:** "Meiorin Case Supreme Court of Canada" What facts related to this precedent setting case? What is a bona fide o requirement (BOR), and what does it have to do with preventing p and potential discrimination?

OB in Action Cases

Students can see key concepts in action with an end-of-chapter case, complete with follow-up questions.

Experiential Exercise

Perception Group Exercise

PURPOSE This exercise is meant to help familiarize you with the OB concept of social perception. Approx. Timing: 20 minutes.

END-OF-TEXT PEDAGOGY

VIDEO CASES

OB 4TH EDITION VIDEO SEGMENTS

(AVAILABLE ON KINICKI 4th EDITION DVD AND WITHIN CONNECT)

PLEASE GO TO connect TO VIEW THE VIDEOS. INSTRUCTORS, PLEASE NOTE THAT THESE SEGMENTS ARE AVAILABLE ON DVD FOR CLASSROOM VIEWING. ANSWERS ARE PROVIDED WITHIN THE CONNECT INSTRUCTOR SITE.

Video Cases

This resource offers the opportunity for situational analysis in the classroom or individual study. The instructor's package, including a DVD and questions for discussion and videos, is available on Connect™. The video case studies are grouped to align with each unit of study within the text.

CORRESPONDING TEXT UNIT	VIDEO TITLE/TIME/ SOURCE	VIDEO DESCRIPTION/ QUESTIONS
Unit #1 Introduction to Organizational Behaviour	**Managing Religious Diversity at Work** 3:42 min. McGraw-Hill Management video library	The video describes how Ford Motor Company manages religious diversity in the workplace. It discusses the pros and cons of recognizing and allowing for religious expression in today's diverse organizations. 1. Do you anticipate more or less demand for a meditation-type room located onsite within an organization? 2. Why would Ford Motor Company offer a prayer room on Fridays especially?
Unit #1 Introduction to Organizational	**Talent Management at Aviva** 4:08	Ramona Tobler, VP HR business partner for underwriting and finance at Aviva, talks about the company's talent management system and how it is create conversations about emplo

CASE STUDIES

These cases were written by Victoria Digby solely to provide material for class discussion. The author does not intend to illustrate either effective or ineffective handling of a managerial situation. The author may have disguised certain names and other identifying information to protect confidentiality.

▶ **WALLIER SPECIALTY ITEMS, INC. – Unit 1 Case Study**

Mark Nash's company was faced with extraordinary, rapid growth. Over the past 12 months, sales had doubled at Wallier Specialty Items Inc. in Dawson Creek, B.C., and were expected to quadruple by the start of the next fiscal year. Nash, the Vice President of New Business Development at Wallier was very pleased with the strategic decisions the executive management team had made over the last 18 months to boost the company into the current circumstances of increased sales and high growth.

One day he was going over the sales forecast models when it struck him that although the growth was indeed exciting, it was also unprecedented and straining the current resources. It was not uncommon to hear customers complaining about the long wait times on the phone to get answers to their questions or employees who were becoming increasingly irritable number of overtime hours they were mandated to

feeling overwhelmed. Personally, I think you ter control over their behaviour. Before we latest strategic action, did you inform your anticipating an increase in demand? Have yo sis of how much time it should take to fulfill a or deliver inner-office mail? People in my department don't waste time. I tell them what they have to do and follow-up with them often to ensure they get things done. I think my job is to push them beyond their comfort level," said department manager Paul Grafton.

Another manager, Pat Wong, spoke up, "Paul, I think Karen is saying that even with months of advanced warning and preparation, the volume of orders we're experiencing can sometimes be so large that the staff can't keep up . . . when faced with natural occurrences like illness or emergencies, it can create quite a dilemma throughout the office

Case Studies

An appendix containing additional cases is great for more in-depth individual study or group assignments.

McGraw-Hill Connect™ is a web-based assignment and assessment platform that gives students the means to better connect with their coursework, with their instructors, and with the important concepts that they will need to know for success now and in the future.

With Connect, instructors can deliver assignments, quizzes and tests online. Nearly all the questions from the text are presented in an auto-gradeable format and tied to the text's learning objectives. Instructors can edit existing questions and author entirely new problems. Track individual student performance—by question, assignment or in relation to the class overall—with detailed grade reports. Integrate grade reports easily with Learning Management Systems (LMS) such as WebCT and Blackboard. And much more.

By choosing Connect, instructors are providing their students with a powerful tool for improving academic performance and truly mastering course material. Connect allows students to practise important skills at their own pace and on their own schedule. Importantly, students' assessment results and instructors' feedback are all saved online, so students can continually review their progress and plot their course to success.

Connect also provides 24/7 online access to an eBook—an online edition of the text—to aid them in successfully completing their work, wherever and whenever they choose.

INSTRUCTOR SUPPORT

Video Cases

Each unit includes current and relevant video cases from CEO TV and other sources, helping instructors highlight such important topics as flextime, motivating employees, and diversity. Video teaching notes are available in the Instructor's Resource Manual and are downloadable from the Instructor section Connect.

Instructor Resources

Connect follows the text chapter by chapter, with additional materials and quizzes that enhance the text and/or classroom experience. A secured Instructor Resource Library stores essential course materials and saves prep time before class. This area houses all the Instructor supplements needed for your OB course: an Instructor's Resource Manual, written by the text author; PowerPoint® Presentations; EZ Test Computerized Test Bank; additional Case Studies; and Video Notes and teaching material.

MANAGEMENT ASSET GALLERY FOR INSTRUCTORS AND STUDENTS

Management Asset Gallery is a one-stop-shop for a wealth of McGraw-Hill management assets, making it easier for instructors to locate specific materials to enhance their courses, and for students (Student Asset Gallery) to supplement their knowledge. The Instructor Asset Gallery includes non-text-specific management resources (Self-Assessments, Test Your Knowledge exercises, videos*, Manager's HotSeat, and additional group and individual exercises) along with supporting PowerPoint® and Instructor Manual materials.

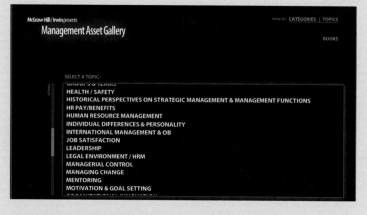

The Manager's HotSeat is a resource within the Asset Gallery that allows students to watch over 14 real managers apply their years of experience to confront daily issues such as ethics, diversity, teamwork, and the virtual work-place. Students are prompted for their feedback throughout each scenario and then submit a report critiquing the manager's choices, while defending their own. The Manager's HotSeat is ideal for group or classroom discussions.

*The Management in the Movies videos are not licensed for distribution outside of the USA, however adopting instructors are able to access the Instructor Notes.

SUPERIOR LEARNING SOLUTIONS AND SUPPORT

The McGraw-Hill Ryerson team is ready to help you assess and integrate any of our products, technology, and services into your course for optimal teaching and learning performance. Whether it's helping your students improve their grades, or putting your entire course online, the McGraw-Hill Ryerson team is here to help you do it. Contact your iLearning Sales Specialist today to learn how to maximize all of McGraw-Hill Ryerson's resources!

For more information on the latest technology and Learning Solutions offered by McGraw-Hill Ryerson and its partners, please visit us online: **www.mcgrawhill.ca/he/ solutions**.

ACKNOWLEDGEMENTS

Anyone who has written a textbook knows the amount of hard work and endless hours of research, thinking, and writing behind a computer screen required to make the final product. It is not a solo effort by any means, and is dependent upon a high level of cooperation that must exist between the head office team and the author. It is for this reason that I would first like to thank McGraw-Hill Ryerson's publisher, Kim Brewster, for her amazing patience, guidance, and support over the years. A huge thanks to Developmental Editor Chris Cullen for sticking with me on this project, as well as his diplomatic communication skills in finding the resources to keep all on schedule. To my Permissions Editor, Tracy Leonard, I want to extend my appreciation for helping find photos, sources, and other resources for the book—you made me laugh when I thought at times there was no hope, and I appreciate it. To Supervising Editor for Editorial, Design and Production, Cathy Biribauer, I'd like to extend my thanks for keeping me in the loop by having all materials so readily accessible during the final stages of production. To my 'other set of eyes', proofreader/quality controller/editor extraordinaire, Janice Dyer, a big thank you, as she was vital in maintaining the kind of quality control I expected on this project.

To the reviewers from across the country who agreed to provide direction on pre- and post-sets of manuscripts, I thank you. It only goes to show you how perception varies depending on where you are at the moment; these individuals were helpful, insightful, and professional in their suggestions. They presented 'ah ha' moments for me that I hadn't even seen. It's never easy to receive critique from others, but they made it palatable. It is because of them that the book found new avenues to explore and new heights to climb. My sincere appreciation goes to:

Marcelle Allen, *Seneca College*
Ian Anderson, *Algonquin College*
Stan Arnold, *Humber College*
Joanne Boothby, *Grant MacEwan University*
Anna Bortolon, *Conestoga College*
Melanie Brydges Down, *University of Manitoba*
Jane Deighan, *SAIT*
Carolyn Gaunt, *Cambrian College*
Stephen Janisse, *St. Clair College*
Barbara Kelly, *Conestoga College*
Garth Maguire, *Okanagan College*
Richard McFadden, *Georgian College*
Barbara Neil, *NAIT*
Grace O'Farrell, *University of Winnipeg*
Ron Velin, *Langara College*

Being a professor and lecturer while authoring a textbook is a treat because material can be tested on current students who provide helpful insight into what material is relevant and what is not. To that end, I'd like to thank my MGMT3041 and MOS2181 OB students for giving me the opportunity to be their teacher and share in their lives and work experiences. I enjoy what I do and feel so blessed to have the opportunity to be their teacher.

As this edition unfolded there were times when work–family conflict became a challenge and staying on task became an issue. But with the help of one individual and one organization, I was able to find my balance. The individual who I dedicate this book to is my life partner, Paul, who was my constant unconditional support, confidante, and advisor . . . all my love and deepest thanks.

The organization that provided me with the opportunity to regain perspective was Rayjon Sharecare Inc. out of Sarnia, Ontario. They allowed me to join a small contingent on an eight-day awareness trip through Haiti while I was on break between semesters and drafting the first manuscript. The trip allowed for reflection to gain insight into what I wanted for this text. Naturally, every author hopes to receive positive feedback, but it became evident to me that writing this book was already paying a return by helping me become a better employee, a more informed teacher for my students, and a more knowledgeable individual, and for that I am grateful. It is for this reason that I want faculty and students to know that their adoption and use of this textbook will allow all of the Canadian author residuals to be donated to Rayjon so they may be able to continue helping the children in the Red Zone areas, especially in St. Marc, Haiti. In addition, I welcome correspondence from school charities, especially those that promote international travel opportunities. Students or faculty looking for supportive donations at schools that have adopted this text are encouraged to contact me directly at vdigby@rogers.com. I look forward to hearing from you. With your help, we can change the world one person at a time, and make a difference.

I conclude by acknowledging the help received from my sons, MJ and Drew, who have kept me grounded and current in so many ways. They were my audience when I needed a quick opinion from a young person on something I was writing or creating. Their time, comments, and honesty are appreciated and I love you both. And to Buckey, our big fluffy dog that slept on the rug in my office for hours at a time, month after month, keeping me company while I worked on the computer . . . I owe you a big walk around the block! Finally, to all my other family and friends who have given me inspiration and support during this process, I extend my most sincere appreciation.

—*Victoria Digby,*
August 2012

"A lot of people in our industry haven't had very diverse experiences. So they don't have enough dots to connect, and they end up with very linear solutions without a broad perspective on the problem. The broader one's understanding of the human experience, the better design we will have."

Steve Jobs (founder of Apple)

Organizational Behaviour and People-Centred Management

FACING AN OB CHALLENGE

I just finished my first year as a business student and I'm facing a tough decision; I have an opportunity for a full-time job working in a factory starting immediately that would pay me $18/hour plus benefits. That's a lot of money and I could certainly live on that kind of income for a long time. The problem is that while I value education, I need money now and lots of it. So, I'm thinking about fast-tracking my studies by only taking certain classes—like accounting, marketing, and entrepreneurship—and forgetting about all the other 'fluff' courses. For example, why do I have to take this Organizational Behaviour course? How is it going to help me in my future job? My family said to hang in there and take the entire program so I can graduate, claiming that classes like OB will help me. I don't know what to do. Any advice?

—*CONFUSED IN CANADA*

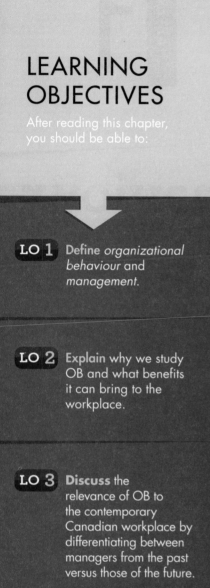

LEARNING OBJECTIVES

After reading this chapter, you should be able to:

LO 1 Define *organizational behaviour* and *management*.

LO 2 Explain why we study OB and what benefits it can bring to the workplace.

LO 3 Discuss the relevance of OB to the contemporary Canadian workplace by differentiating between managers from the past versus those of the future.

LO 4 Summarize the history of OB in a timeline by incorporating three significant landmarks of theory development, including distinguishing characteristics of each.

LO 5 Infer and predict the challenges that at least four contemporary OB issues may present to both non-managerial employees and management in the future.

The Transformation of the Canadian Workplace

The questions posed by the student in Facing an OB Challenge are good ones to ask. Why not take the high-paying job now? Why study a wide variety of courses outside of the core business courses ... especially a course titled Organizational Behaviour? Is a post-secondary education that important to complete? Let's address these questions one at a time. First, the money is tempting, no doubt, especially if *Confused in Canada* is in debt and cash strapped. But while $18/hour may be tempting now, is this enough to satisfy financial obligations in the future? What about job satisfaction based on non-monetary things, such as self-worth, feelings of making a contribution, and working well with others? As minimum wage rates increase in the future, as they have for many years, will the hourly rate at the factory increase as well or fall behind? What sort of salaries are students from your school earning upon graduation and how do they compare? While there are no guarantees in this world, *Confused in Canada* needs to consider whether the current hourly rate is a reasonable criterion to use to decide on a career choice.

Secondly, why study Organizational Behaviour (OB)? Assuming that students like *Confused in Canada* are in school to broaden their perspective and general understanding and to prepare for the world of work, then no other course will do that better than OB. The goal for each student should go beyond the short-range objective of just landing a job; rather, students should look long-term to consider how they are going to succeed at that job by understanding people, learning about behaviour, developing soft skills that build interpersonal relationships, and understanding the context of the workplace ... these are the areas that give workers the most challenge. If students can learn about these things prior to entering the world of work, then they are less likely to make mistakes around their own work behaviours and should experience greater success in future employment.

Third and last, as a student learning business principles, *Confused in Canada* is lucky to be studying during one of the most transformational times in Canadian business history. *Confused in Canada* needs to reflect on whether her job will be replaced by robots or if the entire factory will be moved offshore. Being prepared for the economic changes to come, as well as the increased competition from the global workforce, would be wise factors for *Confused in Canada* to consider. For the last three decades, the Canadian economy has been slowly shifting its economic dependency away from the traditional routine-oriented manufacturing base toward a knowledge-based idea-driven creative economy. According to a report completed by Rick Miner, president and CEO of Miner & Miner Management Consultants in Toronto, "Without effective action, we face a future with large numbers of unskilled workers looking for jobs that require skills they do not possess and a large number of jobs that will go unfilled. By 2031, 77 percent of jobs will require post-secondary education, be it an apprenticeship, diploma, degree, or a professional qualification. About 60 percent of current Canadian workers have such credentials and that proportion is expected to increase slightly to 66 percent by 2031 as younger people finish their studies and enter the workforce."[1] More formal education will become the standard, not less, and *Confused in Canada* needs to be aware of this.

But why the shift in the first place ... where are the jobs going? It used to be China, Mexico, and India. But as these economies have become more affluent with an emerging middle class, the current shift is to send manufacturing to developing countries where the cost of labour is significantly below the poverty line: Sri Lanka, Philippines, Bangladesh, Cambodia, and Vietnam. It's difficult for Canadian manufacturing to compete without introducing changes like more affordable super-robotics in place of labour.

Realize that the shift is happening slowly, but have no doubt it is happening, and all Canadians need to take note—both employees and employers. Naturally, the talent needed to fuel this new kind of knowledge-based creative economy will be offered to Canadians first, but if they are unable to adapt, conform, and be productive under the new expectations, then business will look elsewhere to fill the gap.

So, what can Canadians do to prepare? The Miner report makes three main suggestions:

1. Gain greater understanding of how the Canadian workplace is changing and develop new skills through increased training and post-secondary education.

2. Appreciate the need for reinvention and creativity when designing our jobs.

3. Support the development and promotion of unique Canadian talent from those who have been marginalized in the past—embrace the diversity they bring to the workplace.

This is only a small snapshot of the Canadian work environment today, but nonetheless it is a significant one. The challenge of building a knowledge-based creative economy that is more tech-savvy, inclusive, and sustainable is cause enough to make us all think hard about whether we're prepared to accept a role in this newly transformed workplace. Are you ready?

This is a significant question to reflect upon. As a future employee and possible manager, you need to appreciate the environment that will surround your job, and identify which segments of that workplace can be influenced by your behaviour. As you read this book, you will be invited at times to consider whether or not your own employer (past, present, or future) actually treats employees as valuable assets. Part of the overarching mission of this book is to help you understand both *why* you should value employees and then *how* to actually do it. We contend that knowledge of organizational behaviour is key to unlocking the true potential of employees and optimizing organizational performance.

Studying organizational behaviour will help you understand the Canadian work environment, which is the first step in being better prepared for this new knowledge-based creative economy. Learning organizational behaviour is like placing your cupped hands against the window of a business and looking inside at all of the different behaviours that are occurring at the same time and wondering why . . . Why are people behaving that way? Why does the company have those policies and procedures? Why don't these individuals get along? This text, the cases at the end of the book, the exercises at the end of each chapter, as well as those on the Connect site are designed to help you understand the possible meanings behind such behaviours, and the broad implications they can have on the entire

organization. Further, organizational behaviour will clearly identify workplace expectations waiting for you upon completion of your studies. It is the mission of this book to help increase the number of people-centred organizations who are run by people-centred managers who use an organization's human, financial, technological, and other resources to compete effectively.

We'll begin your journey by providing the fundamentals of organizational behaviour and move on from there. Keep in mind, if at any time you need to review the big picture of what you are studying and how it fits into the larger scheme of things, just open the inside front cover to regain perspective. We have included a flowchart there for review.

What Is Organizational Behaviour? [LO 1]

Organizational behaviour, commonly referred to as OB, investigates three interdependent systems— the individual, the group, and the combination of both individuals and groups within an organizational context—to develop a better understanding of the workplace, especially when managing people. OB involves the study of what people think and feel and the resulting effect on individual and group behaviour within organizations. Figure 1.1 uses the metaphor of three trees, with each tree representing an interdependent system. Deep in the ground, where the roots find nourishment, are research contributions from the behavioural sciences: psychology, sociology, cultural anthropology, political science. Notice how each tree has its own branches and leaves; this shows the many factors that help the transformation process between using the many inputs (external factors like resources, markets, government, legal, history, and competition) to create the positive outputs from each system.

> **Organizational behaviour**
>
> A field of study that investigates three interdependent systems—the individual, the group, and the overall organizational context—to develop better understanding of the workplace, especially when managing people.

We'll first learn about *individual behaviour* and the eight primary topics that contribute to such outputs as creating positive membership behaviour, high task performance, and positive affective responses. Then we'll move on to the second system, *group behaviour*, that will introduce five topics that contribute to such outputs as effective communication, encouraging collaboration, and adaptability. The last area of study, *individual and groups in organizations*, will explore an additional five topics that contribute to such outputs

FIGURE 1.1 A Model of Organizational Behaviour

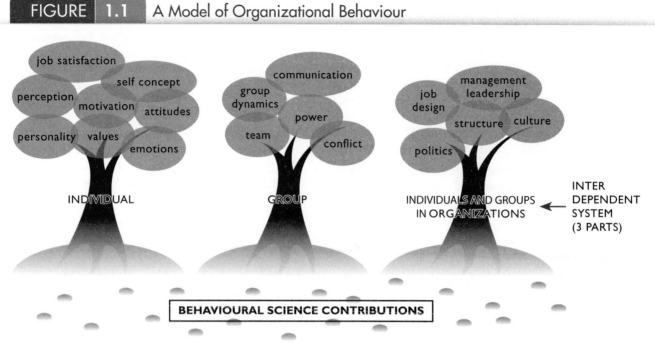

SOURCE: J. Kelly, J.B. Prince, & B. Ashforth, *OB*, 2nd Ed., Prentice-Hall, Toronto (1991) p. 24.

as increased productivity, goal attainment, and effective use of resources.

OB is more than common sense. It gains its credibility as an academic discipline by being research-driven (see Appendix 1). OB researchers investigate unanswered questions relating to effective *management* of behaviour in organizations, and the results are intended to be used by managers and other employees to improve workplace effectiveness. Research evidence indicates that people-centred practices are strongly associated with much higher profits and significantly lower employee turnover. In order for any team of managers and other employees to contribute to organizational goals and objectives, they must all work together and reinforce such practices.

OB is not an everyday job category such as accounting, marketing, or finance. Students of OB typically do not get jobs in organizational behaviour per se. OB is a horizontal discipline that cuts across virtually every job category, business function, and professional specialty.

Management

The process of working with and through others to achieve organizational objectives effectively, efficiently, and ethically.

foster greater satisfaction at their job. In addition, new knowledge can be applied directly and immediately—such as stress reduction techniques—to promote on-the-job satisfaction, which can lead to greater productivity. OB knowledge can help people have greater confidence that their firm is moving in the right direction by understanding the policies and procedures that are reinforced.[2]

Other benefits for individuals studying OB include:

- The ability to identify and analyze fundamental behaviours that occur within the workplace—this can contribute to greater overall cooperation and understanding.

- The ability to evaluate and help other employees develop sensitivity toward organizational structure, corporate strategy, business culture, standard practices, and leadership—this can promote greater understanding, stimulate dialogue, and result in higher performance.

- The ability to identify and demonstrate the knack to operate within an ethical, legal, and socially responsible context—this emphasizes the fact that people-friendly behaviours don't have to be sacrificed to accomplish corporate goals.

LO 2 Why Study Organizational Behaviour?

Anyone who plans to make a living in a large or small, public or private, profit or not-for-profit organization needs to study organizational behaviour. OB provides the foundation for the steps to take when individuals need to

But what about those employees who are offered a team-leadership opportunity or an entry-level supervisory position, or those who have clear managerial aspirations? Why do they need to study OB? It is important for them to study

OB Helps to Separate the Best from the Rest

The Great Recession of 2008–2010 presented companies across the globe with extreme challenges. Many didn't survive, but among those that did, some fared much better than others. Why? Geoff Colvin, an editor at *Fortune* magazine, has a short answer: the winners invested in their people. This conclusion was drawn from a study conducted with the Hay Group. Their work involved reviewing *Fortune*'s "Most Admired Companies" list year after year, which revealed that the top three companies in any particular industry made consistent and significantly greater investments in their employees than did their competitors. Their competitive edge was investing in their people.

Being people-oriented, respecting the human capital within an organization, and valuing contributions is nothing new. As far back as 1999, various firms began tracking Canadian employee needs and wants on the job. Each year the results are remarkably consistent. The most common response, without a doubt, is "being treated with respect." *Canadian HR Reporter* reported that 7,000 people who entered a contest in 2010 said the same thing. What these researchers also discovered when they looked back on previous contests and other surveys was that "being respected" remained a top response despite economic conditions. In good times or bad, people want to be supported, appreciated, and valued. The payoff? Reaping the rewards of having an engaged workforce and earning a competitive edge.

SOURCES: W. Lea, "A Better Way to Treat Your Employees," *Inc. Magazine*, February 16, 2012, www.inc.com/wendy-lea/treat-your-employees-like-humans-increase-productivity.html; G. Colvin, "How Are Most Admired Companies Different? They Invest in People and Keep Them Employed—Even in a Downturn," *Fortune*, March 22, 2010, p 82; and D. Crisp, "Strategic HR—Respect, Good Leadership (ethics) and Quality People," *Canadian HR Reporter*, September 12, 2011, p 8.

OB because they'll need to know what employees want and how to effectively predict and manage others' behaviour (see the Skills & Best Practices feature box). Professor Henry Mintzberg, a respected management scholar from McGill University, Montreal, observed that any kind of management role is vital to our society, as social institutions give them the authority to either serve us well or squander the talents and resources of the organization.[3]

It should be pointed out that we are discussing management in this chapter, not leadership. There is a difference, and we'll explore those differences later, in Chapter 9. For now, let's take a look at the skills that contemporary managers need to have in the workplace, and the future direction of management.

LO 3 The Transformation Toward People-Centred Management

It's important for all employees to understand how management is taking on new behaviours, as this will have a direct impact on the kinds of behaviours that individual employees will be expected to demonstrate on the job. As we've already discussed in broad terms, today's workplace is indeed undergoing immense and permanent changes.[4] Organizations are being "reengineered" for greater speed, efficiency, and flexibility.[5] Entrepreneurial spirit is needed in both small and large businesses. Teams are pushing aside the individual as the primary building block of organizations.[6] Costs are being managed by use of contract workers. Command-and-control management is giving way to participative management and empowerment (we'll discuss these concepts in greater detail in Chapter 8).[7] Ego-centred leaders are being replaced by customer-centred leaders. Employees are increasingly being viewed as internal customers. Clearly, such dynamic changes create a mandate for a new kind of manager in the 21st century. Table 1.1 contrasts the characteristics of past and contemporary managers. This change in management style is not just a good idea; it is an absolute necessity in the new workplace.

Indeed, many elements of organizational behaviour are transforming, and we're going to discuss them in greater detail throughout the rest of this text. For now, let's remain focused on the wide-ranging aspects of OB. We can better understand where the field of organizational behaviour is today and where it appears to be headed by appreciating where it has been. This next section will examine the evolution of understanding and managing people.

The History of Organizational Behaviour LO 4

To understand behaviour in organizations, it is necessary to draw upon a diverse array of disciplines, including psychology, management, sociology, organization theory, social psychology, statistics, anthropology, general systems theory, economics, information technology, political science, vocational counselling, human stress management, psychometrics, ergonomics, decision theory, and ethics. This rich heritage has spawned many competing perspectives and theories about human work behaviour. Figure 1.2 shows the three significant landmarks of OB development, Scientific Management, Human Relations Movement, and Contingency Approach, which we will discuss in the next sections.

TABLE 1.1

THE CHARACTERISTICS OF PAST AND CONTEMPORARY MANAGERS

	PAST MANAGERS	CONTEMPORARY MANAGERS
Primary role	Order giver, privileged elite, manipulator, controller	Facilitator, team member, teacher, advocate, sponsor, coach
Learning and knowledge	Periodic learning, narrow specialist	Continuous lifelong learning, generalist with multiple specialties
Compensation criteria	Time, effort, rank	Skills, results
Cultural orientation	Monocultural, monolingual	Multicultural, multilingual
Primary source of influence	Formal authority	Knowledge (technical and interpersonal)
View of people	Potential problem	Primary resource
Primary communication pattern	Vertical	Multidirectional
Decision-making style	Limited input for individual decisions	Broad-based input for joint decisions
Ethical considerations	Afterthought	Forethought
Nature of interpersonal relationships	Competitive (win–lose)	Cooperative (win–win)
Handling of power and key information	Hoard and restrict access	Share and broaden access
Approach to change	Resist	Facilitate

FIGURE 1.2 — Three Significant Landmarks of OB Theory Development

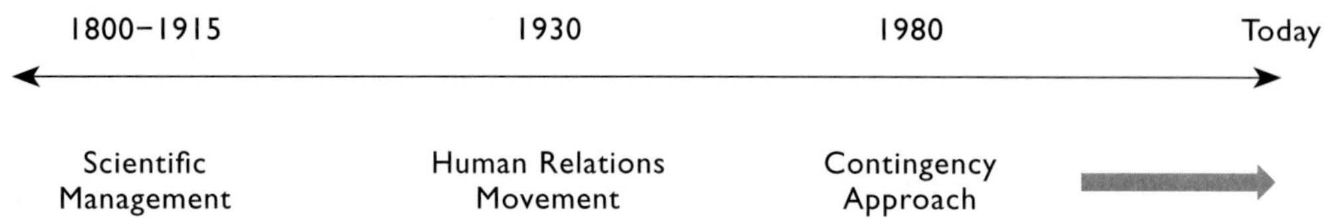

1800–1915	1930	1980	Today
Scientific Management	Human Relations Movement	Contingency Approach	

SCIENTIFIC MANAGEMENT

The Industrial Revolution that started with the development of steam power and the creation of large factories in the late 18th century, which lead to significant changes in the production of textiles and other products.[8] The factories that evolved created tremendous challenges for organizations and management that had not been confronted before. Managing such large pools of material, people, and information over large distances created the need for methods for dealing with the new management issues.

Frederic Taylor began to create a science of management (commonly referred to as *scientific management*) that used research to determine the optimum degree of specialization and standardization of work tasks. His model was the machine with its cheap, interchangeable

Scientific management

A body of research by Frederic Taylor (1856–1915) that involved systematically analyzing human behaviour at work to increase productivity and efficiency.

parts, each of which did one specific task. Taylor attempted to use the machine mind-set as a template to standardize individual work movements and breaks. This involved disassembling each task into its most minute unit and figuring out the one best way to do each job.

The overall goal of Taylor's research was to remove human variability. The results of his efforts were profound, as productivity increased dramatically. Of course, this did not come about without resistance. First, the old line managers resisted the notion that management was a science to be studied, not something one was born with (or inherited). Then, many workers resisted what some considered to be the "dehumanization" of work. Nevertheless, the industrial engineer with his stopwatch and clipboard standing over employees, measuring each little part of the job and their movements, became a hated figure and lead to much sabotage and group resistance.

The core elements of scientific management remain popular today as organizations remain focused on increasing the productivity of their workforce and striving to find the best way to manage an organization to achieve its goals. Some results of the scientific management movement include: the creation of a personnel department, implementation of quality control factors, introducing procedures for operations, striving for greater workplace efficiency, and recognizing the need for formalized management within an organizational structure.[9]

THE HUMAN RELATIONS MOVEMENT

A unique combination of factors during the 1930s fostered the *human relations movement*. First, following legalization of union–management collective bargaining in North America in the early 20th century, management began looking for new ways of handling employees. Until then, management was based on a scientific management approach that focused on the worker as a machine to be managed for maximum efficiency. Second, behavioural scientists conducting on-the-job research started calling for more attention to the "human" factor. Managers who had lost the battle to keep unions out of their factories heeded the call for better human relations and improved working conditions.

> *Human relations movement*
>
> Research that started calling attention to the "human" factor within the workplace.

The human relations movement gathered momentum through the 1950s, as academics and managers alike made stirring claims about the powerful effect that individual needs, supportive supervision, and group dynamics apparently had on job performance.

The Writings of Mayo and Follett Essential to the human relations movement were the writings of Elton Mayo and Mary Parker Follett. Australian-born Mayo advised managers to attend to employees' emotional needs in his 1933 classic, *The Human Problems of an Industrial Civilization*. Follett was a true pioneer, not only as a woman management consultant in the male-dominated industrial world of the 1920s, but also as a writer who saw employees as complex combinations of attitudes, beliefs, and needs. Mary Parker Follett was way ahead of her time in telling managers to motivate job performance instead of merely demanding it, a "pull" rather than "push" strategy.[10]

McGregor's Theories In 1960, Douglas McGregor wrote a book entitled *The Human Side of Enterprise*, which has become an important philosophical base for the modern view of people at work. Drawing upon his experience as a management consultant, McGregor formulated two sharply contrasting sets of assumptions about human nature (see Table 1.2). His *Theory X* assumptions were pessimistic and negative and, according to McGregor's interpretation, typical of how managers traditionally perceived employees. To help managers break with this negative tradition, McGregor formulated *Theory Y*, a modern and positive set of assumptions about people. McGregor believed managers could accomplish more through others by viewing them as self-energized, committed, responsible, and creative beings.

> *Theory X*
>
> Negative, pessimistic assumptions about human nature and its effect on productivity.

> *Theory Y*
>
> Positive assumptions about employees being responsible and creative.

New Assumptions about Human Nature Modern research methods have shown that the human relationists embraced some naive and misleading conclusions. Despite its shortcomings, the human relations movement opened the door to more progressive thinking about human nature. Rather than continuing to view employees as passive economic beings, managers began to see them as active social beings and took steps to create more humane work environments.

THE CONTINGENCY APPROACH

Since the 1980s, OB experts have focused their attention on emphasizing the fit between organizational processes and various characteristics of the situation. Throughout the later part of the 20th century, it became clear that there in fact was no one best way to approach a workplace; rather, an appropriate style depended on the demands of the situation. Hence,

TABLE 1.2

MCGREGOR'S THEORY X AND THEORY Y

OUTDATED (THEORY X) ASSUMPTIONS ABOUT PEOPLE AT WORK	MODERN (THEORY Y) ASSUMPTIONS ABOUT PEOPLE AT WORK
1. Most people dislike work; they avoid it when they can.	1. Work is a natural activity, like play or rest.
2. Most people must be coerced and threatened with punishment before they will work. People require close direction when they are working.	2. People are capable of self-direction and self-control if they are committed to objectives.
3. Most people actually prefer to be directed. They tend to avoid responsibility and exhibit little ambition. They are interested only in security.	3. People generally become committed to organizational objectives if they are rewarded for doing so.
	4. The typical employee can learn to accept and seek responsibility.
	5. The typical member of the general population has imagination, ingenuity, and creativity.

SOURCE: Adapted from D. McGregor, *The Human Side of Enterprise* (New York: McGraw-Hill, 1960), Ch 4.

the ***contingency approach*** calls for using management concepts and techniques in a situationally appropriate manner, instead of trying to rely on one best way. If, for example, you were trying to determine the most effective leadership style to use in a certain situation, you would have to consider the abilities of the followers; or, if you were trying to determine the appropriate level of pay increase for an employee, you would consider if productivity is contingent on the need for more money. Harvard's Clayton Christensen put it this way: "Many of the widely accepted principles of good management are only situationally appropriate."[11]

OB specialists embrace the contingency approach because it helps them realistically interrelate individuals, groups, and organizations. Moreover, the contingency approach sends a clear message to managers in today's global economy: Carefully read the situation and then apply lessons learned from published research studies.[12]

We can see how complex organizational behaviour can be and why it should be studied with great depth and scope.

> ### Contingency approach
>
> Using management tools and techniques in a situationally appropriate manner; avoiding the "one best way" mentality.

LO 5 Contemporary Issues in OB

The field of OB is a dynamic work in progress, not static and in final form. As such, OB is being redirected and reshaped by various forces both inside and outside the discipline. In this section, we explore four contemporary issues affecting OB:

- Workplace diversity
- The ethics challenge
- The Internet and e-business revolution
- Globalization

WORKPLACE DIVERSITY

How well do you appreciate and value diversity? Before we begin this section, you are encouraged to complete the Self-Assessment Exercise to better understand the concepts we're about to discuss. ***Diversity management*** is one of the most important social issues facing Canadian organizations today. Policies, activities, and organizational changes are developed and aimed at managing individual differences to enable all people to perform to their maximum potential. According to Statistics Canada, Canada's population growth between 2006 and 2011 was the highest among the G8 countries and can be attriuted predominately to an increase in the number of immigrants and non-permanent residents.[13] Earlier census statistics found that the number of foreign-born residents in Canada between 2001 and 2006 represented virtually one in five (19.8 percent) of the total population, the highest proportion since 1931.

> ### Diversity management
>
> Policies, activities, and organizational changes aimed at managing individual differences to enable all people to perform up to their maximum potential.

What Is Your Attitude Toward Diversity?

INSTRUCTIONS: Complete the following survey items by considering either your current job or one that you have held in the past. If you have never worked, ask a friend who is working to complete the questionnaire for his or her organization. Read each item and circle your response by using the rating scale shown below. Compute your total score by adding up your responses, then compare it to the scoring norms.

		Strongly Disagree	Disagree	Neutral	Agree	Strongly Agree
1	The minorities in this organization do not have a greater difficulty getting along with others.	1	2	3	4	5
2	If one of my coworkers were racist, I would confront that person and let him or her know of my disapproval.	1	2	3	4	5
3	Workers who are prejudiced have no place in this organization.	1	2	3	4	5
4	I feel that women do not have a more difficult time handling positions of authority relative to men.	1	2	3	4	5
5	I would feel just as comfortable with an Asian or Aboriginal supervisor as I do with a white supervisor.	1	2	3	4	5
6	It seems that most minorities in supervisory positions are just as effective relative to other supervisors.	1	2	3	4	5
7	I feel that diversity is good for this organization even if it means I will have a supervisor who is a minority.	1	2	3	4	5
8	Most of the minority supervisors in this organization possess the same leadership qualities as those supervisors who are white.	1	2	3	4	5
9	All employees are held to the same performance standards, regardless of gender or race.	1	2	3	4	5
10	I believe that increasing the hiring of women and minorities can only help this organization.	1	2	3	4	5

Scoring Norms

1–18 Unfavourable attitudes
19–36 Moderate attitudes
37–50 Favourable attitudes

SOURCES: Adapted from M. Montei, G. Adams, and L. Eggers, "Validity of Scores on the Attitudes Toward Diversity Scale," *Educational and Psychological Measurement*, April 1996, pp 298–99.

The number of foreign-born residents in Canada has nearly tripled during the past 80+ years and is expected to continue rising; this is four times faster than the Canadian-born population. Now you can see why diversity management is of such interest to OB experts. We'll reference Statistics Canada data again later, as well as when we talk about globalization (Chapter 14).

Diversity represents the multitude of individual differences and similarities that exist among people.[14] The many different dimensions or components of diversity make all of us unique. Figure 1.3 shows the diversity wheel and its four layers. Personality is at the centre of the diversity wheel because it represents a stable set of characteristics that are responsible for a person's individual identity. We further discuss the dimensions of personality in Chapter 3.

> **Diversity**
>
> The host of individual differences that make people different from and similar to each other.

The next layer of diversity consists of a set of internal dimensions such as age, race, and gender that are referred to as the primary dimensions of diversity.[15] These dimensions, for the most part, are not within our control, but strongly influence our attitudes, expectations, and assumptions about others, which in turn influence our behaviour.

The next layer of diversity is composed of external, or secondary, dimensions such as religion and marital status. They represent individual differences that we have a greater ability to influence or control. These dimensions also exert a significant influence on our perceptions, behaviour, and attitudes. The final layer of diversity includes organizational dimensions such as job title, management status, and seniority. For example,

FIGURE 1.3 The Four Layers of Diversity

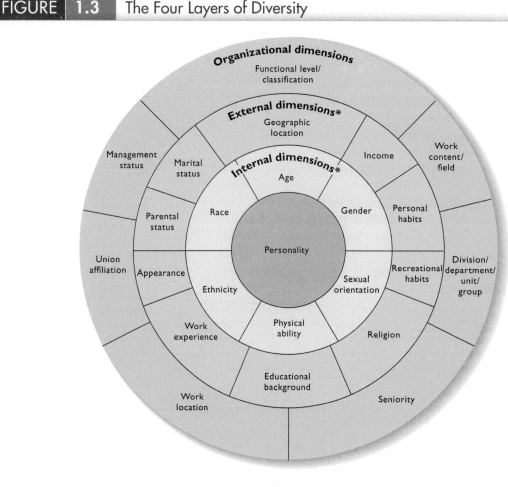

*Internal Dimensions and External Dimensions are adapted from Loden and Rosener, *Workforce America!* (Homewood, IL: Business One Irwin, 1991).
SOURCE: L. Gardenswartz and A. Rowe, *Diverse Teams at Work: Capitalizing on the Power of Diversity* (New York: McGraw-Hill, 1994), p 33. Copyright 1994. Reproduced with permission of The McGraw-Hill Companies.

Loblaws Companies Ltd. recently set a goal to raise representation of female store managers, and within twelve months it doubled that number. With 31,582 employees, this kind of commitment to diversity placed Loblaws on the *Globe and Mail* list of the Top 45 Best Diversity Employers.[16]

One of the most well-known problems faced by women and visible minorities in the workplace is the *glass ceiling*. The glass ceiling represents an invisible barrier that blocks certain workers, primarily qualified women and visible minorities, from advancing into top management positions. It can be particularly demotivating because employees can look up and see coveted top management positions through the transparent ceiling, but are unable to obtain them. One study found that the barrier is much greater for minorities, and called it a "concrete ceiling."[17]

Diversity management involves activities aimed at managing individual differences to enable people to perform to their maximum potential, including but not limited to those required for employment equity (see the Law and Ethics at Work feature box for more on this topic). It focuses on changing an organization's culture, policies, and procedures so that employees can perform at their highest level of productivity. To attract and retain the best workers, companies need to adopt policies and programs that meet the needs of a diverse group of workers. Programs such as daycare, eldercare, flexible work schedules, less rigid relocation policies, and mentoring programs are likely to help workers from all backgrounds to perform their job duties at an optimal level.

A landmark study of the diversity practices used by 16 organizations that successfully manage diversity uncovered 52 different practices, 20 of which were used by the majority of the companies sampled. The practices were classified into three main types: accountability, developmental, and recruitment.[18] Table 1.3 shows the top practices associated with each type. We discuss them in relative order of importance.

Accountability Practices Accountability practices relate to the manager's responsibility to treat diverse employees fairly. Table 1.3 reveals that companies predominantly accomplish this objective by creating administrative procedures aimed at integrating diverse employees into the management ranks (practices numbered 3, 4, 5, 6, 8, 9, and 10). In contrast, work and family policies (practice 7) focus on creating an environment that fosters employee commitment and productivity. Moreover, organizations are increasingly attempting to build an accountability component into their diversity programs to motivate managers to effectively manage diversity.

Developmental Practices The use of developmental practices to manage diversity is relatively new compared with the historical use of accountability and recruitment

> **Glass ceiling**
>
> Invisible barrier blocking qualified women and minorities from top management positions.

EMPLOYMENT EQUITY ACT IN CANADA

LAW AND ETHICS AT WORK

In Canada, legislation covering federal workers and those in some provinces requires employers to actively pursue employment equity. Employment equity involves aiming to increase the number of employees from groups that have historically been underrepresented in an organization's workforce. In particular, the legislation requires that steps be taken to increase the representation of qualified women, visible minorities, Aboriginal people, and persons with disabilities at all levels of an organization. The Canadian Human Rights Commission is responsible for ensuring compliance with the Act. To this end, the Commission conducts audits to determine whether employers meet the statutory requirements of the Act.

SOURCE: The Government of Canada *Employment Equity Act*: www.chrc-ccdp.ca/employment_equity/default-en.asp.

TABLE 1.3

COMMON DIVERSITY PRACTICES

ACCOUNTABILITY PRACTICES	DEVELOPMENT PRACTICES	RECRUITMENT PRACTICES
1. Top management's personal intervention	1. Diversity training programs	1. Targeted recruitment of non-managers
2. Internal advocacy groups	2. Networks and support groups	2. Key outside hires
3. Emphasis on employment equity statistics, profiles	3. Development programs for all high-potential managers	3. Extensive public exposure to diversity
4. Inclusion of diversity in performance evaluation goals, ratings	4. Informal networking activities	4. Corporate image as liberal, progressive, or benevolent
5. Inclusion of diversity in promotion decisions, criteria	5. Job rotation	5. Partnerships with educational institutions
6. Inclusion of diversity in management succession planning	6. Formal mentoring program	6. Recruitment incentives such as cash supplements
7. Work and family policies	7. Informal mentoring program	7. Internships
8. Policies against racism, sexism	8. Entry development programs for all high-potential new hires	8. Publications or PR products that highlight diversity
9. Internal audit or attitude survey	9. Internal training (such as personal safety or language)	9. Targeted recruitment of managers
10. Active employment equity committee, office	10. Recognition events, awards	10. Partnership with non-traditional groups

SOURCE: Abstracted from Tables A.10, A.11, and A.12 in A.M. Morrison, *The New Leaders: Guidelines on Leadership Diversity in America* (San Francisco: Jossey-Bass, 1992). Reprinted with permission of John Wiley & Sons, Inc.

practices. Developmental practices focus on preparing diverse employees for greater responsibility and advancement. These activities are needed because most non-traditional employees have not been exposed to the types of activities and job assignments that develop effective leadership and social networks.[19] Table 1.3 indicates that diversity training programs, networks and support groups, and mentoring programs are among the most frequently used developmental practices. Certainly this is the case at the law firm of Fraser Milner Casgrain, as shown in the photo at right.

Law associate Denise Williams, left, is a recipient of a diversity scholarship program launched by the 1,250-person law firm Fraser Milner Casgrain. Partner Kate Broer, right, helps co-chair the national diversity and inclusion initiative that has led to the firm recently winning numerous national diversity awards in Canada for six years in a row.

Recruitment Practices Recruitment practices focus on attracting diverse job applicants at all levels who are willing to accept challenging work assignments. This focus is critical because people learn the leadership skills needed for advancement by successfully accomplishing work assignments with increasing responsibility. As shown in Table 1.3, targeted recruitment of non-managers (practice 1) and managers (practice 9) are commonly used to identify and recruit workers in groups that are often underrepresented in the workforce. Consider this business case: A Canadian firm wants to become more aggressive in developing new global markets, as well as exploring new local markets of a diverse nature. But how? By recruiting and hiring internationally trained workers, doors can open to global markets and in such diverse cities as Montreal, Vancouver, and Toronto, they are able to open doors in local markets. Recently, the Toronto Region Immigrant Employment Council (TRIEC) commissioned a survey asking a random sampling of 462 employers about their experiences with recently recruited and hired skilled immigrants. Of those who said they had hired a skilled immigrant to help open up new local markets, 84 percent felt it had been effective. Of those who had hired a skilled immigrant to help open up global markets, a whopping 94 percent said it had been effective. Such hiring practices as these can provide a pool of rich talent for the firm when looking to fill the gap in their management ranks.[20]

In summary, effective workforce diversity management requires a number of OB skills, including managing change (Chapter 13), understanding cultural differences when communicating (Chapter 7), avoiding misunderstandings that lead to conflict (Chapter 8), managing the challenges around political issues (Chapter 8), and most of all, exhibiting strong leadership skills (Chapter 10). Understanding diversity is an underlying theme that runs throughout every chapter of this text. Diversity in Canada will resurface again when we discuss globalization (Chapter 14) and is highlighted in the Focus on Diversity feature box. Consider, for example, our discussion about the inclusion of older workers within federally regulated workplaces.

THE ETHICS CHALLENGE

Here are four good reasons to care about business ethics:

1. Bernard Ebbers, the Canadian ex-patriot and former CEO of WorldCom, is serving a 25 year sentence for his orchestration of an $11 billion accounting fraud to cover up a massive debt. The 2002 bankruptcy case earned Ebbers the title of being the tenth most corrupt CEO of all time by *Time* magazine.[21]

2. Conrad Black, the former Canadian media baron and ex-CEO of Hollinger International Inc., recently served out his four years in a US federal prison and was fined for obstruction of justice, $80 million in tax evasion, and three counts of mail fraud. Fallout from the case lead to a loss of $2 billion in shareholder value.[22]

3. Garth Drabinsky, the convicted former head of live-theatre company Livent Inc., was found guilty in 2009 of financial irregularities and fraud against shareholders and sentenced to seven years behind bars. He and his partner were ordered to pay close to $40 million in damages.[23]

4. Frank Dunn, Douglas Beatty, and Michael Gollogly, all former senior executives at Nortel Networks Corporation, were fired 'for cause' in 2004 and faced numerous RCMP criminal charges in 2012 alleging their involvement in an elaborate multi-billion dollar

CANADIAN WORKFORCE WILL NOW INCLUDE OLDER WORKERS

Until very recently in Canada, if you were one of the 800,000 employees working for any of the 12,000 federally regulated employers in this country (i.e., banking, transport, and communications) and you turned 60–65 years old beginning December 2012, you were mandated to retire; even if you didn't want to leave the firm, you had no choice because that was the law. All that changed in late 2011, when the section of the Canadian Human Rights Act that permitted mandatory retirement at the age of 60–65 (depending on the industry) was officially repealed by the federal government.

All Canadian jurisdictions, with the exception of New Brunswick, have now abolished mandatory retirement, although there are some exceptions in some provinces for particular occupations. Human rights groups and labour unions have long argued the need to kill mandatory retirement because of its discriminating nature. Economists believe that eliminating mandatory retirement will help solve Canadian labour shortages as the Baby Boomer population ages. The final result of this repealed law means the Canadian workforce is even more age diverse than it was in the recent past. That is good news for those who want to continue working well past the age of 65.

SOURCE: K. Carlson, "Tories end forced retirement, decades of 'age discrimination'" *National Post,* Dec. 18, 2011. news.nationalpost.com/2011/12/18/tories-end-forced-retirement-decades-of-age-discrimination/

accounting fraud to mask falling Nortel sales. The debacle resulted in more than 60,000 employees losing their jobs.[24]

Thanks to the highly-publicized criminal acts of these and other executives, corporate officers in Canada, as well as those involved with public trading in the US, are now subject to high accountability standards and harsh penalties from the likes of the RCMP, the Ontario Securities Commission, Revenue Canada, and the Securities and Exchange Commission.

Everyone needs to join in the effort to stem this tide of unethical conduct. A variety of individual and organizational factors contribute to unethical behaviour. At an individual level, ethics is a unique combination of personality characteristics, values, and moral principles. At the organizational level, ethics is guided by ethical codes (or lack thereof), culture, size, structure, perceived pressure for results, and corporate strategy.[25] OB is an excellent vantage point for better understanding and improving workplace ethics. If OB can provide insights about managing human work behaviour, then it can teach us something about avoiding misbehaviour.

Ethics involves the study of moral issues and choices. It is concerned with right versus wrong, good versus bad, and the many shades of grey in supposedly black-and-white issues. Moral implications spring from virtually every decision, both on and off the job. All employees are challenged to have more imagination and the courage to do the right thing to make the world a better place.

> **Ethics**
>
> Study of moral issues and choices.

In the final analysis, ethics come down to individual motivation. Organizational climate, role models, structure, and rewards can all point employees in the right direction. But individuals must want to do the right thing. Bill George, the respected former CEO of Medtronic, the maker of life-saving devices such as heart pacemakers, gave this call to action: "Each of us needs to determine...where our ethical boundaries are and, if asked to violate (them), refuse...If this means refusing a direct order, we must be prepared to resign."[26] Rising to this challenge requires strong personal values (more about values in Chapter 4) and the courage to adhere to them during adversity.[27]

Since ethics is such an important issue today, it is worth noting that feature boxes dedicated to law and ethics at work are provided throughout each chapter of this textbook. We'll continue our discussion about ethics when discussing decision making in Chapter 8.

THE INTERNET AND E-BUSINESS REVOLUTION

Experts on the subject draw an important distinction between e-commerce (buying and selling goods and services over the Internet) and *e-business*, using the Internet to facilitate every aspect of running a business.[28] Says one industry observer: "Strip away the highfalutin talk, and at bottom, the Internet is a tool that dramatically lowers the cost of communication. That means it can radically alter any industry or activity that depends heavily on the flow of information."[29]

> **E-business**
>
> Running an entire business via the Internet.

Relevant information includes everything from customer needs and product design specifications, to prices, schedules, finances, employee performance data, and corporate strategy. Intel has taken this broad view of the Internet to heart. This builder of human capital is striving to become what it calls an e-corporation, one that relies primarily on the Internet to not only buy and sell things, but to facilitate all business functions, exchange knowledge among its employees, and build partnerships with outsiders as well. Intel is on the right track, according to this survey finding: "Firms that embraced the Internet averaged a 13.4 percent jump in productivity...compared with 4.9 percent for those that did not."[30]

E-business has significant implications for OB because it eventually will seep into every corner of life, both on and off the job. Thanks to the Internet, individuals are able to make quicker and better decisions because of speedy access to vital information (discussed in greater detail in Chapter 7). The Internet also allows individuals to seemingly defy the laws of physics by being in more than one place at the same time. For example, employees can be sitting in their home office while receiving emails on their smartphone, while at the same time participating in an online net-meeting with colleagues from around the world. In short, organizational life will never be the same because of email, e-learning,[31] e-management, e-leadership, virtual teams, and virtual organizations. You will learn more about virtual teams (Chapter 6), email (Chapter 7), and virtual organizations (Chapter 12) in later chapters.

GLOBALIZATION

Globalization refers to the major trend whereby firms are extending their operations to new markets abroad. When we speak of operations, we need to consider the inclusion of human capital as well, since talent can be exported or imported to meet the human resource needs of a firm (see the International OB feature box for more on this topic). This poses many challenges. For example, it is very likely that the future Canadian labour force will be comprised of many different people from

> **Globalization**
>
> The extension of business operations to markets around the globe.

IMPORTING TALENT FROM AROUND THE WORLD

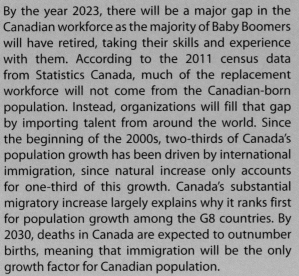

By the year 2023, there will be a major gap in the Canadian workforce as the majority of Baby Boomers will have retired, taking their skills and experience with them. According to the 2011 census data from Statistics Canada, much of the replacement workforce will not come from the Canadian-born population. Instead, organizations will fill that gap by importing talent from around the world. Since the beginning of the 2000s, two-thirds of Canada's population growth has been driven by international immigration, since natural increase only accounts for one-third of this growth. Canada's substantial migratory increase largely explains why it ranks first for population growth among the G8 countries. By 2030, deaths in Canada are expected to outnumber births, meaning that immigration will be the only growth factor for Canadian population.

According to a report from Citizenship and Immigration Canada, 182,000 temporary foreign workers were recruited and selected in 2012. The total number of temporary foreign workers in Canada exceeds 300,000, with increases expected well into 2015. Here are other Canadian population facts resulting from immigration:

- The strongest population growth between 2006 and 2011 occurred in Saskatchewan, specifically Saskatoon and Regina. Prior to this time period, the province experienced 10 straight years of declining population. Saskatchewan saw its growth exceed the national average between 2006 and 2011 by receiving more than 28,000 immigrants, according to the 2011 census. The main factors behind the turnaround are being attributed to a substantial increase of immigrants, with only a slight increase in interprovincial migration. In contrast, the population

growth during this same time period in the United States and France was mainly a result of natural increase (more births than deaths), with migratory increase proportionately lower than Canada.

- Population growth is up in all Atlantic provinces, with immigration being the main factor overall. Population growth in these provinces still remains below the national average.

- Between 2006 and 2011, Ontario experienced its lowest population growth since the 1981–1986 census period. Ontario received approximately 96,000 fewer immigrants, in addition to migratory losses to the other provinces and territories that were approximately twice as large.

- In 2011, more than one Canadian in three (35 percent) were living in one of Canada's three largest Census Metro Areas (CMAs): Toronto, Montreal, or Vancouver. The population growth of these three CMAs was due mainly to immigration, since each year a majority of immigrants choose to settle in these areas.

- In 2011, the population share of the Prairie provinces and British Columbia combined reached 30.7 percent, a proportion which for the first time exceeded that of the Atlantic provinces and Quebec combined. The population share of Canada's Western provinces now exceeds that of the Eastern provinces due to a larger influx of immigrants on average to the Prairie provinces.

SOURCES: "The Canadian Population in 2011: Population Counts and Growth" Census 2011 Analytical Products Statistics Canada website: www12.statcan.gc.ca/census-recensement/2011; and "INTERVIEW: Immigration: The new normal," *HR Professional Magazine*, October 2011, p 45, www.hrpromag.com.

many different cultures other than Canada (we'll discuss this in greater detail in Chapters 13 and 14). The implication for the workplace is that foreign employees with Canadian workplace visas or newly-acquired Canadian citizenship papers may not be aware of Canadian national values, cultural traditions, or workplace behaviours. The chances for misunderstanding and conflict in the workplace are increased under such conditions.

In the case of exporting Canadian human capital, expatriate managers struggle to find effective methods of managing employees in countries as diverse as Kazakhstan, Bangladesh, and Indonesia. Cross-cultural training is essential, and specific knowledge regarding motivation, decision making, communication, and leadership practices in the country of operation is required to help maintain smooth day-to-day operations. Globalization means that organizations manage people all over the world—people speaking different languages, governed by different political systems, under widely differing social, ethical, and behavioural norm. This situation has created a major challenge for managers from Western countries who are deployed in other parts of the world. Managerial approaches based on OB knowledge from North America will not necessarily apply in other cultures. One general research finding of great importance in global management relates back to our earlier discussion about the contingency theory. There is rarely one best way to manage people; the specific situation must be considered.

To Summarize

Overall, today's managers need considerable knowledge of organizational behaviour to effectively manage the individuals and groups they are responsible for. Business realities such as the Internet, e-business, workforce diversity, ethical business practices, and globalization are just some of the factors having a major impact on organizational behaviour. But just as important are other factors that we'll be discussing in future chapters, including demographics and global economics (explored in greater detail when forces of change are discussed in Chapter 13); generational differences (covered in

our discussion of motivation in Chapter 5); different communication styles (addressed in Chapter 7); external forces affecting sustainability (discussed when we look at the kinds of contemporary organizational structures from Chapter 12); as well as legal and legislative changes affecting organizational behaviour (featured in every chapter). All of these factors collectively influence individual employee behaviour, group behaviour, as well as organizational behaviour.

A Road Map to Learning OB

OB is a broad and growing field, and we have a lot of ground to cover. To make the trip as instructive and efficient as possible, we will use a theory–research–practice strategy. For virtually all major topics in this text, we begin by presenting the underlying theoretical framework (often with graphical models showing key variables and how they relate) and defining key terms. Next, we explore the latest research findings for valuable insights using five different sources of research. We encourage you to take a quick look at the beginning of the Appendices to understand the differences. Finally, we round out the discussion with illustrative practical examples and, when applicable, how-to-do-it advice.

Summary of Learning Objectives

 Define *organizational behaviour* and *management*. Organizational behaviour (OB) is a field of study dedicated to better understanding and managing people at work, both individually and in groups. Management is the process of working with and through others to achieve organizational objectives efficiently and ethically.

 Explain why OB is studied and what benefits it can bring to the workplace. OB can assist individual development toward positive membership behaviour and positive affective responses, and can encourage greater task performance. OB can help groups communicate better and work more effectively in collaboration, and as a result, have greater productivity. OB can assist the entire organization by facilitating the adaptation to change process, ensuring that resources are used effectively, and helping achieve corporate goals.

 Discuss the relevance of OB to the contemporary Canadian workplace by differentiating between managers from the past versus those of the future. Managers from the past were primarily order-givers, the privileged elite with a primary role to control and manipulate. Their primary means for influencing others was to use their formal authority. In contrast, the contemporary manager is more participative in nature, inviting employees into the decision-making process. They are interpersonal and knowledgeable, believing people to be their greatest resource.

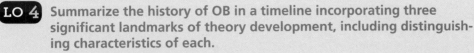

LO 4 Summarize the history of OB in a timeline incorporating three significant landmarks of theory development, including distinguishing characteristics of each.

- Scientific management (late 1800s–1915)—Involved systematically analyzing human behaviour at work to increase productivity and efficiency. Frederic Taylor's research played a significant role during this phase.

- The human relations movement (1930s)—Recognized the powerful effect that individual needs, supportive supervision, and group dynamics apparently have on job performance. This movement called attention to the human factor that exists in the workplace.

- The contingency approach (1980–present)—Uses management tools and techniques in a situationally appropriate manner; avoids the "one best way" mentality.

LO 5 Infer and predict the challenges that at least four contemporary OB issues may present to both non-managerial employees and management in the future.

- Workplace diversity—Diversity is the host of individual differences that make people different from each other. Integration of women, visible minorities, Aboriginal people, and people with disabilities into the Canadian workforce is something that organizations will continue to strive for in the future. Non-managerial employees will find themselves working alongside people of diversity who speak differently, who may not understand Canadian values or appreciate the corporate values, who may not identify with the behaviours of the corporate culture, and who may be unaware of Canadian employment laws. This could create more opportunity for misunderstanding and conflict in the workplace. Managers may find themselves having to educate non-managerial employees on how to get along in a more diverse work environment. Managers themselves may need training in the same area.

- Ethics in the workplace—With the media giving so much attention to prominent CEOs who have been found guilty of cons, schemes, tax evasion, or conspiracy to commit fraud, there is a clear need for greater awareness of business ethics. Individuals need to realize that ethics starts from within. When faced with pressure from certain people or groups, individuals need to do the ethical thing. Organizations need to live up to their vision and values statements, have better corporate governance, and hire people who value ethical behaviour.

- E-business and the Internet—E-business involves using the Internet to more effectively and efficiently manage every aspect of a business. The Internet is reshaping how people communicate. The ability to be in two places at one time allows for multi-tasking and time savings. Individuals will need training and support; management will be expected to provide both. Organizations will be forced to provide the latest resources that support e-business and the Internet so that they will be able to compete.

- Globalization—Globalization is the extension of business operations to markets around the globe. The contingency approach to OB is particularly relevant here, as it suggests that it is better to use management tools and techniques in a situationally appropriate manner than to rely on one best way to manage. The importing and exporting of human capital into and out of the Canadian market will allow individuals to explore new worlds and strengthen their skills. As the world's labour force becomes more intermingled, there will be a need for more customized people-solutions to fit the situation as values between people in different markets will vary.

Discussion Questions

1. How would you respond to a fellow student who says each of the following: OB is just a bunch of common sense, why do I need to buy a book or attend a class? OB means being nice to everyone on the job!

2. Have you ever worked with a Theory X manager (see Table 1.2)? What sorts of experiences did you witness on the job when the manager disciplined others? Communicated with others? In the end, how did this manager make you feel?

3. How has technology changed the skills and role of the employee? The manager?

4. Describe some of the demands that a diverse workforce and increased global operations make on managers. What are some of the opportunities that these trends offer to an organization?

5. If the Canadian government enforced more criminal laws against CEOs and if Revenue Canada cracked down more on tax fraud, do you think we would see more ethical behaviour in business? Why or why not?

Google Searches

1. **Google Search:** "the best workplaces in Canada 20__" AND "Canada's best diversity employers" Review the top 25 organizations on both lists. Do any organizations appear on both lists? What does it take to make the best place to work list? What criteria are used to make the best diversity employer list?

2. **Google Search:** "Conference Board of Canada—employability skills 2000+" Review the three areas for skill development: Fundamental, Personal Management, and Teamwork. How can OB help an individual to achieve these skills?

3. **Google Search:** "Canadians working overseas 20__" AND "What you need to know to work overseas" Based on what you find, do you believe that Canada is the only country experiencing large exchanges of labour to and from other countries? Explain your answer based on the evidence from your search.

4. **Google Search:** "Time Magazine Top 10 Crooked CEO's" Who was ranked the #1 worst CEO of all time? What did this person do to earn such a ranking? Review the full list of the top 10 of all time. What other names appear on the list? Identify the industries they worked in, the type of crime they committed, and look for patterns between the different cases.

Experiential Exercise

TV Group Exercise

PURPOSE   This exercise will help familiarize you with organizational behaviour concepts. It demonstrates OB concepts within contemporary settings and familiar pop culture shows to help you to relate to and understand the concepts.
Approx. Timing: two 15-minute segments

ACTIVITY ASSIGNMENT:

- Work in small groups.
- Choose a popular television show from the list below.

- For homework, individually watch the agreed-upon show, take notes, and be prepared to share your observations with your other group members on the following:
    1. A brief plot summary and situation description
    2. A list of the main characters
    3. Examples of individual workplace behaviour, group behaviour, contemporary organizational situations and responses, and any other OB-related concepts discussed in Chapter 1
- Share your observations with one another, and create a master list of observations.
- Distribute the master list to the entire class.

POSSIBLE TV SHOWS			
The Big Bang Theory	The Office	NCIS-LA	Suits
Dragon's Den	30 Rock	Undercover Boss	Shark Tank

Discussion Questions

1. Given this exercise, how pervasive would you say organizations are in our society? Do you think this has always been the case?
2. Predict what role organizations will play in our future society.
3. Are the situations shown in the TV shows realistic, or are they distorted for entertainment purposes?
4. What possible danger can people run into if they assume that what they see on TV is in fact the way people behave in real life when working?

OB In Action Case Study

HR Metric Service–Benchmarking Standards

A few years ago, the British Columbia Human Resources Management Association (BC HRMA) identified a gap between the way in which HR professionals were basing their organizational decisions around human capital issues and providing such benchmarking data for their members. "We recognized that business intelligence in most functions of the organization, such as computer systems or finance, had and used data to get budgets and resources, present to the executive and demonstrate their results. This was sorely lacking in the HR field," says Ian Cook, director, HR Metrics Service, a leading Canadian resource for providing up-to-date HR business data. HR analytics have always lacked consistency or have been inapplicable to Canada's small- to medium-sized enterprises.

To address such concerns, the BC HRMA set out to build a quick, efficient, accurate, and user-friendly analytics service for human resources. A collaborative venture by the Human Resources Professionals Association (HRPA), the BC HRMA, the Human Resources Management Association of Manitoba (HRMAM), and the Human Resources Institute of Alberta (HRIA), this all-Canadian analytics subscription service lets organizations benchmark their own HR statistics against competitors and peers in their industry sector and geographic region. The not-for-profit, shared service also allows them to compare against the best-in-class across all industry sectors.

Organizations that subscribe to the service provide quarterly data on a minimum of 20 key HR statistics via an easy-to-use online questionnaire. These include productivity, retention, workforce demographics, compensation, revenue per full-time equivalent (FTE), labour cost per FTE, vacancy rate, first-year turnover, diversity ratio, and more. HR Metrics Service crunches the numbers, identifies flows and patterns, and generates customized analytics and benchmarking reports every quarter.

"What we've built is a set of standards that's trackable and audited," Cook says. "You've got the whole backstory, so it's hard for someone to say it's wrong. In financial reporting, GAAP and IFRS state categorically how certain numbers must be treated. HR didn't have the same kinds of standards. We had five ways of looking at turnover. Which was the right number?"

- The City of Ottawa has long been using internal analytics; however, they needed a better handle on a previously under-measured area for the city: talent management. With the help of HR Metrics Service, they were able to determine how their retention and turnover rates compared to a standard.

- Moneris Solutions Corporation, a large North American payment processing company, was interested in assessing their turnover and first-year resignation rates compared with other organizations, particularly in the mission-critical areas. HR Metrics Service was able to help them determine their productivity levels and other lead indicators.

Discussion Questions

1. How can analytics help address any of the contemporary management concerns described in this chapter?
2. How can analytics help predict and explain individual behaviour as well as that of management?
3. Do you anticipate more or less demand for HR analytic services in the future? Explain your reasoning.

SOURCE: M. Morra, "Down To the Crunch. HR Metrics Service Aims To Become The Standard," *HR Professional*, November/December 2011, pp. 24–26, 35–37.

The CONNECTion Zone   McGraw Hill connect™

- The Presentation Assistant
- Ethical OB Dilemma
- Video Case

Practise and learn online with Connect.

Social Perception and Attribution Factors Influencing Individual Behaviour

FACING AN OB CHALLENGE

Can you convince employers not to judge a book by its cover? I wish it was a little easier to get a job even though I have a different kind of look. I have pink hair and several tattoos on my arms and hands . . . another is on my neck. I also have a few facial piercings—my tongue and lip have studs and I have a few lip-rings. I prefer to wear spacers in my ears and some eye makeup; but that's about it. So, what's the big deal?

—*DON'T BE HATIN'*

LO 1 Define *social perception* and *causal attributions.*

LO 2 Explain perception in terms of the four-stage social cognition processing sequence.

LO 3 Illustrate six managerial implications of social perceptions.

LO 4 Examine the managerial challenges and recommendations of sex-role, age, racial/ethnic, and disability stereotypes.

LO 5 Compare and contrast fundamental attribution bias and self-serving bias.

Assessing Your Perception

Being different from others around you . . . what's the big deal? Well, being unique by choice or by birth doesn't matter—the point is you're different, and that distinction can be unsettling for some people. The media is full of stories about people who experience discrimination and persecution for no particular reason other than the fact that they are different from those around them: the colour of their skin, the way they talk, the clothes they wear. Such bias can be eliminated if we take the time to understand people from their point of view, try to see the world from their skin, their shoes, their life. It would help people get along better with others if they took a moment to assess their own attitudes first before judging someone else's behaviour. That is why we have included the self-assessment exercise Assessing Your Perception—to help you determine whether you have the skill to consider the world from others' point of view.

By completing the self-assessment on perspective taking, you have begun the process of uncovering the importance of considering things from different points of view and the role such consideration plays in understanding individual behaviour. So how important is the perception process? It can be the source of communication distortion and conflict between people from different cultures. Our perceptions and feelings are influenced by information we receive from newspapers, magazines, television, Internet, Facebook, radio, family, and friends. We all use information stored in our memories to interpret the world around us, and our interpretations, in turn, influence how we respond and interact with others.

What Is Perception?

As human beings, we constantly strive to make sense of our surroundings. The resulting knowledge influences our behaviour and helps us navigate our way through life. Think of the perceptual process that occurs when you meet someone for the first time. Your attention is drawn to the individual's physical appearance, mannerisms, actions, and reactions to what you say and do. You ultimately arrive at conclusions based on your perceptions of this social interaction. The brown-haired, green-eyed individual turns out to be friendly and fond of outdoor activities. You further conclude that you like this person and then ask him or her to go to a concert, calling the person by the name you stored in memory.

The perception process influences much more than the impressions people make about each other. For example, companies use their knowledge about perceptions when marketing their products, and political candidates use it to get elected.[1]

Moreover, inaccurate perceptions and stereotypes can influence whether or not you get hired, promoted, or fired. Perceptions also impact the grade you receive when giving an oral presentation in class, and whether or not a person wants to date or marry you. The point we are trying to make is that the perception process influences a host of managerial activities, organizational processes, and quality-of-life issues. In this chapter, you will gain a fundamental understanding of how perception works and how you can use it to enhance your future personal and professional success.

Let's begin our exploration of the perceptual process and its associated outcomes. In this chapter we focus on (1) an information-processing model of perception, (2) stereotypes, and (3) how causal attributions are used to interpret behaviour.

Assessing Your Perception

INSTRUCTIONS: Indicate the extent to which you agree or disagree with each statement. Perspective taking skills play a big part in your ability to lead others, to get along with others, to communicate effectively, and to have satisfying interpersonal relationships in both your personal and professional lives. For how to keep score, see question #1.

1 Before criticizing somebody, I try to imagine how I would feel if I were in his/her place.
- ❏ Does not describe me at all (score 1 point)
- ❏ Does not describe me well (score 2 points)
- ❏ Describes me somewhat (score 3 points)
- ❏ Describes me well (score 4 points)
- ❏ Describes me very well (score 5 points)

2 If I'm sure I'm right about something, I don't waste much time listening to other people's arguments.
- ❏ Does not describe me at all
- ❏ Does not describe me well
- ❏ Describes me somewhat
- ❏ Describes me well
- ❏ Describes me very well

3 I sometimes try to understand my friends better by imagining how things look from their perspective.
- ❏ Does not describe me at all
- ❏ Does not describe me well
- ❏ Describes me somewhat
- ❏ Describes me well
- ❏ Describes me very well

4 I believe that there are two sides to every question and try to look at them both.
- ❏ Does not describe me at all
- ❏ Does not describe me well

- ❏ Describes me somewhat
- ❏ Describes me well
- ❏ Describes me very well

5 I sometimes find it difficult to see things from the other person's point of view.
- ❏ Does not describe me at all
- ❏ Does not describe me well
- ❏ Describes me somewhat
- ❏ Describes me well
- ❏ Describes me very well

6 I try to look at everybody's side of a disagreement before I make a decision.
- ❏ Does not describe me at all
- ❏ Does not describe me well
- ❏ Describes me somewhat
- ❏ Describes me well
- ❏ Describes me very well

7 When I'm upset at someone, I usually try to "put myself in his/her shoes" for a while.
- ❏ Does not describe me at all
- ❏ Does not describe me well
- ❏ Describes me somewhat
- ❏ Describes me well
- ❏ Describes me very well

Scoring Key

Sense of meaningfulness (use score for #1–2)	_____
Sense of choice (use score for #3–4)	_____
Sense of competence (use score for #5–6)	_____
Sense of progress (use score for #7)	_____
Overall score (add all items)	_____

Arbitrary Norms

The range of possible scores is from 7 to 35 (low perspective taking: 7–15; moderate perspective taking: 16–25; high perspective taking: 26–35). The average score in studies across Canadian groups of people is approximately 20. Also keep in mind that women tend to score about 1.5 points higher than men on this perspective-taking scale.

SOURCES: M.H. Davis, "A multidimensional approach to individual differences in empathy," *JSAS Catalog of Selected Documents in Psychology,* 10 (1980), 85.

AN INFORMATION-PROCESSING MODEL OF PERCEPTION

Perception is a cognitive process that enables us to interpret and understand our surroundings. One of this process's major functions is recognition of objects. For example, both people and animals recognize familiar objects in their environments. You would recognize a picture of your best friend; dogs and cats can recognize their food dishes or a favourite toy. Reading involves recognition of visual patterns representing letters in the alphabet. People must recognize objects to meaningfully interact with their environment.[2] But since OB's principal focus is on people, the following discussion emphasizes social perception rather than object perception.

The study of how people perceive one another has been labelled *social cognition* and *social information processing*. In contrast to the perception of objects, social cognition is the study of how people make sense of other people and themselves. It focuses on how ordinary people think about people. Research on social cognition also goes beyond naive psychology. The study of social cognition entails a fine-grained analysis of how people think about themselves and others, and it leans heavily on the theory and methods of cognitive psychology.[3]

Let's now examine the fundamental processes underlying perception.

Perception

The process of interpreting one's environment.

Social cognition

How people perceive one another.

LO 2 FOUR-STAGE SEQUENCE

Perception involves a four-stage information-processing sequence, as illustrated in Figure 2.1. The first three stages in this model describe how specific social information is observed and stored in memory. The fourth stage involves turning mental representations into real-world judgments and decisions. To practise using this model, you may want to turn to the Experiential Exercise located at the end of this chapter.

Stage 1: Selective Attention/Comprehension People are constantly bombarded by physical and social stimuli in the environment. Since they do not have the mental capacity to fully comprehend all this information, they selectively perceive subsets of environmental stimuli. This is where attention plays a role. *Attention* is the process of becoming consciously aware of something or someone. Attention can be focused on information either from the environment or from memory. Regarding the latter situation, if you sometimes find yourself thinking about totally unrelated events or people while reading a textbook, your memory is the focus of your attention.

Attention

Being consciously aware of something or someone.

Salient Stimuli Research has shown that people tend to pay attention to salient stimuli. Something is *salient* when it stands out from its context. For example, a 2-metre-long alligator living in the bathtub of someone's apartment would certainly be salient to guests or even the tenants living in the apartment across the hall, but not to those visiting a reptile attraction at a local zoo. One's needs and goals often dictate which stimuli are salient. For a driver whose gas gauge is on empty, a Petro-Canada sign is more salient than a McDonald's or Tim Horton's sign. The reverse would be

FIGURE 2.1 Social Perception Model

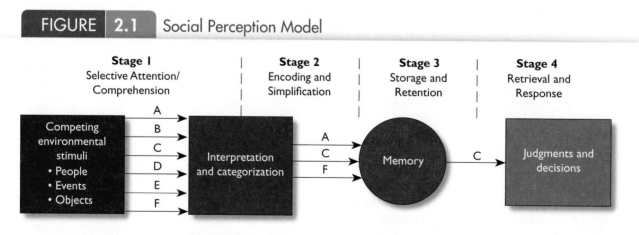

SOURCE: Adapted in part from B.J. Pannett and S. Withane, "Hofstede's Value Survey Module: To Embrace or Abandon?," *Advances in International Comparative Management*, vol 5, ed S.B. Prasad (Greenwich, CT: JAI Press, 1990), pp 69–89.

true for a hungry driver with a full gas tank. Moreover, research shows that people have a tendency to pay more attention to negative than positive information. This leads to a negativity bias.[4] This bias helps explain the gawking factor that slows traffic to a crawl following a car accident.

Stage 2: Encoding and Simplification Observed information is not stored in memory in its original form; encoding is required. Encoding means interpreting or translating raw information into mental representations. To accomplish this, perceivers assign pieces of information to cognitive categories. "By category we mean a number of objects that are considered equivalent. Categories are generally designated by names, e.g., dog, animal."[5] People, events, and objects are interpreted and evaluated by comparing their characteristics with information contained in schemata (or schema in singular form).

Schemata A **schema** represents a person's mental picture or summary of a particular event or type of stimulus. Cognitive-category labels are needed to make schemata meaningful. For example, picture your image of a sports car. Does it contain a smaller vehicle with two doors? Is it red? If you answered yes, you would tend to classify all small, two-door, fire-engine-red vehicles as sports cars because this type of car possesses characteristics that are consistent with your "sports car schema."

schema

Mental picture of an event or object.

Encoding Outcomes We use the encoding process to interpret and evaluate our environment. Interestingly, this process can result in differing interpretations and evaluations of the same person or event. This is where perceptual errors can occur. Table 2.1 describes five common perceptual errors that

can occur in an educational setting. Since these perceptual errors often distort the evaluation of job applicants and of employee performance, managers need to guard against them. Can you think of common office examples where these same perceptual errors could apply? We'll discuss perceptual errors in greater detail a bit later in this chapter.

Stage 3: Storage and Retention This phase involves storage of information in long-term memory. Long-term memory is like the hard drive of your computer. Documents are stored in different files within folders and they are located safely in various locations within your computer. As you know, files can sometimes interact and affect one another—especially if a virus is "hiding" inside one. Some files won't open unless another type of file is present on the hard drive. Well, long-term memory similarly consists of separate but related categories. Like the individual files located within computer folders that are holding unique data, the connected categories of your memory contain different types of information that pass between them. Finally, long-term memory is made up of three compartments containing categories of information about events, semantic materials, and people.[6]

Event Memory This compartment of memory is composed of categories containing information about both specific and general events. These memories describe appropriate sequences of events in well-known situations, such as going to a restaurant, going on a job interview, going to a grocery store, or going to a movie.

Semantic Memory Semantic memory refers to general knowledge about the world. In so doing, it functions as a mental dictionary of concepts. Each concept contains a definition (e.g., a good leader) and associated traits (outgoing), emotional states (happy), physical characteristics (tall), and behaviours (works hard). Just as there are schemata for general events, concepts in semantic memory are stored as schemata.

Person Memory Categories within this compartment contain information about a single individual (a peer) or groups of people (the support staff). These memories help a person evaluate and compare characteristics of a new person or object to the information stored in memory.

Is this consistent with your "sports car schema?" If it is, you'll likely classify all small, two-door, red vehicles as sports cars. Can you think of another example of a common schema in today's culture?

TABLE 2.1

COMMONLY FOUND PERCEPTUAL ERRORS

PERCEPTUAL ERROR	DESCRIPTION	EXAMPLE
Halo	A rater forms an overall impression about an object and then uses that impression to bias ratings about the object.	Rating a professor high on the teaching dimensions of ability to motivate students, knowledge, and communication because he or she is punctual in getting to class.
Leniency	A personal characteristic that leads an individual to consistently evaluate other people or objects in an extremely positive fashion.	Rating a professor high on all dimensions of performance regardless of his or her actual performance. Hesitating to say negative things about others.
Central tendency	The tendency to avoid all extreme judgments and rate people and objects as average or neutral.	Rating a professor average on all dimensions of performance regardless of his or her actual performance.
Recency effects	The tendency to remember recent information. If the recent information is negative, the person or object is evaluated negatively.	Evaluating a professor negatively because lectures over the last three weeks were done poorly, although he or she has given good lectures for 12 to 15 weeks.
Contrast effects	The tendency to evaluate people or objects by comparing them with characteristics of recently observed people or objects.	Rating a good professor as average because you compared his or her performance with three of the best professors you have ever had in university, from whom you are currently taking courses.

Stage 4: Retrieval and Response   People retrieve information from memory when they make judgments and decisions. These judgments and decisions are based on either the process of drawing on, interpreting, and integrating categorical information stored in long-term memory, or retrieving a summary judgment that was already made. For instance, consider how you would feel after your closest colleague at work tells you in confidence that eight years ago your new boss was accused (but not found guilty) of workplace bullying. How long would you hold on to that information in your memory? Do you think that you would always have that knowledge sitting there in the background every time you had to deal with your new boss, just waiting to see any evidence of similar behaviour?

LO 3 MANAGERIAL IMPLICATIONS

Social cognition is the process through which we all observe, interpret, and prepare our responses to people and events. A wide variety of managerial activities, organizational processes, and quality-of-life issues are thus affected by perception. Let's consider the effects of perception on hiring, performance appraisal, leadership, communication, interpersonal influence, workplace aggression, bullying and antisocial behaviour, as well as overall physical and psychological well-being.

Hiring   Interviewers make hiring decisions based on their impression of how an applicant fits the perceived requirements of a job. Unfortunately, many of these decisions are made on the basis of implicit cognition. *Implicit cognition* represents any thoughts or beliefs that are automatically activated without our conscious awareness. The existence of implicit cognition leads people to make biased decisions without an understanding that it is occurring.[7]

Such a tendency was exhibited for many years by the government of British Columbia when they placed false barriers up for females who wanted to become forest firefighters.[8] The infamous gender discrimination case(s) south of the border against Walmart is covered by the media off-and-on, even to this day. You can avoid biased beliefs from influencing the recruitment or selection process by training decision makers to understand and reduce this type of hidden bias. For example, one study demonstrated that training improved interviewers' ability to obtain high-quality job-related

Implicit cognition

Any thought or belief that is automatically activated without conscious awareness.

information and to stay focused on the interview task. Trained interviewers provided more balanced judgments about applicants than did non-trained interviewers.[9] In addition, you can reduce bias by using structured as opposed to unstructured interviews, and by relying on evaluations from multiple interviewers rather than just one or two people.

Performance Appraisal Faulty perceptions about what constitutes good versus poor performance can lead to inaccurate performance appraisals, which erode work motivation, commitment, and loyalty. Therefore, it is important for managers to accurately identify the employee behaviours and results indicative of good performance at the beginning of a performance review cycle. These characteristics can then serve as analytic benchmarks for evaluating employee performance. Managers are advised to use more objectively-based measures of performance as much as possible. For example, if supervisors want to assess the strength of their employees' work ethic, they could look at the attendance pattern of particular employees—do they arrive late in the morning or leave early? These are quantifiable facts and therefore are considered to be objective in nature. But what if the organization wants to measure qualitative factors like cooperative nature, pleasant disposition, eagerness to assist others, and positive attitude? These factors are much harder to measure and can be left to personal interpretation by a supervisor; they are subjective in nature. This type of assessment can be filled with bias and political intent (office politics will be discussed in Chapter 9). Because memory for specific employee performance deteriorates over time, anyone in a position of evaluating another individual needs a mechanism for accurately recalling employee behaviour (work teams where employees evaluate each other will be discussed in Chapter 6). Research reveals that individuals can be trained to more accurately rate performance.[10]

Leadership Research demonstrates that employees' evaluations of leader effectiveness are influenced strongly by their schemata of good and poor leaders. Leaders will have a difficult time influencing employees when they exhibit behaviours contained in employees' schemata of poor leaders. A team of researchers investigated the behaviours contained in our schemata of good leaders. Good leaders were perceived as exhibiting the following behaviours: (1) assigning specific tasks to group members; (2) telling others that they had done well; (3) setting specific goals for the group; (4) letting other group members make decisions; (5) trying to get the group to work as a team; and (6) maintaining definite standards of performance.[11]

Perception colours our interpretation of management behaviours. An employee whose manager multitasks while talking to her is likely to believe that their conversation is not very important. Have you ever been treated this way?

Communication and Interpersonal Influence Managers must remember that social perception is a screening process that can distort communication, both coming and going. Because people interpret oral and written communications by using schemata developed through past experiences, your ability to influence others is affected by information contained in others' schemata regarding age, gender, ethnicity, appearance, speech, mannerisms, personality, and other personal characteristics. It is important to keep this in mind when trying to influence others or when trying to sell your ideas.

Workplace Aggression, Bullying, and Antisocial Behaviour Research revealed that aggressive, bullying, and antisocial behaviour at work are based on employees' perceptions of the work environment. Employees behaved aggressively toward co-workers and displayed antisocial behaviours such as swearing, making fun of someone, and taking home organizational property without consent when they believed that they were treated unfairly.[12] It is very important for managers to treat employees fairly, remembering that perceptions of fairness are in the eye of the beholder. We will speak more about the effects of workplace aggression and recent legislation around workplace bullying in Chapter 8.

Physical and Psychological Well-Being The negativity bias can lead to both physical and psychological problems. Specifically, research shows that perceptions of fear, harm, and anxiety are associated with the onset of illnesses such as asthma and depression.[13] Attempt to avoid the tendency of giving negative thoughts too much attention.

LO 4 # Stereotypes

We'll now examine one of the most important and potentially harmful perceptual outcomes associated with personal perception: stereotypes.

STEREOTYPE FORMATION AND MAINTENANCE

"A *stereotype* is an individual's set of beliefs about the characteristics or attributes of a group."[14] Consider the beliefs some have around how a person looks in terms

> **Stereotype**
>
> Beliefs about the characteristics of a group.

of their weight. What constitutes obese and why is there such a negative bias against people of a certain weight? The International OB feature box discusses how body weight stereotyping is leading to a shift in ideas as weight-based bias goes global.

However, stereotypes are not always negative; for example, the belief that engineers are good at math is certainly part of a stereotype, but you don't see organizations creating hiring policies around such beliefs. Stereotypes may or may not be accurate. Engineers may in fact be better at math than the general population, but being a certain weight does not mean a person is lazy or unsuccessful in life. In general, stereotypic characteristics are used to differentiate a particular group of people from other groups; it is here where bias, prejudice, and discrimination can take place. This is what we want to all attention to.[15]

It is important to remember that stereotypes are a fundamental component

BODY IDEALS SHIFTING AS WEIGHT-BASED BIAS GOES GLOBAL

INTERNATIONAL OB

A new study published in the journal *Current Anthropology* found that the number of societies without negative views about overweight individuals has shrunk in the past few decades. The change comes on the heels of increased global desire for slimness. Places like Paraguay, Puerto Rico, and Samoa, that once valued bigger bodies, now associate overweight with laziness. Since the 1980s, social scientists have been studying the self-perceptions of teenage girls on the South Pacific island of Fiji; the body weight that was once revered and celebrated 25 years ago has teenage girls declaring the need to control their weight through induced vomiting because they are "too fat." According to the researcher who conducted the global study, the greatest surprise was the speed with which attitudes and perceptions about weight-based bias are changing, perhaps from Western ideas and media. "It's this moral judgment that creates prejudice and discrimination," said anthropologist Alexandra Brewis.

Consider the Citizens Medical Centre in Victoria, Texas that issued a controversial hiring policy in 2012 stating that it will not hire anyone with a body mass index (BMI) of 35 or higher. That's the equivalent

of someone who is 1.6 metres tall (5 feet 5 inches) and weighs 95 kilograms (210 pounds). The policy states an employee's physique "should fit with a representational image or specific mental projection of the job of a health-care professional," including an appearance that is "free from distraction."

These negative stereotypes that overweight people are lazy, unhealthy, or unprofessional carry stigma and broad implications that can permeate our entire society. In some regions, they are considered biased, prejudicial, and discriminating.

In Britain, an all-party parliamentary group recently released a report called *Reflections on Body Image*, suggesting that MPs are considering putting "appearance-based discrimination" on the same legal basis as race and sex discrimination. Do you agree that stereotyping is a form of moral judgment that can lead to prejudice and discrimination?

SOURCES: K. Goldhar and S. Higgins, "Outlawing Weight Discrimination, *CBC Radio–The Current*, June 1, 2012; A. Silliker. "U.S. Hospital Balks at Hiring Obese Workers," *Canadian HR Reporter*, May 21, 2012, p 1; and S. Pappas. "Slim is in as Fat Stigma Goes Global," *LiveScience*, March 30, 2011, www.livescience. com/13478-fat-stigma-spreads.html

of the perception process and we use them to help process the large amount of information that bombards us daily. As such, it is not immoral or bad to possess stereotypes. That said, however, inappropriate use of stereotypes can lead to poor decisions; create barriers for women, older individuals, people of colour, or people with disabilities; and undermine loyalty and job satisfaction. In other words, negative stereotyping can lead to workplace barriers through discrimination. When this happens, then personal prejudice occurs, meaning that a shortcut in judgment is made about someone without being fair. Can you see how negative stereotyping can lead to discrimination because of personal prejudices? When this happens in the workplace, opportunities are not equal to all who apply for jobs, and that is not only unethical, but also illegal (see the Law and Ethics at Work feature box). It's important to recognize errors in perception and shortcuts to processing our perceptions as they can lead to dangerous practices within an organization—especially when they unconsciously evolve into formalized policies and procedures.

Stereotyping is a four-step process, as illustrated in Figure 2.2. It begins by categorizing people into groups according to various criteria, such as gender, age, race, and occupation. Next, we infer that all people within a particular category possess the same traits or characteristics (e.g., all women are nurturing and older people have more job-related accidents). Then, we form expectations of others and interpret their behaviour according to our stereotypes. Finally, stereotypes are maintained by overestimating the frequency of stereotypic behaviours exhibited by others, incorrectly explaining expected and unexpected behaviours, and differentiating minority individuals from oneself.[16] It is hard to stop people from using stereotypes because these four steps are self-reinforcing. The good news, however, is that researchers have identified a few ways to break the chain of stereotyping. Research shows that the use of stereotypes is influenced by the amount and type of information available to individuals and their motivation to accurately process information.[17] People are less apt to use stereotypes to judge others when they encounter salient information that is highly inconsistent with a stereotype. For instance, you are unlikely to

CANADA'S BARRIER-REMOVAL LEGISLATION

When it comes to offering jobs or promotional opportunities to visible minorities, the *Canadian Charter of Rights and Freedoms* provides clear protection for all from discriminating business practices. But that wasn't always the case. When the Charter was first drafted in the early 1980s, persons with disabilities were not included among the protected classes of persons enumerated in Section 15. As a result of an intense and effective lobbying effort by a number of groups, the government relented and added the category "mental and physical disability." Section 15 now reads:

Every individual is equal before and under the law and has the right to the protection and equal benefit of

the law without discrimination and, in particular, without discrimination based on race, national or ethnic origin, colour, religion, sex, age, mental or physical disability.

Today, employees with disabilities, as well as all visible minorities, can find protection under the Charter or Canadian Human Rights Legislation. Do you think it was necessary to modify Section 15?

SOURCE: Adapted from the Council of Canadians with Disabilities, Law Reform Analysis, May 14, 1999, www.ccdonline.ca; Canadian Human Rights Commission, www.chrc-ccdp.ca/legislation_policies/human_rights_act-en.asp; and The Canadian Charter of Rights and Freedoms – The Canadian Encyclopedia, www.thecanadianencyclopedia.com/index.cfm?PgNm=TCE&Params=A1ARTA0001270.

FIGURE 2.2 Four-Step Process of Stereotyping

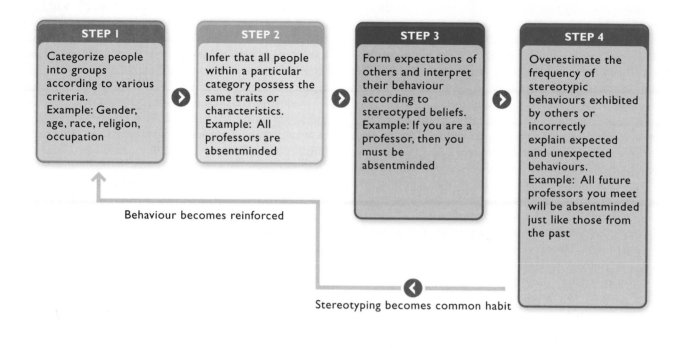

STEP 1

Categorize people into groups according to various criteria. Example: Gender, age, race, religion, occupation

STEP 2

Infer that all people within a particular category possess the same traits or characteristics. Example: All professors are absentminded

STEP 3

Form expectations of others and interpret their behaviour according to stereotyped beliefs. Example: If you are a professor, then you must be absentminded

STEP 4

Overestimate the frequency of stereotypic behaviours exhibited by others or incorrectly explain expected and unexpected behaviours. Example: All future professors you meet will be absentminded just like those from the past

Behaviour becomes reinforced

Stereotyping becomes common habit

assign stereotypic "professor" traits to a new professor you have this semester if she rides a Harley-Davidson, wears leather pants to class, and has a pierced nose.

People are also less likely to rely on stereotypes when they are motivated. Let's consider, for example, a situation where you are looking for a job and you really need the money badly because of all of the school debt you've incurred. To your delight, an opening comes up at a company in your town that involves working alongside another individual. After a successful interview, where you claim to be a team player, they offer you the position. On the first day, you're introduced to your new colleague, a female Canadian Aboriginal. You've never worked with an Aboriginal individual before. This has you seriously concerned and cautious because of stereotype comments made by colleagues, friends, and/or family over the years. Rather than quit because of this, you decide to give the job a chance. After one week, you decide to stay at the job. Working alongside your new colleague turns out to be a non-issue because the motivation to earn money to pay off debts takes precedence over your possibly stereotypical behaviour.

Sex-role stereotype

Beliefs about appropriate roles for men and women.

We'll now turn our attention to four common forms of stereotypes: sex-role, age, racial and ethnic, as well as disability. It's important for you to become familiar with these different stereotypes so you can avoid them in your own behaviour, and also be aware in case you witness such behaviour in a future work environment.

Sex-Role Stereotypes A *sex-role stereotype* is the belief that differing traits and abilities make men and women particularly well suited to different roles. A recent survey of 61,647 people—50 percent female and 50 percent male—sheds light on common sex-role stereotypes. Results revealed that women were labelled as moody, gossipy, emotional, and catty. A similar set of negative stereotypes was not uncovered when it came to perceptions about men. When asked who would be more likely to lead effectively, males were preferred by a two-to-one margin by both men and women.[18] Researchers suggest that this pattern of results is related to gender-based expectations or stereotypes that people have about men and women.[19] The key question, however, is whether or not these stereotypes influence the hiring, evaluation, and promotion of people at work.

A meta-analysis of 19 studies comprising 1,842 individuals found no significant relationships between applicant gender and hiring recommendations.[20] A second meta-analysis of 24 experimental studies revealed that men and women received similar performance ratings for the same level of task performance. Stated differently, there was no pro-male bias. These experimental results were further supported in a field study of female and male professors.[21] Unfortunately, results pertaining to promotion decisions are not as promising. A field study of 682 employees in a multinational Fortune 500 company demonstrated that gender was significantly related to promotion potential ratings. Men received more favourable evaluations than women, in spite of controlling for age, education, organizational tenure, salary grade, and type of job.[22] Another study of 448 upper-level managers showed that gender bias influenced the performance ratings and promotional opportunities for women, particularly when women work in non-traditional jobs. The researchers conducting this study concluded that sex-role stereotypes partially explain these findings.[23]

Age Stereotypes Age stereotypes reinforce age discrimination because of their negative orientation. For example, long-standing age stereotypes depict older workers as less satisfied, not as involved with their work, less motivated, not as committed, less productive, and more apt to be absent from work than younger co-workers. Older employees are also perceived as being more accident prone. OB researcher Susan Rhodes sought to determine whether age stereotypes were supported by data from 185 different studies. She discovered that as age increases, so do employees' job satisfaction, job involvement, internal work motivation, and organizational commitment. Moreover, older workers are not more accident prone.[24]

Results are not as clear-cut regarding job performance. A meta-analysis of 96 studies representing 38,983 people and a cross-section of jobs revealed that age and job performance are unrelated.[25] Some OB researchers, however, believe that this finding does not reflect the true relationship between age and performance. They propose that the relationship between age and performance changes as people grow older.[26] This idea was tested on data obtained from 24,219 individuals. In support of this hypothesis, results revealed that age is positively related to performance for younger employees (25 to 30 years of age) and then plateaus: older employees are not less productive. Age and experience also better predict performance for

more complex jobs than other jobs, and job experience has a stronger relationship with performance than age.[27]

Another study examined memory, reasoning, spatial relations, and dual tasking for 1,000 doctors, ages 25 to 92, and 600 other adults. The researchers concluded "that a large proportion of older individuals scored as well or better on aptitude tests as those in the prime of life. We call these intellectually vigorous individuals 'optimal agers.'"[28]

What about turnover and absenteeism? A meta-analysis containing 45 samples and a total of 21,656 individuals revealed that age and turnover are negatively related.[29] That is, older employees quit less often than younger employees quit. Similarly, another meta-analysis of 34 studies encompassing 7,772 workers indicated that age is inversely related to both voluntary (a day at the beach) and involuntary (sick day) absenteeism.[30] Contrary to stereotypes, older workers are ready and able to meet their job requirements. Moreover, results from the two meta-analyses suggest that decision makers should focus more attention on the turnover and absenteeism among younger workers than among older workers.

Racial and Ethnic Stereotypes Racial and ethnic stereotypes are typically unfavourable and particularly problematic because they are automatically triggered and lead to racial bias without our conscious awareness.[31] For example, if British people tend to be reserved, it is fairly easy to interpret this reserve as snobbishness and arrogance. These kind of stereotypes are often activated by obvious language differences, facial features, or skin colour.[32] This practice came to light after 9–11 when Canadian and United States border customs officers were accused of using racial profiling on the job. In 2011, a Rogers Communications customer service agent accused Toronto police of racial profiling and discrimination after he was targeted and arrested on bogus charges that were later dropped.[33]

According to Statistics Canada Census data, despite being more highly educated than non-visible minorities, visible minorities have higher unemployment rates than their counterparts, namely 9.5 percent to 7.1 percent. As a follow-up to the census data, The Canadian Centre for Justice Statistics in Ottawa compiled a report from their own study and found that the proportion of visible minorities who felt they had experienced discrimination was twice that of non-visible minorities. Overall, 81 percent of visible minorities who felt that they had experienced discrimination believed that it was because of their race or ethnic origin.[34]

When it comes to ethnic stereotyping within organizations, it becomes harder to prove that higher unemployment rates are a direct result of stereotyping. Many anecdotal stories suggest that it may be occurring, but on a subtle level. Take, for instance, the case involving the United Parcel Service (UPS) at their Mississauga, Ontario sorting plant. The UPS manager claimed that he had to fire eight Muslim women because they refused to follow the dress code that was put into place for health and safety reasons. The women, all part-time workers, refused to hike their ankle-length skirts above the knee over their long pants. The UPS manager told the Human Rights tribunal that was investigating the complaint that the way the women dressed was a safety hazard, as workers were expected to climb ladders up to six metres high. The women claimed their dismissal was more than that. The discrimination case was settled with the mediation assistance of both the tribunal and the Worker's Action Centre organization, but the terms of the agreement were kept secret.[35]

In a fairly recent UN report, Canada was cited as not doing enough in the area of racial and Aboriginal issues, including providing training and employment opportunities.[36] John Sims, deputy minister of the Department of Justice, was the head of the 20-person delegation that presented Canada's case in Geneva. In his response, Sims said, "Canada recognized that no country, including Canada, has a perfect human rights record." He acknowledged Canada's efforts and challenges when it came to areas like Native rights.[37]

On a more positive note, a paper by Professor Krishna Pendakur, of Simon Fraser University, suggests that changes in visible minority labour market performance across cities will fare well in Canada's future. As more natural integration takes place, barriers to employment opportunities because of racial and ethnic stereotyping will decrease.[38] Enlightened employers like Correctional Services Canada (see the Focus on Diversity feature box) have developed ways to accommodate visible minorities and different religious groups.

Disability Stereotypes   People with disabilities not only face negative stereotypes that affect their employability, but they also can be stigmatized by the general population. These trends create a host of problems for people with disabilities. For example, Canadians with disabilities are more likely to be unemployed, and they are also

CORRECTIONAL SERVICE OF CANADA HIRES FIRST FEMALE MUSLIM PRISON GUARD

The Correctional Service of Canada (CSC) is responsible for the supervision of offenders serving sentences of two or more years and for their safe reintegration into society. CSC has a little more than 16,000 employees; approximately 5,100 of these are correctional officers. In late 2010, CSC reported hiring its first female Muslim correctional officer who, after a nine-week training program in Ontario, was assigned as a guard in a men's federal penitentiary. After processing the recruit's application, the CSC formed a working group to identify ways to address both the employer's and employee's needs. A special hijab head covering as well as a breathing apparatus that works with the hijab were developed. The employee worked with CSC to develop a schedule for prayers during break times as well as developing other mutually agreeable practices related to her job.

As an employer, the CSC strives to create a diverse workforce that reflects both the prison population and Canadian society at large. According to CSC national spokesman Graham Andrews, 6 percent of the staff are visible minorities, 7.9 percent are aboriginal, 4.6 percent are people with disabilities, and 47.6 percent are women. CSC drew both criticism and applause for taking steps to accommodate the religious and cultural practices of the new female Muslim employee. Some felt the CSC acted politically correct, while others believed religious faith should not be a factor on the job for any employee.

SOURCES: "A Career With The Correctional Service of Canada – Join Us!" Government of Canada - CSC website www.csc-scc.gc.ca/text/index-eng.shtml; "Corrections Canada Hires First Female Muslim Guard," *QMI Agency/Toronto Sun*, December 10, 2010, www.torontosun.com/news/canada/2010/12/10/16507931.html; "Accommodation – Muslim Guard Gets Exceptions" *London Free Press*, Dec 13, 2010, p B3.

FOCUS ON DIVERSITY

far more likely to be living at the bottom of the income scale. Among adults aged 25 to 54 with disabilities, 47 percent have a personal income below $15,000, compared with only 25 percent of those without disabilities. Lower income and high unemployment rates are largely the result of lower educational attainment among adults with disabilities. In fact, Canadian adults with a disability are nearly two times less likely to obtain university credentials as compared to those without a disability.[39]

Martha Johnson, an IT specialist at TD Canada Trust, says the bank works hard to assist employees with disabilities.

In Ontario, organizations that provide goods or services to the public or a third party are required to have physically accessible workplaces as per the Accessibility Standards for Customer Service under the *Accessibility for Ontarians with Disabilities Act* (AODA). The customer service standard came into effect January 1, 2012 for the private sector; it had already been established in the public sector a year prior. This standard may be the first of its kind in the country, but similar legislation is likely to follow in other jurisdictions according to Jennifer Miller, principal at Accessibility Consultants and Trainers. Under AODA, an organization could be fined up to $100,000 per day or part of a day that an offence occurs, and directors and officers may be fined up to $50,000. To avoid legal issues with high financial impact, employers need to take the accommodation of disabilities seriously and follow their obligation to accommodate under the *Canadian Human Rights Act*.[40]

Being aware of the myths around disability stereotypes is important when designing a successful business model; see the Skills and Best Practices feature box for more on how one franchise owner has lowered his turnover rate by hiring individuals with intellectual disabilities.

Causal Attributions

Another very important perception relates to the causes of observed behaviour. Attributions are perceptions regarding the causes of observed behaviour. Rightly or wrongly, we constantly formulate cause-and-effect explanations for our own and others' behaviour. Attributional statements such as the following are

Skills & Best Practices

Understanding Perceptual Process Can Assist Business Model Design

Organizations that are aware of the perceptual process and its outcomes enjoy a competitive edge. Take, for example Mark Wafer, a Toronto-based Tim Horton's franchise owner who, 17 years ago, hired an employee with an intellectual disability. Over the years, Wafer has hired more than 50 people with intellectual disabilities, and his stores experience a 45 percent lower turnover rate compared to industry averages.

"This is not because I am a better operator, it is simply because we have created an inclusive workplace where people with disabilities are treated as equals," said Wafer, who is partly deaf.

Wafer, who owns seven franchise stores, has become an advocate, encouraging other companies to hire people with disabilities as part of their business model.

Wafer believes that too often business owners, hiring managers, and human resource managers buy into the myths and misconception that people with disabilities will work slower, be sick more often, show up late, work in a less safe manner, or that accommodations will cost too much. "They are just that—myths! Telling owners to hire a person with a disability, that it is the right thing to do, simply doesn't work," said Wafer. "We have to show them how they will benefit and how their company will be stronger, be more profitable, (and) have higher staff morale."

SOURCES: "Workers with Disabilities – Tim Horton's Franchisor Serves Jobs," *Canadian HR Reporter,* June 6, 2011, p 12; "Workplace Bias Towards Hiring Canadians With Disabilities," *The National Benefit Authority,* November 7, 2011, www.disabilityliving.ca/disability-canada-workplace-bias-towards-hiring/; and "A Hire Awareness," National Disability Employment Awareness Month 2010, www.ndeam.ca/home.shtml.

common: "Joe drinks too much because he has no willpower; but I need a couple of drinks after work because I'm under a lot of pressure." Formally defined, *causal attributions* are the perceived causes of behaviour. It is important to understand how people formulate attributions, because they profoundly affect organizational behaviour. For example, a supervisor who attributes an employee's poor performance to a lack of effort might reprimand that individual. However,

Causal attributions

Suspected or inferred causes of behaviour.

training might be deemed necessary if the supervisor attributes the poor performance to a lack of ability.

Generally speaking, people formulate causal attributions by considering the events preceding an observed behaviour. Attribution theory proposes that behaviour can be attributed either to internal factors within a person (such as ability), or to external factors within the environment (such as a difficult task). See Figure 2.3

FIGURE 2.3 Causal Attributions Around Three Dimensions

CONSENSUS: Suri looks at a new student in class and compares the student to her current friends.

She's not like us and she dresses differently!

DISTINCTIVENESS: Suri observes the new student answering questions during class one day and is impressed with the responses.

Wow, that new girl sure answered that question well—better than anyone else in class!

CONSISTENCY: Suri decides the new student is smart because every time she gives a response during class, the teacher agrees with her.

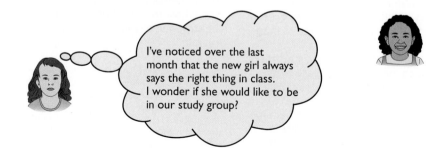

I've noticed over the last month that the new girl always says the right thing in class. I wonder if she would like to be in our study group?

for an example of how people make causal attributions after gathering information about three dimensions of behaviour: consensus, distinctiveness, and consistency.[41] These dimensions vary independently, thus forming various combinations and leading to differing attributions.

- *Consensus* involves a perceiver comparing an individual's behaviour with that of his or her peers. There is high consensus when the individual acts like the rest of the group and low consensus when the individual acts differently.

- *Distinctiveness* is determined by a perceiver comparing an individual's behaviour on one task with the individual's behaviour on other tasks. High distinctiveness means the individual performs the task in question in a significantly different manner than he or she performed other tasks. Low distinctiveness means stable performance or quality from one task to another.

- *Consistency* is determined when a perceiver judges if an individual's performance on a given task is consistent over time. High consistency implies that the individual performs a certain task the same, time after time. Unstable performance of a given task over time would mean low consistency.

It is important to remember that consensus relates to other *people*, distinctiveness relates to other *tasks*, and consistency relates to *time*. The question now is: How does information about these three dimensions of behaviour lead to internal or external attributions?

People attribute behaviour to external causes (environmental factors) when they perceive high consensus, high distinctiveness, and low consistency. Internal attributions (personal factors) tend to be made when observed behaviour is characterized by low consensus, low distinctiveness, and high consistency. So, for example, when all employees are performing poorly (high consensus), when the poor performance occurs on only one of several tasks (high distinctiveness), and the poor performance occurs during only one time period (low consistency), a supervisor will probably attribute an employee's poor performance to an external source such as peer pressure or an overly difficult task. In contrast, performance will be attributed to an employee's personal characteristics (an internal attribution) when only the individual in question is performing poorly (low consensus), when the inferior performance is found across several tasks (low distinctiveness), and when the low performance has persisted over time (high consistency). Many studies support this predicted pattern of attributions.[42]

ATTRIBUTIONAL TENDENCIES

Researchers have uncovered two attributional tendencies that distort one's interpretation of observed behaviour—*fundamental attribution bias* and *self-serving bias*.

Fundamental Attribution Bias The *fundamental attribution bias* reflects the tendency to attribute behaviour to personal characteristics as opposed to situational factors. This bias causes perceivers to ignore important environmental forces that often significantly affect behaviour. For example, consider a scenario involving a sales clerk we'll call Pat at a retail store, who is being evaluated by his supervisor two weeks before Christmas. Let's say there is a shortage of help because of a firing and another clerk is expected to be away ill for the next week, leaving no one to straighten up the merchandise on the floor or circulate around asking "may I help you" kinds of questions to potential customers. The clerks who are scheduled, including Pat, pick up the slack and do the best they can under the circumstances. It doesn't come as a surprise when customer complaints around poor customer service and messy merchandise presentations are received. If the supervisor attributes these complaints solely to Pat's personal characteristic deficiencies, then the supervisor has ignored all the situational factors that played a role during this time period. Such a fundamental attribution bias is not an accurate judgment of the situation.

> *Fundamental attribution bias*
>
> Ignoring environmental factors that affect behaviour.

Self-Serving Bias The *self-serving bias* represents **LO 5** one's tendency to take more personal responsibility for success than for failure. Employees tend to attribute their successes to internal factors (high ability and/or hard work) and their failures to uncontrollable external factors (tough job, bad luck, unproductive co-workers, or an unsympathetic boss).[43] For example, if you were to go for a job interview and not get the job, would you say the interview questions were too difficult or unfair, or the timing of the interview disadvantaged you? If this happened, then you would be using self-serving bias to explain the situation, especially if you were out the night before partying, were unable to answer questions during the interview because you didn't do any research prior to the visit, wore ripped jeans and a ball cap on your head, and answered your cell phone during the interview! Instead, you blame the lack of a job offer from this firm on factors you believe could not be controlled; you believe you were a victim of someone else's bias.

> *Self-serving bias*
>
> Taking more personal responsibility for success than failure.

But what if you are offered a promotion at your job? If you believe you have earned the promotion because of your hard work and good work ethic, then telling you that no one else applied or wanted the job wouldn't be a factor for consideration. Instead, you attribute the promotion to the fact that you were the best candidate for the job. You believe you controlled all the variables in this situation.

MANAGERIAL APPLICATION AND IMPLICATIONS

Attribution models can be used to explain how managers handle poorly performing employees. One study revealed that managers gave employees more immediate, frequent, and negative feedback when they attributed their performance to low effort. This reaction was even more pronounced when the manager's success was dependent on an employee's performance. A second study indicated that managers tended to transfer employees whose poor performance was attributed to a lack of ability. These same managers also decided to take no immediate action when poor performance was attributed to external factors beyond an individual's control.[44]

The preceding situations have several important implications for managers. First, managers tend to disproportionately attribute behaviour to internal causes.[45]

This can result in inaccurate evaluations of performance, leading to reduced employee motivation. No one likes to be blamed because of factors they perceive to be beyond their control. Further, because managers' responses to employee performance vary according to their attributions, attributional biases may lead to inappropriate managerial actions, including promotions, transfers, layoffs, and so forth. This can dampen motivation and performance. Attributional training sessions for managers are in order. Basic attributional processes can be explained, and managers can be taught to detect and avoid these biases. Finally, employees' attributions for their own performance have dramatic effects on subsequent motivation, performance, and personal attitudes such as self-esteem. For instance, people tend to give up, develop lower expectations for future success, and experience decreased self-esteem when they attribute failure to a lack of ability. In contrast, employees are more likely to display high performance and job satisfaction when they attribute success to internal factors such as ability and effort.[46] Fortunately, attributional realignment can improve both motivation and performance. The goal of attributional realignment is to shift failure attributions away from ability and toward attributions of low effort or some other external cause (e.g., lack of resources).

Summary of Learning Objectives

 Define *perception* and *causal attributions*. Perception is a cognitive process that enables you to interpret and understand your surroundings. It is possible that during the cognitive process of gathering information, certain external variables can have a salient stimuli effect, or perhaps internal bias can cause errors in judgment. Causal attributions are suspected or inferred causes of behaviour. Attribution theory is based on the premise that people attempt to infer causes for observed behaviour. Rightly or wrongly, we constantly formulate cause-and-effect explanations for our own and others' behaviour.

 Explain perception in terms of the four-stage social cognition processing sequence. Social perception, also referred to as social cognition, is the study of how people perceive one another, and it is best explained with a four-stage process. The four stages are selective attention/comprehension, encoding and simplification, storage and retention, and retrieval and response. During social cognition, salient stimuli are assigned to cognitive categories and stored in long-term memory.

LO 3 **Illustrate six managerial implications of social perceptions.** Social perception affects hiring decisions, performance appraisals, leadership perceptions, communication processes, workplace aggression and antisocial behaviour, and physical and psychological well-being. Inaccurate

schemata or racist and sexist schemata may be used to evaluate job applicants. Similarly, faulty schemata about what constitutes good versus poor performance can lead to inaccurate performance appraisals. Invalid schemata need to be identified and replaced with appropriate schemata through coaching and training. Further, managers are advised to use objective rather than subjective measures of performance. With respect to leadership, leaders will have a difficult time influencing employees when they exhibit behaviours contained in employees' schemata of poor leaders. Because people interpret oral and written communications by using schemata developed through past experiences, an individual's ability to influence others is affected by information contained in others' schemata regarding age, gender, ethnicity, appearance, speech, mannerisms, personality, and other personal characteristics. It is very important to treat employees fairly, as perceptions of unfairness are associated with aggressive and antisocial behaviour.

LO 4 **Examine the managerial challenges and recommendations of sex-role, age, racial/ethnic, and disability stereotypes.** The key managerial challenge is to reduce the extent to which stereotypes influence decision making and interpersonal processes throughout the organization. Training can be used to educate employees about the problem of stereotyping and to equip managers with the skills needed to handle situations associated with managing employees with disabilities. Because mixed-group contact reduces stereotyping, organizations should create opportunities for diverse employees to meet and work together in cooperative groups of equal status. Hiring decisions should be based on valid individual differences, and managers can be trained to use valid criteria when evaluating employee performance. Minimizing differences in job opportunities and experiences across groups of people can help alleviate promotional barriers. It is critical to obtain top management's commitment and support to eliminate stereotyping and discriminatory decisions.

LO 5 **Compare and contrast fundamental attribution bias and self-serving bias.** Fundamental attribution bias involves emphasizing personal factors more than situational factors while formulating causal attributions for the behaviour of others. Self-serving bias involves personalizing the causes of one's successes and externalizing the causes of one's failures.

Discussion Questions

1. Why is it important for decision-makers to have a working knowledge of perception and attribution?

2. Have you ever been stereotyped by someone? If so, what were the conditions under which you experienced it and how did it make you feel?

3. Can you think of an example of salient stimuli?

4. Can you think of an example of someone you know who has used self-serving bias? Try and recall the situation for your classmates.

5. Is it possible for individuals NOT to constantly formulate cause-and-effect explanations for their own and others' behaviour? Explain.

Integration of OB Concepts—Discussion Questions

1. Review Chapter 1. Discuss the role of social perception and its effects on workplace diversity.

Google Searches

1. **Google Search:** "common stereotypes about Canadians" Identify at least three stereotypes and share them with your classmates. Discuss how such stereotype makes people feel.

2. **Google Search:** "self serving bias" Identify at least two examples from various sites that can help clarify this concept. Share your examples with the rest of the class.

3. **Google Search:** Compare and contrast Section 15 of the "Canadian Charter of Rights and Freedoms" to the purpose of the *Canadian Human Rights Act* under the "Canadian Human Rights Commission." How do these documents support one another, especially when it comes to fair treatment in the workplace?

4. **Google Search:** "Gender discrimination at Walmart" OR "Paying to Hire Older Workers In Australia until 2016" Identify the kinds of discrimination cases over the last five years brought before the courts involving Walmart. What were the major concerns of the complainants and are they still happening? How much is the federal government in Australia paying for organizations to hire a person over the age of 50? Do you agree with public funds being used in such a way? In your opinion, should Canada institute the same policy?

5. **Google Search:** "Meiorin Case Supreme Court of Canada" What were the facts related to this precedent setting case? What is a bona fide occupational requirement (BOR), and what does it have to do with preventing perceptual bias and potential discrimination?

Experiential Exercise

Perception Group Exercise

PURPOSE   This exercise is meant to help familiarize you with the OB concept of social perception. Approx. Timing: 20 minutes.

ACTIVITY ASSIGNMENT:

Work in teams of three or four members each. Each person should have his or her own sheet of paper to write responses.

■ Step #1: Without speaking or discussing with anyone, silently recall the first day of organizational behaviour class. Write as much as you can remember about that first day. What occurred? Who said what? Who sat where? What topics did people speak about? Who spoke the most? The least? Focus on as many "people-events" as possible. From your perspective, try and list in order of occurrence all that happened. Write your own reflection on the paper in front of you. Do not share at this point. (5 minutes)

- Step #2: Take turns in your team reading out loud your written responses. As each member goes through the list of events, cross off near-identical events on your own sheet. (5 minutes)

- Step #3: After all members of the teams have read their lists, create a new master list of those events that occurred that were unique and only mentioned by one or a few. When complete, add up the number of unusual and/or unique events to arrive at a total. (3 minutes)

- Step #4: Answer the following questions: (7 minutes)

  1. How is it possible that your team members would have different perceptions of the same event?

  2. Turn to Figure 2.1 and consider the social perception model to explain the differences in your responses.

OB in Action Case Study

Lockout at Electro-Motive Diesel Inc.

SCENARIO BACKGROUND:

Ralph Zapke is a full-time tenured unionized employee at Electro-Motive Diesel Inc. (EMD), a Canadian subsidiary of a large US transnational corporation located in London, Ontario that makes locomotives. In early 2012, Zapke joined 420 other unionized employees on a picket line due to a lock out by EMD. The issue came to a head in January when the management at EMD asked unionized workers to take 50 to 55 percent wage and benefit cuts under a new contract offer to keep their jobs in London. Zapke's pay would be reduced to $18 per hour if such cuts were made. He doesn't want to be out on the street protesting the lockout because that's not how he defines himself, and he doesn't feel comfortable being confrontational with his employer. Zapke enjoys working at EMD and wishes the whole thing would go away. He is worried about what is going to happen and fears the worst, "I think they want to starve us out."

RALF ZAPKE

Soft-spoken Ralf Zapke is 49 years old and joined EMD 19 years ago as a welder. He is near the top of the pay scale, earning $32.91/hour. Before joining EMD at the age of 30, he worked for ten years at the old Stelco plant in Hamilton (now named US Steel Canada), but left when he learned about the EMD opportunity. For the first ten years at EMD, his training and hard work paid off; the company was pleased with his welding work and approached him to apply for a new position as an overhead crane operator. At first he wasn't sure he wanted the job. It was intimidating just thinking about being in a glass-floored cab 12 metres (40 feet) in the air, especially given his fear of heights, not to mention the skill of maneuvering a 30-tonne engine onto a locomotive platform. However, the welding fumes at Stelco were getting to him. "I had been sucking in smoke for 25 years of my life, so I decided it was a good time to make a change (to accept the crane operator position at EMD). I got over the height thing. I got very good at my job to the point where they made me a trainer, training the new recruits coming in on the crane crew."

Zapke finds it hard to believe that in his nineteenth year at EMD he is in this difficult situation. Not only is he in a lock out situation at his job, but he is also using his sick benefits battling cancer. Not knowing what the future holds or the kind of wages he will have to go back to once the strike is over—"If I have a job to go back to"—Zapke and his wife, Lise, put their two-bedroom bungalow up for sale two weeks into the lock out. The couple plan to move closer to Lise's job. She earns about $16 an hour working part-time at the Beer Store.

EMD INC.

EMD Inc., a locomotive manufacturing plant, is a privately owned Canadian subsidiary of Caterpillar Inc. located in Peoria, Illinois. EMD has been operating in London for over 60 years and has enjoyed relatively stable labour relations with its employees. At the time of strike, the plant was employing 700 people, with nearly 500 unionized members represented by the CAW. Management faced increasing pressure from their US parent company to cut costs at the plant, resulting in an offer to its unionized workers to take up to a 55 percent wage cut or face possible layoffs. The workers voted to reject the offer (twice), resulting in the firm locking the workers out. EMD was purchased by Caterpillar three years earlier. According to the purchasing department at EMD, at the time of the lockout Caterpillar Inc. had more than $7 billion in orders on the books for the next three years: 300 locomotives in 2012, 700 in 2013, and 800 in 2014.

Three weeks into the lockout, a top executive at EMD Inc. made a public statement that the London factory lockout was not hurting the firm's ability to meet demand, "Our employees and suppliers have done a great job taking care of our customers, but we have to be prepared for recovery in the developed world beyond 2012 and continuing growth in emerging markets." Around the same time, the following financial performance data was reported in the media:

- D. Oberhelman, CEO Caterpillar Inc.: approximately $10 million (US) annual salary

- EMD Inc.: $4.9 billion (US) in profit on $60.1 billion (US) in revenue last year (highest in their corporate history)

- Revenue forecast: $68–$72 billion (US)

THE FOLLOW-UP

Six months after EMD locked out the workers, Bob Scott, the CAW chairperson for the London EMD plant, was quoted as saying only 70 of the 481 former EMD workers had found work. Further, the media reported that Caterpillar had offered contract employment in Muncie, Indiana and Brazil to some of the same men and women that worked at the London plant. When contacted, one worker defended his move when asked why he took the job in Muncie, saying he had a family in London to support and good-paying work was tough to come by. "When you have the skill set I do, it is very specific to this industry. I have a trade and I have to apply that trade. I will work where I can," said the former worker. He was training workers on site and said there were about six other former EMD employees doing similar work. They were making more than $330 a day at the time of this writing (approximately $41/hour over an eight-hour day).

CANADIAN WORKER DEMOGRAPHIC & STATISTICS

Older workers who face a sudden layoff rarely match their previous earnings upon re-employment and, as a result, many retire early, according to a study by the Institute for Research on Public Policy (IRPP) in Montreal. The 2011 study *Labour Force Participation of Older Displaced Workers In Canada: Should I Stay or Should I Go?*, reported that one-quarter of workers laid off between the ages of 45 and 59 leave the workforce within five years. Among those aged 60–64, the proportion rises to nearly 70 percent. This is due largely to the inability to find a new job with a comparable salary. The implication of the study is clear: Canada is losing people, perhaps forever, from the labour force because it seems the only way they can get a job now is to take a tremendous wage cut. David Gray, a co-author of the study, said, "A lot of them simply throw in the towel and try to finesse an early retirement." Workers aged 45 to 64 who find a job after they have been laid off typically see earning losses of about 40 percent relative to earnings in their previous job. Older laid-off workers tend to have more difficulty finding a new position if they held a high degree of seniority at their previous job. The higher up they were, the longer they were likely working with that particular company, and the less likely they are to find work in that area.

Discussion Questions

1. Looking at the big picture, after so many years of having relatively stable labour relations, can you identify the various kinds of possible internal and/or external pressures facing EMD management that would cause them to react in such a way toward the 420 workers?

2. Why is Ralf Zapke worried and what are some of the possible outcomes of the situation he finds himself in?

3. Why are there so few workers in Canada over the age of 55? In your opinion, is it their choice to self-select out of the labour market OR is age discrimination taking place among employers?

SOURCES: N. De Bono, "Some EMD Workers Back With Cat," *The London Free Press,* June 26, 2012, p A4; D. Carruthers, "Managers Move Into Electro-Motive," *The London Free Press*, January 4, 2012, p A1j and A. Silliker, "Lack of Comparable Earnings Drives Older Displaced Workers To Retire Early," *Canadian HR Reporter*, March 28, 2011, p N3.

The CONNECTion Zone   Mc Graw Hill connect™

■ The Presentation Assistant
■ Ethical OB Dilemma
■ Video Case

Practise and learn online with Connect.

CHAPTER 3

Self Concept, Personality, and Emotions

I put my foot in my mouth all the time, especially at work. I told my last boss that one of her newly hired executives was a dummy—and I got fired. A month into another job, I humiliated a partner in front of the whole team. I didn't intend to personally attack any of these people. I just saw the damage they were doing to the company and didn't respect them for that. I am, however, tired of coming across as arrogant and a loose cannon. Sometimes I just get blinded by other people's stupidity. My current boss has offered to hire a coach. But that would embarrass me too much. One executive who fired me told me I was the most competent person he's ever worked with, but that was clearly not enough.

—MY FAULT EVERYONE'S A DUMMY?

People Are Different

To some employees, the world would be a much better place if everyone acted and thought just like they did. As unrealistic as this may sound, it doesn't stop people from trying to limit diverse opinions, perspectives, or types of personalities throughout an organization. While a workplace filled with different kinds of people has its challenges, it also presents a compelling (exciting) opportunity for managers to view individual differences among employees in a fresh new way. Rather than limiting diversity, as in the past, today's decision makers need to better understand and accommodate organizational diversity and individual employee differences.[1]

This chapter explores the following important dimensions of individual differences: (1) self-concept, (2) personality traits, (3) intelligence, and (4) emotions. The conceptual model in Figure 3.1 shows the relationship between self-concept, personality, and key forms of self-expression. Considered as an integrated package, these factors provide a foundation for better understanding yourself and others as unique and special individuals.

Understanding Self-Concept

Self is the core of one's conscious existence. Awareness of self is referred to as one's self-concept. Individualistic North American cultures have been called self-centred. Not surprisingly, when people ages 16 to 70 were asked in a recent survey what they would do differently if they could live life over again, 48 percent chose the response category "Get in touch with self."[2] To know more about self-concept is to understand more about life in general.[3]

Sociologist Viktor Gecas defines *self-concept* as "the concept the individual has of himself as a physical, social, and spiritual or moral being."[4] In other words, because you have a self-concept, you recognize yourself as a distinct human being. A self-concept would be impossible without the capacity to think. This brings us to the role of cognitions. *Cognitions* represent "any knowledge, opinion, or belief about the environment, about oneself, or about one's behaviour."[5] Among many different types of cognitions, those involving anticipation, planning, goal setting, evaluating, and setting personal standards are particularly relevant to OB.

Importantly, ideas of self and self-concept vary from one historical era to another, from one socioeconomic group to another, and from culture to culture.[6] How well a person detects and adjusts to different cultural notions of self can spell the difference between success and failure in international dealings. Keeping this cultural qualification in mind, we will explore three topics invariably mentioned when behavioural scientists discuss self-concept: self-esteem, self-efficacy, and self-monitoring.

> **Self-concept**
>
> A person's self-perception as a physical, social, and spiritual being.

> **Cognitions**
>
> A person's knowledge, opinions, or beliefs.

LEARNING OBJECTIVES

After reading this chapter, you should be able to:

LO 1 Define *self-esteem* and *self-efficacy*.

LO 2 Explain what is meant by self-monitoring and discuss how it relates to the social learning model of self-management.

LO 3 Relate the one Big Five personality dimension that is most positively correlated with job performance.

LO 4 Compare and contrast internal and external locus of control.

LO 5 Summarize the theory of emotional intelligence and explain how it relates to appreciating individual differences between people.

FIGURE | 3.1 | Studying Individual Differences

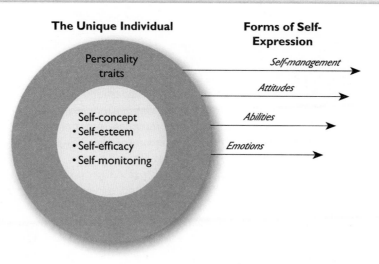

LO 1 SELF-ESTEEM

Self-esteem is beliefs about one's own self-worth based on an overall self-evaluation.[7] Self-esteem is measured by having survey respondents indicate their agreement or disagreement with both positive and negative statements. A positive statement on one general self-esteem survey is: "I feel I am a person of worth, the equal of other people."[8] Among the negative items is: "I feel I do not have much to be proud of."[9] Those who agree with the positive statements and disagree with the negative statements have high self-esteem. They see themselves as worthwhile, capable, and acceptable. People with low self-esteem view themselves in negative terms. They do not feel good about themselves and are hampered by self-doubts.[10]

Self-esteem

One's overall self-evaluation.

Employment and Self-Esteem What researchers call *organization-based self-esteem* makes paid employment a prime determinant of overall self-esteem in modern life.[11] Identifying yourself with a collective group of individuals who are gainfully employed can be very rewarding and fulfilling, especially when others around you are out of work. Consequently, unemployment can have a devastating impact on people's self-esteem. Consider the tens of thousands of individuals who lost their jobs during the 2008/09 financial crisis and those who have lost their jobs when companies started moving operations and jobs to places outside of Canada. Imagine how low their self-esteem must be, knowing that finding a career job in the near future will be a very difficult task. They may learn from Arthur J. Fiacco, a 56-year-old executive who was laid off without any warning:

I had never felt so lonely and helpless. I had been working since I was 16 years old. . . . A job isn't just about working. A job helps define who we are. It is what we talk with our neighbours about. It is the place we go. It is how we are introduced. It is one of the first things people ask about when we meet them. And most important, we measure ourselves from our very first job onward. Without a job, I felt I had lost my identity.[12]

Fiacco eventually turned things around by building a successful consulting business. He says now, "I am making a contribution and feel good. . . . I have learned to listen to what others are trying to tell me."[13]

Life-Span and Gender Perspectives A recent meta-analysis of 80,433 people showed that self-esteem is stable over the course of one's life. The biggest changes happen in the first 10 years of adulthood, with little significant change after age 30. A particularly interesting result was that self-esteem does not change much during adolescence, and the differences between men and women are small at best.[14] While this suggests that self-esteem is consistent over time, it begs the question: Can it be improved?

LOW SELF-ESTEEM

popular view that high self-esteem is the key to better performance. The conclusion:

> . . . self-esteem and school or job performance are correlated. But long overdue scientific scrutiny points out the foolishness of supposing that people's opinion of themselves can be the cause of achievement. Rather, high-esteem is the result of good performance.[18]

Bottom line: Research is mixed on the relationship between self-esteem and performance. However, research continues. A recent study showed that self-esteem positively affects performance when the task at hand is relevant to one's self-esteem. In other words, if getting an A in your OB course is part of your evaluation of your self-worth, then you will be motivated to work harder and presumably perform better.[19] Research also shows a moderately positive correlation between self-esteem and life satisfaction, especially in Western cultures. (See the International OB feature box for more on cross-cultural differences for self-esteem.) The next topic, self-efficacy, sheds more light on the issue of performance.

Can General Self-Esteem Be Improved? The short answer is yes. More detailed answers come from research. In one study, youth-league baseball coaches who were trained in supportive teaching techniques had a positive effect on the self-esteem of young boys. A control group of untrained coaches had no such positive effect.[15] Another study led to this conclusion: "Low self-esteem can be raised more by having the person think of desirable characteristics possessed rather than of undesirable characteristics from which he or she is free."[16] Research also shows that supportive clinical mentors improved medical residents' self-esteem.[17] Yet another comprehensive study threw cold water on the

SELF-EFFICACY ("I CAN DO THAT.")

Have you noticed how those who are confident about their ability tend to succeed, while those who are preoccupied with failing tend to fail? *Self-efficacy* is a person's belief about his or her

Self-efficacy

Belief in one's ability to do a task.

CROSS-CULTURAL DIFFERENCES FOR SELF-ESTEEM

What are the cross-cultural implications for self-esteem? Self-esteem is a concept that has been called uniquely Western. In a survey of 13,118 students from 31 countries worldwide, a moderately positive correlation was found between self-esteem and life satisfaction. But the relationship was stronger in individualistic cultures (e.g., Canada, New Zealand, Netherlands, and the United States) than in collectivist cultures (e.g., Korea, Kenya, and Japan). The researchers concluded that individualistic cultures socialize people to focus more on

themselves, while people in collectivist cultures "are socialized to fit into the community and to do their duty. Thus, how a collectivist feels about him- or herself is less relevant to . . . life satisfaction."[20] Global managers and employees working in multi-cultural work environments, whether in Canada or abroad, need to remember to de-emphasize self-esteem when doing business in collectivist ("we") cultures, as opposed to emphasizing it in individualistic ("me") cultures.[21] Chapter 14 discusses cultural differences in greater detail.

chances of successfully accomplishing a specific task. According to one OB writer, "Self-efficacy arises from the gradual acquisition of complex cognitive, social, linguistic, and/or physical skills through experience."[22]

Helpful nudges in the right direction from parents, role models, and mentors are central to the development of high self-efficacy. Consider the medical resident study mentioned previously. Mentor guidance and social support improved the resident's clinical self-efficacy.[23] Now consider, which would you prefer—a surgeon who is confident (high self-esteem) or one who is good (high self-efficacy)?

The relationship between self-efficacy and performance is a cyclical one. Efficacy–performance cycles can spiral upward toward success or downward toward failure.[24] Researchers have documented a strong link between high self-efficacy expectations and success in widely varied physical and mental tasks, anxiety reduction, addiction control, pain tolerance, illness recovery, and avoidance of seasickness in naval cadets.[25] In contrast, those with low self-efficacy expectations tend to have low success rates. Chronically low self-efficacy is associated with a condition called learned helplessness, the severely debilitating belief that people have no control over their environment.[26] Although self-efficacy sounds like some sort of mental magic, it operates in a very straightforward manner, as the following model will show.

Mechanisms of Self-Efficacy A basic model of self-efficacy is displayed in Figure 3.2. It draws upon the work of psychologist Albert Bandura.[27] Let's explore this model with a simple illustrative task. Imagine you have been told to prepare and deliver a 10-minute talk to an OB class of 50 students on the workings of the self-efficacy model in Figure 3.2. Your self-efficacy assessment would involve thinking and reviewing the interaction between your perceived abilities and those opportunities and obstacles around you.

As you begin to prepare for your presentation, the four sources of self-efficacy beliefs come into play. Because prior experience is the most potent source, according to Bandura, it is listed first and connected to self-efficacy beliefs with a solid line.[28] Past success in public speaking would boost your self-efficacy. But bad experiences with delivering speeches would foster low self-efficacy. Regarding behaviour models as a source of self-efficacy beliefs, you would be influenced by the success or failure of your classmates in delivering similar talks. Their successes would tend to bolster you (or perhaps their failure would if you were very competitive and had high self-esteem). Likewise, any supportive persuasion from your classmates that you

will do a good job would enhance your self-efficacy. Physical and emotional factors also might affect your self-confidence. A sudden case of laryngitis or a bout of stage fright could cause your self-efficacy expectations to plunge. Your cognitive evaluation of the situation then would yield a self-efficacy belief—ranging from high to low expectations for success. Importantly, self-efficacy beliefs are not merely boastful statements based on bravado (swagger); they are deep convictions supported by experience.

Moving to the *behavioural patterns* portion of Figure 3.2, we see how self-efficacy beliefs are acted out. In short, if you have high self-efficacy about giving your 10-minute speech you will work harder, more creatively, and longer when preparing for your talk than will your low self-efficacy classmates. The results would then take shape accordingly. People program themselves for success or failure by enacting their self-efficacy expectations. Positive or negative results subsequently become feedback for a person's base of personal experience.

Managerial Implications On-the-job research evidence encourages managers to nurture self-efficacy, both in themselves and in others. In fact, a meta-analysis encompassing 21,616 subjects found a significant positive correlation between self-efficacy and job performance.[29] To illustrate this point, let's take the case example discussed in the Law and Ethics at Work feature box, where a manager receives information suggesting employees waste time on the job. That translates into money being wasted in the mind of the manager and prompts a reaction; in this instance, it's critical for the manager not to overreact with coercive (tough) tactics. To get people back on track, management should reflect on the best way to help the employees understand the need for behaviour change. By providing employees with the right tools, employees can monitor their own behaviour and thus maintain positive self-efficacy, which in turn will lead to better job performance.

Self-efficacy requires constructive action in each of the following managerial areas:

1. **Recruiting/selection/job assignments** Design interview questions to probe job applicants' general self-efficacy as a basis for determining orientation and training needs. Pencil-and-paper tests for self-efficacy are not in an advanced stage of development and validation. Take care to not hire solely on the basis of self-efficacy, because studies have detected below-average self-esteem and self-efficacy among women and protected minorities.[30]

FIGURE 3.2 Self-Efficacy Beliefs Pave the Way for Success or Failure

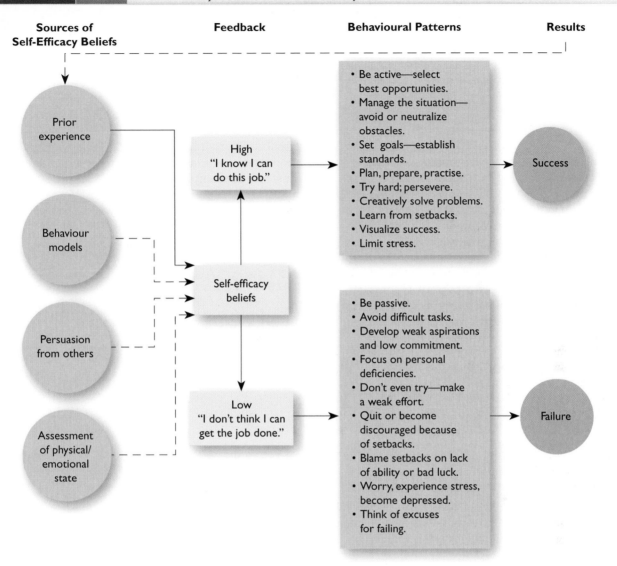

SOURCES: Adapted from discussion in A. Bandura, "Regulation of Cognitive Processes through Perceived Self-Efficacy," *Developmental Psychology,* September 1989, pp 729–35; and R. Wood and A. Bandura, "Social Cognitive Theory of Organizational Management," *Academy of Management Review,* July 1989, pp 361–84.

2. **Job design** Complex, challenging, and autonomous jobs tend to enhance perceived self-efficacy.[31] Boring, tedious jobs generally do the opposite.

3. **Training and development** Improve employees' self-efficacy expectations for key tasks through guided experiences, mentoring, and role modelling.[32]

4. **Self-management** Provide broad and formalized organizational training of employees on how to manage their own personal behaviour as well as how to enhance self-efficacy expectations.[33]

5. **Goal setting and quality improvement** Goal difficulty needs to match the individual's perceived self-efficacy.[34] As self-efficacy and performance improve, goals and quality standards can be made more challenging.

6. **Creativity** Supportive managerial actions can enhance the strong linkage between self-efficacy beliefs and workplace creativity.[35]

7. **Coaching** Those with low self-efficacy need lots of constructive pointers and positive feedback.[36]

EMPLOYERS NEED TO FIND WAYS TO BUILD EMPLOYEE SELF-EFFICACY

Imagine you are a manager and you've just read a recent Gallup poll stating that employees acknowledge that they waste an average of about one hour a day at work. This has you concerned. Are your employees wasting hours at work each week or are they being productive? You decide to ask a colleague his opinion on how to monitor such activity in the workplace. He suggests installing NetVizor, the latest software that lets employers secretly monitor all computer and Internet activities of every employee on their network. But is it legal?

In banking, insurance, telecommunications, and travel, as many as 80 percent of employees may be subject to some level of monitoring. While it is an offence under the Criminal Code in Canada to intercept private communications, the Personal Information Protection and Electronic Documents Act (PIPEDA) introduced in 2004 makes it clear that Canadian companies have to justify surveillance and have written policies regarding Internet and phone use or face a possible civil lawsuit before the federal court.

Several decisions from the Canadian federal privacy commissioner clearly identify that employers must act in compliance with the purposes and limited collection provisions of PIPEDA that allow individuals the right to privacy so as to, in essence, monitor their own behaviour without coercive means from management.

SOURCES: A. Gahtan, "Big Brother or Good Business?," *WebWorld*, March 1997, p. 24; J. Allinson, "Companies Will Have To Justify Surveillance," *London Free Press*, December 27, 2003; J. Allinson, "Written Policies are must for Internet, phone use," *London Free Press*, January 8, 2004; and M. Cywinski, "Management Tip-employees acknowledged in Self-Monitoring 2007 that they wasted an average of about an hour a day at work, but . . . ," *Canadian Management Centre PodCast Series*, January 24, 2008, (www.cmctraining.org/wordpress/?author=2).

---

8. **Leadership** Leadership talent emerges when top management gives high self-efficacy managers a chance to prove themselves under pressure.

9. **Rewards** Small successes need to be rewarded as stepping-stones to a stronger self-image and greater achievements.

LO 2 SELF-MONITORING

Self-monitoring is the extent to which people observe their own self-expressive behaviour and adapt it to the demands of the situation.[37]

Consider these contrasting scenarios:

1. You are rushing to an important meeting when a co-worker pulls you aside and starts to discuss a personal problem. You want to break off the conversation, so you glance at your watch. He keeps talking. You say, "I'm late for a big meeting." He continues. You turn and start to walk away. The person keeps talking as if he never received any of your verbal and non-verbal signals that the conversation was over. You think, "What's his problem?"

2. Same situation. Only this time, when you glance at your watch, the person immediately says, "I know,

you've got to go. Sorry. We'll talk later." You think, "What a considerate person!"

In the first all-too-familiar scenario, you are talking to a *low self-monitor*. The second scenario involves a *high self-monitor*. But more is involved here than an irritating situation: a significant and measurable individual difference in self-expression behaviour, called self-monitoring, is highlighted.

Experts on the subject offer this explanation:

Individuals high in self-monitoring are thought to regulate their expressive self-presentation for the sake of desired public appearances, and thus are highly responsive to social and interpersonal cues of situationally appropriate performances. Individuals low in self-monitoring are thought to lack either the ability or the motivation to so regulate their expressive self-presentations. Instead, their expressive behaviours are thought to functionally reflect their own enduring and momentary inner states, including their attitudes, traits, and feelings.[38]

> **Self-monitoring**
> Observing one's own behaviour and adapting it to the situation.

> **Low self-monitor**
> Low personal awareness levels of related patterns of self-expression on how to adapt to situations.

> **High self-monitor**
> High personal awareness levels of how to adapt related patterns of self-expression to fit situations.

How Good Are You at Self-Monitoring?

INSTRUCTIONS: In an honest self-appraisal, mark each of the following statements as True (T) or False (F), and then consult the scoring key.

_____ 1 I guess I put on a show to impress or entertain others.

_____ 2 In a group of people I am rarely the centre of attention.

_____ 3 In different situations and with different people, I often act like very different persons.

_____ 4 I would not change my opinions (or the way I do things) to please someone or win their favour.

_____ 5 I have considered being an entertainer.

_____ 6 I have trouble changing my behaviour to suit different people and different situations.

_____ 7 At a party I let others keep the jokes and stories going.

_____ 8 I feel a bit awkward in public and do not show up quite as well as I should.

_____ 9 I can look anyone in the eye and tell a lie with a straight face (if for a right end).

_____ 10 I may deceive people by being friendly when I really dislike them.

Scoring Key

Score one point for each of the following answers:
1. T; 2. F; 3. T; 4. F; 5. T; 6. F; 7. F; 8. F; 9. T; 10. T

Score:

1–3 = Low self-monitoring

4–5 = Moderately low self-monitoring

6–7 = Moderately high self-monitoring

8–10 = High self-monitoring

SOURCE: Excerpted and adapted from M. Snyder and S. Gangestad, "On the Nature of Self-Monitoring: Matters of Assessment, Matters of Validity," *Journal of Personality and Social Psychology*, July 1986, p 137.

In organizational life, both high and low self-monitors are subject to criticism. High self-monitors are sometimes called *chameleons,* who readily adapt their self-presentation to their surroundings. Low self-monitors, on the other hand, are often criticized for being insensitive to others. Importantly, within an OB context, self-monitoring is like any other individual difference—not a matter of right or wrong or good versus bad, but rather a source of diversity that needs to be adequately understood.

A Matter of Degree Self-monitoring is not an either–or proposition; it is a matter of degree, a matter of being relatively high or low in terms of related patterns of self-expression. If you haven't done so already, complete Self-Assessment Exercise #1 to determine how good you are at self-monitoring. It is meant to help

you better understand yourself. Review your score. Does it surprise you in any way? Are you unhappy with the way you present yourself to others? What are the ethical implications of your score (particularly with regard to items 9 and 10)?

Research Insights and Practical Recommendations According to field research, there is a positive relationship between high self-monitoring and career success. Among 139 MBA graduates who were tracked for five years, high self-monitors enjoyed more internal and external promotions than did their low self-monitoring classmates.[39] Another study of 147 managers and professionals found that high self-monitors had a better record of acquiring a mentor (someone to act as a personal career coach and professional sponsor).[40] These results mesh well with an earlier study that found managerial success (in terms of speed of promotions) was tied to political savvy (knowing how to socialize, network, and engage in organizational politics).[41]

The foregoing evidence and practical experience lead us to make these practical recommendations:

■ *For high, moderate, and low self-monitors:* Become more consciously aware of your self-image and how it affects others.

■ *For high self-monitors:* Don't overdo it by turning from a successful chameleon into someone who is widely perceived as insincere, dishonest, phony, and untrustworthy. You cannot be everything to everyone.

■ *For low self-monitors:* You can bend without breaking, so try to be a bit more accommodating while being true to your basic beliefs. Don't wear out your welcome when communicating. Practise reading and adjusting to non-verbal cues in various public situations. If your conversation partner is bored or distracted, stop—he or she is not really listening.

SELF-MANAGEMENT: A SOCIAL LEARNING MODEL

Albert Bandura, the expert psychologist introduced earlier, extended his self-efficacy concept into a comprehensive model of human learning. According to Bandura's *social learning theory*, an individual acquires new behaviour through the interplay of environmental cues and consequences and cognitive processes.[42] When you consciously control this learning process yourself, you are engaging in self-management.

The practical model displayed in Figure 3.3 is derived from social learning theory. Since the focal

---

FIGURE 3.3 A Social Learning Model of Self-Management

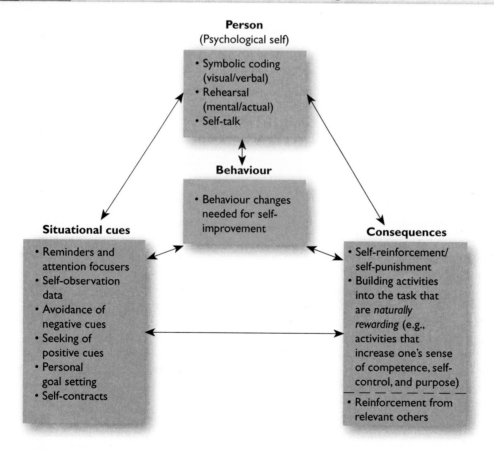

Person
(Psychological self)
- Symbolic coding (visual/verbal)
- Rehearsal (mental/actual)
- Self-talk

Behaviour
- Behaviour changes needed for self-improvement

Situational cues
- Reminders and attention focusers
- Self-observation data
- Avoidance of negative cues
- Seeking of positive cues
- Personal goal setting
- Self-contracts

Consequences
- Self-reinforcement/self-punishment
- Building activities into the task that are *naturally rewarding* (e.g., activities that increase one's sense of competence, self-control, and purpose)
- Reinforcement from relevant others

SOURCE: Adapted in part from B.J. Pannett and S. Withane, "Hofstede's Value Survey Module: To Embrace or Abandon?," *Advances in International Comparative Management,* vol 5, ed. S.B. Prasad (Greenwich, CT: JAI Press, 1990), pp 69–89.

point of this model is behaviour change, let's begin by discussing the behaviour component in the centre of the triangle.[43]

Changing Your Behaviour

In today's fast-paced Internet age, corporate hand-holding is pretty much a thing of the past when it comes to career management. Employees are told things such as, "You own your own employability." The new age of career self-management challenges you to do a better job of setting personal goals, having clear priorities, being well organized, skilfully managing your time, and developing a self-learning program.[44] Next, a supportive environment is needed for the target behaviour.

Managing Situational Cues

When people try to give up a nagging habit such as smoking, the cards are stacked against them. Many people (friends who smoke) and situations (after dinner, when under stress at work, or when relaxing) serve as subtle yet powerful cues telling the individual to light up another cigarette. If the behaviour is to be changed, the cues need to be rearranged so they trigger alternative behaviour. The work of journalist and author Charles Duhigg, in his book *The Power of Habit,* speaks about this very process: Identify the cue(s) that trigger the habit, recognize the steps in your routine and how you currently reward the need(s). If you want to break a habit, Duhigg suggests focusing attention on what reward is truly being desired. This is key, otherwise you could be demonstrating behaviour that is the complete opposite to what is desired.[45] Six techniques for managing situational cues are listed in the left column of Figure 3.3.

Reminders and attention focusers do just that. For example, many students and employees cue themselves about deadlines and appointments with notes stuck all over their work areas, refrigerators, and dashboards. Self-observation data, when compared against a goal or standard, can be a potent cue for improvement. Those who keep a weight chart near their bathroom scale will attest to the value of this tactic. Successful self-management calls for avoiding negative cues while seeking positive cues.

Arranging Support for the Psychological Self

Referring to the person portion of the self-management model in Figure 3.3, three cognitive supports for behaviour change are symbolic: coding, rehearsal, and self-talk. These amount to psychological, as opposed to environmental, cues. Yet, according to Bandura, they prompt appropriate behaviour in the same manner. Each requires a brief explanation:

- **Symbolic coding** The human brain stores information in visual and verbal codes. People commonly rely on acronyms (or verbal code) to recall names, rules for behaviour, and other information. An acronym that is often heard in managerial circles is the KISS principle, standing for "Keep It Simple, Stupid."

- **Rehearsal** Mental rehearsal of challenging tasks can increase one's chances of success. Job-finding seminars for students are very popular on campuses today because they typically involve mental and actual rehearsal of tough job interviews. This sort of manufactured experience can build the confidence and self-efficacy necessary for real-world success.[46]

- **Self-talk** According to an expert on the subject, "*self-talk* is the set of evaluating thoughts that you give yourself about facts and events that happen to you."[47] Personal experience tells us that self-talk tends to be a self-fulfilling prophecy. Negative self-talk tends to pave the way for failure, whereas positive self-talk often facilitates success. Replacing negative self-talk ("I'll never get a raise") with positive self-talk ("I deserve a raise and I'm going to get it") is fundamental to better self-management.

> **Self-talk**
>
> Evaluating thoughts about oneself.

> Athletes, such as UFC Welterweight Champion and Canadian Georges St-Pierre, use a combination of visualization and self-talk techniques when competing as a way of supporting themselves during a challenging time.

Consequences The completion of self-contracts and other personal achievements calls for self-reinforcement. This means that individuals must be realistic and honest with themselves when controlling the reinforcers. Self-reinforcement strategies need to be resourceful, creative, and positive:

> *Self-granted rewards can lead to self-improvement. But as failed dieters and smokers can attest, there are short-run as well as long-run influences on self-reinforcement. For the overeater, the immediate gratification of eating has more influence than the promise of a new wardrobe. The same sort of dilemma plagues procrastinators. Consequently, one needs to weave a powerful web of cues, cognitive supports, and internal and external consequences to win the tug-of-war with status-quo payoffs. Primarily because it is so easy to avoid, self-punishment tends to be ineffectual (weak). As with managing the behaviour of others, positive instead of negative consequences are recommended for effective self-management.*[48]

In addition, it helps to solicit positive reinforcement for self-improvement from supportive friends, co-workers, and relatives. To practise applying the social learning model to real-life types of situations, refer to the two scenarios in the Experiential Exercise section at the end of this chapter.

Personality Dynamics

Individuals have their own way of thinking and acting, their own unique style or *personality*. **Personality** is defined as the combination of stable physical and mental characteristics that give individuals their identity. These characteristics or traits—including how one looks, thinks, acts, and feels—are the product of interacting genetic and environmental influences.[49] In this section, we introduce the Big Five personality dimensions and discuss key personality dynamics, including locus of control, attitudes, intelligence, and mental abilities.

Personality

Stable physical and mental characteristics responsible for a person's identity.

THE BIG FIVE PERSONALITY DIMENSIONS

When it comes to personality, the Big Five identifies the following key five dimensions: extraversion, agreeableness, conscientiousness, emotional stability, and openness to experience (see Table 3.1 for descriptions). Standardized personality tests determine how positively or negatively a person scores on each of the Big Five. For example, someone scoring negatively on extraversion would be an introverted person prone to shy and withdrawn behaviour.[50] Someone scoring negatively on emotional stability would be nervous, tense, angry, and worried. The various scores on the Big Five reveal a personality profile as unique as fingerprints. You are invited to complete Self-Assessment #2 titled "Your Own Big Five Profile" to determine your own set of Big Five scores.

But one important question lingers: Are personality models ethnocentric and unique to the culture in which they were developed? At least as far as the Big Five model goes, cross-cultural research evidence points in the direction of "no." Specifically, the Big Five personality structure held up very well in a study of women and men from Canada, Russia, Hong Kong, Poland, Germany, and Finland.[51]

TABLE 3.1

THE BIG FIVE PERSONALITY DIMENSIONS

STABLE PHYSICAL AND MENTAL CHARACTERISTICS RESPONSIBLE FOR A PERSON'S IDENTITY	
1. Extraversion	Outgoing, talkative, sociable, assertive
2. Agreeableness	Trusting, good-natured, cooperative, soft-hearted
3. Conscientiousness	Dependable, responsible, achievement-oriented, persistent
4. Emotional stability	Relaxed, secure, unworried
5. Openness to experience	Intellectual, imaginative, curious, broad-minded

SOURCE: Adapted from M.R. Barrick and M.K. Mount, "Autonomy as a Moderator of the Relationships between the Big Five Personality Dimensions and Job Performance," *Journal of Applied Psychology*, February 1993, pp 111–18.

Your Own Big Five Profile

INSTRUCTIONS: Using the scale below, indicate to what extent each of the following statements describes you.

	1 Not at all like me	2 A little bit like me	3 Somewhat like me	4 Like me	5 Very much like me
1 I talk to many different people at parties.	1	2	3	4	5
2 I don't mind being the centre of attention.	1	2	3	4	5
3 I sympathize with other people's feelings.	1	2	3	4	5
4 I take time out for others.	1	2	3	4	5
5 I am always prepared.	1	2	3	4	5
6 I pay attention to details.	1	2	3	4	5
7 I am relaxed most of the time.	1	2	3	4	5
8 I am not easily bothered by things.	1	2	3	4	5
9 I enjoy hearing new ideas.	1	2	3	4	5
10 I enjoy thinking about things.	1	2	3	4	5

Scoring Key:

Add Q1 and Q2 = _____ Extraversion Score
Add Q3 and Q4 = _____ Agreeableness Score
Add Q5 and Q6 = _____ Conscientiousness Score
Add Q7 and Q8 = _____ Emotional Stability Score
Add Q9 and Q10 = _____ Openness to Experience Score

Interpretation:

A score greater than 8 indicates a high level of that particular personality factor. A score between 6 and 8 indicates a moderate level on that factor, and a score less than 6 indicates a low level on that factor.

SOURCE: L.R. Goldberg, J.A. Johnson, H.W. Eber, R. Hogan, M.C. Ashton, C.R. Cloninger, & H.C. Gough, "The International Personality Item Pool and the Future of Public-domain Personality Measures," *Journal of Research in Personality, 40,* 2006, pp 84–96.

LO 3 **Personality and Job Performance** Those interested in OB want to know the connection between the Big Five and job performance. Ideally, Big Five personality dimensions that correlate positively and strongly with job performance would be helpful in the selection, training, and appraisal of employees. A meta-analysis of 117 studies involving 23,994 subjects from many professions offers guidance.[52] Among the Big Five, *conscientiousness* has the strongest positive correlation with job performance and training performance. According to the researchers, "those individuals who exhibit traits associated with a strong sense of purpose, obligation, and persistence generally perform better than those who do not."[53] Not surprisingly, entrepreneurs score high on conscientiousness.[54] Another recent finding: Extraversion (an outgoing personality) correlates positively with promotions, salary level, and career satisfaction. And, as you might expect, neuroticism (low emotional stability) is associated with low career satisfaction.[55]

Another expected finding was that extraversion is associated with success for managers and salespeople. Also, extraversion is a stronger predictor of job performance than agreeableness, across all professions. The researchers concluded, "It appears that being courteous, trusting, straightforward, and soft-hearted has a smaller impact on job performance than being talkative, active, and assertive."[56] Not surprisingly, in a recent study, a strong linkage between conscientiousness and performance was found among those with polished social skills.[57] As an added bonus for extraverts, a recent positive psychology study led to this conclusion: "All you have to do is act extraverted and you can get a happiness boost."[58] So the next time you are on the job, go initiate a conversation with someone and be more productive and happier!

The Proactive Personality As suggested by the above discussion, someone who scores high on the Big Five dimension of conscientiousness is probably a better and safer worker. Researchers Thomas S. Bateman and J. Michael Crant took this important linkage an additional step by formulating the concept of the *proactive personality*. They define and characterize the proactive personality in these terms: "Someone who is relatively unconstrained by situational forces and who effects environmental change. Proactive people identify opportunities and act on them, show initiative, take action, and persevere until meaningful change occurs."[59] In short, people with proactive personalities are "hardwired" to change the status quo. In a review of relevant

> **Proactive personality**
>
> Action-oriented person who shows initiative and perseveres to change things.

studies, Crant found the proactive personality to be positively associated with individual, team, and organizational success.[60]

Successful entrepreneurs exemplify the proactive personality.[61] Those wanting to get ahead would do well to cultivate the initiative, drive, courage, and perseverance of someone with a proactive personality—and managers would do well to hire them. Matt Glotzbach, product management director for Google Enterprise, is a good case in point:

> *My first morning at Google, I put my name and address on one form online, and it went everywhere it needed to go electronically. That's how this place works. I went to a staff meeting that afternoon and got assigned to figure out how Google could launch Enterprise (applications for corporations) in Europe. I was told to come back with the answer at the end of the week. It was like, "Hey, New Guy, you don't know anything about our business yet, and you don't have any international experience, but here are some people who can help you. Go figure it out." We launched in Europe a few months later.*[62]

Glotzbach's experience suggests that Bateman and Crant were correct in that "people who were inclined to control their environment so they could get what they wanted were likely to start new businesses." People with proactive personalities truly are valuable *human capital*.

There Is No "Ideal Employee" Personality A word of caution is in order here. The Big Five personality dimensions of conscientiousness and extraversion and the proactive personality are generally desirable in the workplace, but they are not panaceas (cure-all). Given the complexity of today's work environments, the diversity of today's workforce, and recent research evidence,[63] the quest for an ideal employee personality profile is sheer folly. Just as one shoe does not fit all people, one personality profile does not fit all job situations. Good management involves taking the time to get to know each employee's unique combination of personality traits, abilities, and potential, and then creating a productive and satisfying person–job fit.

Personality Assessment Instrument While there are several assessment instruments available on the market to identify employee personality type, the Myers-Briggs Type Indicator (MBTI) is a fairly popular instrument. If you are a post-secondary student, the majority of career/counselling offices provide personality assessments at little to no cost. You would be well advised to investigate your own school to determine the kind of assessments available. For business application and with assistance from Psychometrics Canada, Inc., the Canadian distributor of the instrument, organizations can have a trained professional arrive on-site to work with employees or to help screen new applicants. The results of the test can help individuals understand their own preferences, biases, and behaviour. If team-orientation is desired by the firm, then test results can be used to help facilitate a better transition between members. To determine your own personality type, go to the Connect site and complete the personality self-assessment listed under the 'Build Your Management Skills'.

LO 4   LOCUS OF CONTROL: SELF OR ENVIRONMENT?

Individuals vary in terms of how much personal responsibility they take for their behaviour and its consequences. Julian Rotter, a personality researcher, identified a dimension of personality he labelled *locus of control* to explain these differences. He proposed that people tend to attribute the causes of their behaviour primarily to either themselves or environmental factors,[64] producing different behaviour patterns.

People who believe they control the events and consequences that affect their lives are said to possess an *internal locus of control*. For example, these people tend to attribute positive outcomes, such as getting a passing grade on an exam, to their own abilities. Similarly, an "internal" tends to blame negative events, such as failing an exam, on personal shortcomings—not studying hard enough, or perhaps just not being good at math. Many entrepreneurs eventually succeed because their internal locus of control helps them overcome setbacks and disappointments.[65] They see themselves as masters of their own fate and not as simply lucky. Likewise, when people with an internal locus of control must shoulder a heavy workload, they look for solutions rather than wait for someone to bring them a solution.

On the other side of this personality dimension are those who believe their performance is the product of circumstances beyond their immediate control. These individuals are said to possess an *external locus of control* and tend to attribute outcomes to environmental causes, such as luck or fate. Unlike internals, an "external" would attribute

| **Internal locus of control** |
| Attributing outcomes to one's own actions. |

| **External locus of control** |
| Attributing outcomes to circumstances beyond one's control. |

a passing grade on an exam to something external (an easy test or a good day), and attribute a failing grade to an unfair test or problems at home.

Research Lessons Researchers have found important behavioural differences between internals and externals:

- Internals display greater work motivation.
- Internals have stronger expectations that effort leads to performance.
- Internals exhibit higher performance on tasks involving learning or problem solving, when performance leads to valued rewards.
- There is a stronger relationship between job satisfaction and performance for internals than for externals.
- Internals obtain higher salaries and greater salary increases than externals.
- Externals tend to be more anxious than internals.[66]

Tempering an Internal Locus of Control with Humility   Do you have an internal locus of control? Odds are high that you do, judging from the "typical" OB student we have worked with over the years. Good thing, because it should pay off in the workplace with opportunities, raises, and promotions. But before you declare yourself Grade A executive material, here is one more thing to toss into your tool kit: a touch of humility. *Humility* is "a realistic assessment of one's own contribution and the recognition of the contribution of others, along with luck and good fortune that made one's own success possible."[67] Humility has been called the silent virtue. How many truly humble people brag about being humble? Two OB experts recently offered this instructive perspective:

| *Humility* |
| Considering the contributions of others and good fortune when gauging one's success. |

Humble individuals have a down-to-earth perspective of themselves and of the events and relationships in their lives. Humility involves a capability to evaluate success, failure, work, and life without exaggeration. Furthermore, humility enables leaders to distinguish the delicate line between such characteristics as healthy self-confidence, self-esteem, and self-assessment, and those of over-confidence, narcissism, and stubbornness. Humility is the mid-point between the two negative extremes of arrogance and lack of self-esteem. This depiction allows one to see that a person can be humble and competitive or humble and ambitious at the same time, which contradicts common—but mistaken—views about humility.[68]

Abilities (Intelligence) and Performance

Although experts do not agree on a specific definition, *intelligence* represents an individual's capacity for constructive thinking, reasoning, and problem solving.[69] When employers engage in hiring potential candidates, traits such as these become of interest as the right person is sought and selected. But what is the best way to find such candidates to hire? Historically, intelligence was believed to be an innate capacity, passed genetically from one generation to the next. So, for example, if a

Intelligence

An individual's capacity for constructive thinking, reasoning, and problem solving.

firm hired the son or daughter of a prominent business person, then it was assumed that the child would perform at the same successful level as the parent. Of course, such a hiring practice is riddled with bias and discourages diversity. The Focus on Diversity feature box takes this discussion of hiring and bias a bit further.

For now, contemporary research shows that intelligence (like personality) goes beyond genetics and is also a function of environmental influences, such as sleep deprivation and nutrition.[70] Organic factors have more recently been added to the formula as a result of mounting evidence of the connection between alcohol and drug abuse by pregnant women and intellectual development problems in their children.[71]

Researchers have produced some interesting findings about abilities and intelligence in recent years. A unique five-year study documented the tendency of people to "gravitate into jobs commensurate with their abilities."[72] This prompts the vision of the labour

APPLICANT TRACKING SYSTEMS CAN BIAS SELECTION PROCESS

During the recruitment stage of the hiring process, organizations complete a series of steps to find the best candidate. These steps can include sourcing candidates, screening potential candidates, managing and then tracking resumés, and so on. To help make the process more efficient and accurate, Canadian HR specialists have turned to technology. Applicant tracking systems, or ATS, have become popular among large organizations with thousands of employees, as well as with smaller firms that may only have one or two HR professionals for all HR tasks. However, ATS tend to screen out groups of potentially valuable applicants who don't know how to prepare an application that will get through the system's filters.

"Applicant tracking systems have an unintended impact on immigrants—when a person first arrives in Canada, they often don't understand how recruitment works . . . and don't understand that the way to apply for jobs online is to put keywords from the posting itself into your application letter and resumé," explains Michael Bach, Director

of Diversity, Equity, and Inclusion at KPMG. Bach believes Aboriginal Canadians and people in remote and northern towns, who have limited access to computers and the Internet, are also disadvantaged by ATS.

An employer that relies only on its ATS may miss an applicant who has great job skills, but who doesn't know how modern recruiting and screening systems are based on keyword searches. Bach believes that people in a position to hire others should not depend only on computerized systems to find employees. He also suggests going beyond the traditional career fairs, open houses, and campus recruiting events; instead, organizations should try reaching out to underrepresented groups to find new talent. By working with local community groups, an organization can show applicants how to prepare cover letters and resumés that the ATS will recognize.

SOURCE: S. Bury, "ATS: Can You Rely On Software To Find The Perfect Job Candidate?" *HR Professional*, January 2012, p. 36.

market acting as a giant sorting or sifting machine, with employees tumbling into various ability bins. Meanwhile, a steady and significant rise in average intelligence among those in developed countries has been observed over the last 70 years. Why? Experts at a North American psychology conference concluded, "Some combination of better schooling, improved socioeconomic status, healthier nutrition, and a more technologically complex society might account for the gains in IQ scores."[73] So if you think you're smarter than your parents and your teachers, you're probably right!

Two Types of Abilities By examining the relationships between measures of mental abilities and behaviour using an empirical approach, researchers have statistically isolated major components of intelligence. Using this procedure, pioneering psychologist Charles Spearman proposed in 1927 that all cognitive performance is determined by two types of abilities. The first can be characterized as a general mental ability needed for all cognitive tasks. The second is unique to the task at hand. For example, an ability to complete crossword puzzles is a function of broad mental abilities, as well as the specific ability to perceive patterns in partially completed words.

Seven Major Mental Abilities Through the years, much research has been devoted to developing and expanding Spearman's ideas on the relationship between cognitive abilities and intelligence.[74] One research psychologist listed 120 distinct mental abilities. Table 3.2 defines the seven most frequently cited mental abilities. Of the seven abilities, personnel selection researchers have found verbal ability, numerical ability, spatial ability, and inductive reasoning to be valid predictors of job performance for both minority and majority applicants.

DO WE HAVE MULTIPLE INTELLIGENCES?

Howard Gardner, a world-renown professor of education, offered a new paradigm for human intelligence in his 1983 book, *Frames of Mind: The Theory of Multiple Intelligences*.[75] He subsequently identified eight different intelligences that vastly broaden the long-standing concept of intelligence. Gardner's concept of multiple intelligences (MI) includes not only cognitive abilities, but also social and physical abilities and skills:

- **Linguistic intelligence** Potential to learn and use spoken and written languages.
- **Logical-mathematical intelligence** Potential for deductive reasoning, problem analysis, and mathematical calculation.
- **Musical intelligence** Potential to appreciate, compose, and perform music.
- **Bodily-kinesthetic intelligence** Potential to use mind and body to coordinate physical movement.

TABLE 3.2

MENTAL ABILITIES ABILITY DESCRIPTION

STABLE PHYSICAL AND MENTAL CHARACTERISTICS RESPONSIBLE FOR A PERSON'S IDENTITY	
1. Verbal comprehension	The ability to understand what words mean and to readily comprehend what is read.
2. Word fluency	The ability to produce isolated words that fulfill specific symbolic or structural requirements (such as all words that begin with the letter b and have two vowels).
3. Numerical	The ability to make quick and accurate arithmetic computations such as adding and subtracting.
4. Spatial	The ability to perceive spatial patterns and to visualize how geometric shapes would look if transformed in shape or position.
5. Memory	Having good rote memory for paired words, symbols, lists of numbers, or other associated items.
6. Perceptual speed	The ability to perceive figures, identify similarities and differences, and carry out tasks involving visual perception.
7. Inductive reasoning	The ability to reason from specifics to general conclusions.

SOURCE: Adapted from M.D. Dunnette, "Aptitudes, Abilities, and Skills," in *Handbook of Industrial and Organizational Psychology,* ed. M.D. Dunnette (Skokie, IL: Rand McNally, 1976), pp 478–83.

"Enough with the Beethoven, Mom! How about some Jay-Z?" Some parents strive to develop their baby's multiple intelligences by exposing them to unconventional stimuli. Research tells us the vote is still out on whether or not they are being successful.

- **Spatial intelligence** Potential to recognize and use patterns.

- **Interpersonal intelligence** Potential to understand, connect with, and effectively work with others.

- **Intrapersonal intelligence** Potential to understand and regulate oneself.

- **Naturalist intelligence** Potential to live in harmony with one's environment.[76]

Many educators and parents have embraced MI because it helps explain how a child could score poorly on a standard IQ test yet be obviously gifted in one or more ways (e.g., music, sports, relationship building). Moreover, they believe the concept of MI underscores the need to help children develop in their own unique way and at their own pace. They say standard IQ tests deal only with the first two intelligences on Gardner's list. Meanwhile, most academic psychologists and intelligence specialists continue to criticize Gardner's model as being too subjective and poorly integrated. They prefer the traditional model of intelligence as a unified variable measured by a single test. Others believe MI has important implications for employee selection and training.[77] Ontario company OneSmallWorld has found a way to link MI to innovation and problem solving. See the Skills & Best Practices feature box for more on this topic. Training programs fall short when MI diversity is not taken into consideration. We look forward to breakthroughs in this area as MI attracts OB researchers and practicing managers.

Skills & Best Practices

OneSmartWorld Links Multiple Intelligence to Group Problem Solving

As the Canadian workplace becomes more diverse, there is a greater need for common language to communicate as well as encourage innovation and problem solving. OneSmartWorld (OSW), a firm operating out of Collingwood, Ontario, has discovered a unique way to link types of thinking with technology to effectively solve problems. Imagine a traffic light. This simple metaphor illustrates how the company uses colour to code four primary types of thinking that are key to success and high performance work: creativity (green), understanding (yellow), decision making (red), and personal spirit (white). Each type of thinking is represented by a colour and shape and is arranged in a traffic light format to make it easy to learn and use and impossible to forget.

This universal common language forms the basis of all OneSmartWorld client solutions—the tools, methodologies, and programs. Once all members of a group or team have been identified through an assessment instrument, they are assigned a corresponding colour. This makes it incredibly easy for people in groups to remember their own thinking styles and the styles of others during a meeting where problems are being discussed and solutions are being discovered. It makes it easy to shift into the type of thinking a task or situation requires. Over the years, educational organizations, large and small corporations, and not-for-profit agencies across North America have turned to OneSmartWorld because, as one client stated in this testimonial, ". . . OSW delivered the kind of package we were looking for. It integrated multiple-intelligence, creativity, innovation, resiliency, and a number of components of emotional intelligence. It really was the 'total package' that helped us decide what to bring . . . into the program."

SOURCE: www.onesmartworld.com/content/think-smarter-work-better-together

Emotions: An Evolving OB Topic

In the ideal world of management theory, employees pursue organizational goals in a logical and rational manner; emotional behaviour is seldom factored into the equation. Yet day-to-day organizational life shows how prevalent and powerful emotions can be. Anger and jealousy, both potent emotions, often push aside logic and rationality in the workplace. Managers use fear and other emotions to both motivate and intimidate. For example, consider Microsoft CEO Steve Ballmer's management style prior to his recent efforts to become a kinder, gentler leader: "Ballmer shouts when he gets excited or angry—his voice rising so suddenly that it's like an electric shock . . . by the early 1990s, Ballmer had to have throat surgery to fix problems brought on by shouting."[78]

Less noisy, but still emotion-laden, is the description of Apple founder, Steve Jobs as witnessed by Walter Isaacson in his biography of the late CEO:

> Sometimes I'd look up and there would be tears running down his cheek," Isaacson said. Jobs told him he was always moved by "artistic purity." Sometimes, it was the design of a product, or even the creation of an advertisement that would move him to tears. Other times, it happened as he talked about a person who meant a lot to him.[79]

These corporate leaders would not have achieved what they have without the ability to be logical and rational decision makers *and* be emotionally charged. Too much emotion, however, could have spelled career and organizational disaster for either one of them.

In this final section, our examination of individual differences turns to defining emotions, reviewing a typology of 10 positive and negative emotions, and discussing the topics of emotional contagion, emotional labour, and emotional intelligence.

POSITIVE AND NEGATIVE EMOTIONS

Richard S. Lazarus, a leading authority on the subject, defines *emotions* as "complex, patterned, organismic reactions to how we think we are doing in our lifelong efforts to survive and flourish and to achieve what we wish for ourselves."[80] The word *organismic* is appropriate because emotions involve the *whole* person—biological, psychological, and social. Importantly, psychologists draw a distinction between *felt* and *displayed* emotions.[81] For example, you might feel angry (felt emotion) at a rude

Emotions

Complex human reactions to personal achievements and setbacks that may be felt and displayed.

co-worker, but not make a nasty remark in return (displayed emotion). Emotions play roles in both causing and adapting to stress and its associated biological and psychological problems. The destructive effect of emotional behaviour on social relationships is all too obvious in daily life.

Lazarus's definition of emotions centres on a person's goals. Accordingly, his distinction between positive and negative emotions is goal-oriented. Some emotions are triggered by frustration and failure when pursuing one's goals. Lazarus calls these *negative* emotions. They are said to be goal incongruent. For example, which of the six negative emotions in Figure 3.4 are you likely to experience if you fail the final exam in a required course? Failing the exam would be incongruent with your goal of graduating on time. On the other hand, which of the four *positive* emotions in Figure 3.4 would you probably experience if you graduated on time and with honours? The emotions you would experience in this situation are positive because they are congruent (or consistent) with an important lifetime goal. The individual's goals, it is important to note, may or may not be socially acceptable. Thus, a positive emotion, such as love/affection, may be undesirable if associated with sexual harassment. Oppositely, slight pangs of guilt, anxiety, and envy can motivate extra effort. On balance, the constructive or destructive nature of a particular emotion must be judged in terms of both its intensity and the person's relevant goal.

GOOD (AND BAD) MOODS ARE CONTAGIOUS

Have you ever had someone's bad mood sour your mood? That person could have been a parent, supervisor, co-worker, friend, or someone serving you in a store or restaurant. Appropriately, researchers call this emotional contagion. We, quite literally, can catch another person's good or bad mood or displayed emotions. This effect has been documented in two separate studies. UBC OB Professor Peter Frost talked about it in his book *Toxic Emotions At Work* (we'll be discussing how negative emotions can trigger conflict in Chapter 8), as well as in a study involving 131 bank tellers (92 percent female) and 220 exit interviews with their customers. In the latter study, tellers who expressed positive emotions tended to have more satisfied customers.[82] Two field studies with nurses and accountants as subjects found a strong linkage between the work group's collective mood and the individual's mood.[83] Both foul moods and good moods turned out to be contagious. Perhaps more managers should follow the lead of orchestra director Lorin Maazel:

FIGURE | 3.4 | Positive and Negative Emotions

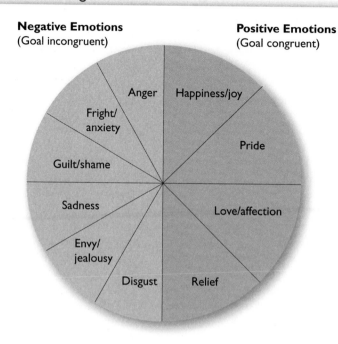

Negative Emotions
(Goal incongruent)

Positive Emotions
(Goal congruent)

SOURCE: Adapted from discussion in R.S. Lazarus, *Emotion and Adaptation* (New York: Oxford University Press, 1991), Chapters 6, 7.

I have noticed in my long career that if I am really tired or I have a flu coming on that it's felt. Everybody gets into that mode, and pretty soon, they're playing as sluggishly as I'm conducting. I have learned to come to rehearsal fresh, energetic, projecting enthusiasm and go-go-go. It's got to be irresistible. If I don't think I'm up to it, I take a cold shower. That's my job—to energize people. If they grind it out and couldn't care less, then they wind up hating you and themselves because it's not why they practised all of their lives. Emotion is what it's all about. Music making without emotion and passion is nothing.[84]

EMOTIONAL LABOUR (IT HAS NOT BEEN A PLEASURE SERVING YOU!)

Although they did not have the benefit of a catchy label or a body of sophisticated research, generations of managers have known about the power of emotional contagion in the marketplace. "Smile, look happy for the customers," employees are told over and over again. But what if the employees are having a rotten day? What if they have to mask their true feelings and emotions? What if they have to fake it?

Researchers have begun studying the dynamics of what they call *emotional labour*. Sociologist Arlie Hochschild defines emotional labour as the management of feeling to create a publicly observable facial and bodily display.[85] Other OB researchers have considered the complexities around emotional labour, and here is what they conclude:

Emotional labour

Management of feeling to create a publicly observable facial and bodily display.

Emotional labour can be particularly detrimental to the employee performing the labour and can take its toll both psychologically and physically. Employees ... may bottle up feelings of frustration, resentment, and anger, which are not appropriate to express. These feelings result, in part, from the constant requirement to monitor one's negative emotions and express positive ones. If not given a healthy expressive outlet, this emotional repression can lead to a syndrome of emotional exhaustion and burnout.[86]

Interestingly, a pair of laboratory studies found no gender difference in *felt* emotions, but the women were more emotionally expressive than the men.[87] This stream of research on emotional labour has major practical implications for productivity and job satisfaction, as well as for workplace anger, aggression, and violence. Taking a lead from Lorin Maazel, who we mentioned just a few paragraphs ago, managers need to be attuned to (and responsive to) the emotional states and needs of their people. They need to understand how emotions affect people and how their own personal emotions affect others in a contagious way. This understanding can be achieved through emotional intelligence.

LO 5 EMOTIONAL INTELLIGENCE

Emotional intelligence is the ability to perceive, express, understand, and regulate emotions. When an individual has the ability to manage himself or herself in a mature and constructive manner, especially when interacting with others, we say that person has high emotional intelligence (EI). Certainly, Gardner's work in 1983 on intrapersonal and interpersonal levels of intelligence began the contemporary discussion around EI; however it was the work of clinical psychologist Dr. Reuven Bar-On that defined the term EI—he referred to his research as the study of emotional social intelligence. Bar-On began investigation into those factors that were related to success in life, such as why some people with moderate IQ do well in life while others with high IQ fail. In 1988, Bar-On placed EI in the context of personality theory, specifically a model of well-being.[88]

Following Bar-On's work, in 1990 psychologists Peter Salovey and John Mayer proposed that the definition of EI should include social communication factors which require accurate perception of content, as well as tone and non-verbal signals such as posture and facial expression.[89] In 1995, Daniel Goleman, a psychologist turned journalist, popularized the concept of emotional intelligence and formulated EI in terms of a theory of job and work performance. He created a stir in education and management circles with the publication of his book, *Emotional Intelligence*. Since then, he's written many articles on the subject, including one that appeared in the *Harvard Business Review* just a few years ago on the correlation between emotional intelligence and effective leadership.[90] The once obscure topic of EI has now become mainstream (refer to Table 3.3 for more details). According to Goleman, traditional models of intelligence (IQ) are too narrow, failing to consider interpersonal competence. Goleman's broader agenda includes "abilities such as being able to motivate oneself and persist in the face of frustrations; to control impulse and delay gratification;

to regulate one's moods and keep distress from swamping the ability to think; to empathize and to hope."[91] Referred to by some as EI and others as EQ, emotional intelligence is said to have four key components: self-awareness, self-management, social awareness, and relationship management.[92] The first two constitute personal competence; the second two feed into social competence.

These emotional intelligence skills need to be well polished in today's pressure-packed workplaces:

> *Unanticipated hot spots often flare up during important meetings. Show patience, career experts say. Take deep breaths, compose your thoughts, restate the question—and use humour to defuse tension. If you avoid blurting out the first thing that comes to mind, "people will see your demeanour as cool and professional," observes [executive and author] David F D'Alessandro.*
>
> *Most people don't do well with the unexpected because they lack a script, notes Dr. [Dory] Hollander. The workplace psychologist recommends acting classes for her clients. A year of lessons helped one female client advance into the executive ranks at a big technology company. The woman used to perform poorly when colleagues tossed out unforeseen questions after presentations. "She looked like she was in pain," Dr. Hollander recalls. Today, the former middle manager acts confidently and appears to enjoy herself, even when she lands on the hot seat. "It really is theatre," her coach concludes.[93]*

Self-assessment instruments like the one located on Connect under 'Building Your Management Skills' link can shed some light on your own EI level. Sample questions include "I believe I can stay on top of tough situations,"[94] and "I am able to admit my own mistakes."[95] Recent research would encourage such EI scores only as starting points for personal development and by themselves are not conclusive.[96] Even Goleman concedes, "It's very tough to measure our own emotional intelligence, because most of us don't have a very clear sense of how we come across to other people. . . ."[97] Honest feedback from others is necessary. Still, the area of emotional intelligence is useful for teachers and organizational trainers because, unlike IQ, social problem solving and the ability to control one's emotions can be taught and learned. Scores on emotional intelligence tests definitely should *not* be used for making hiring and promotion decisions until valid measuring tools are developed.

Emotional intelligence

Ability to manage oneself and interact with others in mature and constructive ways.

TABLE 3.3

DEVELOPING PERSONAL AND SOCIAL COMPETENCE THROUGH EMOTIONAL INTELLIGENCE

Personal Competence: These capabilities determine how we manage ourselves.

Self-Awareness

- Emotional self-awareness: Reading one's own emotions and recognizing their impact; using "gut sense" to guide decisions.
- Accurate self-assessment: Knowing one's strengths and limits.
- Self-confidence: A sound sense of one's self-worth and capabilities.

Self-Management

- Emotional self-control: Keeping disruptive emotions and impulses under control.
- Transparency: Displaying honesty and integrity; trustworthiness.
- Adaptability: Flexibility in adapting to changing situations or overcoming obstacles.
- Achievement: The drive to improve performance to meet inner standards of excellence.
- Initiative: Readiness to act and seize opportunities.
- Optimism: Seeing the upside in events.

Social Competence: These capabilities determine how we manage relationships.

Social Awareness

- Empathy: Sensing others' emotions, understanding their perspective, and taking active interest in their concerns.
- Organizational awareness: Reading the currents, decision networks, and politics at the organizational level.
- Service: Recognizing and meeting follower, client, or customer needs.

Relationship Management

- Inspirational leadership: Guiding and motivating with a compelling vision.
- Influence: Wielding a range of tactics for persuasion.
- Developing others: Bolstering others' abilities through feedback and guidance.
- Change catalyst: Initiating, managing, and leading in a new direction.
- Conflict management: Resolving disagreements.
- Building bonds: Cultivating and maintaining a web of relationships.
- Teamwork and collaboration: Cooperation and team building.

Summary of Learning Objectives

 Define *self-esteem* and *self-efficacy*. Self-esteem is an overall evaluation of oneself, one's perceived self-worth. Self-efficacy is the belief in one's ability to successfully perform a task.

 Explain what is meant by self-monitoring and discuss how it relates to the social learning model of self-management. High self-monitors strive to make a good public impression by closely monitoring their behaviour and adapting it to the situation. Low self-monitors do the opposite by acting out their momentary feelings, regardless of their surroundings. According to the social learning model of self-management, behaviour results from interaction among four components: (a) situational cues, (b) the person's psychological self, (c) the person's behaviour, and (d) consequences. Effective behaviour can be developed by relying on supportive cognitive processes such as mental rehearsal and self-talk. Carefully arranged cues and consequences also help in the self-improvement process.

LO 3 **Relate the one Big Five personality dimension that is most positively correlated with job performance.** The Big Five personality dimensions are extraversion (social and talkative), agreeableness (trusting and cooperative), conscientiousness (responsible and persistent), emotional stability (relaxed and unworried), and openness to experience (intellectual and curious). Conscientiousness is the best predictor of job performance.

LO 4 **Compare and contrast internal and external locus of control.** People with an internal locus of control, such as entrepreneurs, believe they are masters of their own fate. Those with an external locus of control attribute their behaviour and its results to situational forces. In an empowered workplace, a manager would want to hire people with a high internal locus of control because they would be more likely to "blame" themselves rather than others for poor work performance, thus self-managing themselves to higher productivity.

LO 5 **Summarize the theory of emotional intelligence and explain how it relates to appreciating individual differences between people.** Emotional intelligence (EI) is the ability to manage oneself and interact with others in mature and constructive ways. The four key components of EI are self-awareness and self-management (personal competence), and social awareness and relationship management (social competence). Someone with high EI has the ability to see the connection between emotions and behaviour in the workplace—first their own, and then those of others. Since EI goes beyond traditional intelligence, it provides a deeper understanding of individual human behaviour. Old school assumptions around hiring people who have certain personalities or intelligences need to be enriched with a more contemporary understanding of EI so that a more complete picture of how people differ is considered.

Discussion Questions

1. How is someone you know with low self-efficacy, relative to a specified task, "programming himself/herself for failure"? How could that individual develop high self-efficacy?

2. What importance do you attach to self-talk in self-management? Explain.

3. On a scale of 1 (low) to 10 (high), how would you rate yourself on the Big Five personality dimensions? Is your personality profile suitable for your current (or chosen) line of work? Explain.

4. What benefit would there be to employers if they pre-screened all job applicants with a combination of personality assessments and instruments measuring EI levels?

5. Which of the four key components of emotional intelligence is (or are) your strong suit? Which is (or are) your weakest? What are the everyday implications of your EI profile?

6. Describe how you might use your knowledge of intelligences at work.

Integration of OB Concepts—Discussion Questions

1. See Chapter 1 – Discuss the relationship between the Big Five personality dimensions (locus of control, self-monitoring, self-esteem, proactive personality, and general self-efficacy) with each of the characteristics desired for future managers as outlined in Table 1.1.

2. See Chapter 2 – How can perception influence self-concept?

Google Searches

1. **Google Search:** "Good To Great—Jim Collins Level 5 Leadership" Read about the Level 5 leadership qualities as outlined in Collins' book. What sort of personality dimensions does a Level 5 leader have? What type of locus of control would you speculate a Level 5 to have and why?

2. **Google Search:** "The Luck Factor—Change Your Luck, Change Your Life" Read a few paragraphs of what Professor Wiseman's research discovered about 'lucky' individuals. How do lucky people cope with disappointment or bad luck? Are you a lucky person? Working with a partner, answer the following question: Would you say that lucky people have a high or low internal locus on control? Explain.

3. **Google Search:** "What is Your Emotional Intelligence Quotient?" and complete the self-assessment located on Connect under the 'Building your Management Skills' link. What did you score? Do you agree with the EQ results? Explain your response. Compare your results with group members and discuss the differences between people.

4. **Google Search:** "How To Become An Expert—The 10,000 Hour Rule" Determine who coined this phrase and explain what it has to do with intelligence. Relate your findings to how individual behaviour is affected when a person applies the 10,000 hour rule to their job, skill, or ability. What does this tell you about people who succeed and those that don't? Is it all about being born with a high IQ?

Experiential Exercise

Managing Situational Cues

PURPOSE   This exercise is meant to strengthen student understanding of the Social Learning Model of Self-Management (Figure 3.3). Approx. Timing: 15 minutes.

ACTIVITY ASSIGNMENT

- The two individuals described below want to achieve a new goal.
- Working in groups, help the individuals through the various factors of the Social Learning Model to achieve a successful outcome.
- Review the Social Learning Model (Figure 3.3) while working through the two situations.

1. SHAKIRA

SCENARIO: Shakira's family doctor says that she is in poor health, 60 pounds over-weight, and is a strong candidate for diabetes. The doctor has ordered Shakira to start eating properly, exercise daily, and lose weight over the next 12 months or face taking medication every day for the rest of her life.

BEHAVIOUR CHANGE: Shakira decides to set a goal of taking her health more seriously—starting now.

SITUATIONAL CUES: Identify at least six cues that have to be rearranged for Shakira to achieve her goal.

CONSEQUENCES: List at least three consequences (or rewards) that Shakira can implement.

2. XIN (pronounced "Shin")

SCENARIO: Xin works 50–60 hours per week, on average. Sometimes there is so much to do that the only time work can get done is for Xin to stay late at night or work on weekends to get caught up. Xin is getting concerned about being able to sustain such a level of performance; besides, no one else in the office works the same kind of hours. One day, a colleague in the next office mentions to Xin that the HR Department is offering a time management seminar. Xin wonders if attending this seminar might help decrease the number of hours spent at the office each week.

BEHAVIOUR CHANGE: Xin decides to set a goal to decrease the number of hours spent working each week.

SITUATIONAL CUES: Identify at least six cues that have to be rearranged for Xin to achieve this goal.

CONSEQUENCES: List at least three consequences (or rewards) that Xin can implement.

OB In Action Case Study

We Are Looking for Honest and Humble People

Consider the following scenario:

University Hospital is a large urban health-care facility located in Calgary, Alberta. The HR department was recently restructured by a new director, Samir Padavan, CHRP, who believes strongly in recruiting and selecting individuals with high levels of self-awareness. One day he is in his office talking to Sally Sparks, a supervisor in the department.

"Samir, do you have a minute? I want to get your opinion on something. It involves one of the medical departments that is looking to hire a new employee. They want to select using an old traditional method and I want to implement a new screening instrument to find the best candidate. It involves an online survey that the candidate would take that includes approximately 240 personality items, followed up by a behavioural interview. I'm getting some push-back from the department because they say self-assessment are a waste of time . . . and behavioural interviews take too much time! Ugh! What do you think?" asks Sparks.

"Old screening techniques can be quick and simple to implement, but can leave too many potential gaps. Behavioural interviews allow us to see traits and values in play. I know they take time to orchestrate, but the results are without question the

best. Screening candidates that have certain kinds of personality traits and high self-awareness levels means that they'll succeed in an empowered workplace. University Hospital is an innovative and caring facility made up of empowered employees who give extra effort toward patient care because that's just who they are. We're light on management and heavy on front-line caregivers. I'd much prefer hiring someone who acts in a professional way, brings managers solutions rather than problems, and looks for opportunities to help this hospital deliver high quality patient care using fewer resources. The last thing we need around here are more employees that need a manager directing their daily tasks or pushing them to higher performance," responds Padavan.

"I totally agree. I was reading a recent study that stated employees who self-reported honesty and humility on assessments correlated positively with supervisor ratings and job performance. It went on to say that conscientiousness and emotional stability are important for job performance. How are these traits going to be identified in a traditional screening and interviewing process? I really need to convince the decision maker in that department that I can help him find the candidate with the best fit . . . they need to trust me on this one," says Sparks.

"Sally, did it ever occur to you that maybe the decision maker is really trying to find an employee that doesn't ask questions and just does as they are told? If you place an independent thinker in that job, it might cause some problems in that department!" states Padavan.

Just then there is a knock at Padavan's door telling him his 2:30 p.m. appointment has arrived. "Sally, go back to that department and ask a few more questions . . . find out what kind of employee they really want to hire . . . then come back and let's talk more. OK?" says Padavan.

"Sounds good. Thanks!" says Sparks as she turns and walks out of his office.

Discussion Questions

1. Is Samir discussing high or low self-monitoring employees for University Hospital?
2. What level of humility would Sally prefer the new candidate to have? Explain.
3. What is Samir suggesting when he states that "maybe the decision maker is really trying to find an employee that doesn't ask questions"? Why would a supervisor want to hire a person who does as he or she is told and doesn't ask questions?
4. What kind of locus of control does a person have if he or she prefers to have others direct them?
5. If a person has a high internal locus of control, what would his or her levels of self-esteem and self-efficacy probably be? Explain.

The CONNECTion Zone   McGraw Hill connect™

- The Presentation Assistant
- Ethical OB Dilemma
- Video Case

Practise and learn online with Connect.

Values, Attitudes, and Job Satisfaction

FACING AN OB CHALLENGE

I am single, in my mid-twenties, and have a good job. This job pays well, and I could potentially have it the rest of my career. My colleagues like me and my supervisor assures me my job is secure. That being said, I do not feel as though I am fulfilling my passion in this position. I could work here for the next 30 years and be financially well off. I do not, however, know what my passion is or what I would do if I left this job. In this economy, it's easy to justify staying in a job even though a person may not be happy. I know jobs are difficult to get and I should be thankful to have one. How do I find my passion?

—WONDERING

LEARNING OBJECTIVES

After reading this chapter, you should be able to:

LO 1 Define *personal values* and relate them to Schwartz's Value Theory.

LO 2 Describe three types of value conflicts.

LO 3 Identify the three components of attitude.

LO 4 Relate organizational commitment to psychological contract.

LO 5 Compare and discriminate between eight variables that have a relationship with job satisfaction.

Self Assessing Values

Having passion for your job is a reasonable request, and you shouldn't have to apologize for wanting it in your life. But where does it come from? Is it something that the employer is responsible for generating, or should employees have it within themselves naturally? These are all good questions, and this chapter will attempt to shed light on the challenges in the contemporary workplace. The overall goal of Chapter 4 is to continue the investigation of individual behaviour so that you get a better idea of how managers and organizations can use knowledge of individual differences to attract, motivate, and retain quality employees. We explore and discuss the impact of personal values and attitudes on important outcomes such as job satisfaction, performance, and turnover. To prepare for these topics, you are invited to complete the "What Do You Value?" Self-Assessment Exercise.

Personal Values

LO 1

Personal values essentially represent the beliefs that give meaning to things in your life. Values are important to your understanding of organizational behaviour because they influence behaviour across different settings. Shalom Schwartz has developed a comprehensive and well-accepted theory of personal values.[1] Let's learn more about personal values by exploring Schwartz's theory, discussing value conflicts, and examining the timely value-related topic of work versus family life conflicts. It is worth noting here that as we move through the text, we'll revisit the concept of values but in different ways. For example, we'll shift away from personal values and eventually focus on collective or shared values when we discuss organizational culture in Chapter 11.

> **Personal values**
> Enduring beliefs that give our lives meaning.

SCHWARTZ'S VALUE THEORY

Schwartz believes that values are motivational in that they "represent broad goals that apply across contexts and time."[2] For example, valuing achievement will likely result in your working hard to earn a promotion at work, just as it will drive you to compete against friends in a weekly golf game. Values are also relatively stable and can influence behaviour outside of our awareness.

Schwartz proposes that there are 10 broad values that guide behaviour. He also identifies the motivational mechanisms that underlie each value (see Table 4.1). It is these motivational mechanisms that give values their ability to influence our behaviour. For example, Table 4.1 shows that the desire for social power, authority, and wealth collectively motivate someone who values power. In contrast, the value of conformity is driven by motives related to politeness, obedience, self-discipline, and honouring one's parents and elders. Not only have these 10 values been found to predict behaviour as outlined in the theory, but they also generalize across cultures.[3] A recent study showed that the 10 basic values are relevant to understanding behaviour across 20 countries.[4]

Figure 4.1 shows the proposed relationships among the 10 values. The circular pattern reveals which ones are most strongly related and which ones are in conflict. In general, adjacent values like self-direction and

What Do You Value?

INSTRUCTIONS: Rate each item in terms of how important it is to you on a scale of 0 (not important) to 100 (very important). Write a number between 0 and 100 on the line to the left of each item.

NOT IMPORTANT				SOMEWHAT IMPORTANT				VERY IMPORTANT		
0	10	20	30	40	50	60	70	80	90	100

_____ 1 An enjoyable, satisfying job

_____ 2 A high-paying job

_____ 3 A good marriage

_____ 4 Meeting new people; social events

_____ 5 Involvement in community activities

_____ 6 My religion

_____ 7 Exercising, playing sports

_____ 8 Intellectual development

_____ 9 A career with challenging opportunities

_____ 10 Nice cars, clothes, home, and so on

_____ 11 Spending time with family

_____ 12 Having several close friends

_____ 13 Volunteer work for non-profit organizations, such as the Canadian Cancer Society

_____ 14 Meditation, quiet time to think, pray, and so on

_____ 15 A healthy, balanced diet

_____ 16 Educational reading, television, self-improvement programs, and so on

Scoring Key

Transfer the numbers for each of the 16 items to the appropriate column; then add up the 2 numbers in each column.

Professional	Financial	Family	Social
1. _____	2. _____	3. _____	4. _____
9. _____	10. _____	11. _____	12. _____

TOTALS

Community	Spiritual	Physical	Intellectual
5. _____	6. _____	7. _____	8. _____
13. _____	14. _____	15. _____	16. _____

TOTALS

The higher the total in any value dimension, the higher the importance you place on that value set. The closer the numbers are in all eight dimensions, the more well-rounded you are.

SOURCE: R.N. Lussier, *Human Relations in Organizations: A Skill Building Approach,* 2nd ed. (Homewood, IL: Richard D. Irwin, 1993). Reprinted by permission of the McGraw-Hill Companies, Inc.

TABLE 4.1

DEFINITION OF VALUES AND MOTIVES IN SCHWARTZ'S THEORY

VALUE	DEFINITION AND UNDERLYING MOTIVES
Power	Social status and prestige, control or dominance over people and resources (social power, authority, wealth)
Achievement	Personal success through demonstrating competence according to social standards (successful, capable, ambitious, influential)
Hedonism	Pleasure and sensuous gratification for oneself (pleasure, enjoying life)
Stimulation	Excitement, novelty, and challenge in life (daring, a varied life, an exciting life)
Self-direction	Independent thought and action choosing, creating, exploring (creativity, freedom, independent, curious, choosing own goals)
Universalism	Understanding, appreciation, tolerance, and protection of the welfare of all people and of nature (broadminded, wisdom, social justice, equality, a world at peace, a world of beauty, unity with nature, protecting the environment)
Benevolence	Preservation and enhancement of the welfare of people with whom one is in frequent personal contact (helpful, honest, forgiving, loyal, responsible)
Tradition	Respect, commitment, and acceptance of the customs and ideas that traditional culture or religion provides the self (humble, accepting my portion in life, devout, respect for tradition, moderate)
Conformity	Restraint of actions, inclinations, and impulses likely to upset or harm others and violate social expectations or norms (politeness, obedient, self-discipline, honouring parents and elders)
Security	Safety, harmony, and stability of society, of relationships, and of self (family security, national security, social order, clean, reciprocation of favours)

SOURCE: From Anat Bradi and Shalom H Schwartz. "Values and Behavior: Strength and Structure of Relations," *Personality & Social Psychology Bulletin,* October 2003, p 1208. Copyright © 2003 by Sage Publications.

FIGURE 4.1 Relationship among Schwartz's Values

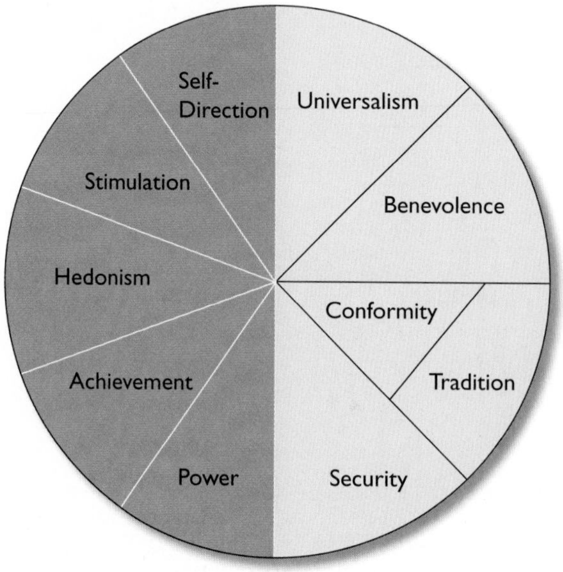

universalism are positively related, whereas values that are further apart (e.g., self-direction and power) are less strongly related. Taking this one step further, Schwartz proposes that values that are in opposing directions from the centre conflict with each other. Examples are power and universalism or stimulation and conformity/tradition. For instance, the drive to live a stimulating life by engaging in activities like sky-diving or mountain climbing would conflict with the desire to live a moderate or traditional life. Research provides partial support for these predictions.[5]

LO 2 VALUE CONFLICTS

Three types of value conflict related to an individual's attitude and overall job satisfaction can directly impact performance. They are intrapersonal value conflict, interpersonal value conflict, and individual–organization value conflict. These sources of conflict are, respectively, from inside the person, between people, and between the person and the organization. Value conflict can lead to higher employee turnover throughout the organization.

Intrapersonal Value Conflict Our discussion of Schwartz's theory of values revealed that people are likely to experience inner conflict and worry when personal values conflict with each other. For individuals who want balance in their life, a worrisome conflict arises when they value, for example, "being highly ambitious and wanting the fancy urban job" (achievement), and at the same time want to "be happy in the end while spending time with family and friends" (security)—all at the same time. A few years ago, Dan Rosensweig, the ex-chief operating officer at Yahoo!, expressed having intrapersonal value conflict to a reporter from *Fast Company* by noting that his "biggest challenge was giving your job everything you have because it deserves it, but at the same time recognizing and appreciating the most important things in your life," such as your family. He commented on feeling "envious of people who were able to find better balance between work and personal life."[6] In general, people are happier and less stressed when their personal values are aligned.

Interpersonal Value Conflict This type of value conflict is often at the core of personality conflicts, and such conflicts can negatively affect a person's career. Consider the case of a former newspaper publisher, Jeffrey Johnson, who was fired by the owner when

"My first mistake was telling the people I work with where we were going on vacation."

his values collided with those of senior management. Senior management wanted Johnson to improve the paper's financial results by cutting costs. Johnson was then asked to eliminate employees from the payroll. The conflict for Mr. Johnson was that he did not believe that the newspaper's problems would be solved by employee layoffs. He wanted to improve the newspaper's financial status by exploring creative ways to generate revenue as opposed to cutting costs.[7] This example highlights how important it is to carefully evaluate the pros and cons of handling interpersonal value conflicts with your superiors.

Individual–Organization Value Conflict Companies actively seek to embed certain values into their corporate cultures. Conflict can occur when values that are publicly announced and believed to be accepted by the organization collide with employees' personal values. OB researchers refer to this type of conflict as value congruence or person–culture fit.[8] *Value congruence or person–culture fit* reflects the similarity between an individual's personal values and the cultural value system of an organization. This is an important type of conflict to consider when accepting future jobs, because positive outcomes such as satisfaction, commitment, performance, career success, reduced stress, and lower turnover intentions are realized when an individual's personal values are similar or aligned with organizational values.[9]

> *Value congruence or person–culture fit*
>
> The similarity between personal values and organizational values.

WORK VS. FAMILY LIFE CONFLICT

A complex web of demographic and economic factors makes the balancing act between job and life very challenging for most of us. Demographically, there are more women in the workforce, more dual-income families, more single working parents, and an aging population that gives mid-career employees daycare and/or eldercare responsibilities.[10] On the economic front, years of downsizing and corporate cost-cutting have given employees heavier workloads. According to data collected by Carleton University Professor Linda Duxbury, a noted pioneer in the field of organizational health, Canadians who are working 60–75 hours per week do not have balance in their lives, and if balance is what we seek, then workload must be addressed.[11]

In this section, we search for better understanding when it comes to work versus family life conflict by introducing a values-based model and discussing practical research insights.

A Values-Based Model of Work/Family Conflict   Pamela L. Perrewé and Wayne A. Hochwarter proposed a model of work/family conflict (see Figure 4.2). This model is meant to help you understand the causes of work/family conflict. Let's start on the left box of the model; here we see *general life values* feeding into family-related values and work-related values. Family values involve enduring beliefs about the importance of family and who should play key family roles (e.g., child rearing, housekeeping, and income earning). Work values centre on the relative importance of work and career goals in one's life.

From here, the model splits in two. *Value similarity* relates to the degree of consensus among family members about family values. While work may be a symptom of conflict between family members, the real cause stems from competing values between family members. For example, if a homemaker launches a business venture despite her spouse's desire to be the sole breadwinner, lack of family value similarity will cause work/family conflict. *Value congruence,* on the other hand, involves the amount of value agreement between employee and employer. In this instance, it's the demands of the job and the expectations of the employer that are the cause of conflict. If, for example, refusing to go on a business trip to stay home for a child's birthday is viewed as disloyalty to the company, then lack of value congruence can trigger work/family conflict within the employee.

At this point, the model converges into actual work/life conflicts. Notice how these "work-family conflicts can take two distinct forms: (1) work interference with family, or (2) family interference with work."[12] For example, suppose two managers in the same department have daughters playing on the same soccer team. One manager misses the big soccer game to attend a last-minute department meeting; the other manager skips the meeting to attend the game. Both may experience work/family conflict, but for different reasons.

FIGURE 4.2   A Values Model of Work/Family Conflict

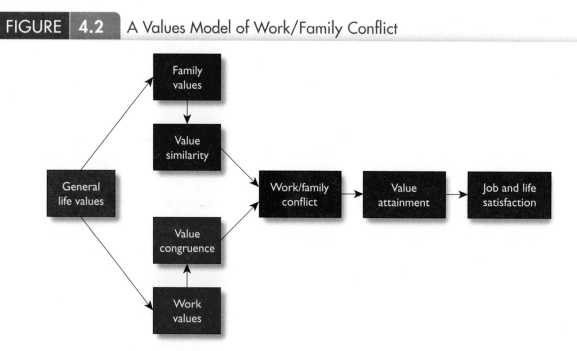

SOURCE: P.L. Perrewé and W.A. Hochwarter, "Can We Really Have It All? The Attainment of Work and Family Values," *Current Directions in Psychological Science,* February 2001, p 30. Published by Blackwell Publishers, Inc. © American Psychological Society.

Work/life balance is a universal concern. Here, Italy's member of the European Parliament Licia Ronzulli takes part with her daughter in a voting session at the European Parliament in Strasbourg, France.

The last two boxes in the model—value attainment and job and life satisfaction—are a package deal. Satisfaction tends to be higher for those who stay true to themselves by living their life according to their values, and lower for those who do not. Overall, this model reflects much common sense. How does your life track through the model? Sadly, for many it is often a painful trip.

Practical Research Insights about Work/Family Conflict
This is a new but very active area of OB research. The evidence typically comes from field surveys of real people in real jobs. Recent practical findings include:

- *Work/family balance begins at home.* Historically, women have shouldered the majority of the standard household chores and child-rearing responsibilities. Fortunately, recent research shows that men are beginning to share more of the work associated with running a home.[13] To help out with the domestic chore of cooking, Google Canada offers new parents a $500 take-out meal reimbursement plan to use during the first three months after the baby's birth. This benefit can be applied to grocery purchases, take-out meals, or home cooking provided by a catering service.[14]

- *An employer's family-supportive philosophy is more important than specific programs.* Many employers offer family-friendly programs, including child and elder daycare assistance, parental leave, telecommuting, and flexible work schedules. However, if employees are afraid or reluctant to take advantage

of those programs because the organization's culture values hard work and long hours above all else, families will inevitably suffer. To be truly family-friendly, the organization needs to provide programs and back them up with a family-supportive philosophy and culture.[15] For example, at construction powerhouse EllisDon Corp., employees are allowed to exercise an unlimited policy that grants employees' requests for days off as they need them, rather than according to an arbitrary vacation schedule. Further, their employee assistance program helps employees line up medical care for family members or emergency child care. Such give-back from the organization to their employees is one of the reasons EllisDon earned a spot on Canada's Top 100 Employers list.[16]

- *Informal flexibility in work hours as well as allowing people to work at home is essential to promoting work/family balance.* Quite simply, flexibility allows people to cope more effectively with competing demands across their personal and work lives.

- *Take a proactive approach to managing work/family conflict.* Two recent meta-analyses of more than 60 different studies and 43,000 people demonstrated that employees' personal lives spill over to their work life and vice versa. This means that employees' job satisfaction, organizational commitment, and intentions to quit are significantly related to the amount of work/family conflict that exists in their lives.[17] We encourage you to identify the sources of work/family conflict and consider how the organization may help you manage your workload. For example, the Toronto business law office of Stikeman Elliott LLP made Canada's Top 100 Employers list for recognizing that after-hours work cannot be avoided, so the firm provides a technology stipend so its lawyers can work from home on top-of-the-line equipment if they request it. Said another way, the employee identifies and manages the need while the firm supports it.[18]

- *Mentors can help.* According to a field survey of 502 respondents (63 percent men), "The results indicate that having a mentor is significantly related to lower levels of work-family conflict ... Such findings suggest another potential benefit of mentoring: a source of social support to reduce employee stress caused by conflicts between the work and family domains."[19] PricewaterhouseCoopers Canada (PwC), for example, has won several awards recently, including Best Employer in Canada, recognizing various elements of the PwC workplace, including their coaching and mentorship program. All senior associates are formally mentored with new associates for on-going feedback and support to develop, excel, and advance careers, as well as to help achieve personal goals. Even the CEO has a dedicated coach![20]

"PwC is different because they really invest in their people," says recent business graduate Fahad Meer, who started working as a summer student in the downtown office and is now an Experienced Associate in the Audit and Assurance Group (AAG) at PwC, Toronto.

■ *Being your own boss is no panacea (ultimate solution).* Self-employment turns out to be a good news/bad news proposition when compared to standard organizational employment. Among the benefits of being self-employed are a stronger sense of autonomy (independence), a higher level of job involvement, and greater job satisfaction. But self-employed people also report higher levels of work/family conflict and lower levels of family satisfaction.[21]

Organizational Response to Work/Family Issues   Organizations have implemented a variety of family-friendly programs and services aimed at helping employees integrate between their work and personal lives. Corporate leaders at EllisDon, PricewaterhouseCoopers, Google, and Stikeman Eliott say employees who know what is expected of them, and how their employers will support them in meeting those expectations, are better equipped to meet the demands of their jobs—even when the demands are heavy, intense, and chronic.

One last consideration in the discussion around organizational response to work/family issues is religious accommodation, which plays a major role in the lives of some employees. If, for example, your

HELPING EMPLOYEES BALANCE WORK/ PERSONAL LIFE

Managers who know Canadian laws have a greater chance of creating a mutually satisfying and balanced work environment for their employees. Employers who have legal savvy know the boundaries of which individual employee requests (which are rooted in personal values) are reasonable and which are not. Canadian laws, such as the federal Human Rights Act or any one of the provincial Human Rights Codes, are basically broad core values of this country that outline specific behaviours and/ or responsibilities on the part of all persons and organizations operating within Canada.

If, for example, an employee were to make a reasonable personal request for time off to observe a religious celebration even though it competed with a corporate value, the employer who is familiar with the Act or an HR Code would know that it's against the law to discriminate on the basis of religious beliefs. Knowing this expectation, the employer would accommodate such a request

as much as possible, thereby minimizing work/ life conflict within the employee and creating a mutually satisfying work environment.

What if an employer is not familiar with the wide variety of religious celebrations? Then it is imperative for both sides to respectively discuss the details around the request and review timelines and policies. The employee needs to be sensitive to work demands by ensuring a reasonable timeline to place the request. The manager needs to understand the legal and ethical obligations to accommodate when and if possible. As Canada becomes more diverse, there is greater incentive for organizations to be familiar with applicable Canadian laws; such action will minimize work/life conflict and keep individual values from competing with corporate values.

SOURCE: Canadian Human Rights Act (1985) website: www. chrc-ccdp.ca/legislation_policies/human_rights_act-en.asp; Ontario Human Rights Commission website: www.ohrc.on.ca; 2011–2012

LAW AND ETHICS AT WORK

organization has a significant number of Muslim male employees, it would be wise not to schedule a staff meeting at noon every Friday—the time they go to prayer. Out of respect for employees who practise their faith, some organizations have built prayer rooms on site, which translates into less time spent away from the office,[22] resulting in a win–win situation. As illustrated in the Law and Ethics at Work feature box, it benefits the entire organization when values are mutually respected.

Attitudes

LO 3

Hardly a day goes by without the media reporting the results of another attitude survey, designed to take the pulse of public opinion. What do we think about candidate X, terrorism, the war on drugs, long-gun registry, or tax increases? Meanwhile, in the workplace, managers conduct attitude surveys to monitor such things as job and pay satisfaction. All this attention on attitudes is based on the realization that our attitudes influence our behaviour. For example, research demonstrated that seniors with a positive attitude about aging had better memory, better hearing, and lived longer than those with negative attitudes.[23] A recent meta-analysis involving more than 50,000 people revealed that overall job attitudes are positively related to performance and negatively associated with indicators of withdrawal—lateness, absenteeism, and turnover.[24] In this section, we discuss the components of attitudes and examine the connection between attitudes and behaviour.

THE NATURE OF ATTITUDES

An *attitude* is defined as "a learned predisposition to respond in a consistently favourable or unfavourable manner with respect to a given object."[25] Consider your attitude toward chocolate ice cream. You are more likely to purchase a chocolate ice cream cone if you have a positive attitude toward chocolate ice cream. In contrast, you are more likely to purchase some other flavour, say vanilla caramel swirl, if you have a positive attitude toward vanilla and a neutral or negative attitude toward chocolate ice cream. Now consider a work example. If you have a positive attitude about your job (i.e., you like what you are doing), you are likely to be more willing to extend yourself at work by working longer and harder.

These examples illustrate that attitudes propel us to act in a specific way in

Attitude

Learned predisposition toward a given object.

a specific context. That is, attitudes affect behaviour at a different level than do values. While values represent global beliefs that influence behaviour across all situations, attitudes relate only to behaviour directed toward specific objects, persons, or situations. Values and attitudes generally, but not always, are in harmony. For example, a manager who strongly values helpful behaviour may have a negative attitude toward helping an unethical co-worker. The difference between attitudes and values is clarified by considering the three components of attitudes: affective, cognitive, and behavioural.[26] It is important to note that your overall attitude toward someone or something is a function of the combined influence of all three components.

Affective Component The *affective component* of an attitude includes the feelings or emotions a person has about a given object or situation. For example:

- *I don't like working with bossy people because they make me feel inferior.*

Affective component

The feelings or emotions a person has about an object or situation.

Cognitive Component The *cognitive component* of an attitude reflects the beliefs or ideas a person has about an object or situation. For example:

- *I work with a person named Pat who I believe is a bossy person.*

Cognitive component

The beliefs or ideas a person has about an object or situation.

Behavioural Component The *behavioural component* refers to how a person intends or expects to act toward someone or something. Attitude Theory suggests that your ultimate behaviour in this situation is a function of all three attitudinal components. For example:

Behavioural component

How a person intends to act or behave toward someone or something.

- *I avoid working with Pat (behavioural) because I believe that Pat is bossy (cognitive) and I don't like working with bossy people who make me feel inferior (affective).*

So, while we observe individual behaviour around the office, we need to understand the two steps that took place before the person acted them out. Greater understanding of behaviour will occur once a clearer picture unfolds around the feelings and beliefs that went before it. If the desire is to correct a person's behaviour, then don't start at the behaviour; rather, go back two steps and clarify the factors that prompted it.

COGNITIVE DISSONANCE—WHEN ATTITUDES AND REALITY COLLIDE

What happens when a strongly held attitude is contradicted by reality? Suppose you are extremely concerned about getting AIDS, which you believe is transferred from contact with body fluids, including blood. Then you find yourself in a life-threatening accident in a foreign country and need surgery and blood transfusions—including transfusions from a blood bank with unknown quality control. Would you reject the blood to remain consistent with your beliefs about getting AIDS? According to social psychologist Leon Festinger, this situation would create cognitive dissonance.

Many business students probably recall learning about cognitive dissonance from their marketing class when discussing consumer behaviour. But it also applies to OB; in this instance, **cognitive dissonance** represents the psychological discomfort people experience when their attitudes or beliefs are incompatible with their behaviour.[27] Festinger proposed that people are motivated to maintain consistency between their attitudes and beliefs and their behaviour. He theorized that people will seek to reduce the "dissonance" or psychological tension through one of three main methods:

> *Cognitive dissonance*
>
> Psychological discomfort experienced when attitudes and behaviour are inconsistent.

1. **Change attitude or behaviour, or both** This is the simplest solution when confronted with cognitive dissonance. Let's take an example of a person who is anti-smoking. What will this employee do if the company she works for co-sponsors a sporting event with Imperial Tobacco Group and she is expected to attend the event on behalf of the company? If the employee attends, she will feel like a hypocrite (two-faced). If she refuses to attend, it could mean a reprimand (discipline) from the employer. What to do? To avoid the dissonance, the employee changes her attitude toward cigarette smoking, saying that people have the right to smoke if they want to. The employee considers that perhaps she has been *overreacting toward the whole thing*.

2. **Belittle the importance of the inconsistent behaviour** This happens all the time. In our example, the employee could belittle the belief that attending the event means supporting cigarette smoking. *It's a sporting event, not a smoking event. And besides, it's just a one-time thing.*

3. **Find consonant (hormonious) elements that outweigh dissonant (harsh) ones** This approach entails rationalizing away the dissonance. The employee attends the sporting event because she believes there are no other options. *After all, it could mean the employee's job and she can't afford to lose this great paying job because of family obligations and responsibilities.*

HOW STABLE ARE ATTITUDES?

In one landmark study, researchers found the job attitudes of 5,000 middle-aged male employees to be very stable over a five-year period. Positive job attitudes remained positive; negative ones remained negative. Even those who changed jobs or occupations tended to maintain their prior job attitudes.[28] More recent research suggests the previous study may have overstated the stability of attitudes because it was restricted to a middle-aged sample. This time, researchers asked: What happens to attitudes over the entire span of adulthood? General attitudes were found to be more susceptible to change during early and late adulthood than during middle adulthood. Three factors accounted for middle-age attitude stability: (1) greater personal certainty, (2) perceived abundance of knowledge, and (3) a need for strong attitudes. Thus, the conventional notion that general attitudes become less likely to change as the person ages was rejected. Elderly people, along with young adults, can and do change their general attitudes because they are more open and less self-assured.[29]

Because our cultural backgrounds and experiences vary, our attitudes and behaviour vary. Attitudes are translated into behaviour via behavioural intentions. Let's examine an established model of this important process.

ATTITUDES AFFECT BEHAVIOUR VIA INTENTIONS

Building on Leon Festinger's work on cognitive dissonance, Icek Ajzen and Martin Fishbein delved further into understanding the reason for discrepancies between individuals' attitudes and behaviour. Ajzen ultimately developed and refined a model focusing on intentions as the key link between attitudes and planned behaviour. His theory of planned behaviour in Figure 4.3 shows three separate but interacting determinants of one's intention (a person's readiness to perform a given behaviour) to exhibit a specific behaviour.

Importantly, this model only predicts behaviour under an individual's control, not behaviour due to circumstances beyond one's control. For example, this model can predict the likelihood of someone skipping work if the person says his or her intention is to stay in bed tomorrow morning. But it would be a poor model for predicting getting to work on time, because uncontrolled circumstances such as traffic delays or an accident could intervene.

Determinants of Intention Ajzen explains the nature and roles of the three determinants of intention as follows:

The first is the attitude toward the behaviour *and refers to the degree to which a person has a favourable or unfavourable evaluation or appraisal of the behaviour in question. The second predictor is a social factor termed* subjective norm; *it refers to the perceived social pressure to perform or not to perform the behaviour. The third antecedent of intention is the degree of* perceived behaviour control, *which... refers to the perceived ease or difficulty of performing the behaviour and it is assumed to reflect past experience as well as anticipated impediments and obstacles.* [30]

To bring these three determinants of intention to life, let's return to our lazy soul who chose to stay in bed rather than go to work. This person feels overworked and underpaid, and thus has a favourable attitude about skipping work occasionally. The person's perceived subjective norm is favourable because he sees co-workers skipping work with no ill effects (in fact, they collect sick pay). Regarding perceived behaviour control, this person is completely in charge of acting on his intention to skip work today. So he turns off the alarm clock and pulls the covers over his head. Sweet dreams!

Intentions and Behaviour Research Lessons and Implications According to Ajzen's model of planned behaviour, someone's intention to engage in a given behaviour is a strong predictor of that behaviour. A meta-analysis of 34 studies of employee turnover involving more than 83,000 employees validated this direct approach. The researchers found stated behavioural intentions to be a better predictor of employee turnover than job satisfaction, satisfaction with the work itself, or organizational

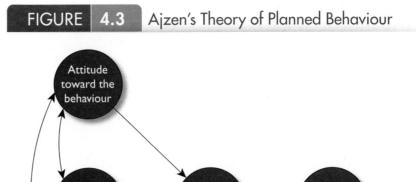

FIGURE **4.3** Ajzen's Theory of Planned Behaviour

SOURCE: Reprinted from I. Ajzen, "The Theory of Planned Behaviour," *Organizational Behaviour and Human Decision Processes,* Figure 1, p 182. Copyright 1991, with permission from Elsevier Science.

commitment.[31] Another study took these findings one step further by considering whether or not job applicants' intention to quit a job before they were hired would predict voluntary turnover six months after being hired. Results demonstrated that intentions to quit significantly predicted turnover.[32] Consider the following:

The quickest and possibly most accurate way of determining whether individuals who are already employed by the firm will quit their job is to have an objective third party, like a supplier, ask if they intend to quit. As for seasonal or part time contract workers, perhaps now you can understand why your summer employer asked if you planned on returning to school in the fall. Your stated intention was an accurate indicator of your future behaviour.

Research demonstrates that Ajzen's model accurately predicts intentions to choose a career versus becoming a homemaker, weight loss intentions, voting intentions for political candidates, using Internet services to facilitate the shipping of products, nurses' willingness to work with older patients, and attending on-the-job training sessions.[33] Understanding this simple model can also help you succeed while studying at school. For example:

> Consider using Ajzen's model when establishing a working group for your next project. Before forming a group, you may want to ask each potential member their final grade intention for the project. Asking the questions, "What grade do you want to earn on this project?" or "How many hours per week do you plan on working on this project?" may actually provide you with a clearer picture of how a fellow student is going to behave over the next few months.

From a practical standpoint, Ajzen's theory of planned behaviour has important managerial implications. Managers are encouraged to use prescriptions derived from the model to implement intervention techniques aimed at changing employees' behaviour. According to this model, changing behaviour starts with the recognition that behaviour is modified through intentions, which in turn are influenced by three different determinants (see Figure 4.3). Managers can thus influence behavioural change by doing or saying things that affect the three determinants of employees' intentions to exhibit a specific behaviour.[34] For example, if full-time employees are paranoid that they are going to lose their job because of downsizing, then they may act out with hostility toward part-time workers. As a case in point, a study showed that employees had lower perceptions of job security and more negative attitudes toward temporary workers when they had the behavioural belief that temporary workers posed a threat to their jobs.[35]

Ultimately, a manager would want to intervene by first asking the full-time workers, *"How do you feel about having temporary workers on site?"* Once this attitude is confirmed, then the manager could ask, *"Do you believe your job security to be threatened by temporary workers? If so, in what way(s)?"* This second question gets to the heart of the subjective norms and beliefs. Finally, to help change behaviour, the manager could ask the full-timers, *"What experiences have you had in the past being replaced by temporary workers? Are you aware that your performance at work is being negatively affected by your beliefs toward temporary workers? Is this what you want? Is this your intention? If not, then your behaviour needs to change. What can I do to help?"*

Employee beliefs can be influenced by the information management provides on a day-by-day basis, organizational cultural values, role models, and rewards that are targeted to reinforce certain beliefs. If a manager wants employee participation in decision making, then inviting them into the process by providing ongoing information and relevant data would be beneficial in maintaining favourable attitudes toward the process. In another example, management can foster the belief that teamwork is valued by setting and rewarding team-based goals instead of individual goals. Beliefs can also be modified through education and training.

Three Key Work Attitudes

Work attitudes such as organizational commitment, job involvement, and job satisfaction have a dual interest to managers. On the one hand, they represent important outcomes that managers may want to enhance. On the other, they are indicative of other potential problems. For example, low job satisfaction may be a symptom of an employee's intention to quit. It is therefore important for managers to understand the causes and consequences of key work attitudes.

What is your attitude toward work? Is work something meaningful that defines and fulfills you, or is it just a way to pay the bills? People have a multitude of attitudes about things that happen to them at work, but OB researchers have focused on a limited number of them. This next section specifically examines two work attitudes—organizational commitment and job involvement—that have important practical implications. Then the third work attitude, job satisfaction, is thoroughly discussed in the final section of this chapter.

ORGANIZATIONAL COMMITMENT

Before discussing a model of organizational commitment, it is important to consider the meaning of the term *commitment*. What does it mean to commit? Common sense suggests that commitment is an agreement to do something for yourself or another individual, group, or organization.[36] Formally, OB researchers define commitment as "a force that binds an individual to a course of action of relevance to one or more targets."[37] This definition highlights that commitment is associated with behaviour and can be aimed at multiple targets or entities. For example, people can be committed to their job, family, girl- or boyfriend, faith, friends, career, organization, or a variety of professional associations. Let's now consider in greater depth the application of commitment to a work organization.

Organizational commitment reflects the extent to which an individual identifies with an organization and is committed to its goals. It is an important work attitude because committed individuals

Organizational commitment

Extent to which an individual identifies with an organization and its goals.

are expected to display a willingness to work harder to achieve organizational goals and a greater desire to stay employed at an organization. Figure 4.4 presents a model of organizational commitment that identifies its causes and consequences.

A Model of Organizational Commitment   Examine Figure 4.4. It looks complicated, but we're going to thoroughly dissect this model to make sense of it.

The centre of Figure 4.4 shows that organizational commitment is composed of three separate but related components: (1) affective commitment, (2) normative commitment, and (3) continuance commitment. John Meyer and Natalie Allen, a pair of commitment experts, define these components as follows:

■ *Affective commitment* refers to the employee's emotional attachment to, identification with, and involvement in the organization. Employees with a strong affective commitment continue employment

with an organization because they want to do so (strong desire).

For example: Marcus is the co-founder of the accounting firm Diamond, Marcus & Company. He has worked for this organization for over 25 years. He is loyal and committed to this firm because he has invested so much of himself and his time to ensuring its success.

■ *Continuance commitment* refers to an awareness of the costs associated with leaving the organization. Employees whose primary link to the organization is based on continuance commitment remain because they need to do so (too costly to leave job).

For example: George Cortez has two more years before he can retire with a full pension. He has worked for the same company for over 30 years.

FIGURE **4.4**   A Model of Organizational Commitment

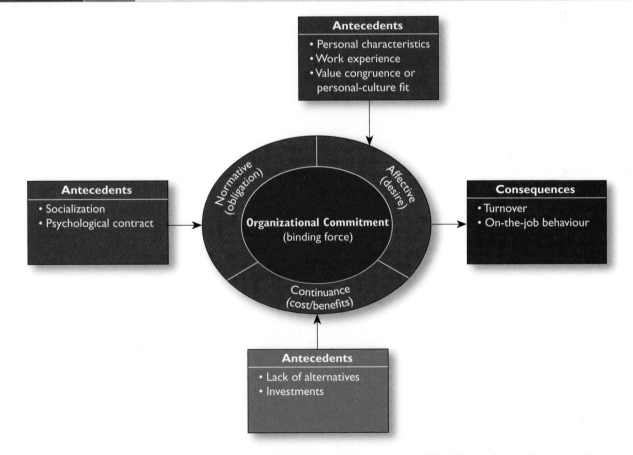

SOURCE: Adapted from J.P. Meyer and L. Herscovitch, "Commitment in the Workplace: Toward a General Model," *Human Resource Management Review,* Autumn 2001, p 317.

He has over 238 sick days in 'the bank'. If he stays with the firm for the next two years, the company will pay him full salary for up to 150 days of his banked sick days. If he leaves the firm prior to two years, he will lose the sick-days offer. George stays committed to the job because he does not want to lose the offer that translates into $50,000 cash.

■ *Normative commitment* reflects a feeling of obligation to continue employment. Employees with a high level of normative commitment feel that they ought to remain with the organization (feel an obligation to stay).[38]

For example: Jessica Zelina was hired by the Georgian College Marketing Department 18 months ago; fresh out of the two-year Business Marketing program at Georgian, she spent two work terms of her education in the marketing department. They liked her because she was a graduate of the college. Over several months, Jessica was mentored by the manager and given many training and development opportunities. Recently Jessica was contacted by a headhunter to apply as a field sales representative at Kraft Canada. The posting is tempting, but Jessica feels obligated to stay at Georgian a bit longer since the people have been so kind at giving her a chance to start her career.

Figure 4.4 also reveals that these three components combine to produce a *binding force* that influences the consequences (the box on the far right in the model) of employee turnover and on-the-job behaviour such as performance, absenteeism, and organizational citizenship, which is discussed later in this chapter.

Going back to the model, notice how each of the three components of commitment has its own separate set of antecedents that influence it. In the current context, an antecedent is something that causes the component of commitment to occur. So, for example, *affective commitment* (the desire to stay at a job) is related to a variety of personal characteristics such as personality and locus of control (recall our discussion in Chapter 3), past work experience, and value congruence, which was discussed earlier in this chapter.[39]

Continuance commitment (can't afford to leave the job because of high cost) reflects a ratio of the costs and benefits associated with leaving an organization. Antecedents are anything that affects the costs and benefits of leaving. Examples are a lack of job/career alternatives and the amount of real and psychological investments a person has in a particular organization

or community. Continuance commitment would be high if individuals have no job alternatives, have many friends in the community, and don't want to leave or can't afford to leave a job because they need the extended health benefits.

Finally, *normative commitment* (the feeling that they have to stay at their job out of obligation) is influenced by the socialization process and what is termed the psychological contract. ***Psychological contracts*** represent an individual's perception about the terms and conditions of a reciprocal exchange between the person and another party.[40] In a work environment, the psychological contract represents employees' beliefs about what they are entitled to receive in return for what they provide to the organization. Research shows that an employer's breach of the psychological contract is associated with lower organizational commitment, job satisfaction, and performance, and greater intentions to quit.[41]

LO 4

Psychological contract

An individual's perception about the terms and conditions of a reciprocal exchange with another party.

Research and Practical Applications Organizational commitment matters. A meta-analysis of 183 studies and almost 26,000 individuals uncovered a significant and strong positive relationship between organizational commitment and job satisfaction.[42] This finding encourages managers to increase job satisfaction to elicit higher levels of commitment. In turn, another meta-analysis involving 26,344 individuals revealed organizational commitment is significantly correlated with job performance.[43] This is an important finding because it implies managers can increase productivity by enhancing employees' organizational commitment.

Finally, a third meta-analysis summarizing results across 67 studies and 27,500 people uncovered a significant negative relationship between organizational commitment and turnover.[44] This finding underscores the importance of paying attention to employees' organizational commitment, because high commitment helps reduce the costs of employee turnover. In summary, managers are encouraged to focus on improving employees' organizational commitment.

So, how do companies increase employees' organizational commitment? Interestingly, they use a variety of methods. Consider the different approaches used by Genentech and the Container Store. Genentech provides employees with a six-week paid sabbatical for every six years of service, and the Container Store pays employees 50 percent to 100 percent more than the industry average. The Container Store also relies on a flexible schedule that allows parents to drop off and pick up their children at daycare or school.[45] All told, people are more likely to be committed to their organizations when they believe that the organization truly cares about their welfare and well-being.

Managers can also increase each of the three components of employee commitment through the following activities:

- *Enhance affective commitment* by hiring people whose personal values are consistent with the organization's values. A positive, satisfying work environment should also increase employees' desire to stay. Deeley Harley-Davidson Canada is following this advice. About 65 percent of the staff are committed to riding and have successfully earned their motorcycle licenses. If employees are successful at taking a riding course, Deeley's picks up the tab, which then allows any of the employees to book one of the 15 demo bikes that are available for the staff either for the week or weekend, at no cost. Deeley's Harley-Davidson has been on Canada's Top 100 Employers list for three years in a row.[46]

- *Enhance continuance commitment* by offering employees a variety of progressive benefits and human resource programs. For instance, Telus Corporation gives their employees an annual $500 "life balance account" for anything they choose that helps keep their life in check—yoga classes, family camping trip, etc., no strings attached.[47] Ceridian Canada introduced an animal health-insurance subsidy plan after employee focus groups and surveys showed the company which programs employees value most.[48] Can you think of some examples through your own work experience where the organization offered incentives to stay with the firm?

- *Increase normative commitment* by making sure that management follows up on its commitments and by trying to enhance the level of trust throughout the organization. We provide specific recommendations for building and maintaining trust in Chapter 6. Have you ever felt this level of commitment toward an organization—for example, your old Scouts' club, a church group, or a former employer?

JOB INVOLVEMENT

Job involvement is defined as "the degree to which one is cognitively preoccupied with, engaged in, and concerned with one's present job."[49] This work attitude manifests itself through the extent to which people are immersed in their job tasks. Think of the passion you have toward your job—do you feel emotionally connected to the work? Do you feel physically engaged, so much so that even if you're not feeling great, you still show up for work because it actually helps make you feel better in the end? Are you cognitively engaged enough to feel like you make a difference when you work? If you answered yes to all three of these questions, then you have a high level of job involvement. Consider Jarrod Clarke's testimonial about working at Sunshine Village at Banff, Alberta:

I love my job at Sunshine so much I intend to return next season. The staff here are great! My supervisor told me on my first day, "Have fun at work, or I'll make you do it again until you do." Sunshine has supplied me with a comfortable working environment so I wake up happy to go to work. Furthermore, I get to work outside in one of the most scenic surroundings in the world! As for the perks, this position has allowed me to ride at eight mountains across Alberta and BC for free, and I have more trips planned. I also get regular ride breaks at work, so during the middle of most work days, I get to ride for a few hours. We get discounts on food and equipment and cheap deals on staff trips, such as going to Flames hockey games, ski-doo runs, heli-skiing, overnight staff trips, plus more.[50]

Management Implications The results from a meta-analytic study involving thousands of people provide more information about job involvement.[51] In this study, job involvement was positively associated with job satisfaction, organizational commitment, and intrinsic motivation, and negatively related to intentions to quit. There are three key managerial implications associated with these results:

1. Managerial attempts to improve either of the two work attitudes discussed in this section are likely to positively affect the other work attitude.

2. Managers can increase employees' job involvement by providing work environments that fuel intrinsic motivation. We discuss specific recommendations for doing this in the section on intrinsic motivation in Chapter 5.

3. Improving job involvement can reduce employee turnover.

Job Involvement and Performance Past results pertaining to the relationship between job involvement and performance are controversial. While an earlier meta-analysis failed to uncover a significant relationship between job involvement and performance, poor measures of job involvement used in past studies may have biased the results. A more recent study corrected this problem and found a positive relationship between job involvement and performance.[52] Managers are thus encouraged to increase employees' job involvement as a viable strategy for improving job performance.

> **Job involvement**
>
> Extent to which individuals are immersed in their present job.

Results from three recent studies shed additional insight about the importance of job involvement. First, job involvement was found to remain relatively stable over five years. This suggests that managers may want to include an assessment of an individual's job involvement during the hiring process.[53] Second, job involvement was negatively associated with employees' psychological detachment from their work.[54] Individuals are thus more likely to stay productive and focused at work when they possess high job involvement. Finally, job involvement was significantly associated with absenteeism when employees were dissatisfied with their jobs.[55] This finding underscores the importance of the interrelationship among key work attitudes. Managers are encouraged to consider the interplay among organizational commitment, job involvement, and job satisfaction when trying to motivate and retain employees. Let's now turn our attention to job satisfaction, the work attitude that is most frequently investigated by OB researchers.

JOB SATISFACTION

Job satisfaction essentially reflects the extent to which individuals like (or dislike) their job. Formally defined, *job satisfaction* is an emotional response toward various facets of one's job. This definition implies that people can be relatively satisfied with one aspect of their job and dissatisfied with one or more other aspects. For example, a recent survey of job satisfaction across generational groups uncovered the following trends: Traditionalists, Baby Boomers, Gen-Xers, and Gen-Ys are most satisfied with their employers

> **Job satisfaction**
>
> An affective or emotional response to one's job.

and least satisfied with compensation; Baby Boomers have lower satisfaction with employers, the jobs they perform, and compensation than the other three groups; and Traditionalists have higher job satisfaction than the other groups across all aspects of satisfaction.[56] Decision makers need to understand these finer distinctions, especially those with a multi-generational workforce. For more on this specific topic, consider the data provided in the Focus on Diversity feature box.

Although researchers have not reached consensus about the exact number of dimensions that constitute job satisfaction, they do agree that it has five predominant causes. It is important to understand these various causes because each one offers a different solution for stopping the decline in job satisfaction uncovered in recent employee surveys.[57] We believe that knowledge about the causes of job satisfaction can help managers use a multi-faceted approach toward increasing this key work attitude. Let's now examine the five major causes of job satisfaction.

THE FIVE MAJOR CAUSES OF JOB SATISFACTION

The five predominant models of job satisfaction focus on different causes: (1) need fulfillment, (2) discrepancy, (3) value attainment, (4) equity, and (5) dispositional/genetic components. The distinctions between them can be very small at times, but a brief review of each model should provide greater insight into the variety of methods that can be used to increase employees' job satisfaction.[58] See Figure 4.5 for an overview of the five causes.

FIGURE 4.5 Five Causes of Job Satisfaction

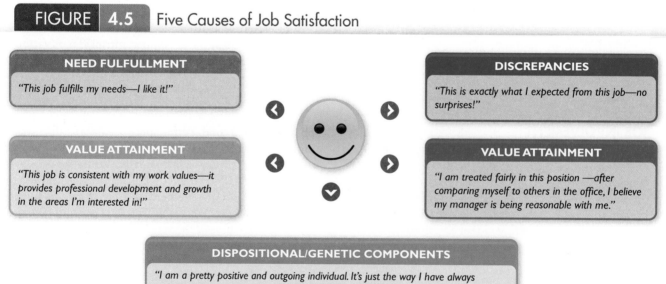

NEED FULFULLMENT
"This job fulfills my needs—I like it!"

DISCREPANCIES
"This is exactly what I expected from this job—no surprises!"

VALUE ATTAINMENT
"This job is consistent with my work values—it provides professional development and growth in the areas I'm interested in!"

VALUE ATTAINMENT
"I am treated fairly in this position —after comparing myself to others in the office, I believe my manager is being reasonable with me."

DISPOSITIONAL/GENETIC COMPONENTS
"I am a pretty positive and outgoing individual. It's just the way I have always been. So I come to work ready to have a positive and productive day."

MULTI-GENERATIONAL WORKPLACE CHALLENGE

When individual values collide with those of others in the workplace, it can lead to lower job satisfaction. The Conference Board of Canada recently sponsored a two-day event in Quebec titled *Managing Generational Difference*. Included in the day were presentations, round table discussions, and panels comprised of executive representatives and diversity leaders from major Canadian corporations, including Jazz Air, CN Railway, Canadian Blood Services, J.D. Irving, NAV, and IBEW. What they all had in common was the need to understand the challenges and implications of having four rather distinctive generations in the workplace at one time that are often required to work with one another.

Knowledge of generational differences in work values is important because there is strong evidence that having a good fit between a person's values and those of the organization leads to positive work attitudes and behaviours, including reduced chances of quitting. This means that an organization may have to consider relating accommodation issues, job designs, shifting leadership styles, and benefit preferences to the generational mix of their workforce. Look at the data below and try to relate it to your own work experience. As the years progress, how would you see this chart changing, and why?

Generation and Year of Birth	Est. Size of Work force (2010)	Traits	To Them Work Is	Work Ethic	Employment goals	Communication	Time at Work Is Defined	Need Most in the workplace
Traditionalists 1925–1945	2.4%	• Conservative • Believe in discipline • Respect for authority • Loyal • Patriotic	If you want a roof and food	Loyal and dedicated	Retirement	Face-to-face	Punch clock	"I want to stay involved"
Baby Boomers 1946–1964	37.4%	• Idealistic • Break the rules • Time stressed • Politically correct	An exciting adventure	Driven	Second career Low mobility expectation	Telephone Fax	Visibility in the office	"Stop ignoring me"
Generation X 1965–1980	32.4%	• Pragmatic • Self-sufficient • Skeptical • Flexible • Media/info/tech savvy • Entrepreneurial	A difficult challenge	Balanced	Work/Life Balance	Email	Why does it matter if I get it done today?	"Nobody tells me anything"
Millenials (Gen-Ys or the Net Gen) 1981–1996	27.9%	• Confident • Well-educated • Self-sufficient • Tolerant • Team builders • Socially and politically conscious	To make a difference	Eager but anxious	Unrealistic	IM/Text messaging	Is it 5 p.m.? I have a life.	"This is fun! Did I do a good job?" OR "Did I do a great job? This is fun!"

SOURCES: Adapted from J.C. Meister and K. Willyerd, *The 2020 Workplace* (New York: Harper Collins, 2010), pp 54–55; R. Alsop, *The Trophy Kids Grow Up* (San Francisco: Jossey-Bass, 2008) p. 5; "Generations in the Workplace in the United States & Canada," *Catalyst Canada Inc.* (Quick Takes, Toronto, July 2011) www.catalyst.org/publications/434/generations-in-the-workplace-in-the-united-states-canada; and Statistics Canada, "Labour Force Characteristics by Selected Age Groups in Canada: 2010 Annual Average and 2011 Average from January to May," *Labour Force Survey, CANSIM,* June 2011.

Need Fulfillment These models propose that satisfaction is determined by the extent to which the characteristics of a job allow employees to fulfill their needs. Organizations are aware of the premise associated with this model of satisfaction and have responded by providing creative benefits to help satisfy employees' needs. A survey of 975 employers, for example, revealed the percentage of companies that provide the following services on the premises to make employees' lives easier: ATM (41 percent), banking services (24 percent), dry cleaning/laundry service (21 percent), credit union (19 percent), travel services (18 percent), company store (16 percent), entertainment discounts and ticket purchase (15 percent), and mail services (14 percent).[59] Although need fulfillment models generate a great degree of controversy, it is generally accepted that need fulfillment is correlated with job satisfaction.[60] What sorts of services have you experienced at a job that you felt were very convenient and that you liked?

Have you ever considered working in a diamond mine near the Arctic Circle as a satisfying job? Employees at Diavik rank the company one of Canada's best employers.

Discrepancies These models propose that satisfaction is a result of *met expectations*. Met expectations represent the difference between what people expect to receive from a job, such as good pay and promotional opportunities, and what they actually receive. When expectations are greater than what is received, people will be dissatisfied. In contrast, this model predicts that employees will be satisfied when they attain outcomes above and beyond expectations. If realistic expectations are stated during the interview and hiring stages, then clearly employees know what to expect when they start the job. But if the employer fails to clarify expectations of the job or if employees fail to clarify their understanding of the expectations of the job, then a discrepancy occurs, causing job dissatisfaction. A meta-analysis of 31 studies that included 17,241 people demonstrated that met expectations are significantly related to job satisfaction.[61] Many companies use employee attitude or opinion surveys to assess employees' expectations and concerns.

> **Met expectations**
>
> The extent to which one receives what one expects from a job.

Value Attainment The idea underlying *value attainment* is that satisfaction results from the perception that a job allows for fulfillment of an individual's important work values.[62] For example, geotechnical engineer Richard LeBreton works for one of Canada's Top 100 Employers: Diavik Diamond Mines Inc., a subsidiary of Rio Tinto. The mine is located on an isolated island that sits 300 kilometres northeast of Yellowknife and 200 kilometres

> **Value attainment**
>
> The extent to which a job allows fulfillment of one's work values.

south of the Arctic Circle. In winter, temperatures at the site reach −40°C. As harsh as these conditions may sound, LeBreton was willing to move from Montreal to the Northwest Territories to accept the job offer four years ago because, as LeBreton says, "The work itself is a prime opportunity to develop outstanding experience in my field. I pinch myself every day. (Living this far north) has enriched my life experience. There's a sense of adventure, going to a remote location. It has an exotic feel to it."[63]

Compare LeBreton's work experience at Diavik to those employees working at the Foxconn Technology plant in mainland China discussed in the International OB Feature Box. What would cause the factory worker experience to be so unsatisfying to employees?

In general, research consistently supports the prediction that value fulfillment is positively related to job satisfaction. Managers can thus enhance employee satisfaction by structuring the work environment and its associated rewards and recognition to reinforce employees' values. A bit confused? Think of *value attainment* as those psychological rewards felt from the job itself—for example, flex time when requested, or leaving early once the job is completed, or the freedom of discretion to come and go on the job without asking permission. On the other hand, think of *needs fulfillment* as those creative benefit packages that an organization develops for all the employees in the entire organization to take advantage of, regardless of the job or position.

Equity   In this model, satisfaction is a function of how fairly an individual is treated at work. Satisfaction results from a person's perception that work outcomes, relative to inputs, compare favourably with a significant other's outcomes/inputs. A meta-analysis involving 190 studies and 64,757 people supported this model. Employees' perceptions of being treated fairly at work were highly related to overall job satisfaction.[64] Managers are therefore encouraged to monitor employees' fairness perceptions and to interact with employees in such a way that they feel equitably treated. Naturally, the problem with fairness is that it is very subjective. As a result, it's wise to assess reality from the employees' perspective.

In other words, how an individual defines fair management treatment is the starting point for discussion, not the other way around. Do you think the *equity* sounds similar to *discrepancy?* If so, this may help: Not all discrepancies are a result of feeling a lack of fairness. When an individual feels something isn't fair, it may have nothing to do with unfulfilled expectations or false promises that were made at the time of hiring. It's a fine distinction, but nonetheless an important one.

Dispositional/Genetic Components   Have you ever noticed that some of your co-workers or friends appear to be satisfied across a variety of job circumstances, whereas

INTERNATIONAL OB

FOXCONN CEO PREFERS ROBOTS TO HUMANS

The China-based company, Foxconn Technology, has had a long reputation of exhausting employee workloads, humiliating discipline, and cramped dormitories for its workers. Despite Apple's efforts to end the grueling conditions at the Foxconn factories (where iPhones are made), a report by the Hong Kong workers' rights group Students and Scholars Against Corporation Misbehaviour says workers at the world's 10th largest employer are still clocking up to 80 hours of overtime a month; have been told to sit only on a third of the stools that have been provided so that they remain 'nimble' enough to do the work; sweep lawns; and write confession letters, which are then pinned up on notice boards or read out to colleagues.

When details began to circulate in early 2012 about anticipated layoffs, employee transfers, and backing out on an agreement to pay severance, it resulted in a protest from 150 of the 32,000 employees at its Wuhan factory located in the southern Guangdong province. Most of the protesters climbed to the factory roof and threatened to jump off the three-story high building if their demands were not met. Company representatives said negotiations to settle the dispute were successful, and most of the protesting workers agreed to return to the assembly line; about 45 resigned. Coincidentally, it was around this same time that Foxconn CEO, Terry Gou, publicly announced his desire to install more than one million robots within the next few years throughout the company's Chinese factories.

According to the official Xinhua news agency, Gou also stated, "As human beings are also animals, to manage one million animals gives me a headache."

Foxconn, the single largest private employer in mainland China, earned worldwide media attention in 2010 at their Shenzhen campus because of the numerous large nets the employer installed around the perimeter of the factory to catch the dozens of employee suicide attempts that were occurring annually. Foxconn manufactures iPads, iPhones, Xboxes and many other products that make up the world's $150 billion consumer-electronics industry—the firm's output accounts for nearly 40 percent of that revenue. Altogether, the company employs about one million people, nearly half of whom work at the 20-year-old Shenzhen plant. Workers make $200 a month at Foxconn's Guangdong plant and $175 at their Jiangsu plant. These wages are still considered too high by many companies that have chosen to move their operations to Cambodia and Bangladesh instead, where pay is around $135 per month.

SOURCES: J. Markoff "Skilled Work, Without the Worker," *The Toronto Star* August 26, 2012 *The N.Y. Times* section pp 1 and 6; J. Garside, "Apple's efforts fail to end grueling conditions at Foxconn factories," *Guardian News and Media Ltd.* May 30, 2012, www.guardian.co.uk; P. Gupta and E Chan "Apple, Foxconn revamp China work conditions," *Reuters* (San Francisco) March 29, 2012, www.reuters.com; D. Barboza, "Foxconn Resolves a Dispute With Some Workers in China," *New York Times,* January 12, 2012, www.nytimes.com/2012/01/13/technology/foxconn-resolves-pay-dispute-with-workers.html?ref=technology&pagewanted=print; and J. Johnson, "My Gadget Guilt," *Wired Magazine,* March 2011, pp 96–103.

others always seem dissatisfied? This model of satisfaction attempts to explain this pattern.[65] Specifically, the dispositional/genetic model is based on the belief that job satisfaction is partly a function of both personal traits and genetic factors. As such, this model implies that stable individual differences are just as important in explaining job satisfaction as are characteristics of the work environment. Although only a few studies have tested these propositions, results support a positive, significant relationship between personal traits and job satisfaction over time periods ranging from two to 50 years.[66] Genetic factors were also found to significantly predict life satisfaction, well-being, and general job satisfaction.[67] Overall, researchers estimate that 30 percent of an individual's job satisfaction is associated with dispositional and genetic components.[68]

Pete and Laura Wakeman, founders of Great Harvest Bread Company, have used this model of job satisfaction while running their company for more than 25 years:

Our hiring ads say clearly that we need people with "strong personal loves as important as their work." This is not a little thing. You can't have a great life unless you have a buffer of like-minded people all around you. If you want to be nice, you can't surround yourself with crabby people and expect it to work. You might stay nice for a while, just because—but it isn't sustainable over years. If you want a happy company, you can do it only by hiring naturally happy people. You'll never build a happy company by "making people happy"— you can't really "make" people any way that they aren't already. Laura and I want to be in love with life, and our business has been a good thing for us in that journey.[69]

Although Pete and Laura's hiring approach is consistent with the dispositional and genetic model of job satisfaction, it is important to note that hiring "like-minded" people can potentially lead to discriminatory decisions. Managers are advised not to discriminate on the basis of race, gender, religion, colour, national origin, and age.

THE RELATIONSHIP BETWEEN JOB SATISFACTION AND EIGHT OTHER FACTORS

LO 5

Thousands of studies have examined the relationship between job satisfaction and other organizational variables, making it an area with significant managerial implications. Because it is impossible to examine them all, we will consider a subset of the more important variables from the standpoint of managerial relevance. Table 4.2 summarizes the pattern of

TABLE 4.2

SUMMARY OF JOB SATISFACTION CORRELATES

VARIABLES RELATED TO SATISFACTION	DIRECTION OF RELATIONSHIP	STRENGTH OF RELATIONSHIP	MEANING
Motivation	Positive	Moderate	Managers can potentially enhance employee motivation through increasing job satisfaction.
Job involvement	Positive	Moderate	Managers can potentially enhance employee job involvement through increasing job satisfaction.
Organizational citizenship behaviour	Positive	Moderate	Manager behaviour can potentially influence employee willingness to exhibit citizenship behaviour, which can increase job satisfaction.
Absenteeism	Negative	Weak	Managers will not see much decrease in absenteeism by increasing job satisfaction alone.
Withdrawal cognitions	Negative	Strong	Indirectly, managers can help to reduce employee turnover significantly by enhancing job satisfaction.
Turnover	Negative	Moderate	Managers are encouraged to try and reduce turnover by attempting to increase employee job satisfaction.
Perceived stress	Negative	Strong	Managers are strongly urged to reduce the negative effects of stress by improving job satisfaction.
Job Performance	Positive	Moderate	Managers can potentially enhance job performance through increasing job satisfaction.

results. Let us now consider eight key correlates of job satisfaction.

1. **Motivation** A recent meta-analysis of nine studies and 1,739 workers revealed a significant positive relationship between motivation and job satisfaction. Because satisfaction with supervision is also significantly correlated with motivation, managers are advised to consider how their behaviour affects employee satisfaction.[70] Managers can potentially enhance employees' motivation through various attempts to increase job satisfaction.

2. **Job Involvement** Job involvement represents the extent to which employees are personally involved with their work role. A meta-analysis involving 27,925 individuals from 87 different studies demonstrated that job involvement is moderately related with job satisfaction.[71] Managers are thus encouraged to foster satisfying work environments to fuel employees' job involvement.

3. **Organizational Citizenship Behaviour** *Organizational citizenship behaviours (OCBs)* consist of employee behaviours that are beyond the call of duty. Examples include "such gestures as constructive statements about the department, expression of personal interest in the work of others, suggestions for improvement, training new people, respect for the spirit as well as the letter of housekeeping rules, care for organizational property, and punctuality and attendance well beyond standard or enforceable levels."[72] Managers certainly would like employees to exhibit these behaviours. A meta-analysis of 7,031 people in 21 separate studies revealed a significant and moderately positive relationship between organizational citizenship behaviours and job satisfaction.[73] Moreover, additional research demonstrated that employees' citizenship behaviours are determined more by leadership and characteristics of the work environment than by an employee's personality.[74] It thus appears that managerial behaviour significantly influences an employee's willingness to exhibit citizenship behaviours. This relationship is important to recognize because employees' OCBs are positively correlated with their conscientiousness at work, organizational commitment, performance ratings, and promotions.[75] We discuss this topic further in Chapter 9.

Organizational citizenship behaviours (OCBs)

Employee behaviours that exceed work-role requirements.

4. **Absenteeism** Absenteeism is not always what it appears to be, and it can be costly. For example, a survey of 700 managers indicated that 20 percent of them called in sick because they simply did not feel like going to work that day. The top three reasons given for the bogus excuse of being sick were doing personal errands, catching up on sleep, and relaxing.[76] While it is difficult to provide a precise estimate of the cost of absenteeism, one study projected it to be $789 per employee.[77] This would suggest that absenteeism costs $236,700 for a company with 300 employees. Imagine the costs for a company with 100,000 employees! Because of these costs, managers are constantly on the lookout for ways to reduce it. One recommendation has been to increase job satisfaction. If this is a valid recommendation, there should be a strong negative relationship between satisfaction and absenteeism. In other words, as satisfaction increases, absenteeism should decrease. A researcher tracked this prediction by synthesizing three separate meta-analyses containing a total of 74 studies. Results revealed a weak negative relationship between satisfaction and absenteeism.[78] It is unlikely, therefore, that managers will realize any significant decrease in absenteeism by increasing job satisfaction. Remember, here we are talking about a relationship between job satisfaction and absenteeism . . . earlier we were talking about job involvement and absenteeism. It may be beneficial to review the distinctions between these two types of work attitudes.

5. **Withdrawal Cognitions** Although some people quit their jobs impulsively or in a fit of anger, most go through a process of thinking about whether or not they should quit.[79] *Withdrawal cognitions* encapsulate this thought process by representing an individual's overall thoughts and feelings about quitting. What causes employees to think about quitting their job? Consider the Skills & Best Practices Feature Box involving the payroll services firm, Ceridian Canada. Notice how their research study illustrated performance reviews as a predictor when identifying discontent with compensation and/or promotion promises from management. Ceridian takes great effort to keep in touch with their employee values, attitudes, and levels of job satisfaction. Results from another study on withdrawal cognitions showed that managers can indirectly help to reduce employee turnover by enhancing employee job satisfaction.[80]

Withdrawal cognitions

Overall thoughts and feelings about quitting a job.

Skills & Best Practices

Performance Reviews Matter

To help reduce withdrawal cognitions and turnover, Ceridian Canada Ltd. performs individual performance reviews every 6 months for employees, supported by training for all managers in how to conduct effective performance reviews. In a survey conducted with Harris Decima, Ceridian learned that commitments made during a performance review must be fulfilled to maintain long-term employees. Thirty-two percent of workers who were expecting a salary increase, promotion, or bonus within a year said they would look for a new job it they did not receive one within the year, 13 percent would definitely start looking, and 19 percent would probably start looking. This was most prevalent among workers 18–24 years of age, who had a household income of $40K or less, and/or who had been in their current position for less than two years.

Ceridian sponsors its own in-house employee satisfaction survey every 12 months. In addition, an outside consultant conducts confidential employee satisfaction and engagement surveys annually. With numerous benefits and incentive packages, Ceridian is able to show they care about maintaining overall high levels of employee job satisfaction.

In another Canadian survey employees were asked, "How effective are annual or semi-annual performance reviews in helping you improve your performance?" Thirteen percent responded very effective and 44 percent said somewhat effective—in other words, almost two-thirds of employees responding said that performance reviews are effective. These results are consistent in suggesting that employees welcome and benefit from performance reviews, despite the common belief that they don't. One last key finding from this survey indicated that 11 percent of respondents stated they don't receive reviews. Does this last statistic surprise you?

SOURCES: "Mixed reviews for performance reviews," *Canadian HR Reporter*, July 12, 2012, website: www.hrreporter.com; "Performance Reviews," *HR Professional Magazine*, January 2012, p. 12; R. Yerema and K. Leung, *Canada's Top 100 Employers 2012, Mediacorp Canada Inc.*, October 6, 2011, website: www.eluta.ca/top-employer-ceridian-canada.

6. **Turnover** Recent statistics show that turnover is on the rise for managers, salespeople, manufacturing workers, and chief financial officers.[81] This is a problem because turnover disrupts organizational continuity and is very costly. Costs of turnover fall into two categories: separation costs and replacement costs.

   Separation costs may include severance pay, costs associated with an exit interview, outplacement fees, and possible litigation costs, particularly for involuntary separation. Replacement costs are the well-known costs of a hire, including sourcing expenses, HR processing costs for screening and assessing candidates, the time spent by hiring managers interviewing candidates, travel and relocation expenses, signing bonuses (if applicable), and orientation and training costs.[82]

   Experts estimate that the cost of turnover for an hourly employee is roughly 30 percent of annual salary, whereas the cost can range up to 150 percent of yearly salary for professional employees.[83]

   Although there are various things a manager can do to reduce employee turnover, many of them revolve around attempts to improve employees' job satisfaction.[84] This trend is supported by results from a meta-analysis of 67 studies covering 24,556 people. Job satisfaction has a moderate negative relationship with employee turnover.[85] Given the strength of this relationship, managers are advised to try to reduce employee turnover by increasing employee job satisfaction.

7. **Perceived Stress** Stress can have very negative effects on organizational behaviour and an individual's health. Stress is positively related to absenteeism, turnover, coronary heart disease, and viral infections. Based on a meta-analysis of 32 studies covering 11,063 individuals, perceived stress has a strong negative relationship with job satisfaction.[86] Managers should attempt to reduce the negative effects of stress by improving job satisfaction.

8. **Job Performance** One of the biggest controversies within OB research centres is the relationship between job satisfaction and job performance. Although researchers have identified eight different ways in which these variables are related, the dominant beliefs are either that satisfaction causes performance, or performance causes satisfaction.[87] A team of researchers recently attempted to resolve this controversy through a meta-analysis of data from 312 samples involving 54,417 individuals.[88] There were two key findings from this study. First, job satisfaction and performance are moderately related. This is an important finding because it supports

the belief that employee job satisfaction is a key work attitude managers should consider when attempting to increase employees' job performance. Second, the relationship between job satisfaction and performance is much more complex than originally thought. It is not as simple as satisfaction causing performance or performance causing satisfaction. Rather, researchers now believe both variables indirectly influence each other through a host of individual differences and work-environment characteristics.[89]

There is one additional consideration to keep in mind regarding the relationship between job satisfaction and job performance. Researchers believe the relationship between satisfaction and performance is understated due to incomplete measures of individual-level performance. For example, if performance ratings used in past research did not reflect the actual interactions and interdependencies at work, inaccurate measures of performance lowered the reported relationships between satisfaction and performance. Examining the relationship between aggregate measures of job satisfaction and organizational performance is one way to correct this problem.

In support of these ideas, a team of researchers recently conducted a meta-analysis of 7,939 business units in 36 companies. Results uncovered significant positive relationships between business-unit-level employee satisfaction and business-unit outcomes of customer satisfaction, productivity, profit, employee turnover, and accidents.[90] As a result, it appears that managers can positively affect a variety of important organizational outcomes, including performance, by increasing employee job satisfaction.

Summary of Learning Objectives

LO 1 Define *value system,* *terminal values,* and *instrumental values.* A value system is an enduring organization of one's personal beliefs about preferred ways of behaving and desired end-states. An individual can have an intense value system or a weak value system. Personal values can be categorized in two dimensions: terminal and instrumental values. A terminal value is an enduring belief about a desired end-state (e.g., happy, full of wisdom). An instrumental value is an enduring belief about how one should behave (e.g., obedient, honest).

LO 2 Describe three types of value conflicts. (1) Intrapersonal value conflict can be likened to the internal conflict individuals feel when they are torn between two opposite desires/feeling (e.g., "I want a high paying job because I value large amounts of money, but I don't want to work nights or weekends because I'll miss time with my family, whom I love"). (2) Interpersonal value conflict occurs when the values that an individual is feeling conflict with external values from another individual (e.g., "My boss tells me to bury the costs so that our bottom line looks more positive, but that goes against my personal values of being an ethical accountant"). (3) Individual–organizational value conflict is classic whistle-blower behaviour (e.g., if an employee sees that the organizational culture is moving toward dishonesty and infectious greed, then the person will feel compelled to blow the whistle by going to the board of directors or the media).

LO 3 Identify the three components of attitude. The three components of attitude are affective, cognitive, and behavioural. The affective component represents the feelings or emotions one has about a given object or situation. The cognitive component reflects the beliefs or ideas one has about an object or situation. The behavioural component refers to how one intends or expects to act toward someone or something.

Relate organizational commitment to psychological contract. Organizational commitment reflects how strongly a person identifies with an organization and is committed to its goals. Organizational commitment is composed of three related components: affective commitment, continuance commitment, and normative commitment. In turn, each of these components is influenced by a separate set of antecedents. An antecedent is something that causes the component of commitment to occur. Once an individual feels strong commitment toward the organization, it will be easier to establish a psychological contract between the two parties. A psychological contract represents employees' beliefs about what they are entitled to receive in return for what they provide to the organization.

 Compare and discriminate between eight variables that have a relationship with job satisfaction. Eight major variables that have a relationship with job satisfaction are: motivation (moderate positive relationship), job involvement (moderate positive), organizational citizenship behaviour (moderate positive), absenteeism (weak negative), withdrawal cognitions (strong negative), turnover (moderate negative), perceived stress (strong negative), and job performance (moderate positive). Strong relationships imply that managers can significantly influence the variable of interest by increasing job satisfaction.

Discussion Questions

1. Can you think of a situation when a person's attitude(s) might not predict his or her work behaviour?

2. Why do you think a store manager would have greater impact on employee turnover than the actual neighbourhood location of the store?

3. Imagine that you work with a fellow employee who continues to take credit for work you complete. You decide to approach the person and give him a piece of your mind! The final decision to behave this way toward someone gives you a bad attitude. Explain which of the three behavioural components of attitude you are exhibiting at this time.

4. Use Ajzen's theory of planned behaviour (Figure 4.3) to analyze how managers can reduce voluntary turnover. Be sure to explain what managers can do to affect each aspect of the theory.

5. "What's the matter with today's generation? They just don't have the same ambition or work ethic as the employees we hired 50 years ago. Their personal values are clashing with our corporate values." How does this quote make you feel? Do you agree or disagree with the statement? You may want to refer to the chart within the Focus on Diversity Feature Box to explain your response.

Integration of OB Concepts—Discussion Questions

1. See Chapter 2 – What role do perceptions play in the determination of job satisfaction?

2. See Chapter 3 – How might the factors from Chapter 3 (Big Five personality, locus of control, self-esteem, and self-efficacy) influence occupational choice,

job satisfaction, and/or organizational commitment? If personality influences job satisfaction and organizational commitment, how can HR professionals attract and nurture high levels of these attitudes for their organization?

Google Searches

1. **Google Search:** "Canadian Family Caregiver Leave Act (Employment Standards Amendment)" What is this Act trying to give employees the ability to do? Why do you think the government would have to legislate such behaviour? Wouldn't every organization voluntarily offer such a benefit to their employees? What does this say about what the Canadian government values? What does this say about corporate values?

2. **Google Search:** "Equity and Human Rights Services Religious Accommodation" Notice how many post-secondary educational institutions in Canada have produced a calendar of religious accommodation. Go to one of the sites and review the organizational policy recognizing diverse faiths and their respective holy dates. Are you familiar with all these religious faiths and their celebrations? What are your impressions of an organization having a policy for such occasions?

3. **Google Search:** "Duty to Accommodate FAQs—Canadian Human Rights Commission" OR "Service Canada Fails in Its Duty to Accommodate Nathalie Cyr" What does it mean for an employer to accommodate? Do you think a Canadian organization would intentionally discriminate against an individual applicant whose values differ from the corporate values?

4. **Google Search:** "Canada's Top 100 Employers for 201_" Each year this list is generated and the Globe and Mail writes a feature article on it to highlight the best employers to work for in Canada. Select one firm from the list and identify the various criteria that employees use to rank their employer nomination. Then go through the entire Top 100 list and find at last 5 unique benefits companies offer their employees. Share your findings.

5. **Google Search:** "Workopolis.ca" Find a current job posting in your field and try to identify the kind of word cues listed in the ad that identify the corporate values of that firm. List the values. Now consider how that firm will identify such values in candidates that apply for a job. Will a resumé alone help identify good prospective candidates? A face-to-face interview? Cognitive tests? Personality tests? A behavioural event interview?

Experiential Exercise

Behavioural-Event Interviewing Goes Beyond Words—A Design Exercise

PURPOSE   This exercise is meant to have students design a behavioural-event interview process that would help an organization identify individual-organizational fit. Approx. Timing: 25 minutes.

ACTIVITY ASSIGNMENT:

Scenario: You are the HR Director at ABC Inc. You and your staff are looking for certain kinds of candidates for a number of positions that have opened up at the firm.

Prior to today, you had your staff ask the various managers in each of the departments where these positions exist to provide a list of the kinds of characteristics desired. Below is that list.

Directions: Given the following list and the type of value being desired, write at least one behavioural question and/or design at least one event that would help you find the best candidate for that position. An example has been provided for you.

What the Manager Wants	The Kind of Value(s) Being Desired	At least One Behavioural Question and/or At least One Event To Help Ensure Candidate Values Won't Compete With Corporate Values
Example: The manager of CreativeServices Dept. is looking for a person that can work well with different types of individuals.	• Diversity of individuals • Respect for others who differ	Q: What kinds of people frustrate you? Event #1: Have an interviewing panel made up of a diverse group of people; be sure to monitor the responses toward the different members of panel; consider eye contact, tone of voice, and language choice Event #2: Have a candidate job-shadow with different kinds of people within the firm; monitor behaviour variations among the differing types
The manager of programming wants a person who won't be looking at the clock all the time, who will work late if necessary, and who will be willing to adjust their personal schedule to fit the client's needs.	• Work ethic to serve clients • Loyalty to client needs • Task-completion oriented rather than time-oriented	
The manager in account services is looking for a person who is social, articulate, good at speaking in front of people, and who knows how to do presentations well	• Likes people • Open to speaking with others without prompts • Extraverted	
The manager in payroll accounting is looking for a person who pays attention to detail and doesn't have to be told all the time what to do at their job when they see a mistake	• High self-monitoring • Patient • Shows initiative without prompts	

OB In Action Case Study

High Liner Foods Responds To Employee Survey To Boost Satisfaction

BACKGROUND

High Liner Foods Inc. is a processor and marketer of value-added frozen seafood products, including the popular High Liner, Fisher Boy, Mirabel, Sea Cuisine, Royal Sea, FPI, and Viking brands. Originally founded in 1899 as a salt fish operation in Lunenburg, Nova Scotia, the publicly-traded company has additional locations in Canada, as well as in Massachusetts and New Hampshire. With revenues of $585 million, this company has grown to employ 1,042 full-time employees worldwide. Other statistics include:

- Employee turnover is 2.19 percent.
- The longest serving employee has worked 50.9 years at the company.
- Four hundred annual job applications were received most recently.
- Twenty new jobs were created in Canada in the previous year.
- A total of 43 percent of employees are women.
- The average age of all employees is 50 years old.
- The percentage of the workforce on a contract basis is 2.3 percent.

SURVEY RESULTS

When it comes to employee engagement, High Liner Foods (HLF) believes in staying on top of employee attitudes. They achieve this goal by administering their own in-house employee satisfaction survey every 6 months. Based on the results of one satisfaction survey collected in 2010, HLF learned that their employees wanted more information about the company and its business strategies. After speaking to outside consultants, the executive decision was made to first improve the communication system at the Lunenburg location, one of the most modern and diversified food processing plants in the world, covering over 250,000 square feet and housing 535 employees. The solution was to create and manage a High Liner TV station featuring company and community events, employee benefits information, job postings, corporate office messages, inventory levels, and annual production and sales figures.

The responsibility for operating and maintaining the in-house TV station rested with the Human Resources Department. With the help and cooperation of High Liner's Information Services department, broadcasting and other technical problems were kept to a minimum. Besides the HLF data that was requested by employees, added features to the station included streamed CBC News feeds for top regional, national, and world news stories. Current and forecasted weather as well as sports scores were also displayed on selected screens throughout the facility.

After a few months of operation, a follow-up survey revealed very positive feedback from HLF employees about the in-house TV station. Employees responded that they were better informed about the company, production processes, and company events, and they found the content entertaining as they relaxed in the company cafeteria. The company expanded the in-house TV station to include communicating new initiatives around employee wellness programs, such as quitting smoking and better nutrition. The in-house TV station allowed High Liner to distribute a greater variety of real-time information to their employees, which had a positive impact on the production process. Having received such positive results from the Luneburg plant, the High Liner TV station was expanded to other HLF facilities throughout Canada and the US.

LAUNCHING INTRANET SITE

The recent move from an in-house TV station to include a new corporate intranet site was natural for HLF. As computer use continues to increase around the HLF global facilities, the blending of the old technology with the new facilitated a positive work atmosphere by generating greater communication. When High Liner was recently nominated as one of Canada's top 100 employers, the strength of their employee engagement (surveys conducted twice per year), as well as their ability to fairly distribute company information to all employees (using the in-house TV station together with the intranet site), were mentioned as contributing factors to its success.

"Because the system is so easy to use, we are able to constantly change and update the information we distribute. This keeps it fresh and relevant for our employees," says Natalie Shannon, HR Systems Specialist at HLF. "It is an excellent business tool and there are no limits to what we can do with it."

Discussion Questions

1. Why would greater communication to all employees (about corporate operations and other company activities) have a positive impact on the production process?

2. By responding so actively to the employee survey results, which of the five causes of job satisfaction would you say HLF helped fulfill?

3. What sort of organizational commitment must HLF employees have if they nominate their own company for an Employer of The Year award? What sort of attitude must they have toward their jobs? Their employer? Explain.

4. Do you believe there is any correlation between the average age of all HLF employees and the amount of job involvement they seek from their employer?

SOURCES: R. Yerema and K. Leung, "High Liner Foods Inc.–Chosen as one of Canada's Top 100 Employers for 2012," October 6, 2011, website: www.eluta.ca; "High Liner Foods–Digital Signage Employee Communication System," Omnivex website: www.omnivex.com/casestudies/; High Liner Foods Inc. Corporate website–About High Liner Tab, www.highlinerfoods.com.

The CONNECTion Zone   McGraw Hill connect™

- The Presentation Assistant
- Ethical OB Dilemma
- Video Case

McGraw Hill connect™

Practise and learn online with Connect.

CHAPTER 5

Foundations of Motivation

I have been out of school for more than a year now. I have a two-year college diploma followed by a three-year university degree, but I cannot find a professional job. Currently, I am working at the same service job I had while I was in school. If I were to leave and take a lower-paying entry job somewhere else, I'd have to move back home. My friends have had the same problem finding a good job this past year. We know the economy and our lack of experience are to blame. But there is a lack of hope, and every day I become more upset with my situation, though I try to be grateful for what I have. What can I do to regain motivation and be more positive about my professional future?

—*STUCK*

Understanding Motivation

Whether encouraging self-reflection on personal motivation ("Can you tell me what motivates you?") or trying to determine effective motivational techniques in the workplace ("What can I do to motivate that employee to achieve higher performance?"), the topic of motivation has long been one of management's most difficult and important duties. As you will read in this chapter, an employee's motivation is a function of several components, including an individual's needs, the extent to which a work environment is positive and supportive, perceptions of being treated fairly (creating a strong relationship between performance and the receipt of valued rewards), the use of accurate measures of performance, and the setting of specific goals. As you study the various theories and practices of motivation, keep in mind that each one offers different recommendations about how to motivate employees. Table 5.1 gives you an overall summary of what we'll be discussing.

The term *motivation* derives from the Latin word *movere*, meaning "to move." In the present context, **motivation** represents "those psychological processes that cause the arousal, direction, and persistence of voluntary actions that are goal directed."[1] Researchers have proposed two general *theories of motivation* to explain the psychological processes underlying employee motivation: content theories and process theories. *Content theories of motivation* focus on identifying internal factors such as instincts, needs, satisfaction, and job characteristics that energize employee motivation. These theories do not explain how motivation is influenced by the dynamic interaction between individuals and the environment in which they work. This limitation led to the creation of process theories of motivation. *Process theories of motivation* focus on explaining the process by which internal factors and cognitions (the process of acquiring knowledge) influence employee motivation.[2] We'll explore both of these theories in greater detail over the next several sections, but first let's discuss the content theories of motivation.

Content (Need) Theories of Motivation

Most content theories of motivation revolve around the notion that an employee's needs influence motivation. **Needs** are physiological or psychological deficiencies that arouse behaviour. They can be strong or weak, and are influenced by environmental factors. Thus, human needs vary over time and place. The general idea behind need theories of motivation is that unmet needs motivate people to satisfy them. Conversely, people are not motivated to pursue a satisfied need. Let's now consider four popular content theories of motivation: (1) Maslow's need hierarchy theory, (2) Alderfer's ERG theory, (3) McClelland's need theory, and (4) Herzberg's motivator–hygiene model.

Motivation

Psychological processes that arouse and direct goal-directed behaviour.

Theories of motivation

Include two psychological processes: content and process.

Content theories of motivation

Identify internal factors influencing motivation.

Process theories of motivation

Identify the process by which internal factors and cognitions influence motivation.

LO 1

LO 2

Needs

Physiological or psychological deficiencies that arouse behaviour.

TABLE 5.1

THEORIES AND APPROACHES TO MOTIVATION

1. **CONTENT (NEED) THEORIES** (focus on internal factors that energize employee motivation)
   - **Maslow's Need Hierarchy**—There are five basic needs: physiological, safety, belonging (love), esteem, and self-actualization; needs are satisfied in a one-directional manner starting with lowest-level needs first.
   - **Alderfer's ERG Needs Model**—There are three basic needs: existence, relatedness, and growth; needs influence individual behaviour differently at different times throughout life.
   - **McClelland's Need/Behaviour Relationship**—There are three needs: achievement, affiliation, and power; needs can influence behaviour.
   - **Herzberg's (Two-Factor) Motivator-Hygiene**—Identified factors responsible for job satisfaction (motivators like achievement, recognition, responsibility, characteristics of the work, and advancement) vs. dissatisfaction (hygiene factors like work environment, company policy, technical supervision, salary, and interpersonal relations with one's supervisor).

2. **PROCESS THEORIES** (focus on explaining the process that internal factors and cognitions influence employee motivation)
   - **Adams Equity Model**—Motivation is a function of fairness in social exchanges.
   - **Vroom's Expectancy Model**—People are motivated to behave in ways that produce valued outcomes.
   - **Goal Setting**: People are motivated to achieve a certain outcome and focus their energy toward accomplishing the end result.

3. **JOB DESIGN PRACTICES**
   - **Mechanistic Approach**—Jobs are designed using scientific management principles (highly specialized and standardized), which targets efficiency and employee productivity.
   - **Motivational Approaches**—There are four motivational techniques: job enlargement, job rotation, job enrichment, and job characteristics model (JCM).
   - **Biological Approach**—Based on biomechanics, work physiology, and ergonomics, the focus is on designing a work environment to reduce employees' physical strain, fatigue, and health complaints.
   - **Perceptual-Motor Approach**—Examines human factors in engineering, perceptual and cognitive skills, and information processing to examine error rates, accidents, and workers' feedback about facilities and equipment.

4. **TIME SHIFTING APPROACHES**
   - **Alternative Work Schedules**—There are four types of schedules: flextime, compressed work week, job sharing, and telecommuting.

MASLOW'S NEED HIERARCHY THEORY

In 1943, psychologist Abraham Maslow published his now-famous *need hierarchy theory* of motivation. Although the theory was based on his clinical observation of a few individuals, it has subsequently been used to explain the entire spectrum of human behaviour. Maslow proposed that motivation is a function of five basic needs. These needs are:

1. **Physiological** Basic need entails having enough food, air, and water to survive.

2. **Safety** The need to be safe from physical and psychological harm. For example, how safe do social media users feel in terms of organizations creeping through their webpages, especially when organizations are screening job applicants? Or how much psychological harm occurs when an organization spies on its employees? The need to feel safe from harm has become a real priority in today's workplace. However, there is concern that some organizations are using monitoring devices as negative motivational tools or as an excuse to catch employees doing something wrong. See the next Law & Ethics At Work and the International OB feature boxes for more on this. The OB Ethical Dilemma on Connect also picks up on this theme.

> *Need hierarchy theory*
>
> Five basic needs— physiological, safety, belonging (love), esteem, and self-actualization— influence behaviour.

EMPLOYEE SURVEILLANCE—FOR SAFETY OR MONITORING PURPOSES?

LAW AND ETHICS AT WORK

When an employer uses electronic surveillance equipment in the workplace, is it doing so for employee safety reasons or for purposes of monitoring employee behaviour? The Canadian courts have no problem with keeping the workplace safe; but when organizational surveillance equipment is used as a monitoring device to catch employees doing something wrong, that is when they take notice.

If employees believe their workplace is physically unsafe or that they are being psychologically targeted by someone in the workplace (e.g., an unauthorized individual using an employee computer terminal illegally on off-times), then they may express their concern to the employer and request to have their workplace monitored in some way. But what if an employer installs video cameras around the office at workstations, or even installs keystroke monitoring software on all work computers, claiming all action to be in the name of workplace safety. Is it legal? In short, federal, and provincial privacy commissions in Canada have held that monitoring of employee computer use, particularly surreptitious (sneaky) monitoring, should only be undertaken in limited circumstances, and usually as a last resort after other less privacy-invasive attempts have been made to deter any unwanted conduct.

Video surveillance is deemed to be at the top end of what is considered privacy invasive, and therefore typically receives greater scrutiny by the courts. Clearly, private areas like bath and change rooms should not have such equipment installed.

Privacy laws are continually evolving. The trend in Canada is moving toward increasing privacy rights for employees. Employers need to balance safety needs in the workplace with respecting employees' rights to privacy. Here is what the most current court decisions are indicating when it comes to the Canadian workplace:

- Employers must be reasonable in their approach and provide clear warnings to employees that cameras are installed in certain areas of the organization . . . and employee computer use may be subject to monitoring as well.

- A company-wide policy should be developed, publicized, and enforced, and that what is stored on the computer is the property of the employer (downloading files, Internet, emails, etc.). Keep the policy clear in terms of what types of uses are permitted and prohibited. Be sure to include that the employer can randomly access such monitoring devices when necessary.

- Identify the consequences for failing to abide by the policy.

SOURCE: B. Burgess, "Debunking common misconceptions around employee privacy," *Canadian HR Reporter*, August 15, 2011, p 21–22.

3. **Belonging (love)** The desire to belong. To love and be loved. Includes the needs for affection and social interaction.

4. **Esteem** Need for reputation, prestige, and recognition from others. Also includes need for self-confidence and strength.

5. **Self-actualization** The desire for self-fulfillment—to become the best one is capable of becoming.

Maslow said these five needs are arranged in the hierarchy as shown in Figure 5.1. In other words, he believed human needs generally emerge in a predictable stair-step fashion. Accordingly, when one's physiological needs are relatively satisfied, one's safety needs emerge, and so on up the need hierarchy, one step at a time. Once a need is satisfied, it activates the next higher need in the hierarchy. This process continues until the need for self-actualization is activated.[3]

Although research does not clearly support this theory of motivation, two key managerial implications of Maslow's theory are worth noting. First, it is important for managers and team leaders to focus on satisfying employee needs related to self-concepts—self-esteem and self-actualization—because their satisfaction is significantly associated with a host of important outcomes such as academic achievement, physical illness, psychological well-being (e.g., anxiety disorders, depression), criminal convictions, drug abuse, marital satisfaction, money and work problems, and performance at work.[4]

KEEPING EMPLOYEES SAFE IN GERMANY

It's been years pending, and still German employees wait for the passing of a bill that will protect their rights and private interests from employers who cross the line. Hidden video cameras, creeping through Internet sites, and undercover spying—sounds like a scene from a James Bond movie. But for some Germans it's just another day at work. A series of workplace spying scandals over the last several years involving well-known organizations like the telecommunications firm Deutsche Telekom, the discount retailer Lidl, and the national railway operator Deutsche Bahn resulted in the drafting of a new privacy type of bill.

While the passing of the bill is anxiously anticipated, once it becomes law it will better regulate workplace privacy. "It's a balanced compromise among the various interests and will foster more trust in the workplace between employer and employee," said Interior Minister Thomas de Maiziere. Up until the writing of the bill, such behaviour was not regulated in Germany in terms of what capacity and under what conditions an employer could use video surveillance to collect information about (the) employee. Further, once the bill is passed, German employers will be banned from using Facebook as a screening tool for new applicants or for current employees being promoted.

Not everyone is on board. Those employers who are in favour of workplace surveillance say that spying can actually help to keep the workplace safe, arguing that it deters theft, corruption, and criminal activity. In addition, they also believe that by investigating applicant Facebook sites prior to hiring, they are able to screen undesirables away from their company, once again making the workplace safer.

When employers spy in the workplace, what does that tell you about their attitudes toward employees? What is motivating the employer?

SOURCES: S. Meyer, "S. Meyer, Evidon CEO, On Germany's Impending New Privacy Law," *ExchangeWire EMEA* Blog, April 12, 2012; S. Harman, "Germany Weighs Bill To Outlaw Spying On Employees," *DW-World.DE*, Deutsche Welle, October 25, 2010, website: www.dw-world.de/dw/article/0,,594207700.html; and A. Dugdale, "German Privacy Law Would Ban Firms From Using Facebook To Vet Potential Employees," *Fast Company*, August 23, 2010.

FIGURE 5.1 Maslow's Need Hierarchy

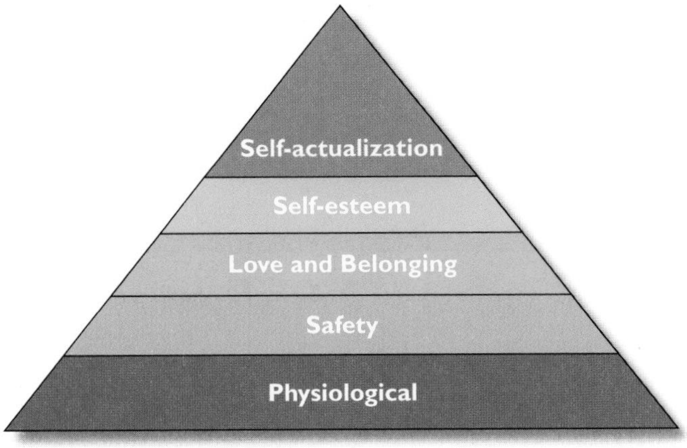

Self-actualization

Self-esteem

Love and Belonging

Safety

Physiological

Second, a satisfied need may lose its motivational potential. Therefore, managers and team leaders are advised to motivate others by devising programs or practices aimed at satisfying emerging or unmet needs. Many companies have responded to this recommendation by offering employees targeted benefits that meet their specific needs.[5] Results from a nationwide survey conducted by the Society for Human Resource Management can help in this pursuit. Findings revealed that employee wants and desires vary by age. The Focus on Diversity feature box summarizes the survey results by presenting the top five things employees are looking for from their jobs across various age and generational

groups. Managers and team leaders are encouraged to use customized surveys to assess the specific needs of employees.[6]

ALDERFER'S ERG THEORY

Clayton Alderfer developed an alternative theory of human needs in the late 1960s (see Figure 5.2). Alderfer's theory differs from Maslow's in three major respects. First, a smaller set of core needs is used to explain behaviour. From lowest to highest level, they are existence needs (E)—the desire for physiological and materialistic well-being; relatedness needs (R)—the

EMPLOYEES' NEEDS AND DESIRES VARY BY AGE

Alderfer's ERG theory is consistent with the finding that individual differences influence our need states at different times in our lives. Managers and team leaders are advised to motivate others by devising programs or practices aimed at satisfying emerging or unmet needs. Consider the table below and notice how the need for compensation diminishes as an individual ages. Why is that? What type of need becomes more important as we age?

AGE	GENERATION TYPE	TOP FIVE NEEDS and DESIRES
17–36 years	Millenials (Gen-Ys) (Note: The Digitals are those born after 1996 who have yet to enter the workforce)	1. Compensation 2. Other benefits 3. Extended health care and medical benefits 4. Job security 5. Flexibility to balance work/life issues
37–56 years	Generation X	1. Compensation 2. Extended health care and medical benefits 3. Retirement benefits 4. Other benefits 5. Job security
57–66 years	Baby Boomers	1. Feeling safe in work environment 2. Retirement benefits 3. Other benefits 4. Extended health and medical benefits 5. Meaningfulness of job

SOURCE: Data extrapolated from E. Esen, *SHRM 2006 Job Satisfaction Survey Report* (Alexandria, VA: Society for Human Resource Management, 2006).

FIGURE 5.2 Comparing Maslow's Need Theory to Alderfer's ERG Theory

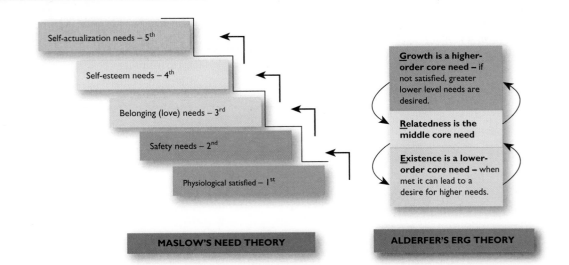

desire to have meaningful relationships with significant others; and growth needs (G)—the desire to grow as a human being and to use one's abilities to their fullest potential; hence, the label *ERG theory*. Second, ERG theory does not assume needs are related to each other in a stair-step hierarchy as does Maslow. Alderfer believed that more than one need may be activated at a time. Finally, ERG theory contains a frustration-regression component. That is, frustration of higher-order needs can influence the desire for lower-order needs.[7] For example, employees may demand higher pay or better benefits (existence needs) when they are frustrated or dissatisfied with the quality of their interpersonal relationships (relatedness needs) at work.

Research on ERG theory has provided mixed support for some of the theory's key propositions.[8] That said, however, there are two key managerial implications associated with ERG. The first revolves around the frustration-regression aspect of the theory. Managers and team leaders should keep in mind that employees may be motivated to pursue lower-level needs because they are frustrated with a higher-order need. For instance, the solution for a stifling work environment may be a request for higher pay or better benefits.

Second, ERG theory is consistent with the finding that individual and cultural differences influence our

ERG theory

Three basic needs—existence, relatedness, and growth—influence behaviour.

need states. People are motivated by different needs at different times in their lives. This implies that managers should customize their reward and recognition programs to meet employees' varying needs. Consider how Marc Albin, CEO of Albin Engineering Services, Inc. handles this recommendation.

To identify which parts of individual employees' egos need scratching, Albin takes an unconventional approach.

"My experience in managing people is, they're all different," says Albin. "Some people want to be recognized for their cheerful attitude and their ability to spread their cheerful attitude. Some want to be recognized for the quality of their work, some for the quantity of their work. Some like to be recognized individually, others want to be recognized in groups."

Consequently, at the end of each employee-orientation session, Albin emails his new hires and asks them how and in what form they prefer their strokes.

"It helps me understand what they think of themselves and their abilities, and I make a mental note to pay special attention to them when they're working in that particular arena," he says. "No one has ever said, 'Just recognize me for anything I do well.'"[9]

MCCLELLAND'S NEED THEORY

In the late 1940s, David McClelland, a well-known psychologist, studied the relationship between needs and behaviour. Although he is most recognized for his research on the need for achievement, he also investigated the needs for affiliation and power. Let's consider each of these needs.

The Need for Achievement The *need for achievement* is defined by the following desires:

> *To accomplish something difficult. To master, manipulate, or organize physical objects, human beings, or ideas. To do this as rapidly and as independently as possible. To overcome obstacles and attain a high standard. To excel one's self. To rival and surpass others. To increase self-regard by the successful exercise of talent.*[10]

> **Need for achievement**
>
> Desire to accomplish something difficult.

Achievement-motivated people share three common characteristics: (1) they prefer working on tasks of moderate difficulty; (2) they prefer situations in which performance is due to their efforts rather than other factors, such as luck; and (3) they desire more feedback on their successes and failures than do low achievers.

The Need for Affiliation People with a high *need for affiliation* prefer to spend more time maintaining social relationships, joining groups, and wanting to be loved. Individuals high in this need are not the most effective managers or leaders because they have a hard time making difficult decisions without worrying about being disliked.[11]

> **Need for affiliation**
>
> Desire to spend time in social relationships and activities.

The Need for Power The *need for power* reflects an individual's desire to influence, coach, teach, or encourage others to achieve. Consider the Skills & Best Practices feature box that describes the managers at the City of Mississauga who felt the need to restore their sense of power and status in the workplace. People with a high need for power like to work and are concerned with discipline and self-respect. There is a positive and negative side to this need. The negative face of power is characterized by an "if I win, you lose" mentality. In contrast, people with a positive orientation to power focus on accomplishing group goals and helping employees obtain the feeling of competence. Chapter 9 provides more information about the two faces of power. Because effective managers must positively influence others, McClelland proposes that top managers should have a high need for power coupled with a low need for affiliation. He also believes that individuals with high achievement motivation are not best suited for top management positions. Several studies support these propositions.[12]

> **Need for power**
>
> Desire to influence, coach, teach, or encourage others to achieve.

Skills & Best Practices

City of Mississauga Managers Feel Power and Status Under Attack

A few years ago, the City of Mississauga hired an outside consultant and a change agent to introduce a new kind of open-concept physical layout and a more team-oriented workplace design throughout the corporate offices. The intent was to increase productivity, improve customer service, and stimulate collegiality among workers. The plan fit nicely into the overall corporate objectives, as managers were taken out of their offices and placed into large open spaces along with employees. However, the changes were not well received by some departments and middle-managers.

Why? Because they felt their power and status had been reduced. As one manager put it, "We work years to become managers and now you want to take away one of the very few perks (that are left)."

To overcome the resistance for those managers who insisted on restoring their status and power walls, the employer installed glass rather than opaque walls. Clearly, the personal office space represents far more than privacy to the managers—it is about power, status, and recognition. You take that away, you take away their motivation.

SOURCE: D. Scrisp, "Changing People The Hard Part," *Canadian HR Reporter*, April 25, 2011, p 11.

Managerial Implications Given that adults can be trained to increase their achievement motivation,[13] organizations should consider the benefits of providing achievement training for employees. Moreover, achievement, affiliation, and power needs can be considered during the selection process for better placement. For example, a study revealed that individuals' need for achievement affected their preference to work in different companies. People with a high need for achievement were more attracted to companies that had a pay-for-performance environment than were those with a low achievement motivation.[14] Finally, managers should create challenging task assignments or goals because the need for achievement is positively correlated with goal commitment and job involvement.[15] Moreover, challenging goals should accompany a more autonomous work environment and employee empowerment to capitalize on the characteristics of high achievers.

HERZBERG'S MOTIVATOR–HYGIENE THEORY

Frederick Herzberg's two-factor theory is based on a landmark study in which he interviewed 203 accountants and engineers.[16] These interviews sought to determine the factors responsible for job satisfaction and dissatisfaction. Herzberg found separate and distinct clusters of factors associated with job satisfaction and dissatisfaction. Job satisfaction was more frequently associated with achievement, recognition, characteristics of the work, responsibility, and advancement. These factors were all related to outcomes associated with the content of the task being performed. Herzberg labelled these factors *motivators* because each was associated with strong effort and good performance. He hypothesized that motivators cause a person to move from a state of no satisfaction to satisfaction (see Figure 5.3). Therefore, Herzberg's theory predicts managers can motivate individuals by incorporating motivators into an individual's job.

Herzberg found job dissatisfaction to be associated primarily with factors in the work context or environment. Specifically, company policy and administration, technical supervision, salary, interpersonal relations with one's supervisor, and working conditions were most

> **Motivators**
>
> Job characteristics associated with job satisfaction.

FIGURE 5.3 Herzberg's Motivator–Hygiene Model

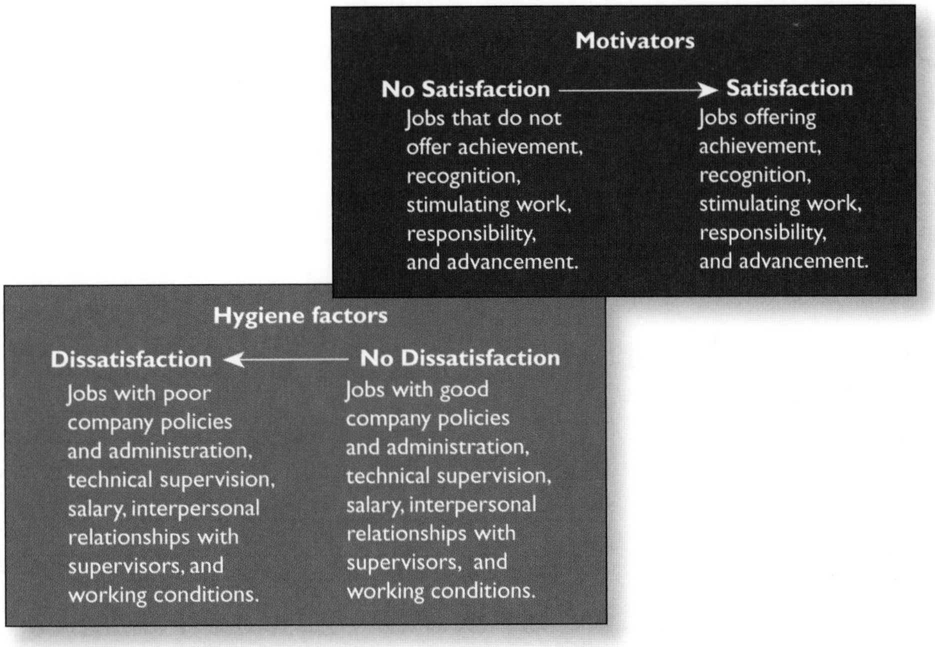

Motivators

No Satisfaction ⟶ Satisfaction

Jobs that do not offer achievement, recognition, stimulating work, responsibility, and advancement.

Jobs offering achievement, recognition, stimulating work, responsibility, and advancement.

Hygiene factors

Dissatisfaction ⟵ No Dissatisfaction

Jobs with poor company policies and administration, technical supervision, salary, interpersonal relationships with supervisors, and working conditions.

Jobs with good company policies and administration, technical supervision, salary, interpersonal relationships with supervisors, and working conditions.

SOURCE: Adapted in part from D.A. Whitsett and E.K. Winslow, "An Analysis of Studies Critical of the Motivator–Hygiene Theory," *Personnel Psychology,* Winter 1967, pp 391–415.

frequently mentioned by employees expressing job dissatisfaction. Herzberg labelled this second cluster of factors **hygiene factors**. He further proposed that they were not motivational. At best, according to Herzberg's interpretation, individuals will experience no job dissatisfaction when they have no grievances about hygiene factors (refer to Figure 5.3). In contrast, employees are likely to quit when poor hygiene factors lead to job dissatisfaction.

The key to adequately understanding Herzberg's motivator–hygiene theory is recognizing that he believes that satisfaction is not the opposite of dissatisfaction. Herzberg concludes that "the opposite of job satisfaction is not job dissatisfaction, but rather no job satisfaction; and similarly, the opposite of job dissatisfaction is not job satisfaction, but no dissatisfaction."[17] Herzberg thus asserts that the dissatisfaction–satisfaction continuum contains a zero midpoint at which dissatisfaction and satisfaction are absent. Conceivably, an organization member who has good supervision, pay, and working conditions but a tedious and unchallenging task with little chance of advancement would be at the zero midpoint. That person would have no dissatisfaction (because of good hygiene factors) and no satisfaction (because of a lack of motivators).

Herzberg's theory has generated a great deal of research and controversy.[18] Research does not support the two-factor aspect of his theory nor the proposition that hygiene factors are unrelated to job satisfaction. On the positive side, however, Herzberg correctly concluded that people are motivated when their needs for achievement, recognition, stimulating work, and advancement are satisfied.[19] As you will learn in a later section of this chapter, Herzberg's theory has important implications for how managers and team leaders can motivate employees through job design.

Process Theories of Motivation

We now explore the three most common process theories of motivation: (1) equity theory, (2) expectancy theory, and (3) goal-setting theory.

EQUITY THEORY OF MOTIVATION

Defined generally, *equity theory* is a model of motivation that explains how people strive for fairness and justice in social exchanges or give-and-take relationships.

> *Hygiene factors*
>
> Job characteristics associated with job dissatisfaction.

> *Equity theory*
>
> Holds that motivation is a function of fairness in social exchanges.

As a process theory of motivation, equity theory explains how an individual's motivation to behave in a certain way is fuelled by feelings of inequity or a lack of justice. Psychologist J. Stacy Adams pioneered application of the equity principle to the workplace. Central to understanding Adams's equity theory of motivation is an awareness of key components of the individual–organization exchange relationship. This relationship is essential in the formation of employees' perceptions of equity and inequity.

The Individual–Organization Exchange Relationship Adams points out that two primary components are involved in the employee–employer exchange: *inputs* and *outcomes*. Employees' inputs, for which they expect a just return, include education/training, skills, creativity, seniority, age, personality traits, effort expended, and personal appearance. On the outcome side of the exchange, the organization provides such things as pay/bonuses, fringe benefits, challenging assignments, job security, promotions, status symbols, and participation in important decisions.

Negative and Positive Inequity On the job, feelings of inequity revolve around people's evaluation of whether they receive adequate rewards to compensate for their contributions. People perform these evaluations by comparing the perceived fairness of their employment exchange to that of relevant others. This comparative process, which is based on an equity norm, generalizes across countries.[20] People tend to compare themselves to other individuals with whom they have close interpersonal ties (such as friends) or to similar others (such as people performing the same job or individuals of the same gender or educational level) rather than dissimilar others. For example, do you consider the average top-100 CEO in Canada a relevant comparison to yourself? If not, then you should not feel inequity because Canada's 100 best paid CEOs make an average of $8.4 million.[21] For someone working at minimum wage, the contrast is beyond extreme. As of this writing, by noon January 3rd, the best-paid CEOs pocket what takes a minimum wage worker the entire year to earn![22]

Three different equity relationships are illustrated in Figure 5.4: (A) equity, (B) negative inequity, and (C) positive inequity. Try and think of a time when you found out that a person at work was earning more than you per hour—even though you both had pretty much the same job. How did that make you

FIGURE 5.4 Negative and Positive Inequity

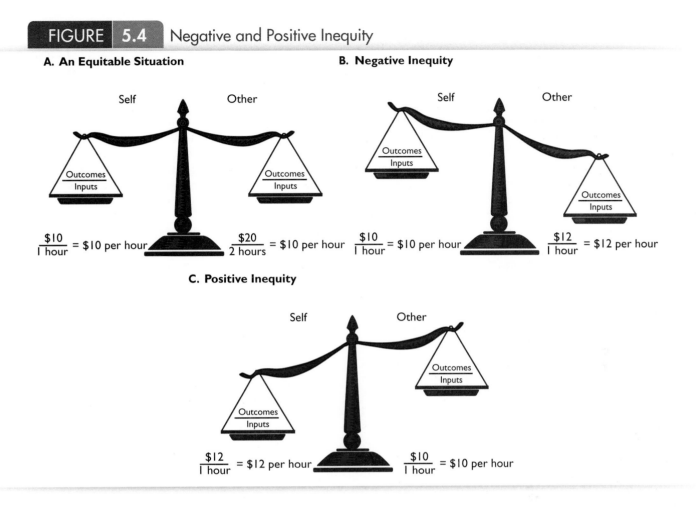

A. An Equitable Situation

Self   Other

$$\frac{\$10}{1\ hour} = \$10\ per\ hour \qquad \frac{\$20}{2\ hours} = \$10\ per\ hour$$

B. Negative Inequity

Self   Other

$$\frac{\$10}{1\ hour} = \$10\ per\ hour \qquad \frac{\$12}{1\ hour} = \$12\ per\ hour$$

C. Positive Inequity

Self   Other

$$\frac{\$12}{1\ hour} = \$12\ per\ hour \qquad \frac{\$10}{1\ hour} = \$10\ per\ hour$$

feel? To understand this situation, refer to Figure 5.4 as we walk you through the theory. In the example, assume the two people in each of the equity relationships have equivalent backgrounds (equal education, seniority, and so forth) and perform identical tasks; only their hourly pay rates differ. Equity exists for people when their ratio of perceived outcomes to inputs is equal to the ratio of outcomes to inputs for a relevant co-worker (part A in Figure 5.4). Because equity is based on comparing *ratios* of outcomes to inputs, inequity will not necessarily be perceived just because someone else receives greater rewards. If the other person's additional outcomes are due to greater inputs, a sense of equity may still exist. However, if the comparison person enjoys greater outcomes for similar inputs, *negative inequity* will be perceived (part B in Figure 5.4). On the other hand, a person will experience *positive inequity* when the outcome to input ratio is greater than that of a relevant co-worker (part C in Figure 5.4).

Dynamics of Perceived Inequity Managers can derive practical benefits from Adams's equity theory by recognizing that (1) people have varying sensitivities to perceived equity and inequity, and (2) inequity can be reduced in a variety of ways.

Thresholds of Equity and Inequity Have you ever noticed that some people become very upset over the slightest inequity, whereas others are not bothered at all? Research shows that people respond differently to the same level of inequity due to an individual difference called equity sensitivity. *Equity sensitivity* reflects an individual's "different preferences for, tolerances for, and reactions to the level of equity associated with any given situation."[23] Equity sensitivity spans across a continuum. On one side are those people who have a *higher tolerance* for negative inequity (Figure 5.4 B); they are tolerant

Negative inequity

Comparison in which another person receives greater outcomes for similar inputs.

Positive inequity

Comparison in which another person receives lesser outcomes for similar inputs.

Equity sensitivity

An individual's tolerance for negative and positive equity.

when their outcome/input ratio is lower than ratios from the other person who they are comparing themselves against. In contrast, along the same continuum, some other people are more sensitive because of their loyalty to a strict norm of reciprocity (this task earns this reward always, no matter who does it), and are quickly motivated to resolve both negative and positive inequity (either Figure 5.4 B or C). And finally, on the complete opposite side of the continuum are those people who have *no tolerance* for negative inequity (Figure 5.4 B). They actually expect to obtain greater output/input ratios than others and become upset when this is not the case.[24]

Reducing Inequity If people perceive inequity, then only they can alter it by attempting to alter outcomes or adjusting inputs. For example, negative inequity might be resolved by asking for a raise or a promotion (i.e., raising outputs) or by reducing inputs (i.e., working fewer hours or exerting less effort). It is also important to note that equity can be restored by altering equity ratios behaviourally or cognitively, or both. A cognitive strategy entails psychologically distorting perceptions of one's own or one's comparison person's outcomes and inputs (e.g., conclude that the other person you're comparing yourself to has more experience or works harder). You may recall we talked about cognitive dissonance in Chapter 4.

LO 3 EXPECTANCY THEORY

Expectancy theory holds that people are motivated to behave in ways that produce desired combinations of expected outcomes. Generally, expectancy theory can be used to predict motivation and behaviour in any situation in which a choice between two or more alternatives must be made. For instance, it can be used to predict whether to quit or stay at a job; whether to exert substantial or minimal effort at a task; and whether to major in IT, human resources, insurance, finance, marketing, accounting, or general business.

> *Expectancy theory*
>
> Holds that people are motivated to behave in ways that produce valued outcomes.

Victor Vroom formulated a mathematical model of expectancy in his 1964 book, *Work and Motivation.*[25] Vroom's theory is summarized as follows:

> *The strength of a tendency to act in a certain way depends on the strength of an expectancy that the act will be followed by a given consequence (or outcome) and on the value or attractiveness of that consequence (or outcome) to the actor.*[26]

Motivation, according to Vroom, boils down to the decision of how much effort to exert in a specific task situation. This choice is based on a two-stage sequence of expectations (effort → performance, and performance → outcome). First, motivation is affected by an individual's expectation that a certain level of effort will produce the intended performance goal. For example, if you do not believe increasing the amount of time you spend studying will significantly raise your grade on an exam, you probably will not study any harder than usual. Motivation is also influenced by employees' perceived chances of getting various outcomes as a result of accomplishing their performance goal. Finally, individuals are motivated to the extent that they value the outcomes received.

Vroom used a mathematical equation to integrate the above concepts into a model of motivational force or strength. For our purposes however, it is sufficient to define and explain the three key concepts within Vroom's model—*expectancy, instrumentality,* and *valence.*

Expectancy An *expectancy*, according to Vroom's terminology, represents an individual's belief that a particular degree of effort will be followed by a particular level of performance. In other words, it is an effort → performance expectation. For example, suppose you have not memorized the keys on a computer keyboard. No matter how much effort you exert, your perceived probability of typing 30 error-free words per minute likely would be zero. If you decide to memorize the letters on a keyboard as well as practise a couple of hours a day for a few weeks (high effort), you should be able to type 30 words per minute without any errors. In contrast, if you do not memorize the letters on a keyboard and only practise an hour or two per week (low effort), there is a very low probability (say, a 20 percent chance) of being able to type 30 words per minute without any errors.

> *Expectancy*
>
> Belief that effort leads to a specific level of performance.

Instrumentality An *instrumentality* is a performance → outcome perception. It represents a person's belief that one lower level outcome leads to another higher level outcome occurring. In other words, a particular outcome is contingent on accomplishing a specific level of performance. Performance is instrumental when it leads to something else. For example, passing exams with the necessary grade level is instrumental to graduating; or, completing all required tasks as directed by the boss is instrumental to securing a pay raise. Hopefully, one outcome leads to another with greater certainty.

> *Instrumentality*
>
> A performance → outcome perception.

The concept of instrumentality can be seen in practice by considering the national debate regarding CEO pay. Amid complaints that CEOs make too much money, especially if their firm is losing tens of millions of dollars, more corporate boards are linking CEO pay to specific performance targets.

Valence   As Vroom used the term, *valence* refers to the positive or negative value people place on outcomes. Valence mirrors our personal preferences. For example, most employees have a positive valence for receiving additional money or recognition. In contrast, job stress and being laid off would likely result in negative valence for most individuals.

> *Valence*
>
> The value of a reward or outcome.

This is rather complicated, to say the least, and you might be asking yourself: Do people really think this way? Do they consciously look at expectancy, percentage chances of achieving certain performances or outcomes, and then measure the valence of a reward or outcome? Simply stated—probably not. It's more likely that people take all three into consideration when living their lives. Use yourself as an example: Think about the kinds of expectancies you have about your own school achievement. You probably have an idea of what sorts of opportunities will come your way if you achieve what you set out to do, and of the value of such opportunities for yourself.

Research on Expectancy Theory and Managerial Implications   Many researchers have tested expectancy theory. In support of the theory, a meta-analysis of 77 studies indicated that expectancy theory significantly predicts performance, effort, intentions, preferences, and choice.[27] Another summary of 16 studies revealed that expectancy theory correctly predicts occupational or organizational choice 63.4 percent of the time, significantly better than chance predictions.[28]

Nonetheless, expectancy theory has been criticized for a variety of reasons. For example, the theory is difficult to test, and the measures used to assess expectancy, instrumentality, and valence have questionable validity.[29] In the final analysis, however, expectancy theory has important practical implications for individual managers and organizations as a whole (see Table 5.2).

Managers are advised to enhance effort that leads to performance expectancies by helping employees accomplish their performance goals. Managers can do this by providing support and coaching, and by increasing employees' self-efficacy. It is also important for managers to influence employees' instrumentalities and to monitor valences for various rewards. This raises the issue of whether organizations should use monetary rewards as the primary method to reinforce performance.

TABLE 5.2

MANAGERIAL AND ORGANIZATIONAL IMPLICATIONS OF EXPECTANCY THEORY

IMPLICATIONS FOR MANAGERS	IMPLICATIONS FOR ORGANIZATIONS
Determine the outcomes that employees value.	Reward people for desired performance and do not keep pay decisions secret.
Identify good performance so appropriate behaviours can be rewarded.	Design challenging jobs.
Make sure employees can achieve targeted performance levels.	Tie some rewards to group accomplishments to build teamwork and encourage cooperation.
Link desired outcomes to targeted levels of performance.	Reward managers for creating, monitoring, and maintaining expectancies, instrumentalities, and outcomes that lead to high effort and goal attainment.
Make sure changes in outcomes are large enough to motivate high effort.	Monitor employee motivation through interviews or anonymous questionnaires.
Monitor the reward system for inequities.	Accommodate individual differences by building flexibility into the motivation program.

Although money is certainly a positive reward for most people, there are many issues to consider when deciding on the relative balance between monetary and non-monetary rewards. For example, research shows that some workers value interesting work, recognition, and group welfare more than money.[30]

In summary, there is no one best type of reward. Individual differences and need theories tell us that people are motivated by different rewards. Managers should therefore focus on linking employee performance to valued rewards regardless of the type of reward used to enhance motivation.

MOTIVATION THROUGH GOAL SETTING

Regardless of the nature of their specific achievements, successful people tend to have one thing in common: their lives are goal oriented. As a process model of motivation, goal-setting theory explains how the simple behaviour of setting goals activates a powerful motivational process that leads to sustained, high performance. This section explores the theory and research pertaining to goal setting.

LO 4 **Goals: Definition and Background** Edwin Locke, a leading authority on goal setting, and his colleagues define a **goal** as "what an individual is trying to accomplish; it is the object or aim of an action."[31] The motivational effect of performance goals and goal-based reward

> **Goal**
>
> What an individual is trying to accomplish.

plans has been recognized for a long time. At the turn of the century, Frederick Taylor attempted to scientifically establish how much work of a specified quality an individual should be assigned each day. He proposed that bonuses be based on accomplishing those output standards. More recently, goal setting has been promoted through a widely used management technique called *management by objectives* (MBO).

Management by Objectives (MBO) First introduced in the 1950s, MBO is a management system that incorporates participation into decision making, goal setting, and objective feedback.[32] The central idea of MBO, getting individuals employees to "own" a piece of a collective effort, is evident in this recent bit of advice from Google executive Paul Russell:

> *Help your people map out their goals. Ask them to apply those aspirations to what they do every day. You'll build their sense of affiliation with the company and make them feel they belong. And they'll believe that they don't have to leave to accomplish their ambitions.*[33]

How Does Goal Setting Work? Despite abundant goal-setting research and practice, goal-setting theories are surprisingly scarce. An instructive model was formulated by Locke and his associates. According to Locke's model, goal setting has four motivational mechanisms: (1) directs attention, (2) regulates effort, (3) increases persistence, and (4) helps to foster development and application of strategies and plans.

Goals Direct Attention Goals direct a person's attention and effort toward goal-relevant activities and away from goal-irrelevant activities. If, for example, you have a term project due in a few days, your thoughts and actions tend to revolve around completing that project.

Goals Regulate Effort Not only do goals make us selectively perceptive, they also motivate us to act. The instructor's deadline for turning in your term project would prompt you to complete it, as opposed to going out with friends, watching television, or studying for another course. Generally, the level of effort is proportionate to the difficulty of the goal.

Goals Increase Persistence Within the context of goal setting, persistence represents the effort on a task over an extended period of time: It takes effort to run 100 metres; it takes persistence to run a 26-mile marathon. Persistent people tend to see obstacles as challenges to be overcome rather than as reasons to fail.

"I'm moving you into this office because it overlooks the unemployment office. I thought you could use the motivation."

Irish professional golfer Rory McIlroy's impressive record places him among the top PGA-touring earners in the world.

A difficult goal that is important to an individual is a constant reminder to keep giving effort in the appropriate direction. This is illustrated by Rory McIlroy's determination, the Irish professional golfer, who at the age of 22 won the US Open with a record score of 16-under par. Born in Ireland on May 4, 1989, Rory tweeted after playing in his first Masters, "It's repetition of affirmations that leads to belief—and once that belief becomes a deep conviction, things begin to happen." Later, he went on to say, "Your success only makes you more motivated to do better. I have become a very good player, but I still have a lot of years to progress and I just want to keep improving and hopefully one day I will be able to compete with Tiger (Woods)."[34]

Goals Foster the Development and Application of Task Strategies and Action Plans If you are here and your goal is out there somewhere, you face the problem of getting from here to there. For example, think about the challenge of starting a business. Do you want to earn profits, grow larger, or make the world a better place? To get there, you have to make a tremendous number of decisions and complete a myriad of tasks. Goals can help because they encourage people to develop strategies and action plans that enable them to achieve their goals.

Practical Lessons from Goal-Setting Research Research has consistently supported goal setting as a motivational technique. Setting performance goals increases individual, group, and organizational performance. Further, the positive effects of goal setting were found in six other countries or regions outside of Canada: Australia, the Caribbean, England, West Germany, the United States, and Japan. Goal setting works in different

cultures. Reviews of the many goal-setting studies conducted over the past few decades have given managers five practical insights.

1. **Specific high goals lead to greater performance** *Goal specificity* pertains to the quantifiability of a goal. In accordance with available research evidence, goals should be SMART—an acronym that stands for specific, measurable, attainable, results oriented, and time bound. For example, a goal of selling nine cars a month is more specific than asking a salesperson to do his best. Results from more than 1,000 studies involving over 88 different tasks and 40,000 people demonstrated that performance is greater when people have specific, high goals.[35]

> **Goal specificity**
> Quantifiability of a goal.

2. **Feedback enhances the effect of specific, difficult goals** Feedback plays a key role in all of our lives. Feedback lets people know if they are headed toward their goals or if they are off course and need to redirect their efforts. Goals plus feedback is the recommended approach.[36] Goals inform people about performance standards and expectations so that they can channel their energies accordingly. In turn, feedback provides the information needed to adjust direction, effort, and strategies for goal accomplishment. While face-to-face feedback may be something past generations preferred, future generations (who have grown up with interactive technology) will expect instant and continuous feedback for their just-in-time performance reviews.

3. **Participative goals, assigned goals, and self-set goals are equally effective** Both managers and researchers are interested in identifying the best way to set goals. Should goals be cooperatively set, assigned, or set by the employee? A summary of goal-setting research indicated that no single approach is consistently more effective than others in increasing performance.[37] Managers are advised to use a contingency approach by picking a method that seems best suited for the individual and situation at hand.

4. **Action planning facilitates goal accomplishment** An action plan outlines the activities or tasks that need to be accomplished to achieve a goal. They can also include dates associated with completing each task, resources needed, and obstacles that must be overcome. Managers can use action plans as a vehicle to have performance discussions with employees, and employees can use them to monitor progress toward goal achievement. An action plan also serves as a cue to remind employees of what they should be working on, which turn leads to

goal-relevant behaviour and success.[38] Finally, managers are encouraged to allow employees to develop their own action plans because this autonomy fuels higher goal commitment and a sense of doing meaningful work.[39]

5. **Goal commitment and monetary incentives affect goal-setting outcomes** *Goal commitment* is the extent to which an individual is personally committed to achieving a goal. In general, individuals are expected to persist in attempts to accomplish a goal when they are committed to it. Researchers believe that goal commitment moderates the relationship between the difficulty of a goal and performance. That is, difficult goals lead to higher performance only when employees are committed to their goals. Conversely, difficult goals are hypothesized to lead to lower performance when people are not committed to their goals. A meta-analysis of 21 studies based on 2,360 people supports these predictions.[40] It is also important to note that people are more likely to commit to high goals when they have high self-efficacy about successfully accomplishing their goals.

> **Goal commitment**
>
> Amount of commitment to achieving a goal.

Like goal setting, the use of monetary incentives to motivate employees is seldom questioned. Unfortunately, research uncovers some negative consequences when goal achievement is linked to individual incentives. Empirical (observed data) studies demonstrate that goal-based bonus incentives produce higher commitment to easy goals and lower commitment to difficult goals. People are reluctant to commit to high goals that are tied to monetary incentives. People with high goal commitment offer less help to their co-workers when they receive goal-based bonus incentives to accomplish difficult individual goals. Individuals also neglect aspects of the job that are not covered in the performance goals.[41]

These findings underscore some of the dangers of using goal-based incentives, particularly for employees in complex, interdependent jobs requiring cooperation. Managers need to consider the advantages, disadvantages, and dilemmas of goal-based incentives prior to implementation.

LO 5 Motivating Employees through Job Design

Job design is used when a manager suspects that the type of work an employee performs or characteristics of the work environment are causing motivational problems. *Job design,* also referred to as *job redesign,* "refers to any set of activities that involve the alteration

> **Job design**
>
> Changing the content or process of a specific job to increase job satisfaction and performance.

of specific jobs or interdependent systems of jobs with the intent of improving the quality of employee job experience and their on-the-job productivity."[42] A team of researchers examined the various methods for conducting job design and integrated them into an interdisciplinary framework that includes four major approaches: (1) mechanistic, (2) motivational, (3) biological, and (4) perceptual-motor.[43] As you will learn, each approach to job design emphasizes different outcomes. This section discusses these four approaches to job design and focuses most heavily on the motivational methods.

THE MECHANISTIC APPROACH

The mechanistic approach draws from Frederick Taylor's research in industrial engineering and *scientific management* (see History of OB in Chapter 1). Taylor, a mechanical engineer, developed the principles of scientific management while working at both Midvale Steel Works and Bethlehem Steel in Pennsylvania. He observed very little cooperation between management and workers, and found that employees were underachieving by engaging in output restriction, which Taylor called "systematic soldiering." Taylor's interest in scientific management grew from his desire to improve upon this situation.

Because jobs are highly specialized and standardized when they are designed according to the principles of scientific management, this approach to job design targets efficiency and employee productivity. An assembly line worker whose job is predictable day in and day out would be an example of a person who works at a mechanistic type of job. The tasks and expectations of the job do not change over time, therefore the employee's proficiency at completing the task is high. The job itself is designed for repetitious routine types of work.

Designing jobs using the principles of scientific management has both positive and negative consequences. Positively, employee efficiency and productivity are increased. On the other hand, research reveals that simplified, repetitive jobs also lead to job dissatisfaction, poor mental health, higher levels of stress, and low sense of accomplishment and personal growth.[44] These negative consequences paved the way for the motivational approach to job design.

It is worth noting here that you will come across similar but not identical concepts and terms in Chapter 12 when we discuss designing organizations. Motivation guides job design and organic principles guide structure design. We encourage you to remember this fine distinction as we continue our discussion.

MOTIVATIONAL APPROACHES

The motivational approaches to job design attempt to improve employees' affective and attitudinal reactions such as job satisfaction and intrinsic motivation, as well as a host of behavioural outcomes such as absenteeism, turnover, and performance. In support of motivational approaches, Daniel Pink, a contemporary author and journalist, has popularized the cognitive performance (Candle Problem) test results of Gestalt psychologist Karl Duncker (1945).[45] Pink writes about the changing world of work where the mechanistic approaches of the 20th century do not work anymore and can do harm instead. Pink asserts that contingent motivators, like incentives, were commonly used in the past to increase employee performance; as a result, such motivators facilitated rigid thinking because of their emphasis on focusing attention quickly.[46] Pink states that these results—which Duncker called 'functional fixedness'—are counterproductive and not the kind of creative thinking needed for the 21st century workplace.

To build upon what Pink is referring to, we will now discuss four key motivational techniques: (1) job enlargement, (2) job enrichment, (3) job rotation, and (4) a contingency approach called the job characteristics model.

Job Enlargement   This technique was first used in the late 1940s in response to complaints about tedious and overspecialized jobs. *Job enlargement* involves putting more variety into a worker's job by combining specialized tasks of comparable difficulty. Some call this *horizontally loading* the job. Researchers recommend using job enlargement as part of a broader

Job enlargement

Putting more variety into a job.

Daniel Pink has coined the term "Motivation 3.0". Pink believes contingent motivators just don't work anymore and instead supports instrinsic motivational approaches for decision making in the 21st century.

approach that uses multiple motivational methods, because it does not have a significant and lasting positive effect on job performance by itself.[47]

An example of job enlargement would be a contemporary customer service representative for a packaged good firm who loads up the SUV in the morning with boxes of product, drives to retail stores to meet with clients, notices if stock is low on store shelves and replenishes it, places an electronic order to head office on behalf of the retailer for a larger future shipment, and then issues the paperwork for signature and payment purposes. Traditionally, several employees would have completed these tasks: one person loaded trucks with boxes, another employee delivered boxes to retailers, another employee acted as the customer rep taking orders from clients, and then another employee back in the office issued the paperwork. Today, job enlargement significantly improves work efficiency and flexibility.

Job Rotation   As with job enlargement, job rotation's purpose is to give employees greater variety in their work. *Job rotation* calls for moving employees from one specialized job to another. Rather than performing only one job, workers are trained and given the opportunity to perform two or more separate jobs on a rotating basis. By rotating employees from job to job, managers believe they can stimulate interest and motivation while providing employees with a broader perspective of the organization.

Job rotation

Moving employees from one specialized job to another.

Other proposed advantages of job rotation include increased worker flexibility and easier scheduling, because employees are cross-trained to perform different jobs. Organizations also use job rotation as a vehicle to place new employees into jobs of their choice. The idea is that turnover is reduced and performance increases because people self-select their jobs. Ability Beyond Disability, an 800-person firm that provides health care for people with disabilities in more than 100 locations, is a good example:

> *Within days after an interview, a successful applicant is on the payroll, undergoing extensive training and visiting the employer's group homes to see the real world of caring for people with disabilities. For about two months, sometimes three, the new hires—called intern floaters—are exposed to a wide variety of jobs in a variety of settings before they commit to a particular post. . . . New hires have choices and are urged to "try different areas" within the organization, to sample many types of direct care before taking a regular post.[48]*

Managers at Ability Beyond Disability are happy with the results from the rotation program. Employee retention is up, turnover is down, and there is a reduction in staffing needs. Despite these types of positive experiences, it is not possible to draw firm conclusions about the value of job rotation programs because they have not been adequately researched.

Job Enrichment   Job enrichment is the practical application of Herzberg's motivator–hygiene theory of job satisfaction that we discussed earlier in this chapter. Specifically, *job enrichment* entails modifying a job such that an employee has the opportunity to experience achievement, recognition, stimulating work, responsibility, and advancement. These characteristics are incorporated into a job through vertical loading. Rather than giving employees additional tasks of similar difficulty (horizontal loading), vertical loading consists of giving workers more responsibility. In other words, employees take on tasks normally performed by their supervisors. Going back to our earlier example, if we want to also enrich the job of the contemporary customer service representative for a packaged good firm, we could have that same person responsible for assessing the efficiency of the entire supply chain for that particular client. If the client had a problem, the customer service rep would have the authority to approach the delivery truck driver directly or even call the warehouse supervisor and make inquiries.

> *Job enrichment*
>
> Building achievement, recognition, stimulating work, responsibility, and advancement into a job.

The Job Characteristics Model   Two OB researchers, J. Richard Hackman and Greg Oldham, played a central role in developing the job characteristics approach. These researchers tried to determine how work can be structured so that employees are internally or intrinsically motivated. To determine your own preference, you may want to complete the Self-Assessment Exercise, "Are You Intrinsically Motivated At Work?"

Intrinsic motivation occurs when an individual is "turned on to one's work because of the positive internal feelings that are generated by doing well, rather than being dependent on extrinsic or external factors (such as incentive pay or compliments from the boss) for the motivation to work effectively."[49] These positive feelings power a self-perpetuating cycle of motivation. As shown in Figure 5.5, internal work motivation is determined by three psychological states. In turn, these psychological states are fostered by the presence of five core job dimensions. The object of this approach is to promote high intrinsic motivation by designing jobs that possess the five core job characteristics shown in Figure 5.5. Let's examine the core job dimensions.

In general terms, *core job dimensions* are common characteristics found

> *Intrinsic motivation*
>
> Motivation caused by positive internal feelings.

> *Core job dimensions*
>
> Job characteristics found to various degrees in all jobs.

FIGURE 5.5   The Job Characteristics Model

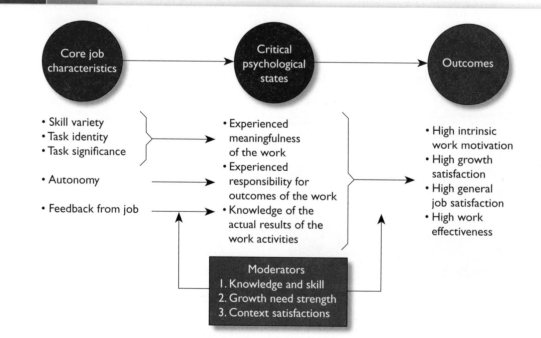

SOURCE: From J.R. Hackman and G.R. Oldham, *Work Redesign,* © 1980, p. 90. Reprinted by permission of Pearson Education, Inc., Upper Saddle River, NJ.

Are You Intrinsically Motivated at Work?

INSTRUCTIONS: The following survey was designed to assess the extent to which you are deriving intrinsic rewards from your current job. If you are not working, use a past job or your role as a student to complete the survey. There are no right or wrong answers to the statements. Circle your answer by using the rating scale provided. After evaluating each of the survey statements, complete the scoring guide.

	STRONGLY DISAGREE	DISAGREE	NEITHER AGREE or DISAGREE	AGREE	STRONGLY AGREE
1 I am passionate about my work.	1	2	3	4	5
2 I can see how my work tasks contribute to my organization's corporate vision.	1	2	3	4	5
3 I have significant autonomy in determining how I do my job.	1	2	3	4	5
4 My supervisor/manager delegates important projects/tasks to me that significantly impact my department's overall success.	1	2	3	4	5
5 I have mastered the skills necessary for my job.	1	2	3	4	5
6 My supervisor/manager recognizes when I competently perform my job.	1	2	3	4	5
7 Throughout the year, my department celebrates its progress toward achieving its goals.	1	2	3	4	5
8 I regularly receive evidence/information about my progress toward achieving my overall performance goals.	1	2	3	4	5

Scoring Key

Sense of meaningfulness (add items 1–2) _____

Sense of choice (add items 3–4) _____

Sense of competence (add items 5–6) _____

Sense of progress (add items 7–8) _____

Overall score (add all items) _____

Arbitrary Norms

For each intrinsic reward, a score of 2–4 indicates low intrinsic motivation, 5–7 represents moderate intrinsic motivation, and 8–10 indicates high intrinsic motivation. For the overall score, 8–19 is low, 20–30 is moderate, and 31–40 is high.

to a varying degree in all jobs. Three of the job characteristics shown in Figure 5.5 combine to determine the experienced meaningfulness of work, which includes:

- **Skill variety** The extent to which the job requires individuals to perform a variety of tasks that require them to use different skills and abilities.

- **Task identity** The extent to which the job requires individuals to perform a whole or completely identifiable piece of work. In other words, task identity is high when people work on a product or project from beginning to end and see a tangible result.

- **Task significance** The extent to which the job affects the lives of other people within or outside the organization.

- **Autonomy** The extent to which the job enables individuals to experience freedom, independence, and discretion in both scheduling and determining the procedures used in completing the job.

- **Feedback** The extent to which individuals receive direct and clear information about how effectively they are performing the job.[50]

Hackman and Oldham recognized that everyone does not want a job containing high amounts of the five core job characteristics. They incorporated this conclusion into their model by identifying three attributes that affect how individuals respond to job enrichment. These attributes are concerned with the individual's knowledge and skill, growth need strength (representing the desire to grow and develop as an individual), and context satisfactions (see the box labelled Moderators in Figure 5.5). Context satisfactions represent the extent to which employees are satisfied with various aspects of their job, such as satisfaction with pay, co-workers, and supervision.

Several practical implications are associated with using the job characteristics model to enhance intrinsic motivation. Managers may want to use this model to increase employee job satisfaction. Research overwhelmingly demonstrates a moderately strong relationship between job characteristics and satisfaction.[51] Employee job satisfaction can occur as a result of

designing more autonomy into employees' jobs, such as allowing employees to select from a variety of work schedules that meet their needs like working flexible hours using compressed work weeks and telecommuting from home.[52] Research supports this investment, as autonomy is positively associated with job performance and proactive work behaviours.[53]

Moreover, research suggests that managers can enhance employees' intrinsic motivation, initiative, creativity, innovation, and commitment to their performance goals by increasing the core job characterstics.[54] Two separate meta-analyses also support the practice of using the job characteristics model to help managers reduce absenteeism and turnover.[55] On the negative side, however, job redesign appears to reduce the quantity of output just as often as it has a positive effect. Caution and situational appropriateness are advised. For example, one study demonstrated that job redesign works better in less complex organizations (small plants or companies).[56] Nonetheless, managers are likely to find noticeable increases in the quality of performance after a job redesign program. Results from 21 experimental studies revealed that job redesign resulted in a median increase of 28 percent in the quality of performance.[57]

BIOLOGICAL AND PERCEPTUAL-MOTOR APPROACHES

We've grouped two approaches together: biological and perceptual-motor. First, the biological approach to job design is based on research from biomechanics, work physiology, and ergonomics, and focuses on designing the work environment to reduce employees' physical strain, fatigue, and health complaints. For example, a

Google employees are offered a variety of alternative office environments. Would you like to work in this type of office?

host of companies, including Google, Skype, and Sprint Nextel Corporation, are experimenting with work station practices by allowing employees to sit away from their desks, opting instead for alternative furniture over traditional chairs. To date, researchers have identified both pros (e.g., improved concentration) and cons (e.g., lower back strain, no arm support) for such work stations.[58]

The perceptual-motor approach is derived from research that examines human factors in engineering, perceptual and cognitive skills, and information processing. This approach to job design emphasizes the reliability of work outcomes by examining error rates, accidents, and workers' feedback about facilities and equipment.[59] Toyota Motor Company (TMC) applies such principles in developing standard procedures and training of its manufacturing plants around the world. As a recent example, to prepare workers in China, the company taught 3,000 detailed assembly-line tasks by displaying videos above workstations simulating factory setups. The videos taught workers how to perform tasks as basic as holding a screw or air gun in the way that is most efficient, delivers consistent quality, and is least tiring. As the company simplified jobs for inexperienced workers in places like China, it discovered solutions that could be applied anywhere in the world. Today you can find these video displays in other TMC plants, including their two Canadian plants.[60]

The frequency of using both the biological and perceptual-motor approaches to job redesign is increasing in light of the number of workers who experience injuries related to overexertion or repetitive motion. *Repetitive motion disorders (RMDs)* are a family of muscular conditions that result from repeated motions performed in the course of normal work or daily activities. "RMDs include carpal tunnel syndrome, bursitis, tendonitis, epicondylitis, ganglion cyst, tenosynovitis, and trigger finger. RMDs are caused by too many uninterrupted repetitions of an activity or motion, unnatural or awkward motions such as twisting the arm or wrist, overexertion, incorrect posture, or muscle fatigue."[61]

Data from the Canadian Centre for Occupational Health and Safety (CCOHS) shows that RMDs (sometimes referred to as work-related musculoskeletal disorders or WMSDs) are recognized as leading causes of significant human suffering, loss of productivity, and economic burdens on society. Workplaces looking to be proactive and ensure RMD/WMSD policies are up-to-date may consider hiring a consultant for a risk assessment analysis of work conditions, said Dhananjai Borwankar, a technical specialist at CCOHS. RMD/ WMSD information is always being updated and the online resource called "OSH Answers" covers a variety of workplace injuries.[62]

The problem with RMD/WMSD injuries is that they don't occur immediately and therefore may go unnoticed by supervisors and maybe even the employee themselves in the workplace. If there is no immediate concern, people tend not to recognize the hazard and this is where it is important to be proactive as an organization. Training is key at all levels throughout the organization.

Time Shifting Approaches

This last section has been included to discuss alternative work arrangements that are becoming more frequently used to motivate employees. We will focus on four time shifting options: flextime, telecommuting, compressed workweek, and job sharing.

Flextime is an alternative work schedule that allows employees to select their choice of morning arrival or afternoon departure as long as a middle core of hours is covered. This type of schedule is offered to Cisco Canada employees and helped to earn it the title of one of Canada's Best Employers by Macleans.[63] A review of research concluded that flextime has a positive effect on productivity, job satisfaction, and satisfaction with work schedule, and that it lowers employee absenteeism.[64]

Telecommuting allows employees to work from their home using electronic communication to complete their work. This saves commuting time and allows employees the chance to shift how and when they work. For example, Skype a meeting, tap into company network system via laptop connection, smartphone instant messaging, or scan and fax documents into the cloud. Loyaltyone in Toronto was recognized for allowing their employees this option.[65] Telecommuting has a positive effect on job satisfaction and job performance and can result in lower stress and turnover.[66] There is growing popularity of organizations using telecommuting, however management is still sometimes reluctant to introduce these programs into their workplace because employees cannot be physically watched. Telecommuting takes trust between manager and employee.[67] Telecommuting is discussed further in Chapter 7 when we discuss how contemporary

Repetitive motion disorders (RMDs)

Muscular disorder caused by repeated motions.

Flextime

Alternative work schedule that allows employees to determine hours of work around a core timeframe.

Telecommuting

Alternative work schedule that allows employees to work from home rather than in an office.

communication technology is altering the traditional work and place connection.

Compressed workweeks allow employees to cover a full work week into a compressed week. For some, it may mean working four 10-hour shifts Monday to Thursday and taking Friday off. Others may work three or four days straight—like firefighters—and then get the next few days off. The Co-operators in Guelph, Ontario offer this option to their employees who in turn recognized the company for its flexibility.[68] According to research, there is a positive effect on job satisfaction and satisfaction with work schedule, but no effect on absenteeism or productivity.[69]

Job sharing is when two part-time employees divide the work of one full-time

> **Compressed workweek**
>
> Alternative work schedule that allows full time employees to work a 40 hour week in less than 5 days.

> **Job sharing**
>
> Alternative work schedule that allows two part time employees to share one full time job.

job. It allows those employees (who only want to work part-time) the option of having personal time as well as keeping their hand in a career. Parents with young children may find this alternative schedule motivating because it allows them to work a morning shift so they stay connected to their employer and maintain skills and knowledge, but in the afternoon they get to go home, allowing the family time needed to watch the children. There is no empirical data on job sharing.[70] Anecdotal reports suggest that job sharing demands high levels of cooperation between the parties involved. If things are not communicated and coordinated well, problems can occur. The issue of performance reviews also surfaces. How can two people sharing one job be assessed accurately?

Summary of Learning Objectives

LO 1 Define *motivation* and *theories of motivation.* Motivation represents psychological processes that arouse and direct goal-directed behaviour. There are two theories of motivation: need and process. Need theories attempt to pinpoint internal factors that energize behaviour. Process theories go one step further in explaining motivation by identifying the process by which various internal factors influence motivation. These models are also cognitive in nature. That is, they are based on the premise that motivation is a function of employees' perceptions, thoughts, and beliefs.

LO 2 Contrast Maslow's, Alderfer's, and McClelland's need theories. Maslow proposed that motivation is a function of five basic needs arranged in a prepotent (greater in power) hierarchy. The concept of a stair-step hierarchy has not stood up well under research. Alderfer concluded that three core needs explain behaviour—existence, relatedness, and growth (ERG). He proposed that more than one need can be activated at a time, and frustration of higher-order needs can influence the desire for lower-level needs. McClelland argued that motivation and performance vary according to the strength of an individual's need for achievement. High achievers prefer tasks of moderate difficulty, situations under their control, and a desire for more performance feedback than low achievers. Top managers have a high need for power coupled with a low need for affiliation.

LO 3 Explain Vroom's expectancy theory and review its practical implications. Expectancy theory assumes motivation is determined by one's perceived chances of achieving valued outcomes. Vroom's expectancy model of motivation reveals how effort → performance expectancies and performance → outcome instrumentalities influence the degree of effort expended to achieve desired (positively valent) outcomes. Managers are advised to enhance effort → performance expectancies by helping employees accomplish their performance goals. With respect to instrumentalities and valences, managers should attempt to link employee performance and valued rewards.

LO 4 Explain how goal setting motivates an individual and review the five practical lessons from goal-setting research. Four motivational mechanisms of goal setting are: (1) goals direct one's attention, (2) goals regulate effort, (3) goals increase one's persistence, and (4) goals encourage development of goal-attainment strategies and action plans. Research identifies four practical lessons about goal setting. First, specific high goals lead to greater performance. Second, feedback enhances the effect of specific, difficult goals. Third, participative goals, assigned goals, and self-set goals are equally effective. Fourth, action planning facilitates goal accomplishment. Five, goal commitment and monetary incentives affect goal-setting outcomes.

LO 5 Summarize the various approaches to job design, including mechanistic, motivational, biological, and perceptual-motor. Job design is changing the content or process of a specific job to increase job satisfaction and performance. The mechanistic approach is based on industrial engineering and scientific management and focuses on increasing efficiency, flexibility, and employee productivity. Motivational approaches aim to improve employees' affective and attitudinal reactions and behavioural outcomes. Job enlargement, job enrichment, job rotation, and a contingency approach called the job characteristics model are motivational approaches to job design. The biological approach focuses on designing the work environment to reduce employees' physical strain, fatigue, and health complaints. The perceptual-motor approach emphasizes the reliability of work outcomes.

Discussion Questions

1. Why should the average manager be well versed in various motivational theories?

2. Which of the four types of motivational job design is most likely to be used in the future? Explain your rationale.

3. Could managers' attempts to treat their employees as equals still lead to misperceptions of inequity? Explain.

4. According to goal commitment, difficult goals can lead to higher performance. How does this fit with expectancy theory? Explain where these two concepts could possibly disagree.

5. There are many media stories recounting the unethical behaviour of various organizations' employees. In your opinion, what do you believe is the motivation for these people to behave in such a manner? Try relating your answer to one of the two motivational theories: content (need) or process.

Integration of OB Concepts—Discussion Questions

1. See Chapter 2–What role does social perception play in the determination of an employee having the 'right' level of motivation to perform their job well? Explain how an attribution error could be made by a supervisor about the lack of motivation and/or performance of an employee.

2. See Chapter 3–If a person has a low self-concept, how can their motivation and on-the-job performance be affected?

3. See Chapter 4–If an employee does not value a certain task, how motivated will the person be to perform his or her duties? Explain how a positive or negative attitude can affect an employee's motivation to do the job well.

Google Searches

1. **Google Search:** "The Canadian Centre for Occupational Health and Safety—work-related musculoskeletal disorders (WMSDs)" Review the risk factors for WMSDs. For each risk factor, try to determine the type of occupation/job that would cause such an injury. Share your responses with the class. Continue to read prevention techniques for each.

2. **Google Search:** "Globe and Mail Executive Compensation Survey 201__" OR "Canadian Centre for Policy Alternatives–Canada's CEO Elite 100 for 201_" Review the compensation paid in fiscal 201_ to the CEOs of the 100 largest companies. How does this information make you feel when compared to the annual salary of a minimum wage earner? Do you feel a sense of positive or negative inequity with these figures? Explain.

3. **Google Search:** "Best Employers in Canada 201__" This annual survey is conducted by several organizations, including *The Globe & Mail*. A list has been published each year since 2000. Review the latest list and compare the top five firms to those that have made the top five over the last few years. Are there any repeats? If so, who? Read through the website to determine how a company is nominated for such a list. If the company you worked for appeared on this list, would you find it motivating enough to perform at a higher level overall? Explain.

4. **Google Search:** "Canadian Employment Law Articles–2011 Resources" Review the list of cases. Find those that deal with employees who were fired for lack of performance while claiming to be injured, ill, harassed, suffering in some way, etc. As a class exercise, have several teams read their particular case and summarize for the class. Be prepared to identify both the employer's and employee's perspectives. Conclude with the final court decision. After listening to several cases, identify a pattern of how Canadian courts feel about termination of employees who employers claim are lazy or lacking in performance. Discuss.

Experiential Exercise

Intrinsic Motivation and Extrinsic Rewards Exercise

PURPOSE This exercise is meant to help you understand the differences between intrinsic motivation and extrinsic rewards. Approx. Timing: 12 minutes.

ACTIVITY:

■ Individually complete the chart below.

■ After a few minutes, form a small group for discussion purposes.

■ Share your responses with the other group members. Try and come to a consensus.

■ Share your group's responses with the rest of the class.

	INTRINSIC MOTIVATING FACTOR or EXTRINSIC REWARD?
Compensation	
Fear of losing job from downsizing	
Freedom to express oneself	
Fun and enjoyment on the job	
Peer recognition	
Public recognition from boss	
Training and development opportunities	
New iphone with data plan	
Job promotion with more responsibility, authority, and prestige	
International travel opportunities	
Confidence in work completed means a lack of anxiety	

OB In Action Case Study

Design a Motivating Job Using The JCM

Scenario:

Ahmed Haagsma is 19 years old and a full-time student working part-time at the Target store in the Nanaimo North Town Centre in suburban Nanaimo, British Columbia. It's been two months since Ahmed began working for the new retailer and he enjoys the experience of helping customers. Yet, not everyone he works with is as pleased with the new employer and working conditions. Already Ahmed is hearing complaints in the employee lunchroom from fellow workers: *"Things were better under Zellers! At least there was a collective agreement to take our concerns to. Where do we go now if we have concerns about our job?"* and another, *"This is exactly what happened to Woolco employees back in the 1980s when Walmart came to Canada; all the union-ized Woolco employees were let go and had to reapply for their old jobs at the new Walmart store, only to get their old jobs back but with more responsibility and less pay. How is this progress?,"* and one last comment, *"I guess we should just be thankful we have a job, it's better than nothing, eh? How's that for being motivated!?!"*

Ahmed has never worked in retail before and is looking forward to earning some much-needed cash, although earning the standard minimum wage. He hopes to hang in there long enough to gain valuable experience and earn a promotion with higher pay next year.

The first few months working the sales floor prove to be a steep learning curve for Ahmed. His role involves helping people, providing guest assistance, and presenting merchandise in an appealing attractive manner. The household merchandise area is his primary responsibility when working, and he has only been pulled over a few times to work in men's wear because of staff shortages. For the most part, when he reports to work, he knows where he is working and what he will be doing. He welcomes this type of routine at first because it gives him added confidence knowing the job so well, but after a few months Ahmed finds himself getting bored. The interest he once held for the job is decreasing, so he decides to apply for a logistics position, basically a stock person filling shelves. He works in that position for four weeks and then becomes bored with it. When a position within guest services area opens he thinks he will apply and, to his delight, he gets the job.

Ahmed likes his new role at the beginning because it gets him out from the back of the store and talking to customers up front. But after two weeks of being a customer service person, he begins to get frustrated working with the public who are not always the most polite and some days are downright nasty. He isn't bored with the job, but wishes he could get out from behind the counter once in a while. Ahmed notices many of the full-time and part-time workers are quitting their jobs and looking at other stores in the mall for employment. He talks to his store colleagues in the lunchroom all the time; some are satisfied with their jobs, but others are bored or frustrated too. All they do is complain to each other every time they work. Ahmed decides to take his concerns to management.

The next day, Ahmed makes an appointment to speak to the store manager about what he believes to be the primary reason so many employees are unsatisfied with their jobs. "It has to do with the lack of motivation on the job," says Ahmed. "Is that so?" states the store manager, "And what do you suggest we do to correct the problem?" The store manager welcomes Ahmed's comments and asks him for input about how the jobs can be made more interesting and in the long-run decrease the employee turnover rate at the store.

Discussion Questions

1. Which content theory of motivation seems to apply to Ahmed's situation at Target?
2. Identify at least three factors for Ahmed to consider when making a recommendation to the store manager about designing a motivating job.
3. Imagine that you are Ahmed. Use the Job Characteristics Model—JCM (see Figure 5.5) to create at least five new approaches to solving the problem that he and the other employees are having with their job.

The CONNECTion Zone Mc Graw Hill connect™

- The Presentation Assistant
- Ethical OB Dilemma
- Video Case

McGraw Hill connect™
Practise and learn online with Connect.

"Coming together is a beginning. Keeping together is progress. Working together is success."

Henry Ford (Inventor and 20th century industrialist)

CHAPTER
6

Fundamental Concepts of Group Behaviour

FACING AN OB CHALLENGE

I have been told that working with others is a skill that must be learned and appreciated by employees; but I don't like working with others. Don't get me wrong, it's not that I can't do it, it's just that I don't enjoy it and would prefer not to because no one has the same expectations as me. Whenever I have worked with others in the past, they always burned me and I actually do worse than if I just worked on my own. I've talked to my friends about this—one is in accounting and the other is an IT specialist— and they agree with me totally. In some fields there is just no need for teams because working alone is actually just as productive. Am I right?

— *NOT A TEAM PLAYER*

LO 1 List and define the five
stages of Tuckman's
theory of group
development.

LO 2 Contrast roles and
norms, emphasizing
reasons why norms
are enforced in
organizations.

LO 3 Examine the process
of how a work
group becomes a
team, emphasizing
various teamwork
competencies.

LO 4 Explain why trust is
a key ingredient to
building an effective
team, referring to both
self-managed and
virtual teams.

LO 5 Summarize at least two
threats to group and team
effectiveness.

Working with Others

This chapter begins Unit 3, which shifts the focus away from individual behaviour toward group behaviour. It's important to recognize that we don't study OB in a vacuum; it is the study of the organization and its members in a social environment. Any student who has worked with others on a school project will know the challenges that working with others can bring. Not everyone appreciates the value of teamwork or understands how it can improve the final product.

This chapter will help you see the value of teamwork, how it's being applied throughout the work world, and how it can assist the organization overall. Our discussions will first look at the fundamental building blocks behind formal and informal groups, and then we'll move on to how groups develop, followed by the various roles and norms that exist within groups. Since some people believe that groups and teams are the same, we'll spend time explaining the differences, specifically discussing self-managed teams and the more contemporary virtual teams. To wrap things up, we'll explain what factors nurture teamwork, as well as those that can threaten team effectiveness.

Fundamentals of Group Behaviour

Drawing from the field of sociology,[1] we define a *group* as two or more freely interacting individuals who share collective norms and goals and have a common identity.[2] Organizational psychologist Edgar Schein shed light on this concept by drawing helpful distinctions between a group, a crowd, and an organization:

> *The size of a group is thus limited by the possibilities of mutual interaction and mutual awareness. Mere aggregates of people do not fit this definition because they do not interact and do not perceive themselves to be a group even if they are aware of each other as, for instance, a crowd on a street corner watching some event. A total department, a union, or a whole organization would not be a group in spite of thinking of themselves as "we," because they generally do not all interact and are not all aware of each other. However, work teams, committees, subparts of departments, cliques, and various other informal associations among organizational members would fit this definition of a group.[3]*

Take a moment now to think of various groups of which you are a member. Does each "group" satisfy the four criteria in Figure 6.1? You may want to complete the Self-Assessment Exercise "How Autonomous Is Your Work Group?" to characterize your group experience.

FORMAL AND INFORMAL GROUPS

Individuals join groups, or are assigned to groups, to accomplish various purposes. If the group is formed by a manager to help the organization accomplish its goals, then it qualifies as a *formal group*. Within an organization, formal groups typically wear such labels as work group, committee, or task force. An example of a formal group would be a corporate board responsible for governing an organization; it has legitimate authority and assigned responsibilities, and the decisions it makes affect the organization directly

> *Group*
>
> Two or more freely interacting people with shared norms and goals and a common identity.

> *Formal group*
>
> Formed by the organization.

How Autonomous Is Your Work Group?

INSTRUCTIONS: Think of your current (or past) job and work group. Characterize the group's situation by selecting one number on the following scale for each statement. Add your responses for a total score.

STRONGLY DISAGREE					STRONGLY AGREE	
1	2	3	4	5	6	7

Work Method Autonomy

1 My work group decides how to get the job done. _____

2 My work group determines what procedures to use. _____

3 My work group is free to choose its own methods when carrying out its work. _____

Work Scheduling Autonomy

4 My work group controls the scheduling of its work. _____

5 My work group determines how its work is sequenced. _____

6 My work group decides when to do certain activities. _____

Work Criteria Autonomy

7 My work group is allowed to modify the normal way it is evaluated so some
of our activities are emphasized and some de-emphasized. _____

8 My work group is able to modify its objectives (what it is supposed to accomplish). _____

9 My work group has some control over what it is supposed to accomplish. _____

Total score = _____

Norms

9–26 = Low autonomy

27–45 = Moderate autonomy

46–63 = High autonomy

SOURCE: Adapted from an individual autonomy scale in J.A. Breaugh, "The Work Autonomy Scales: Additional Validity Evidence," *Human Relations*, November 1989, pp 1033–56.

FIGURE 6.1 Four Sociological Criteria of a Group

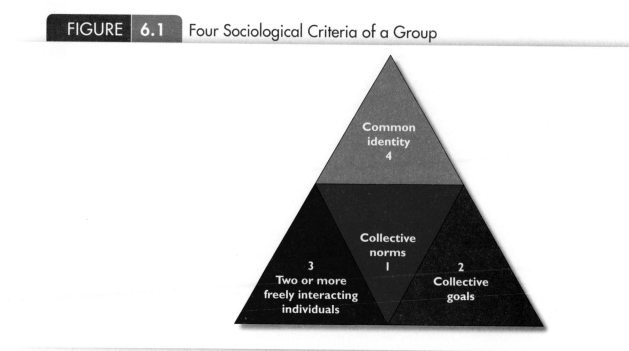

(see the International OB feature box). An *informal group* exists when the members' overriding purpose of getting together is friendship or common interests.[4] Formal and informal groups often overlap, such as when a group of corporate auditors heads for the tennis courts after work.

Informal group

Formed by friends or those with common interests.

SOCIAL NETWORKING IS BLURRING THE FORMAL/INFORMAL BOUNDARIES

Social relationships are complex, alive, and dynamic; they have little regard for arbitrary boundaries. The desirability of overlapping formal and informal groups has its problems. Some managers firmly believe personal friendship can foster group activity on the job, while others view workplace "bull sessions" as a serious threat to productivity. Both situations are common, and it is the manager's job to strike a workable balance, based on the maturity and goals of the people involved. Additionally, there is the ethics-laden issue of managers being friends with the people they oversee.

As social networking sites such as Facebook, Twitter, and LinkedIn continue to mushroom, organizational leaders are generally left scratching their heads. Their unanswered questions typically include: How can we profit from this? How can we embrace and/or control it? Is it a good or bad thing? What are the implications of this massive connectivity for productivity, privacy,

harassment, confidentiality, protection of intellectual property, and information systems security? The lines between formal and informal groups have been blurred almost beyond recognition. Still, managers need to establish some boundaries. We will say more about this topic in Chapter 7 when we discuss organizational communication, including the answer to the question: Should managers be friends on social network sites like Facebook with those who report to them? You may also want to read the Ethical OB Dilemma case on Connect—it talks about this very issue.

TUCKMAN'S FIVE-STAGE GROUP DEVELOPMENT PROCESS

LO1

All groups go through a maturation process, such as what you would find in any life-cycle situation (e.g., humans, organizations, products). While there is general agreement among theorists that the group development process occurs in identifiable stages, they disagree about the exact number, sequence, length, and nature of those stages.[5]

A model often referred to is the one proposed in 1965 by educational psychologist Bruce W. Tuckman. His original model involved only four stages (forming, storming, norming, and performing). The five-stage model evolved when Tuckman and a doctoral student

GLOBAL BOARDS ARE FORMAL GROUPS

The board of directors for any global organization can be considered as a formal group that oversees governing responsibilities covering broad organizational issues that cut across cultural divides. Gone are the days when a group of like-minded, grey-haired men from similar backgrounds could provide adequate guidance and oversight for an organization. The board is a formal group whose legitimate authority requires it to be taken seriously as its decisions impact many. See the Diversity feature box in this chapter for more on global boards.

SOURCES: Y. Arguden, "Global Boards Help Make Companies Global," *Harvard Business Review,* Nov. 9, 2011; online blog: http://blogs.hbr.org/cs/2011/board_diversity_and_global_age.html; T. Palmer and I. Vamer, "A Comparison of the International Diversity on Top Management Teams of Multi-national firms based....," *Singapore Management Review,* January 1, 2007 and *All Business online,* a Dun & Bradstreet Company, http://www.allbusiness.com/public-administration/national-security-international/4019164-1.html.

added "adjourning" in 1977.[6] A word of caution is in order. Somewhat akin to Maslow's need hierarchy theory, Tuckman's theory has been repeated and taught so often and for so long that many have come to view it as documented fact, rather than merely a theory. Even today, it is good to remember Tuckman's own caution that his group development model was derived more from group therapy sessions than from natural-life groups. Still, many in the OB field like Tuckman's five-stage model of group development because of its easy-to-remember labels and common sense appeal.

Let's briefly examine each of the five stages in Tuckman's model. Notice in Figure 6.2 how individuals give up a measure of their independence when they join and participate in a group.[7] Also, the various stages are not necessarily of the same duration or intensity. For instance, the storming stage may be practically non-existent or painfully long, depending on the clarity of the goal and the commitment and maturity of the members. Since the model is not static, it's theoretically possible to go backwards, especially for those groups that make it to the performing stage but experience a significant change. Consider a group that adds a new member or perhaps loses a member; in this case, the group is theoretically forced back into the forming stage all over again, and yet is still expected to perform as if nothing has changed. This situation becomes a complicated challenge for members of the group as adjustments have to be made, but it is also a time of patience for management that has to understand the dynamics the group is experiencing at a possibly demanding time.

You can make this five-step process come to life by relating the various stages to your own experiences with work groups, committees, athletic groups, social or religious groups, or class project groups. You may even wish to practise Tuckman's theory in a practical way by completing the Experiential Exercise at the end of this chapter; applying it to a group contract situation may help make sense of the theory, too.

Stage 1: Forming During this "ice-breaking" stage, group members tend to be uncertain and anxious about such things as their roles, who is in charge, and the group's goals. Mutual trust is low, and there is a good deal of holding back to see who takes charge and how. In life-and-death situations, such as those sometimes faced by a surgical group or airline cockpit crews, the period of uncertainty can be dangerous. If the formal leader (e.g., a supervisor) does not assert (declare) authority, an emergent (evolving) leader will eventually step in to fulfill the group's need for leadership and direction. Leaders typically mistake this honeymoon period as a mandate for permanent control. But later problems may force a leadership change.

Stage 2: Storming This is a time of testing. Individuals test the leader's policies and assumptions as they try to determine how they fit into the power structure.[8] Subgroups take shape and subtle forms of rebellion, such as procrastination, occur. Many groups stall in stage 2 because power politics erupts into open rebellion.

Stage 3: Norming Groups that make it through stage 2 generally do so because a respected member, other than the leader, challenges the group to resolve its power struggles so something can be accomplished. Questions about authority and power are resolved through unemotional, matter-of-fact group discussion. The group moves on

FIGURE | 6.2 | Tuckman's Five-Stage Theory of Group Development

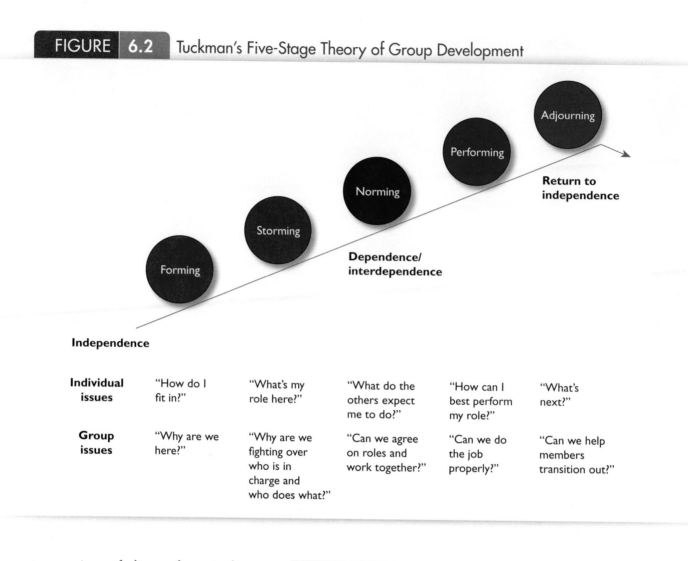

	Forming	Storming	Norming	Performing	Adjourning
Individual issues	"How do I fit in?"	"What's my role here?"	"What do the others expect me to do?"	"How can I best perform my role?"	"What's next?"
Group issues	"Why are we here?"	"Why are we fighting over who is in charge and who does what?"	"Can we agree on roles and work together?"	"Can we do the job properly?"	"Can we help members transition out?"

to experience feelings of esprit de corps because members believe they have found their proper roles. *Group cohesiveness,* defined as the "we feeling" that binds members of a group together, is the principal by-product of stage 3.[9]

Stage 4: Performing   Activity during this vital stage is focused on solving task problems. As members of a mature group, contributors get their work done without hampering others. There is a climate of open communication, strong cooperation, and lots of helping behaviour. Conflicts and job boundary disputes are handled constructively and efficiently.[10] Cohesiveness and personal commitment to group goals help the group achieve more than any one individual acting alone could.

Stage 5: Adjourning   The work is done; it's time to move on to other things. Having worked so hard to get along and get something done, many members feel a compelling sense of loss. The return to independence can be eased by rituals celebrating "the end" and

> *Group cohesiveness*
>
> A "we feeling" binding group members together.

"new beginnings." Parties, award ceremonies, graduations, or mock funerals can provide the needed punctuation at the end of a significant group project. Leaders need to emphasize valuable lessons learned in group dynamics to prepare everyone for future group efforts.

PATTERNS ESTABLISHED EARLY

The initial time spent on upfront planning and organizing the opening stages of group development are well worth the effort, since it is here where core patterns and agreements are determined. At least theoretically, the group will try and abide by such terms until a crisis midpoint occurs and the group members realize they have to start working harder if a deadline is to be met. This point is well illustrated in the 1988 research conducted by professor and OB expert Connie Gersick, who identified a sequence of behaviour a bit different from Tuckman's, and perhaps more appropriate for projects and student group assignments where meeting a deadline is very important.[11] She called it the *punctuated equilibrium model* of group development because of the time spent by the group experiencing stable equilibrium with a punctuated (interruption) period that causes a disturbance to the group. Once resolved, the group progresses on to the deadline. Gersick's research found that from the opening moments of a group's existence, its members try to do two things: (1) develop strategies to complete a task, and (2) develop the structure and processes for interpersonal relationships. Gersick reported:

> ... lasting patterns can appear as early as the first few seconds of a group's life ... The sheer speed with which recurring patterns appear suggests that they're influenced by material established before the group convenes. Such material includes members' expectations about the task, each other and the context and their repertoire of behaviour routines and performance strategies.

Management Implications   No one wants to be part of a group that is set up for failure before it even starts. That is why managers need to create the right sort of conditions for group members from the outset so they can generate team identity and loyalty, such as establishing open communication, building camaraderie, and developing trust. This can be accomplished if management philosophically supports the group process by giving them the opportunity to self-manage, puts into place the necessary resources that create a healthy working climate, and provides time for the group to develop cohesiveness. By planning early on, managers prepare the necessary conditions for positive interpersonal interaction that will also facilitate future decision making.

LO 2   GROUP MEMBER ROLES

Four centuries have passed since William Shakespeare had his character Jacques speak the following memorable lines in Act II of *As You Like It*: "All the world's a stage, And all the men and women merely players; They have their exits and their entrances; And one man in his time plays many parts ....." This intriguing notion of all people as actors in a universal play has not been lost by sociologists, who have developed a complex theory of human interaction based on *roles*. According to an OB scholar, "roles are sets of behaviours that persons expect of occupants of a position."[12] As described in Table 6.1 both task and maintenance roles need to be performed if a work group is to accomplish anything.[13]

Punctuated equilibrium model
Group development process consisting of stable periods interrupted by punctuated situations.

Roles
Expected behaviours for a given position.

Task versus Maintenance Roles   *Task roles* enable the work group to define, clarify, and pursue a common purpose. Meanwhile, *maintenance roles* foster supportive and constructive interpersonal relationships. In short, task roles keep the group on track, while maintenance roles keep the group together.

A project group member is performing a task function when the member says at an update meeting, "What is the real issue here? We don't seem to be getting anywhere." Another individual who says, "Let's hear from those who oppose this plan," is performing a maintenance function. Importantly, each of the various task and maintenance roles may be played in varying combinations and sequences by either the group's leader or any of its members.

Task roles
Task-oriented group behaviour.

Maintenance roles
Relationship-building group behaviour.

Checklist for Managers   The task and maintenance roles listed in Table 6.1 can serve as a handy checklist for managers and group leaders who wish to ensure proper group development. Roles that are not always performed when needed, such as those of coordinator, evaluator, and gatekeeper, can be performed in a timely manner by the formal leader or assigned to other members. The task roles of initiator, orienter, and energizer are especially important because they are goal-directed roles. Research studies on group goal setting confirm the motivational power of challenging goals. As with individual goal setting, difficult but achievable goals are associated with better group results.[14] Also in line with individual goal-setting theory and research, group goals are more effective if group members clearly understand them and are both individually and collectively committed to achieving them. Initiators, orienters, and energizers can be very helpful in this regard.

International managers need to be sensitive to cultural differences regarding the relative importance of task and maintenance roles. In Japan, for example, cultural tradition calls for more emphasis on maintenance roles, especially the roles of harmonizer and compromiser:

> Courtesy requires that members not be noticeable or disruptive in a meeting or classroom. If two or more members discover that their views differ—a fact that is tactfully taken to be unfortunate—they adjourn to find more information and to work toward a stance that all can accept. They do not press their personal opinions through strong arguments, neat logic, or rewards and threats. And they do not hesitate to shift their beliefs if doing so will preserve smooth interpersonal relations. (To lose is to win.)[15]

TABLE 6.1

Functional Roles Performed by Group Members—A Checklist

TASK-ROLES ASSIGNED	DESCRIPTION	NAME OF INDIVIDUAL	✔
Initiator	Suggests new goals or ideas.		
Information seeker/giver	Clarifies key issues.		
Opinion seeker/giver	Clarifies pertinent values.		
Elaborator	Promotes greater understanding through examples or exploration of implications.		
Coordinator	Pulls together ideas and suggestions.		
Orienter	Keeps group headed toward its stated goal(s).		
Evaluator	Tests group's accomplishments with various criteria such as logic and practicality.		
Energizer	Prods group to move along or to accomplish more.		
Procedural technician	Performs routine duties (e.g., handing out materials or rearranging seats).		
Recorder	Performs a "group memory" function by documenting discussion and outcomes.		
MAINTENANCE-ROLES ASSIGNED	DESCRIPTION	NAME OF INDIVIDUAL	✔
Encourager	Fosters group solidarity by accepting and praising various points of view.		
Harmonizer	Mediates conflict through reconciliation or humour.		
Compromiser	Helps resolve conflict by meeting others half way.		
Gatekeeper	Encourages all group members to participate.		
Standard setter	Evaluates the quality of group processes.		
Commentator	Records and comments on group processes/dynamics.		
Follower	Serves as a passive audience.		

SOURCE: Adapted in part from discussion in K.D. Benne and P. Sheats, "Functional Roles of Group Members," *Journal of Social Issues,* Spring 1948, pp 41–49.

GROUP NORMS

Norms are more encompassing than roles. While roles involve behavioural expectations for specific positions, norms help organizational members determine right from wrong and good from bad. According to one respected group of management consultants: "A *norm* is an attitude, opinion, feeling, or action—shared by two or more people—that guides their behaviour."[16] Although norms are typically unwritten and seldom discussed openly, they have a powerful influence on group and organizational behaviour.[17] For instance, consider Alberta-Pacific (Al-Pac) Forest Industries Inc. in Boyle, Alberta. A norm at their pulp facility equates group productivity with physical activity. Voted one of Canada's Top 100 Employers several years in a row as well as one of Alberta's Top Employers, Al-Pac encourages its employees to enjoy the outdoors whenever possible. On any given day, if the weather permits, employees can be observed fishing on their lunch hour in the trout pond located right on the 16-hectare property site, or organizing an informal baseball game on the company ball field, or participating with others in a daily health-walk around the many groomed trails.[18]

At Al-Pac and elsewhere, group members positively reinforce those who adhere to current norms with friendship and acceptance. On the other hand, non-conformists often experience criticism and even rejection by group members. Anyone who has experienced the "silent

> **Norm**
>
> Shared attitudes, opinions, feelings, or actions that guide social behaviour.

When individuals violate group norms, they may find themselves left out of important meetings, isolated from decision making, or given the silent treatment by members—a sort of punishment from the group for non-conforming.

1. **Explicit statements by supervisors or co-workers** For instance, a group leader might explicitly set norms about not drinking alcohol at lunch.

2. **Critical events in the group's history** At times there is a critical event in the group's history that establishes an important precedent. For example, a key recruit may decide to work elsewhere because a group member has said too many negative things about the organization. Hence, a norm against such "sour grapes" behaviour might evolve.

3. **Primacy** The first behaviour pattern that emerges in a group often sets group expectations. For example, if the first group meeting is marked by very formal interaction between supervisors and employees, then the group often expects future meetings to be conducted in the same way.

4. **Carryover behaviours from past situations** Carryover of individual behaviours from past situations can increase the predictability of group members' behaviours in new settings and facilitate task accomplishment. For instance, students and professors carry fairly constant sets of expectations from class to class.[20]

treatment" from a group of friends knows what a potent social weapon ostracism (isolation) can be.[19] Norms can be put into proper perspective by understanding how they develop and why they are enforced.

How Norms Are Developed Experts say norms evolve in an informal manner as the group or organization determines what it takes to be effective. Norms can affect performance either positively or negatively. Generally speaking, norms develop in various combinations of the following four ways:

Enforcing Norms Norms tend to be enforced by group members when they:

- Help the group or organization survive
- Clarify or simplify behavioural expectations
- Help individuals avoid embarrassing situations
- Clarify the group's or organization's central values and/or unique identity[21]

Table 6.2 provides examples of how to enforce norms.

TABLE 6.2

Four Reasons Norms Are Enforced

NORM	REASON FOR ENFORCEMENT	EXAMPLE
"Make our department look good in top management's eyes."	Group/organization survival	After vigorously defending the vital role played by the Human Resources Management Department at a divisional meeting, a staff specialist is complimented by her supervisor.
"Success comes to those who work hard and don't make waves."	Clarification of behavioural expectations	A senior manager takes a young associate aside and cautions him to be a bit more patient with co-workers who see things differently.
"Work well with others, not a lone star."	Avoidance of embarrassment	A project group member is ridiculed by her peers for dominating the discussion during a progress report to top management.
"Customer service is our top priority."	Clarification of central values/ unique identity	Two sales representatives are given a surprise Friday afternoon party for having received prestigious best-in-the-industry customer service awards from an industry association.

Transition from Work Group to Team

Jon R. Katzenbach and Douglas K. Smith, management consultants at McKinsey & Company, say it is a mistake to use the terms 'group' and 'team' interchangeably. After studying many different kinds of teams—from athletic to corporate to military—they concluded that successful teams tend to take on a life of their own. Katzenbach and Smith define a *team* as "a small number of people with complementary skills who are committed to a common purpose, performance goals, and approach for which they hold themselves mutually accountable."[22] As psychology researcher J. Richard Hackman puts it, "To reap the benefits of teamwork, one must actually build a team. Calling a set of people a team or (pressuring) them to work together is insufficient . . . action must be taken to establish a team's boundaries, to define the task as one for which members are collectively responsible and accountable, and to give members the authority to manage."[23]

We can see evidence of this when speaking about professional sports teams. Take the Toronto Maple Leafs, for example. This NHL team has not won the Stanley Cup since the 1966–67 season. It takes more than wearing the same uniform to become a team, and one athlete cannot carry the entire team; members

> **Team**
>
> Small number of people with complementary skills who hold themselves mutually accountable for common purpose, goals, and approach.

have to develop a collective team mindset. Thus, a group becomes a team when the following criteria are met:

1. *Leadership* becomes a shared activity.
2. *Accountability* shifts from strictly individual to both individual and collective.
3. The group develops its own *purpose* or mission.
4. *Problem solving* becomes a way of life, not a part-time activity.
5. *Effectiveness* is measured by the group's collective outcomes and products.[24]

Relative to Tuckman's theory of group development covered earlier—forming, storming, norming, performing, and adjourning—teams are task groups that have matured to the *performing* stage. Because of conflicts over power and authority and unstable interpersonal relations, many work groups never become an effective team.[25] Katzenbach and Smith clarify the distinction this way: "The essence of a team is common commitment. Without it, groups perform as individuals; with it, they become a powerful unit of collective performance."[26]

When Katzenbach and Smith refer to "a small number of people" in their definition, they mean between two and 25 team members. They found that effective teams typically have fewer than 10 members. This conclusion was echoed in a survey of 400 workplace team members in Canada and the United States: "The average North American team consists of 10 members. Eight is the most common size."[27]

TEAM COMPETENCIES, TYPES OF TEAMS, TEAMWORK, AND TRUST

Teams are required on a day-to-day basis to get the job done in organizations of all sizes and types. Take, for example, Whole Foods Market, that uses teams in all seven of their Canadian stores. *BusinessWeek* columnists Jack and Suzy Welch offer this perspective:

> *It is the excitement of being part of something bigger than yourself and the thrill of building something—a product, a service, or a team. It is the fun of laughing, debating, sweating it out with fellow travelers—friends and allies in the never-ending competition for customers and profits . . . it just doesn't get any better.*[28]

Cooperation, trust, and camaraderie energize organizations. Judging from a recent survey that asked corporate leaders to look ahead five years, we all need to polish our ability to work in teams. The survey results indicated that "teamwork/collaboration" (74 percent) was among the top three most important knowledge/skill areas, just behind "critical thinking/problem solving (78 percent)

A goal from one player doesn't make a successful team. What criteria must the Toronto Maple Leafs develop to become a more effective team?

and "information technology application" (77 percent).[29] Jeff Vijungco, director of recruiting at Adobe Systems, tells how he finds team players: "I actually count the number of times a candidate says 'I' in an interview. We'd much rather hear 'we'."[30] Forming workplace teams and urging employees to be team players are good starting points on the road to building effective teams. But by themselves, they are not enough; teams need to develop certain abilities, called *competencies,* that will help them to perform at higher levels. Let's turn our attention to learning more about team competencies.

Teams serve many purposes. At Whole Foods Market, all employees belong to teams. In each of their seven Canadian stores, team members meet regularly to discuss issues, solve problems, and appreciate each other's contributions.

DEVELOPING TEAMWORK COMPETENCIES

The five critical team competencies that must be developed for higher performance include:[31]

1. **Orients team to problem-solving situation** Can the team arrive at a common understanding of the situation or problem?
2. **Organizes and manages team performance** Can the team establish specific, challenging, and accepted team goals?
3. **Promotes a positive team environment** Can the team create and reinforce norms of tolerance, respect, and excellence?
4. **Facilitates and manages task conflict** Can the team encourage desirable conflict and discourage undesirable team conflict?
5. **Appropriately promotes perspective** Can the team defend stated preferences, withstanding pressure to change position for another that is not supported by knowledge-based arguments?

The ability to work with others in a team environment and the competencies we just mentioned need to be modelled and taught. Referring back to the Toronto Maple Leafs example, what competencies must the team develop to perform at a higher level?

TYPES OF TEAMS — 1. SELF-MANAGED TEAMS

Have you ever thought you could do a better job than your boss? Well, if the trend toward self-managed work teams continues to grow in Canada as it has grown in the US, then it's very possible that you may get your chance. Entrepreneurs and artisans often boast of not having a supervisor. In general, the same cannot be said for employees working in offices and factories. But things are changing in North America. It's common business knowledge that self-managed work teams exist in US-owned firms located in offices across Canada—such as Kraft Foods Inc., 3M, and Quaker Canada—but current statistics on the depth and scope of use across this country is very limited. However, according to US facts, an estimated half of the employees at Fortune 500 companies are working on teams,[32] and a growing share of those teams are self-managing. For example, at a General Mills cereal plant, "teams ... schedule, operate, and maintain machinery so effectively that the factory runs with no managers present during the night shift."[33] More typically, managers are present to serve as trainers and facilitators.

Self-managed teams are defined as groups of workers who are given administrative oversight for their task domains. Administrative oversight involves delegated activities such as planning, scheduling, monitoring, and staffing. These chores are normally performed by managers. In short, employees in these unique work groups act as their own supervisor. Accountability is maintained indirectly by outside managers and leaders. According to a recent study of a company with 300 self-managed teams, 66 "team advisors" relied on these four indirect influence tactics:

> **Self-managed teams**
>
> Groups of employees granted administrative oversight for their work.

- **Relating** Understanding the organization's power structure, building trust, showing concern for individual team members
- **Scouting** Seeking outside information, diagnosing teamwork problems, facilitating group problem solving
- **Persuading** Gathering outside support and resources, influencing team to be more effective and to pursue organizational goals
- **Empowering** Delegating decision-making authority, facilitating a team decision-making process, coaching[34]

Self-managed teams are sometimes referred to as semi-autonomous work groups, independent work groups, and super-teams.

Managerial Resistance   Something much more complex is involved than what this apparently simple label suggests. The term *self-managed* does not mean simply turning workers loose to do their own thing. Indeed, an organization embracing self-managed teams should be prepared to undergo revolutionary changes in management philosophy, structure, staffing and training practices, and reward systems. Moreover, the traditional notions of managerial authority and control are turned on their heads. Not surprisingly, many managers strongly resist giving up the reins of power to people they view as subordinate (not equivalent). They see self-managed teams as a threat to their own job security.

Manager Role With Teams   We spoke earlier of the kinds of roles that can be found in groups. Are there roles in teams? In short, yes. Team members have to assume the same kinds of roles to accomplish a task. Within this model is a change in roles for management, as well. The new roles for management assume a number of different behaviours, including being in a more supportive position for the team, finding the resources the team needs to accomplish its tasks, being a corporate liaison for the team when it comes to interacting with other departments, helping to mediate interpersonal conflicts within the team to get them back on task, and ensuring deadlines are met. But such behaviours can be difficult for some managers, especially if they're new. Business professor Linda A. Hill framed the challenge for new managers this way:

> … (T)he new manager must figure out how to harness the power of a team. Simply focusing on one-to-one relationships with members of the team can undermine that process.

> … (M)any new managers fail to recognize, much less address, their team-building responsibilities. Instead, they conceive of their people-management role as building the most effective relationships they can with each individual subordinate, erroneously equating the management of the team with managing the individuals on the team.

> … They attend primarily to individual performance and pay little or no attention to team culture and performance. They hardly ever rely on group forums for identifying and solving problems. Some spend too much time with a small number of trusted subordinates, often those who seem most

supportive. New managers tend to handle issues, even those with team-wide implications, one-on-one. This leads them to make decisions based on unnecessarily limited information.[35]

Cross-Functionalism   A common feature of self-managed teams, particularly among those above the shop floor or clerical level, is **cross-functionalism**.[36] In other words, specialists from different areas are put on the same team. Mark Stefik, a manager for a large research centre, explains the wisdom of cross-functionalism:

> Something magical happens when you bring together a group of people from different disciplines with a common purpose. It's a middle zone, the break-through zone. The idea is to start a team on a problem—a hard problem, to keep people motivated. When there's an obstacle, instead of dodging it, bring in another point of view: an electrical engineer, a user interface expert, a sociologist, whatever spin on the market is needed. Give people new eyeglasses to cross-pollinate ideas.[37]

> *Cross-functionalism*
> Team made up of technical specialists from different areas.

Cross-functionalism is seeping down into college and university programs as well, to help students see the big picture and polish their team skills.[38] The world does not operate in a vacuum, and neither should the learning process. So, by encouraging students from programs that serve different functional areas of an organization to work together on projects or assignments, they are being better prepared for the real-world work environment.

Here again, we see strength in diversity; teams comprised of individuals with differences actually strengthen the perspective as gaps are filled in along the way. For more on cross-functional teams, you may want to read the OB in Action case study about LavaLife located at the end of this chapter.

Earlier, we reviewed in the International OB feature box how global boards are the formal governing bodies of an organization. Clearly even they should be comprised of diverse people with different backgrounds, expertise, and perspective. But are they? See the Focus on Diversity feature box for more on this discussion.

Are Self-Managed Teams Effective?   Research evidence among companies with self-managed teams suggests the most commonly delegated tasks are work scheduling and dealing directly with outside customers. The least common team chores are hiring and firing.[39] Most of today's self-managed teams remain bunched at the shop-floor level in factory settings. Experts predict growth of the practice in the managerial ranks and in service operations.[40] Much of what we know about

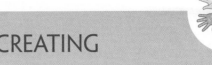

STILL FINDING RESISTANCE WHEN CREATING TEAMS OF DIFFERENCES

When a diverse group of individuals is sitting around a boardroom table, rather than looking at their differences as barriers to overcome, step back and reframe their differences as being an opportunity to bring a different perspective that helps narrow the potential gaps in viewpoints. Just like a cross-functional team, companies need to have a broad perspective from a variety of areas sitting on their boards if they wish to grow globally. And yet, there is still resistance to do so in many large first-world organizations.

For example, Japanese companies usually have only Japanese directors. Toyota, for instance, has an all-Japanese board. Although most European and American companies have people from both sides of the Atlantic on their boards, few directors are from emerging markets. TOTAL, a large energy firm, has 12 French directors and only one each from Sweden, Canada, and Britain; wind energy giant GDF Suez has 18 French directors and one each from Canada, Belgium, and Britain; the multi-national conglomerate General Electric has 13 Americans, two Canadians, and one British person on its board.

By contrast, one study involving organizations in emerging markets showed that firms with global ambitions tend to appoint a greater proportion of their directors from abroad to gain a bigger international footprint. Why do you think there is such a resistance to include diverse people within formal groups?

SOURCE: Y. Arguden, "Global Boards Help Make Companies Global," *Harvard Business Review,* Nov. 9, 2011. See online blog: http://blogs. hbr.org/cs/2011/board_diversity_and_global_age.html.

self-managed teams comes from testimonials and case studies. Fortunately, a body of higher-quality field research is slowly developing across North America. A review of three meta-analyses covering 70 individual studies concluded that self-managed teams have:

- A positive effect on productivity
- A positive effect on specific attitudes relating to self-management (e.g., responsibility and control)
- No significant effect on general attitudes (e.g., job satisfaction and organizational commitment)
- No significant effect on absenteeism or turnover[41]

Although encouraging, these results do not qualify as a sweeping endorsement of self-managed teams. Nonetheless, experts say the trend toward self-managed work teams will continue in North America because of a strong cultural bias in favour of direct participation. Managers need to be prepared for the resulting shift in organizational administration.

TYPES OF TEAMS – 2. VIRTUAL TEAMS

Virtual teams are a product of modern times. They take their name from ***virtual reality*** computer simulations, where "it's almost like the real thing." Thanks to evolving information technologies such as the Internet, teleconferencing, Skype and shareware, you can be a member of a team without really being there.[42] Traditional team meetings are location specific—team members are either physically present or absent. Virtual teams, in contrast, convene electronically with members reporting in from different locations, different organizations, and even different time zones.

Because virtual teams are so new, there is no agreed-upon definition. Our working definition of a ***virtual team*** is a physically dispersed task group that conducts its business through modern information technology.[43] Advocates say virtual teams are very flexible and efficient because they are driven by information and skills, not by time and location.[44] People with needed information and/or skills can be team members, regardless of where or when they actually do their work. On the negative side, lack of face-to-face interaction not only diminishes need for human interaction, but it can weaken trust, communication, and accountability. See the Law and Ethics feature box for a discussion on the social deviance that can occur in virtual teams.

> **Virtual team**
>
> Information technology allows group members in different locations to conduct business.

Research Insights As one might expect with a new and ill-defined area, research evidence to date is a bit spotty.

SOCIAL DEVIANCE IN VIRTUAL TEAMWORK

LAW AND ETHICS AT WORK

If a member of a self-managed work team decides to work from home, how do the other members of the team back in the office know in fact that the member is actually working? In the age of the moveable workplace, where employees do much from home or "on the road," the issue of trustworthiness among team members raises an interesting ethical dilemma.

A body of research suggests that the communication tools routinely used between virtual team members can actually promote untrustworthy social behaviour (e.g., email versus telephone). In other words, the lack of trust that can develop between members may be functionally determined by the type of communication tool preferred and the frequency of its use, and not incidentally as some believe. But let's take this even further: What if a team member visits a personal friend in the evening on a business trip—is this being socially deviant, and is there a need for the rest of the team to be aware of it? Does the private life of members diminish once they become part of a virtual team, (since it's possible for the employee to cast an indirect light on the company/team)? These questions speak to the issue of how much autonomy and privacy one should expect when working for a virtual team-oriented organization. Could you work on a virtual team?

SOURCES: R. Sainsbury and R. Baskerville, "Distrusting Online: Social Deviance in Virtual Teamwork," *System Sciences*, 6(4), January 2006, p. 121a; and R. Audi, *Business Ethics and Ethical Business*, Oxford University Press, 2009, pp 88–89.

Here is what we have learned so far from recent studies of computer-mediated groups:

- Virtual groups formed over the Internet follow a group development process similar to that for face-to-face groups.[45]

- Internet chat rooms create more work and yield poorer decisions than face-to-face meetings and telephone conferences.[46]

- Successful use of groupware, software that facilitates interaction among virtual group members (e.g., Net Meeting, Webex), requires training and hands-on experience.[47]

- Inspirational leadership has a positive impact on creativity in electronic brainstorming groups.[48]

- Conflict management is particularly difficult for asynchronous virtual teams (those not interacting in real time) that have no opportunity for face-to-face interaction.[49]

- Having at least one member of a team working remotely "prompts the group to be more disciplined in its coordination and communication—yielding a better and more productive experience for all members … But turn that isolate into a pair—by adding a coworker at the same location—and the team suffers."[50]

Practical Considerations Virtual teams may be in fashion, but they are not a cure-all. In fact, they may be a giant step backward for those not well versed in modern information technology and group dynamics.[51] Managers who rely on virtual teams agree on one point: *Meaningful face-to-face contact, especially during early phases of the group development process, is absolutely essential.* Virtual group members need "faces" in their minds to go with names and electronic messages.[52] It may be advantageous to approach this type of group first as a self-managed team. Additionally, virtual teams cannot succeed without some old-fashioned factors such as top-management support, hands-on training, a clear mission, specific objectives, effective leadership, organized schedules, and deadlines.[53]

TEAM BUILDING HELPS TEAMWORK

Team building is a catch-all term for a host of techniques aimed at improving the internal functioning of teams. Whether conducted by company trainers or hired consultants (and done on-site or off-site), team-building workshops strive for greater cooperation, better communication, and less dysfunctional conflict. Team builders discourage lectures and routine classroom discussions; they prefer active versus passive learning. They also place greater emphasis on how teams get the job done, rather than on the task itself. Experiential learning

> **Team building**
>
> Experiential learning aimed at improving internal functioning of teams.

techniques such as interpersonal trust exercises, conflict role-play sessions, and competitive games are common.[54] Some prefer off-site gatherings to get participants away from their work and out of their comfort zones.

One such company is Canadian Outback Adventures and Events (COAE). With three operation-centre locations across the country, COAE has grown over the last 20 years to become one of North America's premiere corporate team building companies. Currently, their top team building activity and corporate event themes include: The Amazing Chase, The Apprentice, Iron Chef BBQ Challenge, Cake Creators Culinary Team Building, Whitewater Rafting, Secret Agent 007, GPS Geocache Challenge, X-Games, Urban Olympics, and CI: The Crime Investigators.[55] But since the 2008–09 deep recession, organizations have cut back lavish off-site team-building initiatives. Less costly team-building activities, such as volunteering to build a Habitat for Humanity home, can be both effective and socially responsible. Jeffrey Katzenberg, CEO of Dreamworks Animation SKG, the studio that gave us *Shrek*, prefers celebrations for team building: "When a movie opens, when a DVD comes out, or when awards are won, all of those milestones are celebrated in a big way."[56]

Team building allows team members to wrestle with simulated or real-life problems. Outcomes are then analyzed by the group to determine what group processes need improvement. Learning stems from recognizing and addressing faulty group dynamics. For instance, perhaps one subgroup withheld key information from another, thereby hampering group progress. With cross-cultural teams becoming commonplace in today's global economy, team building is more important than ever.[57]

The bottom line: Without clear goals, proper leadership, careful attention to details, and transfer of learning back to the job, both on-site and off-site team-building sessions can become an expensive disappointment.[58] You don't want people returning to their desks the day after a teambuilding activity wondering why they had to attend or thinking what a waste of time it was.

TRUST: A KEY INGREDIENT OF TEAMWORK LO 4

These have not been good times for trust in the corporate world. Years of mergers, layoffs, bloated executive bonuses, and corporate criminal proceedings have left many people justly cynical about trusting management. According to *Canadian Business Magazine*, which conducts an annual Best Workplace survey, "trust is tops."[59] Building a caring and trusting workplace culture is often mentioned by employees when asked what makes their organization such a great place to work. Here are some principles that have emerged from the survey:[60]

1. Determine where your organization is on the trust continuum. Is it relatively easy to have open conversations about how business decisions affect employee trust, or is trust simply not talked about at the executive table?

2. Managers need to understand that every interaction is an opportunity to build trust, and that missteps can quickly break trust.

3. Focus on a few key trust-building changes and pursue these consistently and relentlessly, recognizing that transforming a culture is evolutionary, not revolutionary.

Definition of Trust *Trust* is defined as reciprocal faith in others' intentions and behaviour.[61] Experts on the subject explain the reciprocal (give-and-take) aspect of trust as follows:

> *Trust*
>
> Reciprocal faith in others' intentions and behaviour.

> When we see others acting in ways that imply that they trust us, we become more disposed to reciprocate by trusting in them more. Conversely, we come to distrust those whose actions appear to violate our trust or to distrust us.[62] In short, we tend to give what we get: Trust begets trust; distrust begets distrust.

According to Patrick Lencioni's best-seller book, *The Five Dysfunctions of a Team,* trust is the first and

Whitewater rafting through the Rocky Mountains is a popular team-building activity in western Canada.

most important part of having a successful team.[63] If there is an absence of trust within the team and members are unwilling to be vulnerable with each other, this can pose an enormous threat to the success of the team and sabotage the ability to achieve its goals.

How to Build Trust   Management professor/consultant Fernando Bartolomé offers the following six guidelines for building and maintaining trust:

1. **Communication** Keep team members and employees informed by explaining policies and decisions and providing accurate feedback. Be candid about your own problems and limitations. Tell the truth.[64]

2. **Support** Be available and approachable. Provide help, advice, coaching, and support for team members' ideas.

3. **Respect** Delegation, in the form of real decision-making authority, is the most important expression of managerial respect. Actively listening to the ideas of others is a close second. Empowerment is not possible without trust.[65]

4. **Fairness** Be quick to give credit and recognition to those who deserve it. Make sure all performance appraisals and evaluations are objective and impartial.

5. **Predictability** Be consistent and predictable in your daily affairs. Keep both expressed and implied promises.

6. **Competence** Enhance your credibility by demonstrating good business sense, technical ability, and professionalism.[66]

Threats to Group and Team Effectiveness   LO 5

No matter how carefully managers staff and organize task groups and teams, group dynamics can still go haywire. Here we discuss two major threats to group effectiveness—groupthink and social loafing—and we provide information that can help managers and team members alike take necessary preventive steps.

GROUPTHINK

Modern managers can all too easily become victims of groupthink, just like professional politicians, if they passively ignore the danger. Professor and OB expert Irving Janis defines *groupthink* as "a mode of thinking that people engage in when they are deeply involved in a cohesive in-group, when members' strivings for unanimity (harmony) override their motivation to realistically appraise alternative courses of action."[67] He adds, "Groupthink refers to a deterioration of mental efficiency, reality testing, and moral judgment that results from in-group pressures."[68] Members of groups victimized by groupthink tend to be friendly and tightly knit.

> *Groupthink*
>
> Janis's term for a cohesive in-group's unwillingness to realistically view alternatives.

According to Janis's model, there are eight classic symptoms of groupthink. The greater the number of symptoms, the higher the probability of groupthink:

1. **Invulnerability** An illusion that breeds excessive optimism and risk taking.

2. **Inherent morality** A belief that encourages the group to ignore ethical implications.

3. **Rationalization** Protects pet assumptions.

4. **Stereotyped views of opposition** Causes the group to underestimate opponents.

5. **Self-censorship** Stifles critical debate.

6. **Illusion of unanimity** Silence is interpreted to mean consent.

7. **Peer pressure** Loyalty of dissenters is questioned.

8. **Mindguards** Self-appointed protectors against unpleasant information.[69]

In short, policy and decision-making groups can become so cohesive that strong-willed executives are able to gain unanimous support for poor decisions.

Janis believes that prevention is better than cure when dealing with groupthink (see the Skills & Best Practices feature box for his preventive measures).[70]

Farcus

by David Waisglass
Gordon Coulthart

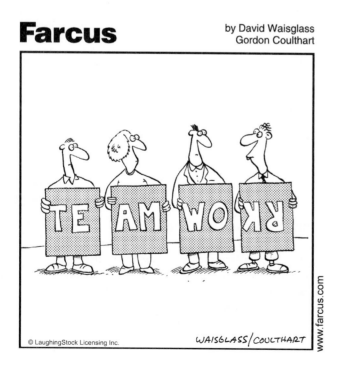

© LaughingStock Licensing Inc.

WAISGLASS/COULTHART

www.farcus.com

Skills & Best Practices

How to Prevent Groupthink

1 Assign each member of the group to the role of critical evaluator. This role involves actively voicing objections and doubts.
2 Do not use policy committees to rubber-stamp decisions that have already been made.
3 Have different groups with different leaders explore the same policy questions.
4 Use subgroup debates and outside experts to introduce fresh perspectives.
5 Give someone the role of devil's advocate when discussing major alternatives. This person tries to uncover every conceivable negative factor.
6 Once a consensus has been reached, encourage everyone to rethink their position to check for flaws.

SOURCE: Adapted from discussion in I.L. Janis, *Groupthink,* 2nd ed. (Boston: Houghton Mifflin, 1982), ch 11.

SOCIAL LOAFING

Is group performance less than, equal to, or greater than the sum of its parts? For example, can three people working together accomplish less than, the same as, or more than they would working separately? An interesting study conducted more than a half century ago by a French agricultural engineer named Ringelmann found the answer to be "less than."[71] In a rope-pulling exercise, Ringelmann reportedly found that three people pulling together could achieve only two and a half times the average individual rate. Eight pullers achieved less than four times the individual rate. This tendency for individual effort to decline as group size increases has come to be called *social loafing*.[72] Let's briefly analyze this threat to group effectiveness and synergy with an eye toward avoiding it.

Social Loafing Theory and Research Among the theoretical explanations for the social loafing effect are: (1) equity of effort ("Everyone else is goofing off, so why shouldn't I?"); (2) loss of personal accountability ("I'm lost in the crowd, so who cares?") (3) motivational loss due to the sharing of rewards ("Why should I work harder than the others when everyone gets the same reward?"); and (4) coordination loss as more people perform the task ("We're getting in each other's way.").

Laboratory studies refined these theories by identifying situational factors that moderate the social loafing effect. Social loafing occurs when

■ The task is perceived to be unimportant, simple, or not interesting[73]

> **Social loafing**
>
> Decrease in individual effort as group size increases.

■ Group members think their individual output is not identifiable[74]

■ Group members expect their co-workers to loaf[75]

But social loafing did *not* occur when group members in two laboratory studies expected to be evaluated.[76] Also, research suggests that self-reliant "individualists" are more prone to social loafing than are group-oriented "collectivists." But individualists can be made more cooperative by keeping the group small and holding each member personally accountable for results.[77]

Practical Implications These findings demonstrate that social loafing is not an inevitable part of group effort. Management can curb this threat to group effectiveness by making sure the task is challenging and perceived as important. Additionally, it is a good idea to hold group members personally accountable for identifiable portions of the group's task.[78] A few strategies worth considering when monitoring for social loafing include implementing self-assessments ("Do you think your contributions are having a positive effect on the team?"), paying for performance ("In order to get this reward, you must produce this outcome"), or using a *360-degree feedback* evaluation instrument (secure anonymous feedback on team performance from all members of team, as well as the manager, subordinates, clients, peers, etc.).

> **360-degree feedback**
>
> Comparison of anonymous feedback from one's superior, subordinates, and peers with self-perceptions.

List and define the five stages of Tuckman's theory of group development. The five stages in Tuckman's theory are forming (the group comes together), storming (members test the limits and each other), norming (questions about authority and power are resolved as the group becomes more cohesive), performing (effective communication and cooperation help the group get things done), and adjourning (group members go their own way).

 Contrast roles from norms, emphasizing reasons why norms are enforced in organizations. While roles are specific to the person's position, norms are shared attitudes that differentiate appropriate from inappropriate behaviour in a variety of situations. Norms evolve informally and are enforced because they help the group or organization survive, clarify behavioural expectations, help people avoid embarrassing situations, and clarify the group's or organization's central values.

 Examine the process for how a work group becomes a team, emphasizing various teamwork competencies. A team is a mature group where leadership is shared, accountability is both individual and collective, the members have developed a common purpose, problem solving is a way of life, and effectiveness is measured by collective outcomes. Five teamwork competencies are (1) orients team to problem-solving situations; (2) organizes and manages team performance; (3) promotes a positive team environment; (4) facilitates and manages task conflict; and (5) appropriately promotes perspective.

LO 4 **Explain why trust is the key ingredient to building an effective team, referring to both self-managed and virtual teams.** Trust contributes to teambuilding by allowing a reciprocal faith in others' intentions and behaviour. By having trust, the internal functioning of work groups is improved. Self-managed teams need to have built-in trust with one another because they have administrative oversight for their task domains; there is no manager per se to turn to for answers. They must have trust in one another as they rely less on management and become more co-dependent. Mutual trust among the membership will allow for open communication, especially during stressful times. Virtual teams need trust to get work done, since they don't have the physical cues to indicate that work is getting done as promised. Dividing up the work within a virtual team assumes that all members are competent and able to complete their portion of a task. That assumption can sometimes be based on blind trust.

 Summarize at least two threats to group and team effectiveness. Two major threats to group and team effectiveness are groupthink and social loafing. Groupthink results when people are deeply involved in a cohesive in-group, when members' strivings for harmony override their motivation to realistically appraise alternative courses of action. This can be dangerous because it can blind the group to minority opinion from dissenters, lead the group to rationalize their behaviour on the basis of false assumptions, and act as a type of censorship that stifles debate. One possible technique to use to minimize groupthink is to assign a member the role of devil's advocate or critical evaluator. Social loafing results when individual effort decreases within a group as the group itself gets larger. This is particularly applicable when intuition would lead us to believe that more is better when applied to assigning membership to a group. Social loafing is a threat to group effectiveness because it leads members to false expectations that authority and responsibility to perform is equally felt throughout the group. This may not be the case, and therefore sets the team up for disappointment. Ongoing assessment and evaluation can minimize social loafing.

Discussion Questions

1. Describe the kind of values, skills, and behaviours you would look for in members of a virtual team. Explain. Do the same for a self-managed team. Explain. Compare and contrast your answers.

2. What is your opinion about managers being friends with the people they supervise (in other words, overlapping formal and informal groups)?

3. In your personal relationships, how do you come to trust someone? How fragile is that trust? Explain.

4. Why is it important to identify clear goals first to make team-building activities successful?

5. Have you ever witnessed groupthink or social loafing firsthand? Explain the circumstances and how things played out.

Integration of OB Concepts—Discussion Questions

1. See Chapter 2 – What role does social perception play in all of the stages of group development? Consider the perceptual process and possible bias that can occur.

2. See Chapter 3 – Explain how teamwork may be more difficult for people who have a certain kind of personality and/or self-concept.

3. See Chapters 4 and 5 – Describe how personal values can affect individual motivation, especially when it comes to being assigned to work with others in a team-like atmosphere.

Google Searches

1. **Google Search:** "Stanford Prison Experiment" What is this research study about? What happened to individual behaviour when groups were formed? Was there evidence of groupthink among the guards? Can you draw a parallel to the workplace—do you think some employees feel hopeless/powerless as they become intimidated by authority, thus lowering their self-esteem? Why was it so hard for the prisoners to resist or quit? Do you think that we are the sole determinants of our behaviour or are we influenced by people and situations around us?

2. **Google Search:** "Summer Olympics 2012" OR "Winter Olympic 2010_2014" Look for the team sports only and the Canadian gold winners of these games.

What were some of the challenges these teams faced when preparing for their race? Identify behaviours, values, and skills that made these athletes a high performing team.

3. **Google Search:** "Canadian Outback Adventures & Events" OR "The Great Canadian Adventure Company" Search the various sites and record five of your favourite team building retreats/activities. Share your responses with the class.

Experiential Exercise

Combining Tuckman's Model with a Team Contract Exercise

PURPOSE: This exercise is meant to assist you with the specifics of group development by combining Tuckman's various stages of group development with the contents of a team operating agreement (courtesy of Microsoft online downloadable templates). You will be able to see theoretical principles applied in a practical exercise. Review Figure 6.2 before beginning this exercise. Approx. Timing: 25 minutes.

ACTIVITY ASSIGNMENT:

- Form small groups and review both Figure 6.2 and the Team Operating Agreement (TOA) below.
- Identify which parts of the agreement correlate best with which stage of Tuckman's model. An example is provided to get you started. Fill in the rest of the table.
- Reflect on which stage(s) is the most important for the TOA.
- Share your responses with the class after 10 minutes.

Team Operating Agreement (TOA)

The Terms of The Contract	Tuckman's Stage	Explain Your Reasoning
1.0 Purpose of the Team Operating Agreement (TOA) This TOA serves as the guidelines and ground rules to help the project team work most productively together over the course of the project. The TOA is a living document and may be updated as the need arises throughout the project. Any updates will be discussed with and ratified by the project team members.	*Example:* Forming Stage	*The forming stage is where team members need to clarify their purpose and address the question "Why are we here?"*
2.0 Team Communications • The project's SharePoint site will house the most up-to-date version of project documents. All team members will be given access.		

(Continued)

The Terms of The Contract	Tuckman's Stage	Explain Your Reasoning
• Meeting agendas will be emailed to project team members. Meeting minutes will be posted to the project SharePoint site within 48 hours after meetings. • Team members will appreciate the sensitive nature of information discussed during this project and will share with care. • "Sidebar" conversations between team members during team meetings will not be allowed. • All communication will be open and courteous. No "overtalking" or interrupting.		

3.0 Decision Making
1. Consensus means that everyone can live with the decision. It doesn't mean everyone has to agree 100 percent.
2. The team will use thumbs up/down voting to make decisions quickly and move on.
   • Thumbs up = agree with no further discussion
   • Thumbs sideways = agree, but have further questions
   • Thumbs down = cannot agree to the solution proposed
3. Members may abstain from voting.
4. No decision is made if there are any thumbs-down votes.
5. Meeting minutes will document the decisions made.		

4.0 Meetings • Project subteam leaders will report their status at each team meeting. • Project team members will meet (frequency, date, time, and locations of meetings). During each meeting, a "parking lot" will be used to record topics that require discussion at a later date. • Meetings will start on time and end on time. • Sending "stand ins" to meetings will not be allowed unless approved by the project manager prior to meetings. • It is the responsibility of each team member to stay current with the project team activities, even if they miss a meeting.		

(Continued)

The Terms of The Contract	Tuckman's Stage	Explain Your Reasoning
5.0 Personal Courtesies • Each team member represents a specific area of expertise or business unit. Team members will bring their individual perspectives to the team and will also consider what is best for the company. • All cell phones and other communication devices must be silenced during meetings and used on an exception basis only.		

Reviewed and approved by:

_____

Project Manager Date

_____

Project Team Member Name Date

_____

Project Team Member Name Date

_____

Project Team Member Name Date

OB In Action Case Study

Cross-Functional Teams at Lavalife

BACKGROUND

Founded in 1987, Lavalife was started in Toronto by Bruce Croxon, Dave Chamandy, Ed Lum, Nick Paine, and Rasool Verjee. These five young entrepreneurs began experimenting with Interactive Voice Response (IVR) technology by applying it to phone-based classified services that included personals, pets, furniture, and apartments. By 1988, the *teleclassifieds* (as they were called) became *telepersonals,* including a phone-based personals service allowing singles to meet and talk via phone. By 1994, traditional dial-up systems (CompuServe, AOL, Prodigy) began to provide Internet access, enabling the World Wide Web to enter private homes. With the growth of the Internet, Lavalife was able to launch *webpersonals* in 1997, allowing singles to come together online in new ways. Throughout the next decade, Lavalife expanded its brand to over 40 cities across North America and Australia. Its popularity fueled more growth, and by the time Lavalife celebrated its 20th anniversary, more new products and initiatives were being introduced. The company grew from four to over 400 employees in two decades, with an estimated value of $180 million.

THE NEED FOR TEAMS

To maintain growth and innovation, Lavalife believes in aligning work to the success of the organization. They believe that finding the right people to capture diverse perspectives and expertise is key. Jamie Erickson, VP of Human Resources and Organization Development, has turned to cross-functional teams over the last several years to accomplish corporate goals. "Cross-functional teams are an art in this organization," says Erickson. At Lavalife, cross-functional teams are regularly used on complex organization priorities, such as the consolidation of their call centres in North America, which involved teams from marketing, IT, legal, finance, and HR.

As teams are formed at Lavalife, member roles are defined and clarified based on a detailed project plan that clearly states deliverables, responsibilities, milestones, and timelines. SMEs (subject matter experts) act as a liaison to get information from the various functional groups that are needed for effective decision making. By designating only one person for overall accountability for a project, communication is streamlined and consistent, leaving no excuses for activities falling through the cracks. According to Erickson, "If the project doesn't have alignment with organization goals, then functional silos do become a challenge." Due to strong alignment between the work of cross-functional teams and organization strategy, competition between functional and organizational interest is rare at Lavalife.

It's important to hold people accountable to the project plan and the SMEs help accomplish that through ongoing communication with the team. What Lavalife doesn't want are members of cross-functional teams perceiving their work on the team to be secondary to their 'normal' job. At Lavalife, "if (team members) meet regularly as a collective, conversations start to happen outside the meeting rooms" and this is a very effective way to accomplish goals. Lavalife has employees located in various geographical locations, which can pose a challenge to some teams; however technology is making it easier to maintain strong connections through video-conferencing, Web-based group communication, and improved project management software.

Finding ways to get team members to connect in a friendly community-building kind of way is welcomed at Lavalife. Humour in a team setting can help to break down barriers. For example, Erickson says that his HR team is comfortable saying, "excuse me, but for the non-IT speaking population, could you put that in terms that I can understand?" And his own group responds positively to requests of "please don't speak in OD (organizational development) language, speak in real people speak!"

Today, Lavalife has over 450 employees and offers its voice services in over 60 markets across Canada, the United States, and Australia, in addition to lavalifeWEB, lavalifePRIME, lavalifeMOBILE, and *CLICK,* an online magazine. While the original entrepreneurs are no longer involved with the company (Croxon can often be seen on CBC's *Dragons' Den*), Lavalife looks forward to celebrating its 30th anniversary in 2017.

Discussion Questions

1. How do SMEs help keep the cross-functional team cohesive, productive, and accountable?

2. What benefit does Lavalife's work environment receive when team roles are specifically defined based on project plans?

3. How can humour contribute to team building, and why would Lavalife welcome it during team meetings?

SOURCES: Lavalife Ltd. corporate website: www.corp.lavalife.com; S. Nador, "The Fine Art of Team Selection," *Canadian HR Reporter* (2001), www.nvisionconsulting.ca; and National Speakers Bureau, Bruce Croxon biography, www.nsb.com.

The CONNECTion Zone   McGraw Hill connect™

- The Presentation Assistant
- Ethical OB Dilemma
- Video Case

Practise and learn online with Connect.

CHAPTER 7

Communicating in the Digital Age

FACING AN OB CHALLENGE

I really enjoy Facebook and how easy it is to communicate with people, but I graduate within the next year and I'm getting worried that a potential employer is going to see photos of me on the Internet that aren't the most flattering. It's not like I haven't done my part to protect my reputation—I learned about data mining years ago and deleted all of the photos and inappropriate 'wall' postings that I didn't want others to see or read. It's other people's websites, social network sites, and Instagram pages where my face is tagged and my name appears that concern me . . . oh yeah, and even an ex-girlfriend's blogsite (we broke up on bad terms) that I have no control over. Do I have reason to be worried?

—FREAKING OUT

LO 1 Illustrate the various
components of
the perceptual
process model of
communication.

LO 2 Describe the various
barriers to effective
communication.

LO 3 Contrast the
communication styles
of assertiveness,
aggressiveness, and
non-assertiveness.

LO 4 Explain the formal and
informal communication
channels.

LO 5 Summarize the various
factors involved in
maintaining effective
communication as
organizations move
toward using more digital
devices in the workplace.

Communication in the Workplace

In the previous chapter we spoke of how communicating within social network sites is blurring the formal/informal boundaries of the workplace. The concerns raised by the individual in *Facing an OB Challenge* build upon this topic and are real as individuals become more aware of the long-lasting effects of using the Internet and social networking sites. In the age of digital communication, an individual's behaviour and choice of communication media can become a search site for potential employers. Past behaviour communicated through online photos, as well as a list of Facebook friends or personal Tweets, may be taken out of context and held as evidence of a person's values, behaviour, and/or communication style. Students of OB would be well served to data mine their own history of communication to see what others can discover about them.

When we consider how organizations are benefitting form such temporary technology, a different view comes into focus. Some companies are taking a page from social networking sites to make the performance evaluation process more fun and useful. For example, a Canadian management consulting firm, Accenture, has developed a Facebook-style program called Performance Multiplier in which, among other things, employees post status updates, photos, and two or three weekly goals that can be viewed by fellow staffers. Even more immediate, new software from a Toronto startup called Rypple lets people post Twitter-length questions about their performance in exchange for anonymous feedback. What Rypple's and Accenture's tools do is create a process in which evaluations become dynamic—and more democratic. Rypple, for example, gives employees the chance to post brief, 140-character questions, such as "What did you think of my presentation?" or "How can I run meetings better?" The queries are emailed to managers, peers, or anyone else the user selects. Short anonymous responses are then aggregated and sent back, providing a quick-and-dirty 360-degree review. The basic service is free. But corporate clients can pay for a premium version that includes tech support, extra security, and analysis of which topics figure highest in employee posts.[1]

Modern information technology is connecting us and transforming our lives in unprecedented ways. There are positives, negatives, and unintended consequences of living in a wired world. It is important for all of us to understand the underlying communication process and the dynamics of communicating as technology continues to evolve (see the Law and Ethics at Work feature box for more on this topic).

The study of communication is fundamentally important because every managerial function and activity involves some form of direct or indirect communication. Whether planning, organizing, directing, or leading, managers find themselves communicating with and through others. This implies that everyone's communication skills affect both personal and organizational effectiveness.[2] For example, one study found that 70 percent of "preventable hospital mishaps" result from a lack of communication between employees, particularly during handoffs (i.e., shift changes) of patient care.[3] This sort of communication breakdown leads to lower productivity and product quality, and higher labour costs and turnover.[4]

This chapter will help you understand how all employees can improve their communication skills and how management can design more effective communication programs. We discuss (1) basic dimensions of the communication processes, focusing on a perceptual process model and barriers to effective communication; (2) interpersonal communication; and (3) communicating in the information technology age.

LO 1 Basic Dimensions of the Communication Process

Communication is defined as "the exchange of information between a sender and a receiver, and the inference (interpretation) of meaning between the individuals involved."[5] Employees who understand this process can analyze their own communication patterns

> **Communication**
>
> Interpersonal exchange of information and understanding.

and managers can design communication programs that fit organizational needs. This section reviews a perceptual process model of communication and discusses the barriers to effective communication.

A PERCEPTUAL PROCESS MODEL OF COMMUNICATION

Communicating is not simple or straightforward—it is fraught with miscommunication. While recognizing

LAW AND ETHICS AT WORK

EMPLOYERS MUST TREAD CAREFULLY WITH SOCIAL MEDIA CHECKS

Consider this scenario: The HR manager of a Canadian organization is looking to fill a position in her firm. While holding one dozen resumés in hand, she walks over to a computer, sits down, and types in one potential candidate's name at a time into Google or Facebook to see what comes up. If the applicant is Russian, then she searches Vkontakte.ru; for Chinese applicants, she searches RenRen.com; and if the applicants are from Brazil or India, she searches Orkut.

This growing trend among Canadian employers prompted the Office of the Information and Privacy Commissioner of Alberta to release *Guidelines for Social Media Background Checks*. British Columbia is currently the only other province in Canada with such guidelines around social network sites, blogs, micro-blogging (such as Twitter), and file sharing sites, including photographs and video. "Employers don't realize the risk involved," claims Tara Perverseff, an officer within the Alberta Privacy Commissioner's office. While collecting personal information about a candidate, employers could be finding inaccurate and out-of-date information that is irrelevant and perhaps prejudicial. Also, the large amount of personal information collected from these sites, such as gender, race, or age, could be used for screening purposes and thus discriminating, which becomes a human rights issue. Last is the action of collecting third party information without consent, and this becomes a privacy issue. Recognize that these Canadian laws only apply to Canadian applicants, but even this area is somewhat cloudy when applied to international applicants.

To avoid risk, Canadian organizations should consider a few factors during the recruitment and selection process:

- Clearly identify on their website that by submitting a resumé, candidates are consenting to a background check, which will include social media.
- Alternatively, choose to not participate and forbid hiring professionals to use social media in the early stages of the screening process. Instead, use social media only after a conditional hire has been made and appropriate disclosures and consent have been received.
- Consider the business purpose of conducting social media background checks and what they are going to gain that they cannot get through traditional means.
- Establish policies that protect against any human rights violations or significant invasion of personal privacy—if a claim is filed, the company recruiters will have to prove they weren't influenced.

Canadian employers need to consider what information they're collecting. "Before we used social media, you interviewed the person, you checked references, you talked to previous employers—you didn't go through their garbage or follow them on the street and listen to a conversation they were having with their mom. Our office would argue (potential employers) just don't need it," says Perverseff.

SOURCES: A. Silliker, "Tread carefully with social media checks," *Canadian HR Reporter*, January 30, 2012, p 1; and R. Pickell, "Checking social media sites when hiring? Proceed with caution," *Canadian HR Reporter*, March 28, 2011, p D7.

this, researchers have begun to examine communication as a form of social information processing in which receivers interpret messages by cognitively processing information. This view led to the development of a *perceptual model of communication* that depicts communication as a process in which receivers create meaning in their own minds. Let us briefly examine the elements of the perceptual process model shown in Figure 7.1.

Sender The sender is an individual, a group, or an organization that desires or attempts to communicate with a particular receiver. A receiver may be an individual, a group, or an organization.

Encoding Communication begins when a sender encodes an idea or thought. Encoding translates mental thoughts into a code or language that can be understood by others. People typically encode using words, numbers, gestures, non-verbal cues such as facial expressions, or pictures. The output of encoding is a message.

Selecting a Medium People can communicate through a variety of media, including face-to-face conversations, telephone calls, electronic mail or email, voice mail, video conferencing, written memos or letters, photographs or drawings, meetings, bulletin boards, computer output, and charts or graphs. Choosing the appropriate media depends on many factors, including the nature of the message, its intended purpose, the type of audience, proximity to the audience, the time horizon for disseminating (distributing) the message,

> **Perceptual model of communication**
>
> Process in which receivers create their own meaning.

personal preferences, and the complexity of the problem/situation at hand.

All media have advantages and disadvantages and should be used in different situations. Face-to-face conversations, for example, are useful for communicating sensitive or important issues that require feedback and intensive interaction. In contrast, telephones are convenient, fast, and private, but lack non-verbal cues. Although writing memos or letters can be time-consuming, they are good media to use when it is difficult to arrange a meeting with another person, when formality and a written record are important, and when face-to-face interaction is not necessary to enhance understanding. Electronic communication, which is discussed later in this chapter, can be used to communicate with a large number of dispersed (widely placed) people and is potentially a very fast medium when recipients regularly check their email.[6]

Decoding and Creating Meaning Decoding is the receiver's version of encoding. Receivers give messages their meaning. Decoding consists of translating verbal, oral, or visual aspects of a message into a form that can be interpreted. Receivers rely on social information processing to determine the meaning of a message during decoding. Decoding is a key contributor to misunderstanding in interracial and intercultural communication. Consider this cross-cultural experience of a *Wall Street Journal* reporter on assignment in China.

> *I was riding the elevator a few weeks ago with a Chinese colleague here in the Journa's Asian*

FIGURE 7.1 Communication Process in Action

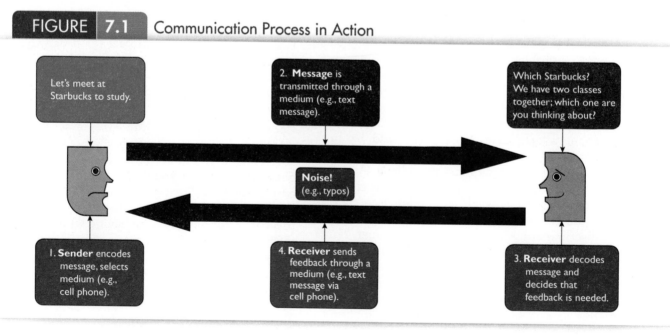

headquarters. I smiled and said, "Hi." She respond-ed, "You've gained weight." I might have been ap-palled, but at least three other Chinese co-workers also have told me I'm fat. I probably should cut back on the pork dumplings. In China, such an inti-mate observation from a colleague isn't necessarily an insult. It's probably just friendliness.[7]

This example highlights how decoding and creating meaning are influenced by cultural norms and values.

Feedback   Two people are in a meeting room. The sender is giving a 10 minute presentation and the receiver is listening to it. "Well, what did you think of my presentation?" asks the sender. "Thanks for showing me your presentation. It went well. I think the message is clear and concise. However, there are just a few things that I'd like to recommend to make it even better. Are you interested in hearing them?" says the receiver. This is an example of feedback—the receiver expresses a reaction to the sender's message. The receiv-er's response to a message is the heart of the feedback loop.

Noise   *Noise* represents anything that interferes with the transmission and under-standing of a message. It affects all linkages of

the communication process. Noise includes factors such as a speech impairment, poor telephone connections, illegible handwriting, inaccurate statistics in a memo or report, poor hearing and eyesight, environmental noises, people talking or whistling, and physical distance between sender and receiver. Supervisors and managers can improve communication by encouraging employees to try to minimize the noise levels around their work sta-tions and reduce office distractions and noise.[8]

BARRIERS TO EFFECTIVE COMMUNICATION   `LO 2`

There are two key components of effective communi-cation. First, senders need to accurately communicate their intended message. Second, receivers need to correspondingly perceive and interpret the message accurately. Anything that gets in the way of the accur-ate transmission and reception of a message is a bar-rier to effective communication. It is important to be aware of and avoid these barriers when com-municating. Some barriers actually are part of the communication process itself. Table 7.1 identifies and explains common barriers at each level of the communication process. Awareness of these barriers is a good start-ing point to improve the communication process.

> *Noise*
>
> Interference with the transmission and understanding of a message.

TABLE 7.1

BARRIERS WITHIN THE COMMUNICATION PROCESS ITSELF

Sender—no message gets sent. Have you ever had an idea but were afraid to voice it because you feared criticism? Obviously no message got sent. But the barrier need not be for psychological reasons. Suppose as a new manager you simply didn't realize (because you weren't told) that supervising your subordinates' expense accounts was part of your responsibility. In that case, it may be understandable why you never call them to task about fudging their expense reports—why, in other words, no message got sent.

Encoding—the message is not expressed correctly. No doubt you've sometimes had difficulty trying to think of the correct word to express how you feel about something. If English is not your first language, for example, then you may have difficulty expressing to a supervisor, co-worker, or subordinate what it is you mean to say.

Medium—the media is blocked. You never get through to someone because his phone always has a busy signal. The computer network is down and the email message you sent doesn't go through. These are instances of a medium being blocked.

Decoding—the recipient doesn't understand the message. Your boss tells you to "lighten up" or "buckle down," but because English is not your first language, you don't understand what the messages mean. Or perhaps you're afraid to show your ignorance when someone is throwing computer terms at you and says that your computer connection has "a bandwidth problem."

Receive—no message gets received. Because you were talking to a co-worker, you weren't listening when your supervisor announced today's work assignments, and so you have to ask her to repeat the announcement.

Feedback—the recipient doesn't respond enough. No doubt you've had the experience of giving someone street directions, but since they only nod their heads and don't repeat the directions back to you, you don't really know whether you were understood. The same thing can happen in many workplace circumstances.

SOURCE: R. Kinicki and A. Kinicki, *Organizational Behaviour*, 9th ed. (New York, NY: McGraw-Hill, 2010), p. 405.

Trying to communicate via cell phone while sitting in a café is likely to be affected by noise. The person's cell phone conversation can also represent noise to someone at the next table.

General barriers can also influence and distort communication such as: (1) personal barriers, (2) physical barriers, and (3) semantic barriers (see Figure 7.2).

Personal Barriers Have you ever communicated with someone and felt totally confused? This may have led you to wonder: is it them or is it me? *Personal barriers* represent any individual attributes that hinder communication. Let's examine nine common personal barriers that foster miscommunication.

> *Personal barriers*
>
> Any individual attribute that hinders communication.

1. **Variable skills in communicating effectively** Some people are simply better communicators than others. They have the speaking and listening skills, the ability to use gestures for dramatic effect, the vocabulary to alter the message to fit the audience, the writing skills to convey concepts in simple and concise terms, and the social skills to make others feel comfortable.[9] In contrast, others lack these skills. Don't worry, communication skills can be enhanced with training.[10]

2. **Variations in how information is processed and interpreted** Did you grow up in the country, in the suburbs, or in a city? Did you attend private or public school? What were your parents' attitudes toward you doing chores and playing sports? Are you from a loving home or one spoiled with fighting, yelling, and lack of structure? Answers to these questions are relevant because they make up the different frames of references and experiences people use to interpret the world around them. This means that these differences affect our interpretations of what we see and hear.

3. **Variations in interpersonal trust** Communication is more likely to be distorted when people do not trust each other. Rather than focusing on the message, a lack of trust is likely to cause people to be defensive and question the accuracy of what is being communicated.

4. **Stereotypes and prejudices** We noted in Chapter 2 that stereotypes are over-simplified beliefs about specific groups of people. They potentially distort communication because their use causes people to misperceive and recall information. It is important for all of us to be aware of our potential stereotypes and to recognize that they may subconsciously affect the interpretation of a message.

5. **Big egos** Our egos, whether due to pride, self-esteem, superior ability, or arrogance, are a communication barrier. Egos can cause political battles, turf wars, and pursuit of power, credit, and resources. Egos influence how we treat others, as well as our receptiveness to being influenced by others. Have you ever had someone put you down in public? Then you know how ego can influence communication.

6. **Poor listening skills** How many times have you been in class when a student asks the same question that was asked minutes earlier? How about going to a party and meeting someone who only talks about himself and never asks questions about you? This experience certainly doesn't make people feel important or memorable. It's hard to communicate effectively when one of the parties is not listening. We discuss listening skills in a later section of this chapter.

7. **Natural tendency to evaluate others' messages** What do you say to someone after watching the latest movie in a theatre? What did you think of

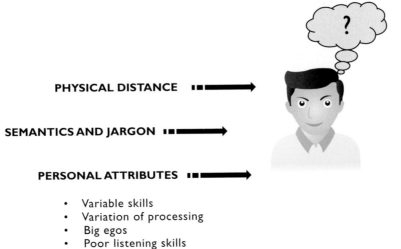

PHYSICAL DISTANCE

SEMANTICS AND JARGON

PERSONAL ATTRIBUTES

- Variable skills
- Variation of processing
- Big egos
- Poor listening skills
- Stereotypes
- Variation of trust
- Inability to listen with understanding
- Tendency to evaluate others' message
- Non-verbal cues, gestures, behaviour

the movie? The person might say, "It was great, best movie I've seen all year." You then may say, "I agree," or alternatively, "I disagree, that movie stunk." The point is that we all have a natural tendency, according to renowned psychologist Carl Rogers, to evaluate messages from our own point of view or frame of reference, particularly when we have strong feelings about the issue.[11]

8. **Inability to listen with understanding** Listening with understanding occurs when a receiver can "see the expressed idea and attitude from the other person's point of view, to sense how it feels to him, to achieve his frame of reference in regard to the thing he is talking about."[12] Try to listen with understanding; it will make you less defensive and can improve your accuracy in perceiving messages.

9. **Non-verbal communication** Communication accuracy is enhanced when facial expressions and gestures are consistent with the intent of a message. Interestingly, people may not even be aware of this issue. We discuss more about this important aspect of communication later in this chapter.

Physical Barriers The distance between employees can interfere with effective communication. It is hard to understand someone who is speaking to you from 20 metres away. Time zone differences between the East and West Coasts also represent physical barriers. Work and office noise are additional barriers. The

quality of telephone lines or crashed computers represent physical barriers that impact our ability to communicate with information technology.

In spite of the general acceptance of physical barriers, they can be reduced. For example, employees from Atlantic Canada can agree to call their West Coast peers prior to leaving for lunch. In the case of a small confining space that discourages communication, walls can be torn down; or if the office is too noisy, maybe doors can be installed or walls built to block it out. It is important that all employees attempt to manage the noise barrier around their work station or the situation in general by choosing a medium that optimally reduces the physical barrier at hand.

Semantics

The study of words.

Semantic Barriers *Semantics* is the study of words. When your boss tells you, "We need to complete this project right away," what does it mean? Does "we" mean just you? You and your co-workers? Or you, your co-workers, and the boss? Does "right away" mean today, tomorrow, or next week? These are examples of semantic barriers. Semantic barriers show up as encoding and decoding errors because these phases of communication involve transmitting and receiving words and symbols. These barriers are partially fuelled by the use of slang ("that's cool!" means something is good) and acronyms ("I drive an SUV" means sports utility vehicle).[13] As text messaging becomes more popular, catchphrases are changing at a frenetic (wild) pace.[14] For example, what does the following statement say? "Hope 2 c u tmr haha if u make it. TTYL." Here is what it says exactly: "I hope to see you tomorrow—I mean, if you make it. Talk to you later." With the rise in texting, IM, and Twitter types of communication, speed is paramount—but so is fitting everything you want to say into a limited space.

Jargon is another key semantic barrier. *Jargon* represents language or terminology that is specific to a particular profession, group, or company. The use of jargon has been increasing as our society becomes more technologically oriented. (For example, "The CIO wants the RFP to go out ASAP" means "The Chief Information Officer wants the Request for Proposal to go out as soon as possible.") It is important to remember that words that are ordinary to you may be mysterious to outsiders. If you want to be understood more clearly, it is important to carefully choose your language.

Semantic barriers are more likely in today's multicultural workforce. Their frequency is also fuelled by the growing trend to outsource customer service operations to foreign countries, particularly India. Unfortunately, some North Americans are incensed (angry) over having to communicate with customer-service employees working in such call centres. In response to complaints from North American customers, Indian outsources such as Wipro have instituted training programs aimed at reducing cross-cultural semantic barriers:

> *In a training class at Wipro, students identify Indian stereotypes and Western stereotypes. The point is to identify shallow images as barriers to good communication so they can be overcome.*
>
> *The class reviews cultural differences—big and small. As a "high-context" culture where what is communicated is more internalized (say, in a family), Indians can seem to be beating around the bush to North Americans who are part of a low-context culture in which communications need to be more explicit, "If you like to talk and you're dealing with a low-context person," explains instructor, Roger George, "you might want to keep it simple and get to the point."*[15]

Semantic barriers also are related to the choice of words we use when communicating. Consider the case of using profanity at work. Some use profanity a lot in the workplace because they believe it shows passion. To others it is offensive. It is important to note that the use of profanity is unprofessional to some people, and its use can create emotional responses that interfere with effective communication.

Choosing your words more carefully is the easiest way to reduce semantic barriers. These barriers can also be decreased by attentiveness to mixed messages and cultural diversity. Mixed messages occur when people's words imply one message while their actions or non-verbal cues suggest something different. Obviously, understanding is enhanced when a person's actions and non-verbal cues match the verbal message.

CHOOSING MEDIA: A CONTINGENCY PERSPECTIVE

We now turn our attention to discussing the *how* of the communication process. Specifically, Figure 7.3 shows how employees and managers can determine the best method or medium to use when communicating across the various formal and informal channels of communication.

Employees can choose from many different types of communication media (for example, telephone, email, voice mail, cell phone, express mail, text messaging, video, blogs, and so forth). Fortunately, research tells us that employees can help reduce information overload and improve communication effectiveness through their choice of communication media. If people use an inappropriate medium, then decisions may be based on inaccurate information, important messages may not reach the intended audience, and employees may become dissatisfied and unproductive.

Media selection is a key component of communication effectiveness. The following section explores a contingency model designed to help all employees select communication media in a systematic and effective manner. Media selection in this model is based on the interaction between information richness and difficulty of the problem/situation at hand.

Media Richness Respected organizational theorists Richard Daft and Robert Lengel define *media richness* in the following manner:

> *Richness is defined as the potential information-carrying capacity of data. If the communication of an item of data, such as a wink, provides substantial new understanding, it would be considered rich. If the (standard position) provides little understanding, it would be low in richness.*[16]

Media richness is based on four factors: (1) feedback (ranging from fast to very slow); (2) channel (ranging from the combined visual and audio characteristics of a video conference to the limited visual aspects of a computer report); (3) type of communication (ranging from personal to impersonal); and (4) language source (ranging from the natural body language and speech contained in a face-to-face conversation to the numbers contained in a financial statement).

Jargon

Language or terminology that is specific to a particular profession, group, or company.

Media richness

Capacity of a communication medium to convey information and promote understanding.

FIGURE **7.3** Contingency Model for Selecting Communication Media

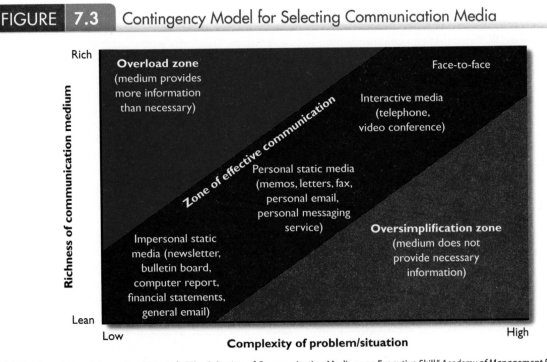

SOURCES: Adapted from R. Lengel and R.L. Daft, "The Selection of Communication Media as an Executive Skill," *Academy of Management Executive*, August 1988, p 226; and R.L. Daft and R.H. Lengel, "Information Richness: A New Approach to Managerial Behavior and Organization Design," *Research in Organizational Behavior*, eds. B.M. Staw and L.L. Cummings (Greenwich, CT: JAI Press, 1984), p 199.

Face-to-face is the richest form of communication. It provides immediate feedback and allows for the observation of multiple language cues, such as body language and tone of voice. Although high in richness, telephone and video conferencing are not as informative as the face-to-face medium. In contrast, newsletters, computer reports, and general email are lean media because feedback is very slow, the channels involve only limited visual information, and the information provided is generic or impersonal.

Contingency Recommendations Figure 7.3 graphically shows the contingency model for selecting media. As shown, there are three zones of communication effectiveness. Effective communication occurs when the richness of the medium is matched appropriately with the complexity of the problem or situation. Media low in richness—impersonal static and personal static—are better suited for simple problems; media high in richness—interactive media and face-to-face—are appropriate for complex situations. Sun Microsystems, for example, followed this recommendation when communicating with employees about upcoming layoffs. The organization used a series of face-to-face sessions to deliver the bad news and provided managers with a set of slides and speaking points to help distribute the necessary information.[17]

On the other hand, ineffective communication occurs when the richness of the medium is either too high or too low for the complexity of the problem or situation. For example, district sales managers would fall into the *overload zone* if they communicated monthly sales reports through richer media. Conducting face-to-face meetings or telephoning each salesperson would provide excessive information and take more time than necessary.

The *oversimplification zone* represents another ineffective choice of communication medium. In this situation, media with inadequate richness are used to communicate complicated or emotional issues. For example, Radio Shack Corporation (now called The Source) used email to notify 400 employees at its headquarters that they were being let go. Worse yet, a London-based body-piercing and jewellery store used a text message to fire an employee. This choice of medium is ineffective in this context because it does not preserve privacy and it does not allow employees to ask questions. Further, dismissing employees in this manner can lower morale among remaining employees and damage a company's image.[18]

Research Evidence The relationship between media richness and problem/situation complexity has not been extensively researched because the underlying theory is relatively new. Available evidence indicates that employees and managers used richer sources when confronted with ambiguous events (those that can be interpreted in more than one way) and complicated events, and miscommunication increased when rich media were used to transmit information that was traditionally communicated through lean media.[19] Moreover, a meta-analysis of more than 40 studies revealed that media usage was significantly different across organizational levels. Upper-level executives/managers spent more time in face-to-face meetings than did lower-level managers.[20] This finding is consistent with recommendations that flow from the contingency model just discussed.

Interpersonal Communication

The quality of interpersonal communication within an organization is very important. People with good communication skills help groups to make more innovative decisions and are promoted more frequently than individuals with less developed abilities.[21] While there are a host of communication abilities and skills under the umbrella of communication skills, we focus on five that you can control: assertiveness, aggressiveness, non-assertiveness, non-verbal communication, and active listening. We will also include some discussion around gender differences in communication. To get things started, complete Self-Assessment Exercise #1 "What Is Your Business Etiquette?" Being sensitive to such items can be considered as a fundamental aspect of good interpersonal communication.

LO 3 | **ASSERTIVENESS, AGGRESSIVENESS, AND NON-ASSERTIVENESS**

Table 7.2 describes the styles of assertiveness, aggressiveness, and non-assertiveness and identifies non-verbal and verbal behaviour patterns associated with each one.

An *assertive style* is expressive and self-enhancing and is based on the "ethical notion that it is not right or good to violate our own or others' basic human rights, such as the right to self-expression or the right to be treated with dignity and respect."[22] In terms of language choice, when speaking with an individual who has an assertive communication style, the pronoun preference is "I"—they will begin conversations speaking for themselves, such as, "I think"; "I feel"; "I need to understand."

In contrast, an *aggressive style* is expressive and self-enhancing, and strives to take unfair advantage of others. The pronoun preference you'll hear when speaking to a person who is aggressive will be "You"—for example, "You were wrong"; "You don't know what you're talking about"; "Let me tell you the real story." They have no problem delivering their message to others without engaging in a dialogue. Consensus is really not a goal that aggressive style communicators strive for. Research studies indicate that when it comes to effective communication, assertiveness is more effective than aggressiveness in both work-related and consumer contexts.[23]

A *non-assertive style* is characterized by timid and self-denying behaviour. Non-assertiveness (sometimes called passive) is ineffective because it gives the other person an unfair advantage. There is neither movement on nor resolution to an issue because the passive style communicator prefers to sit back and wait for others to move or speak first; they allow the interests of others to be discussed and known before their own.

Here's a quick quiz to see if you can understand the three contrasting communication styles. Which style did Carol Bartz, the very successful former CEO of Autodesk, display upon taking the top spot at struggling Yahoo?

Just a few minutes after being introduced at a hastily arranged conference call, the self-described straight shooter told analysts she intends to ensure Yahoo gets "some friggin' breaking room" so the company can "kick some butt."[24]

If you guessed aggressive communication style, you are right. Only time will tell if Bartz's in-your-face style will turn things around at Yahoo, or if it will instead build resentment, mistrust, and resistance. OB experts do know one thing for sure: employees may improve their communication competence by trying to be more assertive and less aggressive or non-assertive. This can be achieved by using the appropriate non-verbal and verbal behaviours listed in Table 7.2.

Refer to Table 7.2 as you attempt the following two exercises. Try applying what is being discussed to the context of two office scenarios:

Scenario #1: **How should a team leader, supervisor, or manager communicate daily events with employees?**
Answer: To encourage dialogue and an ongoing open approach with each other, these people should attempt to use the non-verbal behaviours of good eye contact, a strong,

Non-assertive style

Timid and self-denying behaviour.

Assertive style

Expressive and self-enhancing behaviour, but does not take advantage of others.

Aggressive style

Expressive and self-enhancing behaviour, but takes unfair advantage of others.

What Is Your Business Etiquette?

INSTRUCTIONS: Business etiquette is one component of communication competence. Test your business etiquette by answering the following questions. After circling your response for each item, calculate your score by reviewing the correct answers. Next, use the norms at the end of the test to interpret your results.

1 The following is an example of a proper introduction: "Ms. Boss, I'd like you to meet our client, Mr. Smith."
  True   False

2 If someone forgets to introduce you, you shouldn't introduce yourself; you should just let the conversation continue.
  True   False

3 If you forget someone's name, you should keep talking and hope no one will notice. This way you don't embarrass yourself or the person you are talking to.
  True   False

4 When shaking hands, a man should wait for a woman to extend her hand.
  True   False

5 Who goes first through a revolving door?
  a. Host   b. Visitor

6 It is all right to hold private conversations, either in person or on a cell phone, in office bathrooms, elevators, and other public spaces.
  True   False

7 When two Canadian businesspeople are talking to one another, the space between them should be approximately
  a. 0.5 metre   c. 2 metres
  b. 1 metre

8 Business casual attire requires socks for men and hose for women.
  True   False

9 To signal that you do not want a glass of wine, you should turn your wine glass upside down.
  True   False

10 If a call is disconnected, it's the caller's responsibility to redial.
  True   False

11 When using a speakerphone, you should tell the caller if there is anyone else in the room.
  True   False

12 You should change your voice mail message if you are going to be out of the office.
  True   False

Answers

1. **False.** Clients always take precedence, and people with the greatest authority or importance should be introduced first.

2. **False.** You should introduce yourself. Say something like "My name is _____. I don't believe we've met."

3. **False.** It's OK to admit you can't remember. Say something like "My mind just went blank. Your name is?" Or offer your name and wait for the other person to respond with his or hers.

4. **False.** Business etiquette has become gender neutral.

5. **a. Host.** This enables the host to lead his or her guest to the meeting place.

6. **False.** Not only is it rude to invade public areas with your conversation, but you never know who might hear details of your business transaction or personal life.

7. **b. 1 metre.** Closer than this is an invasion of personal space. Farther away forces people to raise their voices. Because communication varies from country to country, you should also inform yourself about cultural differences.

8. **True.** An exception to this would be if your company holds an event at the beach or the pool.

9. **False.** Just wave your hand over it when asked, or say "No thank you."

10. **True.** The person who initiated the call should redial if the connection is broken.

11. **True.** If you must use a speakerphone, you should inform all parties who's present.

12. **True.** You should record a greeting such as "I'm out of the office today, March 12. If you need help, please dial at extension X."

Arbitrary Norms

Low business etiquette (0–4 correct): Consider buying an etiquette book or hiring a coach to help you polish your professional image.

Moderate business etiquette (5–8 correct): Look for a role model or mentor and look for ways you can improve your business etiquette.

High business etiquette (9–12 correct): Good for you. You should continue to practise good etiquette and look for ways to maintain your professional image.

SOURCE: Adapted from material contained in M. Brody, "Test Your Etiquette," *Training & Development*, February 2002, pp 64–66. Copyright © February 2002 from *Training & Development* by M. Brody. Reprinted with permission of American Society for Training & Development.

TABLE 7.2

COMMUNICATION STYLES

COMMUNICATION STYLE	DESCRIPTION	NON-VERBAL BEHAVIOUR PATTERN	VERBAL BEHAVIOUR PATTERN
Assertive	Pushes hard without attacking; permits others to influence outcome; expressive and self-enhancing without intruding on others	• Good eye contact • Comfortable but firm posture • Strong, steady, and audible voice • Facial expressions matched to message	• Direct but not forceful and unambiguous language • No attributions or evaluations of other's behaviour • Appropriately serious tone • Selective interruptions to ensure understanding • Use of "I" statements and cooperative "we" statements
Aggressive	Takes advantage of others; expressive and self-enhancing at other's expense	• Glaring eye contact • Moves or leans too close • Threatening gestures (pointed finger; clenched fist) • Loud voice • Frequent interruptions	• Swear words and abusive language • Attributions and evaluations of other's behaviour • Sexist or racist terms • Explicit threats or put-downs
Non-assertive	Encourages others to take advantage of self; inhibited; self-denying	• Little eye contact • Downward glances • Slumped posture • Constantly shifting weight • Wringing hands • Weak or whiny voice	• Qualifiers ("maybe," "kind of") • Fillers ("uh," "you know," "well") • Negaters ("It's not really that important"; "I'm not sure")

SOURCE: Adapted in part from J.A. Waters, "Managerial Assertiveness," *Business Horizons*, September–October 1982, pp 24–29.

steady, and audible voice, and selective interruptions. When speaking to employees, they should avoid non-verbal behaviours that can be interpreted as aggressive, such as glaring and threatening gestures. They should also avoid non-assertive behaviours such as little eye contact, slumped posture, and a weak or whiny voice. Appropriate verbal behaviours include direct and unambiguous language. The use of "I" messages instead of "you" statements minimize defensiveness, such as: *"Youngsook, I was disappointed with your report because it contained typographical errors,"* rather than *"Youngsook, your report was poorly done."* When "I" statements are used, it basically describes personal feelings about someone's performance or behaviour instead of delivering blame. We'll spend more time discussing the language of conflict in the next chapter.

Scenario #2: **How do you say *no* to someone?**

Answer: We all get asked to do things we really don't want to do. Employees may be asked by their supervisor to share office resources or ideas, or may be told to take a three-day professional development course that employees feel they don't need. The communication goal in these cases is to say *no* in an assertive manner. Use "I" statements whenever possible to speak for yourself, and remember that it is okay to say *no*. Keep these four points in mind: 1) Don't feel pressured to say *yes* or *no* on the spot. Take time to think over the request; 2) Be honest and start the response saying *no*. It's easier to be steadfast in a commitment to saying no if you start out by saying the word up front; 3) Use non-verbal assertive behaviours to reinforce words, such as shaking your head back and forth while saying the word *no* or looking into the requester's eyes as you say no—but don't glare; and 4) Use verbal assertive behaviours such as saying *no* in a firm direct voice.

SOURCES OF NON-VERBAL COMMUNICATION

Non-verbal communication is "any message, sent or received independent of the written or spoken word. [It] includes such factors as use of time and space, distance between persons when conversing (talking), use of colour, dress, walking behaviour, standing, positioning, seat arrangement, office locations and furnishings."[25]

Experts estimate that 65 percent to 90 percent of every conversation is partially interpreted through non-verbal communication.[26] It is therefore important to ensure that your non-verbal signals are consistent with your intended verbal messages. Because of the prevalence of non-verbal communication and its significant effect on organizational behaviour (including, but not limited to, perceptions of others, hiring decisions, work attitudes, turnover, and the acceptance of one's ideas in a presentation), it is important that all employees become consciously aware of the sources of non-verbal communication. Take a look at Figure 7.4 and try to guess what is being communicated in each of the pictures. You may want to compare your impressions with a friend to see if they are the same.

Body Movements and Gestures   Body movements, such as leaning forward or backward, and gestures, such as pointing, provide additional non-verbal information that can either enhance or detract from the communication process. Open body positions, such as legs that are not crossed and arms relaxed along the side, communicate openness, warmth, and availability for communication. *Defensiveness* is communicated by gestures such as folded arms, crossed hands, and crossed legs. Although it is both easy and fun to interpret body movements and gestures, it is important to remember that body-language analysis is subjective, easily misinterpreted, and highly dependent on the context and cross-cultural differences.[27] As a result, all employees need to be careful when trying to interpret body movements. Inaccurate interpretations can create additional "noise" in the communication process.

Touch   Touching is another powerful non-verbal cue. People tend to touch those they like. A meta-analysis of gender differences in touching indicated that women do more touching during conversations than men.[28] Touching conveys an impression of warmth and caring and can be used to create a personal bond between people. Be careful about touching people from diverse cultures, however, as norms for touching vary significantly around the world.[29]

Facial Expressions   Facial expressions convey a wealth of information. Smiling, for instance, typically represents warmth, happiness, or friendship, whereas frowning conveys dissatisfaction or anger. Do you think these interpretations apply to different cross-cultural groups? A summary of relevant research revealed that the association between facial expressions and emotions varies across cultures.[30] A smile, for example, does not convey the same emotion in different countries. Therefore, managers, supervisors, and team leaders need to be careful in interpreting facial expressions among diverse groups of employees.

> *Non-verbal communication*
>
> Messages sent through means other than spoken or written words.

FIGURE 7.4 Non-verbal Communication

Try and guess what is being communicated in each of the photographs below.

Hand Gestures:

Facial Expressions:

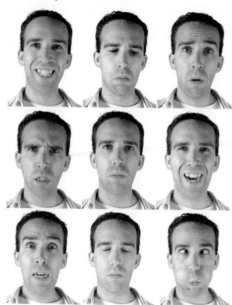

Body Movements:

Eye Contact & Touch:

Eye Contact Eye contact is a strong non-verbal cue that varies across cultures. Westerners are taught at an early age to look at their parents when spoken to. In contrast, Asians are taught to avoid eye contact with a parent or superior to show obedience and subservience (passive).[31] Once again, supervisors should be sensitive to different orientations toward maintaining eye contact with diverse employees.

Practical Tips It is important to have good non-verbal communication skills in light of the fact that they are related to the development of positive interpersonal relationships. Communication experts offer the following advice to improve non-verbal communication skills:[32]

Positive non-verbal actions that help communication:

- Maintaining appropriate eye contact
- Occasionally using affirmative nods to indicate agreement
- Smiling and showing interest
- Leaning slightly toward the speaker
- Keeping your voice low and relaxed
- Being aware of your facial expressions

Actions to avoid:

- Licking your lips or playing with your hair or moustache
- Turning away from the person you are communicating with
- Closing your eyes and displaying uninterested facial expressions such as yawning
- Excessively moving in your chair or tapping your feet
- Using an unpleasant tone and speaking too quickly or too slowly
- Biting your nails, picking your teeth, or constantly adjusting your glasses

ACTIVE LISTENING

Some communication experts contend that listening is the keystone communication skill for employees involved in sales, customer service, or management. In support of this conclusion, listening effectiveness is positively associated with customer satisfaction and negatively associated with employee intentions to quit. Poor communication between employees and management is also cited as a primary cause of employee discontent and turnover.[33] Listening skills are particularly important for all of us because we spend a great deal of time listening to others. You are encouraged to complete Self-Assessment Exercise #2 "Active Listening Skills Inventory" before moving on further.

Listening involves much more than hearing a message. Hearing is merely the physical component of listening. *Listening* is the process of *actively* decoding and interpreting verbal messages. Listening requires cognitive attention and information processing; hearing does not. With these distinctions in mind, we examine listening styles and offer some practical advice for becoming a more effective listener.

> *Listening*
>
> Actively decoding and interpreting verbal messages.

Listening Styles Communication experts believe that people listen with a preferred listening style. While people may lean toward one dominant listening style, we tend to use a combination of two or three. There are five dominant listening styles: appreciative, empathetic, comprehensive, discerning, and evaluative.[34] Let's consider each style.

Appreciative listeners listen in a relaxed manner, preferring to listen for pleasure, entertainment, or inspiration. They tend to tune out speakers who provide no amusement or humour in their communications. *Empathetic* listeners interpret messages by focusing on the emotions and body language being displayed by the speaker, as well as the presentation media. They also tend to listen without judging. *Comprehensive* listeners make sense of a message by first organizing specific thoughts and actions and then integrating this information by focusing on relationships among ideas. These listeners prefer logical presentations without interruptions. *Discerning* listeners attempt to understand the main message and determine important points. They like to take notes and prefer logical presentations. Finally, *evaluative* listeners listen analytically and continually formulate arguments and challenges to what is being said. They tend to accept or reject messages based on personal beliefs, ask a lot of questions, and can become interruptive.

You can improve your listening skills by first becoming aware of the effectiveness of the different listening styles you use in various situations. This awareness can then help you to modify your style to fit a specific situation. For example, if you are watching the comedy channel on TV, then an appreciative style would be appropriate. If you are a journalist hired to cover an upcoming debate between the candidates running for prime minister, then you may want to focus on using a comprehensive and discerning style. In contrast, an evaluative style may be more appropriate if you are listening to a sales presentation.[35]

Becoming a More Effective Listener Effective listening is a learned skill that requires effort and motivation—it takes energy and desire to really listen to others. Unfortunately, although it may seem like there are no rewards for listening, there are negative consequences when you don't. Think of a time, for example, when

Active Listening Skills Inventory

INSTRUCTIONS: This self-assessment is design to help you gauge your strengths and weakness on various dimensions of active listening. Think back to face-to-face conversations you have had with a co-worker or client in the office, hallway, factory floor, or other setting. Indicate the extent that each category to the right describes your behaviour during those conversations. Answer each item as truthfully as possible so that you get an accurate estimate of where your active listening skills need improvement.

Question	Never	Infrequently	Sometimes	Frequently	Always
1 I keep an open mind about people's point of view until they have finished talking.					
2 When listening, I mentally sort out people's ideas in a way that makes sense to me.					
3 I stop speakers and give my opinion when I disagree with something they have said.					
4 People can tell when I'm not concentrating on what they are saying.					
5 I don't evaluate what people are saying until they have finished talking.					
6 When someone takes a long time to present a simple idea, I let my mind wander to other things.					
7 I jump into conversations to present my views rather than wait and risk forgetting what I wanted to say.					
8 I nod my head and gesture to show I'm interested in the conversation.					
9 I keep focused on what people are saying to me, even when they don't sound interesting.					
10 Rather than organizing people's ideas, I expect them to summarize the ideas for me.					
11 I say things like "I see" or "uh-huh" so people know that I'm really listening to them.					
12 While listening, I concentrate of what is being said, and regularly organize the information.					
13 While people are talking, I quickly determine whether I like or dislike their ideas.					
14 I pay close attention to what people are saying even when they are explaining something I already know.					
15 I don't give my opinion until I'm sure others have finished talking.					

Feedback:

As a basis for comparison in assessing your listening skills, you obtained a score of____out of 75 (each response is worth from 1 to 5 points). Responses are organized according to six dimensions of active listening: avoiding, interruption, postponing evaluation, showing interest, maintaining interest, and organizing information.

SOURCE: Adapted from *Active Listening Skills Inventory*, © 2000, Steven L. McShane.

someone did not pay attention to you by looking at her watch or doing some other activity, such as typing on a keyboard. How did you feel? You may have felt put down, unimportant, or offended. In turn, such feelings can erode the quality of interpersonal relationships, as well as fuel job dissatisfaction, lower productivity, and result in poor customer service. Listening is an important skill that can be improved by avoiding the 10 habits of bad listeners, while cultivating the 10 good listening habits (see Table 7.3).

In addition, a communication expert suggests that we can all improve our listening skills by adhering to the following three fundamental recommendations:[36]

1. Attend closely to what's being said, not to what you want to say next.
2. Allow others to finish speaking before taking your turn.
3. Repeat back what you've heard to give the speaker the opportunity to clarify the message.

WOMEN AND MEN COMMUNICATE DIFFERENTLY

Women and men have communicated differently since the dawn of time. These differences can create communication problems that undermine productivity and interpersonal communication. Gender-based differences in communication are partly caused by linguistic (language use) styles commonly used by women and men. Deborah Tannen, a communication expert, explains it this way:

Linguistic style refers to a person's characteristic speaking pattern. It includes such features as directness or indirectness, pacing and pausing, word choice, and the use of such elements as jokes, figures of speech, stories, questions, and apologies. In other words, linguistic style is a set of culturally learned signals by which we not only communicate what we mean but also interpret others' meaning and evaluate one another as people.[37]

Linguistic style not only helps explain communication differences between women and men, but it also influences our perceptions of others' confidence, competence, and abilities. Increased awareness of linguistic styles can thus improve communication accuracy and your communication competence (see the Focus on Diversity feature box for more on this topic). This section strives to increase your understanding of interpersonal communication between women and men by discussion alternative explanations for differences in linguistic styles, various communication differences

TABLE 7.3

THE KEYS TO EFFECTIVE LISTENING

KEYS TO EFFECTIVE LISTENING	THE BAD LISTENER	THE GOOD LISTENER
1. Capitalize on thought speed	Tends to daydream	Stays with the speaker, mentally summarizes the message, weighs evidence, and listens between the lines
2. Listen for ideas	Listens for facts	Listens for central or overall ideas
3. Find an area of interest	Tunes out uninteresting speakers or subjects	Listens for any useful information
4. Judge content, not delivery	Tunes out dry or monotone speakers	Assesses content by listening to entire message before making judgments
5. Hold your fire	Gets too emotional or worked up by something said by the speaker and enters into an argument	Withholds judgment until comprehension is complete
6. Work at listening	Does not expend energy on listening	Gives the speaker full attention
7. Resist distractions	Is easily distracted	Fights distractions and concentrates on the speaker
8. Hear what is said	Shuts out or denies unfavourable information	Listens to both favourable and unfavourable information
9. Challenge yourself	Resists listening to presentations of difficult subject matter	Treats complex presentations as exercise for the mind
10. Use handouts, overheads, or other visual aids	Does not take notes or pay attention to visual aids	Takes notes as required and uses visual aids to enhance understanding of the presentation

SOURCES: Derived from N. Skinner, "Communication Skills," *Selling Power,* July/August 1999, pp 32–34; and G. Manning, K. Curtis, and S. McMillen, *Building the Human Side of Work Community* (Cincinnati, OH: Thomson Executive Press, 1996), pp 127–54.

GENDER DIFFERENCES IN COMMUNICATION

Research demonstrates that women and men communicate differently in a number of ways. Below are ten different communication patterns that vary between genders. There are two important issues to keep in mind about the tendencies identified: (1) They are not stereotypes for all men and women. Some men are less likely to boast about their achievements, and some women are less likely to share the credit. The point is that there are always exceptions to the rules; and (2) Your linguistic style influences perceptions about your confidence, competence, and authority.

These judgments may, in turn, affect your future job assignments and subsequent promotability. For example, there could be a male who downplays any uncertainties he has about issues and asks very few questions. He does this even when he is unsure about an issue being discussed. In contrast, there could be a female who is more forthright at admitting when she does not understand something and tends to ask a lot of questions. This could lead some people to perceive the male as more competent than the female because he displays confidence and acts as if he understands the issues being discussed.

1. Men are less likely to ask for information or directions in a public situation that would reveal their lack of knowledge.
2. In decision making, women are more likely to downplay their certainty; men are more likely to downplay their doubts.
3. Women tend to apologize even when they have done nothing wrong. Men tend to avoid apologies as signs of weakness or concession.
4. Women tend to accept blame as a way of smoothing awkward situations. Men tend to ignore blame and place it elsewhere.
5. Women tend to temper criticism with positive buffers. Men tend to give criticism directly.
6. Women tend to insert unnecessary and unwarranted thank-yous in conversations. Men may avoid thanks altogether as a sign of weakness.
7. Women tend to ask "What do you think?" to build consensus. Men often perceive that question to be a sign of incompetence and lack of confidence.
8. Women tend to give directions in indirect ways, a technique that may be perceived as confusing, less confident, or manipulative by men.
9. Men tend to usurp (take) ideas stated by women and claim them as their own. Women tend to allow this process to take place without protest.
10. Women use softer voice volume to encourage persuasion and approval. Men use louder voice volume to attract attention and maintain control.

SOURCE: From Dayle M. Smith, *Women at Work: Leadership for the Next Century*, 1st ed. Copyright@ 2000. Reproduced by permission of Pearson Education, Inc., Upper Saddle River, New Jersey.

between women and men, and recommendations for improving communication across the gender divide.

Why Do Linguistic Styles Vary Between Women and Men?
Although researchers do not completely agree on the cause of communication differences between women and men, there are two competing explanations that involve the well-worn debate between nature and nurture. The first is based on researchers who believe that interpersonal differences between women and men are due to inherited biological differences between the sexes. More specifically, this perspective, which also is called the *Darwinian perspective* or *evolutionary psychology*, attributes gender differences in communication to drives, needs, and conflicts associated with reproductive strategies used by women and men. For example, proponents would say that males

communicate more aggressively, interrupt others more than women, and hide their emotions because they have an inherent desire to possess features attractive to females to compete with other males for purposes of mate selection. Although males may not be competing for mate selection during a business meeting, evolutionary psychologists propose that men cannot turn off their biologically-based determinants of behaviour.[38]

In contrast, the second explanation, based on social role theory, contends that females and males learn ways of speaking as children growing up. Research shows that girls learn conversational skills and habits that focus on rapport and relationships, whereas boys learn skills and habits that focus on status and hierarchies. Accordingly, women come to view communication as a network of connections in which conversations are negotiations for closeness. This orientation leads

Men and women possess different communication styles. Do you think that these differences can impede brainstorming sessions like the one shown here?

women to seek and give confirmation and support more so than men. Men, on the other hand, see conversations as negotiations in which people try to achieve and maintain the upper hand. It thus is important for males to protect themselves from others' attempts to put them down or push them around. This perspective increases a male's need to maintain independence and avoid failure.[39]

Improving Communication between Women and Men
Author Judith Tingley suggests that women and men should learn to 'genderflex', which entails the temporary use of communication behaviours typical of the other gender to increase the potential for influence.[40]

In contrast, Deborah Tannen recommends that everyone needs to become aware of how linguistic styles work and how they influence our perceptions and judgments. She believes that knowledge of linguistic styles help to ensure that people with valuable insights or ideas get heard. Consider how gender-based linguistic differences affect who gets heard at a meeting:

Those who are comfortable speaking up in groups, who need little or no silence before raising their hands, or who speak out easily without waiting to be recognized are far more like to get heard at meetings. Those who refrain from talking until it's clear that the previous speaker is finished, who wait to be recognized, and who are inclined to link their comments to those of others will do fine at a meeting where everyone else is following the same rules but will have a hard time getting heard in a meeting with people whose styles are more like the first pattern. Given the socialization typical of boys and girls, men are more likely to have

learned the first style and women the second, making meetings more congenial for men than for women.[41]

Knowledge of these linguistic differences can help managers devise methods to ensure that everyone's ideas are heard and given fair credit both in and out of meetings. Furthermore, it is useful to consider the organizational strengths and limitations of your linguistic style. You may want to consider modifying a linguistic characteristic that is a detriment (negative effect) to perceptions of your confidence, competence, and authority. In conclusion, cross-gender communication can be improved by remembering that women and men have different ways of saying the same thing.

THE GRAPEVINE LO 4

There are two types of communication channels within an organization: formal and informal. The formal channels are authorized and used by all employees in a common and open manner. Formal channels follow structural etiquette in a public manner; as a result, the process takes time to "get the message out." Examples include staff notices, public forums, minutes of meetings, client briefing reports, and all other types of documents approved and/or written by management. Information received through formal channels can be considered accurate.

An *informal communication channel* does not follow the chain of command; it skips management levels and bypasses lines of authority. The *grapevine* represents the unofficial communication system of the organization and covers all types of communication media. For example, people can just as easily pass along information with email, face-to-face conversations, or telephone calls. Although the grapevine can be a source of inaccurate rumours, it functions positively as an early warning signal for organizational changes, a way to create organizational changes and to embed organizational culture, a mechanism for fostering group cohesiveness, and a way to get employee and customer feedback. For example, research shows that employees and consumers use the grapevine as a frequent source of information. Its use has increased with the advent of the Internet and instant messaging.

People who consistently pass along grapevine information to others are called *liaison individuals* or gossips:

Informal communication channel

Does not follow the chain of command or legitimate organizational structure.

Grapevine

Unofficial communication system that follows no chain of authority or formal structure.

Liaison individuals

Those who consistently pass along grapevine information to others.

About 10 percent of the employees on an average grapevine will be highly active participants. They serve as liaisons with the rest of the staff members who receive information but spread it to only a few other people. Usually these liaisons are friendly, outgoing people who are in positions that allow them to cross departmental lines.[42]

Effective managers monitor the pulse of work groups by regularly communicating with known liaisons.

In contrast to liaison individuals, *organizational moles* use the grapevine for a different purpose. They obtain information, often negative, to enhance their power and status. They do this by secretly reporting their perceptions and hearsay about the difficulties, conflicts, or failure of other employees to people with influence within the organization. This enables moles to switch attention away from themselves and to position themselves as more capable than others. Management should attempt to create an open, trusting environment that discourages mole behaviour because it can destroy teamwork, create conflict, and impair productivity.

> **Organizational moles**
>
> Those who use the grapevine to enhance their power and status.

Research about the grapevine provides the following insights: (1) it is faster than formal channels; (2) it is about 75 percent accurate; (3) people rely on it when they are insecure, threatened, or faced with organizational changes; and (4) employees use the grapevine to acquire the majority of their on-the-job information.[43]

The key recommendation for all employees is to understand the grapevine and listen to what is going on within it to remain informed. However, do not participate in it, otherwise you become part of the problem. For managers, the same advice applies, plus one additional recommendation: Do not try and control the grapevine—there are too many variables to keep track of and it's a waste of energy. Besides, there are other more important things to do for the organization.

Communication in the Age of Information Technology

Imagine how a universal language would make worldwide communication much easier. While there may be no universally understood written and spoken languages, a universal digital language of 1s and 0s is reshaping the way we live, work, and play. Digitized words (wireless email on a smartphone), pictures (video clips on YouTube or images on Instagram), sounds (talking on an iPhone or listening to music with your iPad), and motions (hitting and throwing on a Wii game) are conveniently packaged and readily shared communication content. In turn, the transmission of digitized content has been revolutionized by technologies such as the Internet, communication satellites, and Wi-Fi. Put it all together and we have virtually immediate access to unprecedented amounts of information and globe-spanning communication opportunities.

The purpose of this concluding section is to explore how the digital communication revolution is affecting organizational behaviour, both positively and negatively. For example, in the Skills & Best Practices feature box, we highlight the results of a recent Canadian survey that explored the various organizational applications as well as those implications related to social media usage. Beyond this, however, our focus is not on the technological fine points of digital communication innovations (e.g., cloud computing, mobile Internet, texting, blogging, and social networking on Facebook and Twitter),[44] but rather on how digital communication affects how we act and interact in work settings. For instance, researchers want to know if "peers rate each other differently depending on what medium they use. It turns out people are far more likely to trash their colleagues via email than when (they are) filling out paper forms."[45] Also, we are interested in assessing the impact of communication technology on employee productivity. For example,

(a) recent study found that in one organization the employees with the most extensive personal digital networks were 7 percent more productive than their colleagues—so Wikis and Web 2.0 tools may indeed improve productivity. In the same organization, however, the employees with the most cohesive face-to-face networks were 30 percent more productive. Electronic tools may well be suited for information discovery, but face-to-face communication . . . best supports information integration.[46]

More and faster digital communication does not necessarily mean *better* communication.

After highlighting two strategic concerns for management, we discuss eight norms of the Internet Generation, the dynamics of work-connecting technologies, and some unintended consequences of today's communication and information technologies.

STRATEGIC CONCERNS: SECURITY, SABOTAGE, AND PRIVACY

Because much of today's communication involves complex Internet-linked computer systems, careless and malicious actions can wreak havoc in terms of costly downtime and lost or stolen data. Of course, this

Skills & Best Practices

Mobile and Social Media Use in Canadian Private Companies

According to a recent *PwC Business Insights Survey* of 400 Canadian private companies CEO's, mobile and social media platforms are transforming the way business gets done in some areas. For example, three-quarters of the survey's respondents said they have plans to invest in mobile while 72 percent said they plan to use social media in the future. Other findings include 47 percent of respondents planning to use social media for sales and marketing purposes; 34 percent plan to use social media in their organizations to attract and retain talent and 16 percent said they want to use social media to foster internal new-idea collaboration. What are the implications of such statistics? From an overall industry perspective, the majority of Canadian private businesses are embracing such media as part of their daily practices in some sort of way.

From an employee perspective, the implications are pretty clear: those applicants who have technical knowledge and skills in using mobile or social media will be highly desirable when it comes to seeking positions in the sales and marketing areas of organizations. In addition, there is an opportunity for growth in the human resource departments of organizations who will be demanding employees that can assist in transforming the recruitment/selection processes using such technology. The skill of communicating and collaborating with others using mobile and social media will be a positive.

From an employer's point of view, businesses need to make an investment in social media in order for them to be effective and stay ahead of their competitors. How? First, by attracting the best applicants with such tech saavy skills. Second, by giving consumers an active voice to be part of the development process when collaborating on the kinds of products and services they want. Third, the ability to innovate and create with peers and companies in real time which means bringing new ideas to market sooner rather than later. As Tahir Ayub, PwC's Canadian private company services leader says, "They need to innovate by embracing and using social media and other digital technologies because it's a business imperative."

SOURCE: One-third of employers using social media to recruit, retain *Canadian HR Reporter* October 23, 2012 http://www.hrreporter.com/articleview/16516-one-third-of-employers-using-social-media-to-recruit-retain

---

includes mobile devises like smartphones that have the capability to access data from remote sites. Any discussion of digital communication and information technology must necessarily address the twin concerns of security and privacy. Failure in those areas compromises the integrity and reliability of the entire electronic communication process. Experts say the losses resulting from Internet crime are estimated to be well above the hundreds of millions; because companies are reluctant to acknowledge Internet fraud for fear of bad publicity, only a small fraction gets reported. While some fraud is unintentional, a survey with disturbing results conducted by the mega-research firm of Harris Interactive for SailPoint Technologies reported that some employees actually would consider profiting from proprietary information (see the International OB feature box for key findings).

Key findings in a global study from Cisco found that 7 out of 10 young employees frequently ignore IT policies.[47] The three-part Cisco report found that the desire for on-demand access to information is so ingrained in the incoming generation of employees that many young professionals take extreme measures to access the Internet, even if it compromises their company or their own security.. Such behaviour includes secretly using neighbours' wireless connections, sitting outside of business locations to access free WiFi networks, and borrowing other people's devices without supervision. "The role of IT in any business is to successfully bring together technology architectures and business architectures," says Rebecca Jacoby, CIO of Cisco. "As workforces become increasingly mobile, the shift in IT infrastructure means that security and policy are no longer an add-on but the highest priority." These younger employee demands are placing greater pressure on recruiters, hiring managers, IT departments, and corporate cultures to allow more flexibility in the hope the next wave of talent can provide an edge over competitors.

HERE COMES THE HUGE INTERNET GENERATION

We now merge our discussion of security and privacy with something we spoke about in Chapter 4—the emergence of the Gen Y generation into the Canadian workforce. Gen Y (sometimes called Digitals or the New Generation) are demanding new balance in their lives and they're bringing a new style and attitude to

EMPLOYEES WILLING TO EXPOSE COMPANIES TO INTERNAL SABOTAGE AND THEFT

An alarming number of employees would be willing to expose their companies to internal sabotage and theft, according to a survey of 3,484 employees in Great Britain, Australia, and the United States. Forty eight percent of British, 29 percent of Australian, and 22 percent of American employees who have access to their employers' or clients' private data say they would feel comfortable doing something with that data, intentionally or accidentally. Further, 27 percent of British, 12 percent of Australian, and 10 percent of American employees with access admitted they would forward electronic files to a non-employee. One-quarter (24 percent) of British workers also said they would be comfortable profiting from proprietary information by selling it online.

EXCERPT: "Possibility of internal sabotage 'alarming'" HR By The Numbers, *Canadian HR Reporter*, August 15, 2011, p 4 news.

---

the workplace. They are the biggest population bulge since the Baby Boomers, and all 6.7 million of them live their lives in a hyped-up world of multi-media, multi-tasking, and constant change that was shaped by the Internet and digital communication technologies.[48] Author, consultant, and University of Toronto professor Don Tapscott, in his book *Grown Up Digital: How the New Generation Is Changing Your World*, offers this overview of Gen Y:

> As talent, the Net Gen (Gen Y) is already trans-forming the workforce. The biggest generation ever is flooding into a talent vortex being created by the expansion of the global economy, the mobility of labour, and the fastest and biggest generational retirement ever. They are bringing new approaches to collaboration, knowledge sharing, and innovation in businesses and governments around the world. There is strong evidence that those organizations that embrace these new ways of working experience better performance, growth, and success. To win the battle for talent, organizations need to rethink many aspects of how they recruit, compensate, develop, collaborate with, and supervise talent. I believe the very idea of management is changing.[49]

Years of focus groups and interviews with nearly 10,000 people worldwide (with an emphasis on young people) let Tapscott and his research team to identify eight Net Gen norms (see Table 7.4). These norms reflect general patterns of experiences, attitudes, preferences, and expectations. Net Gen members expect the same instant access to comprehensive information and people—and the accompanying empowerment—in their work lives

as they had growing up and going to school. Change-resistant managers who stubbornly stand in the way of Net Gen's digital lifelines will get run over.

How many of the eight New Gen norms in Table 7.4 are evident in this recent situation?

> Like just about every twenty-something, Jamie Varon, 23, had her heart set on working at Twitter. She had already applied for a position through the company's website. And asked a contact at Google to put in a good word for her. And showed up at the company's headquarters with a bag of cookies in an attempt to charm a recruiter into talking to her. But she still hadn't landed an interview. What Varon did next made her feel a little crazy. But then, it's a crazy time to be looking for a job. She created a website called twittershouldhireme.com, including her resumé, recommendations, and a blog tracking her quest. Within 24 hours the company contacted her. She had a lunch meeting set up at Twitter, and in the meantime got two job offers from tech companies that had noticed her site.[50]

THE TWO FACES OF TELECOMMMUTING/ TELEWORKING

Digital communication has significantly altered the traditional linkages between work, place, and time. This is especially true for knowledge workers who do not produce tangible products such as cars or provide tangible services such as haircuts. Thanks to advances in telecommunications technology and Internet tools such as Web conference, many variations of telecommuting are possible.[51] Rather than the person physically traveling

TABLE 7.4

WHAT MAKES THE INTERNET GENERATION TICK? EIGHT NORMS

1. **Freedom.** A desire to experience new and different things takes precedence over long-term commitments. Flexible work hours and locations, a say in how things are done, and freedom of choice are desirable.

2. **Customization.** Everything from personalized cell phone ring tones to lifestyle choices to unique Facebook layouts make life interesting and fun.

3. **Scrutiny.** With both trash and treasure on the Internet, Net Geners (Gen Ys) have learned to be skeptical, check things out, and ask probing questions.

4. **Integrity.** New Geners (Gen Ys) care about Integrity—being honest, considerate, transparent, and abiding by their commitments. Trust in employers, people, and a product is important. Some ethical elasticity (i.e., pirating music and plagiarizing) when in cyberspace is an open issue.

5. **Collaboration.** Relationships are a key importance. They know how to work and play with others and are eager to offer up opinions and suggestions. Volunteering is valued.

6. **Entertainment.** A job should not be a life sentence; it should be both challenging and fun. The Internet is a productivity tool, personal communication device, information source, and a "fun tool of choice." Multi-tasking is a way of life to keep things moving and interesting.

7. **Speed.** "They're used to instant response. 24/7. Video games give them instant feedback; Google answers their inquiries within nanoseconds." Rapid-fire texting, instant messaging, and Tweeting are far faster and superior to email and slow organizational decision making. Fast, accurate, and helpful feedback on job performance is demanded.

8. **Innovation.** An impatience for new and different user experience is evident. "In the workplace, innovation means rejecting the traditional command-and-control devising work processes that encourage collaboration and creativity."

SOURCE: Quoted and adapted from discussion in D. Tapscott, *Grown Up Digital: How the Net Generation is Changing Your World* (New York: McGraw-Hill, 2009), pp 73–96.

to and from an office, *telecommuting* allows the work to travel electronically to and from the person's home. Wireless Internet access and cell phones have further evolved telecommuting into *teleworking* (connecting to the office from practically anywhere). All this has altered the traditional work and place connection, as employees can now perform their work in various locations rather than always physically gathering in one place. Because of computerized memory capabilities, the traditional work and time connection also has been altered. Employees in different locations and time zones can work simultaneously (called synchronous communication) and team members can work on the same project at different times (asynchronous communication).

Use and Benefits An expert recently listed the benefits of telecommuting: "(1) increases employee productivity, (2) increases employer attractiveness, (3) decreases operating costs, (4) increases operationality during a crisis, and (5) contributes to green initiatives."[52] Additionally, telecommuting can bring homebound, disabled, recovering, or semi-infirmed and confined people into the workforce.

Problems The benefits of telecommuting/teleworking have been documented primarily through testimonial claims rather than through rigorous research. While IBM reported saving $100 million in capital

> **Telecommuting/ Teleworking**
>
> Shifting work generally performed from the office to home or some other convenient location using advanced communication technologies.

facilities and equipment costs by letting 42 percent of its employees work from home, there are managerial doubts and negative research evidence accumulating. According to *BusinessWeek*, "(w)ell into the work-from-anywhere era, managers are beginning to ask: Are the underlings working remotely . . . or remotely working?"[53] Working from home, the grocery store, or the beach takes self-discipline. There also are career implications.

A survey of 1,300 executives from 71 countries found a general belief that people who telework are less likely to get promoted.[54] This is the 'out of sight, out of mind' dilemma. Another problem is a sense of professional isolation among teleworkers. In a recent study, "a matched sample of 261 professional-level teleworkers and their managers revealed that professional isolation negatively impacts job performance."[55]

SUSTAINING EFFECTIVE COMMUNICATION IN THE DIGITAL AGE

LO 5

The challenge that lies ahead for all contemporary organizations is how to maintain effective interpersonal communication while moving toward greater usage of electronic devices in the workplace. The notion of using capital assets (i.e., computers connected to the Internet, email systems, webcams and video conferencing equipment, smartphones, webinars, podcasts)

Telecommuting from home is a benefit that can be very motivating for some employees.

to enhance productivity has a clear accounting and economic advantage; however, the intrusive nature of some of these devises presents a balancing act that employees are going to have to either get used to or learn to control. Undoubtedly, the employer's mandate to find greater efficiencies in day-to-day operations will only continue, and at times compete with, the personal interests of employees who wish to keep their work lives somewhat separate from their personal lives. Being on call 24/7 may appeal to some, but not all, employees.

We're in a transitional phase between Baby Boomers who are holding on to many of the senior jobs in the workforce and who have witnessed the birth, evolution, and workplace application of these devises, and Gen Y (Net Gen) adults who have grown up with these items and consider electronic communication devises as standard issue. In fact, to many in this age group, there is an unmistakable preference for instant communication— and why not? From their perspective, it's affordable, available, and desirable.

As the use of electronic communication devises increases, employers will have to find ways to help some senior employees to overcome their feelings of fear and anxiety at using these items in the workplace. Developing and communicating policies around these issues, along with providing training, can certainly help this effort. For younger employees, the challenge will be to rein in their behaviour so they can maintain focus on their job. Because using these devises is second nature to many, these employees will see a short email chat or text-message exchange as not at all distracting. Again, training workshops that identify organizational objectives and expectations should support such employees.

Summary of Learning Objectives

LO 1 Illustrate the various components of the perceptual process model of communication. Communication is a process of consecutively linked elements. This model of communication depicts receivers as information processors who create the meaning of messages in their own mind. Because receivers' interpretations of messages often differ from those intended by senders, miscommunication is a common occurrence. The various components are: (1) the sender who encodes; (2) the message; (3) the medium; (4) the receiver who decodes; (5) create meaning; (6) feedback from receiver to sender; and (7) noise that can distort message.

LO 2 Describe at least eight barriers to effective communication. Every element of the perceptual model of communication is a potential process barrier. Personal barriers that commonly influence communication include: (1) the ability to effectively communicate; (2) the way people process and interpret information; (3) the level of interpersonal trust between people;

(4) the existence of stereotypes and prejudices; (5) the egos of the people communicating; (6) the ability to listen; (7) the natural tendency to evaluate or judge a sender's message; and (8) the inability to listen with understanding. Physical barriers pertain to distance, physical objects, time, and work and office noise. Semantic barriers show up as encoding and decoding errors because these phases of communication involve transmitting and receiving words and symbols. Cultural diversity is a key contributor to semantic barriers.

LO 3 **Contrast the communication styles of assertiveness, aggressiveness, and non-assertiveness.** An assertive style of communication is expressive and self-enhancing and is based on the ethical notion that it is not right or good to violate our own or others' basic human rights, such as the right to self-expression or the right to be treated with dignity and respect. In contrast, an aggressive style is expressive and self-enhancing, and strives to take unfair advantage of others. A non-assertive style is characterized by timid and self-denying behaviour. Non-assertiveness is ineffective because it gives the other person an unfair advantage. Employees may improve their communication competence by trying to be more assertive and less aggressive or non-assertive.

LO 4 **Explain the formal and informal communication channels.** There are two types of communication channels: formal and informal. The formal channels are authorized and used by all employees in a common and open manner. Formal channels follow structural protocol in a public manner; as a result, the process takes time to "get the message out." Examples include staff notices, public forums, minutes of meetings, client briefing reports, and all other types of documents approved and/or written by management. Information received through formal channels can be considered as accurate. An informal channel does not follow the chain of command; it skips management levels and bypasses lines of authority. The grapevine is an example of an unofficial communication channel. Information received through this channel travels quickly throughout the organization, it is estimated to be only about 75 percent accurate, and it is commonly referred to as office gossip.

LO 5 **Summarize the various factors involved in maintaining effective communication as organizations move toward using more digital devices in the workplace.** The challenges that lie ahead for all contemporary organizations include how to maintain effective interpersonal communication, minimize distractions, and improve productivity while moving toward greater use of digital devices in the workplace. The notion of using capital assets (i.e., computers connected to the Internet, electronic mail, video conferencing equipment, smartphones) to enhance productivity has a clear accounting and economic advantage. However, the intrusive nature of some of these devises presents a balancing act that employees are going to have to either get used to or learn to control. As the use of electronic communication devises increases, employers will have to find ways to help senior employees to overcome their feelings of fear and trepidation (cautionary behaviour) toward using these items in the workplace. Developing and communicating policies around these issues, along with training, can certainly help this effort. For younger employees, the challenge will be to rein in their behaviour so they maintain focus on their job. Because use of these devices is second nature to younger employees, they will see a short email chat or text-message exchange as not distracting at all. Again, training workshops that identify organizational objectives and expectations should support these employees.

Discussion Questions

1. What are some sources of noise that interfere with communication during a class lecture, an encounter with a professor in her office, or a movie?

2. Which barrier to effective communication is most difficult to reduce: process barriers or personal barriers? Explain.

3. What are the behavioural differences between hearing a song through your iPod and actively listening to a classroom presentation by your professor?

4. Review the "Practical Tips—Advice to Improve Non-Verbal Communication Skills" and explain the reasons behind avoiding each of the six negative behaviours. For example, what does it mean when a receiver looks away from the speaker?

5. Discuss the pros and cons of the existence of the grapevine in organizations. Suppose an organization wanted to 'kill' the grapevine. How easy do you think this would be?

Integration of OB Concepts—Discussion Questions

1. See Chapter 2 – What role does perception play in the communication process?

2. See Chapter 2 – Based on what this chapter says about Deborah Tannen's work around the communication style preferences between men and women, what role does perception play in gender differences? What effect might these misunderstandings and inaccurate perceptions have on gender stereotypes?

3. See Chapter 4 – How do the values of the various generations differ when it comes to the various types of communication? Review the Focus on Diversity feature box in Chapter 4 for help.

4. See Chapter 6 – Explain the role of effective communication at every stage of the group development process. Try to identify if or how the choice of language changes throughout.

Google Searches

1. **Google Search:** "Non-Verbal Communication Social Experiment" AND "Non-verbal Communication Functions" AND "Gestures Around The World" AND "Secrets of Body Language" Go to YouTube.ca and watch a few minutes of each. If non-verbal communication makes up such a large portion of every conversation (65–90 percent), how can the benefits from non-verbal communication be conveyed in the digital world? Discuss and share some possible solutions.

2. **Google Search:** "Deborah Tannen – The Official Website" Review the site of this well-known socio-linguistic professor and expert on the differences between men and women. Various samples are available for download/listening: *You Just Don't Understand* (Women and Men in Conversation) Simon & Schuster 1991 and *Talking From 9–5* (Women and Men At Work) Simon & Schuster 2004. Listen to these samples for free or purchase an audiobook for less than $7. Can you think of an example in your own life where a female

would describe a situation differently from how a male would describe the same situation? Share your examples with the class.

3. **Google Search:** "English Homonyms" AND "Canadianisms Contrasted and Compared to the US" Review both fun and lengthy lists. Does the English language have built-in barriers to effective communication? If you were a recent immigrant to Canada and heard Canadians speaking, do you think you would be confused and misunderstand the intention of a message? Explain and give examples where possible.

4. **Google Search:** "Social Networks, Data Leaks, and Operation Security – Israeli Defense Forces – March 4, 2010 Blogger" Read this article, summarize it, and share it with the class. Relate this article to the International OB feature box discussed in this chapter. Should corporations block such sites? Would it make a difference? Is any organization protected from such possible breach in unauthorized disclosure of confidential client or company plans?

Experiential Exercise

Corporate Canada Using Digital Media–A Group Exercise

PURPOSE: This exercise demonstrates the extent of use of digital communication tools by corporate Canada. You will need computer access to complete this assignment. Approx. Timing: 25–30 minutes.

ACTIVITY ASSIGNMENT

- Work in groups of 4–5 students each.
- Go to Google and search the website of each company listed in the table below.
- Review the home pages of these organizations and determine what kinds of digital tools they use.
- Compare and contrast the various sites. Make notes and fill in the table below.
- Which organization has the most variety? Which has the least?
- Are there any surprises in your findings? Which organization in your opinion is the most effective in their use? Be prepared to support your reasoning.
- Discuss among your team and, if time permits, share your findings with class.

Company	Twitter	Facebook	Blog	YouTube	Online Newsletter	Intranet Login Page	Contact List via Emails	Other (Webcast or Podcasts, RSS Feeds, etc.)
General Motors Canada								
Molson (Coors)								
Canadian HR Reporter								
Maple Leaf Entertainment								
Cisco Systems								
TD Canada Trust								
Your own school								

Go Ahead, Use Facebook

Wendy Wilkes is giving a presentation about Unilever's information technology to 30 new hires—most of them barely out of school—and they are not happy. They don't like the company-issued mobile phones and laptops (or lack thereof). The employee website is so 1990s since it doesn't have interactive features, such as Facebook. And they can't download iTunes or instant-messaging software to communicate with people outside the company.

Wilkes can certainly identify with their gripes. The 27-year-old manager also joined the maker of such consumer staples as Lipton, Slim-Fast, and Vaseline right out of college. In school, she was accustomed to using her Hotmail account from any computer. But from her desktop at work she has access to corporate email only. Not to mention that instant messaging—the foundation of her social life in school—is forbidden with anyone outside the company. "It was the amount of lockdown that surprised me the most," she says.

For anyone born after 1985, entering the workforce is a technological shock. Raised on Myspace.com and Wikipedia, these workers can't comprehend why they should have to wait 18 months for a company to build corporate software when they can download what they need instantly. "Technology is an important thing in my personal and work life, and I think the two of them should be connected," says Amy Johannigman, a 22-year-old college senior who worked at a company one summer where the use of social-networking sites was discouraged, camera phones verboten (forbidden), and the interns were told to limit personal emails.

Revolt In The Ranks

Corporate policy isn't stopping Johannigman's contemporaries. Sure, there are official policies against using gear the tech department hasn't sanctioned, but the sheer number of workers who are ignoring the rules makes enforcement nearly impossible. Consulting firm Forrester Research even coined a term for workers ignoring corporate policy and taking technology into their own hands: *Technology Populism*.

At Unilever, half of the desktop software and services used by employees come from outside the company, and a lot of it shouldn't be there—Skype and iTunes, to name just a couple. "We can't stop them," says Chris Turner, Unilever's chief technology officer. "They're not accepting no as an answer."

Neither did Wilkes. She joined Unilever with a degree in information management and soon became a member of the marketing department's support team, where she experienced Unilever's rigid rules firsthand. So Wilkes put together some ideas about how employees could be more productive using consumer technology and sent her thoughts to Turner.

About six months later, Turner offered Wilkes a new job, basically in her words, to "get involved in trying to make a difference." Now Wilkes is one of 13 so-called "consumerization architects" whose job is to spread the use of popular—and in many cases free—technology. For example, Wilkes is looking into letting employees install webcams so they can confer by videoconference and cut down on travel time.

Unilever is still testing how to give employees more digital freedom. It may move users outside the corporate firewall and allow them to connect via their own computers, provided they're using certain security technologies. Anecdotal evidence suggests that the savings could be millions of dollars. "We see this as a real opportunity to start altering the cost model to deliver IT," says Turner.

Turner's ideas are unpopular with some people in his own department. But, as he points out, the social and economic forces are overwhelming.

SOURCE: Reprinted from R. King, "Go Ahead, Use Facebook," August 25–September 1, 2008 issue of *BusinessWeek* by special permission. Copyright @ 2009 by The McGraw-Hill Companies, Inc.; Seven Twitter tools are discussed in R. Scoble, "Brand New Day," *Fast Company,* May 2009, p 52.

Discussion Questions

1. Have you ever been frustrated with out-of-date information technology in the workplace? If so, explain how it hampered your communication.

2. From a strategic standpoint, what are the arguments against uncontrolled information technology in the workplace?

3. As a top-level manager, what information technology policies would you put in place? What would you do to enforce those policies?

4. What is your personal stance on *Technology Populism?* What are the implications of your position for organizations?

5. What evidence of Net Gen (the Digital) norms (see Table 7.4) can you find in this case? Are they potentially positive or disruptive to organizational success? Explain.

6. How can Unilever's Wendy Wilkes give employees more digital freedom without endangering the company? Explain in terms of specific tools such as Skype, Webcam videoconferencing, iPods, Facebook, and Twitter.

The CONNECTion Zone Mc Graw Hill connect™

- The Presentation Assistant
- Ethical OB Dilemma
- Video Case

Practise and learn online with Connect.

CHAPTER 8

Conflict and Negotiation

I am having problems with my employees and need some advice. I have repeatedly caught workers conducting personal business on company time or calling in sick and then being seen at a social activity around town. I'm tired of employees sneaking out of the office to do personal errands. I have people on teams not getting along with one another for whatever reason. Oh, and one more thing—the office gossip has got to stop because it's hurting people. These things have become very annoying. How do I correct this?

—CONFLICTED AND CONCERNED

Conflict in the Workplace

Make no mistake—conflict is an unavoidable aspect of modern life. The workplace is comprised of individuals who have their own agenda items, timelines, and ideas of how to conduct their life and work priorities. At times, these can conflict with other competing factors, making the contemporary workplace ripe for conflict. The following major trends work together to make organizational conflict an expected part of the workplace:

- Constant change
- Greater employee diversity
- More teams (virtual and self-managed)
- Less face-to-face communication (more electronic interaction)
- A global economy with increased cross-cultural dealings

Dean Tjosvold, at Hong Kong's Lingnan University, notes that "Change (leads to) conflict, conflict (leads to) change"[1] and challenges us to do better with this realistic perspective:

> *Learning to manage conflict is a critical investment in improving how we, our families, and our organizations adapt and take advantage of change. Managing conflicts well does not insulate us from change, nor does it mean that we will always come out on top or get all that we want. However, effective conflict management helps us keep in touch with new developments and create solutions appropriate for new threats and opportunities.*[2]

As outlined in this chapter, conflict management and negotiation tools that can bring about resolution are available if you develop the ability and will to use them frequently. The choice is yours: Be aware of how to resolve conflict, or have conflict manage you.[3]

LO 1 Conflict: A Modern Perspective

A complete review of the conflict literature provides this consensus definition: "*conflict* is a process in which one party perceives that its interests are being opposed or negatively affected by another party."[4] The word *perceives* reminds us that sources of conflict can be real or imagined; the resulting conflict is the same. Conflict can escalate (strengthen) or de-escalate (weaken) over time. "The conflict process unfolds in a context, and whenever conflict, escalated or not, occurs, then the people arguing or third parties can attempt to manage it in some manner."[5] Therefore, current and future managers need to understand the dynamics of conflict and know how to handle it effectively (both as a person in an argument and as third parties). This call to action is supported by a recent survey asking employees what their manager's New Year's resolution should be. The number one response was, "Deal with workplace conflicts faster."[6]

> **Conflict**
>
> One party perceives its interests are being opposed or set back by another party.

THE LANGUAGE OF CONFLICT: METAPHORS, PRONOUNS, AND MEANING

Conflict is a complex subject for several reasons. Primary among them is the reality that conflict often carries a lot of emotional baggage.[7] Fear of losing or fear of change quickly raises the emotional stakes in a conflict. Conflicts

LO 1 Define *conflict, functional conflict,* and *dysfunctional conflict.*

LO 2 Identify the various antecedents (causes) of conflict.

LO 3 List two approaches an employee or manager can take to respond to each of the following: personality conflicts, intergroup conflict, and cross-cultural conflicts.

LO 4 Compare and contrast the five alternative styles for handling conflict.

LO 5 Assess the value of having third party interventions for conflict resolution, including the ADR and two negotiation processes.

also vary widely in magnitude. Conflicts have both participants and observers. Some observers may be interested and active, others disinterested and passive. Consequently, the term *conflict* can take on vastly different meanings, depending on the circumstances and one's involvement. For example, consider these three metaphors and accompanying workplace expressions:

- Conflict as war: "We shot down that idea."

- Conflict as opportunity: "What are all the possibilities for solving this problem?"

- Conflict as journey: "Let's search for common ground."[8]

Anyone viewing a conflict as war will try to win at all costs and wipe out the enemy. For example, Donald Trump has said, "In life, you have fighters and non-fighters. You have winners and losers. I am both a fighter and a winner."[9] Alternatively, those seeing a conflict as an opportunity and a journey will tend to be more positive, open-minded, and constructive. In a hostile world, combative and destructive war-like thinking often prevails. But typical daily workplace conflicts are *not* war. So when dealing with organizational conflicts, you are challenged to rely less on the metaphor and language of war, and more on the metaphors and language of *opportunity* and *journey*. You need to carefully monitor your choice of words in conflict situations.[10]

While explaining the three metaphors, conflict experts Kenneth Cloke and Joan Goldsmith made this observation that you should keep in mind for the balance of this chapter:

> *Conflict gives you an opportunity to deepen your capacity for empathy and intimacy with your opponent. Your anger transforms the "Other" into a stereotyped demon or villain. Similarly, defensiveness will prevent you from communicating openly with your opponents, or listening carefully to what they are saying. On the other hand, once you engage in dialogue with that person, you will resurrect the human side of their personality—and express your own as well.*

> *Moreover, when you process your conflicts with integrity, they lead to growth, increased awareness, and self-improvement. Uncontrolled anger, defensiveness, and shame defeat these possibilities. Everyone feels better when they overcome their problems and reach resolution, and worse when they succumb and fail to resolve them. It is a bitter truth that victories won in anger lead to long-term defeat. Those defeated turn away, feeling betrayed and lost, and carry this feeling with them into their next conflict.*

> *Conflict can be seen simply as a way of learning more about what is not working and discovering how to fix it. The usefulness of the solution depends on the depth of your understanding of the problem. This depends on your ability to listen to the issue as you would to a teacher, which depends on halting the cycle of escalation and searching for opportunities for improvement.*[11]

In Chapter 7 we mentioned the pronoun usage by people with certain communication styles, especially when they are involved in a conflicting situation. For purposes of a quick review, "You" is preferred by those who wish to deliver an angry message to the person they believe guilty of unacceptable behaviour; further, they are neither open to dialogue nor wishing to resolve an issue with anything less than aggressiveness. In contrast, the pronoun "I" is the preferred language for those wishing to speak for themselves using an assertive style; they are speaking to not escalate a situation. Instead, they are inviting further discussion between conflicting parties.

As you learn more about how individuals prefer to handle conflict, try to keep this simple *You* vs. *I* language rule in mind. It will help you understand the connection between communication and conflict, especially during a heated debate when it can be difficult to remain calm and rational. During such an episode, language choice can be the furthest thing from a person's mind. To explore the challenge of communicating in conflict, turn to the end of this chapter and complete the Experiential Exercise.

A CONFLICT CONTINUUM

Ideas about managing conflict underwent an interesting evolution during the 20th century. Initially, scientific management experts such as Frederick W. Taylor believed all conflict ultimately threatened management's authority, and thus had to be avoided or quickly resolved. Later, human relationists recognized the inevitability of conflict and advised both employees and managers to not only understand it, but also to learn to live with it. Emphasis remained on resolving conflict whenever possible.

Beginning in the 1970s, OB specialists realized conflict had both positive and negative outcomes, depending on its nature and intensity. This perspective introduced the revolutionary idea that organizations could suffer from *too little* conflict. Figure 8.1 illustrates the relationship between conflict intensity and outcomes.

Work groups, departments, or organizations experiencing too little conflict tend to be plagued by apathy, lack of creativity, indecision, and missed deadlines. Excessive conflict, on the other hand, can erode organizational performance because of political infighting, dissatisfaction, lack of teamwork, and turnover. Workplace

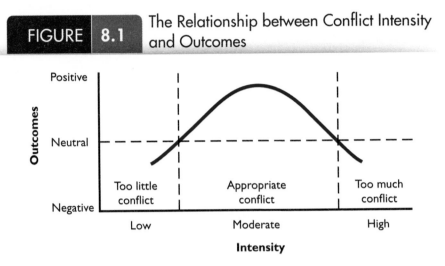

FIGURE 8.1 The Relationship between Conflict Intensity and Outcomes

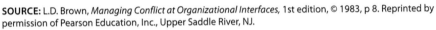

SOURCE: L.D. Brown, *Managing Conflict at Organizational Interfaces,* 1st edition, © 1983, p 8. Reprinted by permission of Pearson Education, Inc., Upper Saddle River, NJ.

The best CEOs I work with know how to exert pressure, say no, and start and win a fight when necessary. So much for teamwork? Actually, collaboration and confrontation aren't mutually exclusive. There's aggression—a basic survival mechanism—and then there's its tamer, more socially adaptive cousin, assertiveness, which can be deployed usefully, including with people working on the same side."

The need to be assertive comes up all the time. It's essential in negotiating contracts, rejecting bad work, criticizing a strategy, or firing (or defending) an employee. Yet some people will do almost anything to avoid confrontation...

aggression and violence can be the result of excessive conflict.[12] Appropriate types and levels of conflict energize people in constructive directions.[13]

FUNCTIONAL VERSUS DYSFUNCTIONAL CONFLICT

The distinction between *functional conflict* and *dysfunctional conflict* revolves around whether the organization's interests are served. According to one conflict expert,

> *Some [types of conflict] support the goals of the organization and improve performance; these are functional, constructive forms of conflict. They benefit or support the main purposes of the organization. Additionally, there are those types of conflict that hinder organizational performance; these are dysfunctional or destructive forms. They are undesirable and should be eliminated.[14]*

Functional conflict is commonly referred to in management circles as constructive or cooperative conflict.[15] In terms of what we just discussed about the language of conflict, those engaging in functional conflict apply a win–win attitude to solve problems and find common ground. Karen Duncum, owner of Star Performance Consulting, is against avoiding conflict and instead recommends turning conflict into cooperation (see the Skills & Best Practices feature box discussing Duncum's approach). Organizational psychologist Kerry Sulkowicz recently drew an important distinction between aggressiveness and assertiveness when giving this advice about functional conflict:

Functional conflict

Serves an organization's interests.

Dysfunctional conflict

Threatens the interests of an organization.

The key, oddly enough, is to empathize with the person you're confronting. To that end, gather useful facts rather than impressions, offer alternatives along with your objections, and limit comments to the deed, not the does. Your opponent won't hear anything you say after an attack on his or her character. And don't be self-righteous. Or gloat if you prevail. Nobody likes a poor winner.[16]

ANTECEDENTS (CAUSES) OF CONFLICT   LO 2

Certain situations produce more conflict than others. By knowing the causes of conflict, individuals are better able to anticipate conflict and take steps to resolve it if it becomes dysfunctional. The following situations tend to produce either functional or dysfunctional conflicts:

- Incompatible personalities or value systems
- Overlapping or unclear job boundaries
- Competition for limited resources
- Inter-department/inter-group competition
- Inadequate communication
- Interdependent tasks (e.g., one person cannot complete his assignment until others have completed their work)
- Organizational complexity (conflict tends to increase as the number of hierarchical layers and specialized tasks increase)

Skills & Best Practices

- Unreasonable or unclear policies, standards, or rules
- Unreasonable deadlines or extreme time pressure
- Collective decision making (the greater the number of people participating in a decision, the greater the potential for conflict)
- Unmet expectations (employees who have unrealistic expectations about job assignments, pay, or promotions are more prone to conflict)
- Unresolved or suppressed conflicts[17]

An antecedent of conflict: layoff survivors who typically complain about being overworked trying to meet unrealistic deadlines with limited resources.

Employees should be aware of these situations and avoid or resolve them. Proactive supervisors, managers, and team leaders should carefully read these early warnings and take appropriate action to manage them.

DESIRED CONFLICT OUTCOMES

Within organizations, conflict management is more than simply a mission to find agreement. If progress is to be made and dysfunctional conflict minimized, a broader agenda is in order. Tjosvold's cooperative conflict model (discussed in this chapter's introduction) calls for three desired outcomes:

1. **Agreement** But at what cost? Equitable and fair agreements are best. An agreement that leaves one party feeling exploited or defeated will tend to breed resentment and subsequent conflict.
2. **Stronger relationships** Good agreements enable conflicting parties to build bridges of goodwill and trust for future use. Moreover, conflicting parties who trust each other are more likely to keep their end of the bargain.
3. **Learning** Functional conflict can promote greater self-awareness and creative problem solving. Like the practice of management itself, successful conflict handling is learned primarily by doing. Knowledge of the concepts and techniques in this chapter is a necessary first step, but there is no substitute for hands-on practice. In a controversial world, there are plenty of opportunities to practise conflict management.[18]

FIGURE 8.2 Three Types of Organizational Conflict

Personality   Intergroup   Cross-cultural

 # Types of Conflict

Certain causes of conflict deserve a closer look. This section explores the nature and organizational implications of three common forms of conflict (see Figure 8.2): (1) personality conflict, (2) inter-group conflict, and (3) cross-cultural conflict. Our discussion of each type of conflict includes some practical tips.

PERSONALITY CONFLICTS

As discussed in Chapter 3, your *personality* is the package of stable traits and characteristics creating your unique identity. According to experts on the subject:

> Each of us has a unique way of interacting with others. Whether we are seen as charming, irritating, fascinating, nondescript, approachable, or intimidating depends in part on our personality, or what others might describe as our style. [19]

Given the many possible combinations of personality traits, it is clear why personality conflicts are inevitable. We define a **personality conflict** as interpersonal opposition based on personal dislike, disagreement, or different styles.

Workplace Incivility: The Seeds of Personality Conflict Somewhat akin to physical pain, chronic personality conflicts often begin with seemingly insignificant irritations. A pair of OB researchers recently offered this cautionary overview of the problem and its consequences:

> Incivility, or employees' lack of regard for one another, is costly to organizations in subtle and pervasive ways. Although uncivil behaviours occur commonly, many organizations fail to

Personality conflict

Interpersonal opposition driven by personal dislike or disagreement.

recognize them, few understand their harmful effects, and most managers and executives are ill-equipped to deal with them. Over the past eight years, as we have learned about this phenomenon through interviews, focus groups, questionnaires, experiments, and executive forums with more than 2,400 people across Canada and the US. We have found that incivility causes its targets, witnesses, and additional stakeholders to act in ways that erode organizational values and deplete organizational resources. Because of their experiences of workplace incivility, employees decrease work effort, time on the job, productivity, and performance. Where incivility is not curtailed, job satisfaction and organizational loyalty diminish as well. Some employees leave their jobs solely because of the impact of this subtle form of deviance. [20]

Vicious cycles of incivility need to be avoided, or broken early, with an organizational culture that places a high value on respect for coworkers. You may wish to go to Connect and take the self-assessment titled "Workplace Incivility: Are You Part of the Problem?" See the Law & Ethics feature box for more on the topic of what happens when incivility escalates within the workplace. In the end, managers and leaders need to act as caring and courteous role models. A positive spirit of cooperation, as opposed to one based on negativism and aggression, also helps. Proactive steps need to be taken because of these troubling statistics:

- From April 1, 2008 to March 31, 2009, Ontario Ministry of Labour Inspectors made 417 field visits and issued 351 orders related to violence in the workplace. [21]

WHEN INCIVILITY ESCALATES – BILL 168

Most people think of violence as a physical assault. However, with the 2010 amendment to the Occupational Health and Safety Act – Bill 168, Ontario has broadened the definition of workplace violence to include any act in which a person is abused, threatened, intimidated, or assaulted in the person's employment. Workplace violence includes:

- *Threatening behaviour* – such as shaking fists, destroying property, or throwing objects
- *Verbal or written threats* – any expression of intent to inflict harm
- *Harassment* – any behaviour that demeans, embarrasses, humiliates, annoys, alarms, or verbally abuses a person and that is known or would be expected to be unwelcome, including words, gestures, intimidation, bullying, or other inappropriate activities
- *Verbal abuse* – swearing, insults, or condescending language
- *Physical attacks* – hitting, shoving, pushing, or kicking

Being uncivil to the point of spreading hurtful rumours, engaging in disturbing gossip, spiteful office pranks, contributing to psychological trauma, or anger-related incidents—all of these would be covered by Bill 168. Most Canadian jurisdictions have a "general duty provision" in their Occupational Health and Safety legislation. Quebec has legislation regarding "psychological harassment" holding employers responsible for their employees' conduct.

The location of uncivil behaviour (and if escalated to violent incidents) is not limited to occur within a traditional workplace. Off-site business-related functions (conferences, trade shows), social events related to work, in clients' homes, or away from work but resulting from work (a threatening telephone call to your home, for example), are all included in current legislation.

SOURCES: Canadian Centre for Occupational Health and Safety– *Violence In the Workplace; OSH Answers, Health Promotion/Wellness/Psychosocial* 9/03/2012, ccohs.ca/oshanswers/psychosocial/violence.html; Industrial Accident Prevention Association – Resource Articles, *Just How Wide Spread Is Workplace Violence?* March 2011, www.iapa.ca/main/articles/2009_workplace_violence.aspx; and J. McCarthy, consultant, "Harassment in the Workplace," Family Services Canada Employee Assistance Programs, *Solutions Newsletter*, Issue 35, www.familyserviceseap.com/_files/solutions_newsletters/solutions35.pdf

---

- 38 percent of Canadian education workers polled reported being targets of verbal abuse, physical threats, and other forms of intimidation by students. Half of the teachers of grades 7–9 students stated that they were bullied by students, and 20 percent of the respondents indicated that they were upset enough by the bullying that they sought professional help.[22]

- A diverse occupational sample of 180 workers in the Canadian prairies found that 40 percent reported experiencing at least 1 of 45 specific acts indicative of psychological harassment or bullying on a weekly basis for at least six months. An additional 10 percent of the sample reported experiencing five or more such acts on a weekly basis for at least six months. [23]

- More than half of the 308 respondents to a recent national survey given to Canadian HR professionals stated that their departments have heard of anywhere from one to five incivility-related complaints within the past six months. One-fifth of the respondents heard of six to 10 such complaints.[24]

Some organizations have resorted to workplace etiquette training.[25] Constructive feedback or skillful behaviour shaping can keep a single irritating behaviour from becoming a full-blown personality conflict (or worse). Another promising tool for nipping workplace incivility in the bud is to offer the employee exhibiting incivility a *day of contemplation*, defined as "a paid day off where an employee showing lack of dedication to the job is granted the opportunity to rethink their commitment to working at your company."[26] This tactic, also called decision-making leave, is not part of the organization's formal disciplinary process, nor is it a traditional suspension without pay. A day of contemplation is a one-time-only-per-employee option.

> *Day of contemplation*
>
> A one-time-only day off with pay to allow a problem employee to reflect and recommit to the organization's values and mission.

Dealing with Personality Conflicts Personality conflicts are a potential minefield for organizations. Traditionally, the workplace dealt with personality conflicts by either

TABLE 8.1

HOW TO DEAL WITH PERSONALITY CONFLICTS

TIPS FOR EMPLOYEES HAVING A PERSONALITY CONFLICT	TIPS FOR THIRD-PARTY OBSERVERS OF A PERSONALITY CONFLICT	TIPS FOR MANAGERS WHOSE EMPLOYEES ARE HAVING A PERSONALITY CONFLICT
Communicate directly with the other person to resolve the perceived conflict (emphasize problem solving and common objects, not personalities).	Do not take sides in someone else's personality conflict.	Investigate and document conflict.
Avoid dragging co-workers into the conflict.	Suggest the parties work things out themselves in a constructive and positive way.	If appropriate, take corrective action (e.g., feedback or behaviour shaping).
If dysfunctional conflict persists, seek help from direct supervisors or human resource specialists.	If dysfunctional conflict persists, refer the problem to the parties' direct supervisors.	If necessary, attempt informal dispute resolution.
		Refer difficult conflicts to human resource specialists or hired counsellors for formal resolution attempts and other interventions.

NOTE: All employees need to be familiar with and follow company policies for diversity, anti-discrimination, and sexual harassment.

ignoring them or transferring one party.[27] These responses can lead to conflict escalation or even possible legal implications, such as accusations of harassment or discrimination. Table 8.1 presents practical tips for both non-managers and managers who are involved in or affected by personality conflicts. Our later discussions of handling dysfunctional conflict and alternative dispute resolution techniques also apply.

INTERGROUP CONFLICT

Conflict among work groups, teams, and departments is a common threat to organizational competitiveness. As we discussed in Chapter 6, cohesiveness—a "we feeling" binding group members together—can be a good or bad thing. A certain amount of cohesiveness can turn a group of individuals into a smooth-running team. Too much cohesiveness, however, can breed groupthink because a desire to get along pushes aside critical thinking. The study of in-groups by researchers has revealed a whole package of changes associated with increased group cohesiveness. For example:

- Members of in-groups view themselves as a collection of unique individuals, while they stereotype members of other groups as being "all alike."

- In-group members see themselves positively and as morally correct, while they view members of other groups negatively and as immoral.

- In-groups view outsiders as a threat.

- In-group members exaggerate the differences between their group and other groups. This typically involves a distorted perception of reality.[28]

Avid sports fans who simply can't imagine how someone would support the opposing team exemplify one form of in-group thinking. Also, this pattern of behaviour is a form *ethnocentrism* (i.e., looking at the world primarily from the perspective of one's own culture, which we will discuss in more detail in Chapter 14). Reflect for a moment on evidence of in-group behaviour in your life. Does your circle of friends make fun of others because of their race, gender, age, nationality, weight, sexual preference, or occupational program choice?[29]

In-group thinking is one more fact of organizational life that virtually guarantees conflict. Employees who are affected by such thinking need to become aware of it and try to avoid it by pointing it out to their group members. Managers cannot eliminate in-group thinking, but they certainly should not ignore it when handling inter-group conflicts.

Research Lessons for Handling Inter-Group Conflict

Sociologists have long recommended the contact hypothesis for reducing inter-group conflict. According to the contact hypothesis, the more the members of different groups interact, the less inter-group conflict they will experience. Those interested in improving race, international, and union–management relations typically encourage cross-group interaction. The hope is that any type of interaction, short of actual conflict, will reduce stereotyping and combat in-group thinking. But research has shown this approach to be naive and limited.

Inter-group friendships are still desirable, but they are readily overpowered by negative inter-group interactions. Thus, the number one priority for managers faced with inter-group conflict is to identify and root out specific negative linkages between (or among) groups. A single personality conflict, for instance, may contaminate the entire inter-group experience. The same goes for an employee who voices negative opinions or spreads negative rumours about another group. Our updated contact model in Figure 8.3 is based on this and other recent research insights, such as the need to foster positive attitudes toward other groups.[30] Notice how conflict within the group and negative gossip from third parties are threats that need to be neutralized if inter-group conflict is to be minimized.

CROSS-CULTURAL CONFLICT

Doing business with people from different cultures is commonplace in our global economy, where world-wide mergers, joint ventures, outsourcing, and alliances are the order of the day.[31] Because of differing assumptions about how to think and act, the potential for cross-cultural conflict is both immediate and huge. Success or failure, when conducting business across cultures, often hinges on avoiding and minimizing actual or perceived conflict. This is not a matter of who is right and who is wrong; rather it is a matter of accommodating cultural differences for a successful business transaction.

By studying cultural traditions and accommodating differences, Walmart has put aside their North American values and styles of communicating to avoided cross-cultural disagreements overseas. Here is a store in Wuhan City, China, decorated in bold red colours with many traditional lanterns in anticipation of the popular Chinese New Year celebration.

Stereotypes also need to be identified and neutralized. Beyond that, cross-cultural conflict can be moderated by using international consultants and building cross-cultural relationships.

FIGURE 8.3 Minimizing Intergroup Conflict: An Updated Contact Model

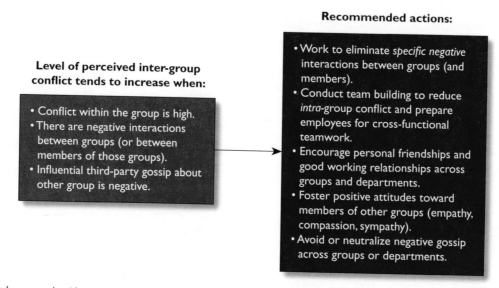

Level of perceived inter-group conflict tends to increase when:

- Conflict within the group is high.
- There are negative interactions between groups (or between members of those groups).
- Influential third-party gossip about other group is negative.

Recommended actions:

- Work to eliminate *specific negative* interactions between groups (and members).
- Conduct team building to reduce *intra*-group conflict and prepare employees for cross-functional teamwork.
- Encourage personal friendships and good working relationships across groups and departments.
- Foster positive attitudes toward members of other groups (empathy, compassion, sympathy).
- Avoid or neutralize negative gossip across groups or departments.

SOURCES: Based on research evidence in G. Labianca, D.J. Brass, and B. Gray, "Social Networks and Perceptions of Intergroup Conflict: The Role of Negative Relationships and Third Parties," *Academy of Management Journal,* February 1998, pp 55–67; C.D. Batson et al., "Empathy and Attitudes: Can Feeling for a Member of a Stigmatized Group Improve Feelings toward the Group?," *Journal of Personality and Social Psychology,* January 1997, pp 105–18; and S.C. Wright et al., "The Extended Contact Effect: Knowledge of Cross-Group Friendships and Prejudice," *Journal of Personality and Social Psychology,* July 1997, pp 73–90.

Using International Consultants In response to broad demand, there is a growing army of management consultants specializing in cross-cultural relations. Competency and fees vary widely, of course. But a carefully selected cross-cultural consultant can be helpful, as this illustration shows:

When electronics-maker Canon planned to set up a subsidiary in Dubai through its Netherlands division, it asked consultant Sahid Mirza of Glocom, based in Dubai, to find out how the two cultures would work together. Mirza sent out the test questionnaires and got a sizable response. "The findings were somewhat surprising," he recalls. "We found that, at the bedrock level, there were relatively few differences. Many of the Arab (executives) came from former British colonies and viewed business in much the same way as the Dutch." But at the level of behaviour, there was a real conflict. "The Dutch are blunt and honest in expression, and such expression is very offensive to Arab sensibilities." Mirza offers the example of a Dutch executive who says something like, "We can't meet the deadline." Such a negative expression—true or not—would be gravely offensive to an Arab. As a result of Mirza's research, Canon did start the subsidiary in Dubai, but it first trained both the Dutch and the Arab executives.[32]

Consultants can also help untangle possible personality, value, and inter-group conflicts from conflicts rooted in differing national cultures. Note that although we have discussed basic types of conflict separately, they typically are encountered in complex, messy bundles. The work completed by researcher Rosalie L. Tung (see the International OB feature box) provides some interesting insight into ways to build cross-cultural relationships.

Managing Conflict

LO 4

As you have seen, conflict has many faces and is a constant challenge for employees who are being given higher performance expectations and for managers who are responsible for reaching organizational goals.[33] Our attention now turns to the five alternative style for handling conflict and how third parties can deal effectively with conflict. Before going further, you may wish to complete Self-Assessment Exercise What is Your Preferred Conflict-Handling Style? to determine your preferred style.

INTERNATIONAL OB

WAYS TO BUILD CROSS-CULTURAL RELATIONSHIPS

Rosalie L. Tung's study of 409 expatriates from Canadian and US multinational firms is very helpful when building cross-cultural relationships. Her survey sought to pinpoint success factors for expatriates (14 percent female) who were working in 51 different countries worldwide. Nine specific ways to facilitate interaction with host-country nationals, as ranked from most useful to least useful by the respondents, are listed below. Good listening skills topped the list, followed by sensitivity to others and cooperativeness rather than competitiveness.

BEHAVIOUR	RANK
Be a good listener	1
Be sensitive to needs of others	2 ⟩ Tie
Be cooperative, rather than overly competitive	2
Advocate inclusive (participative) leadership	3
Compromise rather than dominate	4
Build rapport through conversations	5
Be compassionate and understanding	6
Avoid conflict by emphasizing harmony	7
Nurture others (develop and mentor)	8

SOURCE: Adapted from R.L. Tung, "American Expatriates Abroad: From Neophytes to Cosmopolitans," *Journal of World Business,* Summer 1998, Table 6, p 136.

What is Your Preferred Conflict-Handling Style?

INSTRUCTIONS: Rate each statement using the scale provided.

	Rarely	Infrequently	Sometimes	Frequently	Always
1 I argue my case with my co-workers to show the merits of my position.					
2 I negotiate with my co-workers so that a compromise can be reached.					
3 I try to satisfy the expectations of my co-workers.					
4 I try to investigate an issue with my co-workers to find a solution acceptable to us.					
5 I am firm in pursuing my side of the issue.					
6 I attempt to avoid being "put on the spot" and try to keep my conflict with my co-workers to myself.					
7 I hold on to my solution to a problem.					
8 I use "give and take" so that a compromise can be made.					
9 I exchange accurate information with my co-workers to solve a problem together.					
10 I avoid open discussion of my differences with my co-workers.					
11 I accommodate the wishes of my co-workers.					
12 I try to bring all issues out into the open so that the issues can be resolved in the best possible way.					
13 I propose a middle ground for breaking conflicts.					
14 I go along with suggestions of my co-workers.					
15 I try to keep disagreements with my co-workers to myself to avoid hard feelings.					

SOURCE: The complete instrument may be found in M.A. Rahim, "A Measure of Styles of Handling Interpersonal Conflict," *Academy of Management Journal*, June 1983, pp 368–76.

Scoring Key

Assign a point value to your response for each question. "Rarely" is worth 1 point, "Infrequently" is worth 2 points, "Sometimes" is worth 3 points, "Frequently" is worth 4 points, and "Always" is worth 5 points. Insert your score for each question into the categories below. The category with the highest score represents your preferred conflict-handling style.

Dominating: (Q1) ____ + (Q5) ____ + (Q7) ____ = ____
Compromising: (Q2) ____ + (Q8) ____ + (Q13) ____ = ____
Obliging: (Q3) ____ + (Q11) ____ + (Q14) ____ = ____
Integrating: (Q4) ____ + (Q9) ____ + (Q12) ____ = ____
Avoiding: (Q6) ____ + (Q10) ____ + (Q15) ____ = ____

ALTERNATIVE STYLES FOR HANDLING CONFLICT

People tend to handle negative conflict in patterned ways, referred to as styles. Several conflict styles have been categorized over the years. Conflict specialist Afzalur Rahim has identified five different conflict-handling styles (Table 8.2): integrating, obliging, dominating, avoiding, and compromising.[34] It is worth remembering that there is no single best style; each has strengths and limitations, and is subject to "best fit" based on the situation.

TABLE 8.2

FIVE CONFLICT-HANDLING STYLES

	Low Interest in Satisfying Others' Concerns	Mid Interest in Satisfying Others' Concerns	High Interest in Satisfying Others' Concerns
High Interest in Satisfying Self-Concerns	DOMINATING (Forcing)	-	INTEGRATING (Problem Solving)
Mid Interest in Satisfying Self-Concerns	-	COMPROMISING	-
Low Interest in Satisfying Self-Concerns	AVOIDING	-	OBLIGING (Smoothing)

Integrating (Problem Solving) In this style, the concern for self and others is high; therefore, the problem becomes the primary focus as interested parties take the time to confront an issue and cooperatively identify the problem, generate and weigh alternative solutions, and select a solution. Integrating is appropriate for complex issues plagued by misunderstanding. However, it is inappropriate for resolving conflicts rooted in opposing value systems. Its primary strength is its longer lasting impact because it deals with the underlying problem rather than merely with symptoms. The primary weakness of this style is that it is very time-consuming.

Obliging (Smoothing) "An obliging person neglects his or her own concern to satisfy the concern of the other party."[35] This style, often called smoothing, involves more concern for others rather than for oneself. This is a style rooted in humility, as conflicting parties play down their differences while emphasizing what they have in common. Obliging may be an appropriate conflict-handling strategy when it is possible to eventually get something in return (for example, helping people when they need it and in turn asking for their help in the future when it is important to you). However, it is inappropriate for complex or worsening problems. Its primary strength is that it encourages cooperation. Its main weakness is that it's a temporary fix that fails to confront the underlying problem.

Dominating (Forcing) High concern for self and low concern for others encourages aggressive tactics where the other party's needs are largely ignored. This style is often called forcing because it relies on formal authority to force compliance. Dominating is appropriate when an unpopular solution must be implemented, the issue is minor, there are safety or security issues, or a deadline is very near. It is inappropriate in an open and participative climate. Speed is its primary strength. The primary weakness of this domineering style is that it often breeds resentment.[36]

Avoiding This style has low concern for both self and others' needs. This tactic may involve either passive withdrawal from the problem or active suppression of the issue. Avoidance is appropriate for trivial issues when emotions are flared and things need to calm down, or when the costs of confrontation outweigh the benefits of resolving the conflict. It is inappropriate for difficult and worsening problems because it doesn't address the problem. The main strength of this style is that it buys time in emotionally charged or confusing situations. The primary weakness is that the tactic provides a temporary fix that sidesteps the underlying problem.

Compromising This is a give-and-take approach involving moderate concern for both self and others. Although compromises are a result of mid-regard for self and others' concerns, it is not the ultimate style to use for all situations. Compromise is appropriate when parties have opposite goals or possess equal power. But compromise is inappropriate when overuse would lead to inconclusive action (e.g., failure to meet production deadlines). The primary strength of this tactic is that everyone gets something, but it's a temporary fix that can stifle creative problem solving.[37]

THIRD-PARTY INTERVENTIONS: ALTERNATIVE DISPUTE RESOLUTION

Disputes such as those between employees, between employees and their employer, and between companies too often end up in lengthy and costly court battles. A more constructive, less expensive approach, called alternative dispute resolution, has enjoyed enthusiastic growth in recent years.[38] *Alternative dispute resolution (ADR)*, according to a pair of Canadian labour lawyers, "uses faster, more user-friendly methods of dispute resolution, instead of traditional, confrontational approaches."[39]

The following ADR techniques represent a progression of steps third parties can take to resolve organizational conflicts.[40] They are ranked from easiest and least expensive to most difficult and costly. A growing number of organizations have

> **Alternative dispute resolution (ADR)**
>
> A conflict resolution strategy that involves assistance from a third party; used when both parties are unable to find resolution on their own.

Third party intervention is sometimes necessary to help conflicting parties find resolution. Several strategies are available, including mediation and arbitration techniques.

formal ADR policies involving an established sequence of various combinations of these techniques.

1. **Facilitation** A third party, usually a manager, informally urges disputing parties to deal directly with each other in a positive and practical manner.

2. **Conciliation** A neutral third party informally acts as a communication link between conflicting parties. This is appropriate when conflicting parties refuse to meet face-to-face. The immediate goal is to establish direct communication, with the broader aim of finding common ground and a constructive solution.

3. **Peer review** A panel of trustworthy co-workers, selected for their ability to remain objective, hears both sides of a dispute in an informal and private meeting. Any decision by the review panel may or may not be binding, depending on the company's ADR policy. Membership on the peer review panel is often rotated among employees.[41]

4. **Ombudsman** Someone who works for the organization, and is widely respected and trusted by co-workers, hears grievances on a private basis and attempts to arrange a solution. This approach, more common in Europe than North America, permits someone to get help from an executive with ties to management without relying on the formal chain of command chain.

5. **Mediation** "The mediator—a trained, third-party neutral—actively guides the conflicting parties in exploring innovative solutions to the conflict. Although some companies have in-house mediators who have received ADR training, most also use external mediators who have no ties to the company."[42] Unlike an arbitrator, a mediator does not

render a decision. It is up to the disputants to reach a mutually acceptable decision.

6. **Arbitration** Disputing parties agree ahead of time to accept the decision of a neutral arbitrator in a formal court-like setting, often complete with evidence and witnesses. Statements are classified. Decisions are based on legal merits. Trained arbitrators, typically from outside agencies such as the Arbitration and Mediation Institute of Canada, Inc., are versed in important laws and case precedents.

PRACTICAL LESSONS FROM CONFLICT RESEARCH

Laboratory studies, relying on college students as subjects, have uncovered the following insights about organizational conflict:

- People with a high need to belong tend to rely on a smoothing (obliging) style while avoiding a forcing (dominating) style.[43] Thus, personality traits affect how people handle conflict.

- Disagreement expressed in a demeaning manner produces significantly more negative effects than the same sort of disagreement expressed in a reasonable manner.[44] In other words, how you disagree with someone is very important in conflict situations.

- Threats and punishment by one party in a disagreement tend to produce intensifying threats and punishment from the other party.[45] In short, aggression breeds aggression.

- As conflict increases, group satisfaction decreases. An integrative style of handling conflict leads to higher group satisfaction than does an avoidance style.[46]

- Companies with mandatory or binding arbitration policies are viewed less favourably than companies without such policies.[47] Apparently, mandatory or binding arbitration policies are a turn-off for job applicants who dislike the idea of being forced to do something.

Field studies involving real organizations have given us the following insights:

- Both intra-departmental and inter-departmental conflict decreases as goal difficulty and goal clarity increases. Thus, challenging and clear goals can smooth conflict.

- Higher levels of conflict tend to erode job satisfaction and internal work motivation.[48]

- Conflict tends to move around the organization, as shown in a case study of a public school system.[49]

Thus, team leaders and managers need to be alert to the fact that conflict often begins in one area or level and becomes evident somewhere else. Conflict needs to be traced back to its source if there is to be lasting improvement.

- Samples of Japanese and German managers presented with the same conflict scenario prefer different resolution techniques. Japanese and German managers do not like the idea of integrating the interests of all parties. The Japanese tend to look upward to management for direction, whereas the Germans are more bound by rules and regulations. In cross-cultural conflict resolution, there is no one best approach. Culture-specific preferences need to be taken into consideration prior to beginning the conflict resolution process.[50]

As we transition from conflict to negotiation, take a short break from your reading and reflect on how you can better handle conflict in your daily life.

Negotiating

Formally defined, negotiation is a give-and-take decision-making process involving interdependent parties with different preferences.[51] Common examples include working in a unionized environment, labour–management negotiations over wages, hours, and working conditions, and negotiations between supply chain specialists and vendors involving price, delivery schedules, and credit terms. Self-managed work teams with overlapping task boundaries also need to rely on negotiated agreements. Negotiating skills are more important today than ever.[52] In fact, in a recent survey of 3,600 professional employees in 18 countries, only 52 percent said yes to the question, "Have you ever asked for or negotiated a pay raise?"[53] This section will conclude by addressing practical lessons learned from negotiation research, including the different styles between genders.

TWO BASIC TYPES OF NEGOTIATION

Negotiation experts distinguish between two types of negotiation: *distributive* and *integrative*. Understanding the difference requires a change in traditional thinking:

A distributive negotiation usually involves a single issue—a "fixed-pie"—in which one person gains at the expense of the other. For example, haggling over the price of a rug in a bazaar is a distributive negotiation. In most conflicts, however, more than one issue is at stake, and each party values the issues differently. The outcomes available are no longer a fixed-pie divided among all parties. An agreement can be found that is

better for both parties than what they would have reached through distributive negotiation. This is an integrative negotiation.

However, parties in a negotiation often don't find these beneficial trade-offs because each assumes its interests directly conflict with those of the other party. "What is good for the other side must be bad for us" is a common and unfortunate perspective that most people have. This is the mind-set we call the mythical "fixed-pie."[54]

Distributive The "fixed-pie" metaphor has been associated with *distributive negotiation* because it involves win–lose thinking around a fixed amount of assets. This is illustrated by historical labour-management negotiations when settlements over wage increases seemed impossible. If you have survived a labour strike at your own college or university, then you personally know the characteristics of distributive negotiation. Refer back to Table 8.2 and try visualizing distributive negotiation tactics on an imaginary line between dominating and obliging as negotiators use such tactics as force, persuasion, promises, threats, or just digging in their heels (which can result in a strike) to find resolution. If resolution is still not possible after such tactics, like in our example of a college or university labour issue, then the conflicting parties may decide to seek resolution from an arbitrator (see the earlier discussion about ADR techniques).

> *Distributive negotiation*
>
> Two interdependent parties, each with their own opposite preference, seek to make a decision that will result in one party winning at the expense of the other.

Integrative In contrast *integrative negotiation* works under the belief that a resolution can be found that is mutually satisfying because it calls for a progressive win–win strategy.[55] Individuals can use integrative or added-value negotiation, for example when they are trying to negotiate a settlement for themselves. Integrative negotiation is most appropriate for intergroup and inter-organizational conflict because of the numerous controversial issues on the table for discussion. It encourages joint cooperation and rich dialogue, hence more valued discussion. You can imagine the amount of time and money involved in reaching such resolution. In a laboratory study of joint venture negotiations, teams trained in integrative tactics achieved better outcomes for both sides than did untrained teams.[56] North American negotiators generally are too short-term oriented and are poor relationship builders when negotiating in Asia, Latin America, and the Middle East.[57]

> *Integrative negotiation*
>
> Two interdependent parties with their own preferences and values seek a win–win resolution through greater dialogue and cooperation.

FIGURE | 8.4 | An Integrative Approach: Added-Value Negotiation

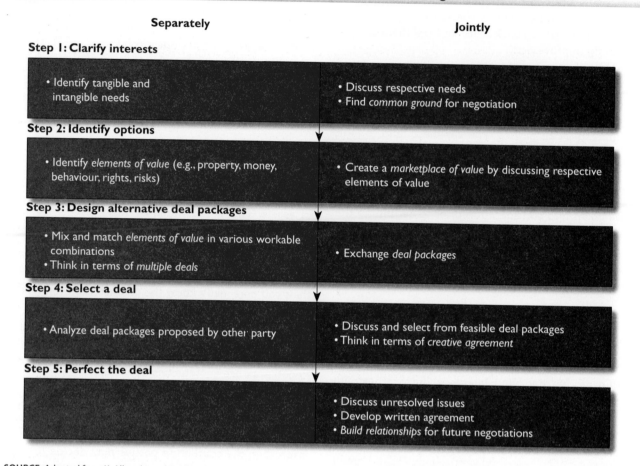

Separately

Jointly

Step 1: Clarify interests

- Identify tangible and intangible needs

- Discuss respective needs
- Find *common ground* for negotiation

Step 2: Identify options

- Identify *elements of value* (e.g., property, money, behaviour, rights, risks)

- Create a *marketplace of value* by discussing respective elements of value

Step 3: Design alternative deal packages

- Mix and match *elements of value* in various workable combinations
- Think in terms of *multiple deals*

- Exchange *deal packages*

Step 4: Select a deal

- Analyze deal packages proposed by other party

- Discuss and select from feasible deal packages
- Think in terms of *creative agreement*

Step 5: Perfect the deal

- Discuss unresolved issues
- Develop written agreement
- *Build relationships* for future negotiations

SOURCE: Adapted from K. Albrecht and S. Albrecht, "Added Value Negotiating," *Training*, April 1993, pp 26–29. Used by permission of VNU Business Publications via The Copyright Clearance Center.

The added-value negotiation techniques illustrated in Figure 8.4 are helpful during integrative negotiation. Notice how dialogue expands under this model, as each side is encouraged to make a collective effort to make this agreement work. Refer back to Table 8.2 and try to visualize integrative negotiation tactics on an imaginary line between integrating and avoiding, as negotiators use such tactics as reframing problems into opportunities, helping the other side save money, building trust during information exchanges to show sincerity in bargaining in good faith, or maybe even helping the other side find more assets (expand the size of the pie).

COMMON BUSINESS NEGOTIATION MISTAKES

Individuals in business are always looking for practical suggestions on how to build a better relationship between themselves and colleagues, clients, or those closest to them. The following list, from the well-respected

Negotiation newsletter, provides several common business negotiation mistakes and pitfalls to avoid:

■ **Mistake #1 – Not identifying enough trades**[58]: Avoid the false assumption that only one party has something of value worth trading. To create value, you need to learn about the other party's interests and preferences. This can be accomplished by:

— ensuring both sides share valuable information about how much they each care about important issues—*"On-time delivery is critical to us,"* you might tell a representative of a technology consulting firm in a negotiation over new business. *"Our old contractor did good work, but couldn't meet deadlines. Now tell me some of your key concerns."*

— listening and asking questions to collect important new information—*You might ask the consulting rep, "What mechanisms does your firm have in place to make sure you meet our deadlines?"*

— presenting more than one offer on the table at a time—*"Here are three options to consider... do any of these interest you?"* If the other party rejects all the options but has fewer objections to the third, then you have learned where there is some potential room to trade. Then you can come back and say, *"OK, if we build on this third option, here are a few more variations on that theme to explore. I'm being flexible here because I want to seal this deal."*

■ **Mistake #2 – Overvaluing your assets**[59]: Contrary to rational thinking, we seem to view almost anything as more valuable once it belongs to us: our home, grandma's wedding ring, the old nameplate from your first office desk. Why? Ownership is accompanied by the threat of loss relative to the status quo. This loss aversion can lead you to overvalue your assets and ask too much for them. Ask yourself these four questions:

— *"Would I want it if it weren't mine?"* When you put yourself in a prospective buyer's shoes, the item you are overpricing might not look as appealing.

— *"How much is it really worth?"* Consult with an expert in the field to improve your estimate of an item's value.

— *"What if it doesn't sell?"* Imagine what will happen if you are unable to make a sale. If it causes financial difficulties, then it's time to rethink your goal.

— *"What other value can I offer?"* Other than price, maybe there is something else of value to offer, such as delivery options, payment plans, matching rights, or an ongoing relationship to a potential buyer.

■ **Mistake #3 – Power tripping**[60]: *"Take it or leave it"* is harsh negotiating language. If people leave the bargaining table feeling that you've disrespected or mistreated them, you may end up the victim of a power backlash.

— Power hungry negotiators may fail to anticipate "irrational" behaviour from their counterparts. *"It's a matter of principle. I'm going to dig in my heels and let everyone know what a bully he is. I realize I have little to gain, but that's not the point."*

— If people can't deliver on the deal, then they may just renege and give up. Suppose a big-box retailer tells a sporting goods supplier that it must submit a lower bid to retain a contract; reluctantly, the supplier delivers a revised bid with a slim-to-none profit margin. It should come as no surprise if the supplier misses delivery targets, sacrifices product quality, or defects to one of the retailer's competitors.

— The powerful will be taken to court. Were the actions of both sides fair and reasonable or was one side overbearing and dominating?

■ **Mistake #4 – Not knowing what you really want**[61]: Errors in judgment and unrealistic expectations of what will satisfy you can bias your thinking. Try to avoid this by being realistic and truly reflective on what it is you're asking for.

— *"If I don't get this deal, I'll be ruined. I have to win at all costs!"* This kind of emotional response doesn't consider how fleeting and weak emotions can be.

— Because our brains are wired to adapt to changing circumstances, we tend to return to a set level of happiness after a boost or a setback. For negotiators who agonize over hard choices, it's important to remember, *"You'll get over it and will likely bounce back enough to take calculated risks again in the future. Just remember to keep it all in perspective."*

■ **Mistake #5 – Binding yourself too tightly to a deal**[62]: When talks get difficult, it can be easy to conclude that you've invested too much to quit and feel trapped in a disappointing deal. This is called an escalation to commitment (we'll talk more about this in Chapter 9) and can become a possible trap when negotiating tactics and contract terms. Accepting a lopsided deal can be a recipe for disaster. Consider the following three steps:

— Play *"What if...?"* Before negotiating, ask yourself how difficult it would be to walk away without a deal, both psychologically and economically.

— Ask yourself *"How difficult will it be for me to back out, or for my counterpart to back out? What will happen to me if they do back out?"*

— It's up to you to negotiate a more balanced deal—and to be prepared to walk away if your counterpart won't cooperate. Begin by pointing out your risk exposure. *"What if I'm unhappy with the completed work? How can we both be protected?"* A negotiator who wants to do a deal will listen and consider making adjustments. If someone won't cooperate, you may need to explore alternatives to the current deal.

ETHICAL PITFALLS IN NEGOTIATION

The success of integrative negotiation, such as added-value negotiation, depends to a large extent on the *quality* of information exchanged, as researchers have documented.[63] Telling lies, hiding key facts, and engaging in the other potentially unethical tactics listed in Table 8.3 erode trust and goodwill. Without the benefits of trust and goodwill, a win–win resolution is not going to be possible.[64] An awareness of these dirty tricks can keep good faith bargainers from being unfairly exploited.[65] Unethical negotiating tactics need to be factored into organizational codes of ethics.

PRACTICAL LESSONS FROM NEGOTIATION RESEARCH

Laboratory and field studies have yielded these insights:

- Negotiators with fixed-pie expectations produce poor joint outcomes because they restrict and mismanage information.[66]

- Personality characteristics can affect negotiating success. Negotiators who scored high on the Big Five personality dimensions of extraversion and agreeableness (refer back to Chapter 3, Table 3.1) tended to do poorly with distributive (fixed-pie, win–lose) negotiations.[67]

- Good and bad moods can have positive and negative effects, respectively, on negotiators' plans and outcomes.[68] So, wait until both you and your boss are in a good mood before you ask for a raise.

- Subjects trained in goal setting and problem solving enjoyed more satisfying and hopeful dialogues on a controversial subject than did those with no particular strategy.[69] Practical implication: don't negotiate without being adequately prepared.

Research in the area of conflict, negotiation, and gender issues continues to draw attention and the results are rather interesting. See the Focus on Diversity feature box for more research results around the differences between genders when it comes to negotiation.

TABLE 8.3

QUESTIONABLE/UNETHICAL TACTICS IN NEGOTIATION

TACTIC	DESCRIPTION/CLARIFICATION/RANGE
Lies	Subject matter for lies can include limits, alternatives, the negotiator's intent, authority to bargain, other commitments, acceptability of the opponent's offers, time pressures, and available resources.
Puffery	Among the items that can be puffed up are the value of the negotiator's payoffs to the opponent, the negotiator's own alternatives, the costs of what the negotiator is giving up or is prepared to yield, importance of issues, and attributes of the products or services.
Deception	Acts and statements may include promises or threats, excessive initial demands, careless misstatements of facts, or asking for concessions not wanted.
Weakening the opponent	The negotiator may cut off or eliminate some of the opponent's alternatives, blame the opponent for their own actions, use personally abrasive statements to or about the opponent, or undermine the opponent's alliances.
Strengthening negotiator's own position	Includes building the negotiator's own resources, such as expertise, finances, position, and alliances. It also includes presentations of persuasive rationales to the opponent or third parties (e.g., the public, the media) or getting mandates for the negotiator's position.
Non-disclosure	Includes partial disclosure of facts, failure to disclose a hidden fact, failure to correct the opponents' misperceptions or ignorance, and concealment of the negotiator's own position or circumstances.
Information exploitation	Information provided by the opponent can be used to exploit their weaknesses, close off their alternatives, generate demands against them, or weaken their alliances.
Change of mind	Includes accepting offers the negotiator had claimed they would not accept, changing demands, withdrawing promised offers, and making threats they promised would not be made. Also includes the failure to behave as predicted.
Distraction	These acts or statements can be as simple as providing excessive information to the opponent, asking many questions, evading questions, or burying the issue. Or they can be more complex, such as the negotiator feigning weakness in one area so that the opponent concentrates on it and ignores another.
Maximization	Includes demanding the opponent make concessions that result in the negotiator's gain and the opponent's equal or greater loss. Also entails converting a win–win situation into win–lose.

SOURCE: Reprinted from H.J. Reitz, J.A. Wall Jr., and M.S. Love, "Ethics in Negotiation: Oil and Water or Good Lubrication?," *Business Horizons*, May–June 1998, p 6. © 1998, with permission from Elsevier.

PRACTICAL LESSONS – GENDER DIFFERENCES

FOCUS ON DIVERSITY

How different are men from women when it comes to handling conflict and negotiating a settlement over a dispute? In terms of conflict, laboratory studies uncovered that men and women at the same level within an organization tend to handle conflict similarly. In short, there was no gender effect.[70] When it came to negotiation, a meta-analysis of 62 studies found a slight tendency for women to negotiate more cooperatively than men. But when faced with a tit-for-tat bargaining strategy (equal responses back and forth), women were significantly more competitive than men.[71] For example, a recent report stated that when it comes to buying a new car, women bargain harder and also do more extensive preparatory work than men.[72]

In regards to negotiating fair compensation, women too often come up short, not getting what they want or deserve. Women often don't ask for the compensation they want or deserve, whereas men are more likely to negotiate for what they want. Several reasons are cited for this phenomena: (1) women are socialized from an early age not to promote their own interests and to focus on the needs of others; (2) women tend to assume that they will be recognized and rewarded for working hard and doing a good job; and (3) some companies' cultures penalize women when they do ask, further discouraging them from doing so.[73] Consequently, women (and any other employees) who feel they are being shortchanged in pay and/or promotions should polish their integrative negotiation skills.

LO 5 SUMMARIZING THE VALUE OF THIRD-PARTY INTERVENTION

When conflicting parties are not able to find resolution on their <u>own</u> and need some assistance, third party intervention can help. ADR offers many different strategies to assist conflicting parties find resolution, including facilitation, conciliation, peer review, use of an ombudsman, mediation, and arbitration. Negotiation differs from ADR as it is more of a give and take. Distributive negotiation is rooted in the assumption that there is a fixed amount of assets, so win–lose tactics include threats, promises, firmness, persuasion, or digging in heels to achieve the desired outcome. Integrative negotiation seeks a win–win resolution using tactics such as reframing problems into opportunities, helping the other side save money, building trust during information exchanges to show sincerity in bargaining in good faith . . . or maybe even helping the other side find more assets (expand the size of the pie).

Conflicting individuals are sometimes so focused on their own emotions that they have difficulty moving on to find a satisfying resolution. By inviting third-party intervention, individuals can determine unbiased parameters or ground rules for arguing so that a neutral perspective can guide discussion toward finding common interests.

A Contingency Approach to Conflict

Three realities exist around organizational conflict. First, various types of conflict are inevitable because they are triggered by different causes. Second, too little conflict may be as counterproductive as too much. Third, there is no single best way to avoid or resolve conflict. Conflict specialists recommend a contingency approach to managing conflict by monitoring causes of conflict and actual conflict. If signs of too little conflict—such as apathy or lack of creativity—appear, then functional conflict needs to be stimulated by looking for possible causes of conflict. On the other hand, when conflict becomes dysfunctional, the appropriate conflict-handling style needs to be used to find resolution and get the workplace back to a healthy place. Training involving role playing can prepare all employees to try alternative conflict-handling styles.

Third-party interventions are necessary when conflicting parties are unwilling or unable to engage in conflict resolution or integrative negotiation. Integrative or added-value negotiation is most appropriate for intergroup and inter-organizational conflict. The key is to get the conflicting parties to abandon traditional fixed-pie thinking and their win–lose expectations.

Summary of Learning Objectives

LO 1   **Define *conflict*, *functional conflict*, and *dysfunctional conflict*.** Conflict is a process in which one party perceives that its interests are being opposed or negatively affected by another party. It is inevitable and not necessarily destructive. Too little conflict, as evidenced by apathy or lack of creativity, can be as great a problem as too much conflict. Functional conflict enhances organizational interests, while dysfunctional conflict is counterproductive.

LO 2   **Identify the various antecedents (causes) of conflict.** Conflict can come from many different sources, including: incompatible personalities or value systems; overlapping or unclear job boundaries; competition for limited resources; inter-group or interdependent group competition; inadequate communication; unreasonable or unclear policies, standards, or rules; unreasonable deadlines; extreme time pressures; unmet expectations; unresolved or hidden conflicts that people are afraid to talk about; and the complexity of the organization.

LO 3   **List two approaches an employee or manager can take to respond to each of the following: personality conflicts, inter-group conflict, and cross-cultural conflicts.** Personality conflicts involve interpersonal opposition based on personal dislike and/or disagreement (or as an outgrowth of workplace incivility). Care needs to be taken with personality conflicts in the workplace because of the legal implications of diversity, discrimination, and sexual harassment. This applies to all employees. As for managers, they should investigate and document personality conflicts, take corrective actions such as feedback or behaviour modification if appropriate, or attempt informal dispute resolution. Difficult or persistent personality conflicts need to be referred to human resource specialists or counsellors. Members of in-groups tend to see themselves as unique individuals who are more moral than outsiders, whom they view as a threat and stereotypically as all alike. In-group thinking is associated with a type of behaviour called ethnocentrism, which means looking at the world primarily from the perspective of one's own culture. International consultants can prepare people from different cultures to work effectively together. Cross-cultural conflict can be minimized by having expatriates build strong cross-cultural relationships with their hosts (primarily by being good listeners, being sensitive to others, and being more cooperative than competitive).

LO 4   **Compare and contrast the five alternative styles for handling conflict.** There is no single best style. (1) Integrating (problem solving) shows high concern for self and the other person's needs. The focus is directed to working the problem. This is a good style for generating a lot of alternative solutions around a complex conflict, but is very time consuming. (2) Obliging (smoothing) is when people neglect their own concerns to satisfy the concerns of the other party. Differences between conflicting parties are played down and cooperation to assist the other side achieve their interests is preferred. This style is appropriate if you are involved with making a decision about something that is not of great priority to you. Obliging works on a cooperative model, but is usually used as a temporary fix, not a long-term solution. (3) Dominating (forcing) is a style that has low concern for others' needs but high concern for oneself. This can cause the other party to become angry, as they feel they aren't having any say over the situation. Dominating styles work during contentious issues, when safety and security are at risk, and when a deadline is very near and a speedy solution is needed. However, it often breeds resentment. (4) Avoiding is when there is low concern for self and others' needs. This is a passive style and appropriate for calming emotionally charged situations, but it is a temporary fix as the real issues don't get addressed. (5) Compromising is a give and take from both sides, involving moderate concern for both self and others. It works best if conflicting parties are from the same political level of the organization or have equal power. The strength of this strategy is that everyone gets something of value, but it does stifle creative problem solving.

LO 5 **Assess the value of having third party interventions for conflict resolution, including the ADR and two negotiation processes.** Sometimes conflicting parties are not able to find resolution on their own and need some assistance. A third party is brought in to help achieve a faster and more user-friendly resolution. ADR offers many different strategies to assist conflicting parties find resolution, including facilitation, conciliation, peer review, using an ombudsman, mediation, and arbitration. Negotiation differs from ADR as it is more of a give and take. There are two basic types of negotiation: distributive and integrative. Both involve people who are interdependent and have their own preferences, but the mindset is different. Distributive negotiation is rooted in the assumption that there is a fixed amount of assets. Here the win–lose tactics can include threats, promises, firmness, persuasion, or digging in heels to achieve desired outcome. This type of negotiation can be found on a line between the conflict-handling styles of dominating and obliging, and is usually associated with historical labour–management wage disputes. Integrative negotiation seeks a win–win resolution around many issues. The negotiators can use a range of tactics, such as reframing problems into opportunities, helping the other side save money, building trust during information exchanges to show sincerity in bargaining in good faith . . . or even helping the other side find more assets (expand the size of the pie). It is most appropriate for inter-group and inter-organizational conflict. Integrative negotiation can be found on a line between the conflict-handling styles of integrating and avoiding, as each side engages in dialogue to reach an agreement.

Discussion Questions

1. What examples of functional and dysfunctional conflict have you observed in organizations? What were the outcomes? What caused the dysfunctional conflict?

2. Which of the six ADR techniques appeals to you the most? Explain your response.

3. In your opinion, why would some individuals be reluctant to invite a third party to help resolve a conflict, while others are quick to drag as many people into the conflict as possible? Try to understand the behaviours of both types of people.

4. Why are some conflicting parties willing to stage a strike to get what they want?

5. If an individual has a conflict-handling preference that involves them depending on the same style in all situations, will this result in creating more or less conflict? Explain your reasoning referring to Table 8.2.

Integration of OB Concepts—Discussion Questions

1. See Chapter 2 – What role does perception play in both identifying a conflict in the workplace as well as an individual selecting their conflict-handling style?

2. See Chapter 3 – Referring to the Big Five Personality Dimensions, does personality influence the way individuals manage conflict? Consider the relationship between personality and approach.

3. See Chapter 7 – What sorts of connections or similarities may exist between an individual's preferred communication style and conflict-handling style?

Google Searches

1. **Google Search:** "The cost of conflict in the workplace – dollars" OR "Centre for Conflict Resolution International – About Workplace Conflict_The Cost of Conflict" In business, activity that affects the bottom line gets the most attention. What is the cost of workplace conflict? Some experts call unresolved conflict the largest reducible cost in many businesses. Search for information that quantifies the cost of workplace conflict on an annual basis in terms of dollars lost or lost productivity from increased absenteeism.

2. **Google Search:** "ADR Institute of Canada Inc." OR "Stitt Feld Handy Group" If you needed to find a third party to help resolve a conflict, who in your province is an available contact or affiliate?

3. **Google Search:** "WATNA/BATNA – best negotiated agreement" AND "walk away point of negotiation" Compare and contrast these two concepts. How do they relate to this chapter and the section on negotiation?

Experiential Exercise

Communicating in Conflict Exercise

PURPOSE: This exercise is to help familiarize you with communicating in conflict language, using the two pronouns "I" vs "You." Approx. Timing: 20 minutes.

ACTIVITY ASSIGNMENT

Below are three statements that were made to people at various times. Working with the student next to you, follow these directions:

- Underline and count the number of "you" (or your) words in each sentence.
- Circle the word(s) that make the sentence harsh and accusatory.
- Rewrite the statement using the word "I" so that the sentence isn't as likely to stir conflict. Try not to use the word "you." Remember, you are not trying to escalate the conflict; instead, find words that communicate your position but not in such an inflaming manner.
- Share your new sentence with the rest of the class.
- Make corrections or enhancements to your rewritten sentence as necessary.

1. **Giving direction to an employee who is doing a task poorly:**

   "No, you are wrong. You have no idea what you're talking about. Thank goodness I'm here otherwise this mess would just continue. Now let me show you how the filing is done correctly."

2. **Disagreeing with someone else's opinion:**

   "Really? You're joking right? You mean that's what you think? (laughing) Oh my goodness. Well I can see **you** (with emphasis) haven't studied this matter in the kind of depth needed for a thorough understanding. But I have and I know what's really going on here."

3. **Explaining your side of a situation:**

   "You know, you have been misleading this office and frankly we're all tired of having two standards around here—your way and then the policy way. Why is it that you can behave one way and the rest of us have to follow a different procedure to get work completed?"

OB In Action Case Study

Selina Lo Sees the Light

Throughout the 1990s, Selina Lo had a reputation as one of the industry's most aggressive and successful salespeople. But anyone who was not part of what Lo deemed the solution, she treated as her personal problem. Her bag of management tools included yelling, fist pounding, and stomach-curdling sarcasm.

David Callisch, director of marketing at switchmaker Alteon WebSystems in the late 1990s, was among those she shot down, rolled over, and put in their place. After two years of working for Lo, who was vice president of marketing at the time, Callisch begged her to please, please let him report to someone else. "I said, 'I can't handle working for you,'" he recalls. "'You cause me huge amounts of anxiety. I don't want to go on like this.'"

"She'd stick her head in your office and bark out a bunch of commands," Callisch says. "We used to call them 'drive-bys.' If we ever wanted to motivate someone, we'd say, 'We're going to tell Selina that you can't do this.' It would put the fear of God into them."

The Big-Cheese Challenge

In 2004, Lo became CEO of Ruckus Wireless, a Wi-Fi start-up in the Western Region. And that was when she realized she needed to change. The first inkling came as she was trying to recruit executives she had known in other jobs. She made them financial offers they couldn't refuse. They refused anyway. They also told her why. "I had heard complaints before," says Lo. "But I always shrugged that off. Hey, stress is part of this profession; it's part of the package. I didn't realize I was making people physically sick."

Lo had also grown accustomed to ripping into her bosses, who generally tolerated it because her fierceness served their companies. But shortly after taking over at Ruckus, she got into a heated argument with a major investor, and even Lo realized she had crossed a line. Dominic Orr, chairman of the board at Ruckus and Lo's boss at Alteon, was present at that investor meeting and calls it a moment of truth. "It became clear that Selina Lo might win—but Ruckus might lose," he says.

The final straw came as Lo found herself for the first time managing people she had recruited and hired. She felt an unfamiliar obligation for the lives and happiness of employees—all employees, not just the engineers and marketers she usually favoured. "When I was VP of marketing, I could go nuts, and the damage would be limited," she says. "When the CEO screams, the impact is much greater. I can't build a company with nervous people."

The Softening

What Lo calls her "directness" is bred in her bones, the result of being raised by hyper-competitive parents in fast-paced Hong Kong. It also stems from being a woman in a male-dominated industry, she says. Changing required a huge effort of will. And she was no stranger to management training. "I tried to do what the books said: be hands-off and let people make their own mistakes," says Lo. "But I hated it, hated it, hated it."

Disenchanted with the classes-and-books route to better leadership, Lo resolved to reform her own way. Impatience, she recognized, was her greatest foe. Lo likes things settled, which means arguments end when she leaves the room. Winner: Selina Lo. At Ruckus, she adopted a group decision-making process that forces her to consider the opinions of others. Now, when a disagreement arises, she quickly convenes a meeting of herself, her disputant, and one or two other people affected by the decision. "If they agree with me, he gets more data points about why I am correct," says Lo. "If they agree with him, I ask myself, Am I being blind or unfair?"

She also gets a group to assist in matters of emotional intelligence. In the past, Lo had always been stingy with praise, because she herself doesn't need it. "In Chinese culture, it's considered bad manners to praise your kid, so I never got that from my parents," she says. "I became very self-driven." At Ruckus, Lo has asked colleagues to help her recognize when and how to dole out the kudos. Before an all-hands meeting, for example, someone might suggest she acknowledge an individual for a job well done. "The process has been like learning to be a parent," she says. "People learn to be good parents without going to school. If you care, over time you figure out how to do it."

Questions for Discussion

1. How did Selina Lo's interpersonal style evolve in terms of the conflict metaphors, pronouns, and meaning discussed in this chapter?
2. What evidence of functional and dysfunctional conflict is apparent in this case?
3. What did Selina Lo need to learn early on about emotional intelligence, as discussed in Chapter 3? How would it have impacted her management style?
4. How would you handle a boss with the win–lose style Selina Lo exhibited early in her career? Explain.
5. Referring to the Chapter 8 International OB feature box as a guide, what lessons about cross-cultural conflict did Selina Lo need to learn early in her career?
6. Which conflict-handing styles are evident in this case? What was their comparative effectiveness?

SOURCE: Excerpted from L. Buchanan, "The Ultimate Business Makeover," *Inc.: The Magazine for Growing Companies,* March 2009. Copyright © 2009 by Mansueto Ventures LLC. Reproduced with permission of Mansueto Ventures LLC via Copyright Clearance Center.

The CONNECTion Zone   McGraw Hill connect™

- The Presentation Assistant
- Ethical OB Dilemma
- Video Case

McGraw Hill connect™

Practise and learn online with Connect.

CHAPTER 9

Power, Politics, and Decision Making

I've recently been offered a supervisory management position at my office and have to decide whether to accept it or reject it. I have ideas on how to improve the way we do things around here, and I know if I take this new job it will give me the power to improve customer service—but I don't know how to handle office politics. From my current position, everybody above me fights all the time. I just want to keep my head down and stick to my job. How can I move into management and stay out of all that political nonsense?

— NOT A POLITICAL PERSON

LO 1 Define *power*,
personalized power,
and *socialized power*.

LO 2 Identify and briefly
describe French and
Raven's five bases of
power, relating factors
to tactics used and
work outcomes (e.g.,
job performance,
job satisfaction, and
turnover).

LO 3 Explain how
uncertainty can trigger
the production of
organizational politics,
which can lead to the
use of personalized
power tactics.

LO 4 Compare and contrast
the rational model of
decision making to
bounded rationality,
decision trees, and
intuition.

LO 5 Infer what causes an
escalation of commitment
and predict what type of
outcome can result.

LO 6 Summarize the pros and
cons of involving groups
in the decision-making
process.

Workplace Complexities

Reading the OB Challenge, you can feel the mixed feelings this individual has regarding the decision to accept or reject an offer to be a supervisor. Unfortunately, this person is confusing petty politics and the pursuit of personal aspirations causing constant disagreement with what could be genuine concern about important workplace issues being openly discussed among office colleagues. We are not saying it's okay to 'be political' or to 'play power games' in the office; rather, individuals must be willing and able to operate effectively in the political environment that exists within all organizations. Their success will depend on their ability to manage and influence not just their own group, but the broader organization within which they operate. Positions provide individuals with legitimate power to make decisions. When decisions are not quick and forthcoming in the manner in which individuals prefer, then they resort to using political avenues to influence others. That is the essence of what we'll be talking about in this chapter.

We'll begin by discussing the fundamental dimensions of power (followed by a natural transition into office politics, as we see how one can influence the other). Understanding the role of politics within an organization is something that is rarely talked about in business classes. However, it does exist and understanding the fundamentals around political action, building network contacts for support, and being aware of political tactics is important.

We'll end our chapter discussions with decision making, because those with power who have the political influence are affecting organizational outcomes all the time. Other than using your "guts" to make decisions, there are several other models worth considering. As organizations strive to remain competitive and profitable, it's critical to emphasize the need for creative decision making to help find new solutions to complex problems . . . and to keep in mind the need for an ethical base when doing so.

The Fundamentals of Power **LO 1**

Power is often related to dependency, and is defined as the ability to influence others to develop a dependent relationship. For example, if employees depend on their manager to sign their paycheque, then the manager has power over the employees. If a manager only has one employee with the ability to complete a certain task and no one else in the organization has the same skill or ability, then the employee has power over the manager. Think of power as potential influence that can exist throughout the entire organization, at all levels, and in all different sorts of positions. When people call upon that power to do something good for the organization and others, it is said that they are using *socialized power*. Knowing the difference between self-serving personalized power and socialized power is important. Let's explore this a bit more.

> *Power*
>
> The ability to influence others to develop a dependent relationship.

Personalized and Socialized Power Recalling our discussion in Chapter 5 about motivation and McClelland's Need Theory, we learned that one of the basic human needs is for power. McClelland stated that this need for power is a learned behaviour, not something individuals are born with. Subsequently, throughout the last half century, researchers have been drawn to the notion of power and what it means to want it. To some, power is bad; but to others, power is necessary for doing something constructive. From this perspective, researchers have drawn a distinction between *socialized power* which is a good thing because it means effort is directed for the purposes of helping others versus *personalized power* which is desired for the sake of personal benefit.[1]

Individuals who pursue personalized power for their own selfish ends give power a bad name. According to research, personalized power is exhibited when people tend to:

■ Focus more on satisfying their own needs

■ Focus less on the needs of others, especially those they are responsible for

■ Act like "the rules" others are expected to follow don't apply to them[2]

Take, for example, Nancy Traversy, co-founder and CEO of the successful children's book publisher Barefoot Books. She decided to quit her job and start her own entrepreneurial journey after she experienced what she perceived to be a double standard of personalized power:

> *I was born in Canada to a family of artists. I studied business, which made me the … (odd) sheep.*

Socialized power
Directed at helping others.

Personalized power
Directed at helping oneself.

After college, I worked for the banking division of Pricewaterhouse in London, (England). One day I was wearing a suit. One of the partners said to me, "Women don't wear trousers" and sent me home to change. It was a formative (influential) experience.[3]

A series of interviews with 25 of the most powerful women in business found a strong preference for socialized power.[4] A good case in point is Sheryl Sandberg, Facebook's chief operating officer, who wrote:

> *My first job was at the World Bank, where I worked on health projects in India— leprosy, AIDS, and blindness. During my first trip to India, I was taken on a tour of a village leprosy home, where I saw people in conditions that I would not have thought possible. I promised myself that going forward, I would work only on things that really mattered. Facebook allows people to … have a real impact on … lives.[5]*

The Focus on Diversity feature box explores in greater detail the differences in perspective on socialized power between the genders.

FOCUS ON DIVERSITY

WOMEN PREFER MORE SOCIALIZED POWER THAN MEN

Is there a difference between the way women and men view power? In one study, a sample of 94 male and 84 female non-managerial and professional employees completed a psychological test. Results indicated that the male and female employees had similar needs for power, but the women had a significantly higher need for socialized power than did their male counterparts. This finding serves today's workplaces well, as women are playing an ever-greater administrative role. Unfortunately, as women gain power in the workplace, greater tension is observed between men and women. The article published in *Training* magazine provides this perspective:

> *Observers view the tension between women and men in the workplace as a natural outcome of power inequities between the genders. Social researchers argue that men still have most of*

the power and are resisting any change as a way to protect their power base. Consultant Susan L. Webb asserts that sexual harassment has far more to do with exercising power in an unhealthy way than with sexual attraction. Likewise, the glass ceiling, a metaphor for the barriers women face in climbing the corporate ladder to management and executive positions, is about power and access to power.

Accordingly, "powerful women were described more positively by women than by men" in a study of 140 female and 125 male college students in Sydney, Australia.

SOURCE: Adapted from R. Kreitner, *Organizational Behaviour*, 9th US. Ed. The McGraw-Hill Companies, Inc. 1221 Ave. of the Americas, New York, N.Y., 2010 pp 443–444.

LO 2 THE FIVE BASES OF POWER

A popular classification scheme for social power originated over 50 years ago with the work of John French and Bertram Raven. They proposed that power arises from five different bases: reward power, coercive power, legitimate power, expert power, and referent power.[6] Each involves a different approach to influencing others.

- **Legitimate power** This base of power is anchored to your formal position or authority. Thus, individuals who obtain influence primarily because of their formal authority to make decisions have *legitimate power*. Legitimate power may express itself in either a positive or negative manner. Here's an example of positive legitimate power that focuses constructively on job performance: *"Pat, as the production coordinator on this project, I have to advise you that this material is late. I need your continued cooperation in the future because if ads are expected to run on time, then I'm going to need the approved copy no later than 24 hours before the deadline. OK? So, how's the family?"* Negative legitimate power tends to be threatening and demeaning to those being influenced. Its main purpose is to build the power holder's ego. For example, *"I suggest you take my advice since I'm the Supervisor in charge of this unit . . . I can make or break your career, you know!"*

  > **Legitimate power**
  > Obtaining influence through formal authority.

- **Reward power** People have *reward power* if they can obtain influence by promising or granting rewards. This concept relates back to our discussions about Vroom's expectancy theory in Chapter 5. An example of reward power is a professor who encourages students to actively participate in class, and in return rewards students with bonus marks: *"If you do this extra work, then I'd be pleased to take it into consideration when calculating your final mark."*

  > **Reward power**
  > Obtaining influence with promised or actual rewards.

- **Coercive power** Threats of punishment and actual punishment give an individual *coercive power*. For instance, consider this heavy-handed tactic by Wolfgang Bernhard, who is now a member of the Board of Management of Daimler AG executive. When he was an executive at Volkswagen, his reputation was well known for being a ruthless cost-cutter. Bernhard's favourite technique was routinely locking staffers in meeting rooms,

  > **Coercive power**
  > Obtaining influence through threatened or actual punishment.

then refusing to open the doors until they had stripped $1,500 in costs from a future model.[7] Another example is, *"Hey Hot Shot! If you don't want to do this job, then let me know and I'll inform the boss. I'm sure we can find ten other people in the unemployment office who would love to do this job at half the salary! So, what'll it be?"*

- **Expert power** Valued knowledge or information gives an individual *expert power* over those who need such knowledge or information. The power of supervisors is enhanced because they know about work schedules and assignments before their employees do. But employees who have a unique skill set that is the best in the region hold the power. In today's high-tech workplace, knowledge is power. For example, *"I know Ahmed is very hard to work with and can be difficult, but he writes better program than any person in this province. We need him!"*

  > **Expert power**
  > Obtaining influence through knowledge or information.

- **Referent power** Also called charisma, *referent power* comes into play when personality becomes the reason for influence. Role models have referent power over those who identify closely with them.[8] They are liked—it's that simple. Certain kinds of leaders can have a lot of referent power over members of the organization (we'll talk more about this in the next chapter). But anyone in the organization who holds true to their word, is considerate of others, and treats people with respect and dignity will be given power by those who feel they deserve it. For example: *"Fred is the best custodian we've ever had—he's competent, he's kind and very dependable. He's helpful to every employee in this building. If Fred says we're wasting too much energy, then I say we listen to him and start using more energy efficient bulbs!"*

  > **Referent power**
  > Obtaining influence through charisma or personal attraction.

RESEARCH FINDINGS: INFLUENCING TACTICS

Remember that power is the potential of influencing others—so how is this achieved? Research initiated by David Kipnis and his colleagues revealed how people influence each other in organizations. Statistical refinements and replications by other researchers over a 13-year period eventually narrowed the findings down to nine influence tactics.[9] The nine tactics, ranked in diminishing order of use in the workplace, are as follows:

1. *Rational persuasion* – Trying to convince someone with reason, logic, or facts.

2. *Inspirational appeals* – Trying to build enthusiasm by appealing to others' emotions, ideals, or values.

3. *Consultation* – Getting others to participate in planning, making decisions, and changes.

4. *Ingratiation* – Getting someone in a good mood prior to making a request; being friendly, helpful, and using praise or flattery.

5. *Personal appeals* – Referring to friendship and loyalty when making a request.

6. *Exchange* – Making express or implied promises and trading favours.

7. *Coalition* – Getting others to support your effort to persuade someone.

8. *Pressure* – Demanding compliance or using intimidation or threats.

9. *Legitimating* – Basing a request on authority or right, organizational rules or policies, or express or implied support from superiors.[10]

These approaches can be considered *generic* influence tactics because they characterize social influence in all directions and in a wide variety of settings. Researchers have found this ranking to be fairly consistent regardless of whether the direction of influence is downward, upward, or lateral.[11]

Some call the first five influence tactics—rational persuasion, inspirational appeals, consultation, ingratiation, and personal appeals—*soft* tactics because they are friendlier and not as coercive as the last four tactics. Exchange, coalition, pressure, and legitimating tactics accordingly are called *hard* tactics because they involve more overt pressure.

THREE POSSIBLE INFLUENCE OUTCOMES

Put yourself in this familiar situation. It's Wednesday and a big project you've been working on for your project team is due Friday. You're behind on the preparation of your computer graphics for your final report and presentation. You catch a friend who is great at computer graphics as he heads out of the office at quitting time. You try this *exchange tactic* to get your friend to help you out: "I'm way behind. I need your help. If you could come back in for two to three hours tonight and help me with these graphics, I'll complete those spreadsheets you've been complaining about." According to

researchers, your friend will engage in one of three possible influence outcomes:

1. *Commitment* – Your friend enthusiastically agrees and will demonstrate initiative and persistence while completing the assignment.

2. *Compliance* – Your friend grudgingly complies and will need prodding to satisfy minimum requirements.

3. *Resistance* – Your friend will say no, make excuses, stall, or put up an argument.[12]

The best outcome is commitment because the target person's intrinsic motivation will energize good performance. However, managers often have to settle for compliance in today's hectic workplace. Resistance means a failed influence attempt.

PRACTICAL RESEARCH INSIGHTS

Laboratory and field studies have taught us useful lessons about the relative effectiveness of influence tactics along with other instructive insights:

- Core influence tactics—rational persuasion, consultation, collaboration, and inspirational appeals—are most effective at building commitment.[13] Do not rely on pressure and coalition tactics.[14]

- Commitment is more likely when the influence attempt involves something important and enjoyable and is based on a friendly relationship.[15]

- Credible (believable and trustworthy) people tend to be the most persuasive.[16]

- In a survey of 101 employees from two different organizations, employees were more likely to resist change when managers used a legitimating tactic and were more apt to accept change when managers relied on a consultative strategy.[17]

- Ingratiation improved short-term but reduced long-term sales goal achievement in a study of 241 sales people.[18] Schmoozing can help today's sales but not tomorrow's.

- Subtle flattery and agreeing with the other person's opinion (both forms of ingratiation) were shown to increase the likelihood of executives being recommended to sit on boards of directors.[19]

- Research involving corporate managers of a supermarket chain showed that influence tactics can be taught. Managers who received 360-degree feedback on two occasions regarding their influence tactics showed an increased use of core influence tactics.[20]

The bottom line: The influence tactics mentioned earlier can be learned and improved to move resisters to

Skills & Best Practices

compliance, and those that are compliant to committed. The Skills & Best Practices feature box provides additional suggestions on increasing your influence. Use this knowledge to achieve better outcomes for you, your team, and your organization.

EMPOWERMENT: FROM POWER SHARING TO POWER DISTRIBUTION

An exciting trend in today's organization centres on giving employees a greater say in the workplace. This trend wears various labels, including "participative management" and "open-book management."[21] Regardless of the label you prefer, it is all about empowerment. Management consultant and writer W. Alan Rudolph offers this definition of *empowerment*: "recognizing and releasing into the organization the power that people already have in their wealth of useful knowledge, experience, and internal motivation."[22]

A study used 45 in-depth interviews to determine the meaning of empowerment from an employee point of view. Interestingly, employees interpreted empowerment in terms of how much personal responsibility and control over their work they experience. Results also showed that employees vary in terms of how much empowerment they desire. Some employees like to have responsibility and freedom, and others do not.[23] Another study involving more than 1,000 employees and 1,772 customers of 91 bank branches showed that employees who feel empowered provide higher quality service than those who do not feel empowered.[24]

Swiss power broker Klaus Schwab sees an erosion of the traditional command and control type of organization in the Web 2.0 world.

Empowerment

Employees being assigned authority and responsibility over tasks once held by their superiors.

Those who dismiss the employee empowerment trend as a passing North American fad need to see it as part of a global movement (see the International OB feature box). Klaus Schwab, a respected Swiss businessman and philanthropist, offers this sweeping perspective:

A general issue will be the changing power equation, which means that everywhere in society and business, the power is moving from the centre to the periphery. Vertical command-and-control structures are being eroded and replaced by communities and different platforms. We are moving into the Web 2.0 world (a slang tech term referencing

CHINESE STUDY RESULTS: EMPLOYEE EMPOWERMENT HAS EFFECT ON TURNOVER

Is empowerment only valued by Canadian OB experts? According to a study conducted by researcher Kai Yao at the School of Management at Fudan University in Shanghai (China), the tendency toward employee turnover is directly linked to employee empowerment as well as other variables such as promotion opportunities (or lack thereof), social relationships within the firm, and work opportunities outside of the current employment experience. In fact, employee empowerment became the moderating variable within the study—statistically, this means that when universally applied to the study, employee empowerment within the Chinese workplace had more of a universal effect on all variables when trying to identify causation.

The Chinese study concluded that the human resource management of an organization could be strengthened, while at the same time decreasing turnover, if they focused on employee empowerment and those other factors that influence individuals to leave. The role of employee empowerment must be taken seriously by employers with Chinese staff members.

SOURCE: K. Yao, "Study on the Moderating Effect of the Employee Psychological Empowerment on the Enterprise Employee Turnover Tendency: Taking Small and Middle Enterprises in Jinan as the Example," *International Business Research*, Vol. 3, No. 3, July 2010.

---

a new world of broad improvements), and this has tremendous implications on the national level and on business models. [25]

A core component of empowerment is progressively pushing decision-making authority throughout the organization at all levels. Steve Kerr, who has served as the chief learning officer at General Electric and is currently the director of Harvard Business School publishing corporation, adds this important qualification: "We say empowerment is moving decision making (throughout the operational levels) where a competent decision can be made."[26]

Of course, it is naive and counterproductive to hand power over to unwilling or unprepared employees. There is an assumption within an empowered work environment that all employees want to be empowered. From our experience, we can attest to the fact that some employees just want to do their job and go home. They don't want any more responsibility or authority; to them, a job is a job. This type of employee would resist the introduction of empowerment in the workplace, and would need to be shown the advantages of it through mentorship or development workshops.

A MATTER OF DEGREE

The concept of empowerment requires some adjustments in traditional thinking. Power is not a fixed-pie situation where one person's gain is another's loss (recall our discussion of distributive negotiation in the last chapter). Remember, the purpose of socialized power is to help others, so the possibility of gains is unlimited.

Empowerment is an extension of socialized power and it requires win–win thinking. Frances Hesselbein, the woman credited with modernizing the Girl Guides organization, put it this way: "The more power you give away, the more you have."[27] People who prefer to maintain control over their organizational territory will view empowerment as a threat to their personal power and are missing the point because of their win–lose thinking.

The second adjustment to traditional thinking involves seeing empowerment as a matter of degree, not as an either–or proposition.[28] Figure 9.1 illustrates how power can be shifted to the hands of non-managers, step by step, throughout all the functional areas of the organization. The overriding goal is to increase productivity and competitiveness in leaner organizations. Each step in this evolution increases the power of employees who traditionally were told what, when, and how to do things. A good role model for the spirit of empowerment is Motorola executive Greg Brown:

He boils his philosophy down to three words: listen, learn, lead. It means you need to understand your business down to the nuts and bolts, let your employees know you won't have all the answers, and focus on just a handful of truly crucial things, even though dozens seem as important.[29]

USING POWER RESPONSIBLY AND ETHICALLY

Two aspects of power responsibility are worth mentioning here: the abuse of power as it relates to dependency, and violating the spirit of socialized power.

FIGURE **9.1** The Evolution of Power: From Domination to Delegation

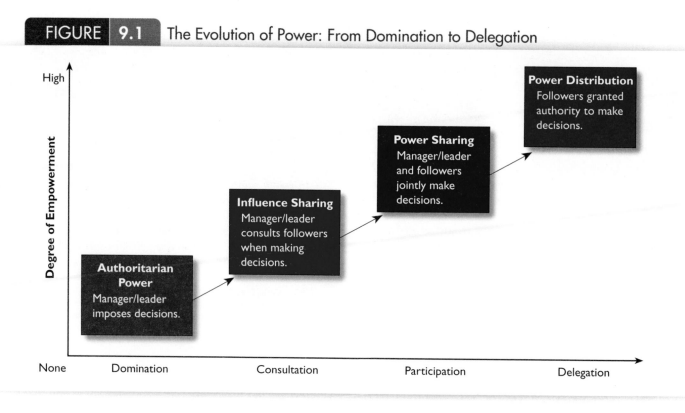

Abuse of Power as it Relates to Dependency When one person exerts power over another person in the office, and does so through harassing and degrading means, then this is an abuse of power. Any type of harassing or bullying behaviour, including racial as well as sexual harassment, is about building up the impression of unstoppable power and control over another in a coercive demeaning way. Victims of this type of abuse in the office may not understand the method of these power games, but the intent is to belittle the self-worth of the person to the point of creating the illusion that success in the firm will only occur if total compliance is given over to the abuser (thus building dependency).

In Chapter 8, we spoke of how conflict can escalate into creating toxic workplaces. Today, most contemporary organizations assign their human resource department to look after complaints from employees reporting abuse. This type of behaviour is something that management must take seriously and remove from the workplace.

If for some reason employees do not want to go to management or some other department within the organization to resolve such an issue, then there are also outside government agencies in most major cities, like the Human Rights Commission, which will hear their complaint on a confidential basis. There are resources at all levels of government worth considering for help, including Human Resources and Skills Development Canada (HRDC) at the federal level, and provincial or territorial Ministries of Labour. Collectively, these departments and ministries have become more vigilant in researching, educating, and providing relevant statistics on the abuse of workplace power to increase awareness and offer solutions to prevent violence in the workplace.

Abuse of Power by Violating the Spirit of Socialized Power People who have power but who do not use it for the purposes of helping others risk losing it. Media continue to cover stories of people in positions of authority who engage in personalized power. You've probably heard these infamous stories: former Canadian citizen Conrad Black served five years of jail time for his misdealings as CEO of Hollinger International; Bernie Madoff is serving 150 years for his $65 billion Ponzi scheme; and Alberta's own Bernard Ebbers, the former ex-CEO of bankrupt WorldCom (now Verizon), is serving 25 years in jail for his misuse of power. And there are dozens of others in similar circumstances. What they have in common is the highly limiting effect personalized power offers to those who engage in it. People who have this type of power are not trusted, as their interests remain focused on themselves rather than on the collective interests of the organization.

Mutuality of Interest At the very heart of interpersonal dealings in today's work organizations is a constant struggle between individual and collective interests. For example, Sid wants a raise, but his company doesn't make enough money to both grant raises and buy needed capital equipment. The downside of such misalignment of interests is evident in the results of a recent survey of 150 senior executives who were asked, "What makes good employees quit?" "Unhappiness with management" was the number one response category (35 percent), followed by "Limited opportunities for advancement" (33 percent), and "Lack of recognition" (13 percent).[30] That's almost a 50 percent preoccupation with self-interest—but is this not understandable? After all, each of us was born not as a cooperating organizational member, but as an individual with instincts for self-preservation. It took socialization in family, school, religion, sports, recreation, and employment to introduce us to the notion of mutuality of interest. Basically, *mutuality of interest* involves win–win situations in which your self-interest is served by cooperating actively and creatively with potential adversaries. A pair of organization development consultants offered this managerial perspective of mutuality of interest:

> *Nothing is more important than this sense of mutuality to the effectiveness and quality of an organization's products and services. Management must strive to stimulate a strong sense of shared ownership in every employee, because otherwise an organization cannot do its best in the long run. Employees who identify their own personal self-interest with the quality of their organization's output understand mutuality and strive to maintain it in their jobs and work relations.*[31]

Figure 9.2 graphically portrays the constant tug-of-war between employees' self-interest and the organization's need for mutuality of interest. It also shows the linkage between this chapter—influence, empowerment, and politics—and other key topics in this book. Decision makers, especially managers, need a complete tool kit of techniques to guide diverse individuals, who are often powerfully motivated to put their own self-interests first, to pursue common objectives. At stake in this tug-of-war between individual and collective interests is no less than the ultimate survival of organizations.

Mutuality of interest

Balancing individual and organizational interests through win–win cooperation.

The Fundamentals of Organizational Politics

Employees are constantly challenged to achieve a workable balance between exercising personalized power that is self-serving, and socialized power that addresses the interests of the organization. If individuals spend too much energy enhancing their own position within the company, then it's safe to say they understand the effect politics can have. We will use the following definition when discussing politics: "*Organizational politics* involves intentional acts of influence to enhance or protect the self-interest of an individual or group."[32] An emphasis on self-interest is key to this concept.

When a proper balance exists, the pursuit of self-interest may serve the organization's interests. Political behaviour becomes a negative force when self-interests erode or defeat organizational interests. For example, researchers have documented the political tactic of filtering and distorting information flowing up to the boss. This self-serving practice places the reporting employee in the best possible light.[33]

Most students of OB find the study of organizational politics intriguing. As we will see, however, organizational politics includes, but is certainly not limited to, dirty dealing. Organizational politics is an ever-present

Organizational politics

Intentional acts of influence to enhance or protect the self-interest of an individual or group.

FIGURE	9.2	The Constant Tug-of-War between Self-Interest and Mutuality of Interest Requires Managerial Action

and sometimes annoying feature of modern work life. "Executives say that they spend 19 percent of their time dealing with political infighting with their staffs, according to a survey by OfficeTeam, a staffing services firm."[34] One expert recently observed, "Many 'new economy' companies use the acronym WOMBAT—or waste of money, brains, and time—to describe office politics."[35] On the other hand, organizational politics can be a positive force in modern work organizations. Skillful and well-timed politics can help you get your point across, neutralize resistance to a key project, or get a choice job assignment.

A recent Accountemps survey asked 572 workers, "How do you deal with office politics?" A majority (54 percent) chose the response "Know what's going on but do not participate," while 16 percent said "Participate directly," and 29 percent said they would not participate.[36] To reflect on your own feelings toward office politics, see Table 9.1 to consider if you are a political shark or a naive individual. We'll revisit this table again shortly. For now, it is important to understand that politics is about knowing how "the game" is played; that is what really counts.[37] Actively playing politics at work is a matter of personal preference and ethics. Roberta Bhasin, a telephone company district manager, put organizational politics into perspective by observing the following:

Most of us would like to believe that organizations are rationally structured, based on reasonable divisions of labour, a clear hierarchical communication flow, and well-defined lines of authority aimed at meeting universally understood goals and objectives.

But organizations are made up of people with personal agendas designed to win power and influence. The agenda—the game—is called corporate politics. It is played by avoiding the rational structure, manipulating the communications hierarchy, and ignoring established lines of authority. The rules are never written down and seldom discussed.

For some, corporate politics are second nature. They instinctively know the unspoken rules of the game. Others must learn. Managers who don't understand the politics of their organizations are at a disadvantage, not only in winning raises and promotions, but even in getting things done. [38]

To that end, 32 percent of 3,447 middle and senior managers responding to an Internet survey said they needed coaching in how to be more politically savvy at work.[39] In the next section we explore this important and interesting area by (1) identifying some basic triggers of political behaviour, (2) exploring the three levels of political action, and (3) discussing eight specific political tactics. It is our intent to provide you with the tools needed to deal effectively with office politics.

TRIGGERS OF POLITICAL BEHAVIOUR   **LO 3**

Political manoeuvring is triggered primarily by uncertainty. Five common sources of uncertainty within organizations are:

1. Unclear objectives
2. Vague performance measures
3. Ill-defined decision processes
4. Strong individual or group competition[40]
5. Uncertainty that results from change

Regarding this last source of uncertainty, organizational development specialist Anthony Raia noted, "Whatever we attempt to change, the political subsystem becomes active. Vested interests are almost always at stake and the distribution of power is challenged." [41]

TABLE 9.1

ARE YOU POLITICALLY NAIVE, POLITICALLY SENSIBLE, OR A POLITICAL SHARK?

CHARACTERISTICS	NAIVE	SENSIBLE	SHARKS
Underlying attitude	Politics is unpleasant.	Politics is necessary.	Politics is an opportunity.
Intent	Avoid at all costs.	Further departmental goals.	Self-serving and predatory.
Techniques	Tell it like it is.	Network; expand connections; use system to give and receive favours.	Manipulate; use fraud and deceit when necessary.
Favourite tactics	None—the truth will win out.	Negotiate, bargain.	Bully, misuse information; cultivate and use "friends" and other contacts.

SOURCE: Reprinted from J.K. Pinto and O.P. Kharbanda, "Lessons for an Accidental Profession," *Business Horizons,* Vol. 38, No. 2, p 45, © 1995, with permission from Elsevier.

Thus, we would expect a field sales representative striving to achieve an assigned quota to be less political than a management trainee working on a variety of projects. While some management trainees stake their career success on hard work, competence, and a bit of luck, many do not. These people attempt to gain a competitive edge through some combination of political tactics. Meanwhile, the salesperson's performance is measured in actual sales, not in terms of being friends with the boss or taking credit for others' work. Thus, the management trainee would tend to be more political than the field salesperson because of greater uncertainty about management's expectations.

Because employees generally experience greater uncertainty during the earlier stages of their careers, are junior employees more political than more senior ones? The answer is yes, according to a survey of 243 employed adults. In fact, one senior employee nearing retirement told the researcher: "I used to play political games when I was younger. Now I just do my job."[42] It is easy to see how the management trainee would resort to as many personalized power tactics as possible to gain the kind of recognition desired, so let's discuss political action and tactics a bit more.

THREE LEVELS OF POLITICAL ACTION

Figure 9.3 illustrates three different levels of political action: the individual level, the coalition level, and the network level.[43] Each level has its distinguishing characteristics.

- *First level*—the individual level. Personal self-interests are pursued by the individual. The political aspects of coalitions and networks are not obvious.

- *Second level*—the coalition level. People with a common interest can become a political coalition by fitting the following definition. In an organizational context, a **coalition** is an informal group bound together by the active pursuit of a single goal. Coalitions may or may not coincide with formal group membership. For example, a group of employees could get together with a target goal of getting a sexual-harassing team leader fired. Once the problem is resolved and the goal reached, the coalition disbands. Experts note that political coalitions have "fuzzy boundaries," meaning they are fluid in membership, flexible in structure, and temporary in duration.[44]

> **Coalition**
>
> An informal group bound together by the active pursuit of a single goal.

- *Third Level*—the network level. Political action involves networks.[45] In most major cities across the country, individuals can join a network of like-minded people (some refer to them as professional social clubs) who help each other achieve opportunities through word of mouth, and make broad connections and contacts that may serve them politically in the future. Unlike coalitions, which pivot on specific goals, networks are loose associations of individuals seeking social support for their general self-interests. Politically, networks are people-oriented, while coalitions are goal-oriented. Networks have broader and longer-term agendas than do coalitions.

POLITICAL TACTICS

Anyone who has worked in an organization has firsthand knowledge of obvious politicking. Blaming someone else for your mistake is an obvious political ploy. But other political tactics are more subtle. Researchers have identified a range of political behaviour.

One landmark study, involving in-depth interviews with 87 people from 30 electronics companies, identified eight political tactics. According to the researchers, "Respondents were asked to describe organizational political tactics and personal characteristics of effective political actors based upon their accumulated experience in *all* organizations in which they had worked."[46]

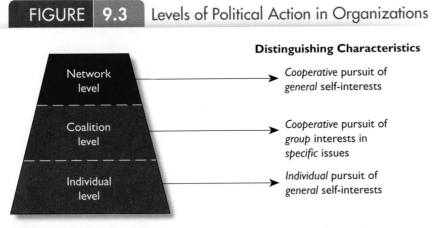

FIGURE 9.3 Levels of Political Action in Organizations

Distinguishing Characteristics

Network level → *Cooperative* pursuit of *general* self-interests

Coalition level → *Cooperative* pursuit of *group* interests in *specific* issues

Individual level → *Individual* pursuit of *general* self-interests

SOURCE: A.T. Cobb, "Political Diagnosis: Applications in Organizational Development," *Academy of Management Review*, July 1986, pp 482–96.

Listed in descending order of occurrence, the eight political tactics that emerged are:

1. Attacking or blaming others (scapegoating)
2. Using information as a political tool
3. Creating a favourable image (impression management)
4. Developing a base of support (network of useful contacts)
5. Praising others (ingratiation)
6. Forming power coalitions with strong allies
7. Associating with influential people
8. Creating obligations (reciprocity)

The researchers distinguished between reactive and proactive political tactics. Some of the tactics, such as scapegoating, were reactive because the intent was to defend one's self-interest. Other tactics, such as building a network of useful contacts, were proactive because they sought to promote the individual's self-interest.

What is your attitude toward organizational politics? How often do you rely on various tactics? Now that you have had a chance to learn a bit more about the different characteristics of politics, refer back to Table 9.1 and compare your tendencies to the others listed. How do you think others view your political actions? What are the career, friendship, and ethical implications of your political tendencies?[47]

Next we will move on to the next discussion, understanding the decision-making process. Since power is about creating dependency or having influence to affect favourable outcomes, and politics is about creating outcomes that fulfill self-interest, then insight into the motives behind the *decisions* people make on a daily basis will enrich your understanding of this process; it's all about outcomes.

The Fundamentals of Decision Making

Decision making entails identifying and choosing alternative solutions that lead to a desired outcome. For example, you may be reading this book as part of an online course that you decided to take because you are working full time. Alternatively, you may be a full-time student reading this book as part of a course you are taking on campus. Identifying and sorting out alternatives like when and how to take a course is the process of decision making.

> **Decision making**
>
> Identifying and choosing solutions that lead to a desired outcome.

Before we begin our discussion, you are encouraged to complete the Self-Assessment Exercise, "What Is Your Decision-Making Style?" Knowing your score may

"Our task, then, is to decide how to decide how to decide."

help you personalize the concepts discussed in the rest of this chapter.

THE RATIONAL MODEL

The *rational model* proposes that individuals use a rational six-step sequence when making decisions: (1) identify the problem or opportunity, (2) gather related information to make an informed decision, (3) formulate alternative solutions, (4) select the best alternative, (5) implement the solution, and (6) monitor and evaluate the solution. According to this model, shown in Figure 9.4, individuals are completely objective and possess complete information to make a decision.[48] Despite criticism for being unrealistic, the rational model is helpful because it breaks down the decision-making process and serves as an anchor when designing future models.[49]

> **Rational model**
>
> A logical and sequential approach to decision making.

Identifying the Problem A problem exists when the actual situation and the desired situation differ. For example, a problem exists when you have to pay rent for your apartment at the end of the month and you don't have enough money. Your problem is not that you have to pay rent; your problem is obtaining the needed funds.

Gathering Related Information To make an informed decision, the decision-maker has to consider related information. Sticking with our rent example, consider all the variables that play into this problem, such as: Have you ever missed a payment in the past? Have you received a warning from the landlord about missed payments in the past, and if so, what are the conditions of the warning? How much money is owed and how much do you actually have? When is the money due? Can it be paid in installments over a few

What Is Your Decision-Making Style?

INSTRUCTIONS: Consider each possible response for a question and then rank them according to how much you prefer each response. Because many of the questions are anchored to how individuals make decisions at work, feel free to use your student role as a frame of reference. For each question, rank the four responses with 1, 2, 4, or 8. Use an 8 for the responses that are **most** like you, a 4 for those that are **moderately** like you, a 2 for those that are **slightly** like you, and a 1 for the responses that are **least** like you. For example, a question might be answered [8], [4], [2], [1].

1	My prime objective in life is to:	❏ have a position with status	❏ be the best in what-ever I do	❏ be recognized for my work	❏ feel secure in my job
2	I enjoy work that:	❏ is clear and well defined	❏ is varied and challenging	❏ lets me act independently	❏ involves people
3	I expect people to be:	❏ productive	❏ capable	❏ committed	❏ responsive
4	My work lets me:	❏ get things done	❏ find workable approaches	❏ apply new ideas	❏ be truly satisfied
5	I communicate best by:	❏ talking with others	❏ putting things in writing	❏ being open with others	❏ having a group meeting
6	My planning focuses on:	❏ current problems	❏ how best to meet goals	❏ future opportunities	❏ needs of people in the organization
7	I prefer to solve problems by:	❏ applying rules	❏ using careful analysis	❏ being creative	❏ relying on my feelings
8	I prefer information:	❏ that is simple and direct	❏ that is complete	❏ that is broad and informative	❏ that is easily understood
9	When I'm not sure what to do:	❏ I rely on my intuition	❏ I search for alternatives	❏ I try to find a compromise	❏ I avoid making a decision
10	Whenever possible, I avoid:	❏ long debates	❏ incomplete work	❏ technical problems	❏ conflict with others
11	I am really good at:	❏ remembering details	❏ finding answers	❏ seeing many options	❏ working with people
12	When time is important, I:	❏ decide and act quickly	❏ apply proven approaches	❏ look for what will work	❏ refuse to be pressured
13	In social settings, I:	❏ speak with many people	❏ observe what others are doing	❏ contribute to the conversation	❏ want to be part of the discussion
14	I always remember:	❏ people's names	❏ places I have been	❏ people's faces	❏ people's personalities
15	I prefer jobs where I:	❏ receive high rewards	❏ have challenging assignments	❏ can reach my personal goals	❏ am accepted by the group
16	I work best with people who:	❏ are energetic and ambitious	❏ are very competent	❏ are open-minded	❏ are polite and understanding
17	When I am under stress, I:	❏ speak quickly	❏ try to concentrate on the problem	❏ become frustrated	❏ worry about what I should do
18	Others consider me:	❏ aggressive	❏ disciplined	❏ imaginative	❏ supportive
19	My decisions are generally:	❏ realistic and direct	❏ systematic and logical	❏ broad and flexible	❏ sensitive to other's needs
20	I dislike:	❏ losing control	❏ boring work	❏ following rules	❏ being rejected
Column Totals		Directive Style	Analytical Style	Conceptual Style	Behavioural Style

SOURCE: © Alan J Rowe, Professor Emeritus. Revised 12/18/98. Reprinted by permission.

Scoring

Total the scores in each of the four columns. The total score for column one represents your directive style, column two your analytical style, column three your conceptual style, and column four your behavioural style. The column with the highest score is your decision-making style preference.

FIGURE 9.4 The Four Stages in Rational Decision Making

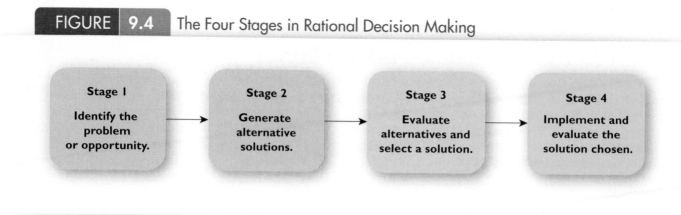

weeks? Is there a clause in the rental agreement that outlines the specifics if a payment is missed? Can you get access to a line of credit or take out a cash advance on a credit card until payday?

Generate Solutions Now that you have considered all the related information, you remember that this will be your second warning for late rent payments, and if you miss again, the warning says that the landlord can evict you. Furthermore, you are only missing $150 to pay the rent in full. So, the next logical step is generating alternative solutions with this context in mind. Since this is not a repetitive or routine decision, there aren't any hard and fast rules or policies that will help you solve this issue. You find yourself in a unique situation, and as a result, you need to create customized alternative solutions around your issue. You consider three possible alternative courses of action: (1) get a credit card cash advance, (2) ask your parents for a $150 short-term loan, or (3) pay the landlord as much as you currently have and then pay the balance once your paycheque comes in next week.

Selecting a Solution According to the rational model, decision-makers want to optimize the outcome by choosing the alternative with the greatest value, such as highest benefit, greatest profit, or lowest cost. This is no easy task. First, assigning values to alternatives is complicated and prone to error. Furthermore, evaluating alternatives assumes they can be judged according to some standards or criteria, such as benefit return, quality assessment, cost saving, profit generated, or the amount of risk involved. Research demonstrates that people vary in their preferences for safety or risk when making decisions.[50] Evaluating alternatives assumes they can be judged according to some standards or

criteria. This further assumes that (1) valid criteria exist, (2) each alternative can be compared against these criteria, and (3) the decision-maker actually uses the criteria. As you know from making your own key life decisions, people frequently violate these assumptions. Finally, consider the ethics of the solution. In our rent example, you choose to ask your parents for a $150 short-term loan. For you, this solution addresses your problem by providing the most benefit with the fewest disadvantages.

Implement the Solution Once you have chosen a solution, you need to implement it. This involves identifying and choosing key action items, giving responsibilities to those who will carry out the action items, and setting realistic timelines for planning purposes. When it comes to implementing the solution, remember what you learned from our discussions about influencing people and politics. Referring back to our rent example, before going home to talk to your parents tonight, you decide to wait until they've had their dinner (so they are more relaxed), you buy some flowers for your mother (because you know she loves receiving them), and you buy your father the latest car magazine (because you know he'll enjoy reading it)—and you also bring home your mid-term mark of 89 percent to let them know how hard you are working at school. These actions should create the kind of favourable setting that makes it easier for you to ask for the loan and for your parents to listen and agree to the request.

Monitor and Evaluate the Solution After the solution is implemented, its effectiveness must be observed, monitored, and evaluated. If the solution is effective, it should reduce the difference between the actual and desired states that created the problem. If the gap is not closed, the implementation was not successful, and one of the following is true: the problem was incorrectly identified, or the solution was inappropriate. Using the rent example one last time, consider: Did you get the money you needed from your parents? Were they receptive to your gifts and the request? Was your timing right when you asked them after dinner, or should you have chosen a better time? If you need money again in the future, will they say yes?

Summarizing the Rational Model The rational model is based on the premise that people optimize when they make decisions. *Optimizing* involves solving problems by producing the best possible solution that provides the highest return or greatest rewards.

> **Optimizing**
>
> Choosing the solution that provides the highest return or rewards.

As noted by decision theorist and Nobel Prize winner Herbert Simon, "The assumptions of perfect rationality are contrary to fact. It is not a question of approximation; they do not even remotely describe the processes that human beings use for making decisions in complex situations."[51] Since decision-makers do not follow these rational procedures, Simon proposed a bounded rationality model of decision making.

LO 4 Non-Rational Model Of Decision Making

In contrast to the rational model's focus on how decisions *should* be made, a non-rational model explains how decisions *actually* are made. OB expert Herbert Simon coined the phrase *bounded rationality* to cover non-rational decision making, which represents the notion that decision-makers are bounded or restricted by a variety of constraints when making decisions. These constraints include: limited capacity of the human mind, problem complexity and uncertainty, amount and timeliness of information at hand, criticality of the decision, and time demands.[52]

> **Bounded rationality**
>
> Decision strategy that takes into consideration constraints such as human limitations, time, problem complexity, and uncertainty.

Simon's bounded rationality model suggests that decision making is characterized by (1) limited information processing, (2) judgmental heuristics, and (3) satisficing. We now explore each of these characteristics.

Limited Information Processing People are limited by how much information they process because of bounded rationality, which makes it difficult for them to identify all possible alternative solutions. In the long run, the constraints of bounded rationality cause decision-makers to fail to evaluate all potential alternatives.

Judgmental Heuristics *Judgmental heuristics* represent rules of thumb or shortcuts that people use to reduce information processing demands.[53] We automatically use them without conscious awareness. Because these shortcuts represent knowledge gained from past experience, they can help decision-makers evaluate current problems. But they also can lead to errors that erode the quality of decisions. There are two common categories of heuristics:

> **Judgmental heuristics**
>
> Rules of thumb or shortcuts that people use to reduce information processing demands.

- *Availability heuristics* represent a decision-maker's tendency to base decisions on information that is readily available in memory.[54] Information is more accessible in memory when it involves an event that recently occurred, when it is most important (e.g., a plane crash), and when it evokes strong emotions (e.g., innocent people being killed). These heuristics are likely to cause people to overestimate the occurrence of unlikely events such as a plane crash or a school shooting.

> **Availability heuristic**
>
> Tendency to base decisions on information readily available in memory.

- *Representativeness heuristics* are used when people estimate the probability of an event occurring. They reflect the tendency to assess the likelihood of an event occurring on the basis of your impressions about similar occurrences. A team leader, for example, may hire a graduate from a particular college or university program because the past three people hired from that school were good performers. Unfortunately, this shortcut can result in a biased decision.

> **Representativeness heuristic**
>
> Tendency to assess the likelihood of an event occurring on the basis of impressions about similar occurrences.

Satisficing People do not always select the optimal solution because they do not have the time, information, or ability to handle the complexity associated with following a rational process. This is not necessarily undesirable. *Satisficing* involves choosing a solution that meets some minimum qualifications, one that is good enough. Satisficing resolves problems by producing solutions that are satisfactory, as opposed to optimal.

> **Satisficing**
>
> Choosing a solution that meets a minimum standard of acceptance.

This person is in a hurry to get to work, so he is satisficing a nutritional breakfast by eating only a single piece of toast before leaving home.

Dynamics of Decision Making

This section examines various dynamics of decision making—personal decision-making styles, the role of intuition (using your gut), decision trees, escalation of commitment, and the role for creativity. An understanding of these dynamics can help all employees make better decisions.

PERSONAL DECISION-MAKING STYLES

By now you have taken the Self-Assessment Exercise and know your own personal decision-making style, which can help you see preferences and patterns that you rely upon, rightly or wrongly. A personal decision-making style is based on the idea that styles vary along two different dimensions: value orientation and tolerance for ambiguity.[55] Value orientation reflects the extent to which an individual focuses on either task and technical concerns versus people and social concerns when making decisions. The second dimension pertains to a person's tolerance for ambiguity, the extent to which people have a high need for structure or control in their life. When the dimensions of value orientation and tolerance for ambiguity are combined, they form four styles of decision making (see Figure 9.5): directive, analytical, conceptual, and behavioural.

1. **Directive** People with a directive style have a low tolerance for ambiguity and are oriented toward task and technical concerns when making decisions. They are efficient, logical, practical, and systematic in their approach to solving problems. People with this style are action-oriented and decisive and like to focus on facts. In their pursuit of speed and results, however, these individuals tend to be autocratic (dominating), exercise power and control, and focus on the short run.

2. **Analytical** This style has a much higher tolerance for ambiguity and is characterized by the tendency to over-analyze a situation. People with this style like to consider more information and alternatives than do directives. They are careful decision-makers who take longer to make decisions, but who also respond well to new or uncertain situations. They can often be autocratic.

3. **Conceptual** People with a conceptual style have a high tolerance for ambiguity and tend to focus on the people or social aspects of a work situation. They take a broad perspective to problem solving and like to consider many options and future possibilities. Conceptual types adopt a long-term perspective and rely on intuition and discussions with others to acquire information. They also are willing to take risks and are good at finding creative solutions to problems. On the downside, however, a conceptual style can foster an unrealistic and uncertain approach to decision making.

4. **Behavioural** People with this style work well with others and enjoy social interactions in which opinions are openly exchanged. Behavioural types are supportive, receptive to suggestions, show warmth, and prefer verbal to written information. Although they like to hold meetings, people with this style have a tendency to avoid conflict and to be too concerned about others. This can lead behavioural types to adopt a "wishy-washy" approach to decision making, to have a hard time saying no to others, and to have trouble making difficult decisions.

Research and Practical Implications   Research shows that very few people have only one dominant decision-making style. Rather, most have characteristics that fall into two or three styles. Studies also show that decision-making styles vary across occupations, job levels, and countries.[56] You can use knowledge of decision-making styles

FIGURE 9.5 Decision-Making Styles

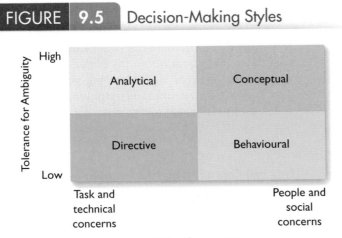

SOURCE: Based on discussion contained in A.J. Rowe and R.O. Mason, *Managing with Style: A Guide to Understanding, Assessing, and Improving Decision Making* (San Francisco: Jossey-Bass, 1987), pp 1–17.

in three ways. First, knowledge of styles can help you to understand yourself. Second, you can increase your ability to influence others by being aware of styles. For example,

if you are dealing with an analytical person, you should provide as much information as possible to support your ideas. Finally, knowledge of styles gives you an awareness of how people can take the same information and yet arrive at different decisions by using a variety of decision-making strategies. It is important to conclude with the reminder that there is no best decision-making style that applies in all situations.

THE ROLE OF INTUITION

Have you ever had a hunch or gut feeling about something? If yes, then you have experienced the effects of intuition. *Intuition* "is a capacity for attaining direct knowledge or understanding without the apparent intrusion of rational thought or logical inference."[57] As a process, intuition is automatic and involuntary. There are two types of intuition and two sources for intuition (see Figure 9.6).[58] We will discuss both briefly and then provide some

> **Intuition**
>
> Making a choice without the use of conscious thought or logical inference.

FIGURE 9.6 A Model of Intuition

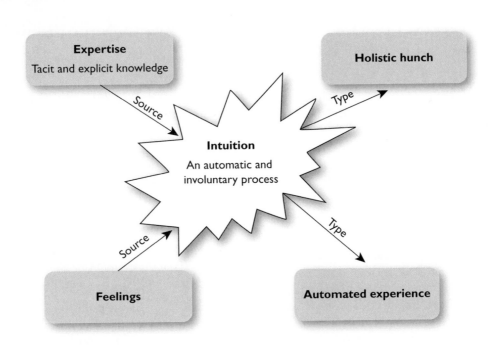

SOURCES: Based in part on E. Sadler-Smith and E. Shefy, "The Intuitive Executive: Understanding and Applying 'Gut Feel' in Decision-Making," *Academy of Management Executive*, November 2004, pp 76–91; and C.C. Miller and R.D. Ireland, "Intuition in Strategic Decision Making: Friend or Foe in the Fast-Paced 21st Century," *Academy of Management Executive*, February 2005, pp 19–30.

pros and cons for using intuition for decision making. The two types of intuition are:

- *A holistic hunch*—making a judgment that is based on a subconscious combination of information stored in your memory. For example: someone says, "It just feels right" or "I can't explain it, but I just know this is not the right thing to do!"
- *Automated experience*—making a choice that is based on a familiar situation and a partially subconscious application of previously-learned information related to that situation. For example: driving a car or riding a bicycle.

There are two sources of intuition:

- *Expertise*—an individual's knowledge regarding an object, person, situation, or decision opportunity based on previous training, experience, and overall skills developed over time. For example: a well-seasoned employee who has been working at the same job for over 20 years.
- *Feelings*—an individual's emotive re-sponse when experiencing a situation, a person, an object, or

decision opportunity. For example: an emotional response when a person cuts you off on the highway.

It is possible to combine the sources; considering the example of being cut off on the highway, your experience (intuitive expertise) would tell you that getting angry to the point of road rage (intuitive feelings) would not be rational nor safe, and so you make the decision to not make rude gestures back to the inconsiderate driver in the other car.

Pros and Cons of Using Intuition when Making Decisions

On the positive side, intuition can speed up the decision-making process.[59] Intuition thus can be valuable in our complex and ever-changing world. Intuition also is a good approach to use when people are faced with limited resources and tight deadlines. On the negative side, intuition is subject to the same type of biases associated with rational decision making. This means that intuition is particularly at risk to both types of heuristics mentioned earlier, as well as accusations from others that such a decision is bold and biased.[60] A final limitation involves the difficulty in convincing others

THE NEED TO FOSTER MORE ETHICS IN BUSINESS

Ethics involves the study of moral issues and choices. It is concerned with right versus wrong, good versus bad, and the many shades of grey in supposedly black-and-white issues. Moral implications spring from virtually every decision we make, both on and off the job. It is critical that decisions be ethical—entire organizations can disappear as a result of unethical decisions.

The early part of the 21st century has been riddled with unprecedented accounting scandals, business fraud, and market debacles (disasters). The one factor consistent with all of these cases was that the CEOs reported to a higher internal moral compass called the board of directors. Further, each board answered to the ultimate authority, their shareholders. When you then consider that each firm was held to operate within the guidelines of the Securities Exchange Commission (SEC) and/or Ontario Exchange

Commission (OEC), not to mention the corporate protocols set by federal tax departments, it begs the following questions: How much more regulation is needed to prevent such situations from occurring again? Do we need more federal tax regulation? More stock market watchdogs? More involved shareholders? Albert Einstein said it best:

> ... *the world is a dangerous place to live; not because of the people who are evil, but because of the people who don't do anything about it...*

The ultimate response is that for every new law put into place, corporations will find a way around it; therefore, ethics must start with each of us—we are the shareholders, we are the regulators, so we must become the moral compass of our workplace.

that a hunch makes sense. In the end, a good intuitive idea may be ignored because people do not understand the idea's underlying logic.

ROAD MAP TO ETHICAL DECISION MAKING: A DECISION TREE

In every chapter of this textbook, we have tried to emphasize the importance of ethics. Clearly, there is growing concern about the lack of ethical behaviour in business. This point is illustrated in a recent poll investigating the perception of corporate behaviour, which revealed that 72 percent of respondents perceived that corporate wrongdoing was rampant, and only 2 percent believed that leaders of large organizations were trustworthy.[61] While this trend partially explains the passage of laws to regulate ethical behaviour, we believe that ethical acts ultimately involve individual or group decisions (see the Law & Ethics feature box). Harvard

Professor Constance Bagley suggests that a decision tree can help people make more ethical decisions.[62] A *decision tree* is a graphical representation of the process underlying decisions, showing the resulting consequences of making various choices. Decision trees are used as an aid in decision making.

Ethical decision making frequently involves trade-offs, and a decision tree helps individuals to navigate through them. Individuals can apply the decision tree shown in Figure 9.7 to any type of decision or action they are contemplating. In this case, the decision tree is considering the action a public corporation is contemplating. Looking at the tree, the first question to ask is whether or not the proposed action is legal. If the action is illegal, do not do it. If the action is legal, then consider the impact of the action on shareholder value. A decision maximizes shareholder value

> **Decision tree**
>
> Graphical representation of the process underlying decision making.

FIGURE 9.7 An Ethical Decision Tree

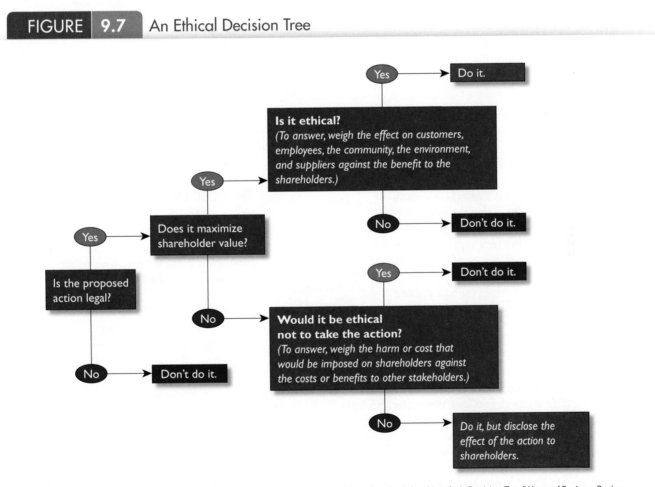

when it results in a more favourable financial position (e.g., increased profits) for an organization.

Whether or not an action maximizes shareholder value, the decision tree shows that employees still need to consider the ethical implications of the decision or action. For example, if an action maximizes shareholder value, the next question to consider is whether or not the action is ethical. The answer to this question is based on considering the positive effect of the action on an organization's other key constituents (e.g., customers, employees, the community, the environment, and suppliers) against the benefit to the shareholders. According to the decision-tree framework, individuals should make the decision to engage in an action if the benefits to the shareholders exceed the benefits to the other key constituents. Individuals should not engage in the action if the other key constituents would benefit more from the action than shareholders.

It is important to keep in mind that the decision tree does not provide a quick formula that individuals can use to assess every ethical question. It does, however, provide a framework for considering the trade-offs between individual, managerial, and corporate actions and ethics. Try using this decision tree the next time you are faced with a significant ethical question or problem.

LO 5 ESCALATION OF COMMITMENT

Escalation situations involve circumstances in which things have gone wrong, but where the situation can possibly be turned around by investing additional time, money, or effort. *Escalation of commitment* refers to the tendency to stick to an ineffective course of action when it is unlikely that the bad situation can be reversed; our opening chapter vignette illustrates this concept. Personal examples include investing more money into an old or broken car, waiting an extremely long time for a bus to take you somewhere that you could just as easily have walked to, or trying to save a disruptive interpersonal relationship that has lasted 10 years. Does this sound like any situations that you've been in?

Several reasons for escalation of commitment have been identified.[63] Research shows that individuals tend to (1) bias facts to support previous decisions and thus discourage change, (2) take more risks out of desperation when a decision is stated in negative terms (to recover losses) rather than positive ones (to achieve gains), and (3) get too ego-involved with the project. Because failure threatens an individual's self-esteem or ego, people tend to ignore negative signs and push forward. Also, peer pressure makes it difficult for individuals to drop a course of action when they publicly supported it in the past.

> **Escalation of commitment**
>
> Sticking to an ineffective course of action when it is unlikely that the bad situation can be reversed.

Breakdown in communication, workplace politics, and organizational inertia (momentum) cause organizations to maintain bad courses of action. Project characteristics—the objective features of a project—have the greatest impact on escalation decisions. For example, because most projects do not reap benefits until some later time period, decision-makers are motivated to stay with the project until the end.[64] Thus, there is a tendency to attribute setbacks to temporary causes that are correctable with additional expenditures.

Reducing Escalation of Commitment It is important to reduce escalation of commitment because it leads to poor decision making for both individuals and groups. Recommended ways to reduce escalation of commitment include:

- Setting minimum targets for performance and having decision-makers compare their performance with these targets
- Having different individuals make the initial and subsequent decisions about a project
- Encouraging decision-makers to become less ego-involved with a project
- Providing more frequent feedback about project completion and costs
- Reducing the risk or penalties of failure
- Making decision-makers aware of the costs of persistence

THE ROLE OF CREATIVITY

You can identify a situation as either a problem or an opportunity. In addition, creative alternatives that you think of when trying to solve a problem can lead to an effective solution that no one has thought of. In light of today's need for sound, strategic, and yet fast-paced decisions, an organization's ability to stimulate its employees' creativity and innovation is becoming increasingly important. Although many definitions have been proposed, *creativity* is defined here as the process of using intelligence, imagination, and skill to develop a new or novel product, object, process, or thought.[65] It can be as simple as locating a new place to hang your car keys, or as complex as developing a pocket-sized microcomputer. There are three broad types of creativity: (1) create something new (creation), (2) combine or synthesize things (synthesis), or (3) improve or change things (modification).

> **Creativity**
>
> Process of using intelligence, imagination, and skill to develop a new or novel idea.

Researchers are not absolutely certain how creativity takes place. Nonetheless, they do know that creativity involves "making remote associations" between unconnected events, ideas, information stored in memory, or physical objects.

Improving Organizational Creativity and Innovation

Organizational creativity is directly influenced by individual characteristics, such as motivation (see Chapter 5). Individuals have to want to apply their knowledge and capabilities to create new ideas, things, or products.[66] In addition, creative people are dissatisfied with the status quo. They look for new and exciting solutions to problems, and because of this they can be perceived as disruptive and hard to get along with. This was certainly the case of Apple's co-founder the late Steve Jobs, who had a reputation for being driven, dynamic, and difficult—yet, there is no denying his creative genius that spilled over into the workplace. Here is what he said when unveiling the first iPad:

> "It's in Apple's DNA that technology alone is not enough. It's technology married with liberal arts, married with the humanities, that yields us the result that makes our heart sing."[67]

Jobs is basically saying that Apple's success goes beyond having technology, that it's the kind of organization that attracts a certain type of passionate yet well-rounded person who thinks differently—and thinking creatively would fit within his expectations.

Organizational creativity is also affected by group and organizational characteristics. Group creativity is fuelled by a cohesive environment that supports open interactions, diverse viewpoints, and playful surroundings.[68] Finally, organizational characteristics such as resources for creativity, a commitment to creativity, and an organizational culture that encourages and rewards creative activity are important for generating organizational creativity.

Group Decision-Making   LO 6

Including groups in the decision-making process has both pros and cons (see Table 9.2). Before recommending that groups be included in the decision-making process, it is important to examine whether groups perform better or worse than individuals. After reviewing 61 years of relevant research, a decision-making expert concluded, "Group performance was generally qualitatively and quantitatively superior to the performance of the average individual."[69] Although subsequent research of small-group decision making generally supported this conclusion, additional research suggests that team leaders, supervisors, and managers should use a contingency approach when determining whether to include others in the decision-making process. They can apply the following three guidelines to help decide whether groups should be included in the decision-making process:

1. If additional information would increase the quality of the decision, involve those people who can provide the needed information.

TABLE 9.2

ADVANTAGES AND DISADVANTAGES OF GROUP DECISION-MAKING

ADVANTAGES	DISADVANTAGES
1. Greater pool of knowledge. A group can bring much more information and experience to bear on a decision or problem than can an individual acting alone.	**1. Social pressure.** Unwillingness to "rock the boat" and pressure to conform may combine to stifle the creativity of individual contributors.
2. Different perspectives. Individuals with varied experience and interests help the group see decision situations and problems from different angles.	**2. Domination by a vocal few.** Sometimes the quality of group action is reduced when the group gives in to those who talk the loudest and longest.
3. Greater comprehension. Those who personally experience the give-and-take of group discussion about alternative courses of action tend to understand the rationale behind the final decision.	**3. Logrolling.** Political wheeling and dealing can displace sound thinking when an individual's pet project or vested interest is at stake.
4. Increased acceptance. Those who play an active role in group decision-making and problem-solving tend to view the outcome as "ours" rather than "theirs."	**4. Goal displacement.** Sometimes secondary considerations such as winning an argument, making a point, or getting back at a rival displace the primary task of making a sound decision or solving a problem.
5. Training ground Less experienced participants in group action learn how to cope with group dynamics by actually being involved.	**5. Groupthink.** Sometimes cohesive in-groups let the desire for unanimity (majority rule) override sound judgment when generating and evaluating alternative courses of action. (Groupthink was discussed in Chapter 6.)

Sticky notes, white boards, and markers—brainstorming can be fun and is used to generate multiple ideas and solutions for solving problems.

Brainstorming *Brainstorming* is defined as a process to generate a quantity of ideas within an open, creative, and non-judgmental context. It is used to help groups generate multiple ideas and *create* alternative courses of action for solving problems. However, it is not appropriate for *evaluating* alternative courses of action or selecting the best solution.

When brainstorming, a group is convened and the problem at hand is reviewed. Individual members are then asked to silently generate ideas/alternatives for solving the problem. Silent idea generation is recommended over the practice of having group members randomly shout out their ideas because it leads to a greater number of unique ideas. Next, these ideas/alternatives are solicited and written on a board or flip chart. Finally, a second session is used to critique and evaluate the alternatives. Here are seven rules for brainstorming according to IDEO, a product design company:[73]

> **Brainstorming**
>
> Process to generate a quantity of ideas within an open, creative, and non-judgmental context.

2. If acceptance is important, involve those individuals whose acceptance and commitment are important.

3. If people can be developed through their participation, involve those whose development is most important.[70]

Groupthink occurs when members of a cohesive group attempt to reach agreement to the extent that it overrides minority opinion (recall our discussion of group behaviour in Chapter 6). It is characterized by a deterioration of mental efficiency, reality testing, and moral judgment that results from group pressures to conform and agree.[71] Avoid groupthink as much as possible.

GROUP PROBLEM-SOLVING TECHNIQUES

Groups can experience roadblocks when trying to arrive at a consensus decision. For one, groups may not generate all relevant alternatives to a problem because an individual dominates or intimidates other group members, because of shyness on the part of other members, or because of satisficing due to time and information constraints. To successfully achieve consensus, groups should use active listening skills, involve as many members as possible, seek out the reasons behind arguments, and dig for the facts. At the same time, groups should not horse-trade (e.g. "I'll support you on this decision because you supported me on the last one"), or agree just to avoid "rocking the boat." Voting is not encouraged because it can split the group into winners and losers.[72]

To reduce such roadblocks, decision-making experts have developed several group problem-solving techniques; we will discuss brainstorming, the nominal group technique, and computer-aided decision making. Knowledge of these techniques can help employees to more effectively use group-aided decision making.

1. *Defer judgment.* Don't criticize during the initial stage of idea generation. Phrases such as "we've never done it that way," "it won't work," "it's too expensive," and "our manager will never agree" should not be used.

2. *Build on the ideas of others.* Encourage participants to extend others' ideas by avoiding "buts" and using "ands."

3. *Encourage wild ideas.* Encourage out-of-the-box thinking. The wilder and more outrageous the ideas, the better.

4. *Go for quantity over quality.* Participants should try to generate and write down as many new ideas as possible. Focusing on quantity encourages people to think beyond their favorite ideas.

5. *Be visual.* Use different coloured pens (e.g., red, purple, blue) to write on big sheets of flip chart paper, white boards, or poster board that are displayed on the wall.

6. *Stay focused on the topic.* Use a facilitator to keep the discussion on target.

7. *One conversation at a time.* The ground rules are that no one interrupts another person and there is no dismissing of someone's ideas, no disrespect, and no rudeness.

This technique is effective because it helps reduce interference caused by critical and judgmental reactions to an individual's ideas by other group members. Recent research revealed that people can be trained to improve their brainstorming skills.[74]

> **Nominal group technique (NGT)**
>
> A face-to-face structured process to generate ideas using discussion and voting techniques.

The Nominal Group Technique The *nominal group technique (NGT)* is defined as a face-to-face process to generate a variety of ideas, evaluate options using a combination of discussion/voting techniques, and finally select solutions through consensus. NGT helps groups generate ideas and evaluate and select solutions. NGT is a structured group meeting that follows a specific format.[75]

A group is convened to discuss a particular problem or issue. After the problem is understood, individuals silently generate ideas in writing. Individuals, in round-robin fashion, then offer one idea from their list. The group leader records ideas on a board or flip chart; the group does not discuss the ideas at this stage of the process. Once all ideas are elicited, the group discusses them. Anyone may criticize or defend any item. During this step, clarification is provided, as well as general agreement or disagreement with the idea. Finally, group members anonymously vote for their top choices with a weighted voting procedure (e.g., 1st choice = 3 points; 2nd choice = 2 points; 3rd choice = 1 point). The group leader then adds the votes to determine the group's choice. Prior to making a final decision, the group may decide to discuss the top-ranked items and conduct a second round of voting.

The nominal group technique reduces the roadblocks to group decision making by (1) separating brainstorming from evaluation, (2) promoting balanced participation among group members, and (3) incorporating mathematical voting techniques to reach consensus.

The Delphi Technique This problem-solving method was originally developed by the Rand Corporation for technological forecasting.[76] It is used as a multipurpose planning tool. The *Delphi technique* is a group process that anonymously generates ideas or judgments from physically dispersed experts. Unlike the NGT, experts' ideas are obtained from questionnaires or via the Internet as opposed to face-to-face group discussions.

The Delphi process begins with a manager identifying the issue(s) he or she wants to investigate. For example, a manager might want to inquire about customer demand, customers' future preferences, or the effect of locating a plant in a certain region of the country. Next, participants are identified and a questionnaire is developed. The questionnaire is sent to participants and returned to the manager. In today's computer-networked environments, this often means that the questionnaires are emailed to participants. The manager then summarizes the responses and sends feedback to the participants. At this stage, participants are asked to (1) review the feedback, (2) prioritize the issues being considered, and (3) return the survey within a specified time period. This cycle repeats until the manager obtains the necessary information.

> **Delphi technique**
>
> A group process to anonymously generate ideas from physically dispersed experts.

The Delphi technique is useful when face-to-face discussions are impractical, when disagreements and conflict are likely to impair communication, when certain individuals might severely dominate group discussion, and when groupthink is a probable outcome of the group process.[77]

Computer-Aided Decision Making The increased globalization of organizations, coupled with the advancement of information technology, has led to the development of computer-aided decision-making systems. Many organizations are using a variety of computer, software, and electronic devices to improve decision making. Such systems allow managers to quickly obtain larger amounts of information from employees, customers, or suppliers around the world. For example, Best Buy Co., Google, GE, Intel, and Microsoft all use internal intranets to obtain input from employees. Both Best Buy and Google found that these systems were helpful in estimating the demand for new products and services.[78] Walmart is also well known for using computer-aided decision making to improve decision making. For example, Walmart stores use a new computerized system to schedule its 1.3 million workers. The system creates staffing levels for each store based on the number of customers in the store at any given point in time.[79]

These systems also improve information processing and decision making within virtual teams.[80] For example, this is what hospital administrator and director of staff and community education, Loubna Noureddin, had to say about her organization's computer-aided decision making:

"What I truly like about it is my connection to other hospitals," Noureddin says. "I'm able to understand what other hospitals are doing about specific things. I put my question out, and people can respond, and I can answer back." She explains, for instance, that using the system, she and her colleagues have received guidance from other corporate educators, and even subject matter experts, on how to best train workers in such fields as critical care. "You get many other hospitals logging into the system, and telling us what they do," she says.[81]

Noureddin claims that the system has saved the company time and money.

In conclusion, we expect the use of computer-aided decision making to increase in the future. These systems are well suited for modern organizational life and for the large number of Millennials or Gen Ys entering the workforce.[82]

Summary of Learning Objectives

 Define *power, personalized power,* **and** *socialized power.* Power is the ability to influence others to develop a dependent relationship. Personalized power is when power is directed to helping oneself. Socialized power is when power is directed to helping others.

 Identify and briefly describe French and Raven's five bases of power, relating factors to tactics used and work outcomes (e.g., job performance, job satisfaction, and turnover). French and Raven's five bases of power are (1) reward power (rewarding compliance), (2) coercive power (punishing non-compliance), (3) legitimate power (relying on formal authority), (4) expert power (providing needed information), and (5) referent power (relying on personal attraction). Once individuals have power, they can use up to a possible eight types of influencing tactics to achieve the desired outcome. The eight tactics include: logic, emotional appeals, consultation, praise, personal appeals, exchange, coalition, threats, or reference to rules. Researchers have identified three relationship points between power bases and work outcomes: (1) expert and referent power have a generally positive impact on job performance, increasing job satisfaction and lowering turnover—using these types of power bases has a greater chance of getting commitment from others; (2) reward and positive legitimate power have only a slightly positive impact over the same variables—these power bases will likely result in getting others to be compliant with requests; (3) coercive power has a slightly negative impact on similar work outcomes, meaning you can expect compliance or even total resistance from others.

 Explain how uncertainty can trigger the production of organizational politics, which can lead to the use of personalized power tactics. When a person feels uncertainty, it is typically a result of change where personal interests are at stake and power can be challenged. When faced with such uncertain threats, people will rely on personalized power tactics that will serve their own self-interests. As a result, the focus of energy turns away from serving the interests of the organization as a whole in a social way; instead, they employ political tactics to promote personal success.

 Compare and contrast the rational model of decision making to bounded rationality, decision trees, and intuition. The rational decision-making model consists of identifying the problem, gathering related information, generating alternative solutions, evaluating and selecting a solution, and implementing, monitoring, and evaluating the solution. Research indicates that decision-makers do not live in a perfect rational world and thus do not typically make decisions in such a manner. Rather, they use a bounded rationality model, which means that decision-makers are bounded or restricted by a variety of constraints when making decisions, such as time constraints, ability, etc. There are three types of characteristics of the bounded rationality model: (1) limited information processing, (2) the use of judgmental heuristics, and (3) satisficing. Using intuition is another way of making choices, meaning a dependence on less rational thought or logic. There are two types of intuition: holistic hunch and automated experience. There are two sources of intuition: expertise and feelings. Intuition is helpful because it speeds up the decision-making process, but it can be biased and perceived as illogical. A decision tree helps make decisions, especially in ethical situations, because it is a graphical representation of the process. Through a series of trade-off choices, a person goes through a prescribed sequence until the logical solution emerges. A decision tree is helpful when considering tradeoffs between individual, managerial, or corporate actions.

 Infer what causes an escalation of commitment and predict what type of outcome can result. There are three possible causes of an escalation of commitment: (1) individuals who bias facts to support previous decisions and thus discourage change, (2) individuals who are desperate and so they take more risks when a decision is stated in negative terms, and (3) individuals who have too much ego invested in a project. As individuals or organizations stick to an ineffective course of action when it is unlikely that the bad situation can be reversed, a situation can go from bad to worse.

 Summarize the pros and cons of involving groups in the decision-making process. OB experts suggest using a contingency approach because there are both advantages and disadvantages to using teams in decision making. From a positive perspective, groups (1) collect a greater pool of knowledge, (2) provide for different perspectives, (3) allow for greater comprehension, and (4) encourage greater acceptance. From a negative perspective, groups (1) can push pressure to conform to the point of stifling creativity, (2) can sometimes be dominated by one or a few members, (3) can experience wheeling and dealing in lots of political games, (4) can have misguided priorities and goal achievement, and (5) can experience groupthink.

Discussion Questions

1. How can personalized power be a source of effective or ineffective decision making? Explain.
2. In your opinion, is there such a thing as too much empowerment in the contemporary workplace?
3. What is it about organizational politics that can make individuals feel uneasy? Explain.
4. How can an organization create and sustain an ethical workplace?
5. Describe a situation in which you exhibited escalation of commitment. Why did you escalate a losing situation?

Integration of OB Concepts— Discussion Questions

1. See Chapter 3 – What role does personality play in desire for power? Consider how this would affect individual behaviour choices. Explain why a person with a high internal locus of control would welcome empowerment. Would this also apply to those that are high self-managers? What about those with high self-esteem?
2. See Chapter 5 – What is the role of motivation on people who engage in accumulating extreme power within an organization? How do they use office politics to achieve their goals?

3. See Chapter 6 – How can a team prevent or minimize unethical decision making?

4. See Chapter 8 – Explain how executive conflict handling styles and preferences can affect or influence the way major strategic decisions are made (and the outcomes that occur) within an organization. How can this change, if at all, when group decision-making is involved? Discuss.

Google Searches

1. **Google Search:** "Future car technology" OR "Alternative Fuel Vehicles" OR "Alternative Fuel Cars" You want to buy a new car next year. What kind of car should you buy given the current cost of gasoline? What is the cost of gas predicted to be over the next 10 years? Are there any government incentives to purchase alternative fuel powered cars?

2. **Google Search:** "International Olympic Committee – Site Selection" AND "Olympian Site Selection Scandal" How does the NOC decide where the next Olympic games are going to be held? Based on what you have read, is their process equitable and free of political influence? Where are the next series of games being held?

3. **Google Search:** "Evidence Based Decision Making Model" OR "EBDM Briner, Denyer, Rousseau" Define and explain this model for decision making. How did it come about? Review the model and compare/contrast it with the rational model. Share your observations with the rest in your class. Which model do you believe to be more valid for business application and why?

4. **Google Search:** "Your School _____ Program" OR "Business Programs in the Province of _____" How did you decide what program to go into and which post-secondary school you were going to enroll in? Explain who influenced your decision and how they were able to convince you to a different way of thinking.

5. **Google Search:** "Daniel Kahneman – Thinking Fast And Slow" This bestselling book by a Nobel laureate talks about how we can improve our decision making. What does he mean by Systems #1 thinking? Systems #2 thinking? How does Kahneman feel about intuition when making decisions? According to Kahneman, when is Systems #1 thinking appropriate for use vs. Systems #2 thinking?

Experiential Exercise

Power Influencing Tactics Group Exercise

PURPOSE: This exercise is meant to discover the value and application between the different decision models. Approx. Timing: 20 minutes.

ACTIVITY ASSIGNMENT

- Break into small groups.
- Complete the table below. Read the given problem situation, consider the alternative decision models to use, choose which you believe to be the most appropriate, then explain your reasoning.
- The first two situations have been completed for you. Apply the same kinds of decision models to the third problem situation.

- Be prepared to share your responses with the rest of the class to generate a rich discussion.

The Problem Situation (Read First)	The Appropriate Decision Model to Use (Choose One)	Explain Your Reasoning – Which Decision Model is the Most Appropriate? or Which is the Worst?
#1: It's Sunday morning at 6:30 a.m. and you have received an emergency telephone call to come in to work immediately. You are hungry and wonder what to do about breakfast before leaving the house.	*Satisficing* – Grab a piece of left-over cold pizza from the refrigerator and begin eating while walking out the door to get into car. *Intuition* – From experience, you know that there is no time to waste; you'll have to wait until the emergency is resolved before stopping at a fast-food drive-in restaurant to eat. You have a feeling that it's best to forget about eating for now. *Creative* – Change your perspective to see this as an opportunity to make overtime pay, and if possible, to get employer to pay for breakfast. *Rationale* – Take 10 minutes to reflect on the level of hunger you feel. Review the various choices in the refrigerator and on the cupboard shelves before making your final decision—which may or may not include eating.	
#2: You are deciding whether or not to enrol next year in a new academic program that involves international studies, co-op work placements, and articulation linkages that would lead to earning both a college diploma and university degree upon completion.	*Satisficing* – You ask your friend Skippy what he thinks since he graduated from high school and is going to the local college on a part-time basis while working at Best Buy. Maybe they are hiring at Best Buy and a diploma or degree isn't necessary. *Intuition* – You know from previous experience that just because something sounds good on paper it doesn't mean that it's the right fit for you. You have a feeling that if would be best to go to the open house being held at one of the schools to find out more information. *Creative* – Although you have never considered studying overseas, you keep an open mind and consider approaching the program coordinator at the local post-secondary school to see if you could begin taking a class or two online, just to see if you like it. If you do, then you will consider enrolling full-time in the new program next year.	

	Rationale – You make a short list of all the programs you are interested in, being sure to collect as much information as possible about each. Consider: costs, grad rates, job opportunities for grads, length of study, co-op placements, location of classrooms, technology expectations, etc. You then plan a personal tour of each campus to see how it 'feels'. You prioritize each program and send in your application to at least three because you know that you may not get your first program choice.
#3: *You need transportation for work, school and generally just getting around the city. You want to buy a new car. You have $5,000 saved. You pay your own tuition and book costs. You earned $13,000 working part-time last year at Starbucks. You live at home and will turn 20 next year.*	*Satisficing* – *Intuition* – *Creative* – *Rationale* –

OB In Action Case Study

Bailing Out Corporate Giants

BACKGROUND

Throughout the early months of 2009, Federal Finance Minister of record Jim Flaherty was faced with a controversial decision: *Should the Canadian government bail out the struggling auto manufacturers?* The Big Three domestic automakers (GM, Ford, and Chrysler) were asking for $1 billion in loan guarantees to help tide over the sector until demand from Canada's biggest trading partner, the US, recovered for North American-produced vehicles. GM reported a $2.5 billion third-quarter loss and warned that its cash levels could fall below what was needed to run its business by the end of the year if the economy didn't turn around and if it didn't get government aid.

What was at stake? A threat to potentially hundreds of thousands of jobs, due to the multiplier effect, that could double unemployment and throw this country into an immediate recession the likes of which were being compared to the depression years of the 1930s. It was feared that the economy would not be able to tolerate such a shock and that the effects would be long lasting. Flaherty refused to rush into making a decision, and chose instead to continue discussions with Canada's Big Three on whether taxpayer money should be provided to bail out these large corporations.

The Canadian Auto Workers supported the bailout. As Chris Buckley, then president of CAW Local 222 in Oshawa, told *Canadian Business Magazine*, ". . . it's absolutely disgusting" that Flaherty says he's only monitoring the situation when immediate action is required. Buckley said Canada can't wait for the US bailout decision. "We're asking Flaherty and (Prime Minister Stephen) Harper to react immediately." Ken Lewenza, then national CAW president, agreed that any money for the auto industry should not be viewed as a bailout, but rather as an investment in the Canadian economy.

But Flaherty was quick to respond with a counter-argument. He told a group of economists in Toronto that, ". . . in my own riding, where I was yesterday, in Whitby-Oshawa . . . there are lots of people who say, 'Don't do anything. Don't use my tax money to bail out an enterprise that may not survive. These are not high falutin' rich people saying this to me—these are people on the street." Adam Taylor, the acting federal director of the Canadian Taxpayers Federation, clearly disagreed with a bailout by stating, "Taxpayers cannot afford to continue to bail out mismanaged companies that expect perpetual handouts in good and bad times." The federation claimed that between 2003 and 2008, the Big Three had already received a total of $782 million in loans and future commitments from Canadian taxpayers. As Finance Minister, Flaherty had the legitimate power to authorize a loan, but granting a bailout of such sizable proportions without consultation would be a risky political move. Flaherty was faced with a difficult decision that would bring much criticism.

THE DECISION

By spring 2009, Flaherty felt able to justify a $13 + billion loan to GM and Chrysler (Ford decided it didn't need the money and withdrew their bailout request). In his words, " . . . what is the value of preserving an industry? What is the value of preserving 52,000 jobs in our country? You have to put a value on those, which are pretty substantial values in my view." Between the federal and Ontario governments, $2.9 billion in loans was given to Chrysler. GM received $10.8 billion. In return, the auto makers agreed to pay interest on the loans and both offered stock ownership.

In May of 2011, almost 2 years later, Flaherty spoke to the media about the bailouts and addressed the question of whether it was good for Canadians to offer government loans to these corporate giants. Still supporting his earlier decision, Flaherty held fast to justifying the financial support, but emphasized that there was "not going to be a full recovery of the taxpayers' investments that were made back in 2008–2009—in the sense of cash recovery." Again, he referred to saving thousands of well-paying jobs. At the same press conference held at Chrysler's Etobicoke Casting Plant, Chrysler CEO Sergio Marchionne was celebrating a $1.7 billion repayment of their government loan. Marchionne stated, "They gave us a second chance. Something that happens very rarely in life and they gave us not only the hope for our survival, but also the great opportunity to build the future."

As for GM, they too repaid part of their loan—$1.5 billion plus $83 million in interest . . . not enough for some critics who stated that both GM and the CAW used taxpayer money to pull off the biggest scam in Canadian history. Plus, Ottawa and Ontario were sold about $4.4 billion worth of common shares, resulting in some opponents mockingly renaming General Motors "Government Motors."

UPDATE

By the fall of 2012, auto analysts were looking back on the previous year, noting almost a 2 percent increase in total auto sales from the previous year. The fall rebound especially was the highest sales numbers since 2000. The winner overall? Ford Motor Co. of Canada Ltd., who did not take a bailout.

The CAW negotiated an anticipated four-year contract with the Big Three domestic auto makers (set to expire in 2016) that extended the four-year wage freeze but offered a phased-in annual bonus package totaling $9,000 per worker over four years. The results of the negotiations left Ford pledging to hire 600 more people in Oakville; Chrysler remaining in Windsor despite its negotiation bluff to pull out if the contract terms were too harsh; and GM creating or maintaining 1,750 Canadian jobs while investing $675 million in capital spending.

Discussion Questions

1. Do you think Ford lost or gained more power by not taking the bailout?
2. How did the CAW influence Flaherty's decision?
3. What model of decision making do you think Flaherty used in this case? Explain your reasoning.
4. Based on the latest sales numbers, was Flaherty's decision to bail out both GM and Chrysler of Canada justified?
5. In your opinion, are government bailouts for corporations ethical? Why or why not?

SOURCES: G. Keenan, "Auto Sales Pick Up Speed Even As Economy Sputters," The *Globe and Mail*, October 2, 2012, www.theglobeandmail.com/globe-investor/auto-sales-pick-up-speed-even-as-economy-sputters/article4581844/; C. Vander Doelen, "CAW Deal Cloaked In Secrecy," *The Windsor* Star, October 1, 2012, www.ottawacitizen.com/cars/deal+cloaked+secrecy/7324945/story.html; G. Keenan, "Auto Bailouts Won't Be Repaid In Full," *The Globe and Mail,* May 30, 2011, Report on Business online www.theglobeandmail.com; T. Burgmann and C. Thomas, "Flaherty, CAW spar over auto sector help; Clement wants long-term solution," *The Canadian Press,* November 12, 2008, Canadian Business Online: www.canadianbusiness.com/shared/print.jsp?content=b1112167A&adzone=markets/headline_news; and B. Saporito, "Is General Motors Worth Saving?," *Time Magazine,* November 13, 2008, www.time.com/time/printout/0,8816,1858702,00.html.

The CONNECTion Zone

- The Presentation Assistant
- Ethical OB Dilemma
- Video Case

Practise and learn online with Connect.

CHAPTER 10

Leadership

FACING AN OB CHALLENGE

Last week I was asked by my manager to be in charge of an assignment that involves leading others on a project. I realize this is a real honour to be singled out from the other employees—but I don't feel comfortable in the new role at all. Here are the facts: I'm in my mid 20s. I have some work experience, but not a lot. I don't talk like a leader. I'd rather listen than stand in front of people telling them what to do or how to do it. Aren't leaders supposed to have all the answers? Well, I don't, and I'm not sure I ever will. Maybe I should tell them 'thanks' but find someone else. Is it wrong for me to feel this way?

—NOT READY TO LEAD

LEARNING OBJECTIVES

After reading this chapter, you should be able to:

LO 1 Define *leadership*.

LO 2 Differentiate between being a leader versus a manager.

LO 3 Differentiate between the factors related to Fiedler's contingency theory and House's revised Path-Goal Theory.

LO 4 Compare and contrast the key characteristics between transactional and transformational leadership.

LO 5 Review the principles of servant-leadership.

Assessing Your Leadership Potential

"Not Ready to Lead," the person in the opening OB Challenge, seems to have some misunderstandings about what it takes to become a leader. It's important that people assuming the added responsibility and authority of leadership be fully prepared for what they are about to accept. They should understand the kinds of traits, behaviours, and abilities needed to succeed in a leadership role within a contemporary organization. Before beginning this chapter, we invite you to complete Self-Assessment Exercise #1 to explore your leadership potential. At the end of this chapter, you may also want to complete Self-Assessment Exercise #2 to determine if you are ready to take on a leadership role. Compare and contrast your scores from each; the overall results may provide interesting insights to help improve your leadership skills.

Someone once observed that a leader is a person who finds out which way the parade is going, jumps in front, and yells, "follow me!" The plain fact is that this approach to leadership has little chance of succeeding in today's rapidly changing world. In short, successful leaders are those individuals who can step into a difficult situation and make a noticeable difference. But how much of a difference can leaders make in modern organizations?

OB researchers have discovered that leaders can make a difference. One study, for instance, revealed that leadership was positively associated with net profits for 167 companies over a time span of 20 years.[1] Research also showed that coaches' leadership skills affect the success of their team. Specifically, teams in Major League Baseball and college and university basketball won more games when players perceived the coach to be an effective leader.[2] Rest assured, leadership can make a difference!

When studying leadership principles, there are an unbelievable number of different theories; the number increases significantly if we count those proposed by managerial consultants. Rather than overwhelm you with all these theories of leadership, we have chosen to focus on the historical ones that have received the most research support.

What Does Leadership Involve?

Disagreement about the definition of leadership stems from the fact that it involves a complex interaction among the leader, the followers, and the situation. For example, some researchers define leadership in terms of personality and physical traits, while others believe leadership is represented by a set of prescribed behaviours. In contrast, other researchers define leadership in terms of the power relationship between leaders and followers. According to this perspective, leaders use their power to influence followers' behaviour. Leadership also can be seen as an instrument of goal achievement. In other words, leaders are individuals who help others accomplish their goals. Still others view leadership from a skills perspective.

Figure 10.1 summarizes the four commonalities among the many definitions of leadership: (1) leadership is a process between a leader and followers; (2) leadership involves social influence; (3) leadership occurs at multiple levels in an organization (at the individual level, for example, leadership involves mentoring, coaching, inspiring, and motivating; leaders also build teams, generate cohesion, and resolve conflicts at the group level; finally, leaders build culture and generate change at the organizational level);[3] and (4) leadership focuses on goal accomplishment.[4] Based on these commonalities, *leadership* is defined as a process that uses social influence to enable and seek the participation of subordinates in an effort to reach common organizational goals.[5]

> *Leadership*
>
> A process that uses social influence to enable and seek the participation of subordinates in an effort to reach common organizational goals.

Do You Have What It Takes to Be a Leader?

INSTRUCTIONS: Indicate the extent to which you agree or disagree with each statement listed by circling the number that best represents your skill level. Then, add up your score to determine your leadership skill development.

1 = STRONGLY AGREE
2 = DISAGREE
3 = NEITHER AGREE NOR DISAGREE

4 = AGREE
5 = STRONGLY AGREE

1	I can separate my personal life from work/school.	1—2—3—4—5
2	I'm honest with myself.	1—2—3—4—5
3	I communicate my ideas clearly.	1—2—3—4—5
4	I regularly prioritize what needs to get done.	1—2—3—4—5
5	I am on time for meetings/classes.	1—2—3—4—5
6	I am positive and upbeat.	1—2—3—4—5
7	I am solution-oriented rather than problem-oriented.	1—2—3—4—5
8	I take responsibility for my actions.	1—2—3—4—5
9	I do not blame others for my mistakes.	1—2—3—4—5
10	When working in a group, I work with others to solve and prevent problems.	1—2—3—4—5
11	I don't have to redo things because my work is thorough and complete.	1—2—3—4—5
12	I do not procrastinate on projects/tasks.	1—2—3—4—5
13	I do not get distracted when working on projects/tasks.	1—2—3—4—5
14	I work well in a group.	1—2—3—4—5
15	I am people-oriented, not just results-oriented.	1—2—3—4—5
16	I listen to others beyond just the words being spoken.	1—2—3—4—5
17	When working with a group, I am more concerned with the group's success than my own.	1—2—3—4—5
18	I adjust well to different communication styles.	1—2—3—4—5
19	I praise others when they are doing a good job.	1—2—3—4—5
20	I work at getting ahead, but within appropriate boundaries.	1—2—3—4—5

Total Score = _____

Scoring:

Although there are no hard-and-fast cutoff scores for this assessment, generally speaking, the higher your score out of 100 possible points, the more leadership skills you have developed. Conversely, lower scores (closer to zero) suggest the need for more leadership skill development. To determine which skill needs the most development, consider the following seven qualities:

❑ Personal Stability (#2, 6)
❑ Productivity (#4, 7, 12)
❑ Self-Management (#5, 8, 9)
❑ Boundary Setting (#1, 20)

❑ Communication (#3, 16, 18)
❑ Work Quality (#11, 13)
❑ Teamwork (#10, 14, 15, 17, 19)

SOURCE: Questions for this assessment exercise were adapted from Interlink Training and Coaching, "The Leadership Assessment Tool," www.interlinktc.com/assessment.html, Interlink Training and Coaching, 3655 W. Anthem Way, Box 315, Anthem, AZ, 85086.

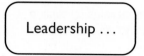

FIGURE 10.1 Leadership Commonalities between Definitions

Leadership . . .
1. is a *process* between a leader and followers
2. involves *social influence*
3. occurs at *multiple levels* in an organization
4. focuses on *goal accomplishment*

There are two components of leadership missing from the definition: the moral and the follower perspectives. Leadership is not a moral concept. History is filled with examples of effective leaders who were killers, corrupt, and morally bankrupt. Barbara Kellerman, a leadership expert, commented on this notion:

"Leaders are like the rest of us; trustworthy and deceitful, cowardly and brave, greedy and generous. To assume that all good leaders are good people is to be willfully blind to the reality of the human condition, and it more severely limits our scope for becoming more effective at leadership."[6]

The point is that good leaders develop a keen sense of their strengths and weaknesses and build on their positive attributes. The second component missing from the definition is the role of followers. You cannot lead without having followers, and you cannot follow without having leaders. The point we're trying to make here is that each needs the other, and the quality of the relationship determines how followers behave. This is why it is important for both leaders and followers to focus on developing a mutually rewarding and beneficial relationship.

PREDICTING EFFECTIVE LEADERSHIP

What is the best predictor of choosing an effective leader? Are there certain traits they must have or specific behaviours they must exhibit? Is there one best approach to use when evaluating effective leadership? OB researchers have been attempting to answer these questions for many years. They began studying leadership in the early part of the 20th century by focusing on the *traits* associated with leadership effectiveness. This perspective was followed by attempts in the 1950s and 1960s to examine the *behaviours* or styles exhibited by effective leaders. This research led to the realization that there is not one best style of leadership, which in turn spawned various *contingency* approaches to leadership in the 1960s and 1970s. Contingency approaches focused on identifying the types of leadership behaviours that are most effective in different settings. The *transformational* approach is the most popular perspective for

studying leadership today. Research based on this approach began in the early 1980s and adheres to the idea that leaders transform employees to pursue organizational goals through a variety of leader behaviours. We conclude this chapter with a unique philosophy called the *servant-leadership* approach, which has proven to have both academic and practical application. See Table 10.1 for a summary of the different major leadership approaches that will be discussed in this chapter.

LEADING VERSUS MANAGING   LO 2

Before we start exploring the various predictors of finding an effective leader, we must first make the distinction between leadership and management to fully understand what leadership is all about. Bernard Bass, a leadership expert, concluded that "leaders manage and managers lead, but the two activities are not synonymous."[7] Bass tells us that although leadership and management overlap, each entails a unique set of activities or functions. Broadly speaking, managers typically perform functions associated with planning, investigating, organizing, and control, and leaders deal with the interpersonal aspects of a manager's job. Leaders inspire others, provide emotional support, and try to get employees to rally around a common goal. Leaders also play a key role in creating a vision and strategic plan for an organization. Managers, in turn, are charged with implementing the vision and strategic plan. Table 10.2 summarizes the key characteristics associated with being a leader and a manager.[8] There are several conclusions to be drawn from the information presented in Table 10.2:

1. Good leaders are not necessarily good managers, and good managers are not necessarily good leaders.
2. Effective leadership requires effective managerial skills at some level. For example, good managerial skills turn a leader's vision into actionable items and successful implementation.
3. Today's leaders need to be effective at both leading and managing.

While this may seem like a huge task, the good news is that a recent meta-analysis of leadership interventions shows that people can be taught to be more effective leaders and managers.[9] EllisDon, one of the largest building contractors in Canada and one of Canada's Top 100 Employers, trains its corporate leaders at EllisDon University (EDU).

TABLE 10.1

APPROACHES TO STUDYING LEADERSHIP

1. TRAIT APPROACHES	• Stogdill and Mann's five traits—intelligence, dominance, self-confidence, level of energy, and task-relevant knowledge
	• Leadership prototypes—intelligence, masculinity, and dominance
	• Kouzes and Posner's four traits—honesty, forward-looking, inspiring, and competent
	• Goleman—emotional intelligence
	• Judge and colleagues' two meta-analyses—importance of extraversion, conscientiousness, and openness; importance of personality over intelligence
	• Kellerman's bad traits—incompetent, rigid, intemperate, callous, corrupt, insular, and evil
2. BEHAVIOURAL APPROACHES	• Ohio State Studies' two dimensions—initiating structure behaviour and consideration behaviour
	• University of Michigan Studies' two leadership styles—job-centred and employee-centred
3. CONTINGENCY APPROACHES	• Fiedler's Contingency Theory—task-oriented style and relationship-oriented style; three dimensions of situational control: leader–member relations, task structure, and position power
	• House's Revised Path–Goal Theory—eight leadership behaviours clarify paths for followers' goals; employee characteristics and environmental factors are contingency factors that influence the effectiveness of leadership behaviours; shared leadership that involves a mutual influence process in which people throughout organization share responsibility for leading
	• Shared Leadership—mutual influence process in which people share responsibility for leading wherever they may be within an organizational structure
4. TRANSFORMATIONAL APPROACH	• Bass and Avolio's four transformational leadership behaviours—inspirational motivation, idealized influence, individualized consideration, and intellectual stimulation
	• Full-Range Theory of Leadership—leadership varies along a continuum from laissez-faire leadership to transactional leadership to transformational leadership
5. A LEADERSHIP PHILOSOPHY	• Greenleaf's servant leadership—providing service to others, not oneself

SOURCE: Adapted and updated August 2012 from A. Kinicki and B. Williams, *Management: A Practical Introduction,* 4th ed. (Burr Ridge, IL: McGraw-Hill/Irwin, 2009), p 410. Reprinted by permission of The McGraw-Hill Companies, Inc.

Skills & Best Practices

AlliedBarton Security Service's Leadership Development Produces Positive Results

AlliedBarton Leadership Boot Camp signals a shift in how the company views and leads employees. It includes three stages. The first, "On-Ramp Preparation," is a six-week process that includes a 360-degree leadership analysis, personal coaching, and a virtual reality leadership video in which participants practise principles and skills. Another two assessments are delivered to understand the employee's level of engagement. The multi-rater feedback establishes a baseline for performance. The second stage, "Residential," includes three-and-a-half days in which participants engage with peers to build execution plans. The final phase, "On-the-Job Application," occurs over a 16-week period, and includes on-the-job implementation of execution plans. Participants meet with direct reports, deliver a plan to engage employees, and complete the multi-rater survey.

Following Boot Camp, account manager turnover was reduced from 32 percent to 21 percent. Financial impact at the time of writing was more than $2 million in turnover reduction savings. Why do you believe this program is so successful?

SOURCE: Excerpted from "Best Practices & Outstanding Initiatives," *Training Magazine*, Feb. 2008, p 118.

TABLE 10.2

CHARACTERISTICS OF BEING A LEADER AND A MANAGER

BEING A LEADER MEANS	BEING A MANAGER MEANS
Motivating, influencing, and changing behaviour	Practising stewardship, directing, and being held accountable for resources
Inspiring, setting the tone, and articulating a vision	Executing plans, implementing, and delivering the goods and services
Managing people	Managing resources
Being charismatic	Being conscientious
Being visionary	Planning, organizing, directing, and controlling
Understanding and using power and influence	Understanding and using authority and responsibility
Acting decisively	Acting responsibly
Putting people first; leaders know, respond to, and act for their followers	Putting customers first; managers know, respond to, and act for their customers
Leaders can make mistakes when	Managers can make mistakes when
1. They choose the wrong goal, direction, or inspiration due to incompetence or bad intentions; or	1. They fail to grasp the importance of people as the key resource; or
2. They overload; or	2. They underlead; they treat people like other resources, numbers; or
3. They are unable to deliver or implement the vision due to incompetence or a lack of follow-through commitment	3. They are eager to direct and to control but are unwilling to accept accountability

SOURCE: Reprinted from P. Lorenzi, "Managing for the Common Good: Prosocial Leadership," *Organizational Dynamics,* vol. 33, no. 3, p 286, © 2004, with permission from Elsevier.

EDU is a division that coordinates senior leaders of the firm sharing their wealth of experience with newly appointed managers who "'thirst for knowledge and further development'."[10] See the previous Skills & Best Practices feature box for another example of leadership development at security services firm AlliedBarton.

Trait and Behavioural Approaches

This section examines the two earliest approaches used to explain leadership. Trait theories focus on identifying the personal traits that differentiate leaders from followers. Behavioural theorists examine leadership from a different perspective. They try to uncover the different kinds of leader behaviours that result in higher work group performance. Both approaches to leadership can teach valuable lessons about leading. After reading each section, which do you believe is the better predictor for finding an effective leader?

TRAIT THEORY

Trait Theory is the successor to what was called the "great man" theory of leadership. This approach was based on the assumption that leaders such as former Prime Minister Pierre Trudeau, Jim Balsillie (former CEO of RIM), or environmentalist Dr. David Suzuki were born with some innate (inborn) ability to lead.

In contrast, trait theorists believe that leadership traits are not innate, but can be developed through experience and learning. A *leader trait* is a physical or personality characteristic that can be used to differentiate leaders from followers.

Before World War II, hundreds of studies were conducted to pinpoint the traits of successful leaders. Dozens of leadership traits were identified. During the postwar period, however, enthusiasm was replaced by widespread criticism. This section reviews a series of studies that provide a foundation for understanding leadership traits. We conclude by integrating results across the various studies and summarizing the practical recommendations of trait theory.

Stogdill's and Mann's Findings Ralph Stogdill in 1948 and Richard Mann in 1959 sought to summarize the impact of traits on leadership. Based on his review, Stogdill concluded that five traits tend to differentiate leaders from average followers: (1) intelligence, (2) dominance, (3) self-confidence, (4) level of energy and activity, and (5) task-relevant knowledge. Among the seven categories of personality traits examined by Mann, intelligence was the best predictor of leadership.[11] Unfortunately, the overall pattern of research findings revealed that both Stogdill's and Mann's key traits did not accurately predict which individuals became leaders in organizations. People with these traits often remained followers.

> **Leader trait**
>
> A physical trait or personality characteristic that can be used to differentiate leaders from followers.

Implicit Leadership Theory (Prototypes) Implicit leadership theory is based on the idea that people have beliefs about how leaders should behave and what they should do for their followers. These beliefs are summarized in what is called a leadership prototype.[12] A leadership prototype is a mental representation of the traits and behaviours possessed by leaders. It is important to understand the content of leadership prototypes because we tend to perceive that someone is a leader when he or she exhibits traits or behaviours that are consistent with our prototypes (recall our discussion of social perception attribution error in Chapter 2). We also tend to identify with leaders and evaluate them as more effective when they behave in prototypical ways. Robert Lord and his colleagues attempted to identify employees' leadership prototypes by conducting a meta-analysis of past studies. Results demonstrated that people are perceived as leaders when they exhibit traits and behaviours associated with intelligence, masculinity, and dominance.[13] Other studies showed that leadership prototypes tend to be shared throughout an organization and are culturally based.[14] In other words, leadership prototypes are influenced by national cultural values. See the International OB feature box for more on cultural differences.

Kouzes and Posner's Research: Is Honesty the Most Critical Leadership Trait? James Kouzes and Barry Posner attempted to identify key leadership traits by asking the following open-ended question of more than 20,000 people around the world: "What values (personal traits or characteristics) do you look for and admire in your

INTERNATIONAL OB

LEADERSHIP LESSONS FROM THE GOLD PROJECT

GLOBE is the acronym for Global Leadership and Organizational Behaviour Effectiveness, an 11-year study involving 170 researchers worldwide. The GLOBE Project was introduced in 2004 and followed up the next year with specific findings about how leadership and leaders' styles vary among nations and cultures. In phase 2, the GLOBE researchers set out to discover which, if any, attributes of leadership are universally liked or disliked. They surveyed 17,000 middle managers working for 951 organizations across 62 countries. Their results identified 22 universally positive leader attributes and 8 negative attributes:

Positive Attributes

Trustworthy, just, honest, foresight, plans ahead, encouraging, positive, dynamic, motive arouser, confidence builder, motivational, dependable, intelligent, decisive, effective bargainer, win-win problem solver, skilled administrator, communicative, informed, coordinator, team builder, excellence-oriented

Negative Attributes

Loner, asocial, non-cooperative, irritable, non-explicit, egocentric, ruthless, dictatorial

These results have important implications for trainers and current and future global managers.[15] Visionary and inspirational charismatic leaders who are good team builders generally do the best. On the other hand, self-centred leaders seen as loners or face-savers generally receive a poor reception worldwide. Local and foreign managers who heed these results are still advised to use a contingency approach to leadership after using their cultural intelligence to read the local people and culture. David Whitwam, the former CEO of appliance maker Whirlpool, frames the challenge this way:

Leading a company today is different from the 1980s and 1990s, especially in a global company. It requires a new set of competencies. Bureaucratic structures don't work anymore. You have to take the command-and-control types out of the system. You need to allow and encourage broad-based involvement in the company. Especially in consumer kinds of companies, we need a diverse workforce with diverse leadership. You need strong regional leadership that lives in the culture. We have a North American running the North American business, and a Latin American running the Latin American business.[16]

superiors?" The top four traits were honesty, forward-looking, inspiring, and competent.[17] The researchers concluded that these four traits constitute a leader's credibility. This research suggests that people want their leaders to be credible and to have a sense of direction.

Goleman's Research on Emotional Intelligence We discussed Daniel Goleman's research on emotional intelligence in Chapter 3 (see Table 3.3). Recall that emotional intelligence is the ability to manage yourself and your relationships in mature and constructive ways. Given that leadership is an influence process between leaders and followers, it should come as no surprise that emotional intelligence is predicted to be associated with leadership effectiveness. While Goleman contends he has evidence to support this conclusion, he has not published it in any academic journals or professional magazine. We agree with others who contend that there presently is not enough research published in OB journals to substantiate the conclusion that emotional intelligence is significantly associated with leadership effectiveness.[18]

Judge's Research: Is Personality More Important than Intelligence? Tim Judge and his colleagues completed two meta-analyses related to the subject of traits and leadership. The first examined the relationship among the Big Five personality traits (see Table 3.1 for a review of these traits) and leadership emergence and effectiveness in 94 studies. Results revealed that extraversion is most consistently and positively related to both leadership emergence and effectiveness. Conscientiousness and openness to experience also are positively correlated with leadership effectiveness.[19] Judge's second meta-analysis involved 151 samples and demonstrated that intelligence is modestly related to leadership effectiveness. Judge concluded that personality is more important than intelligence when selecting leaders.[20]

Kellerman's Research: What Traits Are Possessed by Bad Leaders? Thus far we have been discussing traits associated with "good leadership." Barbara Kellerman believes this approach is limiting because it fails to recognize that "bad leadership" is related to "good leadership." It also ignores the valuable insights that are gained by examining ineffective leaders. Kellerman thus set out to study hundreds of contemporary cases involving bad leadership and bad followers in search of the traits possessed by bad leaders. Her qualitative analysis uncovered seven key traits of bad leaders:[21]

1. *Incompetent.* The leader and at least some followers lack the will or skill (or both) to sustain effective action. With regard to at least one important leadership challenge, they do not create positive change.

   For example, Mary McLeod (nicknamed 'Neutron Mary') at Pfizer had a reputation of being difficult and had strained relationships with her direct reports, bragged about having the CEO under her thumb, encouraged the CEO to become isolated from the rest of the organization, and subtly threatened those that challenged her. Overall, she had a murky vision for HR and in the end was responsible for causing the CEO to lose his job.[22]

2. *Rigid.* The leader and at least some followers are stiff and unyielding. Although they may be competent, they are unable or unwilling to adapt to new ideas, new information, or changing times.

   Richard Fuld, former CEO of Lehman Brothers (global finance firm), held firm to his belief that Lehman was too big to fail. And yet, Lehman Brothers filed for bankruptcy in 2008 with cash flows anticipated to reach $40.5 billion through 2015 and beyond.[23]

3. *Intemperate.* The leader lacks self-control and is aided and abetted by followers who are unwilling or unable effectively to intervene.

   Consider the conviction of 35 year old Gary Foster, a former Citigroup vice-president who embezzled more than $22 million by secretly transferring money from various Citibank accounts to his personal account at another bank.[24]

4. *Callous.* The leader and at least some followers are uncaring and unkind. The needs, wants, and desires of most members of the group or organization, especially subordinates, are ignored or discounted.

   For example, former Ornge CEO Chris Mazza didn't see anything wrong with purchasing a fleet of over-priced medic-helicopters with interiors so cramped that paramedics couldn't perform life-saving procedures on patients.[25]

5. *Corrupt.* The leader and at least some followers lie, cheat, or steal. To a degree that exceeds the norm, they put self-interest ahead of the public interest.

   Consider Canadian-born Bernard Ebbers, the ex-CEO of Worldcom (known today through mergers as Verizon Business), who is still in prison serving 25 years for orchestrating a massive corporate fraud that resulted in a $11 billion bankruptcy.[26]

6. *Insular.* The leader and at least some followers minimize or disregard the health and welfare of "the other," that is, those outside the group or organization for which they are directly responsible.

   To save money, Philip Schoonover, former CEO of Circuit City (now known as The Source), fired 3,400 of the most experienced and productive salespeople because he felt they made too much *money. Meanwhile, Schoonover was reportedly earning an annual salary of nearly $4.5 million.*[27]

7. *Evil.* The leader and at least some followers commit atrocities. They use pain as an instrument of power. The harm done to men, women, and children is severe rather than slight. The harm can be physical, psychological, or both.[28]

Do you know leaders who possess any of these traits? Unfortunately, there are many examples.

Gender and Leadership As illustrated in the Focus on Diversity feature box, women in leadership roles throughout corporate Canada still have a long way to go to reach the proportionate levels of their male counterparts. However, the increase of women in the workforce has generated much interest in understanding the similarities and differences in female and male leaders. Three separate meta-analyses and a series of studies conducted by consultants across the country uncovered the following

differences: (1) men display more task leadership and women display more social leadership;[29] (2) women use a more democratic or participative style than men, and men use a more autocratic and directive style than women;[30] (3) men and women are equally assertive;[31] and (4) women executives, when rated by their peers, managers, and direct reports, score higher than their male counterparts on a variety of effectiveness criteria.[32]

What Are the Takeaways from Trait Theory? We can no longer afford to ignore the implications of leadership traits. Traits play a central role in how we perceive leaders, and they ultimately impact leadership effectiveness. What can be learned from research on traits? Integrating results across past studies leads to the extended list of positive traits shown in Table 10.3. Are traits the best predictor for finding an effective leader? This list provides some guidance regarding the leadership traits you should attempt to cultivate if you want to

THE GAP IN CANADIAN FEMALE CEOS

Whether we're talking about the boardroom or the top executive office, the chance of a woman assuming such roles in corporate Canada is still very low. At the time of this writing, there is only one woman among the highest paid 100 CEOs in publicly-traded companies in Canada: Nancy Southern, who heads a Calgary-based energy and utilities firm, ranked 85th with an annual income of nearly $4.8 million. Catalyst Canada recently reported that women hold just 6.2 percent of top earning positions at the Financial Post 500 list of largest and most influential companies in the country.

According to GovernanceMetrics International, the total percentage of women on Canadian boards was 12.9 percent in 2011, an increase of 0.7 percentage points from 2009. And the percentage of Canadian companies with at least one female director is now reaching 71.8 percent, up from 68.4 percent in 2009. But is that enough? Not at all, according to Sylvie Champoux-Paille a board member at MEDAC, a shareholder rights group, who put forward a proposal for gender parity on boards in Canada. "If we want to have the positive benefits of having women on boards, one is not sufficient. Studies have shown better representation of women can lead to better performance in a financial crisis because women have a different management style and where risk-taking is concerned,

tend to be more cautious and take prudent positions," says Champoux-Paille.

Is there any difference between the boardroom statistics and the presence of Canadian women in senior management positions? No, according to a study titled *Women in Senior Management: Where Are They?* conducted by the Conference Board of Canada, which analyzed data from 1987 to 2009. Results show the proportion of women in senior management positions changed very little. "Since the 1990s, men have consistently been two to three times more likely than women to hold a senior management role in Canada," said the report.

The criteria used to assess whether someone is suitable for a board also work against women. Between 45 percent to 50 percent of board members are CEOs or ex-CEOs. "If we look at women in the CEO function in Canada, we don't have a lot of them. So, when you are using such criteria, there is a gap," says Champoux-Paille.

SOURCES: D. Flavelle, "Only One Woman Among 100 Highest Paid CEOs In Canada," *The Toronto Star,* January 2, 2012, www.thestar.com; S. Dobson, "Women Missing From Boardrooms," *Canadian HR Reporter,* May 9, 2011, p 1; S. Dobson, "Far Too Few Female Execs: Report," *Canadian HR Reporter,* October 10, 2011; and "Women Still Missing From Senior Management Positions In Canada," *HR Professional,* December 2011, p 13.

TABLE 10.3

KEY POSITIVE LEADERSHIP TRAITS

Task competence (Intelligence, knowledge, problem-solving skills).

Interpersonal competence (ability to communicate, demonstrate caring and empathy).

Intuition.

Traits of character (conscientiousness, discipline, moral reasoning, integrity, and honesty).

Biophysical traits (physical fitness, hardiness, and energy level).

Personal traits (self-confidence, sociability, self-monitoring, extraversion, self-regulating, and self-efficacy).

SOURCE: These traits were identified in B M Bass and R Bass, *The Bass Handbook of Leadership* (New York: Free Press, 2008), p 135.

assume a leadership role. Consider personality tests, discussed in Chapter 3, and other trait assessments, as they are continued efforts on the part of OB theorists to try and evaluate personal strengths and weaknesses. Some practitioners find it beneficial to consider the results from such assessments in preparation for a personal development plan.[33]

There are two organizational applications of Trait Theory. First, organizations may want to include personality and trait assessments in their selection and promotion processes—not by themselves, but in combination with other selection tools. It is important to remember that this should only be done with valid measures of leadership traits. Second, enhance management development programs by including identifying and exploring employees' leadership traits. For example, PricewaterhouseCoopers sends targeted groups of managers to developmental programs that include management classes, coaching sessions, trait assessments, and stretch assignments.[34] Many companies also are using information technology to offer developmental classes online.[35]

BEHAVIOURAL STYLES THEORY

We will now consider the behavioural styles of leaders. Are certain behaviours the best way to predict who will succeed in a leadership role or not? This phase of leadership research began during World War II as part of an effort to develop better military leaders. It was an outgrowth of two events: the seeming inability of Trait Theory to explain leadership effectiveness, and the human relations movement (an outgrowth of the Hawthorne Studies). The thrust of early behavioural leadership theory was to focus on leader behaviour instead of on personality traits. It was believed that leader behaviour directly affect work group effectiveness. This led researchers to identify patterns of behaviour (called leadership styles) that enable leaders to effectively influence others.

The Ohio State Studies Researchers at Ohio State University began by generating a list of behaviours exhibited by leaders. Ultimately, the Ohio State researchers

concluded there are only two independent dimensions of leader behaviour: consideration and initiating structure. *Consideration* involves leader behaviour associated with creating mutual respect or trust and focuses on a concern for group members' needs and desires.

Initiating structure is leader behaviour that organizes and defines what group members should be doing to maximize output. These two dimensions of leader behaviour are oriented at right angles to yield four behavioural styles of leadership: low structure–high consideration, high structure–high consideration, low structure–low consideration, and high structure–low consideration.

It initially was hypothesized that a high structure–high consideration style would be the one best style of leadership. Through the years, the effectiveness of the high–high style has been tested many times. Overall, results have been mixed and there has been very little research about these leader behaviours until recently. Findings from a 2004 meta-analysis of 130 studies and more than 20,000 individuals demonstrated that consideration and initiating structure has a moderately strong, significant relationship with leadership outcomes. Results revealed that followers perform more effectively for structuring leaders, even though they prefer considerate leaders.[36] All told, results do not support the idea that there is one best style of leadership, but they do confirm the importance of considerate and structuring leader behaviours. Follower satisfaction, motivation, and performance are significantly associated with these two leader behaviours. Additional research is needed to incorporate them into more contemporary leadership theories.

University of Michigan Studies As in the Ohio State Studies, this research sought to identify behavioural differences between effective and ineffective leaders. Researchers identified two different styles of leadership: employee-centred and job-centred. These behavioural styles parallel the consideration and initiating-structure styles identified by the Ohio State group. In summarizing the results from these studies, one management expert concluded that effective leaders (1) tend to have supportive or employee-centred relationships with employees, (2) use group rather than individual methods of supervision, and (3) set high performance goals.[37]

> **Consideration**
>
> A leader with focused concern for group needs who practises creating mutual respect or trust with followers.

> **Initiating structure**
>
> A leader who organizes and defines what group members should be doing to maximize output.

Marissa Mayers, CEO of Yahoo Inc., enjoys tackling complex problems. She exhibits the kind of positive behaviours desired for leading a troubled firm.

What Are the Takeaways from Behavioural Styles Theory?
By emphasizing leader behaviour, something that is learned, the behavioural style approach makes it clear that leaders are made, not born. This is indeed wonderful news for all students! Given what we know about behaviour shaping and model-based training, leader behaviours can be systematically improved and developed.[38]

Behavioural styles research has also revealed that there is no one best style of leadership. The effectiveness of a particular leadership style depends on the situation at hand. For instance, employees prefer structure over consideration when faced with role ambiguity.[39] Finally, research has also revealed that it is important to consider the difference between how frequently and how effectively managers exhibit various leader behaviours. For example, a manager might ineffectively display a lot of considerate leader behaviours. Such a style is likely to frustrate employees, and possibly result in lowered job satisfaction and performance. Because the frequency of exhibiting leadership behaviours is secondary in importance to effectiveness, managers are encouraged to concentrate on improving the effective execution of their leader behaviours.[40]

Finally, Peter Drucker, an internationally renowned management expert and consultant, recommended a set of nine behaviours managers can focus on to improve their leadership effectiveness (see Table 10.4). The first two practices provide the knowledge leaders need. An example of this occurred when Marissa Mayer was made CEO of Yahoo. When it was announced that she would become the fifth leader in five years to take over the helm of the troubled company, people questioned what her first move would be. In her first interview, Mayer stated, "My first order of business is to meet with the senior leadership team and get a product road map," adding that she was confident she could make Yahoo's services "even more innovative and inspiring in the future."[41]

The next four practices help leaders convert knowledge into effective action, and the last two ensure that the whole organization feels responsible and accountable. Drucker refers to the last recommendation as a managerial rule.

TABLE 10.4

PETER DRUCKER'S TIPS FOR IMPROVING LEADERSHIP EFFECTIVENESS

1. Determine what needs to be done.
2. Determine the right thing to do for the welfare of the entire enterprise or organization.
3. Develop action plans that specify desired results, probable restraints, future revisions, check-in points, and implications for how one should spend his or her time.
4. Take responsibility for decisions.
5. Take responsibility for communicating action plans and give people the information they need to get the job done.
6. Focus on opportunities rather than problems. Do not sweep problems under the rug, and treat change as an opportunity rather than a threat.
7. Run productive meetings. Different types of meetings require different forms of preparation and different results. Prepare accordingly.
8. Think and say "we" rather than "I." Consider the needs and opportunities of the organization before thinking of your own opportunities and needs.
9. Listen first, speak last.

SOURCE: Reprinted by permission of *Harvard Business Review.* Recommendations were derived from "What Makes an Effective Executive," by P. F. Drucker, June 2004, pp 58–63. Copyright 2004 by the Harvard Business School Publishing Corporation, all rights reserved.

Contingency Approaches

So far, we have learned that when HR departments combine both traits and behaviours with other recruitment and selection tools to find an effective leader, they can provide some direction (prediction capabilities) for a company. But you must remember not to use trait and/or behaviours in isolation; rather, they must be combined with other section criteria. What else could be considered? Contingency approaches may help here. Contingency approaches grew out of an attempt to explain the inconsistent findings about traits and behavioural styles. The ability to predict successful leadership as a result of certain traits or behaviours fell short, and the search for other contributing variables needed to be considered. *Contingency approaches* propose that the effectiveness of a particular style of leader behaviour depends on the situation. As situations change, different styles become appropriate. This directly challenges the idea of one best style of leadership. Let's closely examine two alternative contingency approaches of leadership that reject the notion of one best leadership style: (1) Fiedler's Contingency Theory and (2) House's Path–Goal Theory. Read them both and then decide which you think to be the better of the two, or determine under which circumstances you think one would be more beneficial in terms of leadership selection and placement. Remember, we are trying to find and predict who will do the better job if selected to be a leader.

> **Contingency approaches**
>
> The effectiveness of a particular style of leader behaviour will depend on many variables.

LO 3 FIEDLER'S CONTINGENCY THEORY

Fred Fiedler, an OB scholar, developed a contingency model of leadership. It is the oldest and one of the most widely-known models of leadership. Fiedler's model is based on the following assumption:

> *The performance of a leader depends on two interrelated factors: (1) the degree to which the situation gives the leader control and influence—that is, the likelihood that [the leader] can successfully accomplish the job; and (2) the leader's basic motivation— that is, whether [the leader's] self-esteem depends primarily on accomplishing the task or on having close supportive relations with others.*[42]

With respect to a leader's basic motivation, Fiedler believes that leaders are either task-motivated or relationship-motivated. These basic motivations are similar to initiating structure/concern for production and consideration/concern for people.

Fiedler's theory is also based on the premise that leaders have one dominant or preferred leadership style that is resistant to change. He suggests that leaders must learn to manipulate or influence the situation to create a match between their leadership style and the amount of control within the situation at hand. After discussing the components of situational control and the leadership matching process, we review relevant research and managerial implications.[43]

Situational Control Situational control refers to the amount of control and influence leaders have in their immediate work environment. Situational control ranges from high to low. High control implies that the leader's decisions will produce predictable results because the leader has the ability to influence work outcomes. Low control implies that the leader's decisions may not influence work outcomes because the leader has very little influence. There are three dimensions of situational control: leader–member relations, task structure, and position power. These dimensions vary independently, forming eight combinations of situational control (see Figure 10.2).

The three dimensions of situational control are defined as follows:

- Leader–member relations reflect the extent to which the leader has the support, loyalty, and trust of the work group.

- Task structure is concerned with the amount of structure contained within tasks performed by the work group.

- Position power refers to the degree to which the leader has formal power to reward, punish, or otherwise obtain compliance from employees.

Linking Leadership Motivation and Situational Control Fiedler's complete contingency model is presented in Figure 10.2. The last row under the Situational Control column shows that there are eight different leadership situations. Each situation represents a unique combination of leader–member relations, task structure, and position power. Situations I, II, and III represent high control situations. Figure 10.2 shows that task-motivated leaders are hypothesized to be most effective in situations of high control. Under conditions of moderate control (situations IV, V, VI, and VII), relationship-motivated leaders are expected to be more effective. Finally, the results orientation of task-motivated leaders is predicted to be more effective under the condition of very low control (situation VIII).

Research and Managerial Implications Research has provided mixed support for Fiedler's model, suggesting that the model needs theoretical refinement.[44] That said, the major contribution of Fiedler's model is that it prompted others to examine the contingency nature of leadership. This research, in turn, reinforced the notion that there is no one best style of leadership. Leaders are advised to take a mental audit of their own preferred task and relationship orientation, compare it to the one demanded by the situation, and then assess the gap or harmony between the two. If possible, find a different approach to the situation, remembering that leaders have a preference for a style, not a limited ability.

Leaders should try and manipulate the situation to fit their style strengths, but as we've already

FIGURE **10.2** The Representation of Fiedler's Contingency Model

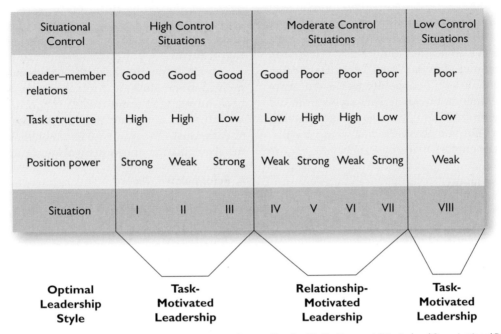

Situational Control	High Control Situations			Moderate Control Situations				Low Control Situations
Leader–member relations	Good	Good	Good	Good	Poor	Poor	Poor	Poor
Task structure	High	High	Low	Low	High	High	Low	Low
Position power	Strong	Weak	Strong	Weak	Strong	Weak	Strong	Weak
Situation	I	II	III	IV	V	VI	VII	VIII

Optimal Leadership Style	Task-Motivated Leadership	Relationship-Motivated Leadership	Task-Motivated Leadership

SOURCE: Adapted from F.E. Fiedler, "Situational Control and a Dynamic Theory of Leadership," in *Managerial Control and Organizational Democracy*, eds. B. King, S. Streufert, and F.E. Fiedler (New York: John Wiley & Sons, 1978), p 114.

mentioned, this isn't always possible. So, it's important for leaders to identify when a preferred leadership style is going to assist efforts or cause a barrier in achieving desired outcomes. If there is a gap, then consider how to compensate for it. This could include voluntarily stepping down. It's not uncommon to find one type of leader during the building phase of an organization, and then a change in leadership during the reorganization of it at another time. Recall the changes made in 2012 at BlackBerry giant Research in Motion (RIM) when co-founders Jim Balsillie and Mike Lazaridis voluntarily stepped aside to make room for Thorsten Heins to take over as President and chief executive officer. The company was trying

To stop the slide in sales, former RIM co-CEOs Mike Lazardis and Jim Balsillie, left, stepped aside in an effort to increase investor confidence in the BlackBerry brand. Thorsten Heins, right, assumed the role of CEO at the Waterloo, Ontario head office. How does Fiedler's contingency model of leadership apply in this situation?

to stem its quick decline from being Canada's largest tech giant as share value fell from the 2007 high of $150 per share to almost $7 by late 2012. Within days of the major announcement, share prices jumped over $2. However, the honeymoon didn't last long because within months of having Heins in the new CEO position, share prices continued to decrease, along with investor confidence, forcing Balsillie to step down from the board. Why? The public perceived there was little difference in the leadership styles from old to new, and having Heins in charge was not making any difference. Do you think Fiedler would be disappointed in the choices made by RIM?[45]

PATH–GOAL THEORY

Path–Goal Theory was originally proposed by Robert House in the 1970s.[46] He developed a model that describes how leadership effectiveness is influenced by the interaction between four leadership styles (directive, supportive, participative, and achievement-oriented) and a variety of contingency factors. *Contingency factors* are internal and external situational variables that cause one style of leadership to be more effective than another. Path–Goal Theory has two groups of contingency variables: employee characteristics and environmental factors. Five important employee characteristics include locus of control, task ability, need for achievement, experience, and need for clarity. Two relevant environmental factors include task structure (independent versus interdependent tasks) and work group dynamics. To gain a better understanding of how these contingency factors influence leadership effectiveness, we consider locus of control (discussed in Chapter 3), task ability and experience, and task structure.

Employees with an internal locus of control are more likely to prefer participative or achievement-oriented leadership because they believe they have control over the work environment. Such individuals are unlikely to be satisfied with directive leader behaviours that exert additional control over their activities. In contrast, employees with an external locus tend to view the environment as uncontrollable, thereby preferring the structure provided by supportive or directive leadership. Employees with high task ability and experience are less apt to need additional direction, and thus would respond negatively to directive leadership. These people are more likely to be motivated and satisfied by participative and achievement-oriented leadership. Oppositely, inexperienced employees would find achievement-oriented leadership overwhelming as they confront challenges associated with learning

a new job. Supportive and directive leadership would be helpful in this situation. Finally, directive and supportive leadership should help employees experiencing role ambiguity. However, directive leadership is likely to frustrate employees working on routine and simple tasks. Supportive leadership is most useful in this context.

About 50 studies have tested various predictions derived from House's original model. Results have been mixed, with some studies supporting the theory and others not.[47] House thus proposed a new version of Path–Goal Theory in 1996 based on these results and the accumulation of new knowledge about OB.

A Reformulated Theory The revised theory is presented in Figure 10.3.[48] There are three key changes in the new theory. First, House now believes that leadership is more complex and involves a greater variety of leader behaviour. He thus identifies eight categories of leadership styles or behaviour (see Table 10.5). Current research and descriptions of business leaders support the need for an expanded list of leader behaviours.[49]

The second key change involves the role of intrinsic motivation (discussed in Chapter 5) and empowerment (discussed in Chapter 9) in influencing leadership effectiveness. House places much more emphasis on the need for leaders to foster intrinsic motivation through empowerment. The final key change in the revised theory is called *shared leadership*. That is, Path–Goal Theory is based on the premise that an employee does not have to be a supervisor or manager to engage in leader behaviour. Rather, House believes that leadership is shared among all employees within an organization.

Shared Leadership A pair of OB scholars noted that "there is some speculation, and some preliminary evidence, to suggest that concentration of leadership in a single chain of command may be less optimal than shared leadership responsibility among two or more individuals in certain task environments."[50] This perspective is quite different from traditional theories and models discussed thus far, which assume that leadership is a vertical, downward-flowing process. In contrast, the notion of shared leadership is based on the idea that people need to share information and collaborate to get things done at work. This, in turn, underscores the need for employees to adopt a horizontal process of influence or leadership. Shared leadership entails a simultaneous, ongoing,

Contingency factors

Internal and external situational variables that influence the appropriateness of a leadership style.

Shared leadership

A simultaneous, ongoing, and mutually influential process in which people throughout an organization share responsibility for leading.

FIGURE 10.3 A General Representation of House's Revised Path–Goal Theory

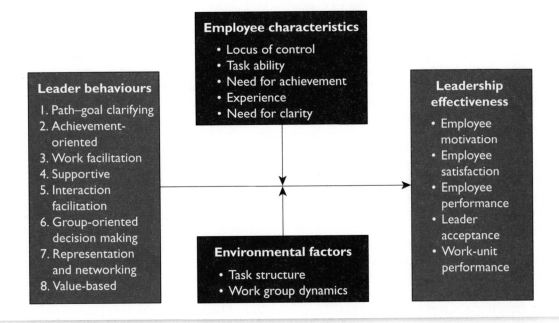

CATEGORIES OF LEADER BEHAVIOUR WITHIN THE REVISED PATH–GOAL THEORY

TABLE 10.5

CATEGORY OF LEADER BEHAVIOUR	DESCRIPTION OF LEADER BEHAVIOURS
Path–goal clarifying behaviours	Clarifying employees' performance goals; providing guidance on how employees can complete tasks; clarifying performance standards and expectations; using positive and negative rewards contingent on performance
Achievement-oriented behaviours	Setting challenging goals; emphasizing excellence; demonstrating confidence in employees' abilities
Work facilitation behaviours	Planning, scheduling, organizing, and coordinating work; providing mentoring, coaching, counselling, and feedback to assist employees in developing their skills; eliminating roadblocks; providing resources; empowering employees to take actions and make decisions
Supportive behaviours	Showing concern for the well-being and needs of employees; being friendly and approachable; treating employees as equals
Interaction facilitation behaviours	Resolving disputes; facilitating communication; encouraging the sharing of minority opinions; emphasizing collaboration and teamwork; encouraging close relationships among employees
Group-oriented decision-making behaviours	Posing problems rather than solutions to the work group; encouraging group members to participate in decision making; providing necessary information to the group for analysis; involving knowledgeable employees in decision making
Representation and networking behaviours	Presenting the work group in a positive light to others; maintaining positive relationships with influential others; participating in organization-wide social functions and ceremonies; doing unconditional favours for others
Value-based behaviours	Establishing a vision, displaying passion for it, and supporting its accomplishment; demonstrating self-confidence; communicating high performance expectations and confidence in others' abilities to meet their goals; giving frequent positive feedback

SOURCE: Descriptions are adapted from R. J. House, "Path–Goal Theory of Leadership: Lessons, Legacy, and a Reformulated Theory," *Leadership Quarterly,* 1996, pp 323–352.

mutual influence process in which individuals share responsibility for leading, regardless of formal roles and titles. This kind of personal leadership allows an opportunity for anyone to assume a leadership role within the context of their own job. Regardless of their position or status, through self-efficacy and empowerment an individual can adopt a horizontal process of leadership.

Shared leadership is most likely to be needed when people work in teams, when people are involved in complex projects, and when people are doing knowledge work—that is, work that requires voluntary contributions of intellectual capital by skilled professionals.[51] Marv Levy, the former CFL football coach of the Montreal Alouettes and member of the NFL Hall of Fame, is a strong believer in shared leadership. He concludes that a head coach "must be willing and desirous of forming a relationship with others in the organization that results in their working together productively and even enjoyably. A head honcho who thinks he can do it all by himself is fooling no one but himself. Working in concert with the team owner, the general manager, the personnel department, etc., allows everyone the opportunity to maximize his talents."[52]

Researchers are just now beginning to explore the process of shared leadership, and the results are promising. For example, shared leadership in teams is positively associated with group cohesion, group citizenship, and group effectiveness.[53] Table 10.6 includes a list of key questions and answers that managers should consider when determining how they can develop shared leadership.

Research and Managerial Implications There are not enough direct tests of House's revised Path–Goal Theory using appropriate research methods and statistical procedures to draw overall conclusions. Future research is clearly needed to assess the accuracy of this model. That said, there are still three important managerial implications. First, effective leaders possess and use more than one style of leadership. Managers are encouraged to familiarize themselves with the different categories of leader behaviour outlined in Path–Goal Theory and to try new behaviours when the situation calls for them. Consider the leader behaviours exhibited by Bob Iger, CEO of Walt Disney Co. He prefers to work behind the

TABLE 10.6

KEY QUESTIONS AND ANSWERS TO CONSIDER WHEN DEVELOPING SHARED LEADERSHIP

KEY QUESTIONS	ANSWERS
What task characteristics call for shared leadership?	Tasks that are highly interdependent.
	Tasks that require a great deal of creativity.
	Tasks that are highly complex.
What is the role of the leader in developing shared leadership?	Designing the team, including clarifying purpose, securing resources, articulating vision, selecting members, and defining team processes.
	Managing the boundaries of the team.
How can organizational systems facilitate the development of shared leadership?	Training and development systems can be used to prepare both designated leaders and team members to engage in shared leadership.
	Reward systems can be used to promote and reward shared leadership.
	Cultural systems can be used to articulate and to demonstrate the value of shared leadership.
What vertical and shared leadership behaviours are important to team outcomes?	Directive leadership can provide task-focused directions.
	Transactional leadership can provide both personal and material rewards based on key performance metrics.
	Transformational leadership can stimulate commitment to a team vision, emotional engagement, and fulfillment of higher-order needs.
	Empowering leadership can reinforce the importance of self-motivation.
What are the ongoing responsibilities of the vertical leader?	The vertical leader needs to be able to step in and fill voids in the team.
	The vertical leader needs to continue to emphasize the importance of the shared leadership approach, given the task characteristics facing the team.

SOURCE: C.L. Pearce, "The Future of Leadership: Combining Vertical and Shared Leadership to Transform Knowledge Work," *Academy of Management Executive: The Thinking Manager's Source*, February 2004, p 48. Copyright 2004 by Academy of Management. Reproduced with permission of Academy of Management via Copyright Clearance Center.

scenes and does not host any Disney TV productions. He is known to say "hello" to everyone he encounters on the Disney campus, and he participates in a Disney team that competes in triathlons to raise money for charity. He loves to study operational statistics and is very interested in studying and using consumers' attitudes to make decisions. Since taking over the helm at Disney, Iger patched up the rocky relationship between Pixar and Disney and ultimately purchased Pixar for $7 billion. He also resolved several contentious issues with former director Roy Disney and Comcast. Iger empowers his employees and allows them plenty of freedom to make decisions. At that same time, he holds people accountable for their work.[54] This example illustrates that Iger uses path–goal clarifying behaviours, achievement-oriented behaviours, work-facilitation behaviours, supportive behaviours, interaction-facilitation behaviours, and representation and networking behaviours.

Second, the theory offers specific suggestions for how leaders can help employees. Leaders are encouraged to clarify the paths to goal accomplishment and to remove any obstacles that may impair employees' abilities to achieve their goals. In so doing, managers need to guide and coach employees during the pursuit of their goals.

Third, a small set of employee characteristics (i.e., ability, experience, and need for independence) and environmental factors (task characteristics of autonomy, variety, and significance) are relevant contingency factors.[55] Managers are advised to modify their leadership style to fit these various employee and task characteristics.

LO 4 The Full-Range Model of Leadership: From Laissez-Faire to Transformational

We want to continue with our objective of trying to find the best predictor for finding an effective leader. If, for example, an HR department has a short list of potential candidates for a leadership role, they may want to conduct formal interviews. But what should they focus on or consider in terms of questions to ask regarding preferences, styles, and philosophy? What sort of experiences or demonstrations of leadership should the HR department look for? What sort of things should be a red flag advising the HR department to stay away?

Having knowledge of the full-range model of leadership may help categorize candidates more easily. A recent model authored by Bernard Bass and Bruce Avolio proposes that leadership behaviour varies along a continuum from laissez-faire leadership (i.e., a general failure to take responsibility for leading) to transactional leadership to transformational leadership.[56]

Examples of laissez-faire leadership include avoiding conflict, surfing the Internet during work, failing to assist employees in setting performance goals, failing to give performance feedback, or being so hands-off that employees have little idea about what they should be doing.[57] Of course, laissez-faire leadership is a terrible way for any manager to behave and should be avoided. Which gender do you think engages in more laissez-faire leadership? A meta-analysis revealed that men display more of this type of leadership than women.[58]

It is important for organizations to identify managers who lead with a laissez-faire style and to train and develop them to use behaviours associated with transactional and transformational leadership. Both transactional and transformational are positively related to a variety of employee attitudes and behaviours and represent different aspects of being a good leader. Let's consider these two important dimensions of leadership.

Transactional leadership focuses on clarifying employees' roles and task requirements and providing followers with positive and negative rewards contingent on performance. Further, transactional leadership encompasses the fundamental managerial activities of setting goals, monitoring progress toward goal achievement, and rewarding and punishing people for their level of goal accomplishment.[59] You can see from this description that transactional leadership is based on using extrinsic motivation (recall our discussion in Chapter 5) to increase employee productivity. That's how leaders at eHealth Ontario thought they would motivate their employees, but it backfired. See the Law and Ethics at Work feature box for the hard lesson learned when external rewards are inconsistent with corporate directives.

On a more positive note, consider how Bijan Khosrowshahi, former CEO of Fuji Fire and Marine Insurance, used transactional leadership to pick up the pace of growth at what had been a slow-moving company:

> He changed reporting lines so more managers talked directly to him. Then he forbade participants from reading prepared reports word-for-word in meetings, as had been customary. To assess talent, he grilled about 40 senior managers on the details of their jobs, discussing issues from reinsurance schemes to the chances of getting business from Toyota Motor Corp. Mr. Khosrowshahi is prodding managers to identify solutions as well as problems, and urging employees to take more initiative. Early on, he solicited volunteers to develop new-product ideas. [Yasunobu] Aoki's team was asked to create a new auto-insurance policy ... When Mr. Aoki presented the

> **Transactional leadership**
>
> Leadership that focuses on clarifying employees' daily roles and providing rewards contingent on performance.

PROMISES OF BONUSES AND MERIT PAY BACKFIRE AT EHEALTH ONTARIO

What happens when a corporate leader goes against company policy by promising bonuses and merit pay increases for work completed? Increased disappointment and lower employee job satisfaction.

In the aftermath of the 2008/09 financial crisis, the Ontario government pledged a two-year wage freeze for all public sector workers. While there was no law passed to enforce such a pledge, the spirit and moral purpose behind the announcement was to ensure the public that ethical management was in place, especially when so many people were still out of work. Ignoring the pledge was the CEO of eHealth Ontario, Sarah Kramer, who allowed promises to pay hundreds of government employees at the agency with bonuses of 7.8 percent and 1.9 percent merit raises as a reward for performance. An Auditor General report at the time criticized the $1 billion spent by the agency trying to develop a public electronic health record system with little to show for it. This resulted in a political scandal which quickly lead to Kramer's "mutually agreed upon" departure. By the spring of 2010, a new president and CEO was hired at eHealth, Greg Reed, who reorganized the management team and revamped the beleaguered (struggling) government agency. Despite new leadership at the top, however, the scandal did not go away. By spring 2011, in response to the outcry, eHealth withdrew its promise of pay increases and bonuses. Reed also turned down his own bonus.

What lesson is learned here? Human resource professionals need to help leaders speak with one voice in matters of reward management. Regardless of how well-intentioned the plan for pay increases and bonuses may be, leaders who do not toe the line when it comes to organizational directives are typically reined in quickly. They need to understand the potential consequences of inconsistent pay decisions, including the potential impact on employee trust and morale and the potential erosion of regulatory compliance that can result.

Do you think it was ethical for the eHealth employees to be promised bonuses and merit pay incentives?

SOURCES: C. Kapel, "Cautionary Tale On Compensation Rescinded," *Canadian HR Reporter*, June 20, 2011, p 15; R. Maurino, "eHealth Bureaucrats To Lose Bonuses and Merit Pay," *The Kitchener-Waterloo Record*, May 21, 2011, www.therecord.com/print/article/535374; and "EHealth Scandal a $1B waste: Auditor," CBC News, October 7, 2009, www.cbc.ca/news/canada/toronto/story/2009/10/07/ehealth-auditor.html.

---

plan to a Fuji committee including Mr. Khosrowshahi, he was taken aback by their tough questions. "That's when I realized this wasn't a game," says Mr. Aoki.[60]

In contrast, *transformational leadership* "engenders trust, seeks to develop leadership in others, exhibits self-sacrifice and serves as moral agents, focusing themselves and followers on objectives that transcend the more immediate needs of the work group."[61] Transformational leaders can produce significant organizational change and results because this form of leadership fosters higher levels of intrinsic motivation, trust, commitment, and loyalty from followers than does transactional leadership. That said, however, it is important to note

> **Transformational leadership**
>
> Leadership wih a vision that transforms the organization through role-modelling and inspiring behaviours, and encourages the pursuit toward achieving organizational goals.

that transactional leadership is an essential prerequisite to effective leadership, and that the best leaders learn to display both transactional and transformational leadership to various degrees. In support of this proposition, research reveals that transformational leadership leads to superior performance when it augments or adds to transactional leadership.[62] Let us return to the example of Fuji's Bijan Khosrowshahi to see how he augmented transactional leadership with transformational leadership so that employees would be inspired to work in new ways.

Mr. Khosrowshahi also worked on boosting morale, scheduling lunches with employees and launching a training program with Tokyo's

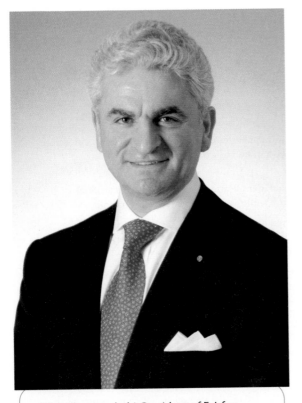

Bijan Khosrowshahi, President of Fairfax International, Toronto uses both transactional and transformational leadership to influence his followers. His leadership style is credited with increased financial performance during his time as CEO of Fuji Fire and Marine Insurance Co. Ltd.

Hitotsubashi University. To commemorate Fuji's improved earnings last year, he gave each of its employees 10,000 yen, or around $95, accompanied by thank-you notes in envelopes decorated with his caricature.

Hiroko Ikeno, an office worker who was a member of Mr. Aoki's team, says Mr. Khosrowshahi is so popular that some colleagues have taped his photo to their PCs.[63]

Khosrowshahi's leadership has helped Fuji's net premiums written (equivalent to revenues) rise for the first time in several years. We now turn our attention to examining the process by which transformational leadership influences followers.

HOW DOES TRANSFORMATIONAL LEADERSHIP TRANSFORM FOLLOWERS?

Transformational leaders transform followers by creating changes in their goals, values, needs, beliefs, and aspirations. They accomplish this transformation by appealing to followers' self-concepts—namely their values and personal identity. Figure 10.4 presents a model of how leaders accomplish this transformation process.

Figure 10.4 shows that transformational leader behaviour is first influenced by various individual and organizational characteristics. For example, research has revealed that transformational leaders tend to have personalities that are more extraverted, agreeable, and proactive and less neurotic than non-transformational leaders.[64] Female leaders are also found to use transformational leadership more than male leaders.[65] It is important to note, however, that the relationship between personality traits and transformational leadership is relatively weak. This suggests that transformational leadership is less trait-like and more susceptible to managerial influence. This conclusion reinforces the notion that an individual's life experiences play a role in developing transformational leadership and that transformational leadership can be learned.[66] Finally, Figure 10.4 shows that organizational culture influences the extent to which leaders are transformational. Cultures that are adaptive and flexible rather than rigid and bureaucratic are more likely to create environments that foster the opportunity for transformational leadership to be exhibited.

Transformational leaders engage in four key sets of leader behaviour (see Figure 10.4).[67] The first set, referred to as *inspirational motivation,* involves establishing an attractive vision of the future, the use of emotional arguments, and exhibition of optimism and enthusiasm. A vision is "a realistic, credible, attractive future for your organization."[68] According to Burt Nanus, a leadership expert, the "right" vision unleashes human potential because it serves as a beacon of hope and common purpose. It does this by attracting commitment, energizing workers, creating meaning in employees' lives, establishing a standard of excellence, promoting high ideals, and bridging the gap between an organization's present problems and its future goals and aspirations. Carl-Henric Svanberg, Ericsson's CEO, understands the importance of establishing an organization's vision. He noted that "[i]n a company this big, you can't just tell everyone, 'Turn left and work fast.' You have to share with them the vision you want to accomplish and get everybody on board and enthusiastic about it. When you get them to march in the same direction, you can really move mountains together."[69]

Idealized influence, the second set of leader behaviours, includes behaviours such as sacrificing for the good of the group, being a role model, and displaying high ethical standards. Home Depot's CEO Frank Blake exhibited idealized influence when he "accepted an annual pay package worth one-quarter of his predecessor's, and he is also finding creative ways to motivate

FIGURE 10.4 A Transformational Model of Leadership

Individual and organizational characteristics	Leader behaviours	Effects on followers and work groups	Outcomes
• Traits	• Inspirational motivation	• Increased intrinsic motivation, achievement orientation, and goal pursuit	• Personal commitment to leader and vision
• Organizational culture	• Idealized influence	• Increased identification and trust with the leader	• Self-sacrificial behaviour
	• Individualized consideration	• Increased identification and cohesion with work group members	• Organizational commitment
	• Intellectual stimulation	• Increased self-esteem, self-efficacy, and intrinsic interests in goal accomplishment	• Task meaningfulness and satisfaction
		• Increased role modelling of transformational leadership	• Increased individual, group, and organizational performance

SOURCE: Based in part on D.A. Waldman and F.J. Yammarino, "CEO Charismatic Leadership: Levels-of-Management and Levels-of-Analysis Effects," *Academy of Management Review,* April 1999, pp 266–85; and B. Shamir, R.J. House, and M.B. Arthur, "The Motivational Effects of Charismatic Leadership: A Self-Concept Based Theory," *Organization Science,* November 1993, pp 577–594.

employees, including giving merit awards for great customer service and assigning store workers more decision-making power."[70] Through their actions, transformational leaders like Frank Blake model the desired values, traits, beliefs, and behaviours needed to realize the vision.

The third set, *individualized consideration,* entails behaviours associated with providing support, encouragement, empowerment, and coaching to employees. These behaviours necessitate that leaders pay special attention to the needs of their followers and search for ways to help people develop and grow. You can do this by spending time talking with people about their interests and by identifying new learning opportunities for them. You also may want to serve as a mentor. Showing interest in people by remembering their names and previous conversations are other simple ways in which you can demonstrate consideration. Finally, treating people with respect and telling them the truth with compassion also represent examples of individualized consideration.

Intellectual stimulation, the fourth set of leadership behaviours, involves behaviours that encourage employees to question the status quo and to seek innovative and creative solutions to organizational problems. These behaviours are consistent with the finding by management expert Roger Martin that successful leaders tend to see problems and opportunities in all their complexity, rather than as either-or choices. In their search for a fresh perspective, these leaders are more likely to bring together people with different viewpoints, rather than break a problem into components so that, for example, the finance staff looks only at the financial implications while the sales managers look only for ways to push their product to new customers.[71]

RESEARCH AND MANAGERIAL IMPLICATIONS

Components of the transformational model of leadership have been the most widely researched leadership topic over the last decade. Overall, the relationships outlined in Figure 10.4 have been generally supported by previous research. For example, transformational leader behaviours were positively associated with the extent to which employees identified with both their leaders and immediate work groups.[72] Followers of transformational leaders also were found to set goals that were consistent with those of the leader, to be more engaged in their work, to have higher levels of intrinsic motivation, and to have higher levels of group cohesion.[73] With respect to the direct relationship between transformational leadership and work outcomes, a meta-analysis of 49 studies indicated that transformational leadership is positively associated with measures of leadership effectiveness and employees' job satisfaction.[74] At the organizational level, a second meta-analysis demonstrated that transformational leadership is positively correlated with organizational measures of effectiveness.[75]

These results underscore four important managerial implications. First, the best leaders are not just transformational—they are both transactional and transformational. Leaders should attempt to use these two types of leadership while avoiding a laissez-faire or wait-and-see style.

Second, transformational leadership not only affects individual-level outcomes like job satisfaction, organizational commitment, and performance, but it also influences group dynamics and group-level outcomes. Managers can thus use the four types of transformational leadership behaviours shown in Figure 10.4 as a vehicle to improve group dynamics and work-unit outcomes. This is important in today's organizations because most employees do not work in isolation. Rather, people tend to rely on the input and collaboration of others, and many organizations are structured around teams. The key point to remember is that transformational leadership transforms individuals as well as teams and work groups. We encourage you to use this to your advantage.

Third, employees at any level in an organization can be trained to be more transactional and transformational.[76] This reinforces the organizational value of developing and rolling out a combination of transactional and transformational leadership training for all employees.

Fourth, transformational leaders can be ethical or unethical. Whereas ethical transformational leaders enable employees to enhance their self-concepts, unethical ones select or produce obedient, dependent, and compliant followers.

The following are suggestions for how top management can create and maintain ethical transformational leadership:

1. Create and enforce a clearly stated code of ethics—this may include minimum standards for employees to follow.
2. Recruit, select, and promote people who display ethical behaviour.
3. Develop performance expectations around the treatment of employees—these expectations can then be assessed in the performance appraisal process.
4. Train employees to value diversity.

5. Identify, reward, and publicly praise employees who exemplify high moral conduct.[77]

Let's go back to the example we talked about when we started this section. If an HR department is interviewing a candidate, you can see how certain responses can offer insight into how that person thinks, the person's style preference, how inclusive the person is with others, the person's philosophy of engagement and providing employee inspiration, and so on. Listen to what the candidate is saying. If a candidate is focused solely on tasks, costs, deadlines, and commitments—with little to no mention of how such things can impact individual employees, human emotion or feelings, or people and team behaviour—then you can predict with some confidence that you're not talking to a transformational individual. In summary, be sure to use all the tools available to help identify the most effective leader possible for your organization.

SERVANT LEADERSHIP

This last section of the chapter talks about servant leadership, which is more a philosophy of managing than a testable theory. It too can be considered by an HR department when interviewing candidates for a leadership role.

The term *servant leadership* was coined by Robert Greenleaf in 1970. Greenleaf believes that great leaders act as servants, putting the needs of others—including employees, customers, and community—as their first priority. **Servant leadership** focuses on increased service to others rather than to oneself.[78] Because the focus of servant leadership is serving others over self-interest, servant-leaders are less likely to engage in self-serving behaviours that hurt others. Embedding servant leadership into an organization's culture requires actions as well as words. For example, John Donahoe, CEO of eBay, is committed to serving customers, "specifically the companies and entrepreneurs who sell goods on the site. Then he visualizes a chain of command through which the CEO can deliver what customers need. On trips around the world he takes along a Flip Video camera and films interviews with eBay sellers to share their opinions with his staff. He has even tied managers' compensation to customer loyalty, measured through regular surveys."[79]

According to Jim Stuart, cofounder of The Leadership Circle, a training school for CEOs, "[l]eadership derives naturally from a commitment to service. You know that you're practising servant leadership if your followers become wiser, healthier, more autonomous—and

> *Servant leadership*
>
> Focuses on increased service to others rather than to oneself.

more likely to become servant-leaders themselves."[80] Servant leadership is not a quick-fix approach to leadership. Rather, it is a long-term, transformational approach to life and work.

Servant-leaders have the characteristics listed in Table 10.7. An example of someone with these characteristics is Sam Palmisano, chairman and CEO of IBM. Here is what he says about his approach to leadership:

> Over the course of my IBM career I've observed many CEOs, heads of state, and others in positions of great authority. I've noticed that some of the most effective leaders don't make themselves the centre of attention. They are respectful. They listen. This is an appealing personal quality, but it's also an effective leadership attribute. Their selflessness makes the people around them comfortable. People open up, speak up, contribute. They give those leaders their very best.[81]

Researchers have just begun to develop measures of servant leadership and to examine relationships between this type of leadership and various outcomes. In support of Greenleaf's ideas, servant leadership was found to be positively associated with employees' performance, organizational commitment, job satisfaction, creativity, helping behaviours, and perceptions of justice. Servant leadership also was negatively related to counterproductive work behaviour.[82] These results suggest that managers would be well served by using the servant leadership characteristics shown in Table 10.7.

THE ROLE OF FOLLOWERS IN THE LEADERSHIP PROCESS

All of the previous theories discussed in this chapter have been leader-centric. That is, they focused on understanding leadership effectiveness from the leader's point of view. We conclude this chapter by discussing the role of followers in the leadership process. Although very little research has been devoted to this topic, it is an important issue to consider because the success of both leaders and followers is contingent on the dynamic relationship among the people involved.[83]

Leaders and followers are closely linked. You cannot lead without having followers, and you cannot follow without having leaders. The point is that each needs the other, and the quality of the relationship determines how we behave as followers. This is why it is important

TABLE 10.7

CHARACTERISTICS OF THE SERVANT-LEADER

SERVANT-LEADERSHIP CHARACTERISTICS	DESCRIPTION
1. Listening	Servant-leaders focus on listening to identify and clarify the needs and desires of a group.
2. Empathy	Servant-leaders try to empathize with others' feelings and emotions. An individual's good intentions are assumed even when he or she performs poorly.
3. Healing	Servant-leaders strive to make themselves and others whole in the face of failure or suffering.
4. Awareness	Servant-leaders are very self-aware of their strengths and limitations.
5. Persuasion	Servant-leaders rely more on persuasion than positional authority when making decisions and trying to influence others.
6. Conceptualization	Servant leaders take the time and effort to develop broader based conceptual thinking. Servant-leaders seek an appropriate balance between a short-term, day-to-day focus: and a long-term, conceptual orientation.
7. Foresight	Servant-leaders have the ability to foresee future outcomes associated with a current course of action or situation.
8. Stewardship	Servant-leaders assume that they are stewards of the people and resources they manage
9. Commitment to the growth of people	Servant-leaders are committed to people beyond their immediate work role. They commit to fostering an environment that encourages personal, professional, and spiritual growth.
10. Building community	Servant-leaders strive to create a sense of community both within and outside the work organization.

SOURCE: These characteristics and descriptions were derived from L. C. Spears, "Introduction: Servant-Leadership and the Greenleaf Legacy," in *Reflections on Leadership: How Robert K Greenleaf's Theory of Servant-Leadership Influenced Today's Top Management Thinkers,* ed L C Spears (New York John Wiley & Sons, 1995). pp 1–14.

for both leaders and followers to focus on developing a mutually rewarding and beneficial relationship.

Followers vary in terms of the extent to which they commit, comply, and resist a leader's influence attempts. For example, one researcher identified three types of followers: helpers, independents, and rebels. "*Helpers* show deference (respect) and comply with the leadership; *independents* distance themselves from the leadership and show less compliance; and *rebels* show divergence (different) from the leader and are at least compliant. Among other types of followers, moderate in compliance, are *diplomats, partisans,* and *counsellors.*"[84] Leaders obviously want followers who are productive, reliable, honest, cooperative, proactive, and flexible. Leaders do not benefit from followers who hide the truth, withhold information, fail to generate ideas, are unwilling to collaborate, provide inaccurate feedback, or are unwilling to take the lead on projects and initiatives.[85]

In contrast, research shows that followers seek, admire, and respect leaders who foster three emotional responses in others: Followers want organizational leaders to create feelings of *significance* (what one does at work is important and meaningful), *community* (a sense of unity encourages people to treat others with respect and dignity and to work together in pursuit of organizational goals), and *excitement* (people are engaged and feel energy at work).[86]

A pair of OB experts developed a four-step process for followers to use in managing the leader–follower relationship.[87] First, it is critical for followers to understand their boss. Followers should attempt to gain an appreciation for their manager's leadership style, interpersonal style, goals, expectations, pressures, and strengths and weaknesses. One way of doing this is to ask your manager to answer the following seven questions:[88]

1. How would you describe your leadership style? Does your style change when you are under pressure?
2. When would you like me to approach you with questions or information? Are there any situations that are off limits (e.g., a social event)?
3. How do you want me to communicate with you?
4. How do you like to work?
5. Are there behaviours or attitudes that you will not tolerate? What are they?
6. What is your approach toward giving feedback?
7. How can I help you?

Second, followers need to understand their own style, needs, goals, expectations, and strengths and weaknesses. The next step entails conducting a gap analysis between the understanding followers have about their boss and the understanding followers have about themselves. With this information in mind, followers are ready to proceed to the final step of developing and maintaining a relationship that fits both parties' needs and styles.

This final step requires followers to build on mutual strengths and to adjust or accommodate the leader's divergent style, goals, expectations, and weaknesses.[89] For example, followers might adjust their style of communication in response to the boss's preferred method for receiving information. Other adjustments might be made in terms of decision making. If the boss prefers a participative approach, then followers should attempt to involve their manager in all decisions regardless of the follower's decision-making style—recall our discussion of decision-making styles in Chapter 9.

Good use of time and resources is another issue for followers to consider. Most managers are pushed for time, energy, and resources and are more likely to appreciate followers who save rather than cost them time and energy. Followers should not waste their manager's time discussing trivial matters.

There are two final points to consider. First, followers may not be able to accommodate a leader's style, expectations, or weaknesses and may have to seek a transfer or quit their job to reconcile the discrepancy. We recognize that there are personal and ethical trade-offs that people may not be willing to make when managing the leader–follower relationship. Second, we can all enhance our boss's leadership effectiveness and our employer's success by becoming better followers. Remember, it is in an individual's best interest to be a good follower because leaders need and want competent employees.

How Ready Are You to Assume the Leadership Role?

INSTRUCTIONS: For each statement, indicate the extent to which you agree or disagree with it by circling one number from the scale provided. Remember, there are no right or wrong answers. After completing the survey, add your total score for the 20 items and record it in the space provided.

1 = **STRONGLY DISAGREE**
2 = **DISAGREE**
3 = **NEITHER AGREE NOR DISAGREE**

4 = **AGREE**
5 = **STRONGLY AGREE**

1	It is enjoyable having people count on me for ideas and suggestions.	1—2—3—4—5
2	It would be accurate to say that I have inspired other people.	1—2—3—4—5
3	It's a good practice to ask people provocative questions about their work.	1—2—3—4—5
4	It's easy for me to compliment others.	1—2—3—4—5
5	I like to cheer people up even when my own spirits are down.	1—2—3—4—5
6	What my team accomplishes is more important than my personal glory.	1—2—3—4—5
7	Many people imitate my ideas.	1—2—3—4—5
8	Building team spirit is important to me.	1—2—3—4—5
9	I would enjoy coaching other members of the team.	1—2—3—4—5
10	It is important to me to recognize others for their accomplishments.	1—2—3—4—5
11	I would enjoy entertaining visitors to my firm even if it interfered with my completing a report.	1—2—3—4—5
12	It would be fun for me to represent my team at gatherings outside our department.	1—2—3—4—5
13	The problems of my teammates are my problems too.	1—2—3—4—5
14	Resolving conflict is an activity I enjoy.	1—2—3—4—5
15	Would cooperate with another unit in the organization even if I disagreed with the position taken by its members.	1—2—3—4—5
16	I am an idea generator on the job.	1—2—3—4—5
17	It's fun for me to bargain whenever I have the opportunity.	1—2—3—4—5
18	Team members listen to me when I speak.	1—2—3—4—5
19	People have asked me to assume the leadership of an activity several times in my life.	1—2—3—4—5
20	I've always been a convincing person.	1—2—3—4—5

Total Score = _____

Norms for Interpreting the Total Score

90–100 = High readiness for the leadership role

40–59 = Some uneasiness with the leadership role

60–89 = Moderate readiness for the leadership role

39 or less = Low readiness for the leadership role

SOURCE: Adapted from A.J. DuBrin, *Leadership: Research Findings, Practice, and Skills* (Boston: Houghton Mifflin in Company, 1995), pp 10–11.

Summary of Learning Objectives

LO 1 **Define *leadership*.** Leadership is a social influence process in which the leader seeks the voluntary participation of subordinates in an effort to reach organizational goals.

LO 2 **Differentiate between being a leader versus a manager.** Leaders play a key role in creating a vision and strategic plan for an organization. Leaders inspire others, provide emotional support, and try to get employees to rally around a common goal. Managers, in turn, are charged with implementing the vision and strategic plan. They look after the day-to-day activities, such as managing resources, executing plans, or controlling costs.

LO 3 **Differentiate between the factors related to Fiedler's contingency theory and House's revised Path-Goal Theory.** Fiedler believed that leaders were either task or relationship motivated. These basic motivations were similar to initiating structure/concern for production versus consideration/concern for people. Fiedler's theory was also based on the premise that leaders had one dominant or preferred leadership style that was resistant to change. He suggested that leaders had to learn to manipulate or influence the leadership situation to create a match between their leadership style and the amount of control within the situation at hand. This differs from House's revised Path–Goal Theory in three ways: (1) leaders are viewed as exhibiting eight categories of leader behaviour (see Table 10.2); (2) leaders are expected to spend more effort fostering intrinsic motivation through empowerment; and (3) leadership is not limited to people in managerial roles but instead is is shared among all employees within an organization. Shared leadership involves a simultaneous, ongoing, mutual influence process in which individuals share responsibility for leading regardless of formal roles and titles. This type of leadership is most likely to be needed when people work in teams, when people are involved in complex projects, and when people are doing knowledge work.

LO 4 **Compare and contrast the key characteristics between transactional and transformational leadership.** Transactional leaders focus on clarifying employees' daily roles and task requirements, and provide followers with positive and negative rewards contingent on performance. They are helpful to keep the organization on schedule and on track. Transformational leaders motivate employees through inspiring modelling efforts, selling the vision, and pursuing organizational goals over their own self-interests. Both forms of leadership are important for organizational success. Individual characteristics and organizational culture are key forerunners of transformational leadership, which is comprised of four sets of leader behaviour. These leader behaviours, in turn, positively affect followers' and work groups' goals, values, beliefs, aspirations, and motivation. These positive effects are then associated with a host of preferred outcomes.

LO 5 **Review the principles of servant-leadership.** Greenleaf coined the term *servant-leader* to describe his philosophy of managing. It's not so much a tested theory, but rather a conceptual framework of eight characteristics that places great leaders into the role as servants, putting the needs of others—including employees, customers, and community—as their first priority. Because the focus of servant leadership is serving others over self-interest, servant-leaders are less likely to engage in self-serving behaviours that hurt others.

Discussion Questions

1. Is everyone destined to be a leader? Explain.
2. Have you ever worked for a transformational leader? Describe how this leader transformed followers.
3. "A leader makes a difference within a corporation." Do you agree with this statement? Explain.
4. Do you agree with the statement, "The best leaders are born, not taught in some classroom"? Explain your reasoning.
5. Think of the best leader you ever had in your life. Write five traits of that person on a piece of paper. Now think of the worst leader you ever had in your life. Write five traits of this person. Compare and contrast the two lists. What kind of leadership style did your best leader display?

Integration of OB Concepts—Discussion Questions

1. See Chapter 3–What role does personality play in the kind of leadership an individual prefers? Review the Big Five Personality Dimensions (Table 3.1) and find links between the two.
2. See Chapter 5–Review the different theories of motivation. What role can a leader play for employees given the different types of motivational factors that can exist within a workplace?
3. See Chapter 9–Consider the five different bases of power. Which would relate best to House's revised Path–Goal? Which would best relate to Greenleaf's servant leadership?

Google Searches

1. **Google Search:** "Canadian Business – Canada's Richest 100 201_" OR "Top Canadian CEO Salaries 201_" OR "Hugh Mackenzie 100 richest CEO's in Canada 201_" Are Canadian CEOs overpaid? These people are the 1 percent wage earners in Canada. Review the kind of compensation levels these people are earning. Who makes the most salary annually? Compare the minimum wage in your province to the amount the top CEO makes in Canada. How many years would it take for a minimum wage earner to make the kind of money earned by the top CEO?
2. **Google Search:** "Globe & Mail Canada's Top 40 Under 40 – 201_" After reviewing the list, compare and contrast the participants. Look for patterns such as gender, age, education/training, field, or related industry. Now look for the secret to their success. What is their philosophy? How would you categorize the leadership style of these individuals? Which are transformational? Which are servant-leaders?
3. **Google Search:** "Conrad Black Hollinger International" OR "Garth Drabinsky Livent Entertainment Group" OR "Bernard Madoff New York Financier" OR

"Edward Liddy and AIG Bonus Payback" OR "Kenneth Lay CEO Enron" Work in groups to research one of the corporate scandals. Present a five-minute presentation summarizing what happened, how it ended, and the lesson you learned from studying the scandal.

4. **Google Search:** "The Seven Habits of Spectacularly Unsuccessful Executives" AND "A Better Boss from Top to Bottom" Draw a line down the middle of a piece of paper. On one side list those behaviours that would be categorized as poor leadership and on the other side list those that would be considered positive leadership. Be prepared to share your list with others.

5. **Google Search:** "Canadian Centre for Policy Alternatives – Top Women CEOs Paid for 201_" OR "Catalyst Canada 201_ report of Top Earning Positions at Financial Post 500" Look at the latest statistics on female CEOs in Canada. Compare the latest numbers to the ones mentioned in the Focus on Diversity feature box. Have things improved recently? Compare and contrast the latest data findings.

Experiential Exercise

Leadership Group Exercise

PURPOSE: This exercise is meant to help you relate chapter theory to real world application. Compare and contrast leadership style of those listed, and try to find reasons for the differences. Approx. Timing: 35 minutes.

ACTIVITY ASSIGNMENT

- Break the class into working groups.
- Assign a pair of leaders from the table below to each working group. Ask the groups to research and then complete their portion of the table.
- Each group should be prepared to share their responses with the class.

	WHO ARE THEY? Compare and contrast backgrounds, interests/hobbies, training, income, gender, religion, etc.	WHY DO THEY BEHAVE A CERTAIN WAY? Identify and categorize leadership style and power preference, including use of political influencing tactics, motivation, and philosophy. Are they focused on tasks or on people—or on both equally?
Corporation: Costco Jim Sinegal–Ex CEO Vs. Craig Jelinek–New CEO		
Corporation: Apple Steve Jobs–Ex CEO Vs. Tim Cook–New CEO		
Larry Page Google CEO Vs. Mark Zuckerberg–Facebook CEO		

(Continued)

Mahatma Gandhi Vs. Adolf Hitler		
Oprah Winfrey Vs. Rosa Parks		
Craig Kielburger Vs. Mother Theresa		
Corporation: Toronto Maple Leafs Ron Wilson–Ex coach Vs. Randy Carlyle (New coach)		

OB In Action Case Study

Maple Leaf Foods

THE BEGINNING

Since the early 1990s, the McCain family has created a corporate powerhouse out of the old Canada Packers. While Michael McCain's father, the late Wallace McCain, can take the credit for the initial purchase of the firm, Michael has modernized the company. As CEO since 1998, Michael has turned Maple Leaf into a giant food conglomerate—but it hasn't always been a smooth process. Take, for example, one of his earlier decisions to become competitive by restructuring the organization. According to a Maple Foods unionized member at the time, McCain decided to move machines from Edmonton to Hamilton where the company claimed it would control its costs by streamlining its supply chain. Then came cutting wages by up to $9 per hour and benefits by 50 percent, eliminating seniority, making workers pay for each minute over 20 minutes spent going to the bathroom each week, introducing a flexible workweek to eliminate weekend overtime pay, and forcing workers to give up a day's seniority for each day absent. Ten years later, the company was able to re-establish a positive relationship with its union, creating ongoing feedback loops with its employees, introducing performance reviews and state-of-the-art performance assessment and development programs for its management team, as well as recognizing initiatives for outstanding performance.

2008 LISTERIOSIS CRISIS

In late August 2008, McCain had to direct all his attention toward a potentially debilitating situation that involved the presence of the infectious listeriosis bacteria. The bottom line: people were dying from food processed at its Toronto plant. McCain found himself in the middle of a crisis that every CEO dreads—having to publicly acknowledge corporate fault and lay claim to the undisputed fact of ultimate responsibility for a serious mishap. But as the person responsible for the interests of 23,000 employees, McCain accepted his role as CEO without hesitation. As the executive team battled the operational issues, McCain resolved to save the jobs of those (300) employees at the Toronto processing plant.

When faced with media doubt about the firm's ability to overcome this crisis, McCain responded with a determined belief that the organization would indeed survive thanks to the support of dedicated people; the quality, depth, and width of product offerings; the benefits received from customer loyalty; and strong brand recognition. In public appearances, McCain openly stated that the company would eventually recover and experience sales equal to pre-crisis levels. McCain's leadership proved to be compelling, as Maple Leaf again began shipping meat from its Toronto plant within several months after the initial outbreak. Maple Leaf reported a 6.3 percent increase in sales over the previous year for the 2009 first quarter and second quarter earnings per share were adjusted to a positive 12 cents per share, rather than a loss of 1 cent per share the previous year. McCain stated at the time that while Maple Leaf had made good progress, there remained significant value creation opportunity with very positive effects on their future financial results. In other words, there was still much more that had to be done to get Maple Leaf back into a market leader position.

JUST WHEN HEADS GOT ABOVE THE WATERLINE

In August 2010, McCain received news that a new shareholder, Greg Boland of West Face, had purchased 10 percent of Maple Leaf Foods. Boland was well known in Canada as an activist; he had no intention of being a silent shareholder. The news could not have come at a worse time for McCain. He had just pulled the company through the fight of its life and survived the listeria outbreak, there was the global financial crisis still threatening investments, and the resurgence of the Canadian dollar on the international currency exchange was making production and exporting more expensive against US rivals. Then came an "ugly divorce" with Maple Leaf's biggest shareholder, Ontario Teacher's Pension Plan, and finally Michael's mentor Wallace McCain, his 80 year old father, was fighting a losing battle to pancreatic cancer. "The coalescing (merging) of challenges," as Michael called it, meant the family was losing its grip on a company that he now conceded "had not delivered" to shareholders for years. Maple Leaf's stock price had been sinking since 2005.

Why didn't McCain acknowledge the sinking share value before this time? Reports show that McCain had been compensated nearly $20 million in the three years leading up to 2010. Further, he had a strong influence over the board because so many members were close friends of his late father. In fact, many shared the same roots from New Brunswick, home to the historical McCain empire. Bottom line: the young McCain was insulated.

With Boland now in the game, McCain had to respond to shareholder concerns, and the two were often at odds. Boland took the lead by using his political acumen to find the support he needed among other shareholders to coax Maple Leaf into making necessary changes, while Michael McCain held steady with the confidence an experienced leader develops over time. The plan was to restructure the company, and all parties were onside. By early 2011, McCain and the other board members agreed to develop one of its critical assets first: its people. By aligning the restructuring plan with a people plan, Maple Leaf was ready to revisit, refocus, and re-launch its long established HR Leadership Edge training policy developed 11 years earlier. McCain turned this responsibility over to Les Dakens, a well-known and respected HR professional, and Cheryl Fullerton, Maple Leaf's HR Director. Together, they would be responsible for designing and implementing a new people strategy for the organization.

In late 2011, as part of a repositioning strategy, McCain had to make a difficult announcement. A series of sweeping changes, including plant closures around the country, would result in 1,550 jobs being lost over the next few years. But it was all part of the company's plan to create "a highly efficient, world-class production and distribution network (meant to) markedly increase our competitiveness and close the cost gap with our US peers," said McCain. Major reforms would be introduced, including improved production facilities and other moves to modernize operations. Pressure from West Face continued, but by this time McCain and Boland had come to a truce. Mutual understanding and appreciation of each other's leadership qualities evolved as McCain described Boland as "Smart as hell!," "Scary bright!," and "Accomplished." Boland credited Michael McCain as being a good listener.

By the fall of 2012, share prices were rebounding close to pre-crisis levels. McCain, at the age of 53, continued to take his place at the helm of Maple Leaf Foods. Also at this time, Boland agreed to join the Maple Leaf board and other new independent directors were appointed.

Four years after the Maple Foods listeriosis outbreak, another Canadian food giant faced a similar crisis. In the fall of 2012, XL Foods Inc., one of Canada's largest beef processors, faced a massive E. coli-related beef recall—the largest in Canadian history. By November 2012, 17 gastrointestinal illnesses in four provinces had been linked to beef from XL's plant in Alberta. As the story unfolded, the media kept comparing XL's response to that of Maple Leaf Foods.

How did Michael McCain's leadership compare? Very favourably. Jeremy Berry, an associate professor of public relations at Mount Royal University in Calgary, stated to the CBC, "If you look at the Maple Leaf example . . . we saw a lot more openness and transparency and really a lot of leadership on a similar file and one that even involved the deaths of more than 20 people and they were still out there and leading."

Leger Marketing did a study of Canadians' perceptions of Mapel Leaf's crisis with Terry Flynn, a professor who teaches crisis management at McMaster University in Hamilton. The study concluded, among other things, that the company had set a new level of crisis leadership in Canada "by which future companies will be measured."

Questions for Discussion

1. How would you describe McCain's leadership style?
2. Identify those behaviours McCain exhibited early on as CEO that suggest he was a transactional leader. (Hint: Uses extrinsic motivation to increase employee productivity.)
3. How did McCain use transformational leadership to deal with the listeria outbreak?
4. Who do you think is more powerful and politically-oriented, Michael McCain or Greg Boland? Explain.

SOURCES: J. Davison, "How Should A Company Manage A Meat Recall Crisis?" *CBC News,* October 9, 2012, www.cbc.ca; J. McNish, "How An Activist Investor Shook Up a Canadian Brand," *Report on Business Magazine– The Globe and Mail,* March 2012, p 44–48; J. Campbell, "Maple Leaf Foods: Building A People Strategy To Align With Business Needs," *HR Professional Magazine,* January 2012, p 30; and Kreitner, Kinicki, Cole, and Digby, *Organizational Behaviour* 3rd Cdn. Edition, p 234.

The CONNECTion Zone Mc Graw Hill connect™

- The Presentation Assistant
- Ethical OB Dilemma
- Video Case

Practise and learn online with Connect.

"Business and human endeavors are systems ... we tend to focus on snapshots of isolated parts of the system and wonder why our deepest problems never get solved."

Peter Senge, Ph.D. (Author – The Fifth Discipline)

Organizational Culture, Socialization, and Mentoring

FACING AN OB CHALLENGE

I've been looking for a full-time job for almost 18 months without success, until yesterday. I finally found a good paying part-time job at a large Canadian blue-chip organization, and I start next week. The person from the HR Department has given me a series of dates when I have to report to work for training. The duties of the position are pretty straightforward; I'm confident I can learn them quickly. I don't know why they feel the need to have every new employee spend three days in orientation sessions before we can begin! I don't mind sitting around getting paid for learning ... but isn't this just a bit over the top?

—READY TO HIT THE GROUND RUNNING

LO 1 Define *organizational culture, espoused values,* and *enacted values.*

LO 2 Describe the four functions of organizational culture.

LO 3 Discuss the four types of organizational culture associated with the competing values framework.

LO 4 Summarize the various methods used by organizations to change organizational culture.

LO 5 Describe the three phases in Feldman's model of organizational socialization and explain how mentoring can assist the socialization process.

Understanding Culture

The question raised in the opening OB Challenge suggests the need for you to understand how a formal socialization process, like three days of orientation and training to help new employees with their transition into the current organizational culture. To ensure a successful experience at a new job, and to indeed help a new employee "hit the ground running," this particular organization is providing an opportunity to learn the location of various resources and how to use workplace tools, and to clarify as well as reinforce job expectations. Three days of orientation and training will deliver a broad perspective of organizational values, philosophy, and practices—within a friendly context—to allow new employees to ask questions, receive clarification of processes, as well as be empowered to self-manage within the company culture.

This chapter will help you understand the important role of organizational culture within the contemporary workplace. After defining and discussing the context of organizational culture, we examine (1) the dynamics of organizational culture, (2) the process of culture change, (3) the organization socialization process, and (4) the embedding of organizational culture through mentoring.

Organizational Culture: Definition and Context

LO 1

Organizational culture is "the set of taken-for-granted implicit assumptions that a group holds and that determines how it perceives, thinks about, and reacts to its various environments."[1] Henry Mintzberg, commonly referred to as the father of OB and professor emeritus at McGill University, calls culture the "meaningful soul of the organization."[2] Jack Lohman, CEO of the Royal BC Museum in Victoria, refers to culture as "the driving spirit of an organization."[3] In other words, it's the set of shared values and beliefs that underlie a company's identity. This definition highlights three important characteristics of organizational culture. First, organizational culture is passed on to new employees through the process of socialization, a topic discussed later in this chapter. Second, organizational culture influences our behaviour at work. Finally, organizational culture operates at different levels.

Figure 11.1 provides a conceptual framework for reviewing the widespread impact organizational culture has on organizational behaviour. It also shows the linkage between this chapter—culture, socialization, and mentoring—and other key topics in this book. To begin with, let's walk through the basics of Figure 11.1. As you can see, culture is created from four key sources: the founder's values, the industry and business environment, the national culture, and the senior leaders' vision and behaviour.[4] The fundamental philosophy and set of values that the company founders brought with them when they first created the company is paramount to setting the tone and is the driving force behind all strategy or future activity. It would be very difficult to separate the founder from the company, as they are so closely aligned. For example, Joseph-Armand Bombardier's vision as a youthful 16-year-old in 1924 of a functioning machine to use for transportation purposes lead to his invention of the first snowmobile made by the company that carries his name, Bombardier Aerospace Inc. With the help of his family, Joseph-Armand used his passion and drive to propel the company into becoming a giant multi-national engineering and manufacturing

> **Organizational culture**
>
> The set of shared values and beliefs that underlie a company's identity.

business, far from its humble beginnings in Valcourt, Quebec. Today, although Joseph-Armand has passed, a family descendant sits on the Board, contributing to the company using the guiding principles, core values, and appreciate for invention that helped create the company almost 100 years ago. With such a strong culture, it's no wonder that Bombardier has recently won numerous industry awards of excellence.[5]

Organizational culture influences the type of organizational structure adopted by a company (we'll talk more about this in Chapter 12) and a host of practices, policies, and procedures implemented in pursuit of organizational goals. These organizational characteristics then affect a variety of group and social processes. This sequence ultimately affects employees' attitudes and behaviour and a variety of organizational outcomes. All told, Figure 11.1 reveals that organizational culture is a background variable influencing individual, group, and organizational behaviour.

There can be more than one dominant culture within an organization, along with subcultures that operate in a different location (building, department, or regional office). Keith Dewar recently became the CEO of the newly formed Crown Corporation Health PEI, which is responsible for the operation and delivery of publicly-funded health services in Prince Edward Island. His new role at the 4,400 employee Health PEI presents plenty of challenges, particularly in bringing together the cultures of several regional health authorities. "Every organization has multiple cultures," says Dewar, "and it's about aligning those, with everybody having a consistent commitment, knowing where they are going as an organization, what they're trying to achieve and their role in that."[6]

When there are multiple cultures within an organization, there are also contrasting sets of philosophical values working in this subculture area; it can operate almost like a separate company. At times, subcultures can provide healthy alternative work environments that allow for creative expression. But, if left unchecked, they can become strong counter-cultures with competing values that work against the main organizational culture. This is what happened at Apple back in the mid 1990s, when Steven Jobs was lured back to oversee the Macintosh Division that was housed physically away from the main head office building. When Jobs came back to Apple after being away for several years, his transformational leadership and infectious energy made the Macintosh Division "pirates" feel empowered and at the same time at odds with the "corporate shirts" as they competed over which product would be launched first to 'save' Apple Inc.[7]

Dynamics of Organizational Culture

To gain a better understanding of how employees use organizational culture, this section begins by discussing the layers of organizational culture. We then review the four functions of organizational culture, the types of organizational culture, and the outcomes associated with organizational culture.

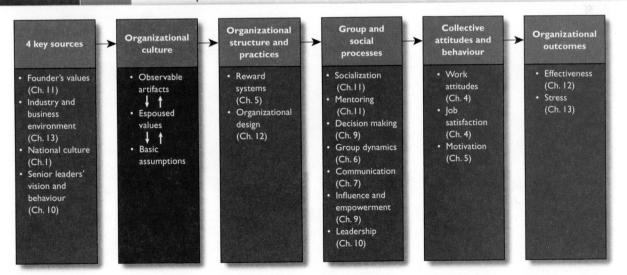

FIGURE 11.1 A Conceptual Framework for Understanding Organizational Culture

SOURCE: Adapted in part from C. Ostroff, A. Kinicki, and M. Tamkins, "Organizational Culture and Climate," in *Handbook of Psychology*, vol. 12, ed Weiner, pp 565–93, © 2003 John Wiley & Sons, Inc. Reprinted with permission of John Wiley & Sons, Inc.

LAYERS OF ORGANIZATIONAL CULTURE

Looking back at Figure 11.1, notice that the second box from the left shows the three fundamental layers of organizational culture: observable artifacts, espoused values, and basic assumptions. Some of these exist within the day-to-day observable behaviours of the organization, while others are found beneath the surface. Looking ahead at Figure 11.2, this illustration may help you understand the complex levels within organizational culture. Each level varies in terms of outward visibility and resistance to change, and each level influences another level.

Observable Artifacts These are the levels that sit above the surface and have the highest visibility; they consist of the physical manifestation (appearance) of an organization's culture. Here are some examples of what we mean by artifacts:

- **Legends and stories** Myths or truths handed down from employee to employee in informal or formal settings about how things came to be at the company. They can also include the historical past and how philosophy and values created the current policies and procedures. For example:

    Canadian retailer Lululemon is first and foremost known as a seller of athletic wear—not just fashionable yoga clothing. The inside legend about the creation of its corporate logo—a stylized "A"—is

now being made public. The published story explains how the symbol was made for the first letter in the name "athletically hip," a corporate name that failed to make the grade, but the executive team liked it so much that they kept it. [8]

- **Language and acronyms** The words used to communicate create an atmosphere of club-like membership that only those who understand are included. This is common in highly tech-oriented work environments, where people talk about Wi-Fi, RSS feeds, C#, etc. Unless you work in the field, these things can be very intimidating. For example:

    "Already services such as PhoneGap are allowing developers to combine an HTML5 core with native APIs to leverage the best of native and open standards." [9]

- **Rituals and ceremonies** These include observable behaviour exhibited by people and groups within the organization. For example:

    Canada's largest general contracting, construction, and project management firm, EllisDon Corporation of Mississauga, hosts numerous events each year for its employees in recognition and appreciation for their hard work, including: end-of-month birthday celebrations, an annual

FIGURE 11.2 Levels of Organizational Culture

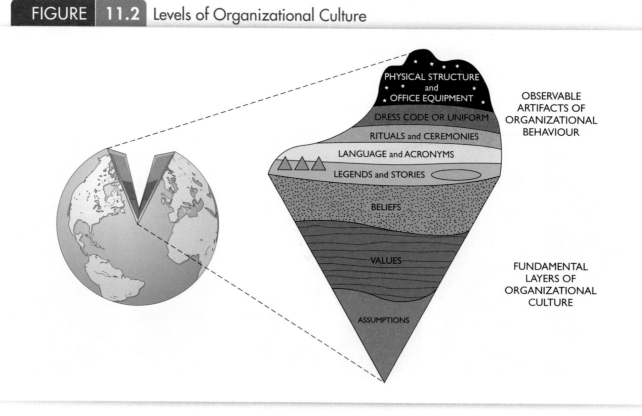

hockey tournament with teams from across the company, regular team lunches, golf tournaments, and annual trips to major sports events.[10]

■ **Dress code or uniform** The acceptable clothing to wear while engaged at work can be a clear indicator of the values of the organization. For example:

> *Observe if the office employees dress casually or formally. Are facial piercings and tattoos banned? A mandatory uniform sets up the expectations of some workplaces; consider Tim Hortons' employees who must wear the same design and style uniform at all times within all stores.*[11]

■ **Physical structure and office equipment** The physical look of the office can include furniture, decorations, equipment, design, colours, and layout. Collectively, they make a statement of the values held by the organization. For example:

> *Consider the unique architecture of the Cirque du Soleil headquarters in Montreal. The unique exterior of the building is only an introduction of the unusual creative expressionism to be found within the interior offices ... values and deep convictions that rest on audacity, imagination, and the type of people drawn to such an organization.*[12]

Observable artifacts are easier to change because they are obvious and tangible in nature. However, not all culture is tangible, as we'll explore in this next section.

Values and Assumptions Going back to Figure 11.2, we now discuss what is below the surface. *Values* possess five key components. "Values (1) are concepts or beliefs, (2) pertain to desirable end-states or behaviours, (3) transcend situations, (4) guide selection or evaluation of behaviour and events, and (5) are ordered by relative importance."[13] It is important to distinguish between values that are espoused versus those that are enacted.

Espoused values represent the explicitly stated values and norms that are preferred by an organization. They are generally established by the founder of a new smaller company and by the top management team in a larger organization. Consider the espoused values of Vancouver-based Lululemon: slogans printed on their shopping bags, advertisements, and websites. It's being community minded, as clearly stated by Executive of the Year Christine Day, Lululemon's CEO since 2008:

> *Day considers Lululemon to be "part of, and contributing to, a bigger macro-trend that affects*

Christine Day, CEO of Lululemon, "... believes in a culture of personal accountability and not compromising your values. (It's) about not accepting mediocrity and being personally accountable for the life you are creating."

Values

Enduring belief in a mode of conductor end-state.

Espoused values

The stated values and norms that are preferred by an organization.

consumers from their early teens to their 70s. Investing in your health will pay big dividends for individuals and society ... elevating the world from mediocrity to greatness."

This quote is layered upon a reference to *Atlas Shrugged*, Ayn Rand's 1957 novel about being unique and the necessity that truly great people strive through all obstacles toward dominance. Day makes no bones about acknowledging the inspiration of the book and the life of its author. "I believe in a culture of personal accountability and not compromising your values. *Atlas Shrugged* is both about not accepting mediocrity and being personally accountable for the life you are creating."[14]

At times the espoused values of the organization are not congruent with the personal values of employees or the national values of their customer. When this happens, it becomes necessary to make adjustments to the organizational culture. See the next International OB feature box discussion about Kal Tires, a family-owned company from Vernon, British Columbia, that expanded into South America but decided to avoid having competing values in the workplace by developing a new hybrid culture.

KAL TIRE'S HYBRID CULTURE HOLDS KEY TO SUCCESS

When the Canadian company Kal Tire decided to leap onto the international scene, few outside of Canada knew about its strong reputation as a solutions supplier of tire services. It knew it had to make adjustments; for example, the company quickly adopted a process of self-evaluation to ensure it was setting best practices and sharing them throughout the company's global network. In addition, it designed a new hybrid culture by placing its international operations in the hands of those who were indigenous to the area. "In Chile, for example, the company may have the name Kal Tire, but it is run by a Chilean, which is as it should be to be a part of the Chilean industry," says Chris Brothen, regional manager in charge of international development and sales. "We don't have a large contingent of expats in our companies around the world. Although we will hopefully add some Canadian concepts to each operation, we're not out to force our values onto (others)," concludes Brothen.

The Kal Tire experience positively correlates with Geert Hofstede's 30-year old cross-cultural comparison research, that in turn was supported by findings from Project Globe (to be discussed further in Chapter 14). The bottom line: Made-in-Canada management policies, cultures, and practices like those made by Kal Tire in BC need to be adapted to local cultures because values that compete can become real roadblocks on the way to international development. Creating a hybrid culture was perhaps Kal Tire's smartest business decision when expanding into the Central and South American markets.

SOURCE: H. Ednie, "Treading New Territory," *The CIM Bulletin,* December 2011/January 2012, Vol. 6 No. 8.

Because espoused values represent aspirations that are explicitly communicated to employees, managers hope that those values will directly influence employee behaviour. Unfortunately, aspirations do not automatically produce the desired behaviours, because people do not always "walk the talk."

Enacted values, on the other hand, represent the values and norms that actually are exhibited or converted into employee behaviour. They represent the values that employees give credit to in an organization, based on their observations of what occurs on a daily basis. Going back to our earlier discussion about Lululemon, CEO Day demonstrates the corporate values through her own lifestyle: she does yoga, hikes, bikes, walks the seawall, and generally lives the outdoor west-coast life.[15] She walks the talk from the top by being a role model for the corporate slogans. To inspire others to do the same, store employees are encouraged to follow Advocates, leaders from the Store Support Centre who actively engage employees to live the values and be passionate about 'doing the right thing' as part of their day-to-day decision making at work and at home, as well as leading the charge within their own communities.[16]

Sometimes organizations say one thing (espouse), but their actions exhibit something completely different (enacted). The following two examples are excellent representations of the difference between espoused and enacted values:

> *A major international corporation hung signs in its hallways proclaiming that trust was one of its driving principles. Yet that same company searched employees' belongings each time they entered or exited the building. In another case, a multinational corporation that claimed to be committed to work/life values drew up an excellent plan to help managers incorporate work/life balance into the business. The company gathered its top 80 officers to review the plan—but scheduled the meetings on a weekend.*[17]

The first company espoused that it valued trust, and then behaved in an untrusting manner by checking employees' belongings. The second company similarly created a mismatch between espoused and enacted values by promoting work/life balance while simultaneously asking managers to attend weekend meetings.

It is important for managers to reduce gaps between espoused and enacted values because they can significantly influence employee attitudes and organizational performance.

Basic Assumptions Think of basic assumptions as the DNA of the organization: you cannot see them, but you know they are important and represent the

Enacted values

The values and norms that are exhibited by employees.

very core of a human being. The same can be said for the basic assumptions found within organizational culture. They constitute organizational values that have become so taken for granted over time that they become assumptions that guide organizational behaviour. They are thus highly resistant to change. When basic assumptions are widely held among employees, people will find behaviour based on an inconsistent value inconceivable. For example, employees at WestJet Airlines would be shocked to see management act in ways that did not value employees' and customers' needs because this is the very core of the organization.

Practical Application of Research on Values Organizations subscribe to a constellation of values rather than to only one, and can be profiled according to their values. Organizations are less likely to accomplish their corporate goals when employees perceive an inconsistency between espoused values (e.g., "We are an organization that values honesty") and the behaviours needed to accomplish the goals (e.g., Employees were directed to shred financial documents while the RCMP was investigating the organization). Similarly, organizational change is unlikely to succeed if it is based on a set of values highly inconsistent with employees' individual values.

LO 2 THE DEVELOPMENT AND FUNCTIONS OF ORGANIZATIONAL CULTURE

Before we address the functions organizational culture creates, let's first take a step back to review *how* culture is developed. While there is no universal process that every organization follows, there are some common patterns worth identifying. When a firm is created, the executive leadership adopts structural features for the entire organization that are typically placed within formal policy documents identifying set responsibilities.

The values and assumptions mentioned earlier form the expectations around employee behaviour, as well as product quality and/or customer service levels. This structure is adopted by all who work for the organization, by explicit (clear and obvious) decision, on the basis of known policies and procedures. We'll talk more about organizational structure and design in Chapter 12, but for now, realize that such structure determines *what* the organization is supposed to do in terms of operations and for what purposes. This occurs within the context of leader philosophy, vision, and shared values. Jim Nowakowski, president and founder of JNE Welding, a Saskatoon-based steel fabricator with 155 employees, states that leaders must be intentional when developing a culture that's healthy and desired. "If you aren't intentional, it forms, whether you like it or not, and it'll form just like anything else—always taking the path of least resistance—and it's not always the path you want to be on."[18]

From here, the culture evolves informally over time within a flexible and fluid set of behaviours. It is entrenched around the interactions of people, daily office events, and general circumstances, and is typically passed on by observation and word-of-mouth. These behaviours are embedded into office procedures, processes, and practices, which are essential for facilitating organizational decisions and movement. Basically it is the organizational culture that determines *how* the organization is to operate. But at this point, we still don't know *why* an organizational culture develops. We now turn our attention to the functions a culture provides.

An organization's culture fulfills four functions: organizational identity, collective commitment, social system stability, and sense-making. As illustrated in Figure 11.3, we can see how these functions help to perpetuate culture. To help bring these four functions to life, we'll consider how each of them has taken shape at the well-known Canadian organization WestJet Airlines Ltd.

WestJet is a particularly instructive example because of its unique culture and phenomenal growth since it began operations out of Calgary in 1996. WestJet is one of Canada's leading passenger airlines. It operates one of the most modern fleets of any large commercial airline in North America. It has also been awarded the title of one of Canada's Most Admired Corporate Cultures for 2005, 2006, 2007, 2008, and 2011 (by Waterstone Human Capital), placing it into the Hall of Fame as one of Canada's best contemporary corporate cultures. In 2011, J.D. Power gave WestJet their highly regarded Customer Service Champion Award, and in 2012, AON Hewitt awarded WestJet as one of the Best Employers in Canada.[19]

1. **Organizational identity** WestJet Airlines helps their members have an organizational identity. It is known as a fun place to work that values employee participation and satisfaction and customer loyalty over corporate profits. Gregg Saretsky, President and CEO, recently stated: "As we expand our reach (to launch a regional airline), we will not lose sight of the importance of our culture, which is built around caring, a simple but powerful concept. We talk a lot about our culture at WestJet and that is because we truly believe it sets us apart from our competitors. WestJetters are encouraged to provide ideas for how we can continue to improve our airline and share thoughts on important business decisions that impact our culture and brand. This culture of inclusion is something we are proud of and was a very important piece of the new short-haul, low-cost, regional airline analysis."[20]

   With the help of their employees, WestJet gets involved with event sponsorships and community partnerships, as demonstrated by their involvement with the Boys and Girls Clubs of Canada,

FIGURE 11.3 Four Functions of Culture

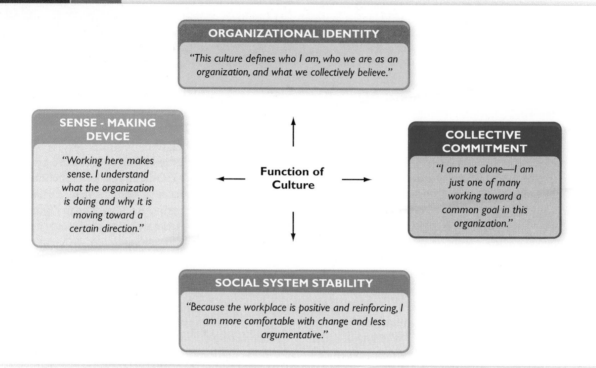

ORGANIZATIONAL IDENTITY

"This culture defines who I am, who we are as an organization, and what we collectively believe."

SENSE - MAKING DEVICE

"Working here makes sense. I understand what the organization is doing and why it is moving toward a certain direction."

Function of Culture

COLLECTIVE COMMITMENT

"I am not alone—I am just one of many working toward a common goal in this organization."

SOCIAL SYSTEM STABILITY

"Because the workplace is positive and reinforcing, I am more comfortable with change and less argumentative."

Big Brothers Big Sisters of Canada, CNIB, Hope Air, Kids Help Phone Canada, Beyond Borders ECPAT Canada, Haiti volunteer support, Make-A-Wish Canada, and Ronald McDonald House Charities Canada.[21]

2. **Collective commitment** An organization of employees that see themselves as part of a collective whole rather than a group of isolated individuals helps to bring more synergy to the workplace. The buy-in to the belief that their collective efforts work in harmony to produce more than what they would produce if they had maintained an individualistic mindset is key to a strong organizational culture.

When WestJet was awarded their most recent title for Best Corporate Culture in Canada by an independent human resource firm, the company was quick to emphasize that the safe and cared-for feeling on every WestJet flight is created by the 8,600 fun and friendly WestJetters who care about each other and 'our' guests every day. "This award belongs to each and every on one of them." In fact, when it came time for the award ceremony in Toronto, the company held an internal nomination contest to decide which WestJetters would attend on behalf of the company.[22] *In other words; they didn't see the success and recognition of WestJet as being the resulting effort of just one person.*

3. **Social system stability** Promoting social system stability reflects the extent to which the work environment is perceived as positive and reinforcing, and the extent to which conflict and change are effectively managed.

According to Ferio Pugliese, Executive Vice-President of People and Culture at WestJet, building relationships with employees is one of its competitive advantages. "The economic engine of any organization . . . is ultimately driven by its people. That's something leaders can never lose sight of— the tremendous power that an engaged workforce can have on productivity." Gregg Saretsky, President, adds, "At WestJet, the learning for me was that a lot of the good (decisions) come from the bottom. Our job is not to lead that change but to support it. It's a notion of servant-leardership."[23]

4. **Sense-making device** Shaping behaviour by helping members make sense of their surroundings is a function of culture that helps employees understand why the organization does what it does and how it intends to accomplish its long-term goals.

WestJetters clearly understand the airline's primary vision: "By 2016, WestJet will be one of the five most successful international airlines in the world, providing our guests with a friendly and caring experience that will change air travel forever." Employees understand their role in making that goal happen and that is why recruitment, training, and ongoing assessment of current employees are such important aspects of their operations. For example, to ensure that new recruits fit into the culture and buy into the values, front-line candidates for jobs must participate in games, team and individual tasks, and presentations in three-hour long group interview sessions.[24]

LO 3 TYPES OF ORGANIZATIONAL CULTURE

Although organizational behaviour researchers have proposed three different frameworks to capture the various types of organizational culture,[25] this section will only discuss the most widely used approach for classifying organizational culture: the Competing Values Framework. It was named as one of the 40 most important frameworks in the study of organizations, and has been shown to be a valid approach for classifying organizational culture.[26]

The *Competing Values Framework* (CVF) provides a practical way to understand, measure, and change organizational culture. It was originally developed by a team of researchers who were trying to classify different ways to assess organizational effectiveness. This research showed that measures of organizational effectiveness vary along two fundamental dimensions or axes. One axis pertains to whether an organization focuses its attention and efforts on internal dynamics and employees or outward toward its external environment and its customers and shareholders. The second is concerned with an organization's preference for flexibility and discretion or control and stability. Combining these two axes creates four types of organizational culture that are based on different core values and different sets of criteria for accessing organizational effectiveness. The CVF is shown in Figure 11.4.[27]

Before beginning our exploration of the CVF, it is important to note that organizations can possess characteristics associated with each culture type. That said, organizations tend to have one type of culture that is more dominant than the others. Let's begin our discussion of culture types by starting in the upper-left-hand quadrant of the CVF.

Clan Culture A *clan culture* has an internal focus and values flexibility rather than stability and control. It resembles a family-type organization in which effectiveness is achieved by encouraging collaboration between employees. This type of culture is very employee-focused and strives to instill cohesion through

> *Competing Values Framework*
>
> A model for identifying, classifying, and categorizing organizational cultures based on effectiveness.

> *Clan culture*
>
> A culture that has an internal focus and values flexibility rather than stability and control.

consensus and job satisfaction and commitment through employee involvement. Clan organizations devote considerable resources to hiring and developing their employees, and they view customers as partners.

Adhocracy Culture An *adhocracy culture* has an external focus and values flexibility. This type of culture fosters the creation of innovative products and services by being adaptable, creative, and fast to respond to changes in the marketplace. Adhocracy cultures do not rely on the type of centralized power and authority relationships that are part of market and hierarchical cultures. They also encourage employees to take risks, think outside the box, and experiment with new ways of getting things done. This type of culture is well suited for start-up companies, those in industries undergoing constant change, and those in mature industries that are in need of innovation to enhance growth.

Market Culture A *market culture* has a strong external focus and values stability and control. Organizations with this culture are driven by competition and a strong desire to deliver results and accomplish goals. Because this type of culture is focused on the external environment, customers and profits take precedence over employee development and satisfaction. The major goal of managers is to drive toward productivity, profits, and customer satisfaction. Employees are expected to react quickly, work hard, and deliver quality work on time. Organizations with this culture tend to reward people who deliver results.

Hierarchy Culture Control is the driving force within a *hierarchical culture*. This culture has an internal focus, which produces a more formalized and structured work environment, and values stability and control over flexibility. This orientation leads to the development of reliable internal processes, extensive measurement, and the implementation of a variety of control mechanisms; for example, companies with a hierarchical culture are more likely to use a Total Quality Management (TQM) program. Effectiveness in a company with this type of culture is likely to be assessed with measures of efficiency, timeliness, and reliability of producing and delivering products and services.

Cultural Types Represent Competing Values It is important to note that certain cultural types reflect opposing core values. These contradicting cultures are found along

> *Adhocracy culture*
>
> A culture that has an external focus and values flexibility.

> *Market culture*
>
> A culture that has a strong external focus and values stability and control.

> *Hierarchical culture*
>
> A culture that has an internal focus and values stability and control over flexibility.

TYPE OF CULTURE	CHARACTERISTICS AND VALUES
Clan	• cohesive team of employees who participate, communicate, and collaborate on various projects; empowerment is an important corporate value • inclusion in decision making has a positive effect on morale; committed to development of employees • **Examples:** *WestJet Airlines Inc.; The Great Little Box Company*
Adhocracy	• highly innovative, creative, and adaptable; cutting edge output that others in the industry are forced to follow • remains flexible in thinking and process to develop new products and designs; concern with needs of the market and what they'll be demanding tomorrow • **Examples:** *National Film Board of Canada; EA Canada (video game developer); Aerospace Industries Association of Canada*
Market	• focus on the external customer needs because of the competitive nature of the market; differentiate themselves to maintain their market share and profitability • goal is to be productive and achieve corporate objectives; value placed on needs of shareholders and customers above employee development or satisfaction • **Examples:** *Labatt Breweries of Canada; Home Depot Canada Ltd.*
Hierarchy	• control process variables to maintain consistency and smooth functioning; focus on capable process, efficiency, and timeliness—not on flexibility • continuity in performance and standardized service/products through employee-enriched training initiatives and customer service programs • **Examples:** *Tim Hortons (TDL) Inc.; TD Bank Group (financial and banking services)*

FIGURE 11.4 Competing Values Framework

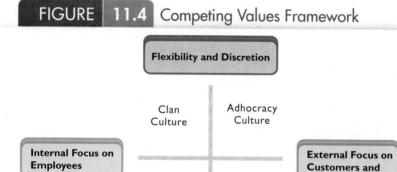

SOURCE: Adapted from K.S. Cameron, R.E. Quinn, J. Degraff, and A.V. Thakor, *Competing Values Leadership* (Northampton, MA: Edward Elgar, 2006), p 32.

the two diagonals in Figure 11.4. For example, the clan culture—upper-left quadrant—is represented by values that emphasize an internal focus and flexibility, whereas the market culture—bottom-right quadrant—has an external focus and concern for stability and control. You can see the same conflict between an adhocracy culture that values flexibility and an external focus, and a hierarchical culture that endorses stability and control along with an internal focus. Why are these contradictions important?

They are important because an organization's success may depend on its ability to possess core values that are associated with competing cultural types. This is difficult to pull off, as demonstrated by the former IT giant Nortel Networks Corporation, a Canadian company, that at its peak in 2000 employed almost 90,000 people and accounted for more than a third of total valuation of all the companies listed on the TSX (Toronto Stock Exchange). In 2009, Nortel filed for bankruptcy protection, seeking to restructure itself to pay its financial obligations.[28] However, it failed to achieve the kind of turnaround needed to stay afloat. Nortel is an example of a company that initially had a culture of adhocracy because of the nature of the products it made and the services it provided in the highly competitive telecommunications industry. However, it was unable to maintain consistent and tighter controls over its own processes, leading to its eventual sell-off.

PERSON-CULTURE CONFLICT, BEHAVIOURS, AND OUTCOMES

You may recall our discussion in Chapter 4 about individual–organization value conflict. Let's now make the connection between employees' personal values and how well they 'fit' into the corporate values embedded into a firm's culture. We stated that if the espoused and enacted values of the organization collide with employees' values, then there would be a conflict. But how would this conflict translate into the workplace?

Certain negative outcomes can be expected, such as lower job satisfaction, lower commitment, higher stress, and lower performance, leading to higher absenteeism or perhaps even higher turnover. This type of conflict and poor 'fit' of values needs to be considered. If, for example, you were applying for a new job, which type of culture would you prefer to work in? Which would be the best 'fit' for you? Before going any further, we suggest completing Self-Assessment Exercise #1 titled *Corporate Culture Preference Scale* to find out which culture type would present the least conflict for you.

We now consider other possible outcomes related to culture. Both managers and academic researchers believe that organizational culture can drive employee attitudes and organizational effectiveness and performance. To test the possibility of such a relationship, various measures of organizational culture have been correlated (compared) with a variety of individual and organizational outcomes. So what have we learned?

A team of researchers recently conducted a meta-analysis to answer this question. Their results are based on 93 studies involving more than 1,100 companies. Figure 11.5 summarizes results in terms of the strength of relationships between eight different organizational outcomes and the culture types of clan, adhocracy, and market (hierarchy was not included due to a lack of research on this type).[29] Results revealed that the eight types of organizational outcomes have significant and positive relationships with clan, adhocracy, and market cultures. The majority of these relationships were of moderate strength, indicating that they are important to today's managers. Closer examination of Figure 11.5 leads to the following five conclusions:

1. Organizational culture is clearly related to measures of organizational effectiveness. This reinforces the conclusion that an organization's culture can be a source of competitive advantage.

2. Employees are more satisfied and committed to organizations with clan cultures. These results suggest that employees prefer to work in organizations that value flexibility over stability and control, as well as those that are more concerned with satisfying employees' needs than customer or shareholder desires.

FIGURE 11.5 The Strength of Relationships Found Within Organizational Culture

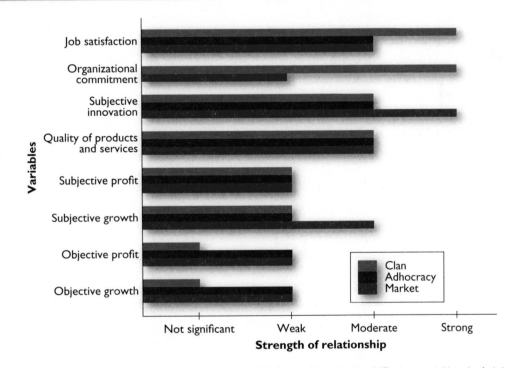

SOURCE: Derived from C. Hartnell, Y. Ou, and A. Kinicki, 2011. "Organizational Culture and Organizational Effectiveness: A Meta-Analytic Investigation of the Competing Values Framework Theoretical Suppositions," *Journal of Psychology*, July 2011, pp 677–694.

Corporate Culture Preference Scale

INSTRUCTIONS: This self-assessment is designed to help you to identify a corporate culture that fits most closely with your personal values and assumptions. Read each pair of statements and choose the statement that describes the organization you would prefer to work in. You might like both statements, or you might not like either statement. In either case, identify which of the two statements is closer to your personal preferences.

I would prefer to work in an organization:

1a	Where employees work well together in teams	**1b**	That produces highly respected products or services
2a	Where top management maintains a sense of order in the workplace	**2b**	Where the organization listens to customers and responds quickly to their needs
3a	Where employees are treated fairly	**3b**	Where employees continuously search for ways to work more efficiently
4a	Where employees adapt quickly to new work requirements	**4b**	Where corporate leaders work hard to keep employees happy
5a	Where senior executives receive special benefits not available to other employees	**5b**	Where employees are proud when the organization achieves its performance goals
6a	Where employees who perform the best get paid the most	**6b**	Where senior executives are respected
7a	Where everyone gets their jobs done like clockwork	**7b**	That is on top of new innovations in the industry
8a	Where employees receive assistance to overcome any personal problems	**8b**	Where employees abide by company rules
9a	That is always experimenting with new ideas in the marketplace	**9b**	That expects everyone to put in 110 percent for peak performance
10a	That quickly benefits from market opportunities	**10b**	Where employees are always kept informed of what's happening in the organization
11a	That can quickly respond to competitive threats	**11b**	Where most decisions are made by the top executives
12a	Where management keeps everything under control	**12b**	Where employees care for each other

SOURCE: Steven L. McShane, *Organizational Behaviour*, 6th Canadian Edition. McGraw-Hill Ryerson Ltd.

Scoring Key for the Corporate Culture Preference Scale

Scoring Instructions: In each space below, write in a "1" if you circled the statement and "0" if you did not. Then add up the scores for each subscale.

Control Culture	_____ (2a)	+	_____ (5a)	+	_____ (6b)	+	_____ (8b)	+	_____ (11b)	+	_____ (12a)	+ _____ = _____

Performance Culture	_____ (1b)	+	_____ (3b)	+	_____ (5b)	+	_____ (6a)	+	_____ (7a)	+	_____ (9b)	= _____

Relationship Culture	_____ (1a)	+	_____ (3a)	+	_____ (4b)	+	_____ (8a)	+	_____ (10b)	+	_____ (12b)	= _____

Responsive Culture	_____ (2b)	+	_____ (4a)	+	_____ (7b)	+	_____ (9a)	+	_____ (10a)	+	_____ (11a)	= _____

Interpreting Your Score: These corporate cultures may be found in many organizational cultures. Also, keep in mind none of these subscales is inherently good or bad. Each is effective in different situations. The four corporate cultures are defined below, along with the range of scores for high, medium, and low levels of each dimension based on a sample of MBA students:

Corporate Culture Dimension and Definition	Score Interpretation
Control Culture: This culture values the role of senior execuves to lead the organization. Its goal is to keep everyone aligned and under control.	High: 3 to 6 Medium: 1 to 2 Low: 0
Performance Culture: This culture values individual and organizational performance and strives for effectiveness and efficiency.	High: 5 to 6 Medium: 3 to 4 Low: 0 to 2
Relationship Culture: This culture values nuturing and well-being. It considers open communication, fairness, teamwork, and sharing a vital part of organizational life.	High: 6 Medium: 4 to 5 Low: 0 to 3
Responsive Culture: This culture values its ability to keep in tune with the external environment, including being competitive ans realizing new opportunities.	High: 6 Medium: 4 to 5 Low: 0 to 3

3. Innovation and quality can be increased by building characteristics associated with clan, adhocracy, and market cultures into the organization.

4. An organization's financial performance (i.e., growth in profit and growth in revenue) is not very strongly related to organizational culture. Managers should not expect to increase financial performance by trying to change their organization's culture.

5. Companies with market cultures tend to have more positive organizational outcomes. Managers are encouraged to consider how they might make their cultures more market-oriented.

Researchers also have investigated the importance of organizational culture within the context of a merger. These studies indicate that mergers frequently fail due to incompatible cultures. As a result of the increasing number of corporate mergers around the world, and the conclusion that 7 out of 10 mergers and acquisitions fail to meet their financial promise, managers within merged companies would be well advised to consider the role of organizational culture in creating a new organization.[30]

In summary, research underscores the significance of organizational culture. It also reinforces the need to learn more about the process of developing, nurturing, and changing an organization's culture. An organization's culture is not determined by fate. It is formed and shaped by the combination and integration of everyone who works in the organization. A change-resistant culture, for instance, can undermine the effectiveness of any type of organizational change. Although it is not an easy task to change an organization's culture, the next section provides a preliminary overview of how this might be done.

The Process of Changing Culture

Before describing the specific ways in which organizational culture can be changed, let's review three factors related to culture change. First, it is possible to change an organization's culture—the process essentially begins with targeting one of the three layers of organizational culture previously discussed (i.e., observable artifacts, espoused values, and basic assumptions for change). Ultimately, culture change involves changing people's minds and their behaviour.[31] But, it can take time, according to Kathy Bardswich, president and CEO of the Co-operators Group based in Guelph, Ontario. Responsible for 6,000 employees along with 4,000 at exclusive agencies, Bardswich acknowledges that culture is something that cannot be changed easily or quickly. "I have to chuckle when I hear a new CEO arrives and within a year or two, he's changed the culture. Well, I don't believe that," says Bardswich, adding that the CEO may have changed symptoms of the culture, but not the entire culture.[32]

Second, it is important to consider the extent to which the current culture is aligned with the organization's vision and competitive business plan before attempting to change any aspect of organizational culture. A *vision* represents a long-term

Vision

Long-term goal describing "what" an organization wants to become.

goal that describes "what" an organization wants to become. A *strategic plan* outlines an organization's competitive business model, long-term goals, and the actions necessary to achieve these goals. Mark Fields, executive vice president of Ford Motor Company, firmly believes that culture, vision, and strategic plans should be aligned. According to Fields, "Culture eats strategy for breakfast. You can have the best plan in the world, and if the culture isn't going to let it happen, it's going to die on the vine."[33]

Finally, it is important to use a structured approach when implementing culture change. Chapter 13 can help you in this regard, as it presents several models that provide specific steps to follow when implementing any type of organizational change. Now consider the specific methods or techniques that can be used to change an organization's culture.

Strategic plan

A long-term plan outlining actions needed to achieve desired results.

Edgar Schein, a well-known OB scholar, notes that changing organizational culture involves a teaching process. That is, organizational members teach each other about the organization's preferred values, beliefs, norms, expectations, and behaviours. This is accomplished by using one or more of the following mechanisms:[34]

1. **Formal statements of organizational philosophy, mission, vision, values, and materials used for recruiting, selection, and socialization** Within the strategic plan are corporate mission and vision statements that often promote organizational values; but a change in these alone may not be enough. Consider the opening message from Bob Paulson after being appointed RCMP Commissioner, when he reminded his 26,000 uniformed and civilian staff what they could expect in terms of his philosophy and new leadership style (see the Law and Ethics feature box

RCMP CULTURE MUST CHANGE

Bob Paulson, RCMP Commissioner, has publicly admitted to an RCMP culture of bullying and a legacy of botched investigations. Paulson made it quite clear when he took over the top position in 2011 that police who indulge in "outrageous conduct" will be dealt with promptly and severely. That would include suspension, taking away the badge, and taking away the gun. It was a tough message, but one that many felt was long overdue.

Over the last decade, the RCMP has been plagued by discipline problems, from the taser-related death of Robert Dziekanski and the perjury charges that followed, to serious allegations of sexual harassment, to charges of physical assault. Paulson says his mandate is to "clear-cut" problems that have taken root so deeply in the police culture that some Mounties are embarrassed to tell others where they work. His assessment of internal dysfunction has gone so far as to suggest that unless the force "gets on it" to urgently regain public trust, they could face the possibility of becoming obsolete.

The force's red serge uniform and Stetson hat have long been the iconic image of Canada, its law-and-order history dating back to the Western frontier. Yet, given how controversies have piled up, public confidence has been shaken. An independent investigation characterized the force as "horribly broken." When asked to comment, Paulson acknowledged many fundamental flaws, but felt the organization was not beyond repair.

The RCMP is working hard to regain its reputation and ethical status. Paulson's open and candid leadership style is said to be refreshing, the kind needed to adjust member attitudes. He publicly reported making proposals to bring in new approaches to discipline and misconduct. Amidst sexual harassment allegations filed in a class-action lawsuit from over 200 current and former RCMP female employees, the force felt compelled to be proactive by immediately training 100 officers to investigate internal complaints of harassment. "I've been talking to the membership about a respectful workplace. I don't think that our numbers are particularly aggravating, but one harassment complaint is one too many," says Paulson. In the end, the effectiveness of Paulson's talk will be determined by the BC Supreme Court as the class-action suit is estimated to take until 2014–15 to wind its way through the justice system.

Paulson knows that the RCMP culture must change: "I have got to be persuasive."

SOURCES: D. Moore, "Hundreds of Women across Canada Come forward to Join RCMP Harassment Class-Action Lawsuit," *The Calgary Herald (The Canadian Press),* July 31, 2012, www.calgaryherald.com/news/Hundreds+women+across+Canada+come+forward+join+RCMP+harassment+class+action+lawsuit/7016415/story.html; T. Wright, "Restoring Image Job No. 1 for RCMP Commissioner," *The PEI Guardian News,* January 26, 2012; C. Freeze, "Top Mountie Delivers Candid, Scathing View of Force at the Brink," *Globe and Mail,* December 19, 2011; and M. Cook, "Proud Call to Duty," *Toronto Star,* December 11, 2011, op/ed page.

LAW AND ETHICS AT WORK

for the full story concerning the RCMP culture). For now, let's look at the Saskatchewan company Cameco Corp, that has a vision to be a dominant nuclear energy company producing uranium fuel and generating clean electricity. Their decisions and actions are guided by four values: safety and environment, people, integrity, and excellence. Together, these values form the foundation of their culture. By pursuing them, Cameco attracts and retains top talent.[35]

2. **The design of physical space, work environments, and buildings** There is something to be said for changing the workspace or context where employees work. To instill the core values of creativity, recall our earlier discussion a few pages back about the unique architecture and work environment of the world renowned Cirque du Soleil Montreal head office building. It has become the benchmark for all future Cirque work spaces, leaving no doubt of the expectations and creative behaviours that must be exhibited.[36]

3. **Slogans, language, acronyms, and sayings** Consider the changes Loblaw Companies Limited made in the early 2000s to their stores across Canada in an attempt to compete against the expansion of Walmart. They switched their name to RCSS (the Real Canadian Superstore), which meant a new logo and store signage, a redesign of the floor plan (physical space), a greater variety of mixed merchandising, and the identification of aisle space (including carrying the new Joe Fresh label). The acronym RCSS appeared on customer bank card statements prior to signage and other changes, which caused some confusion and concern until awareness levels increased.[37]

4. **Deliberate role modelling, training programs, teaching, and coaching by managers and supervisors** Skate Canada is a world renown national organization dedicated to promoting the art of figure skating, but it has had its share of controversy in the past. To avoid such debate, it has taken on a strong initiative to deliberately attract and develop a certain type of coach who will help promote the kind of professional attitudes and expected behaviours within their young athletes. Skate Canada believes that if they are going to make changes, it must first start with the coaches, recognizing their role as being a privilege earned through total commitment. In addition, Skate Canada needs to pass on the organizational expectations, values, and philosophy to the athlete as a role model, teacher, coach, athlete manager, strategist, and volunteer.[38]

5. **Explicit rewards, status symbols (e.g., titles), and promotion criteria** Boeing Canada revisited its reward system to reform its culture. To encourage collaborating with other units to follow ethical rules, pay and bonuses were directly linked to how well executives embraced a set of six leadership attributes such as Living Boeing Values. These values included new criteria such as promoting integrity and avoiding abusive behaviour.[39]

6. **Stories, legends, or myths about key people and events** To outsiders, traditions like hanging plaques around the office of the founder's favourite sayings or rituals like shouting a morning cheer may be perceived as odd. But to insiders, they are very important. If a company decides to take a new direction, it has to review old rituals to consider if they fit into the new culture.

7. **The organizational activities, processes, or outcomes that leaders pay attention to, measure, and control** Flamboyant Canadian entrepreneur Mogen Smed is now the CEO of DIRTT Environmental Solutions. The former Calgary businessman has always believed in the open concept office design—including his own. "Nobody has an office in this company, including me. I just use a sit/stand stool. Yeah, there is some chaos here and a little bit of anarchy but very few meetings . . . ." He isn't about big bureaucracy and prefers to be in the open to interact with his people and be accessible to his clients at all times, claiming, "They call me directly." These are the things that are important to Smed.[40]

8. **Leader reactions to critical incidents and organizational crises** Before he stepped down in early 2012, Jim Balsillie knew that change was needed at RIM. It was reported that Balsillie made a last minute appeal and sought to reinvent the BlackBerry smartphone maker with a radical shift in strategy. This is to be expected from the co-founder: one last attempt to keep control, to fix "it", to protect what he had created before cutting formal ties to the company.[41]

9. **The workflow and organizational structure** Hierarchical structures are more likely to embed an orientation toward control and authority. Leaders from many organizations are increasingly reducing the number of organizational layers in an attempt to empower employees (restructuring is discussed in Chapter 12) and increase employee involvement.

10. **Organizational systems and procedures** An organization can promote achievement and competition through the use of sales contests.[42]

11. **Organizational goals and the associated criteria used for recruitment, selection, development, promotion, layoffs, and retirement of people** In the summer of 2011, Cisco Canada had to cut costs by laying-off 10 percent of its Canadian workforce. It was Cisco's handling of the cuts that demonstrated

why employees actually nominated the company for an award that very year: the rationale was well explained, the process was transparent, and the way forward was made clear, according to David Clarkson, Director of HR. Confidence and trust were crucial in getting employees to buy into Cisco's vision, even during hard times.[43]

It's important to remember that the strength of the culture, in other words, how formalized and embedded the values are across the entire organization, will dictate the success of the culture change initiative. Some organizational cultures have not developed and would be characterized as weak (for example, the kind you would find in a relatively new organization) and others so strong that they would neutralize any management intervention technique. Such was the case at IBM in the 1990s when the company found itself on the brink of near bankruptcy. At the time, Louis Gerstner Jr. attempted to change Big Blue but was met by heavy resistance at all levels—especially when it came to changing the mindset of the IBM employees.[44]

There is also evidence of a strong culture at Walmart Stores Inc., whose founder Sam Walton died in 1992 and yet whose philosophy, values, and vision continue to guide the organization globally.[45] (For example, can you imagine a new store manager taking the helm and deciding that employees would no longer wear the blue Walmart vests?) Another example of a strong culture is found at Apple Inc. Despite the loss of Steve Jobs as the charismatic CEO, it is unlikely that this organization will adopt a new mission, vision, and set of values any time soon. In these examples, the culture sets the norms, the culture establishes the expectations, and the culture controls employee behaviour.

The Organizational Socialization Process

Organizational socialization is defined as "the process by which a person learns the values, norms, and required behaviours which permit him to participate as a member of the organization."[46] Think about your own work experience. Were you properly socialized when starting the job? To determine your own experience with the socialization process, you are invited to complete Self-Assessment Exercise #2, "Were You Adequately Socialized?" This will help you understand the essence of what this section is discussing. As previously mentioned, organization socialization is a key mechanism used by organizations to embed their organizational cultures. In short, organizational socialization turns outsiders into fully functioning insiders by promoting and reinforcing the organization's core values and beliefs. This section introduces a three-phase model of organizational socialization and examines the practical application of socialization research.

FELDMAN'S MODEL OF ORGANIZATIONAL SOCIALIZATION

LO 5

The first year in a complex organization can be confusing for new employees. There is a constant swirl of new faces, strange jargon (language), conflicting expectations, and apparently unrelated events. Some organizations treat new members in a rather haphazard, sink-or-swim manner. More typically, however, the socialization process is characterized by a sequence of identifiable steps.

Organizational behaviour researcher Daniel Feldman proposes a three-phase model of organizational socialization that promotes deeper understanding of this important process. The three phases are (1) anticipatory socialization, (2) encounter, and (3) change and acquisition. Each phase has its associated perceptual and social processes.[47]

Feldman's model also specifies behavioural and affective outcomes that can be used to judge how well an individual has been socialized. The entire three-phase sequence may take from a few weeks to a year to complete, depending on individual differences and the complexity of the situation.

Phase 1: Anticipatory Socialization The *anticipatory socialization phase* occurs before an individual actually joins an organization. It is represented by the information people learn about different careers, occupations, professions, and organizations. For example, anticipatory socialization partially explains the different perceptions you might have about working for the Canadian government versus a video game developer like Toronto's Beanbag Studios. Anticipatory socialization information comes from many sources. For example, an organization's current employees are a powerful source of anticipatory socialization.

Unrealistic expectations about the nature of the work, pay, and promotions are often created during phase 1. Because employees with unrealistic expectations are more likely to quit their jobs in the future, organizations may want to use realistic job previews.[48] A *realistic job preview* (RJP) involves giving recruits a realistic idea of what lies ahead by presenting both positive and negative aspects of the job. RJPs may be verbal, in booklet form, audiovisual, or hands-on. Research supports the practical benefits of

Organizational socialization

Process by which employees learn an organization's values, norms, and required behaviours.

Anticipatory socialization phase

Occurs before an individual joins an organization and involves information people learn about different careers, occupations, professions, and organizations.

Realistic job preview

Presents both positive and negative aspects of a job.

Were You Adequately Socialized?

INSTRUCTIONS: Complete the following survey items by considering either your current job or one you held in the past. If you have never worked, identify a friend who is working and ask that individual to complete the questionnaire for his or her organization. Read each item and circle your response by using the rating scale shown below. Compute your total score by adding up your responses and compare it to the scoring norms.

1 = STRONGLY DISAGREE   4 = AGREE
2 = DISAGREE   5 = STRONGLY AGREE
3 = NEITHER AGREE NOR DISAGREE

1	I have been through a set of training experiences that are specifically designed to give newcomers a thorough knowledge of job-related skills.	1—2—3—4—5
2	This organization puts all newcomers through the same set of learning experiences.	1—2—3—4—5
3	I did not perform any of my normal job responsibilities until I was thoroughly familiar with departmental procedures and work methods.	1—2—3—4—5
4	There is a clear pattern in the way one role leads to another, or one job assignment leads to another, in this organization.	1—2—3—4—5
5	I can predict my future career path in this organization by observing other people's experiences.	1—2—3—4—5
6	Almost all of my colleagues have been supportive of me personally.	1—2—3—4—5
7	My colleagues have gone out of their way to help me adjust to this organization.	1—2—3—4—5
8	I received much guidance from experienced organizational members about how I should perform my job.	1—2—3—4—5

Total Score = _____

Scoring Norms

8–18 = Low socialization

19–29 = Moderate socialization

30–40 = High socialization

SOURCE: Adapted from survey items excerpted from D. Cable and C. Parsons, "Socialization Tactics and Person-Organization Fit," *Personnel Psychology*, Spring 2001, pp 1–23.

using RJPs. A meta-analysis of 40 studies revealed that RJPs are related to higher performance and to lower attrition from the recruitment process. Results also demonstrated that RJPs lower job applicants' initial expectations and lead to lower turnover among those applicants who are hired.[49]

Phase 2: Encounter This second phase begins when the employment contract has been signed. During the *encounter phase*, employees come to learn what the organization is really like. It is a time for recognizing unmet expectations and making sense of a new work environment. Many companies, such as the Ritz-Carlton hotel in Toronto, use a technique called *onboarding* for new employees. This technique involves a combination of orientation and training programs used to socialize employees during the encounter phase. The hotel mandates an extensive two-day experience for all new employees.[50] A recent study found the structured onboarding process

Onboarding

A structured process for new hires involving both orientation and training.

is something all organizations should strive to offer due to its positive impact on employee engagement. Results suggest new employees feel more confident as a result of onboarding as it strengthens their belief that they fit the job and the organization.[51] Onboarding programs help employees to integrate, assimilate, and transition to new jobs by making them familiar with corporate policies, procedures, and culture, and by clarifying work role expectations and responsibilities.[52]

Phase 3: Change and Acquisition The *change and acquisition phase* requires employees to master important tasks and roles and to adjust to their work group's values and norms. Table 11.1 presents a list of socialization processes or tactics used by organizations to help employees or stakeholders through this adjustment process.

> **Change and acquisition phase**
>
> Requires employees to master tasks and roles and to adjust to workgroup values and norms.

TABLE 11.1

SOCIALIZATION TACTICS

TACTIC	DESCRIPTION	EXAMPLE
Collective vs. individual	Collective socialization consists of grouping newcomers and exposing them to a common set of experiences, rather than treating newcomers individually and exposing them to more or less unique experiences.	New student orientation week is a common collective socialization activity organized at many post-secondary schools each fall.
Formal vs. informal	Formal socialization is the practice of segregating a newcomer from regular organization members during a defined socialization period, versus not clearly distinguishing a newcomer from more experienced members.	Military recruits are formally socialized by attending boot camp before they are allowed to work alongside established soldiers.
Sequential vs. random	Sequential socialization refers to a fixed progression of steps that culminate in the new role, compared to an ambiguous or dynamic progression.	The socialization process of doctors involves a lock-step sequence from medical school, to internship, to residency before they are allowed to practise on their own. The same could be said for the trades, where years of training and apprenticeships must be earned prior to receiving journeyman certification.
Fixed vs. variable	Fixed socialization provides a timetable for the assumption of the role, whereas a variable process does not.	It's common for college and university students to spend one fixed year apiece as first-year students, then on to their second year of studies, and so on. It's more the exception than the rule to have students from various years co-mingled within the same classroom or even residency area.
Serial vs. disjunctive	A serial process is one in which the newcomer is socialized by an experienced member, whereas a disjunctive process does not use a role model.	A mentorship–protégé program is a serial socialization process that allows the experienced seasoned employee to help the newer employee adjust to the organization.
Investiture vs. divestiture	Investiture refers to the affirmation of a newcomer's incoming global and specific role identities and attributes. Divestiture is the denial and stripping away of the newcomer's existing sense of self, and the reconstruction of self in the organization's image.	During police training, cadets are socialized through investiture activities such as: requiring them to wear uniforms and maintain an immaculate appearance; addressing them as "officer"; and telling them they are no longer ordinary citizens, but are representatives of the police force. Divestiture processes are likened to fraternity hazing that typically involves denial and degrading techniques.

ADAPTATION: Descriptions were taken from B.E. Ashforth, *Role Transitions in Organizational Life: An Identity-Based Perspective* (Mahwah, NJ: Lawrence Erlbaum Associates, 2001), pp 149–83.

PRACTICAL APPLICATION OF SOCIALIZATION RESEARCH

Past research suggests six practical guidelines for managing organizational socialization:

1. A survey of executives from 100 companies revealed that 65 percent did an average or poor job of socializing new hires.[53] This reinforces the conclusion that managers should avoid a haphazard, sink-or-swim approach to organizational socialization, since formalized socialization tactics positively affect new hires. Formalized or institutionalized socialization tactics were found to positively help employees in both domestic and international operations.[54]

2. Supervisors are encouraged to consider how they might best set expectations regarding ethical behaviour during all three phases of the socialization process.[55]

3. Supervisors play a key role during the encounter phase. Studies of newly hired accountants demonstrated that the frequency and type of information obtained during their first six months of employment significantly affected their job performance, their role clarity, and the extent to which they were socially integrated.[56] Supervisors need to help new hires integrate within the organizational culture. Consider the approach used by John Chambers, CEO of Cisco Systems: "He meets with groups of new hires to welcome them soon after they start, and at monthly breakfast meetings workers are encouraged to ask him tough questions."[57]

4. Support for stage models is mixed. Although there are different stages of socialization, they are not identical in order, length, or content for all people or jobs.[58] Supervisors are advised to use a contingency approach toward organizational socialization. In other words, different techniques are appropriate for different people at different times.

5. Organizations can benefit by training new employees to use proactive socialization behaviours, which encourage new employees to seek information as they proceed through the encounter, change, and acquisition phases of socialization. For example, a study of 140 co-op post-secondary students showed that the use of formalized socialization tactics was associated with newcomers' feedback-seeking and information-seeking behaviours.[59]

6. Supervisors should pay attention to the socialization of diverse employees. Research has demonstrated that diverse employees, particularly those with disabilities, experience different socialization activities than other newcomers. In turn, these different experiences affect their long-term success and job satisfaction.[60]

Embedding Organizational Culture through Mentoring

The modern word *mentor* derives from Mentor, the name of a wise and trusted counsellor in Greek mythology. Terms typically used in connection with mentoring are *teacher, coach, sponsor,* and *peer.* **Mentoring** is defined as the process of forming and maintaining intensive and lasting developmental relationships between a variety of developers (people who provide career and emotional support) and a junior person (the protégé).[61] There are two reasons why mentoring can serve to embed an organization's culture when developers and the protégé work in the same organization: first, mentoring contributes to creating a sense of oneness by promoting acceptance of the organization's core values throughout the organization; and second, the socialization aspect of mentoring promotes a sense of membership.

Not only is mentoring important as a tactic for embedding organizational culture, but research suggests it can significantly influence the protégé's future career. For example, a meta-analysis revealed that mentored employees have higher compensation and more promotions than non-mentored employees. Mentored employees also report higher job and career satisfaction and organizational commitment, and lower turnover.[62] This section focuses on how people can use mentoring to their advantage. We discuss the functions of mentoring, the developmental networks underlying mentoring, and the personal and organizational implications of mentoring.

> **Mentoring**
>
> Process of forming and maintaining developmental relationships between a mentor and a junior person.

FUNCTIONS OF MENTORING

Kathy Kram, a researcher, identifies two general positive functions of the mentoring process. The first function is enhanced career development for protégés, where they gain legitimate sponsorship, exposure and visibility, coaching, protection, and challenging assignments. Mentors can help protégés gain exposure and visibility in the industry by inviting them to participate in local clubs and associations, such as attending a local Rotary International meeting or registering at a highly visible national trade conference. This is certainly the case with Vivek Radhakrishnan, a corporate secretary from India now working at the Bank of Montreal (BMO). His mentor at BMO is Peggy Sum, a former senior vice president with 24 years of Canadian banking industry experience. Although recently retired, the bank brings Sum back specifically to work in a mentorship capacity. "I try to get Vivek in touch with the right people in the industry

Mentors, like former BMO senior VP Peggy Sum, can provide enhanced career development for new employees—the kind she provides for protégé Vivek Radhakrishnan from India.

and in the bank, and show him the right route in his discipline," says Sum. By helping him learn the nuances of the Canadian business work, Sum is providing the kind of career development and professional exposure Radhakrishnan needs to succeed in the banking industry.[63] In addition, when a protégé is faced with organizational decisions that have political overtones, the mentor can coach the individual through the landmines to avoid career disasters. The career development aspect of mentoring is very beneficial for protégé success.

The second function Kram discovered is the psychological, emotional, and social support (called psycho-social) that mentoring provides for the protégé, such as role modelling, acceptance and confirmation, counselling, and friendship. The psycho-social functions clarifies the participants' identities and enhances their self-esteem needs.[64] Having a well-respected mentor on-side during uncertain times can help protégés feel more confident that they won't make a mistake. Further, protégés have someone cheering for them on the sidelines when things go well and congratulations are in order.

BEYOND 1:1 MENTORSHIP—IDENTIFYING DEVELOPMENTAL NETWORKS

Today, the changing nature of technology, organizational structures, and marketplace dynamics require that people seek career information and support from many sources. Contemporary mentoring programs go beyond a one-on-one relationship between the mentor and the protégé. Mentoring is evolving into a process in which protégés seek developmental guidance from a network of people, who are referred to as developers. Figure 11.6 presents a developmental network typology based on integrating the diversity and strength of developmental relationships.[65] To gain a better understanding of this model, we'll spend some time exploring each quadrant. Let's begin by substituting the protégé with yourself and the kind of personal decisions you may be going through within the next year or two while preparing for graduation and getting your first post-grad job.

Along the side of Figure 11.6 we consider the *diversity of developmental relationships*, which reflects the variety of people within the network that a protégé uses for developmental assistance.

> *For example, what kinds of contacts do you have—are they all students? Are they all IT or business teachers? Do you participate in charity work on campus? Are you involved in community activities that allow you to network with industry professionals?*

Consider the two subparts associated with network diversity: (1) the number of different people the protégé is networked with, and (2) the various social systems from which the networked relationships stem (e.g., employer, school, family, community, professional associations, and religious affiliations). As shown in Figure 11.6, developmental relationship diversity ranges from low (few people or social systems) to high (multiple people or social systems).

Across the top of Figure 11.6 are measurements of *developmental relationship strength* that reflect the quality of relationships between protégés and those involved in their developmental network.

> *For example, who at your school would you say you have strong ties to? This is a person with whom you have an ongoing relationship, based on frequent interactions and positive affect—it could be a professor, program advisor, or coach. Now think of the other relationships you have at school that would be considered as weak ties. In contrast, these contacts are based more on superficial relationships—this might be a fellow student who you've been in several classes with throughout the last few years, or a school administrator who you've had occasional contact with over the years. In other words, you know them, but it's not a deep relationship.*

Diversity of developmental relationships

The variety of people in a network used by a protégé for developmental assistance.

Developmental relationship strength

The quality of relationships among protégés and those involved in their development networks.

FIGURE 11.6 Developmental Networks Associated with Mentoring

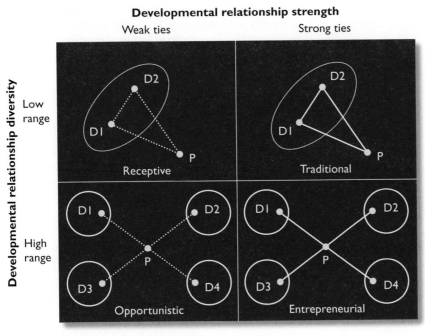

SOURCE: M. Higgins and K. Kram, "Reconceptualizing Mentoring at Work: A Developmental Network Perspective," *Academy of Management Review,* April 2001, p 270. Reprinted by permission of The Academy of Management via The Copyright Clearance Center.

Bringing together diversity and strength of developmental relationships results in four quadrants, each representing a type of developmental network: (1) receptive, (2) traditional, (3) entrepreneurial, and (4) opportunistic.

Quadrant #1: *Receptive* network – composed of a few weak ties from one social system, such as an employer or a professional association. The single oval around D1 and D2 indicates two developers who come from one social system.

An example of this, continuing to use you as the protégé, could be one professor and one student, both from the same program, who you have casually spoken with over the years while in class together. They are weak ties because you only know them from being in class together; you've never spoken with them outside of class. In terms of variety, they are both superficial relationships, not based on any rich experiences that offer a variety of perspective or opinion. This is the weakest quadrant and the worst protégé position to be in.

Quadrant #2: *Traditional* network – contains a few strong ties between a protégé and developers that all come from one social system.

An example of this could be two well-respected professors, both from the same program, who work side-by-side as mentors. They are strong ties because they know you well and you feel comfortable with them. However, in terms of variety, they are too much alike and can't offer a variety of perspectives or opinions on your experience. This position is a bit better for the protégé, but it is still limiting in providing network assistance.

Quadrant #3: *Opportunistic* network – involves having weak ties with multiple developers from different social systems.

An example of this is joining a campus club during the first month of school that gives you the opportunity to interact with many different people from diverse program areas; the only problem is that you only joined to put it on your resumé, you only attended two meetings, you never participated in any activities, and you never became engaged in the spirit of the club. The high degree of diversity this club offers is wonderful, but the relationships are almost non-existent as you don't know anyone well enough. Protégés who engage in this sort of development network are kidding themselves—it may look good on paper, but it is not any better than being in the receptive quadrant.

Quadrant #4: *Entrepreneurial* network – made up of strong ties between several developers (D1–D4) who come from four different social systems, this is the strongest type of developmental network.. In this quadrant, protégés feel close to a variety of contacts.

An example of this would be a professor who you know well; a supervisor who you have worked with for over one year who knows you well; a mentor from a club or organization who you have volunteered with over the last few years; and, finally, a former coach of a team on which you played for two years. This network shows diversity, as well as strong ties, that you can benefit from. This quadrant should be the goal of every student reading this text.

PERSONAL AND ORGANIZATIONAL IMPLICATIONS

Consider the following six key personal and organizational implications of mentoring. First, job and career satisfaction are likely to be influenced by the consistency between individuals' career goals and the type of developmental network at their disposal. For example, people with an entrepreneurial developmental network are more likely to experience change in their careers and to benefit from personal learning than people with receptive, traditional, and opportunistic networks. If this sounds attractive to you, try to increase the diversity and strength of your developmental relationships. In contrast, lower levels of job satisfaction are expected when employees have receptive developmental networks and they want to experience career advancement in multiple organizations. Receptive developmental networks, however, can be satisfying to someone who does not wish to be promoted up the career ladder.[66]

Second, a developer's willingness to provide career and psycho-social assistance is a function of the protégé's ability, potential, and the quality of the interpersonal relationship.[67] This implies that you must take ownership for enhancing your skills, abilities, and developmental networks if you want to experience career advancement throughout your life.[68]

Third, it is important to become proficient at using social networking tools such as Twitter, LinkedIn, and Facebook. Companies like Haliburton in Clairmont, Alberta have joined the Human Resources Institute of Alberta's virtual mentorship program, which urges its participants to use online tools to conduct mentoring across geographical boundaries.[69] These tools not only enable you to increase the breadth of your social network, but they also can increase your productivity.

Fourth, put effort into finding a mentor. A study of 4,559 leaders and 944 human resource professionals from 42 countries showed that 91 percent of those who used a mentor found the experience moderately or greatly beneficial to their career success.[70] That said, another recent study showed that the success of a mentoring relationship from a protégé's perspective is partly determined by the skills and abilities of the mentor.[71]

This leads to the fifth recommendation. If you believe that your mentor is ineffective or, worse yet, causing more harm than benefit, find a new mentor.

Finally, although mentoring can help your career, and some mediocre people advance because of a strong mentor, don't be fooled into thinking that who you know is a replacement for talent, knowledge, and motivation.[72] We strongly encourage you to use your own passion, motivation, talents, and networking skills to achieve your personal and professional goals, which includes creating your own mentoring plan (see the Skills & Best Practices feature box).

Research also supports the organizational benefits of formal mentorship programs. For example, mentoring can assist those organizations looking for creative ways to transfer knowledge, engage employees, and facilitate a learning organization. This is especially relevant when trying to connect experienced baby boomers with younger, less-experienced Gen-Ys. An example

Skills & Best Practices

Building an Effective Mentoring Network

1. *Invest in your relationships.* Devote the time and energy necessary to develop trust and respect in your mentors. Get to know each mentor's personality and background before plunging into specific problems.
2. *Engage in 360-degree networking.* Share information and maintain good relationships with people above, below, and at your level of the organization's hierarchy.
3. *Plan your network.* Assess what competencies you need to build, identify mentors who can help with those competencies, and change mentors as your competencies develop.
4. *Develop diverse connections.* Be open to informal and formal relationships.
5. *Agree on the process.* At the first meeting, the mentor and protégé should agree on how often they will meet and how they will communicate outside the scheduled meetings.
6. *Be ready to move on.* The average mentoring relationship lasts five years. When a relationship is no longer beneficial, the parties should end it and free their time for more productive relationships.

SOURCES: Based on S.C. de Janasz, S.E. Sullivan, and V. Whiting, "Mentor Networks and Career Success: Lessons for Turbulent Times," *Academy of Management Executive,* November 2003, pp 78–91; and N. Anand and J. Conger, "Capabilities of the Consummate Networker," *Organizational Dynamics,* 2007, pp 13–27.

of this can be found at Xerox Canada (see the Focus on Diversity feature box for more details). In addition to these benefits, mentoring also has been found to increase the amount of vertical communication both up and down an organization, and it provides a mechanism for modifying or reinforcing organizational culture.

XEROX CANADA MENTORSHIP BRIDGES GENERATIONAL DIFFERENCES

Xerox Canada developed a formal mentoring program to respond to the desires of Gen-Y employees for greater guidance and direction on how to build a successful career within the company. This fell in line with the corporate desire for increased productivity—Xerox was looking for an innovative way to transfer knowledge from well-experienced baby boomers (expected to retire by 2017), engage employees, and support a high-performing work environment.

From a design perspective, it was important to incorporate elements into the mentorship program that would bridge the diverse needs and values of the two generational groups. To appeal to Baby Boomers' need to add value and differentiate themselves, the program tapped into mentors' desires to share their wealth of experiences.

To align with Gen-Y's expectations, it was important that the program focus on the protégé's individual learning needs—not what the mentor wanted to teach. Gen-Ys value a relationship based on two-way respect and feedback, which became an important part of the formal mentoring program.

How can a formal mentorship program, like the one Xerox has developed, overcome multi-generational workplace challenges such as those discussed in the Chapter 4 Focus on Diversity feature box?

SOURCE: G. Kovary and A. Buahene, "Formal Mentorship Programs Connect Baby Boomers, Gen-Y Employees," *Canadian HR Reporter*, March 26, 2012, p 14. Giselle Kovary and Adwoa K. Buahene are the managing partners and co-founders of n-gen People Performance in Toronto, a training company that delivers learning in the areas of sales and customer service, leadership, team-building, Gen Y, and HR. Giselle can be reached at gkovary@ngenperformance.com and Adwoa can be reached at abuahene@ngenperformance.com. For more information, visit www.ngenperformance.com.

Summary of Learning Objectives

LO 1 Define *organizational culture, espoused values,* and *enacted values.* Organizational culture represents the assumptions that a group holds. It influences employees' perceptions and behaviour at work. It is the shared values and beliefs held throughout the organization. Espoused values represent the explicitly-stated values and norms that are preferred by an organization. Enacted values, in contrast, reflect the values and norms that are actually exhibited or converted into employee behaviour. Employees become cynical when management espouses one set of values and norms and then behaves in an inconsistent fashion.

LO 2 Describe the four functions of organizational culture. The four functions of organizational culture are organizational identity, collective commitment, social system stability, and sense-making device. See the WestJet examples referenced throughout this chapter.

LO 3 Discuss the four types of organizational culture associated with the competing values framework. The competing values framework identifies four different types of organizational culture. A clan culture has an internal focus and values flexibility rather than stability and control. An adhocracy culture has an external focus and values flexibility. A market culture has a strong external focus and values stability and control. A hierarchy culture has an internal focus and values stability and control over flexibility.

 Summarize the various methods used by organizations to change organizational culture. Changing culture involves teaching employees about the organization's new, enhanced, or preferred values, beliefs, expectations, and behaviours. This is accomplished by using one or more of the following 11 mechanisms: (1) formal statements of organizational philosophy, mission, vision, values, and materials used for recruiting, selection, and socialization; (2) the design of physical space, work environments, and buildings; (3) slogans, language, acronyms, and sayings; (4) deliberate role modelling, training programs, teaching, and coaching by managers and supervisors; (5) explicit rewards, status symbols, and promotion criteria; (6) stories, legends, and myths about key people and events; (7) organizational activities, processes, or outcomes that leaders pay attention to, measure, and control; (8) leader reactions to critical incidents and organizational crises; (9) the workflow and organizational structure; (10) organizational systems and procedures; and (11) organizational goals and associated criteria used for recruitment, selection, development, promotion, layoffs, and retirement of people.

 Describe the three phases in Feldman's model of organizational socialization and explain how mentoring can assist the socialization process. The three phases of Feldman's model are anticipatory socialization, encounter, and change and acquisition. Anticipatory socialization begins before an individual actually joins the organization. The encounter phase begins when the employment contract has been signed. The change and acquisition phase involves the period in which employees master important tasks and resolve any role conflicts. Mentorship programs can help protégés to feel included in the organization, and increase understanding of the organization's values, norms, and required behaviours. The relationships that are developed between mentors and protégés provide the psycho-social functions necessary to help new employees establish their identity within the firm and enhance their feelings of competence.

Discussion Questions

1. Respond to the following statement: Organizational cultures are not important to an organization. Do you agree with it? Explain your response.

2. How would the culture of a unionized public sector workplace differ from a non-unionized private sector workplace (e.g., RCMP, Toronto General Hospital, or Transport Canada versus WestJet, Boston Pizza, or TD Canada Trust)?

3. Why is socialization essential to organizational success?

4. Have you ever had a mentor? Provide specific examples of how having a mentor helped your socialization into the organizational culture.

5. How important are formal socialization and mentorship programs, especially in terms of a more diverse Canadian workplace? Explain.

Integration of OB Concepts—Discussion Questions

1. See Chapter 3 – Relate the factors of self-concept (i.e., self-efficacy, self-monitoring, and the social learning model of self-management) to how an organization socializes a new employee. Consider the kind of onboarding initiative that would be used during the encounter stage. How would these self-concept factors affect the design of a formal mentorship program OR how would they influence a mentor–protégé relationship? What do the self-concept factors say about why mentoring is important? (Consider the nine constructive actions to building self-efficacy.)

2. See Chapter 4 – What are some strategies that can be used to avoid individual–organization value conflict? What can a job applicant do during the anticipatory socialization phase to address (1) the concept of value congruence between individual values vs. corporate values, and (2) person–culture fit?

3. See Chapter 9 – Review the ethical decision tree. What might an organizational leader do to create and maintain an ethical organizational culture?

4. See Chapter 10 – Review the International OB "Lessons from the Globe Project" feature box. Consider how a leader creates and maintains an organization's culture in Canada that might lead to conflicts in a country with different work-related values. What are the implications of this for Canadian companies that wish to expand abroad? (For more on this, be sure to read the Chapter 11 Ethical OB Case Study found on Connect).

Google Searches

1. **Google Search:** "Brookfield Renewable Energy buying Brookfield Renewable Power for $3.4 billion" AND "Target buys 220 Zellers" Mergers and acquisitions between organizations have become a common business phenomenon—some work, while some do not. Most often, a corporate takeover may look appealing on paper, yet after the ink dries, the corporate cultures clash. Were these mergers a good blend of cultures? Consider the cultural differences between these organizations.

2. **Google Search:** "CIBC" OR "GoodLife Fitness" OR "Google Canada" Review the websites and try to identify the three layers of organizational culture for each: observable artifacts, espoused values, and/or enacted values.

3. **Google Search:** "Newalta Corporation" This company has been recognized as one of Canada's Best Diversity Employers. Research the details of what Newalta offers by reviewing the corporate website as well as the diversity award website. How have the various unique programs offered by Newalta Corp. bridged the principles of diversity together with mentorship? How do such initiatives effectively embed corporate culture in Newalta?

4. **Google Search:** "Professional Business and Networking Associations in (Name your City)" OR "Business and Professional Women of (Your Town)" Explore the various types of developmental networks that are available in your city. Be prepared to share your list with the class.

Experiential Exercise

Developing a Socialization Process Exercise

PURPOSE: This exercise is to help familiarize you with the OB concept of socialization using Daniel Feldman's three-phase model. Approx. Timing: 20 minutes.

ACTIVITY ASSIGNMENT

- Review the three phases of Feldman's Model of Organizational Socialization.
- Work in small groups to fill in the chart below.
- Be prepared to share your completed chart with the class. Pay close attention to the different techniques and programs recommended as the chart is discussed in class.

Characteristics of Phase	Behaviours New Employee Exhibits in Phase	Event, Program, and/or Strategy to Help New Employees Socialize
#1 – Anticipatory		
#2 – Encounter		
#3 – Change and Acquisition		

OB In Action Case Study

ThyssenKrupp Elevator Canada – Culture Goes On Trial

INTRODUCTION

During a lunchroom break, a male employee at ThyssesnKrupp decided to take up a dare from a fellow colleague for $100 and the Jackass-like prank was videotaped then posted to YouTube. When it came to the attention of the HR manager and other senior management, the employee was fired for violating company policy. The employee argued in court that the organizational culture allowed such behaviour. But would the Ontario Labour Relations Board (OLRB) agree?

BACKGROUND

ThysssenKrupp Elevator Canada was subcontracting elevator installation at a construction site in downtown Toronto where a large office building was being built. All the workers on the site, including those from ThyssenKrupp, and the main contractor of the site, PCL Construction, were male and the culture of the workplace was described as a "macho" environment where pranks were played. There were reportedly pictures of women and provocative calendars hanging on walls, as well as signs displaying vulgar humour. There was little concern about these as access to the building was restricted to people involved in the construction project.

One of ThyssenKrupp's employees at the site was an elevator mechanic. He and several other employees engaged in what he called "picking" on each other and playing pranks to keep things light at work. They also watched pornographic scenes on a worker's iPod and episodes of the television show Jackass, which features individuals doing stupid activities on dares.

ESCALATION OF PRANK BEHAVIOUR

Over a period of a few weeks, the mechanic and other employees performed more and more pranks that copied some of the ones they saw on the Jackass show. Typically these events took place in the basement lunchroom where employees gathered for breaks and meals, to change clothes, and to socialize. Soon, money was being offered on dares to do certain actions. For example, one ThyssenKrupp employee accepted a dare that involved a $60 payment—money collected from fellow employees, including three foremen. The dare involved the employee eating spoiled food found in the common refrigerator of the lunchroom.

A couple of weeks after the first dare, the mechanic was observed playing with a stapler in the lunchroom on a break. One of the foremen walked in and jokingly said, "What are you going to do with that? Why don't you staple your nuts to something?" The mechanic jokingly replied that he'd do it "if you get enough money."

Though he claimed it was intended as a joke, word spread within a few hours, and soon $100 was raised among seven other ThysennKrupp and three PCL employees. Another four people were in the lunchroom later that afternoon watching when the mechanic decided to go ahead with the staple dare. He proceeded to drop his work uniform trousers and staple his scrotum to a wooden plank, which was met by "cheering and high fives," according to the mechanic. With the mechanic's knowledge, the prank was filmed on video. Included on-camera were all those employees present, wearing full worksite uniforms, PCL logos on hats, and TK shirt patches—all easily identifiable and recorded by a worker who was present that day. The mechanic was advised at a later date that the event was posted on YouTube.

Initially, the mechanic did nothing about the YouTube posting, but eventually asked for it to be taken off the site. To ensure this was done, the mechanic went back to YouTube searching for the video clip, but couldn't find it. He assumed it had been removed, however it was not—he just didn't search correctly. In total, the video clip was assessable on YouTube for two weeks, during which time many employees in the construction industry watched it.

It was during these two weeks that ThyssenKrupp became aware of the video after the HR department received an email with a link to the video, and several people discussed it with a ThyssenKrupp executive at a construction labour relations conference. Conference participants insisted the employee was from ThyssenKrupp, and they questioned how the company could allow something like that to happen during work hours.

At this point, ThyssenKrupp management reviewed the video one more time and decided that the mechanic had violated its workplace harassment policy, which prohibited "practical jokes of a sexual nature which cause awkwardness or embarrassment." The mechanic was fired for "a flagrant violation" of ThyssenKrupp's harassment policy and risking the company's reputation.

CULTURE AT FAULT

Upon being fired from his job, the mechanic filed a grievance with the OLRB. He argued that dismissal was too harsh given the culture of the workplace which was accepting of that type of behaviour. He also said no one told him not to do it, no one expressed displeasure, and no one mentioned they were offended. He argued that other employees had done stunts but questioned why he was the only one disciplined for his actions. He also claimed to have never seen the workplace harassment policy, even though it was part of the orientation package.

THE DECISION

In July 2011, the OLRB found the mechanic's misconduct on the employer's premises, plus his permission to record it, "patently unacceptable in almost any workplace." The fact that his employer was easily identified in the video clip contributed to the decision. The fact that the mechanic claimed not to have known about the corporate harassment policy was irrelevant—he should have known better. The OLRB also dismissed as irrelevant that no one protested or objected to the prank during the lunch break, which the mechanic argued was "not during work hours."

The court stated that ThyssenKrupp has an interest in preventing such horseplay and stunts in the workplace. They are in a safety-sensitive industry and such employee misconduct places the firm's reputation in jeopardy.

The seriousness of the mechanic's misconduct also superseded any other factors, such as his claim of being a good employee with a clean record and the argument around the culture. There was no evidence that the company was aware of other pranks, and his role as the principle offender wasn't diminished by the culture, said the board. In dismissing the mechanics grievance, the board stated, "If (ThyssenKrupp) employees want to emulate the principles of Jackass by self-abuse, they may be free to do so when they are not on the (employer's) premises and cannot be identified as being associated with (ThyssenKrupp)."

Discussion Questions:

1. Considering that the mechanic claimed that the ThyssenKrupp culture contributed to such behaviour, which observable artifact would "stunts and pranks" behaviour be classified? (Review the layers of organizational culture discussed in this chapter.)

2. What corporate values did ThyssenKrupp refer to when deciding to terminate the mechanic?

3. Did the OLRB accept the defense that organizational culture contributed to the employee behaviour? Explain their reasoning.

4. In your opinion, does ThyssenKrupp need to change its corporate culture? If not, why not? If so, which of the 11 mechanisms listed in this chapter would you suggest using, and why?

SOURCES: I.U.E.C., Local 50 v. ThyssenKrupp Elevator (Canada) Ltd., 2011 CarswellOnt 7404 (Ont. Lab. Rel. Bd.). Adapted from J. Smith, "Construction Worker Sacked For YouTube Stunt," *Canadian HR Reporter*, October 24, 2011, p 5.

The CONNECTion Zone Connect™

- The Presentation Assistant
- Ethical OB Dilemma
- Video Case

Practise and learn online with Connect.

CHAPTER 12

Organizational Structure and Design

FACING AN OB CHALLENGE

Last year, I started my own business immediately after I graduated and things have been going really well. I do it all: I turned part of my apartment into an office area and set up my smartphone and laptop to interface with the cloud, I contact clients personally, type all invoices, pay all bills, and process shipping orders. I like having total control, but it's becoming too much. If I want my business to grow, I'll have to share decisions related to my company with another person. So, what's the problem? I'm scared another person will mess things up. I've worked hard to build my company and don't want to lose it now. How can I grow my business without losing power or influence?

—CAN'T DO IT ALL ANYMORE

The Fundamentals of an Organization

The question raised by the individual in Facing an OB Challenge is both insightful and very natural; after all, the person has worked hard to get the business started and knows what sacrifices have had to be made to become successful. But the question also shows a realization of what is needed to sustain future operations. Hiring extra help can be too costly for a sole proprietorship. This individual is expressing feelings of uncertainty because hiring help means finding someone who has similar values and a strong work ethic, and who will care about the success of the company, show willingness to plan for the future, and share decision making responsibilities. While this company has experienced growth over the last year, there is no guarantee this will continue. If a commitment is made to hire a full-time person and then business slows down, then what will the owner do? There will be times of feast, where sales revenue is strong as a result of healthy demand and the organization expands its operations, but there will also be times of famine during slow growth phases or poor economic cycles that could result in layoffs. In today's competitive and uncertain marketplace, organizations have to be more flexible and fluid than ever before, especially related to their structure and operations.

In this chapter, we begin our discussion around the fundamentals of an organization, such as the definition and related dimensions. In a manner of speaking, organizations are the chessboard upon which the game of organizational behaviour is played. Therefore, having a working knowledge of how organizations are created, how they grow, and why work is organized the way it is can help managers plan strategically and employees understand the big picture. Being able to recognize the interplay between structure, design, and behaviour is essential to mastering OB.

We'll also explore the various structures in the business world and examine alternative organizational metaphors, then we'll move on to the criteria for assessing organizational effectiveness. We'll end the chapter by discussing the contingency approach to designing organizations. This includes comparing mechanistic versus organic organizations, and new-style versus old-style organizations.

Organizations: Definition and Dimensions **LO 1**

As a necessary springboard for this chapter, we need to formally define the term *organization* and clarify the meaning of organization charts.

WHAT IS AN ORGANIZATION?

According to Chester I. Barnard's classic definition, an *organization* is "a system of consciously coordinated activities or forces of two or more persons."[1] Four common factors of how work is organized are found in the coordination aspect of this definition: (1) coordination of effort, (2) a common goal, (3) division of labour, and (4) a hierarchy of authority.[2] Organization theorists refer to these factors as *organizational structure:*

1. **Coordination of effort** Achieved through creating and enforcing policies, rules, and regulations.

2. **Common goal** An agreed-upon direction for the organization.

3. **Division of labour** When the common goal is pursued by individuals performing different but related tasks.

> *Organization*
>
> A system of consciously coordinated activities of two or more people.

> *Organizational structure*
>
> Four common factors of how work is organized: coordination of effort, common goal, division of labour, and hierarchy of authority.

4. **Hierarchy of authority** Also called the chain of command, this control mechanism is dedicated to making sure the right people do the right things at the right time.[3]

This last factor is especially important in showing how contemporary organizations have moved away from having a traditional perspective of structure. In the historical model, OB experts insisted upon a *unity of command principle*, meaning that each employee reported to only one manager. It was believed that this was how an organization would remain efficient, how communication between employees and their supervisors would be accurate, and if necessary, how corrections to work behaviour could be administered. Can you imagine working at a job where each employee was given his or her own boss? It may sound good on paper, but today's empowered employee (we talked about empowerment in Chapter 9) would probably feel smothered by such constant attention.

When the four common structural factors work together—coordination of effort, a common goal, division of labour, and a hierarchy of authority—it enables an organization to come to life and function successfully.

LO 2 HOW ORGANIZATIONS ARE CREATED

How do organizations come to life? Basically, this question is best addressed by OB expert, Henry Mintzberg[4]: it starts with an entrepreneur type of person who has an idea. This person, as the owner/operator, forms the top manager who recognizes the need to hire employees to complete basic tasks for the organization to reach the goal, called the operating core of the business. As the organization grows, the owner/operator takes on more line managers to oversee the coordination of effort within the operating core—hence the division of labour occurs. The organization may also find that it needs two kinds of staff personnel: (1) analysts who design systems concerned with planning and the control of work tasks, and (2) support staff who provide indirect services to the rest of the organization. As Mintzberg states:

> … not all organizations need all of these parts. Some use few and are simple, others combine all in rather complex ways. The central purpose of structure is to coordinate the work divided in a variety of ways; how that coordination is achieved— by whom and with what—dictates what the organization will look like.[5]

THE GROWTH OF AN ORGANIZATION

The growth of an organization is best explained by way of an illustration called an *organization chart*, showing the formal authority and division of labour relationships. To the casual observer, the term organization chart means the family tree-like pattern of boxes and lines posted on workplace walls. The names and titles of current position holders are usually within each box. To organization theorists, however, organization charts reveal much more. The organization charts in Figure 12.1 show the progression of how an organization grows from the simplest structure to a more complex model. This progression reveals the four basic dimensions of organizational structure mentioned earlier. Mintzberg stated that almost all organizations begin their lives as simple structures, allowing their founding chief executive(s) considerable freedom to set them up the way they want. Just as simple structures were prevalent in the pre-Industrial Revolution, the offspring of industrialization was bureaucracy, which is more complex and has many layers of middle managers. We'll expand on this idea later on in this chapter.

Hierarchy of Authority As Figure 12.1 illustrates, when a new company is created, there is no hierarchy. However, as it grows, adding more line managers and support staff to the chart, there becomes an unmistakable hierarchy of authority that shows who holds the most legitimate power in the company, in this case Pat Smith.[6] As the company acquires more layers of middle managers, it becomes taller and more narrow. We'll discuss this concept of hierarchy of authority a bit later in this chapter.

Division of Labour As the organization grows, the chain of command of who oversees what area becomes more evident. Also, you can see application of division of labour as different managers oversee different functional areas. Further, different support staff support different areas. Working your way from top to bottom, jobs become more specialized at each successive level in the organization. Again, this concept will be discussed later in this chapter when we discuss bureaucracy structures.

Span of Control *Span of control* refers to the number of people reporting directly to a given manager.[7] Spans of control can range from narrow (one manager: two employees or 1:2) to wide (1:50). For example, by the fourth year, Pat Smith in Figure 12.1 is widening the span of control to five. (Staff assistants usually are not included in a manager's span of control.) Raj Sunjie has a narrow span of three. Spans of control exceeding 30 can be found in assembly-line operations where machine-paced and repetitive work substitutes for close supervision. Historically, spans of seven to 10 people were

---

Unity of command principle

A historical belief that each employee should report to a single manager.

Organization chart

A box-and-line illustration showing the chain of formal authority and division of labour.

Span of control

The number of direct reports stated as a ratio.

FIGURE **12.1** Organization Charts that Show Growth

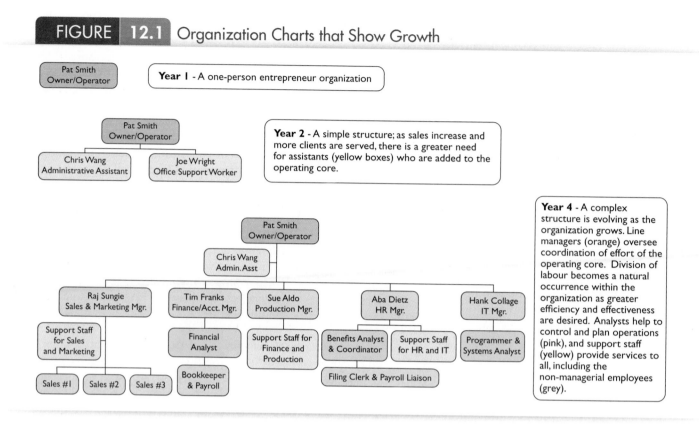

Year 1 - A one-person entrepreneur organization

Year 2 - A simple structure; as sales increase and more clients are served, there is a greater need for assistants (yellow boxes) who are added to the operating core.

Year 4 - A complex structure is evolving as the organization grows. Line managers (orange) oversee coordination of effort of the operating core. Division of labour becomes a natural occurrence within the organization as greater efficiency and effectiveness are desired. Analysts help to control and plan operations (pink), and support staff (yellow) provide services to all, including the non-managerial employees (grey).

considered best. More recently, however, corporate restructuring and improved communication technologies have increased the typical span of control.[8] Despite years of debate, organization theorists have not arrived at a consensus regarding the ideal span of control.

Generally, the narrower (smaller ratio) the span of control, the closer the supervision and the higher the administrative costs; this results in the organization becoming taller and pyramid-like. Recent emphasis on administrative efficiency dictates spans of control as wide as possible, but guarding against inadequate supervision and lack of coordination. Wider spans also complement the trend toward greater worker autonomy and empowerment. In this instance, the organization is flatter and wider. With the increased use of technology in operations and communication, in addition to the growth of the virtual organization, we're seeing the span of control becoming very large. Some industry practitioners have remarked that it can scarcely be called a span of control any longer—it is more a span of 'loose links and alliances'.[9]

Line and Staff Positions The organization chart in Figure 12.1 also distinguishes between line and staff positions. Line managers, such as the president and the five department managers, occupy formal decision-making positions within the chain of command. Staff personnel, such as the analysts and coordinators, do background research and provide technical advice and recommendations to their line managers, who have the authority to make decisions. However, modern trends such as cross-functional teams and reengineering are blurring the distinction between line and staff, as employees are being empowered to make decisions on their own.

DEPARTMENTATION

LO 3

We've covered the fundamentals of what an organization is, how they are created, and how they grow. Now let's take it a step further to try and understand how work is organized. When jobs are grouped together in an organization to gain greater efficiency and maintain effectiveness in customer service, it is called *departmentation*. Departmentation assists in getting work completed through the creation of departments, units, sections, or divisions. While the names can vary from organization to organization, the purpose is the same: to organize and coordinate the flow of work. Figure 12.2 illustrates the basic types of departmentation listed below.

■ **Functional** Work is separated using the major functional areas as guides.

> *Departmentation*
>
> The organizing of work by grouping jobs together to gain greater efficiency and maintain effectiveness in providing customer service.

So, all marketing jobs are housed in the same department, all accounting and finance jobs are grouped in the accounting department, and so on. This is a very common way of organizing work. An example would be how Pat Smith organized the entrepreneurial company after four years, shown in Figure 12.1.[10]

■ **Product** Work that falls within the same product, product line, or service category is grouped together. This is how Proctor & Gamble organizes their work, so that all House and Home products are found under this umbrella division that includes product lines such as Duracell, Swiffer, Tide, and Downy. The Personal and Beauty Division includes product lines such as Venus, Olay, Secret, and CoverGirl.

■ **Matrix** In this model, workers remain in their functional areas but are temporarily assigned to work on time-limited projects with other employees from across the organization. This is a highly cooperative design that requires a great deal of flexibility,

since employees could in fact have more than one supervisor at one time, depending on the task they are working on. The project authority flows horizontally from project managers and works in cooperation with functional department managers on a vertical basis. An example of this is Bayer Healthcare AG, the makers of Bayer aspirin, which regrouped itself many years ago under an umbrella company called Bayer World. This umbrella company combines all the global activities of its four divisions: Animal Health Division, Pharmaceuticals Division, Consumer Care Division, and Medical Care Division. It is possible for a marketing department employee within the Canadian Division of Bayer Healthcare to be living and working in Canada, while at the same time be assigned to a work project in cooperation with the Consumer Care Division of Bayer World (headquarters in Germany) on a consumer campaign.[11] To help firms realize their full potential when introducing a matrix structure, review the six steps outlined in the following Skills & Best Practices feature box.

FIGURE 12.2 Different Departmentation Structures

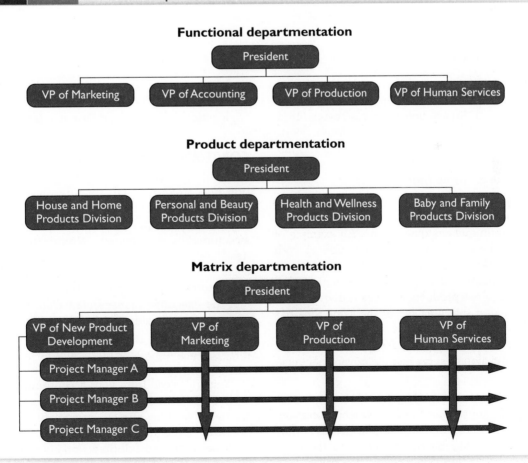

Skills & Best Practices

Realizing the Full Potential of a Matrix Structure

In theory, the matrix organizational structure has many benefits, and yet two global studies identified why so many firms fail in their attempts to implement such a structure. Here are six steps to help firms realize their potential when introducing a matrix structure:

1. **Leaders Connecting At All Levels** In this global economy, connectedness is needed more than ever. When employees are spread out across the globe, in different functional areas, with different backgrounds and cultures, then leaders at all levels need to be working within and across teams to make decisions that are in the best interest of the company as a whole.

2. **Eliminate The White Space** Areas within the matrix where no one is responsible are called *white space*. These are the areas where conflict, wasted time, bad decision-making, and costly, wasteful activities arise.

3. **Collaborate to Compete** Leaders continue to be bred, trained, and rewarded to gain results within their own business rather than optimizing opportunities that benefit the whole. They are maximizing for their own performance metrics, potentially causing unhealthy conflict and turf battles, causing one part of the organization to succeed at the expense of another.

4. **Cultural Intelligence** A deep understanding of different cultures and how people in different cultures respond to different incentives and rewards is critical for successful global operations.

5. **Patience and Presence** Developing cultural intelligence takes time and on-the-ground experience. There is a strong social learning component to global matrix structures that cannot be replaced by classroom experience. Interacting with the team in the field, learning first-hand the values, perceptions, and unwritten rules and behaviours must be dealt with first before discussing business issues at a boardroom table.

6. **New Compensation Models** It is necessary to be sensitive to the different motivation and compensation models that may or may not work in certain cultures. Managers who work in a matrix structure need to understand that exporting the same structural elements to unfamiliar cultures is a recipe for disaster as competing values typically cause conflict.

SOURCE: R. Lash, "Cracking the Matrix Code," *Canadian HR Reporter*, March 28, 2011.

- **Geographic** Workers and tasks are dispersed to the geographic territories where products or services are needed. An example of this is Toyota Motor Corporation, which includes Toyota Motor North America (including Canada), Toyota Motor Philippines, Toyota Motor Thailand, Toyota Motor Europe, Toyota Ghana, Toyota Argentina, etc.[12]

- **Customer** Here, specific product groups are housed in almost self-contained environments to better serve each unique customer group. An example of this would be a company that distributes to both English-speaking Canada and French-speaking Quebec. Another example would be a firm that makes consumer products and has a division that just looks after that area, but at the same time has large government contracts that require totally different service care. The company therefore sets up a separate division to serve just the government customer base.[13]

- **Hybrid** This type is a combination of structures that may include any of the other departmentation structures mentioned so far. For example, the head office of a company may be structured using the functional model for things like centralized payroll and human resources, marketing, and accounting, but the regional offices may be set up by geographical locations to serve the different areas of Canada.[14]

CONTEMPORARY STRUCTURES

LO 4

As the Industrial Age has given way to the Information Age, organizational structures have also changed. Before we discuss the various kinds of contemporary structures developing globally, it's worth noting why structures have changed. Within the organization itself are many operational pressures related to total costs and concerns around contribution to output that will determine profit or loss. These internal pressures fuel the executive management team to review ways to maintain a healthy financial position by lowering costs, increasing profitability, maintaining positive investor or public perception, and keeping an eye on sustainability.

You will recall from your accounting class that the highest operation costs in North America are wages and salaries; this alone attracts immediate executive attention. One of the most common ways to cut labour costs is by not replacing full-time workers when they leave, for whatever reason. Instead, the firm hires contract workers, either on a full-time or part-time basis, to work on a project. The terms of employment, such as pay, hours, location, duties, responsibilities, and length of contract, are covered in the written document that the worker agrees to prior to starting the job. Clearly such contracts allow for no benefit obligations to labour, which provides enormous savings for the organization, in addition to a higher degree of flexibility within the span of control. It is not unusual to find contract workers, some with monthly or multi-year agreements, throughout many of the new contemporary organizational structures.

At the same time an organization is managing internal pressures, it must also deal with the constant barrage of external pressure from numerous market variables that it cannot control. For example, as technological improvements appear within an industry, an organization must adapt or fall behind. Other pressures can include added competition from new entrants threatening market share, environmental impact studies leading to legislative changes in how a firm must operate, new employment laws around health and safety, unstable global economies that affect exports as well as the cost of goods to import, not to mention volatile consumer demand.

All of these internal and external pressures force organizations to adopt new and creative organizational structures. Each has identified strengths and weaknesses, but you may want to explore these further by completing the Experiential Exercise located at the end of the chapter. Let's now look at several contemporary structures that have evolved, including: cross-functional team structures; outsourcing structures; network organizations; virtual organizations; modular structures; and boundaryless organizational structures (see Figure 12.3 for illustrations).

- **Cross-functional team structure** Similar to the matrix model, this wagon-wheel structure has individuals from various departments working together as a team (see Chapter 6). Typically, this group is together for a longer period of time compared to the shorter-lived projects under the matrix structure. Further, the team benefits creatively by having a wider operational perspective. This in turn can contribute to increased communication and cost-effectiveness. An example of this is how Ford Motor Company designed the Mustang over a period of years, where over 30 cross-functional specialty teams worked together from day one to solve design problems and identify quality issues.[15]

- **Outsourcing structure** In this structure, one department within a structure is closed down and the work is redirected to an outside company to complete the task because of lower cost. Contract

workers are often referred to as part-time employees working within the company itself or off-site. In any event, organizations that hire non-full-time employees in any location for any length of time are doing so because they do not have a competitive advantage. It's too costly to operate in the manner they've chosen, so to lower their costs by not absorbing added labour costs (like benefits) or fixed costs (like office furniture) and to maintain a highly flexible structure for the ebb and flow of their company, they outsource part of a function. An example of this would be hiring an outside agency to take care of payroll on a permanent basis because it can operate for less cost.

- **Network organization** In this structure, many departments are contracted out in a cooperative network of suppliers and distributors. The core organization remains structured according to either a functional or product way. However, rather than absorb all the costs from being a full-service company, it's less overhead and more effective to let those companies complete the tasks that they do well for less money. This leaves the core organization to take care of putting it all together, branding, selling, distributing, etc. This structure differs from outsourcing because a network is more than one or two functional parts being contracted out. Instead, there is a series of liaisons between numerous specialist organizations that rely strongly on each other, plus a high degree of coordination within the market. All the assets necessary to produce the finished product or service are present in the network, not held in-house by one firm. The video gaming industry uses this type of structure extensively. Another example would be an advertising agency that has in its core a president, account services personnel, accounting for billing purposes, one art director, and two copy writers, but contracts all other activities to various companies as needed (such as market research, media purchases, final art designs, and coordinating direct mail promotions).[16]

- **Virtual Organization** A virtual organization is a type of network organization with core areas that broker out services over virtual networks that provide flexibility and adaptability for the firm. As the Web provides more accessibility to specialists anywhere in the world, host firms can contract out more and more activity as they need to, resulting in a structure that grows and shrinks as needed, reacts to market demand in real time, and isn't saddled with countless bricks and mortar buildings to staff. The challenge is how to manage geographically-dispersed employees who work within virtual organization structures. Three key points to note in this case

FIGURE 12.3 Contemporary Structures

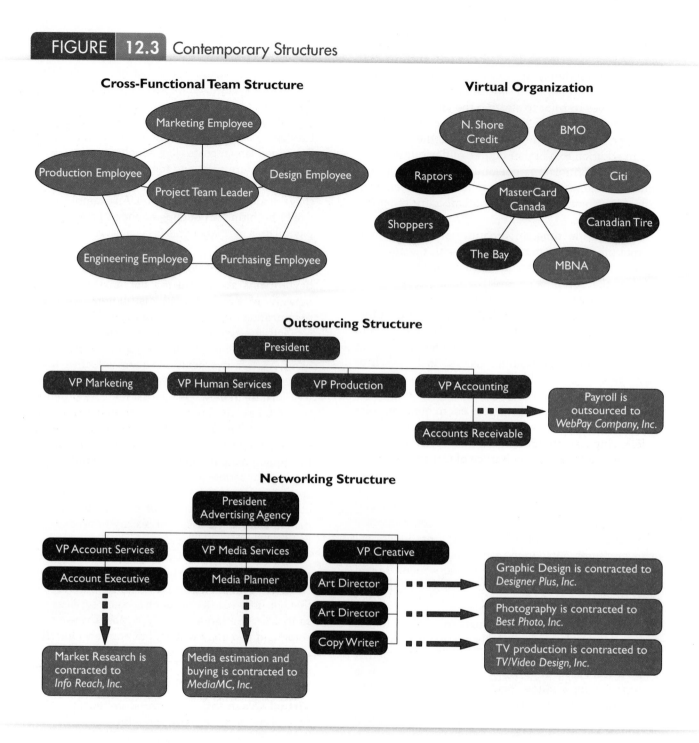

Cross-Functional Team Structure

Marketing Employee

Production Employee

Design Employee

Project Team Leader

Engineering Employee

Purchasing Employee

Virtual Organization

N. Shore Credit

BMO

Raptors

Citi

MasterCard Canada

Shoppers

Canadian Tire

The Bay

MBNA

Outsourcing Structure

President

VP Marketing

VP Human Services

VP Production

VP Accounting

Payroll is outsourced to *WebPay Company, Inc.*

Accounts Receivable

Networking Structure

President Advertising Agency

VP Account Services

VP Media Services

VP Creative

Account Executive

Media Planner

Art Director

Art Director

Copy Writer

Graphic Design is contracted to *Designer Plus, Inc.*

Photography is contracted to *Best Photo, Inc.*

TV production is contracted to *TV/Video Design, Inc.*

Market Research is contracted to *Info Reach, Inc.*

Media estimation and buying is contracted to *MediaMC, Inc.*

are sharing knowledge, building trust, and maintaining connectedness. But how is that done? Steps worth considering include hiring people who can self-manage, having frequent communication with off-site employees, considering leveraging technology for training purposes, finding ways to enable their productivity, and conducting regular audits to ensure compliance with company policies, legal requirements, and ethical standards. An example of a virtual organization would be MasterCard, which acts as the core organization with its own employee base, but is served by a network of thousands of financial institutions and retailers around the world. We'll talk more about virtual organizations when we discuss the globalization of organizations in Chapter 14.

- **Modular Organization** In this structure, an organization has recognized that it lacks flexibility and creativity within its current operations and it is slow to respond to market changes. Through mergers, acquisitions, and restructuring with many suppliers and specialists, all of the various organizations are brought under one corporate umbrella. The new organization emerges as a super-network of interdependent subsidiaries and divisions that can be spread out nationally or even globally. Rather than being one complex tall bureaucracy, the modular approach allows for a more simplistic structure overall that can respond faster to market demands, lower costs through higher efficiencies of operations including workforce reductions, thereby making it more profitable. TELUS Corporation is an example of a modular organizational structure that has evolved since 1999 after dozens of amalgamations, mergers, and acquisitions. The illustrated structure in Fig 12.4 shows the interdependency between the super-network of like-minded organizations.[17] While the modular structure has its benefits, these super-networks are of concern to many, especially to the government of Canada, who seeks to regulate public goods like communication. The following Law and Ethics feature box discusses the role of the Competition Bureau of Canada and how

it monitors the effects of corporate mergers within the Canadian marketplace.[18]

- **Boundaryless Organization** The basic premise behind a boundaryless structure is that if a company wants to truly become competitive globally, then it must take down the barriers that exist between departments, employees, managers, suppliers, divisions, subsidiaries, etc. In many ways, it combines the benefits of the cross-functional team structure with self-managing work groups within a super-network of partners in the supply chain. This structure was first coined in the early 1980s by Jack Welch, former Chairman and CEO of General Electric (GE). When he arrived at GE, Welch couldn't understand the barriers that existed within management where senior managers would never think of talking to anyone outside of their direct reports. Welch said GE had what was called a 'not-invented-here' attitude, which meant employees had nothing to learn from outside the GE organization . . . something Welch felt had to change if GE were to complete globally. The boundaryless structure encompasses both the physical reporting structure of workflow as well as the mindset held by employees. A boundaryless structure lends itself to being a more open system (we'll talk more about this type of system in greater detail later in this chapter).[19]

FIGURE 12.4 A Modular Network Structure

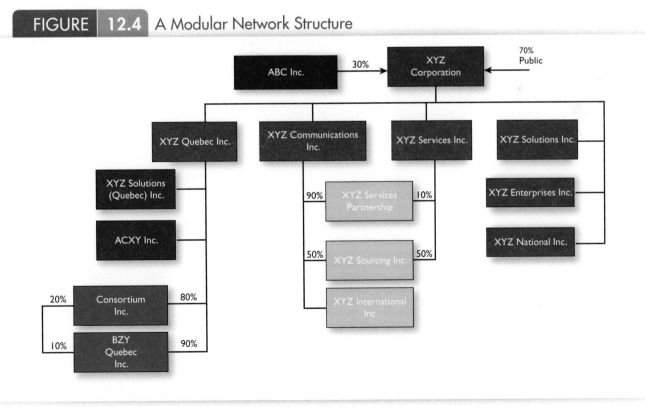

CANADA'S COMPETITION ACT WATCHES SUPER-NETWORK DEVELOPMENT

The Canadian government realizes that businesses may need to expand and grow to achieve lower production costs or to compete more effectively nationally and globally. However, when a dominant company exploits its market power in a way that hurts competition in the marketplace, then the Competition Bureau may enforce the regulations outlined in the Competition Act to level the playing field. Business practices that are intended to reduce competition include, among other things, buying up a competitor's customers and cutting off essential supplies to rival companies. Certainly, mergers and acquisitions that create super-network modular structures are of keen interest to the Bureau. Originally written in 1985, the Competition Act has been amended many times to incorporate issues related to contemporary business practices.

Under the Competition Act, mergers of all sizes and in all sectors of the economy are subject to review by the Commissioner of Competition to determine whether they will likely result in a substantial lessening or prevention of competition. The Commissioner of Competition must be notified of all mergers that exceed certain sized thresholds prior to completion. Failure to notify is a criminal offence.

SOURCE: Competition Bureau of Canada website, www.competitionbureau.gc.ca, Preventing Abuse of Market Power and Reviewing Mergers, June 2012.

Descriptions of Structures Using Organizational Metaphors

The complexity of modern organizations makes them somewhat difficult to describe. Consequently, organization theorists have resorted to the use of metaphors.[20] A metaphor is a figure of speech that characterizes one object in terms of another object. Good metaphors help us understand complicated things by describing them in everyday terms. For example, organizations are often compared to an orchestra. With this metaphor, you could come away with an exaggerated mental image of harmony being associated with large and complex organizations. On the other hand, it realistically encourages you to view managers as facilitators rather than absolute dictators.

We will discuss two types of structures in this section using the metaphor method: (1) the bureaucracy, and (2) the open system.

STRUCTURE #1: ORGANIZATIONS AS MILITARY OR MECHANICAL BUREAUCRACIES

A major by-product of the Industrial Revolution was the factory system of production. People left their farms and cottage industries to operate steam-powered machines in centralized factories. The social unit of production evolved from the family to formally-managed organizations encompassing hundreds or even thousands of people. Managers sought to maximize the economic efficiency of large factories and offices by structuring them according to military principles. At the turn of the 20th century, a German sociologist, Max Weber, formulated what he termed the most rationally efficient form of organization.[21] He patterned his ideal organization after the Prussian army and called it *bureaucracy*.

Weber's Bureaucracy Figure 12.5 summarizes Weber's theory. The following four factors should make bureaucracies the essence of efficiency:

Bureaucracy

A tall organizational structure known for its division of labour, hierarchy of authority, formal framework of rules, and administrative impersonality.

1. **Division of labour** People become better at what they do when they perform standardized tasks over and over again.

   Example: An assembly line worker repeats the same task throughout the entire 8-hour day without much variety or change.

2. **A hierarchy of authority** A formal chain of command ensures coordination and accountability.

   Example: If an employee can't fix a problem, then it is appropriate to take the concern to the next level in the structure to see if it can be solved there. To jump over several management levels to go

FIGURE 12.5 Weber's Four Factors of a Bureaucracy

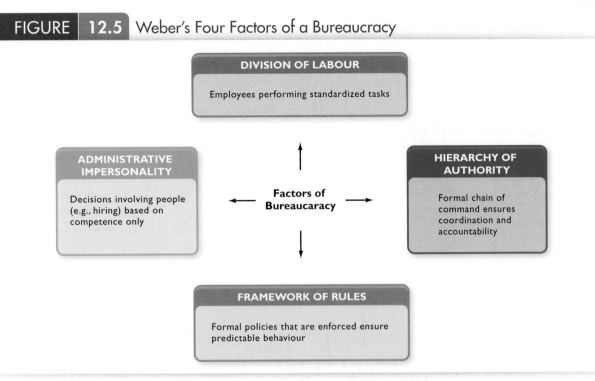

DIVISION OF LABOUR

Employees performing standardized tasks

ADMINISTRATIVE IMPERSONALITY

Decisions involving people (e.g., hiring) based on competence only

Factors of Bureaucaracy

HIERARCHY OF AUTHORITY

Formal chain of command ensures coordination and accountability

FRAMEWORK OF RULES

Formal policies that are enforced ensure predictable behaviour

---

directly to the top executive would be perceived as inappropriate and cause for discipline for not following chain of command.

3. **A framework of rules** Carefully formulated and strictly enforced rules ensure predictable behaviour.

   Example: Formal policies and procedures on how to get work done at the office are provided so there aren't any questions or doubts about what to do. Everything is written down to the finest detail, like when a police officer makes an arrest on the street (i.e., they must follow formal policies and procedures so they don't make any legal mistakes).

4. **Administrative impersonality** Personnel decisions such as hiring and promoting should be based on competence, not favouritism.[22]

   Example: Long and lengthy postings to fill vacant jobs, meant to offer fairness to applicants, allow for proper screening of candidates and intense interviewing processes. It takes time to follow this process in the hopes of finding the best candidate for the job, instead of hiring the boss's relative.

How the Term Bureaucracy Became a Synonym for Inefficiency All organizations possess varying degrees of these characteristics. Thus, every organization is a bureaucracy to some extent. In terms of the ideal metaphor, a bureaucracy should run like a well-oiled machine, and its members should perform with the precision of a polished military unit. But practical problems can arise when bureaucratic characteristics become extreme.

For example, consider the size of the school you are attending right now. Why did you decide to attend this particular school? Did the size of the campus and the potential for large class sizes play a role in the decision you made to apply to one school and not to another? Some students want to feel like they are recognized and appreciated by the school

Traditionally, the Canadian Department of Defense would be considered a bureaucratic system because of its formal chain of command and strict enforcement of procedure and rules.

and to the professors who will teach them. Does this sound like you?

When specialization, rule following, and impersonality cause a patron or client to feel like a number rather than a person, then the organization has become highly complex and bureaucratic.[23]

Another point to emphasize is the inefficiency of large bureaucracies. If you have studied micro-economics, then you've seen the cost-curves that clearly increase as an organization becomes larger and the diseconomies of scale that occur as it takes more resources just to keep the big firm operating.[24] These organizations are tall/narrow in structure, tend to be fixed-cost heavy, and are slow to react to the environment.

A classic example of this would be General Motors prior to their restructuring efforts. Some would currently place Sears into this category

Weber would probably be surprised and dismayed that his model of rational efficiency has become a synonym for inefficiency.[25] Today, bureaucracy stands for being put on hold, waiting in long lines, and getting shuffled from one office to the next. This irony can be explained largely by the fact that organizations with excessive or dysfunctional bureaucratic tendencies often become rigid, inflexible, and resistant to environmental demands and influences.[26]

STRUCTURE #2: THE OPEN SYSTEM

The traditional military/mechanical metaphor is a *closed system* model because it is closed to surrounding environmental influences. It gives the impression that organizations are self-sufficient entities. In contrast, an *open system* depends on constant interaction with the environment for survival. The distinction between closed and open systems is a matter of degree. Because every worldly system is partly closed and partly open, the key question is: How great a role does the environment play in the functioning of the system? For instance, a battery-powered clock is a relatively closed system. Once the battery is inserted, the clock performs its time-keeping function hour after hour until the battery goes dead. The human body, on the other hand, is a highly open system because it requires a constant supply of life-sustaining oxygen and nutrients from the environment. Open systems are capable of self-correction, adaptation, and growth, are typically decentralized, and work in real time. Think of when you cut your finger—the body doesn't debate where to heal the wound. The problem is identified by the central

nervous system and the brain registers the pain, but the solution takes place immediately at the point of injury. Referring to the human body both physically and mentally creates two types of open systems: the biological open system and the cognitive open system.

The Biological Open System This metaphor likens organizations to the human body; hence, it has been labelled the biological model. The biological open system emphasizes interaction between organizations and their environments. OB theorist James D. Thompson explained the biological model of organizations in the following terms:

> *Approached as a natural system, the complex organization is a set of interdependent parts which together make up a whole because each contributes something and receives something from the whole, which in turn is interdependent with some larger environment. Survival of the system is taken to be the goal, and the parts and their relationships presumably are determined through evolutionary processes.*[27]

Unlike the traditional military/mechanical theorists who downplayed the environment, advocates of the biological model characterize the organization as an open system that transforms inputs into various outputs. The outer boundary of the organization is permeable (porous). People, information, capital, and goods and services move back and forth across this boundary. Moreover, each of the five organizational subsystems—goals and values, technical, psycho-social, structural, and managerial—is dependent on the others. Feedback about such things as sales and customer satisfaction or dissatisfaction enables the organization to self-adjust and survive, despite uncertainty and change.[28] In effect, the organization is alive.

The Cognitive Open System A more recent metaphor characterizes organizations in terms of thinking functions. According to respected organization theorists Richard Daft and Karl Weick,

> *This perspective represents a move away from mechanical and biological metaphors of organizations. Organizations are more than transformation processes or control systems. To survive, organizations must have mechanisms to interpret ambiguous events and to provide meaning and direction for participants. Organizations are meaning systems, and this distinguishes them from lower-level systems . . .*

Closed system

A relatively self-sufficient structure that does not seek assistance from outside itself.

Open system

An interactive structure that must constantly interact with its environment to survive as it operates in a self-corrective, adaptable, and real-time manner.

Almost all outcomes in terms of organization structure and design, whether caused by the environment, technology, or size, depend on the interpretation of problems or opportunities by key decision makers.[29]

As it migrates throughout the organization, this interpretation process leads to organizational learning and adaptation.[30] It takes a cooperative culture, mutual trust, and lots of internal cross-communication to fully exploit the organization as a cognitive (thinking) system, or *learning organization*. Recall our earlier discussion of GE and Jack Welch's desire to create a more open boundaryless structure that was able to be more responsive and flexible. This is what he was speaking of—wanting GE to become a learning organization. Another example would be the reaction from Maple Leaf Foods during the outbreak of listeriosis originating from one of its meat packing facilities, (you may recall this OB in Action Case Study from Chapter 10). Maple Leaf credited its vertical coordination strategy in monitoring the quality and safety of product produced because "now they know how and where an animal is raised."[31] The crisis forced Maple Leaf Foods to become a learning organization by constantly being aware and open to internal and external factors impacting their operations, allowing them to adapt successfully.

Learning organization
A type of open system that compares itself to the cognitive abilities of the human body, able to adapt and change according to environmental needs.

Striving for Organizational Effectiveness

In this next section, we provide the tools to assess whether an organization is progressing toward meeting its full potential. This involves an organization reviewing its goals and performance, determining how successful it is at acquiring resources, identifying whether internal processes are straining these resources, and finally considering the concerns from stakeholder groups. Certainly, organizational effectiveness defined in these terms is an important topic for many people, including employees, managers, shareholders, government agencies, interest groups, and OB specialists.

There are many approaches to take in sizing-up performance, and each industry and company will have its own metrics based on key performance drivers. For those studying higher level strategic planning and management systems, a useful approach to creating multiple performance measures is the Balanced Scorecard from Kaplan and Norton (1991).[32] The approach has been updated over the years and is used extensively to align business activities to the vision and strategy of the organization, improve internal and external communications, and monitor organization performance against strategic goals. For those studying general business principles, a generic approach may be helpful in highlighting the broad importance of assessing the performance of the organization that has been structured and designed.

GENERIC EFFECTIVENESS CRITERIA   LO 5

To better understand this complex subject, we will consider four generic approaches to assessing an organization's effectiveness (see Figure 12.6). These effectiveness criteria apply equally well to large or small and profit or not-for-profit organizations. Notice how the circles in Figure 12.6 overlap; that's because the four effectiveness criteria can be used in various combinations. The key thing to remember is "no single approach to the evaluation of effectiveness is appropriate in all circumstances or for all organization types."[33] Because a multidimensional approach is required, we need to look more closely at each of the four generic effectiveness criteria.

Goal Accomplishment   Goal accomplishment is the most widely-used effectiveness criterion for organizations. Key organizational results or outputs are compared with previously-stated goals or objectives. Deviations, either plus or minus, require corrective action. This is simply an organizational variation of the personal goal-setting process discussed in Chapter 5.[34] Effectiveness, relative to the criterion of goal accomplishment, is gauged by how well the organization meets or exceeds its goals.[35] The Canadian retailer, Mountain Equipment Co-op (MEC), publishes an annual accountability report that measures 16 different indicators, compiles a three-year trend projection for each indicator, allows voting members to view past targets against actual numbers within each indicator; and also publishes current year targets. When asked what accountability means to MEC, David Labistour, current CEO said it this way:

We have to . . . do business in a better way and be transparent about what we do. This includes the places where we make our products, the people who make our products, it includes the environmental impact we have with the product we make; this includes the environmental impact of our operations, and it includes our passion for the outdoors and the conservation thereof. We want people to read our Accountability Report and let us know what they think we can do better.[36]

FIGURE | 12.6 | Four Dimensions of Organizational Effectiveness

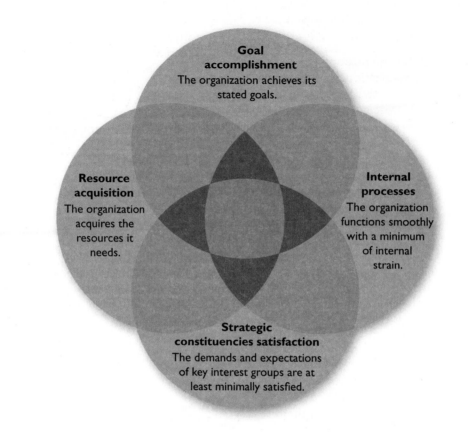

SOURCES: Adapted from discussion in K. Cameron, "Critical Questions in Assessing Organizational Effectiveness," *Organizational Dynamics,* Autumn 1980, pp 66–80; and K.S. Cameron, "Effectiveness as Paradox: Consensus and Conflict in Conceptions of Organizational Effectiveness," *Management Science,* May 1986, pp 539–53.

Resource Acquisition This second criterion relates to inputs rather than outputs. An organization is deemed effective in this regard if it acquires necessary factors of production such as raw materials, labour, capital, and managerial and technical expertise. The Ethical OB Dilemma on the Connect site is an interesting case of the poor resource acquisition decision and further challenges Nokia faced in the smartphone industry as a result. In a different example, charitable organizations such as Habitat for Humanity and The United Way judge their effectiveness in terms of how much money they raise from private and corporate donations.

Internal Processes Some refer to this third effectiveness criterion as the "healthy systems" approach. An organization is said to be a healthy system if information flows smoothly and if employee loyalty, commitment, job satisfaction, and trust prevail. Goals may be set for any of these internal processes. Healthy systems, from a behavioural standpoint, tend to have minimal dysfunctional conflict and destructive political manoeuvring. M. Scott Peck, the physician who wrote the highly regarded book, *The Road Less Traveled,* characterizes healthy organizations in ethical terms:

A healthy organization is one that has a genuine sense of community: It's a place where people are emotionally present with one another, and aren't afraid to talk about fears and disappointments—because that's what allows us to care for one another. It's a place where there is authentic communication, a willingness to be vulnerable,

Vancouver-based MEC follows a cooperative governance model that publishes an annual accountability report on their website of past and current performance for members to view.

a commitment to speaking frankly and respectfully—and a commitment not to walk away when the going gets tough.[37]

Organizations with healthy internal processes tend to be incubators for creativity and innovation. As well, these processes do not compete nor strain company resources, all of which are very important.[38]

Strategic Constituencies' Satisfaction Organizations both depend on people and affect the lives of people. Consequently, many consider the satisfaction of key interested parties to be an important criterion of organizational effectiveness.

A strategic constituency is any group of individuals who have some stake in the organization—for example, resource providers, users of the organization's products or services, producers of the organization's output, groups whose cooperation is essential for the organization's survival, or those whose lives are significantly affected by the organization.[39]

Strategic constituency

Any group of people with a stake in the organization's operation or success.

Strategic constituencies (or stakeholders) generally have competing or conflicting interests.[40] This forces executives to do some strategic juggling to achieve workable balances. This explains Facebook's decision to become an observer for at least 12 months prior to 2014 when considering full membership with the Global Network Initiative (GNI), a non-government organization dedicated to promoting Internet freedom and privacy rights. To ensure their values are congruent, Facebook representatives will attend policy and learning sessions before adopting the GNI principles, which require them to be assessed and audited by an outside third-party.[41] (See the following International OB feature box for more on this topic).

MIXING EFFECTIVENESS CRITERIA: PRACTICAL GUIDELINES

Experts on the subject recommend a multidimensional approach to assessing the effectiveness of modern organizations. This means no single criterion is appropriate for all stages of the organization's life cycle. Nor will a single criterion satisfy competing stakeholders. For example, if goal accomplishment is the only criteria used to measure effectiveness, then profit maximization takes priority over all other factors. This is like saying that as a student, you have only benefited from a class or shown evidence of learning when you earned a grade of 95 percent . . . and that is probably not true. So, reaching a goal or number alone doesn't equal knowledge learned or a standard of effectiveness.

Well-managed organizations mix and match effectiveness criteria to fit the unique requirements of the situation.[42] It's worth stressing that applying all four criteria at once is unrealistic, as organizations don't operate in a perfect world with perfect information and unlimited resources. So, when evaluating an organizations' effectiveness, it's better to prioritize and fit the criteria to a strategic plan.

GLOBAL NETWORK INITIATIVE WELCOMES FACEBOOK

As Facebook continues to evolve into a dominant player of social media, it will have to consider its organizational effectiveness based on strategic constituencies satisfaction. The interest group that has been courting Facebook for some time is the Global Network Initiative (GNI), a non-profit human rights organization dedicated to promoting freedom of expression in the IT area while protecting privacy rights.

Over the last few years, Facebook has been used, along with other social media, by activists in Egypt and Tunisia to organize demonstrations and identify human rights abuses. At the same time, social media has been used to track activists and monitor their activities, which is a great threat to GNI in terms of violating the fundamental human right of privacy. With over 1 billion users worldwide, Facebook is considering whether to join Microsoft, Yahoo!, and Google as an official high profile corporate member—which would add instant credibility to GNI and show a united front of common values between the world's leading IT organizations.

Before joining officially, Facebook has agreed to sign a short-term observer-only contract with GNI, allowing Facebook representatives to learn more about GNI principles. Marne Levine, Facebook vice president for global public policy, stated that the company wants to work with GNI and its members "to promote a free and open Internet. Building a better understanding of the value of the open Internet and its direct impact on job creation, education and good governance, is critical, and precisely where the work of GNI can be useful," said Levine. By 2014–15, Facebook is expected to make their final official membership decision with GNI, showing concern and consideration for an outside interest group.

SOURCES: J. Constine, "Facebook's Amended S-1: 901 Million Users, 500M Mobile, Paid $300M Cash + 23M Shares For Instagram," *TechCrunch*, April 23, 2012 techcrunch.com/2012/04/23/facebooks-amended-s-1-500-million-mobile-users-paid-300m-cash-23-million-shares-for-instagram/; Global Network Initiative website FAQ, www.globalnetworkinitiative.org; A. Ganesan, "Facebook Becomes an Official Observer at Web Freedom Group," *The Economic Times of India*, May 3, 2012; and D. Durbin, "Facebook's Decision to Join Global Network Initiative as an Observer," *Facebook*, May 3, 2012, posting cited online @ 1:10pm.

The Contingency Approach to Designing Organizations

According to the *contingency approach to organization design*, organizations tend to be more effective when they are structured to fit the demands of the situation.[43] The purpose of this section is to introduce you to the contingency approach to organization design by reviewing a landmark study, showing the differences between centralized and decentralized decision making, and comparing new-style and old-style organizations.

MECHANISTIC VERSUS ORGANIC ORGANIZATIONS

A pair of British behavioural scientists, Tom Burns and G.M. Stalker, conducted a landmark contingency design study. In the course of their research, they drew a very useful distinction between what they call mechanistic and organic organizations. *Mechanistic organizations*

> **Contingency approach to organization design**
>
> Creating an effective organization that is a good fit with its environment and the customer it serves.

> **Mechanistic organizations**
>
> Rigid, closed system of command-and-control bureaucracies that follow formal policies and procedures.

are bureaucracies with strict rules, narrowly defined tasks, and top-down communication. They are typically rigid, formalized in terms of following policy and procedure, and comparable to a closed system that operates in a self-sufficient manner. Ironically, it is at the cutting edge of technology that this seemingly out-of-date approach has found a home. In the highly competitive business of Web hosting—running clients' Web sites in high-security facilities humming with Internet servers—speed and reliability are everything. Enter military-style managers who require strict discipline, faithful observance to policies and rules, and flawless execution. But, as *BusinessWeek* observed, "The strictly controlled atmosphere and military themes . . . may be tough to stomach for skilled workers used to a more free-spirited atmosphere."[44] A few examples of mechanistic organizations are Scouts Canada, Girl Guides Canada, RCMP, Tim Horton's, McDonald's, and Walmart. The operations are highly regimented, dependent on large policy manuals for guidance, with strict rules on how to run the business. In the case of fast food chains, much is regimented: recipes, promotions, price-points, uniforms, and how to greet a customer correctly.

In comparison, *organic organizations* are fluid and flexible networks, similar to the open systems mentioned earlier. These kinds of firms rely less on formalized policies and procedures to provide direction, problem solving guidelines, and directions. Typically, you'll find multi-talented individuals working for these firms who are expected to perform a variety of tasks.[45] Examples of organic organizations are Rescan Environmental Services Ltd. (a Canadian-owned environmental consulting firm), Arcis Corp. in Calgary (offers information on earth tremors and seismic solutions to energy), and Next Level Games Inc. of Vancouver (an independent, third-party videogame developer specializing in console video games).[46] All of these organizations are small enough (less than 120 full-time employees) that it's easy to flex what they do, how they operate, and the level of service given a specific customer request. The amount of inter-dependence and inter-communication that takes place on a daily basis is necessary and desired. The type of industry they are in, as well as the context of their work environment, are still fluid enough to keep rigid policies, rules, and fixed thinking away.

A Matter of Degree   Organizations tend to be relatively mechanistic or relatively organic. Pure types are rare because divisions, departments, or units within the same organization may be more or less mechanistic or organic. From an employee's standpoint, what kind of firms have you worked for in the past? Consider taking the next self-assessment, Mechanistic versus Organic Workplace, to determine the answer to this question.

Different Approaches to Decision Making   Decision making tends to be centralized in mechanistic organizations and decentralized in organic organizations. *Centralized decision making* occurs when key decisions are made by top management.

Decentralized decision making occurs when important decisions are made by middle- and lower-level managers and empowered non-managerial employees. Generally, centralized organizations are more tightly controlled, while decentralized organizations are more adaptive to changing situations.[47] Each has its appropriate use. For example,

> *Organic organizations*
>
> A fluid and flexible open systems network structure that relies less on policies and procedures for problem solving and direction.

> *Centralized decision making*
>
> All key decisions are formally made only by top managers who advise others on what to do.

> *Decentralized decision making*
>
> Mid-managers and staff employees are empowered to make important decisions without seeking top management permission or input.

both the Bank of Montreal Financial Group and WestJet are very respected and successful companies, yet the former would gravitate toward a more centralized decision-making model because of SEC compliance regulations around the products they sell, whereas the latter would prefer a more decentralized decision-making model given the numerous independent decisions that have to be made at the customer service level at every WestJet sales counter and on the hundreds of flights that occur daily.

Experts on the subject warn against extremes of centralization or decentralization. The challenge is to achieve a workable balance between the two extremes. A management consultant put it this way:

> *The modern organization in transition will recognize the pull of two polarities: a need for greater centralization to create low-cost shared resources; and, a need to improve market responsiveness with greater decentralization. Today's winning organizations are the ones that can handle the paradox and tensions of both pulls. These are the firms that analyze the optimum organizational solution in each particular circumstance, without prejudice for one type of organization over another. The result is, almost invariably, a messy mixture of decentralized units sharing cost-effective centralized resources.[48]*

Centralization and decentralization are not an either–or proposition; they are more of a balancing act.

Practical Research Insights   When they classified a sample of actual companies as either mechanistic or organic, Burns and Stalker discovered one type is not superior to the other. Each type has its appropriate place, depending on the environment. When the environment is relatively stable and certain, successful organizations tend to be mechanistic. Organic organizations tend to be the successful ones when the environment is unstable and uncertain.[49]

In a more recent study of 103 department managers from eight manufacturing firms and two aerospace organizations, managerial skill was found to have a greater impact on a global measure of department effectiveness in organic departments than in mechanistic departments. This led the researchers to recommend the following contingencies for management staffing and training:

> *If we have two units, one organic and one mechanistic, and two potential applicants differing in overall managerial ability, we might want to assign the more competent*

LO 6

Mechanistic versus Organic?

INSTRUCTIONS: Think of your present (or a past) place of employment. For each characteristic listed, circle the number that best reflects the workplace. Calculate a total score by adding up all eight circled numbers. Compare your score to the scale provided.

---

1 Task definition and knowledge required

NARROW, TECHNICAL 1 2 3 4 5 6 7 BROAD, GENERAL

2 Linkage between individual's contribution and organization's purpose

VAGUE, INDIRECT 1 2 3 4 5 6 7 CLEAR, DIRECT

3 Task flexibility

RIGID, ROUTINE 1 2 3 4 5 6 7 FLEXIBLE, VARIED

4 Specification of techniques, obligations, and rights

SPECIFIC 1 2 3 4 5 6 7 GENERAL

5 Degree of hierarchical control

HIGH 1 2 3 4 5 6 7 LOW (SELF-CONTROL EMPHASIZED)

6 Primary communication pattern

TOP-DOWN 1 2 3 4 5 6 7 LATERAL (BETWEEN PEERS)

7 Primary decision-making style

AUTHORITARIAN 1 2 3 4 5 6 7 DEMOCRATIC, PARTICIPATIVE

8 Emphasis on obedience and loyalty

HIGH 1 2 3 4 5 6 7 LOW

Total score = _____

Scale

8–24 = Relatively mechanistic workplace
25–39 = A mix of both structures
40–56 = Relatively organic workplace

SOURCE: Adapted from discussion in T. Burns and G.M. Stalker, *The Management of Innovation* (London: Tavistock, 1961), pp 119–25.

to the organic unit since in that situation there are few structural aids available to the manager in performing required responsibilities. It is also possible that managerial training is especially needed by managers being groomed to take over units that are more organic in structure.[50]

Another interesting finding comes from a study of 42 voluntary church organizations. As the organizations became more mechanistic (more bureaucratic), the intrinsic motivation (see Chapter 5) of their members decreased. Mechanistic organizations apparently undermined the volunteers' sense of freedom and self-determination. Additionally, the researchers believe their findings help explain why bureaucracy tends to feed on itself: "A mechanistic organizational structure may breed the need for a more extremely mechanistic system because of the reduction in intrinsically motivated behaviour."[51] Thus, bureaucracy creates greater bureaucracy.

Most recently, field research in two factories, one mechanistic and the other organic, found expected communication patterns. Command-and-control (downward) communication characterized the mechanistic factory. Consultative or participative (two-way) communication prevailed in the organic factory.[52]

Both Mechanistic and Organic Structures Have their Places Although achievement-oriented students of OB typically express a distaste for mechanistic organizations, not all organizations or subunits can or should be organic. For example, McDonald's could not achieve its admired quality and service standards without extremely mechanistic restaurant operations. Imagine the food and service you would get if McDonald's employees used their personal preferred ways of doing things and worked at their own pace! On the other hand, the mechanistic structure alienates some employees and stakeholders because they believe it erodes their sense of empowerment, autonomy, and self-managment.

Some mechanistic organizations are trying to change. For example, consider Parks Canada, the large federal government agency that is the guardian of the national parks of Canada. Because of its affiliation with the government of Canada, it tends to have a traditional structure steeped in public sector bureaucracy. It represents a classic mechanistic organization because of its large size, the nature of the service it provides, and the rigid standards it must adhere to. But within Parks Canada, there has been some successful movement toward stakeholder empowerment and sharing decision-making responsibilities by establishing a hybrid management structure that addresses the diverse needs of local Aboriginal groups. This is a big step for the federal government (see the Focus on Diversity feature box for more on Parks Canada).

NEW-STYLE VERSUS OLD-STYLE ORGANIZATIONS

Organization theorists Jay R. Galbraith and Edward E. Lawler III have called for a "new logic of organizing."[53] They recommend a whole new set of adjectives to describe organizations (see Table 12.1). Traditional

TABLE 12.1

NEW-STYLE VERSUS OLD-STYLE ORGANIZATIONS

NEW	OLD
Dynamic, learning	Stable
Information rich	Information is scarce
Global	Local
Small and large	Large
Product/customer oriented	Functional
Team oriented	Job oriented
Skills oriented	Individual oriented
Command/control oriented	Involvement oriented
Lateral/networked	Hierarchical
Customer oriented	Job requirements oriented

SOURCE: From J.R. Galbraith and E.E. Lawler III, "Effective Organizations: Using the New Logic of Organizing," in *Organizing for the Future: The New Logic for Managing Complex Organizations,* eds J.R. Galbraith, E.E. Lawler III, and Associates, 1993, p 298. Copyright © 1993 John Wiley & Sons, Inc. Reprinted with permission of John Wiley & Sons, Inc.

PARKS CANADA NEW MANAGEMENT STRUCTURE AT WOOD BUFFALO PARK

Parks Canada oversees all of Canada's national parks, including Wood Buffalo National Park, which spans the boundary of Alberta and the Northwest Territories. It encompasses 44,807 square kilometres and is Canada's largest national park. Established in 1922 to protect the last free roaming herds of wood bison in northern Canada, Wood Buffalo National Park has been recognized by the UN for its many natural wonders. In 2010, a significant five-year management plan was cooperatively developed by Parks Canada with Wood Buffalo National Park that recognized the need for stronger relationships within the diverse group of stakeholders from local communities in and around the area. The plan set the stage for Parks Canada to establish a management structure with local Aboriginal groups.

Key actions highlighted within the management plan include:

- Building and developing a management structure between Parks Canada and local Aboriginal groups

- Collaborating with local Aboriginal groups and local communities to create a Vision Statement

- Working with the diverse communities around the park to expand partnering opportunities and incorporate Wood Buffalo National Park into their tourism offer

- Engaging local Aboriginal groups in cultural and ecological research and monitoring programs

Parks Canada has worked hard over the past 50 years to earn the reputation as an international leader in working with Aboriginal peoples. "In the past few decades, we have strived to build meaningful relationships with First Nations, Inuit, and Metis peoples to ensure a more holistic stewardship of the land that includes the cultural values and knowledge of its people," says Alan Latourelle, CEO Parks Canada.

This large federal agency demonstrates progressive thinking and policy making within a public sector environment that is typically known for its mechanistic characteristics. Their ongoing effort toward building authentic relationships with diverse groups, especially those living within the Wood Buffalo National Park region of Canada, is worth noting.

SOURCES: M. Keizer, External Relations Manager at Parks Canada, PO Box 750, Fort Smith, NT X0E 0P0–Telephone interview July 17, 2012; H. Tammemagi, "Many of Canada's National Parks Now Honor First Nations People," *Indian Country - Today Media Network,* July 13, 2012, www.indiancountrytodaymedianetwork.com; Parks Canada website, www.pc.gc.ca–May 2012; and National Parks of Canada, Wood Buffalo National Park, Park Management, 2010 Management Plan.

pyramid-shaped organizations, conforming to the old-style pattern, tend to be too slow and inflexible. They are typically bureaucratic and centralized in their decision-making process, but the forces of change are so strong that even the toughest has had to surrender somewhat, as was the case in the Parks Canada example. And that is the challenge for all old-style organizations that succeeded in the old paradigm but are fighting for their life in the new cost-conscious competitive economic model.

Leaner, more open-system and organic-structured organizations are increasingly needed to accommodate a strategic balancing act between cost, quality, and speed. These new-style organizations are customer-focused, dedicated to continuous improvement and learning, and structured around teams. These qualities, along with computerized information technology, will hopefully enable big organizations to mimic the speed and flexibility of small organizations.

Summary of Learning Objectives

LO 1 Define *organization, organizational structure,* and *unity of command.* An organization is a system of coordinated activities of two or more people. Organizational structure is a reference made to four factors: (1) coordination of effort (achieved through policies and rules); (2) a common goal (a collective purpose); (3) division of labour (people performing different but related tasks); and (4) a hierarchy of authority (the chain of command). Unity of command principle is a historical belief that each employee should report to a single manager. This is significant to appreciate because this belief leads to taller, narrower, and eventually more layers of management type of structures that eventually become bureaucracies.

LO 2 Explain the process of how organizations grow and the effect growth has on span of control. Mintzberg states that organizations come to life as a result of an entrepreneur who has an idea. That idea gives way to an owner/operator who recognizes the need to hire employees to complete basic tasks for the organization to reach the goal; they are called the operating core of the business. As the organization grows, the owner/operator takes on more line managers to oversee the coordination of effort within the operating core, hence division of labour occurs. The organization may also find that it needs two kinds of staff personnel: (1) analysts who design systems concerned with planning and the control of work tasks, and (2) support staff who provide indirect services to the rest of the organization. Span of control is typically stated as a ratio and refers to the number of people reporting directly to a given manager. In the past, as organizations grew, the span of control was kept very narrow because of the unity of command principle; hence the organizations were tall and narrow. The more contemporary model is to have a wider span of control (higher ratio), as emphasis has shifted to leanness and efficiency. This trend also complements greater worker autonomy and empowerment; as a result this has created flatter and wider organizational structures.

LO 3 Describe six possible departmentation structures with examples. Departmentation is organizing work by grouping jobs together to gain greater efficiency and maintain effectiveness in providing customer service. The six types of structures discussed include: (1) functional—work separated using functional areas as guides (marketing, accounting/finance, human services, production); (2) product—work grouped together based on product, product line, or service category (car division, truck division, tank division); (3) matrix—workers remain in their functional areas but are temporarily assigned to work on time-limited projects with other employees found throughout the organization (cross-functional teams); (4) geographic—workers and tasks are dispersed to the geographic territories where products or services are needed (Western Region, Atlantic Regions, Quebec); (5) customer—specific product groups are housed in almost self-contained environments to better serve each unique customer group (opening a separate office to serve the needs of just one dominant customer, like Walmart or the Canadian Government); and (6) hybrid—a combination of structures that may include any of the other departmentation structures mentioned above (head offices that are functionally structured but regional offices that are structured in specific geographic areas to serve specific customer needs).

Compare and contrast contemporary structures with bureaucratic and open systems. There are six contemporary structures: cross-functional team structures, outsourcing, network, virtual, modular, and boundaryless organizations. All of the contemporary structures can be considered to be more open than closed systems. This means that each of these structures considers the necessity of the organization to remain in somewhat constant interaction with its environment to survive, so their structures can flex as needed because they are flatter/wider. Open system organizations tend to operate in a self-corrective, adaptable, and real-time manner. In comparison, a bureaucracy tends to be a closed system, as it is slow to respond to the outside environment because it is so big and consuming of its own resources; typically bureaucracies are tall/narrow structures that are slow to change and fixed-cost heavy. Although Weber identified a bureaucracy as the most efficient of all structures, the study of micro-economics provides strong evidence that large structures are especially inefficient.

 Summarize the criteria that can be used to assess organization effectiveness. There are many approaches to take in sizing up performance, and each industry and company will have its own metrics based on the key performance drivers. Experts on the subject of organizational effectiveness recommend a multi-dimensional approach. This means no single criterion is appropriate for all stages of the organization's life cycle. Nor will a single criterion satisfy competing stakeholders. Well-managed organizations mix and match effectiveness criteria to fit the unique requirements of the situation, including: (1) goal accomplishment (satisfying stated objectives), (2) resource acquisition (gathering the necessary productive inputs), (3) internal processes (building and maintaining healthy organizational systems), and (4) strategic constituencies satisfaction (achieving at least minimal satisfaction for all key stakeholders).

LO 6 **Integrate the Burns and Stalker contingency design with old-style and new-style organizations.** British researchers Burns and Stalker found that mechanistic (bureaucratic, centralized) organizations tended to be effective in stable situations. In unstable situations, organic (flexible, decentralized) organizations were more effective. These findings underscored the need for a contingency approach to organization design. New-style organizations are characterized as being more organic as they are dynamic and learning, information rich, global, small and large, product/customer oriented, skills oriented, team oriented, involvement oriented, lateral networked, and customer oriented. Old-style organizations are characterized as being more mechanistic as they tend to be more stable, larger, functional, command/control oriented, hierarchical, and job-requirements oriented.

Discussion Questions

1. Draw an example of an organization chart for your current (or last) place of employment. Does your chart reveal the hierarchy (chain of command), division of labour, span of control, and line-staff distinctions? Does it reveal anything else? Explain.

2. Why is it appropriate to view modern organizations as open systems?

3. If organic organizations are popular with most employees, why can't all organizations be structured in an organic fashion?

4. In your opinion, which of the six organizational structures discussed in this chapter will be most common 20 years from now? Which will be the least common? Explain your response.

Integration of OB Concepts—Discussion Questions

1. See Chapter 3–Which of the Big Five Personality Dimensions would be most likely to work in an organic open organizational structure? Relate the factors of self-concept (i.e., self-efficacy, self-monitoring, and the social learning model of self-management) to organizational structure type. What type of person would be best suited for a mechanistic structured firm? Explain your reasoning for both questions.

2. See Chapter 7–How does organizational structure influence communication?

3. See Chapter 9–How does organizational structure influence empowerment and decision-making responsibilities?

4. See Chapter 10–How does organizational structure influence leader recruitment/selection, leadership success, leadership style, leadership vision, etc.?

5. See Chapter 11–What is the relationship between culture and organizational structure? It's been said that organizational culture can be considered the unofficial structure of the organization; it can also supplement the formal structure or it can substitute for it. Do you agree with this statement? Why or why not?

Google Searches

1. **Google Search:** "_____ college" OR "_____ university" Find the organizational structure of your own institution. See if you can determine where your professor is located on the organizational chart.

2. **Google Search:** "IKEAFANS IKEA Corporate Structure" Working with a team of three people, draw the modular organizational structure of IKEA on a large piece of flipchart paper. Start with Stichting INGKA Foundation, since they own INGKA Holding B.V. Use circles, arrows, and connecting lines to identify relationships between companies. Be prepared to share your drawing with the class. What makes this structure so different and appealing to global organizations? Do you think there will be more or fewer of these sort of structures in the future? Why or why not?

3. **Google Search:** "RIM Organization Chart" AND "Ownership Chart - BCE–Corporate Structure" AND "Ottawa Police Services Organizational Chart" AND "Behaviour Interactive Inc. Management Team" Compare and contrast the four charts. Identify the type of departmentation and structure for each. Relate the two possible metaphors. Which has an open and which has a closed structure? Explain if they are mechanistic or organic in nature. Explain your reasoning.

4. **Google Search:** "Balanced Scorecard–Malcolm Baldrige National Quality Program" OR www.balancedscorecard.org - What Is the Balanced Scorecard? OR "The Balanced Scorecard–Measures That Drive Performance–Harvard Business Review Jan 1992) Summarize this model of organizational effectiveness. Find a graphic of this model. Compare it to and contrast it with the model found in this chapter. Find at least two advantages and disadvantages of each model. Identify appropriate application(s) of each model in terms of business use. Be prepared to share your responses with class.

Experiential Exercise

Strengths and Weaknesses of Structure Type Group Exercise

PURPOSE This exercise is meant to familiarize you with the six departmentation and six contemporary organizational structures discussed in this chapter. By participating in this group activity, you should gain a greater understanding of the concepts and the differences between various departmentation and structure types found in business today. Approx. Timing: 35 minutes.

ACTIVITY ASSIGNMENT

- If necessary, review Figures 12.2, 12.3, and 12.4 before beginning the exercise.
- Work in small groups. Fill in the chart to describe at least two strengths and two weaknesses of each type of departmentation listed.
- After approximately 20 minutes, share your group's responses with the rest of the class.

TYPE	STRENGTHS	WEAKNESSES
Functional Departmentation		
Product Departmentation		
Matrix Departmentation		
Geographic Departmentation		
Customer Departmentation		
Hybrid Departmentation		
Cross Functional Team Structure		
Outsourcing Structure		
Network Structure		
Virtual Structure		
Modular Structure		
Boundaryless Structure		

OB In Action Case Study

The Ongoing Restructuring at Air Canada

BACKGROUND

In January 2001, Air Canada acquired Canada's second largest air carrier, Canadian Airlines. For the next two years, Air Canada tried to make it work, but there were more problems than it could handle: it owed creditors over $900 million, it was running a pension deficit of $1.8 billion, and the company began to consider bankruptcy protection. By April 2003, Air Canada had no choice—it filed for bankruptcy, and for the next 18 months it looked for a buyer who could get it back on its feet. In the fall of 2004, the reorganized Air Canada was placed under a new parent company called ACE Aviation Holdings. As dictated by the financing package, the airline had to review its mission, overall operations, leadership and organizational structure, product offerings, and strategic direction. By 2006, the firm was out of bankruptcy protection and celebrated its 70th anniversary. In 2008, Air Canada was reporting sound financial results as it moved closer to accomplishing higher revenues, planned fleet revamping, higher on-time arrival performance levels, strategic commercial alliances with other North American carriers, and improved fleet/operational efficiencies.

PAINS OF RESTRUCTURING

Years of restructuring at Air Canada had its painful human side. When Air Canada decided to cut costs between 2004–06, it meant closing flight attendant bases in Halifax and Winnipeg that resulted in 345 people losing their jobs. Soon after, another layoff announcement was made eliminating 300 more jobs in Vancouver, with plans to cut 2,000 additional positions across the country. "The loss of jobs is painful in view of our employees' hard work in bringing the airline back to profitability," president and CEO at the time Montie Brewer said. "I regret having to take these actions, but they are necessary to remain competitive going forward," he said. Some people disagreed with the downsizing effort. Joseph D'Cruz, a University of Toronto business professor and airline industry analyst said, "I'm really concerned Air Canada is going to get itself into a vicious cycle. As morale goes down, the treatment that frontline employees offer to passengers is bound to suffer. In the airline business, everything depends on how the frontline employees behave."

The journey has been a long and at times difficult process, but that is common when an organization considers how it needs to be structured and designed to operate effectively and efficiently to remain competitive. Air Canada has had to reinvent itself. Old strategies have been abandoned in favour of a new business template, for example, new brands like A.C. Jetz for sports-team travel and upscale corporate clients, and new subsidiaries like Jazz that appeals to the low-fare traveller. These changes seemed to be working. Or were they? Despite these changes, the airline ended up with a net loss of $249 million in 2010 and was another $24 million in the red for 2011. And this was during a period when the US competitor North American airlines earned $4.1 billion (US), according to data from the International Air Transport Association. Why wasn't Air Canada experiencing the same sort of success?

WHAT WENT WRONG

When Air Canada emerged from bankruptcy protection in 2004, the strategy pitched to investors was to price-match WestJet in the domestic market while leaning on business-class travellers and higher-margin international flights to boost profitability. It worked for a few years. Then fuel prices soared and competition began stealing business. Air Canada was facing high operating costs without higher revenues—estimated costs were roughly 30 percent higher than those of rival WestJet and 50–60 percent higher than some Asian and Persian Gulf carriers.

LEADERSHIP

In 2009, Air Canada announced that Calin Rovinescu was replacing Brewer as president and CEO. Rovinescu was involved in the 2003–04 round of restructuring and had a reputation for slashing costs and debts; and that was what he focused on, but some costs were beyond Air Canada's control. For example, the airline paid roughly $3.4 billion in 2011 for fuel and another $1 billion in airport and navigation fees. In the spring of 2011, the 3,000 member Air Canada Pilots' Association voted against a tentative agreement reached by union negotiators that included plans for a new low-cost carrier to be created, complete with lower wages and benefits for employees. This concerned Rovinescu, who was hoping to create a new low-cost division of Air Canada that would begin to save the airline money, just like the Jetstar subsidiary was designed to do for Quantas. Not surprisingly, Rovinescu's plan wasn't a big hit with Air Canada's unionized workforce—particularly pilots.

Despite Air Canada's dismal financial performance, Robert Milton, the CEO of the holding company ACE Aviation that owned 11 percent of Air Canada at the time, earned more than $82 million for his role in completing the various "value-enhancing transactions" for ACE's shareholders. In 2009, Rovinescu earned $2.6 million; in 2010 and 2011 he earned roughly $4.6 million for each year (long- and short-term stock options plus compensation combined), and in March 2012 was paid a $5 million retention bonus in addition to his annual earnings. (Note: Big salaries such as these are not unusual for executives charged with turning around troubled companies.)

UNION "INCREDIBLY FRUSTRATED"

Having the first offer rejected, the airline was left with no choice but to return to the bargaining table with the pilots' union and made another 'final' offer in March 2012 that didn't include the discount carrier plan like the one offered 12 months earlier. The union membership turned this new offer down and 97 percent voted in favour of going on strike. Almost immediately, the federal government referred Air Canada's two labour disputes to the Canada Industrial Relations Board (CIRB), a move that prevented a work stoppage and effectively forced employees back to work. This came as a relief for weary Canadian travellers going south during March break, but unrest soon resurfaced several weeks later as more than 75 flights had to be grounded after 150 pilots called in sick in one day. Once again, the CIRB stepped in to declare the high volume of sick calls made by pilots amounted to an illegal strike and ordered it stopped or they would face substantial fines. The pilots' union said they did not sanction the job action and that the pilots were acting on their own. It was the third time in less than a month that the airline blamed the pilots' union for a higher-than-normal number of sick calls resulting in flight disruptions.

It's difficult to overstate the level of animosity and distrust that Air Canada workers now had for their bosses. Many felt betrayed after agreeing to over $1 billion in labour concessions during the 2003–04 restructuring, only to be asked for further cuts once those agreements expired in 2009. By August 2012, a federal arbitrator representing the CIRB sided with Air Canada, imposing a retroactive five year collective agreement with the pilot's union until April 2016. The decision was met with a strong reaction from the pilots' group that believed the imposed work rules would only cost more jobs in the future, while demoralizing all Air Canada employees and kicking other important issues years down the road. In contrast, CEO Rovinescu was quoted in the media as saying the new collective agreement "will give Air Canada the flexibility it needs to compete."

THE FUTURE

Rovinescu publicly declared that "things must change at Air Canada." Industry experts have said that asking employees to accept the changes and make sacrifices while top managers make large salaries sends the wrong message. As for Ottawa's involvement, it only delayed the inevitable. Eventually, Air Canada has to face real issues and work with unions to come up with some kind of agreement that both sides can live with. Some have suggested opening the airline industry up to more competition, currently a comfortable duopoly between Air Canada and WestJet. With Air Canada's new discount division slated to be in full operation by 2014, Rovinescu is confident they will be able to compete more efficiently in the expanding vacation destination market, as well as fly to new destinations not currently serviced.

As for the future, it appears that Canadians are stuck with the prospect of watching Air Canada struggle to survive, with Ottawa standing at the bedside ready to administer life support as needed. How many times will Air Canada have to restructure within such a volatile industry? It's anyone's guess.

Discussion Questions

1. What are important effectiveness criteria for Air Canada? (See Fig 12.6 for a reference.)

2. Should Air Canada be organic or mechanistic in nature? Explain your reasoning for what structure they currently have and what you propose.

3. Should decision making be centralized or decentralized at Air Canada? Explain.

4. Conduct a Google search 'Air Canada Organizational Chart' (Air Canada's Structure prior to 2003–04 restructuring tended to be more product focused). Based on what is happening today, what sort of departmentation model or structure would you say Air Canada needs to adopt? Explain.

SOURCES: G. Dixon, "Air Canada to Merge Vacation Business with New Discount Airline," *The Globe and Mail*, October 2, 2012, www.theglobeandmail.com; G. Hughes, "Air Canada Wins in Contract Arbitration With Pilots," *CBC News–The Canadian Press*, July 30, 2012, www.cbc.ca/news/business/story/2012/07/30/air-canada-pilots-arbitration.html; "Air Canada Pilots' Sick Calls Ruled an Illegal Strike," CBC News, April 14, 2012, www.cbc.ca; and C. Sorensen, "Air Canada's Slow Descent," *Macleans*, April 23, 2012, www2.macleans.ca/2012/04/23/a-slow-descent/.

The CONNECTion Zone Mc Graw Hill connect™

- The Presentation Assistant
- Ethical OB Dilemma
- Video Case

Mc Graw Hill **connect**™
Practise and learn online with Connect.

"The rate of change is not going to slow down anytime soon. If anything, competition in most industries will probably speed up even more in the next few decades."

John Kotter (Social Scientist and Professor at Harvard Business School)

Managing Change and Job Stress

FACING AN OB CHALLENGE

I enjoy my job at the credit union very much. I've been working part-time this past year while attending school. I graduate next spring and have been offered a job with the credit union, but I'm scared to take it because it's merging with a large investment bank that has a reputation for expecting employees to be forever-connected Type-A hustlers. That's not who we are at the credit union. We take things slower and are friendlier with our customers ... we build relationships. I'm so worried about my future and what decision I should make that I'm losing sleep, I'm cranky all the time, I've stopped exercising, and I'm stressed out. What should I do?

—NOT IN CONTROL

The Workplace Is Changing

Over the last few chapters we've discussed organizations that go through restructuring, mergers and acquisitions (M&As), the culture change it can bring, and the drive toward new leadership it can create. In a recent study, 25 percent of the 130 Canadian CEOs surveyed are planning to engage in M&As, compared to the global average of 12 percent.[1] That means that the concerns being expressed by the Canadian student in the Facing an OB Challenge are justified. M&As can be very stressful for employees and increase their risk of general anxiety disorder (GAD), according to a recent study from the University of Calgary. Employees who are exposed to M&As are 2.8 times more likely to be diagnosed with GAD within one year than those who are not.[2] This supports the claim that organizational changes can have a direct effect on employee behaviour in some way, at some point.

External environmental factors like increased global competition, startling breakthroughs in information technology, changes in social values, shifting consumer preferences, and calls for greater corporate ethics are also forcing companies to change the way they do business. In addition, matters related to internal corporate factors, such as employees wanting empowerment and demanding safe work environments, customers demanding greater value, and investors wanting more integrity in financial disclosures are also affecting many organizations. The rate of organizational and societal change is clearly accelerating.

As a result, organizations must change to satisfy employees, customers, and shareholders. However, change is also likely to encounter resistance, even when it represents an appropriate course of action. Therefore, it is critical that employees understand the forces of change that are influencing the organizations they work for, and just as important for current and future managers to learn how they can successfully implement and navigate the journey of organizational change.

Specifically, we open this chapter discussion around the forces that create the need for organization change, the models of planned change, reasons for resistance to change, and how to better manage the stress associated with organizational change.

LO 1 Forces of Change

How do organizations know when they should change? Although there is no clear-cut answer to this question, organizations will find the cues that signal the need for change by monitoring the forces for change.

Organizations encounter many different forces that create the need for change, both from external sources and from internal sources. Awareness of the forces of change can help employees understand the responses from their organization. In addition, it can help managers determine when they should consider implementing organizational change in response. The external and internal forces for change are presented in Figure 13.1.[3]

EXTERNAL FORCES

External forces for change originate outside the organization. Because these forces have global effects, they may cause an organization to question the essence of its business and the process by which products and services are produced. There are four key external forces for change: (1) demographic characteristics,

> **External forces for change**
>
> Those forces of change that originate outside the organization.

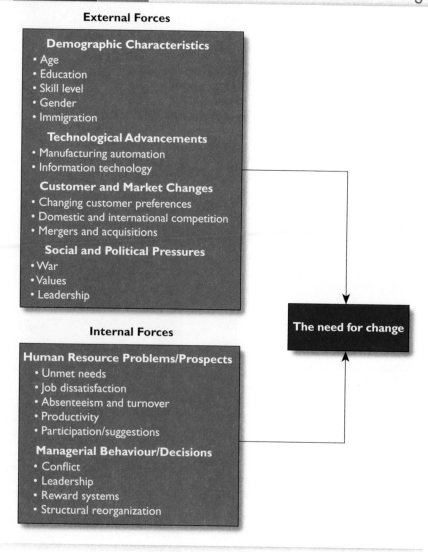

FIGURE 13.1 The External and Internal Forces for Change

External Forces

Demographic Characteristics
• Age
• Education
• Skill level
• Gender
• Immigration

Technological Advancements
• Manufacturing automation
• Information technology

Customer and Market Changes
• Changing customer preferences
• Domestic and international competition
• Mergers and acquisitions

Social and Political Pressures
• War
• Values
• Leadership

Internal Forces

Human Resource Problems/Prospects
• Unmet needs
• Job dissatisfaction
• Absenteeism and turnover
• Productivity
• Participation/suggestions

Managerial Behaviour/Decisions
• Conflict
• Leadership
• Reward systems
• Structural reorganization

The need for change

of new Canadian immigrants (over 38 percent) are from India, Pakistan, Sri Lanka, Bangladesh, and Nepal, and they hold a variety of religious beliefs (e.g., Sikh, Muslim, Buddhist, Hindu). Findings conclude that provincial, regional, and metropolitan differences will also need to be considered when assessing external market factors. The HR challenge will be to identify gaps in current hiring procedures and consider the need for a more diverse workforce. Take, for example, SportsDirect Inc. (SDI) out of Nova Scotia, voted one of Atlantic Canada's Top Employers:

How many ethnic minorities would you guess are currently working for SDI given its location and the focus of its programming content . . . a lot . . . only a few? Your response will probably be tied to the demographic profile of the region which would be predominately Canadians of Western European dissent. Established in 1995, SDI is a Halifax-based Internet publishing and broadcasting company with 55 full-time and 67 part-time employees. This unique online media company provides sports stats, sports fantasy promotional contests (predominately North American) . . . customers include provincial lotteries and gaming sites.[5]

(2) technological advancements, (3) market changes, and (4) social and political pressures. We will now discuss each of these external forces.

Demographic Characteristics Canada has a high degree of multiculturalism, ranging from ethnic to religious diversity. This is something that can be expected to continue and will be a driving external force for organizations looking to hire new employees. Statistics Canada reports that if immigration trends continue, visible minorities will account for about 20 percent of Canada's population by 2017, particularly in the large urban areas of Toronto, Montreal, and Vancouver (almost 96 percent compared to only 2.6 percent for entire Atlantic region).[4] As well, visible minority populations are expected to exceed 50 percent of Toronto's and Vancouver's populations. Survey results show the largest number

In addition to changes in multiculturalism is the age group of the Canadian workforce. A recent report states that Baby Boomers (born after WWII) are making up less of the Canadian workforce, and the ones left working have a declining promotion rate. Filling their positions are Gen-Ys and Gen-Xs. The promotion rates for Gen-Xs is unexpectedly falling as the younger, more aggressive, and tech savvy Gen-Ys are expressing intent to rise quickly through the ranks. Keeping the older Gen-Xs motivated will be an HR challenge.[6] The young members of the labour market entering the workforce during the next 20 years will be even more technologically equipped, and therefore armed with the most powerful tools for business.[7]

Staying with our example of SDI, how many Baby Boomers and Gen Xs would you estimate are employed at the company? The following statistics

would suggest there are few, if any, Baby Boomers: the longest serving SDI employee has 16 years with the company and the average age of all employees is 28.[8]

Technological Advancements The primary drivers of the Industrial Age, machines and capital have long been discussed in economic courses as the labour–capital debate—do we increase productivity and output by hiring more labour? Or, do we invest in more capital assets instead and let the technology increase output? Both manufacturing and service organizations are increasingly using technology as a means to lower total costs in the long run, improve productivity, competitiveness, and customer service. Here is where the clash occurs, because although the Industrial Age still has a strong

Like many, this girl will inherit her parent's old tablet.[15] Here the music stand holds an electronic sheet of music. When it comes to using technology, what expectations will she have as a consumer or future employee? This is behaviour that forces change.

presence in today's workplace, affordable information technology (IT) and supercomputers are allowing us to live in a Knowledge Worker Age.[9] As a management expert stated, "To thrive in the Knowledge Worker Age, we must move beyond effectiveness to a level of greatness . . . accessing a higher level of human genius."[10] Computers can facilitate that genius—a practical example would be the growth of tablets and smartphones. Consider the following data:

It is predicted that global smartphone sales will continue to increase significantly year-on-year with estimates reaching 982 million units in 2015 and 1 billion in 2016.[11] By the time you read this textbook passage, annual smartphone sales will have exceeded those of PCs.[12] The vast majority of owners of smartphones will be 25–34 years of age.[13]

As for tablet use, within 17 months, tablet sales increased 12 percent in Canada. Apple's iPad is clearly the dominant brand of choice among consumers, with almost 50 percent market share.[14]

Thought at first to be primarily for personal use, we have all witnessed different people across generations and cultures using tablets and smartphones for learning, training, or professional purposes. Consider the photo at left of the little girl using a tablet in place of sheet music. Executives are now realizing the potential these tools have for achieving higher contribution levels within organizations. Companies able to leverage the use of computers by blending IT applications across their service networks and overall operations will benefit in the long run through higher productivity.

Customer and Market Changes Customers are simply demanding more than they did in the past. Moreover, customers are likely to shop elsewhere if they do not get what they want because of lower customer switching costs. A recent report stated that Canada's total "Internet Economy" is expected to be 3.6 percent of the country's total GDP by 2016, which translates into $76 billion.[16] What do you think such statistics would mean to Green Beanery, Canada's largest online retailer of coffee and coffee equipment? Consider how the following information would impact a company like the Green Beanery:

The Internet will drive significant economic growth over the next five to 10 years—global research is showing that by 2016, nearly half of the world's population will be Internet users. As the Internet population swells, the Internet economy in the G20 countries is expected to reach $4.2 trillion.[17]

With respect to market changes, service companies are experiencing increased pressure to obtain more productivity because competition is fierce and prices have remained relatively stable.[18] Further, the emergence of a global economy is forcing companies to change the way they do business.[19] Canadian companies have been forging new partnerships and alliances with their suppliers and potential competitors to gain a competitive advantage in the global marketplace.[20]

> For example, a survey by Ernst & Young found that 44 percent of Canadian companies expect to engage in M&As leading up to 2014 (which is an estimated 22 percent increase over the previous year). This statistic is significantly more than only 25 percent of their global counterparts.[21] As for acquisitions outside of Canada, a recent survey found Canadian executives interested in M&A destinations that included US, China, Hong Kong, Singapore, and India. They identify financial services, life sciences (including health care), consumer products, oil and gas, and technology as the most active in acquisitions.[22]

The super-network structures (discussed in Chapter 11) find ways to send operations and production either out to a different source or offshore to lower their total costs.

Social and Political Pressures These forces are created by social and political events, such as social pressure and political pressure (e.g., an increase in demand for green products, or pressure to legislate a ban on the sale of chemical lawn products in certain communities).

In general, social and political pressure is exerted through legislative bodies that represent the Canadian population.[23] Political events can also create substantial change.

> For example, the increased need for oil in North America has attracted a lot of attention at TransCanada Corp, Canada's premier pipeline builder, who remains fully committed to the construction of the Keystone XL pipeline from the tar sands of Canada to the Gulf of Mexico. Although the US initially rejected the pipeline, TransCanada's CEO Russ Girling said, "(the company) will reapply for a permit and expect a new application to be processed by late 2014." Alison Redford, the premier of Canada's oil-rich province of Alberta, said she was disappointed in the US decision because the project is expected to produce many Canadian jobs. Environmental groups, on the other hand, cheered the decision.[24]

Although it is difficult for organizations to predict changes in political forces, many organizations hire consultants to help them detect and respond to social and political changes.

Organizational Crises An organizational crisis may result from an accident, ignored problems that build over time, acts of nature, geopolitical instability, or criminal acts.

> For example, when civil war broke out in Libya in 2011, three Canadian companies—Suncor Energy, SNC-Lavalin, and Pure Technologies—had to move quickly to evacuate employees. While the situation in the Middle East surprised many, such disruptions can happen pretty quickly according to Stephen Cryne, president and CEO of the Canadian Employee Relocation Council. Cryne cited a few past crisis events in Canada: the SARS pandemic (virus) of 2004, the H1N1 Swine Flu pandemic that surfaced in 2009, and the XL E. coli beef recall of 2012.[25]

In each of these situations, an organizational crisis forced significant change upon the firm and its stakeholders. There was no hiding from the forces; they had to be dealt with.

INTERNAL FORCES

Internal forces for change come from inside the organization. These forces can be subtle, such as low job satisfaction, or can manifest in outward signs, such as low productivity or high turnover and conflict. Internal forces for change come from a variety of sources, such as: human resource problems; managerial preferences or decisions; organizational processes, systems, structure, or culture; or insufficient resources in general.

Internal forces for change

Forces of change that originate from inside the organization.

Human Resource Problems or Prospects These problems stem from employee perceptions about how they are treated at work, and the match between individual and organizational needs and desires. In earlier chapters, we discussed the relationship between an employee's unmet needs and job dissatisfaction. Dissatisfaction is a symptom of an underlying employee problem that should be addressed. Unusual or high levels of absenteeism and turnover also represent forces for change. Alberta's labour shortage in the oil sands sector is an example of this:

> The oil sands sector of Alberta is projected to grow its workforce by 73 percent by 2021. Some oil sands operations and occupations are expected to add more than 100 percent of their current workforce by 2021. Demand for more workers is being driven by organizations expanding, retirements, turnover, and replacement of Gen-X & -Y workers who don't feel accepted or valued by their older colleagues.[26]

Managerial Preferences or Decisions Preferences for certain policies, procedures, and directions can be strong internal forces, as the ideology and philosophy of key executives becomes old-style and perhaps counter to external forces. For example, consider the change in focus at RIM only a few months after co-founders Jim Balsillie and Mike Lazaridis stepped down:

CEO Thorsten Heins acknowledged RIM's 'extremely challenging' position in North America, which analysts considered a refreshing departure from the 'stay tuned' mantra of Balsillie. When Heins stated, "BlackBerry cannot succeed if we try to be all things to all people," . . . a senior technology analyst for the industry responded, "This is a good step. At least (RIM) is showing more reality about the marketplace." This is something industry analysts said former company executives never did. [27]

Organizational Processes, Systems, Structure, or Culture

The way an organization is structured, as well as the systems or processes that are in place, may be inadequate to accomplish desired goals and new strategies.

For example, when the Canadian Tourism Commission (CTC) wrote their five-year strategic plan (2012–2016), they identified a lack of innovation and entrepreneurial development among tourism businesses who resist 'selling' Canada using new tools (i.e., social media, apps for smart phones, etc.). Industry members are resistant to new ideas. In order for the CTC to achieve its goal of increased tourism to Canada, it must change the culture within the Canadian tourism industry. [28]

Insufficient Resources
A lack of resources is a very common problem for corporations. Insufficient land, labour, and capital place tremendous pressure on the organization, because it brings into question whether the organization's goals and objectives can be achieved. It's worth mentioning that having resources on site may not be enough if they don't work or they are not reliable and things need to change. For example, a recent survey found malfunctioning office technology as a major source of frustration for employees, such as a laptop that freezes, a printer that refuses to print, or a temperamental (fussy) projector.

"It is not surprising that 62 percent of Canadians find work stressful. What is surprising is the number of respondents who attribute their stress to workplace technology that doesn't work," says Melissa Moore, social media and communications manager at Toshiba of Canada. [29]

Models and Dynamics of Planned Change

Researchers have tried to identify effective ways to manage the change process within organizations. This section identifies three types of change and then reviews three models of planned change: (1) Lewin's change model, (2) a systems model of change, and (3) Kotter's eight steps for leading organizational change and organizational development.

TYPES OF CHANGE

There are three types of change (See Figure 13.2): adaptive, innovative, and radically innovative.

- **Adaptive change** is lowest in complexity, cost, and uncertainty. It involves reimplementation of a change in the same organizational unit at a later time, or imitation of a similar change by a different unit. Adaptive changes are not particularly threatening to employees because they are familiar.

  For example, an adaptive change for a department store would be to rely on 12-hour days during the annual inventory week. The store's accounting department could imitate the same change in work hours during tax preparation time.

- **Innovative changes** fall somewhere in the middle in terms of complexity, cost, and uncertainty. Unfamiliarity, and hence greater uncertainty, makes fear of change a problem with innovative changes.

  For example, an experiment with flexible work schedules by a farm supply warehouse company qualifies as an innovative change if it entails modifying hours of operation and accessibility from other firms in the industry who already use the warehouse.

- **Radically innovative** changes are typically complex and costly, and create high degrees of uncertainty. Changes of this sort are the most difficult to implement and tend to be the most threatening to managerial confidence and employee job security. Radical changes must be supported by an organization's culture. Organizational change is more likely to fail if it is inconsistent with any of the three levels of organizational culture: observable artifacts, espoused values, and basic assumptions (recall our discussion from Chapter 11).

LEWIN'S CHANGE MODEL `LO 2`

Most theories of organizational change originate from the landmark work of social psychologist Kurt Lewin. He developed a three-stage model of planned change that explained how to initiate, manage, and stabilize

FIGURE   **13.2**   A Generic Typology of Organizational Change

Reintroducing a familiar practice

Introducing a practice new to the organization

Introducing a practice new to the industry

Low |————————————————————————————————| High

Degree of complexity, cost, and uncertainty
Potential for resistance to change

the change process.[30] The three stages are unfreezing, changing, and refreezing, as shown in Figure 13.3.

Unfreezing   The focus of this stage is to create the motivation to change. In so doing, individuals are encouraged to replace old behaviours and attitudes with those desired by management. Managers can begin the unfreezing process by disconfirming the usefulness of employees' present behaviours or attitudes. Crises are especially likely to stimulate unfreezing.

For example, the Ornge air ambulance scandal in Ontario saw the provincial auditor detail how senior management and some board members set up a complex web of private companies. The report described an elaborate scheme to misdirect millions of dollars of public money, right under the nose of the government.[31] Leaked documents to the media showed Ornge was running a $14.5 million deficit and absorbing a 654 percent yearly increase in maintenance costs for its new Italian-made helicopters.[32] Once identified, an investigation from the OPP forced Ornge to change its current operations.[33]

Changing   Organizational change, whether large or small, is undertaken to improve some process, procedure, product, service, or outcome of interest to management. Because change involves learning and doing things differently, this stage entails providing employees with new information, new behavioural models, new processes or procedures, new equipment, new technology, or new ways of getting the job done.

Organizational change can be aimed at improvement or growth, or it can focus on solving a problem such as poor customer service or low productivity.

FIGURE   **13.3**   Lewin's Three-Step Change Model

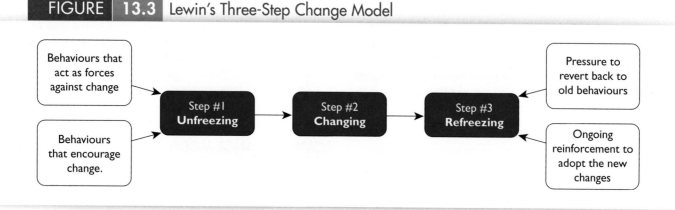

Behaviours that act as forces against change

Behaviours that encourage change.

Step #1 **Unfreezing**

Step #2 **Changing**

Step #3 **Refreezing**

Pressure to revert back to old behaviours

Ongoing reinforcement to adopt the new changes

Change also can be targeted at different levels in an organization.

For example, sending managers to leadership training programs can improve individuals' job satisfaction and productivity. In contrast, installing new information technology may be the change required to increase work group productivity and overall corporate profits.

The point to keep in mind is that change should be targeted at some type of desired end-result.

Refreezing Change is stabilized during refreezing by helping employees integrate the changed behaviour or attitude into their normal way of doing things. This is accomplished by first giving employees the chance to exhibit the new behaviours or attitudes. Once exhibited, positive reinforcement is used to reinforce the desired change. Additional coaching and modelling are also used at this point to reinforce the stability of the change. Extrinsic rewards, particularly monetary incentives (recall our discussion in Chapter 5), are frequently used to reinforce behavioural change. Reinforcement is important otherwise behaviour may revert back, as the same forces that were initially present to resist the change wait to resist again.

For example, let's say you work at a call centre that is receiving negative customer evaluations. The centre wants to improve customer service. Currently, you and the other employees are paid based on the number of calls made per hour; clearly the primary motivation is to place as many calls within an hour as possible. If the centre expects to achieve its goal, the compensation method must change to align it with the goal. Once the new payment system is in place, the centre may also want to introduce a bonus system based on customer satisfaction surveys. Additionally, you and the others may want the opportunity to nominate each other for 'customer service guru of the week'.

A SYSTEMS MODEL OF CHANGE

A systems approach takes a big picture perspective of organizational change. It is based on the notion that any change, no matter how large or small, has a spillover effect throughout an organization.[34]

A systems model of change offers a framework or model to use for diagnosing what to change and for determining how to evaluate the success of a change effort. To further your understanding about this model, we first describe its components and then discuss a brief application. The four main components of a systems model of change are inputs, strategic plans, target elements of change, and outputs (see Figure 13.4).

Inputs All planned strategic organizational changes should be consistent with an organization's mission, vision, and resulting strategic plan. A *mission statement* represents the reason why an organization exists, and an organization's vision is a long-term goal that describes what an organization wants to become. Consider how the difference between mission and vision affects organizational change. Your college or university probably has a mission to educate people. This mission does not necessarily imply anything about change; it simply defines the institution's overall purpose. In contrast, the college or university may have a vision to be recognized as the best in the country. This vision requires the organization to benchmark itself against other world-class higher education institutions and to create plans for achieving the vision.

For example, the vision of Languages Canada, Canada's premier language organization, is to be internationally recognized as the symbol of excellence, representing Canada as the number one destination for quality English and French language training.[35]

An assessment of an organization's internal *S*trengths and *W*eaknesses against its environmental *O*pportunities and *T*hreats (SWOT) is another key input within the systems model. This SWOT analysis is a key component of the strategic planning process. Certainly some but not all threats can be foreseeable. When assessing inputs, consider that extreme situations could occur, resulting in huge unforeseeable change. Building contingencies into the plan when and if possible is encouraged.

Strategic Plans Strategic plans are based on results from a SWOT analysis and identifying long-term goals. Recall our discussion in Chapter 12 that goal accomplishment is the most widely used effectiveness criterion. Combined, these factors help to develop an organizational strategy to attain desired goals such as profits, customer satisfaction, quality, adequate return on investment, acceptable levels of turnover, and employee satisfaction and commitment. When completing a SWOT analysis, the strengths and weaknesses of the internal resources are evaluated against the external market factors that can either be opportunities or threats to the company. We discussed these earlier in this chapter when we looked at internal and external forces of change.

Target Elements of Change *Target elements of change* are the components of an organization that may be changed.

> **Mission statement**
>
> A statement that summarizes the essence or reason why an organization exists.

> **Target elements of change**
>
> Components of an organization that may be changed.

FIGURE   13.4   A Systems Model of Change

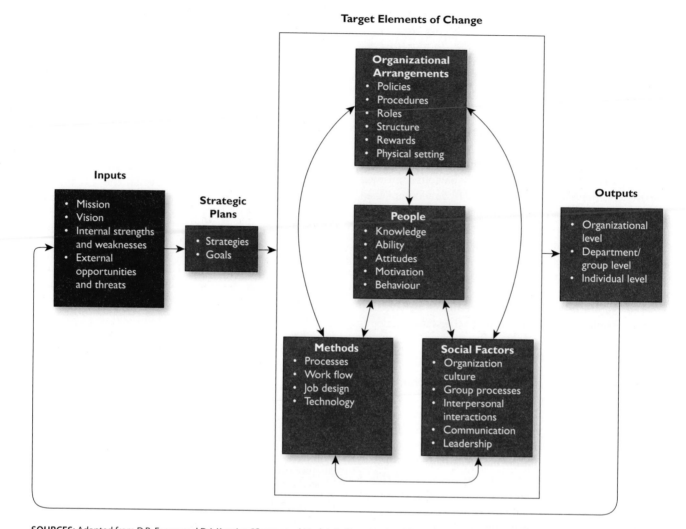

Target Elements of Change

Inputs
- Mission
- Vision
- Internal strengths and weaknesses
- External opportunities and threats

Strategic Plans
- Strategies
- Goals

Organizational Arrangements
- Policies
- Procedures
- Roles
- Structure
- Rewards
- Physical setting

People
- Knowledge
- Ability
- Attitudes
- Motivation
- Behaviour

Methods
- Processes
- Work flow
- Job design
- Technology

Social Factors
- Organization culture
- Group processes
- Interpersonal interactions
- Communication
- Leadership

Outputs
- Organizational level
- Department/ group level
- Individual level

SOURCES: Adapted from D.R. Fuqua and D.J. Kurpius, "Conceptual Models in Organizational Consultation," *Journal of Counselling & Development,* July/ August 1993, pp 602–18; and D.A. Nadler and M.L. Tushman, "Organizational Frame Bending: Principles for Managing Reorientation," *Academy of Management Executive,* August 1989, pp 194–203.

As shown in Figure 13.4, there are four targeted elements of change: organizational arrangements, social factors, methods, and people.[36] Each target element of change contains a subset of more detailed organizational features. For instance, the social factors component includes consideration of an organization's culture, group processes, interpersonal interactions, communication, and leadership. There are two final issues to keep in mind about the target elements of change shown in Figure 13.4. First, the double-headed arrows connecting each target element of change convey the message that change ripples across an organization. Second, the people component is placed in the centre of the target elements of change box because all organizational change ultimately impacts employees.

Outputs   Outputs represent the desired end-results of a change. Once again, these end-results should be consistent with an organization's strategic plan. Figure 13.4 indicates that change may be directed at the organizational level, department/group level, or individual level. Change efforts are more complicated and difficult to manage when they are targeted at the organizational level. This occurs because organizational-level changes are more likely to affect multiple target elements of change shown in the model.

Applying the Systems Model of Change There are two different ways to apply the systems model of change. The first is as an aid during the strategic planning process. Once a group of managers has determined its vision and strategic goals, the target elements of change can be considered when developing action plans to support the accomplishment of goals. The second application involves using the model as a diagnostic framework to determine the causes of an organizational problem and to propose solutions.

LO 3 KOTTER'S EIGHT STEPS FOR LEADING ORGANIZATIONAL CHANGE

John Kotter, an expert in leadership and change management, believes that organizational change typically fails because senior management makes a host of implementation errors. Based on these errors, Kotter proposes an eight-step process for leading change.[37] Unlike the systems model of change, this model is more like Lewin's model of change in that it prescribes how managers should sequence or lead the change process.

Kotter's eight steps, shown in Table 13.1, take Lewin's model of change into account. The first four steps represent Lewin's "unfreezing" stage. Steps 5, 6,

and 7 represent "changing," and step 8 corresponds to "refreezing." The value of Kotter's steps is that they provide specific recommendations about behaviours that managers need to exhibit to successfully lead organizational change. It is important to remember that Kotter's research revealed that it is ineffective to skip steps, and that successful organizational change is 70 percent to 90 percent leadership, and only 10 percent to 30 percent management. Senior managers are thus advised to focus on leading rather than managing change.[38]

CHANGE THROUGH ORGANIZATION DEVELOPMENT

Organization development (OD) is much broader in orientation than any of the previously discussed models. OD constitutes a set of techniques or interventions that are used to implement planned organizational change aimed at increasing "an organization's ability to improve itself as a humane and effective system."[39] OD techniques or interventions apply to each of the change models discussed in this section. For example, OD is used during Lewin's

Organization development

A set of techniques or tools used to implement organizational change.

TABLE 13.1

STEPS TO LEADING ORGANIZATIONAL CHANGE

STEP	DESCRIPTION
1. Establish a sense of urgency	Unfreeze the organization by creating a compelling reason for why change is needed.
2. Create the guiding coalition	Create a cross-functional, cross-level group of people with enough power to lead the change.
3. Develop a vision and strategy	Create a vision and strategic plan to guide the change process.
4. Communicate the change vision	Create and implement a communication strategy that consistently communicates the new vision and strategic plan.
5. Empower broad-based action	Eliminate barriers to change, and use target elements of change to transform the organization. Encourage risk taking and creative problem solving.
6. Generate short-term wins	Plan for and create short-term "wins" or improvements. Recognize and reward people who contribute to the wins.
7. Consolidate gains and produce more change	The guiding coalition uses credibility from short-term wins to create more change. Additional people are brought into the change process as change cascades throughout the organization. Attempts are made to reinvigorate the change process.
8. Anchor new approaches in the culture	Reinforce the changes by highlighting connections between new behaviours and processes and organizational success. Develop methods to ensure leadership development and succession.

SOURCE: The steps were developed by J.P. Kotter, *Leading Change* (Boston: Harvard Business School Press, 1996).

"changing" stage. It is also used to identify and implement targeted elements of change within the systems model of change. Finally, OD might be used during Kotter's steps 1, 3, 5, 6, and 7. In this section, we briefly review the four identifying characteristics of OD, associated research, and practical implications.[40]

Involves Profound Change   Change agents using OD generally desire deep and long-lasting improvement. A change agent can be an event, a process, a material thing, or most commonly, an individual who acts as a catalyst for change. OD consultant and change agent Warner Burke, for example, strives for fundamental cultural change: "By fundamental change, as opposed to fixing a problem or improving a procedure, I mean that some significant aspect of an organization's culture will never be the same."[41] Here is another example of a change agent:

> General Motors Corporation (GM) is a company that continues to undergo changes in product design and development. Since it came out of bankruptcy in 2011, executives have tried to change the culture. To shock the system and fight the bureaucracy, Chairman and Chief Executive Dan Akerson placed a controversial pick, a non-engineer 31-year GM veteran, Mary Barra, in charge of vehicle development . . . to some a risky decision. "She has a bias for action. Mary is a change agent," says Akerson. Barra's predecessor, Bob Lutz, who made great strides in improving the styling and feel of GM cars and trucks, found bureaucratic logjams in engineering harder to eliminate. "(Mary's) got good judgment, great common sense, and she doesn't put up with b.s.," said Lutz. Only time will tell if Ms. Barra will be the kind of change agent GM needs in product development.[42]

Value Loaded   Owing to the fact that OD is rooted partially in humanistic psychology, many OD consultants carry certain values or biases into the client organization. They prefer cooperation over conflict, self-control over institutional control, and democratic and participative management over dictatorial management. In addition to OD being driven by a consultant's values, OD practitioners now believe that there is a broader value perspective that should underlie any organizational change. Specifically, OD should always be customer focused and it should help an organization achieve its vision and strategic goals. This approach implies that organizational interventions should be aimed at helping to satisfy customers' needs and thereby provide enhanced value of an organization's products and services.[43]

A Diagnosis/Prescription Cycle   OD theorists and practitioners have long adhered to a medical model of organization. Like medical doctors, internal and external OD consultants approach the "sick" organization, "diagnose" its ills, "prescribe" and implement an intervention, and "monitor" progress. Figure 13.5 illustrates the OD process in more detail. Consider the following list of OD interventions that can be used to change individual, group, or organizational behaviour as a whole:

- **Survey feedback** A questionnaire is distributed to employees to ascertain their perceptions and attitudes. The results are then shared with them.

- **Process consultation** An OD consultant observes the communication process (interpersonal-relations, decision-making, and conflict-handling patterns) occurring in work groups, and provides feedback to the members involved.

- **Appreciative inquiry of performance** Individuals as well as cross-functional groups use an OD process called *appreciative inquiry* to cooperatively identify opportunities through new perspective and to focus on what is working well within the organization rather than trying to fix what isn't. The idea is to build relationships and explore through collaboration what positive change(s) or action(s) are occurring in the organization and to encourage change in other areas that may not be functioning as well.[44]

- **Team building** Work groups are made more effective by helping members learn to function as a team.

- **Techno-structural activities** These interventions are concerned with improving the work technology or organizational design with people on the job. An intervention involving a work-technology change might be the introduction of email to improve employee communication.[45]

Process Oriented   Ideally, OD consultants focus on the form and not the content of behavioural and administrative dealings. For example, product design engineers and market researchers might be coached on how to communicate more effectively with one another, without the consultant knowing the technical details of their conversations. In addition to communication, OD specialists focus on other processes, including problem solving, decision making, conflict handling, trust, power sharing, and career development.

OD Research and Practical Implications   Before discussing OD research, it is important to note that many of the

FIGURE **13.5** The OD Process

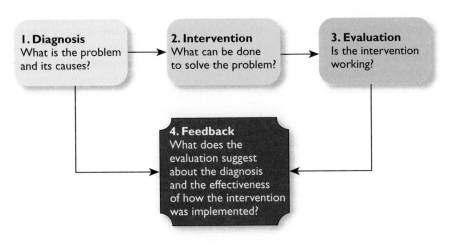

SOURCE: Adapted from W.L. French and C.H. Bell Jr, *Organization Development: Behavioral Interventions for Organizational Improvement* (Englewood Cliffs, NJ: Prentice Hall, 1978).

topics contained in this OB textbook are used during OD interventions. Team building, for example, is commonly used as an OD technique to improve the functioning of work groups. The point is that OD research has practical implications for a variety of OB applications previously discussed. OD-related interventions have led to the following insights:

- A meta-analysis of 18 studies indicated that employee satisfaction with change is higher when top management is highly committed to the change effort.[46]

- A meta-analysis of 52 studies provided support for the systems model of organizational change. Specifically, varying one target element of change creates changes in other target elements. Also, there is a positive relationship between individual behaviour change and organizational-level change.[47]

- A meta-analysis of 126 studies demonstrated that comprehensive interventions using more than one OD technique are more effective in changing job attitudes and work attitudes than interventions that rely on only one human-process or techno-structural approach.[48]

- A survey of 1,700 firms from China, Japan, and Europe revealed that (1) European firms use OD interventions more frequently than firms from China and Japan, and (2) some OD interventions are culture-free and some are not.[49]

There are four practical implications derived from this research: First, planned organizational change works. However, management and change agents are advised to rely on multifaceted interventions. As indicated elsewhere in this book, goal setting, feedback, recognition and rewards, training, participation, and challenging job design have good track records relative to improving performance and satisfaction. Second, change programs are more successful when they are geared toward meeting both short-term and long-term results. Managers should not engage in organizational change for the sake of change; change efforts should produce positive results. Third, organizational change is more likely to succeed when top management is truly committed to the change process and the desired goals of the change program. This is particularly true when organizations pursue large-scale transformation. Finally, the effectiveness of OD interventions is affected by cross-cultural considerations. Managers and OD consultants should not blindly apply an OD intervention that worked in one country to a similar situation in another country.

Understanding and Managing Resistance to Change

It is important for managers, supervisors, and team-leaders to learn to manage resistance because failed change efforts are costly. Costs include decreased employee loyalty, lowered probability of achieving corporate goals, waste of money and resources, and difficulty in fixing the failed change effort. This section examines resistance to change and practical ways of dealing with the problem.

LO 4 | WHY TARGET ELEMENTS RESIST CHANGE IN THE WORKPLACE

No matter how technically or administratively perfect a proposed change may be, there is a good chance it will be met with resistance—but from where and what type? In terms of organizational resistance, we only need to go back and review Figure 13.4, which illustrates the various target elements of change where opposition can be found: six organizational arrangements, four methods, five social factors, and five people elements. To understand the strength of resistance in methods and arrangements, let's use your own school learning environment as an example. Reflect on the following five questions:

1. How are most of your courses taught—a live videoconferencing feed from your home OR totally online OR in a traditional classroom with 45 other students onsite?

2. How many of your courses are delivered using IT and how many of your assignments require using the latest technology?

3. Does your teacher use YouTube, Twitter, Instagram, or Facebook on the SMART Board located at the front of the room while each student refers to the same site using their own tablet computer?

4. Are your papers delivered to an online drop box and are your quizzes taken online and marked immediately by the computer?

5. Do you reference this text material using an eBook reader supplied by your school?

If you answered yes to some of these questions but not all, then it begs the question, "Why not?" What is described above is not that uncommon, and yet it is still not occurring in all schools. Now, looking back at Figure 13.4, it's worth considering what factors under methods and arrangements resist changes in the classroom. Maybe some classrooms are not multi-media

equipped (methods–technology), perhaps your school believes all learning must take place in a classroom (arrangements—policies/procedures), or maybe some believe that teachers can only teach in a classroom (arrangements—roles). In any event, all can be considered possible resistance to change. Some non-people oriented targets, like models and arrangements, can sometimes be easier to change than the social and people elements. To understand why people can be so resistant to change, we now turn our attention to individual and group behaviour.

Individual and group behaviour following an organizational change can take many forms. The extremes range from acceptance to active resistance. *Resistance to change* is an emotional/behavioural response to real or imagined threats to an established work routine; it acts as barriers. Resistance can be as subtle as passive acceptance and as obvious as deliberate sabotage. Here are 11 leading reasons why employees resist change in the first place:[50]

> **Resistance to change**
>
> Emotional/behavioural response to real or imagined work changes that act as barriers.

1. **An individual's predisposition toward change** While some people are distrustful and suspicious of change, others see change as a situation requiring flexibility, patience, and understanding.[51]

2. **Surprise and fear of the unknown** When innovative or radically different changes are introduced without warning, affected employees become fearful of the implications.

3. **Climate of mistrust** Trust involves reciprocal faith in others' intentions. Mutual mistrust can doom an otherwise well-conceived change to failure. Mistrust encourages secrecy, which creates deeper mistrust.

4. **Fear of failure** Intimidating changes on the job can cause employees to doubt their capabilities. Self-doubt works against self-confidence and cripples personal growth and development.

5. **Loss of status and/or job security** Changes that threaten to alter power bases or eliminate jobs generally trigger strong resistance.

6. **Peer pressure** People who are not directly affected by a change may actively resist it to protect the interest of their friends and co-workers.

7. **Disruption of cultural traditions and/or group relationships** Whenever individuals are transferred, promoted, reassigned, or laid-off, cultural and group dynamics are thrown into confusion. This is the case of the disgruntled workers at the Mazda plant in Japan (see the International OB feature box).

8. **Personality conflicts** The personalities of change agents can breed resistance as they engage in

FEWER "JOBS FOR LIFE" IN JAPAN MEANS UNWELCOMED CHANGE

For several decades during Japan's modernization, its major companies guaranteed jobs for life and offered relatively good benefits in return for employee loyalty. Since the early 1990s, the Japanese economy has struggled to regain the kind of growth and power it enjoyed in past decades. The competitive advantages once held in small electronic technologies, as well as in the automobile manufacturing industry, have given way to global competition, leaving Japanese manufacturers with no choice but to change and adapt to new market forces.

Auto makers especially have been pinched by cost-cutting efforts and have responded by increasing dependency on workers called "haken," who are hired on less attractive contracts than regular workers, often through job-referral companies. At Hiroshima-based Mazda Motors Corporation, contract workers are hired on a six-month basis. This two-tiered system of employment leaves some feeling discriminated against and sets the contract workers up to work harder than regular employees, who haken workers believe are people with 'big attitudes' who get 'big money'. This is leading to a social problem in Japan as some contract workers feel strained by this major change in employment tradition. Japanese media report acts of vengeance and violence that have occurred over recent years between haken and regular employees.

SOURCE: Y. Kageyama, "Workers Drive into Crowd at Mazda Plant," AP wireservice, www.thecanadianpress.com, www.MSN.ca, June 22, 2010.

---

political power games that help themselves rather than the organization.

9. **Lack of tact and/or poor timing** Undue resistance can occur because changes are introduced in an insensitive manner or at an awkward time given certain circumstances. An example of this took place at the Gateway Canadian postal facility in Mississauga, Ontario when postal workers refused to handle letters and packages arriving from Japan due to concerns about leaked radiation from a crippled nuclear plant following the 2011 earthquake. Management assessed the situation and introduced a new process to move the mail faster. The union argued that management was more focused on processing mail quickly and ignored the safety of workers by not turning on the numerous radiation detectors located in the facility.[52]

10. **Non-reinforcing reward systems** Individuals resist when they do not foresee positive rewards for changing. For example, employees are unlikely to support change that they think requires them to work longer with more pressure.

11. **Past success** Success can breed smugness. It can also foster a stubbornness to change because people come to believe that what worked in the past will work in the future. IBM experienced this in the mid-1990s, as did Eastman Kodak in the 2000s (see the OB In Action Case Study at the end of this chapter). And who could have predicted the bankruptcy of Zellers, once Canada's dominant discount retail chain?[53]

RESEARCH ON RESISTANCE TO CHANGE

The classic study of resistance to change was reported in 1948 by Lester Coch and John R.P. French. They observed the introduction of a new work procedure in a garment factory, where one set of workers was given no explanation for proposed changes, while another set of workers was given full explanations. The first group faltered, but the latter group experienced an increase in output, no grievances, and no turnover.[54] Since the Coch and French study, participation has been the recommended approach for overcoming resistance to change.

Empirical (evidence from data) research has uncovered additional personal characteristics related to resistance to change:

1. *Commitment to change* is defined as a mind-set "that binds an individual to a course of action deemed necessary for the successful implementation of a change initiative."[55] A series of studies showed that an employee's

> **Commitment to change**
>
> A mind-set of doing whatever it takes to effectively implement change.

commitment to change is a significant and positive predictor of behavioural support for a change initiative.[56] To further illustrate the idea of commitment to change, you are encouraged to complete Self-Assessment Exercise #1 to determine if you have ever demonstrated resistance to change in your current or past work experiences. By taking this assessment, you will get some indication of how committed you were to the change and whether it affected your support for what management was trying to accomplish.

2. **Resilience to change** is a composite characteristic reflecting high self-esteem, optimism, and an internal locus of control (self-esteem and locus of control were discussed in Chapter 3). People with high resilience are expected to be more open and adaptable toward change.[57]

> **Resilience to change**
>
> Composite personal characteristic reflecting high self-esteem, optimism, and an internal locus of control.

3. **Positive self-concept** and tolerance for risk were positively related to coping with change. That is, people with a positive self-concept and a tolerance for risk handled organizational change better than those without such dispositions.[58]

4. **High levels of self-efficacy** (discussed in Chapter 3) are negatively associated with resistance to change.[59] This suggests that those individuals who believe in themselves and their abilities are more likely to be positive about change.

To summarize these four key findings, it's helpful for an organization to implement change if it finds individuals who are committed to change, have strong resilience to change, have a positive self-concept, as well as have high self-efficacy. When resistance is met, there is a growing belief that it is really just employees responding to perceived obstacles within the organization that are preventing them from changing.[60] For example, John Kotter, the researcher who developed the eight steps for leading organizational change that were discussed earlier in this chapter, studied more than 100 companies and concluded that employees generally want to change, but are unable to do so because of obstacles they perceive are preventing successful implementation.

He noted that obstacles in the organization's structure or in a "performance appraisal system [that] makes people choose between the new vision and their own self-interests" prevents change more than an individual's direct resistance.[61] This new perspective implies that a systems model, such as the one shown in Figure 13.4, should be used to determine the causes of failed change. Such an approach would likely reveal that ineffective organizational change is due to faulty organizational processes and systems, as opposed to employees' direct resistance. For example, employees frequently resist change because management has not effectively communicated the rationale to support the change.[62] In conclusion, a systems perspective suggests that people do not resist change, per se; rather individuals' anti-change attitudes and behaviours are caused by obstacles within the work environment.

ALTERNATIVE STRATEGIES FOR OVERCOMING RESISTANCE TO CHANGE

We noted previously that participation has historically been the recommended approach for overcoming resistance to change. More recently, however, organizational change experts have criticized the tendency to treat participation as a cure-all for resistance to change. They prefer a contingency approach because resistance can take many forms and, furthermore, because situational factors vary. Participation + involvement does have its place, but it takes time that is not always available. There are other methods to consider, such as:

- **Education + communication** This method is used in situations when there is a lack of information or inaccurate information and analysis.

- **Participation + involvement** This is helpful when the initiators do not have all the information they need to design the change and when others have considerable power to resist.

- **Facilitation + support** This method is commonly used when people are resisting change because of adjustment problems.

- **Negotiation + agreement** Use this method when someone or some group will clearly lose out in a change and when that group has considerable power to resist.

- **Manipulation + co-optation** This method is helpful when other tactics will not work or are too expensive.

- **Explicit + implicit coercion** This method is used when speed is essential and when the change initiators possess considerable power.[63]

In short, each method has its situational niche, advantages, and drawbacks; there is no universal strategy for overcoming resistance to change.

Does Your Commitment to a Change Initiative Predict Your Behavioural Support for the Change?

INSTRUCTIONS: First, think of a time in which a previous or current employer was undergoing a change initiative that required you to learn something new or to discontinue an attitude, behaviour, or organizational practice. Next, evaluate your commitment to this change effort by indicating the extent to which you agree with the following survey items. Using the rating scale shown below, circle the number that best matches your experience. Once completed, add up the circled numbers to get a final total score for each column. Compare your score to the scoring norms. Finally, assess your behavioural support for the change and reflect on your response.

	Strongly Disagree	Disagree	Neutral	Agree	Strongly Agree
1 I believe in the value of this change.	1	2	3	4	5
2 This change serves an important purpose.	1	2	3	4	5
3 This change is a good strategy for the organization.	1	2	3	4	5
4 I have no choice but to go along with this change.	1	2	3	4	5
5 It would be risky to speak out against this change.	1	2	3	4	5
6 It would be too costly for me to resist this change.	1	2	3	4	5
7 I feel a sense of duty to work toward this change.	1	2	3	4	5
8 It would be irresponsible of me to resist this change.	1	2	3	4	5
9 I feel obligated to support this change.	1	2	3	4	5
Total score	____	____	____	____	____

Scoring Norms

8–18 = Low socialization

19–29 = Moderate socialization

30–40 = High socialization

Behavioural Support for the Change

Overall, I modified my attitudes and behaviour in line with what management was trying to accomplish.

1	2	3	4	5

SOURCES: Survey items were obtained from L. Herscovitch and J.P. Meyer, "Commitment to Organizational Change: Extension of a Three-Component Model," *Journal of Applied Psychology*, June 2002, p 477.

Change Causing Occupational Stress

In our hectic urbanized and industrialized society, change is causing people stress, meaning physical, psychological, or behavioural responses that may trigger negative side effects, including headaches, ulcers, insomnia, heart attacks, high blood pressure, and strokes. Sources of stress can include tight deadlines, role conflict and ambiguity, increasing amounts of financial responsibilities, information overload, too much complexity with technology and systems, traffic congestion, noise and air pollution, family problems, and work overload. Formally defined, **stress** is "an adaptive response, mediated by individual characteristics and/or psychological processes, that is a consequence of any external action, situation, or event that places special physical and/or psychological demands upon a person."[64]

This definition is not as difficult as it seems when we reduce it to three inter-related dimensions of stress: (1) environmental demands, referred to as stressors, that produce (2) an adaptive response, that is influenced by (3) individual differences. We'll talk more about stressors shortly.

For now, however, consider that there is good and bad stress. McGill University professor Dr. Hans Selye, known to many as the father of the modern concept of stress, completed research that emphasized that both positive and negative events can trigger an identical stress response that can be beneficial or harmful. He referred to stress that is positive or produces a positive outcome as **eustress**. An example of eustress would be receiving an award in front of a large crowd, or successfully completing a difficult work assignment that you didn't like but for which you feel a sense of pride and accomplishment once completed. Selye also noted the following:

- Stress is not merely nervous tension.
- Stress can have positive consequences.
- Stress is not something to be avoided. The complete absence of stress is death.[65]

These points make it clear that stress is inevitable. Efforts need to be directed at managing stress, not at somehow escaping it altogether. Because stress and its consequences are manageable, it is important for all employees to learn as much as they can about occupational stress.

A MODEL OF OCCUPATIONAL STRESS

We all experience stress on a daily basis. To an orchestra violinist, stress may stem from giving a solo performance before a big audience. While heat, smoke, and flames may represent stress to a firefighter, delivering a semester presentation or speaking in front of classmates may be stressful for those who are shy. In short, stress means different things to different people. In this section we'll review a model of occupational stress (see Figure 13.6), define stressors, and then apply it to the contemporary workplace.

Stressors *Stressors* are environmental factors that produce stress. There are four major types of stressors: individual, group, organizational, and personal/environmental.

> **Stress**
> Behavioural, physical, or psychological response to stressors.

> **Eustress**
> Stress that is good or produces a positive outcome.

> **Stressors**
> Environmental factors that produce stress.

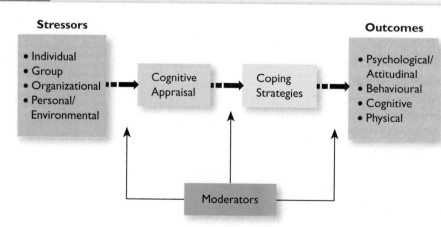

FIGURE 13.6 A Model of Occupational Stress

- **Individual-level stressors** are those directly associated with a person's job duties. Examples include job demands, work overload, role conflict, job characteristics, and work/family conflict.[66] Seventy-five percent of working adults say the most stressful aspect of their job is their immediate boss (bad management).[67] Losing one's job is another important individual-level stressor that is associated with decreased psychological and physical well-being.[68] Finally, sleep-related issues are important stressors. Research shows that most people need about seven hours of sleep per night and that alertness, energy, performance, creativity, and thinking are related to how much we sleep.[69]

- **Group-level stressors** are caused by group dynamics (recall our discussion in Chapter 6) and managerial behaviour. Managers create stress for employees by (1) exhibiting inconsistent behaviours, (2) failing to provide support, (3) showing lack of concern, (4) providing inadequate direction, (5) creating a hyper-productive environment, and (6) focusing on negatives while ignoring good performance. Sexual harassment experiences represent another group-level stressor. A recent meta-analysis of 90 studies involving over 19,000 people demonstrated that harassing experiences are negatively associated with self-esteem, life and job satisfaction, and organizational commitment, and positively associated with intentions to quit, absenteeism, anxiety, depression, and physical symptoms of stress.[70]

- **Organizational stressors** affect many employees. Recall our earlier discussion a few pages back about target elements of change when we used the example of your own classroom learning experience. These non-people elements are indeed organizational stressors. As we mentioned, the increased use of information technology, new processes, policies, changes in roles or structures, poor working conditions like air quality and ventilation—all are sources of organizational stress throughout the organization.

- **Personal and environmental stressors** are caused by factors outside the organization. For example, trying to balance career and family life is stressful. Commuting time, street noise, extreme heat or cold weather, crowds, and pollution are all stressors. Socioeconomic status is another stressor. Stress is higher for people with lower socioeconomic status, which represents a combination of (1) economic status, as measured by income, (2) social status, assessed by education level, and (3) work status, as indexed by occupation. These stressors are likely to become more important in the future.

Cognitive Appraisal of Stressors Cognitive appraisal reflects an individual's overall perception or evaluation of a situation or stressor. It is an important component within the stress process because people interpret the same stressors differently. For example, some individuals perceive unemployment as a positive liberating experience, whereas others perceive it as a negative debilitating (weakening) one.

People make two types of appraisals when evaluating the potential impact of stressors on their lives: primary and secondary appraisals.[71] A **primary appraisal** is an initial response and results in categorizing a situation or stressor as irrelevant, positive, or stressful. A **secondary appraisal** only occurs in response to a stressful primary appraisal. It entails an assessment of what might and can be done to reduce the level of perceived stress. During this evaluation, a person considers which coping strategies are available and which ones are most likely to help resolve the situation at hand. Ultimately, the combination of an individual's primary and secondary appraisal influences the choice of coping strategies used to reduce stress.

> **Primary appraisal**
>
> An initial response to stress to determine whether a stressor is irrelevant, positive, or stressful.

> **Secondary appraisal**
>
> A reassessment of a stressor in terms of what might and can be done to reduce stress.

Coping Strategies Coping strategies are characterized by the specific behaviours and cognitions used to cope with a situation. People use a combination of three approaches to cope with stressors and stress.

1. **Control Strategy** A *control strategy* consists of using behaviours and cognitions to directly anticipate or solve problems. A control strategy has a take-charge tone. Examples include talking to your boss about workload if you feel overwhelmed with your responsibilities. Results from a meta-analysis of 34 studies and more than 4,000 people indicated that control coping is positively related to overall health outcomes.[72]

> **Control strategy**
>
> A coping strategy that directly confronts or solves problems.

2. **Escape Strategy** An *escape strategy* consists of behaviours and cognitions used to avoid or escape situations. Individuals use this strategy when they passively accept stressful situations or avoid them by failing to confront the cause of stress (an obnoxious co-worker, for instance).

> **Escape strategy**
>
> A coping strategy that avoids or ignores stressors and problems.

3. **Symptom Management Strategy** A *symptom management strategy* consists of using methods such as relaxation, meditation, medication, or exercise to manage the symptoms of occupational stress. A vacation, for example, can reduce the symptoms of stress.[73]

> **Symptom management strategy**
>
> A coping strategy that focuses on reducing the symptoms of stress.

Stress Outcomes Theorists contend that stress has psychological/attitudinal, behavioural, cognitive, and physical health outcomes. As discussed earlier, Dr. Selye from Montreal's McGill University has identified the positive effects of certain kinds of stress. However, there is also a large body of research that supports the negative effects of perceived stress on many aspects of our lives. Workplace stress is negatively related to job satisfaction, organizational commitment, organizational citizenship behaviour, positive emotions, performance, and turnover.[74] Research also shows that stress is associated with negative behaviours such as yelling, verbal abuse, and violence toward others. Finally, sufficient evidence supports the conclusion that stress negatively affects our physical health. Stress contributes to the following health problems: lessened ability to ward off illness and infection, high blood pressure, coronary artery disease, tension headaches, back pain, diarrhea, and constipation.[75]

LO 5 MODERATORS OF OCCUPATIONAL STRESS

Moderators are variables that cause the relationships between stressors, perceived stress, and outcomes to be weaker for some people and stronger for others. We will now examine three important moderators: social support, hardiness, and Type A behaviour. A moderator is defined as a variable that causes the relationship between two variables—such as stressors and cognitive appraisal—to be stronger for some people and weaker for others.

Social Support Talking with a friend can be comforting during times of fear, stress, or loneliness. For a variety of reasons, meaningful social relationships help people do a better job of handling stress. *Social support* is the amount of perceived helpfulness derived from social relationships.

Research has shown that people with low social support tend to have poorer cardiovascular and immune system functioning than those with strong social support networks. Further, social support protects against the perception of stress, depression, psychological problems, anxiety, and a variety of other ailments. In contrast, negative social support, which amounts to someone undermining (destabilizing) another person, negatively affects one's mental health.[76] People are well-advised to avoid those who try to undermine them.

Social support research highlights two practical recommendations. First, employees need to be kept informed about external and internal social support systems. Second, participative management programs and company-sponsored activities that make employees feel they are an important part of an extended family can be rich sources of social support.

> **Social support**
>
> Amount of helpfulness derived from social relationships.

Hardiness Suzanne Kobasa, a behavioural scientist, identified a collection of personality characteristics that neutralize occupational stress. This collection of characteristics, referred to as *hardiness*, includes the ability to perceptually or behaviourally transform negative stressors into positive challenges. Hardiness embraces the personality dimensions of commitment, locus of control, and challenge.[77]

> **Hardiness**
>
> A personality characteristic that neutralizes stress.

Commitment reflects the extent to which individuals are involved in whatever they are doing. Committed people have a sense of purpose and do not give up under pressure because they tend to invest themselves in the situation. As discussed in Chapter 3, individuals with an *internal locus of control* believe they can influence the events that affect their lives. People possessing this trait are more likely to foresee stressful events, thereby reducing their exposure to anxiety-producing situations. Moreover, their perception of being in control leads "internals" to use proactive coping strategies. *Challenge* is represented by the belief that change is a normal part of life. Hence, change is seen as an opportunity for growth and development, rather than as a threat to security.

Type A Behaviour Pattern

According to Meyer Friedman and Ray Rosenman (the cardiologists who isolated the Type A syndrome in the 1950s):

> *Type A behaviour pattern is an action-emotion complex that can be observed in any person who is aggressively involved in a chronic, incessant struggle to achieve more and more in less and less time, and if required to do so, against the opposing efforts of other things or persons.*[78]

> **Type A behaviour pattern**
>
> The behaviour of a person who is aggressively involved in a chronic, determined struggle to accomplish more in less time.

While labelling Type A behaviour as "hurry sickness," Friedman and Rosenman noted that Type A individuals frequently tend to exhibit most of the behaviours listed below:

- Hurried speech
- Walk, move, and eat rapidly
- Impatience with rate at which events take place
- Multi-task
- Interrupt others
- Feel guilt during periods of relaxation
- Schedule more in less time[79]

Complete Self-Assessment Exercise #2, *Where Are You on the Type A–B Behaviour Continuum?*, to determine if you have tendencies toward being a Type A or B personality.

Where Are You on the Type A–B Behaviour Continuum?

INSTRUCTIONS: For each question, indicate the extent to which each statement is true of you.

1 = NOT AT ALL TRUE OF ME
2
3 = NEITHER VERY TRUE NOR VERY UNTRUE OF ME
4
5 = VERY TRUE OF ME

1. I hate giving up before I'm absolutely sure that I'm licked.   1—2—3—4—5

2. Sometimes I feel that I shouldn't be working so hard, but something drives me on.   1—2—3—4—5

3. I thrive on challenging situations. The more challenges I have, the better.   1—2—3—4—5

4. In comparison to most people I know, I'm very involved in my work.   1—2—3—4—5

5. It seems as if I need 30 hours a day to finish all the things I'm faced with.   1—2—3—4—5

6. In general, I approach my work more seriously than most people I know.   1—2—3—4—5

7. I guess there are some people who can be nonchalant about their work, but I'm not one of them.   1—2—3—4—5

8. My achievements are considered to be significantly higher than those of most people I know.   1—2—3—4—5

9. I've often been asked to be an officer of some group or groups.   1—2—3—4—5

Total Score = _____

Arbitrary Norms

 9–22 = Type B
23–35 = Balanced Type A and Type B
36–45 = Type A

SOURCE: Taken from R.D. Caplan, S. Cobb, J.R.P. French, Jr., R. Van Harrison, and S.R. Pinneau, Jr., *Job Demands and Worker Health* (HEW Publication No. [NIOSH] 75-160) (Washington, DC: US Department of Health, Education, and Welfare, 1975), pp 253–54.

Because Type A behaviour is a matter of degree, it is measured on a continuum (scale). This continuum has the hurried, competitive Type A behaviour pattern at one end and the more relaxed Type B behaviour pattern at the other. Let's now consider the pros and cons of being Type A.

OB research has demonstrated that Type A employees tend to be more productive than their Type B co-workers. For instance, Type A behaviour yielded a significant and positive correlation with 766 students' grade point averages, the quantity and quality of 278 university professors' performance, and sales performance of 222 life insurance brokers.[80]

On the other hand, Type A behaviour is associated with some negative consequences. A meta-analysis of 99 studies revealed that Type A individuals have higher heart rates and blood pressure than Type B people. Type A people also show greater cardiovascular activity when they encounter the following situations: receipt of positive or negative feedback, receipt of verbal harassment or criticism, and/or tasks requiring mental as opposed to physical work.[81] Unfortunately for Type A individuals, these situations are frequently experienced at work. A second meta-analysis of 83 studies further demonstrated that the hard-driving and competitive aspects of Type A are related to coronary heart disease, but the speed, impatience, and job involvement aspects are not. This meta-analysis also showed that feelings of anger, hostility, and aggression are more strongly related to heart disease than is Type A behaviour.[82]

Do these results signal the need for Type A individuals to quit working so hard? Not necessarily. First, the research indicated that feelings of anger, hostility, and aggression are more detrimental to our health than being Type A. We should all attempt to reduce these negative emotions. Second, researchers have developed stress-reduction techniques to help Type A people pace themselves more realistically and achieve better balance in their lives (these are discussed

Skills & Best Practices

The Top 10 Most and Least Stressful Jobs

According to a survey from the Canadian Centre for Addiction and Mental Health, the odds of having high stress are greater if workers are managers or professionals; if they believe their poor job performance can negatively affect others; or if their poor job performance can result in any physical injury, damage to the company's equipment, or reputation, or cause a financial loss—these jobs score twice as high. Jobs where employees must work long and varied hours are considered stressful jobs. It is important that employees have access to resources to reduce stress. Interventions can help save the annual $17 billion in lost productivity in Canada. Employers should ask themselves, "What am I doing to reduce stress in my most valuable people?"

The top ten *most* stressful jobs are:

1. Enlisted military soldier
2. Firefighter
3. Airline pilot
4. Military general
5. Police officer
6. Event coordinator
7. Public relations executive
8. Senior corporate executive
9. Photojournalist on foreign assignment
10. Taxi driver

The top ten *least* stressful jobs are:

1. Medical records technician
2. Jeweller
3. Hair stylist
4. Dressmaker/tailor
5. Medical laboratory technician
6. Audiologist
7. Precision assembler
8. Dietitian
9. Furniture upholsterer
10. Electrical technician

SOURCES: CareerCast report, "Soldier, Firefighter, Airline Pilot Most Stressful Jobs: Survey," *Canadian HR Reporter,* January 4, 2012, www.hrreporter.com; M. Casserly, "The Most Stressful Jobs of 2012 Aren't For Girls," *Forbes,* January 4, 2012, www.forbes.com/sites/meghancasserly/2012/01/04/the-most-stressful-jobs-of-2012-arent-for-girls/; and M. Torres, "Workers Most Invested In Their Jobs Have Highest Stress Levels, CAMH Study Shows," *Canadian Centre for Addiction and Mental Health,* Press Release for January 25, 2011, www.camh.net/news_events.

in the next section). However, management and team leaders can help Type A people by not overloading them with work despite their apparent eagerness to take an ever-increasing workload. Managers and team leaders need to help rather than exploit Type A individuals.

STRESS-REDUCTION TECHNIQUES

How can organizations help stressed employees? First, employers need to identify if any of the jobs found in their organization are considered high stress and react accordingly (see the Skills & Best Practice feature box). Organizations need to care about employees experiencing high levels of stress because if it causes an employee to leave, for whatever reason, that position will have to be filled and the cost to replace that employee can range from 50 percent to 150 percent of his or her annual salary.[83] Second, consider the recommendations in Table 13.2, which summarizes key findings from the sixth Health Canada report on work–life conflict. Another recent report indicated that employers are in a good position to fight stressful working conditions that lead to depression. With 18–25 percent of the Canadian workforce suffering from depression,

employers are losing billions of dollars from lost productivity and reduced capacity to compete.[84] Third, experts recommend that organizations implement an employee assistance program. *Employee assistance programs* **(EAPs)** consist of a broad array of programs aimed at helping employees to deal with personal problems such as substance abuse, health-related problems, family and marital issues, and other problems that negatively affect their job performance. EAPs are typically provided by employers or in combination with unions. EAPs usually fall under employee benefits, which some employees may not fully understand or feel comfortable engaging in (for more on this topic, see the following Law & Ethics at Work feature box). Alternatively, referral-only EAPs simply provide managers with telephone numbers that they can distribute to employees in need of help. Employees then pay for these services themselves. It's worth emphasizing here that since not all employees will embrace the EAP concept for various reasons (for example, see the next Focus on Diversity feature box on the impact of culture),

> *Employee assistance programs*
>
> Help employees to resolve personal problems that affect their productivity.

TABLE 13.2

RECOMMENDATIONS TO REDUCE STRESS

WHAT CAN EMPLOYEES DO?	WHAT CAN EMPLOYERS DO?
To reduce stress and restore work–life balance, employees should focus on the following:	To reduce work–life conflict and to improve their bottom line, employers need to focus their efforts on the following initiatives:
1. Not attempt to cope by working harder and trying to do it all, nor by reducing the quality of their work (especially at home) or cutting back on sleep. All three of these make things substantially worse, not better.	1. Make work demands and work expectations more realistic.
2. Recognize that no one can balance their life but them. Employees need to educate themselves on how to deal with stress, take advantage of policies and programs in their workplace, delegate tasks, and prioritize.	2. To avoid burnout, increase employees' sense of control over their work and their lives.
3. Put their needs and those of their family first.	3. Provide flexibility around work hours so employees can determine goals and priorities and allocate time accordingly.
4. Consult their family physician if they are experiencing challenges balancing work and family roles. Toughing it out and trying to do it all often make things worse.	4. Focus on creating a more supportive work culture by understanding the circumstances employees face in their work and private lives.
5. Set boundaries between work and personal life and make a concerted effort to reduce the extent to which work intrudes on family/personal life.	5. Increase the number of supportive managers in the organization and decrease the number of non-supportive managers.

SOURCE: C. Higgins & L Duxbury, "Work-Life Conflict in Canada In The New Millennium—Report Six," *Health Canada,* January 2009, pg 27, www.hc.sc.gc.ca, Environmental and Workplace Health Tab; and Reports & Publications—Work Life Balance—Report 6 (January 2009).

MANAGEMENT CANNOT MANDATE COUNSELLING

How should management deal with an employee who is facing a great deal of stress and is failing to achieve a healthy work–life balance? It's important to remember that management cannot mandate that an employee go to counselling. A manager who notices work is not getting completed is obligated to discuss concerns and expectations with employees, but cannot force them to get help. Further, management may elect to review with employees the various benefits of employment that may include cognitive assistance from a trained therapist.

It's important that the employee not feel picked on, isolated, or be identified publicly, as this may cause feelings of prejudice since others are not receiving the same treatment. Failure by management to be sensitive to an employee's rights may cause the employee to claim discrimination or harassment during a vulnerable time.

The solution? Clearly provide literature and resources to all employees, not just one. Under the Canadian Human Rights Act–3.1 Anti-Harassment Policy Statement, employees have the right to work in a non-harassing work environment.

SOURCE: Canadian Human Rights Commission: www.chrc-ccdp .ca/publications/anti_harassment_part3-en.asp#33

---

managers will need to be sensitive to possible resistance by finding an alternative to diffuse employee stress.

How can individuals reduce their stress levels? Reviewing the five recommendations listed earlier in Table 13.2 from Health Canada's extensive study is a good start. One of the recommendations includes taking advantage of organizational policies and programs, such as a human resource information system (HRIS) that is set up to help with early detection of employee burnout. By combining employee vacation time taken, overtime, attendance, vacancy levels in organization, etc., employees and managers may be able to predict and avoid burnout.[85] Second, self-monitor through the three adaptation stages to assess stress levels. Third, use a holistic wellness approach to get centred. Let's explore these last few individual approaches toward stress reduction.[86]

General Adaptation Syndrome The *General Adaptation Syndrome* model was created by scientist Hans Selye and describes a three-stage process that the body goes through in its attempt to maintain balance during stressful episodes.[87] Individuals are advised to self-monitor their own bodily response to stressful situations using these stages as a guide:

- **Alarm Stage** An individual's first reaction when encountering danger is to prepare to deal with the threat (fight or flight response). The nervous system and adrenal glands respond,

> **General Adaptation Syndrome**
>
> A three-stage model that describes body response when exposed to stress.

all to get the body 'energy ready'. If this energy is not used by physical activity, it can be harmful (e.g., gastric ulcers, heart conditions, stroke). Finding an outlet for the adrenaline and other hormones racing through the bloodstream is critical.

- **Resistance Stage** The body shifts into this stage, believing that the threat has been removed and the issue resolved. If the stressful situation continues, then the body adapts by trying to repeat the alarm stage responses. This can leave an individual feeling like there is no end to the threat—just when a balance or a feeling of being in control is believed to be reached, a new threat appears. The body will continue to seek balance until energy is exhausted and it moves an individual into the last stage.

- **Exhaustion Stage** At this point the stress has continued for some time, the body has failed to reach a balance, the individual is feeling no control over the life/situation, and the body has not been successful at resisting the threat because the energy supply is now drained. This stage is considered to be burnout, overload, or adrenal fatigue—stress levels go up and stay up. The attempt to adapt is over and this is the most hazardous to individual health. Chronic stress can damage nerve cells in tissues and organs, thinking and memory can become impaired, and there is a tendency toward anxiety and depression leading to heart issues, high blood pressure, and other illnesses.

SOME EMPLOYEES RESIST COUNSELLING

As the Canadian workplace continues to see an increase in new Canadian immigrants as well as more integration from Canadian Aboriginal people, it is important for managers to remember that not all cultures will welcome stress reduction efforts from the organization. To some, counselling therapy is for the sick and has negative connotations. They would rather find their own way to cope, and in many cases suffer long periods in silence, than discuss it publicly with a stranger.

In the case of Aboriginal employees, the *Journal of Aboriginal Health* reported that community and culture are foundations for resiliency when stressed, not talking to someone in HR. In the case of new Canadians of Chinese descent who have begun working in Canadian organizations, they can find the stress overwhelming just like the rest of us, but may have some resistance to accepting stress reduction techniques. In the Chinese culture, as well with South Koreans, talking openly with a counsellor or psychotherapist is still taboo for their growing anxieties, depression, and stress.

Admitting the need for help is just not done in a face-saving culture. Here in North America, it is becoming more common for firms to offer their employees an intervention of counselling benefits to help with professional and personal issues.

SOURCES: M. McDonald, "Stressed and Depressed, Koreans Avoid Therapy," *The New York Times*, www.nytimes.com/2011/07/07/world/asia/07iht-psych07.html?_r=1&pagewanted=print, July 6, 2011; *Journal of Aboriginal Health*, September 2006, pp 4–7; and R. Kreitner and A. Kinicki, *Organizational Behaviour 8th US Edition*, Chapter 18, p 531.

Holistic Wellness Approach A *holistic wellness approach* encompasses and goes beyond stress reduction by advocating that individuals strive for "a harmonious and productive balance of physical, mental, and social well-being brought about by the acceptance of one's personal responsibility for developing and adhering to a health promotion program."[88] Five dimensions of a holistic wellness approach include:

> **Holistic wellness approach**
>
> Advocates personal responsibility for healthy living.

1. **Self-responsibility** Take personal responsibility for your wellness (e.g., quit smoking).

2. **Nutritional awareness** Become aware of what you take into your system.

3. **Stress reduction and relaxation** Use techniques to relax and reduce the symptoms of stress. A recent study concluded that workers are more likely to call in sick after a stressful day. Tension with co-workers or boss leads to illness.[89]

4. **Physical fitness** Exercise regularly to maintain strength, flexibility, endurance, and a healthy body weight. A review of employee fitness programs indicated that they are positively linked with job performance and job satisfaction.[90]

5. **Environmental sensitivity** Try to identify and eliminate the stressors that are causing your stress.

One stress reduction technique involves exchanging your office chair for an exercise ball to help ease office fatigue and back pain, and strengthen core muscles.

Summary of Learning Objectives

 Discuss the external and internal forces that create the need for organizational change. Organizations encounter both external and internal forces for change. There are five key external forces for change: (1) demographic characteristics, (2) technological advancements, (3) customer and market changes, (4) social and political pressures, and (5) organizational crises. Internal forces for change come from human resource problems; managerial preferences, behaviours, or decisions; poorly designed organizational processes or structures; and insufficient resources.

 Describe Lewin's change model and the systems model of change. Lewin developed a three-stage model of planned change that explained how to initiate, manage, and stabilize the change process. The three stages are unfreezing (creating the motivation to change), changing, and stabilizing change through refreezing. A systems model of change takes a big picture perspective of change. It focuses on the interaction among the key components of change. The three main components of change are inputs, target elements of change, and outputs. The target elements of change represent the components of an organization that may be changed. They include organizational arrangements, social factors, methods, and people.

LO 3 Explain Kotter's eight steps for leading organizational change and the role of organizational development (OD). John Kotter believes that organizational change fails for one or more of eight common errors. He proposes eight steps that organizations can follow to overcome these errors. The eight steps are (1) establish a sense of urgency, (2) create the guiding coalition, (3) develop a vision and strategy, (4) communicate the change vision, (5) empower broad-based action, (6) generate short-term wins, (7) consolidate gains and produce more change, and (8) anchor new approaches in the culture. Organizational development (OD) can assist the change process using tools, change agents, and intervention techniques during steps 1, 3, 5, 6, and 7 of Kotter's model.

 Summarize and explain the 11 reasons why employees resist change. Resistance to change is an emotional/behavioural response to real or imagined threats to an established work routine. Eleven reasons why employees resist change are (1) an individual's predisposition toward change, (2) surprise and fear of the unknown, (3) climate of mistrust, (4) fear of failure, (5) loss of status or job security, (6) peer pressure, (7) disruption of cultural traditions or group relationships, (8) personality conflicts, (9) lack of tact or poor timing, (10) non-reinforcing reward systems, and (11) past success.

LO 5 Compare and contrast the three moderators of occupational stress and identify various kinds of stress-reduction techniques. Recall that a moderator is a variable that causes the relationship between two variables —such as stressors and cognitive appraisal—to be stronger for some people and weaker for others. People use social support, hardiness, and Type A behaviour to help reduce the impact of stressors that are appraised as harmful, threatening, or challenging. Social support represents the amount of perceived helpfulness derived from social relationships. Hardiness is a collection of personality characteristics that neutralize stress. It includes the characteristics of commitment, locus of control, and challenge. The

Type A behaviour pattern is characterized by someone who is aggressively involved in a chronic, determined struggle to accomplish more in less time. Management can help Type A individuals by not overloading them with work despite their apparent eagerness to take on an ever-increasing workload. Organizations can also help reduce stress by: introducing EAP counselling, making work demands and expectations more realistic, increasing employee sense of control, providing flexibility around work hours, creating a more supportive work culture, increasing the number of supportive managers, and decreasing the number of non-supportive managers. Employees can reduce stress by not attempting to do it all, recognizing that they need to take control and balance their life, putting their needs first, consulting their physician if experiencing stress, and setting boundaries. Other stress-reducing techniques include self-monitoring using the General Adaptation Syndrome model and engaging in holistic wellness programs.

Discussion Questions

1. How would you respond to a manager who made the following statement? "Unfreezing is not important; employees will follow my directives."

2. Have you ever gone through a major organizational change at work? If yes, what type of organizational development intervention was used? Was it effective? Explain.

3. Which of the 11 sources of resistance to change mentioned in this chapter do you think is the most common? Which is the most difficult for management to deal with?

4. Why would certain people resist EAP counselling when trying to cope with change?

5. This chapter mentioned that stress is higher for people with lower socio-economic status, which represents a combination of income, education level, and occupation, and that these stressors would become more important in the future. What kinds of reasons can you provide to explain this statement?

6. Why should an organization care about the number of employees facing burn-out and possible depression in their workforce?

Integration of OB Concepts—Discussion Questions

1. See Chapter 3—Relate the factors of self-concept (i.e., self-efficacy, self-monitoring, and the social learning model of self-management) to dealing with change and stressful situations. Explain the role of emotions when it comes to coping with change and avoiding burnout.

2. See Chapter 4—How can values and attitude become a barrier to accepting change? How does low job satisfaction contribute to organizational stress?

3. See Chapter 6—Explain how group think can influence an individual's willingness to accept change. How can group behaviour within a workplace cause an individual greater stress at work?

4. See Chapter 7—Discuss the role of communication during episodes of change.

5. See Chapter 8—Explain how conflict can increase during organizational change.

6. See Chapter 10—Describe how leadership can be a source of stress for employees.

7. See Chapter 11—In what ways can culture be a barrier to change? Explain the roles that socialization and mentoring can have in facilitating organizational change.

Google Searches

1. Google Search: "Job Stress in Canada 201_" AND "Most Stressful Jobs in 201_" AND "Canadian Federal Public Servants Take Double the Sick Days as Private Sector Workers" After reading several articles, determine if stress on the job is real or just imagined. In other words, are employees becoming weaker and less able in the workforce today compared to employees in decades gone by? Explain your response.

2. Google Search: "Workers Drive into Crowd at Mazda Plant" AND "Global Organization for Stress—Stress Facts" AND "International Stress Management Association UK" Based on stress facts and stories you have read, is stress a global issue or is it primarily found only within the Canadian workforce? What do you think would contribute to global stressors?

3. Google Search: "eHealth Scandal a $1b Waste: Auditor CBC" OR "Ornge Scandal" OR "Canada News: Drummond Report: Hospital Amalgamations" As the need for health services continues to increase in this country, there is a shortage of funds and added threats to the system. Review Figure 13.4 and the Systems Model of Change and go through the various stages of the model. Use the Ontario Health industry (and the information your search uncovers) as the case to suggest the need for change.

Experiential Exercise

Why People Resist Change Group Exercise

PURPOSE This exercise is meant to help you to reflect upon those variables that cause employees to become stressed from workplace changes, and as a result experience stress on the job. Approx. Timing: 15 minutes.

ACTIVITY ASSIGNMENT

- Work in small groups.
- Discuss the questions below.
- After 7 minutes of discussion, share your responses with the rest of the class in an open dialogue.

   1. Identify at least five possible reasons why employees resist workplace change. Be sure to explain each reason. For example: *Employees don't like change because they are afraid of the unknown. This causes stress because the unknown causes fear—fear of failure, fear of possible loss of a job, fear of added pressure, etc.*

2. Think of at least four possible ways in which employees can show their resistance toward change. For example: *Employees may show force against the change by calling in sick more often. An increase in absenteeism may occur.*

3. List at least three possible techniques that the organization can use through its management, supervisory, and/or team leadership group to help employees to accept the changes in the workplace. For example: *Management can call a meeting with all employees and show them the financials—nothing like a few pages of actual accounting numbers to present a sobering picture.*

OB In Action Case Study

The Restructuring of Eastman Kodak

Robert Shanebrook, a former long-time Kodak employee, said employees used to consider Kodak to be the Apple Inc. or Google of its time. "We had this self-imposed opinion of ourselves that we could do anything, that we were undefeatable," said Shanebrook. On January 19, 2012, Eastman Kodak Co. filed for bankruptcy protection to allow it to restructure and deal with a $6.8 billion debt. Within the twelve months leading up to the filing, Kodak stock had lost 90 percent of its value. What happened to this once global corporate powerhouse?

BACKGROUND

If you look on the corporate website for Eastman Kodak, it explains the history of the company with the following statement:

> With the slogan "you press the button, we do the rest," George Eastman put the first simple camera into the hands of a world of consumers in 1888. In so doing, he made a cumbersome and complicated process easy to use and accessible to nearly everyone.

There was a time when the word Kodak was synonymous with cameras—its respected long history made it a well-known brand name. But times change, and even 100+ years of being in business weren't enough to keep the forces of change away from the Kodak Corporation.

EXTERNAL FORCES OF CHANGE

Eastman Kodak Company was a very strong market leader in the 1970s. Kodak used the export strategy of designing and producing products in several plants for the US market, and shipping them to domestic and foreign customers, including Canada. However, Kodak began losing its strong leadership position as competition increased from the Japanese.

One of its problem areas of business, for which it was best known to the public, was its photographic products. The Japanese came out with the 35-millimetre camera, while Kodak ignored the market for too long and gave the first move advantage to the Japanese companies. Kodak also unsuccessfully spent years and millions of dollars to develop an instant camera to compete with Polaroid, and got sued in the process for patent infringements. In terms of film, it was losing market share to Fuji and other companies.

On top of the heavy competition, the price of silver rose dramatically. Kodak was in a crisis, because silver was a critical raw material in its photographic products. In the age of the digital camera, Kodak's change was designed to keep the company competitive in the future.

INTERNAL FORCES OF CHANGE

Top managers identified three major factors contributing to problems at Kodak. First, internal operating costs were too high. Second, information at the bottom of the operation was not being shared throughout the company, and managers were not being held accountable for performance. Third, strategic planning was developed by staff specialists but not implemented by the line managers. In other words, the planning process was not working. On the basis of these factors, the company decided to restructure itself from a functional departmentation to a divisional departmentation, which it believed would be more responsive to the global environment. The next decision was how to plan and implement the departmental change. Managers, concerned about making the reorganization a success, decided to use participative management to implement the change.

Fourteen months of intensive preparation and planning took place as teams of managers throughout the layers of the organization were brought in to take part in the process so that the new design became their plan, rather than someone else's. The next step was to appoint people to the top jobs in the new organization. Appointments were based first on assessment of talent, and only then on seniority. Most of the top 150 managers involved in the process had new jobs. But most importantly, the large majority of managers supported the reorganization regardless of their new jobs.

IMPLEMENTING CHANGE

Kodak's reorganization began with a 12 percent reduction of employees over a two-year period. Most left voluntarily for other jobs or retired. Over time, the number of managers was reduced by about 25 percent, and Kodak stopped its habit of promoting managers from within. Over a five-year period, nearly 70 percent of the key managers were new to their jobs.

Next, nearly 30 independent business units were created with the responsibility of developing and implementing their own strategy and worldwide profit performance. The export strategy changed, depending on the business unit, all the way to the direct investment level. The business units were grouped into traditional imaging business, image-intensive information technology, and plastic polymers. Kodak acquired Sterling Drug and expanded into pharmaceuticals as an additional business group.

Manufacturing and R&D were split up and distributed in the business units to achieve better focus on customers, markets, and technology. The relationship between the business units and the different geographic areas where Kodak conducted its business was articulated: in simple terms, each business unit was responsible for developing the strategic thrust of the business, while the geographic unit was responsible for implementing the thrust.

Each business unit was subject to periodic evaluation of its earnings and value. Each was required to generate a return that exceeded an internally established cost of equity, reflecting its own level of risk and market conditions. Businesses unable to attain the required rate of return were put on probation, and if they did not reach the goal, they were taken apart or separated from the rest of the company.

Kodak's reorganization was successful by most measures. It improved its financial position, productivity, and market share. Kodak's performance improved at a rate four times the US average for several years in a row. However, toward the end of the fourth quarter in 2008, the photography company saw its stock fall to its lowest price in at least 34 years, after cutting its yearly sales and profit projections twice. All salary increases planned for 2009 were suspended. The cuts kindled doubt about the success of then-CEO Antonio Perez's four-year restructuring that saw 28,000 jobs eliminated and money invested more in digital products as demand decreased for traditional film. In early 2009, Kodak continued to bash on with plans by merging with Bowe Bell + Howell; their stocks decreased 5.9 percent after the merger was announced. For the next 23 months, Kodak continued to fight for its life.

CASE UPDATE

After weeks of speculation in the markets, Kodak filed for Chapter 11 bankruptcy protection in early 2012. Days before filing, the 131 year-old company was still making last-ditch efforts to sell off some of its patent portfolio. Unfortunately, they were unable to raise the kind of cash needed to cover almost $7 billion debt. However, the protection offered under bankruptcy allowed Kodak to get a $950 million loan to begin restructuring its operations under Perez. Almost immediately, Kodak launched a patent infringement lawsuit against Apple, RIM, and HTC to find the money owed to them.

Around the same time, in a frustrated response to the restructuring, a Kodak employee filed a suit against the company, claiming it should have done a better job safeguarding employees by eliminating the company stock as an investment option. Employees who opted into the stock plans saw their wealth decrease from a high of $31 per share 10 years ago to just 35 cents when the filing occurred. This lawsuit gained attention as it had the chance of turning into a class action piece from all employees who found themselves in a similar situation.

While looking for buyers for its assets, Kodak was also finding ways to cut costs. One of the groups targeted was 16,000 Kodak retirees who were being hit with a $1 billion cut in medical benefits. By May 2012, Kodak faced a desperate situation with key people jumping ship, so the company approached the bankruptcy judge with a request to hand out $13.5 million in bonuses for 300 executives to persuade them to stay with the company while it reorganized.

Discussion Questions

1. What kind of internal and external forces led to Kodak filing for bankruptcy?

2. Which of the 11 reasons mentioned in this chapter would apply to Kodak?

3. Which methods for overcoming resistance to change did Kodak focus on throughout its change?

4. Initially, why didn't Kodak just dictate change from the top CEO position instead of wasting 14 precious months?

5. Did Kodak follow the steps in Lewin's change model?

6. What sort of occupational stress do you think the 300 executives were experiencing to cause their employer to request bonus payments? Explain.

SOURCE: C. Thompson, "Kodak, Under Bankruptcy Protection, Wants to Hand Out $13.5M In Bonuses," *The Huffington Post,* May 14, 2012; N. Brown, "Kodak Retirees Seek Own Bankruptcy Committee," *Reuters Business & Financial News,* March 20, 2012; M. Spector and D. Mattioli, "Kodak Teeters on the Brink," *The Wall Street Journal,* January 5, 2012; and R.N. Lussier, *Human Relations in Organizations: Applications and Skill Building* (New York: McGraw-Hill Ryerson, 2005), pp 503–4.

The CONNECTion Zone Mc Graw Hill connect™

- The Presentation Assistant
- Ethical OB Dilemma
- Video Case

Practise and learn online with Connect.

CHAPTER 14

Developing a Global Organization

FACING AN OB CHALLENGE

I am an international student studying business administration at the post-secondary level in Canada. I am enjoying learning the traditions and culture of the country. I have been on a co-op work assignment this semester and the employer has been very kind to me. I believe they will give positive feedback about my performance on the job. To show appreciation for all they have done to make my experience at the company positive, I want to give the office manager and my teacher a few gift cards. It is customary in my country to do this, but one of my Canadian classmates told me that I could be committing a serious academic offence if I do! Is this true?

—*CONFUSED FROM OVERSEAS*

LEARNING OBJECTIVES

After reading this chapter, you should be able to:

LO 1 Define *ethnocentrism*.

LO 2 Explain what Hofstede concluded about applying Canadian management theories in other countries.

LO 3 Differentiate between five cultural perspectives relevant to individuals becoming cross-culturally competent.

LO 4 Summarize what the GLOBE project has taught us about leadership.

LO 5 Synthesize the four stages of the foreign assignment cycle by identifying an OB trouble spot for each stage.

Understanding Behaviour around the Globe

To answer the Facing an OB Challenge question directly—sharing a box of Timbits with the class or spending time talking with your teacher over a cup of coffee is an acceptable social gesture, but offering a gift of cash would be perceived as bribery, which is an academic offence. This author is reminded of a situation a few months back that involved a colleague who was offered $3,000 from an international student one week before final exams to ensure the student passed a business math course. The gift was left on the professor's desk; 20 Canadian $100 bills were rolled up inside a tea container, and another $1000 in cash and gift cards from various restaurants and retail stores were stuffed inside a large office envelope. When the student was called in and informed by the professor that such behaviour is an academic offense at the college and an illegal act in Canada, the student was shocked, embarrassed, and confused that what was intended to be a sincere offering of appreciation would be misconstrued as an illegal act of bribery.

Students who have an opportunity to travel and study around the world are exposed to various cultural traditions and values. Witnessing the diversity of behaviours allows individuals to grow in cultural understanding and awareness. Before students graduate and move into the world of work, they should be aware of the different values, norms, and business practices that exist around the globe. What works in one country doesn't necessarily work in another. We'll discuss the need to develop what is called 'cultural intelligence' later on in this chapter.

We often hear comments about the global economy. On one level, it seems so grand, so vague, and so distant; but on another level, it is here, it is now, and it is very personal. For example, put yourself into this scenario:

> *It's Saturday morning and your Walmart-purchased alarm clock (made in China) buzzes—it's time to get up. After driving your Japanese Toyota RAV (made in Woodstock Ontario) to TD Canada Trust (that has offices around the world) to deposit your paycheque from London Life (owned by Power Financial Group, a trans-national global organization), you decide to go to Tim Horton's to get a double–double (dominant Canadian firm with franchises in the US and Middle East) before shopping at the local Target store (the US retailer that bought 220 of the former Canadian-owned Zellers stores). You notice that your Samsung smartphone (a South Korean firm) is ringing. It's your friend calling from India. She's using her iphone (made in Brazil by the Chinese firm Foxconn for the US firm Apple) while trekking through the Himalayas. Finally, it's time to have lunch at your favourite local pub and you order a Labatt Blue beer (now co-owned by Belgium-based Interbrew and Brazil's AmBev). After lunch, it's time to finish shopping for your apartment furnishings at IKEA (a Swedish company that builds many products in Poland). It's late and you have to hurry home to begin e-learning for a strategic management exam (from the University of Manchester, England) with your new classmate, Aadon (who is Australian).*

Welcome to the global economy! And you are a big part of it—just check the labels on the products you buy and the clothes you wear. Goods, money, and talent are crossing international borders at an accelerating pace. To illustrate the point, consider the persistent labour shortages in certain industries throughout Canada over the last few decades and how Canadian employers have had to recruit potential candidates from India, the United Kingdom, and South Africa. Top employers and recruitment consultants from Alberta, whose booming oil economy continues to experience a labour shortage, attend the Opportunities Canada Expo (OCE) held in the United Kingdom each year. Similar OCEs are held in South America and Africa. According to Canadian employers who have attended an OCE, participation yields a large pool of qualified international candidates who want to live and work in Canada.[1] For better or worse, even more economic globalization lies ahead.

From an OB standpoint, continued globalization means an exponential increase in both cross-cultural interactions and the demand for managers, supervisors, and employees who are comfortable and effective working with people from other countries and cultures. Competition for businesses and those seeking well-paying jobs in the global economy promises to be very tough. The purpose of this chapter is to help you meet the challenge.

LO 1 Developing a Global Mind-Set

Managing in a global economy is as much about patterns of thinking and behaviour as it is about trade agreements, goods and services, and currency exchange rates. Extended periods in a single dominant culture establish assumptions about how things are and should be. Global employees, whether they work at home for a foreign-owned company or actually work in a foreign country, need to develop a global mind-set (involving open-mindedness, adaptability, and a strong desire to learn).[2] A team of international business professors describes the competencies needed to develop a global mind-set as follows:

1. **Intellectual capital** Knowledge of international business and ability to learn, characterized by global business savvy, cognitive complexity (ability to analyze and connect multiple elements), and cosmopolitan outlook.

2. **Psychological capital** Openness to other cultures and willingness to change, characterized by passion for diversity, thirst for adventure, and self-assurance.

3. **Social capital** Ability to form connections and bring people together, characterized by intercultural empathy, interpersonal impact, and diplomacy.[3]

This next section encourages a global mind-set by defining societal culture and contrasting it with organizational culture, discussing ethnocentrism, exploring ways to become a global employee, and examining the applicability of Canadian management theories in other cultures.

RELATIONSHIP BETWEEN SOCIETAL AND ORGANIZATIONAL CULTURES

Societal culture involves shared values, norms, identities, and interpretations resulting from common experiences of members of collectives that are transmitted over time. Like organizational culture discussed in Chapter 11, societal culture is a social phenomenon that is shared among its members. It is this shared aspect that gives culture its power to influence behaviour.

Typically, when you comply with the expectations of a particular culture you are "rewarded" by its members, and when you don't comply you are "punished" in some way. Culture may be prescriptive (what people should do) and descriptive (what they actually do). Most cultural lessons are learned by observing and imitating role models—family, friends, teachers, co-workers, business leaders—as they go about their daily affairs or are observed in the media. Many factors influence societal cultures, such as economics, technology, politics, laws, ethnicities, and religion. Knowledge of such factors can enhance your global mind-set.

> **Societal culture**
>
> Shared values, norms, identities, and interpretations resulting from common experiences that are transmitted over time.

Peeling the Cultural Onion Culture is difficult to grasp because it is multi-layered. International management experts Fons Trompenaars (from the Netherlands) and Charles Hampden-Turner (from Britain) offer this instructive analogy in their landmark book, *Riding the Waves of Culture*:

> *Culture comes in layers, like an onion. To understand it you have to unpeel it layer by layer. On the outer layer are the products of culture, like the soaring skyscrapers of (Toronto), pillars of private power, with congested public streets between them. These are expressions of deeper values and norms in a society that are not directly visible (values such as upward mobility, "the more-the-better," status, material success). The layers of values and norms are deeper within the "onion," and are more difficult to identify.[4]*

Merging Societal and Organizational Cultures As illustrated in Figure 14.1, both organizational and societal culture influences organizational behaviour. Employees bring their societal culture (based on national values) to work with them in the form of customs and language. Organizational culture, a by-product of societal culture, in turn affects the individual's values, ethics, attitudes, assumptions, and expectations.[5] These cultural differences then influence behaviour at the individual, group, and organizational levels.

FIGURE 14.1 Cultural Influences on Organizational Behaviour[6]

Figure components:
- **Factors influencing societal culture**
  - Economic/technological setting
  - Political/legal setting
  - Ethnic background
  - Religion
- **Societal culture**
  - Customs
  - Language
- **Organizational culture**
- **Individual differences**
  - Personal values/ethics
  - Attitudes
  - Assumptions
  - Expectations
- **Outcomes at 3 levels**
  - Individual
  - Group
  - Organizational

The term societal culture is used here instead of national culture because the boundaries of many modern nation-states were not drawn along cultural lines. The former Soviet Union, for example, included 15 republics and more than 100 ethnic nationalities, many with their own distinct language.[7] Meanwhile, English-speaking Canadians in Vancouver are culturally closer to Americans in Seattle than to their French-speaking compatriots in Quebec.

Once inside the organization's sphere of influence, the individual is further affected by the *organization's* culture. Mixing of societal and organizational cultures can produce interesting dynamics in multinational companies. Proctor & Gamble Canada Inc. (P&G) has won several awards over the last several years as one of Canada's best diversity employers. They continue to strengthen their diversity efforts in a number of ways, such as: (1) recruiting at schools across the country for talented people who represent the richness of Canada's diversity and partnering with Inroad and Career Bridge, organizations that help minorities and newcomers to Canada gain valuable business experience; (2) mandating diversity training for all employees; (3) training managers on various leadership assessment tools that enable them to self-assess and gather input from direct reports to evaluate their leadership and foster continuous improvement in diversity; (4) encouraging a supportive workplace with a number of internal organizations, including Women's Network, French Canadian Network, Gay, Bisexual, & Lesbian Network, Black Professional Network, and Asian Professional Network (APN); and (5) celebrating diversity in the workplace with festivities around cultural events like Chinese New Year and Black History Month.[8] One P&G employee from an Asian country described her experience with the APN internal organization as "beneficial to network with other Asian co-workers" since there are different societal cultures within the large Asian continent, but these individuals are all working in the same organizational culture.[9]

To summarize, merging societal and organizational cultures is an eternal and critical challenge facing managers. Awareness and accommodation of differences is essential to achieve an effective fit between the two and boost performance at all levels—individual, group, and organizational. In the next section, we address a common cause of cross-cultural conflict: ethnocentrism.

ETHNOCENTRISM: REMOVING A CULTURAL ROADBLOCK IN THE GLOBAL ECONOMY

Ethnocentrism, the belief that one's native country, culture, language, and modes of behaviour are superior to all others, has its roots in the dawn of civilization. First identified as a behavioural science concept in 1906 involving the tendency of groups to reject outsiders,[10] the term ethnocentrism generally has a more encompassing (national or societal) meaning today. Worldwide evidence of ethnocentrism is plentiful. For example, ethnocentrism led to deadly ethnic cleansing in Bosnia and Kosovo and genocide in the African nations of Rwanda, Burundi, and Sudan.

Less dramatic, but still troublesome, is ethnocentrism within organizational contexts. The following Law and Ethics at Work feature box addresses the problem that occurs when a workplace takes ethnocentrism to an extreme level by not allowing employment opportunities to certain groups. Experts on the subject have framed the problem this way:

[Ethnocentric managers have] a preference for putting home-country people in key positions

> **Ethnocentrism**
>
> Belief that one's native country, culture, language, and behaviour are superior.

MINORITY EMPLOYMENT PROTECTED UNDER CANADIAN HUMAN RIGHTS LAWS

The Canadian Human Rights Commission provides guidelines for employers when it comes to hiring foreign born Canadian citizens with varied ethnic backgrounds, referred to as 'visible minorities' under the Employment Equity Act. Federally-regulated employers have a duty to consider, include, and accommodate them by providing equal opportunities for employment to members of four designated groups: women, Aboriginal peoples, persons with disabilities, and members of visible minorities.

The Canadian Human Rights Act outlines the legal duties of organizations with respect to anti-discrimination and employment and the provision of services within federal jurisdiction. The idea behind the Act is that people should not be placed at a disadvantage simply because of their race, national or ethnic origin, skin colour, or religion, as well as gender, sexual orientation, marital or family status, age, disability, or conviction for an offence that was pardoned.

A workplace that is sensitive to human rights is considered an organizational culture that ensures that the principles of equal opportunity and non-discrimination are followed. Workplaces that harbour ethnocentrism behaviour would be well advised to educate employees on the possible reputation they create for themselves and the serious implications to the organization when choosing to ignore the rights of minorities.

SOURCE: Canadian Human Rights Commission – Employment Equity and the Canadian Human Rights Act (1977), www.chrc-ccdp.gc.ca.

---

everywhere in the world and rewarding them more handsomely for work, along with a tendency to feel that this group is more intelligent, more capable, or more reliable ... Ethnocentrism is often not attributable to prejudice as much as to inexperience or lack of knowledge about foreign persons and situations. This is not too surprising, since most executives know far more about employees in their home environments. As one executive put it, "At least I understand why our own managers make mistakes. With our foreigners, I never know. The foreign managers may be better. But if I can't trust a person, should I hire him or her just to prove we're multinational?"[11]

Research Insight Research suggests that ethnocentrism is bad for business. A survey of 918 companies with home offices in Japan (309), Europe (337), and the United States (272), found ethnocentric staffing and human resource policies to be associated with increased personnel problems. Those problems included recruiting difficulties, high turnover rates, and lawsuits over personnel policies. Among the three regional samples, Japanese companies had the most ethnocentric human resource practices and the most international human resource problems.[12]

Current and future employees can effectively deal with ethnocentrism through education, greater cross-cultural awareness, international experience, and a conscious effort to value cultural diversity.[13] Pythian Group, a Canadian database administer, found cultural competency training helped attract and retain their talented immigrant employees (see the Skills and Best Practices feature box for more on their efforts). Now take a moment to complete the next Self-Assessment Exercise to assess your own tendency for ethnocentrism.

THE VALUE OF GAINING GLOBAL WORK EXPERIENCE

On any given day in our global economy, a Canadian non-managerial employee or manager can interact with colleagues from several different countries or cultures. If they are to be effective in such multicultural situations, then they need to develop a global mind-set and cross-cultural skills. Notable international management scholars Ming-Jer Chen and Danny Miller coined the term *ambicultural* to describe those employees that effectively integrate Eastern and Western business management knowledge and styles. Like an ambidextrous athlete (e.g., a baseball player that can bat both right- and left-handed, or a basketball player who can shoot both right- and left- handed), ambicultural employees effectively use their diverse knowledge and practices from multiple cultures to perform better in each.

Skills & Best Practices

Managing A Cross-Cultural Workforce

For new internationally-trained professionals (ITP) working at the Pythian Group, the buddy system allows new immigrants to self-manage by being paired with another ITP employee just like them.

Founded almost 16 years ago, the Pythian Group is a private company providing $24 \times 7 \times 365$ fractional IT infrastructure team support on a linear cost-to-effort basis (remote database service) for Oracle, Oracle Applications, MySQL, and SQL server. With headquarters in Ottawa, the company has grown to having offices in North America, Europe, and Asia Pacific. Recently, Pythian won the Employer Excellence Award from Hire Immigrants Ottawa and the Employer Council of Champions, celebrating the firm's skilled immigrant recruitment and retention practice. With 30 percent of their Ottawa office employees coming from outside Canada, the company takes diversity seriously.

Hiring ITPs is essential to helping Pythian reach its goal of hiring the top 5 percent of the world's best performers in the industry. "We want the world's top talent and it doesn't matter where you get your education or gained work experience, talent is talent," says Heidi Hauver, HR Director.

Like other multi-cultural workplaces, Pythian has an established cultural competency training program. However, the relatively new buddy system, although counter-intuitive, has found success not because it pairs ITPs with Canadians already working at Pythian, but rather by pairing ITPs with other ITPs who have just completed their first year of experience. "It helps introduce ITPs to our internal and external programs, helps them socially integrate with our team . . . and when there are questions, they can support each other," says Hauver. "The buddy system really allows ITPs to have a connection right away and form a bond with one of their peers." It lets ITPs self-manage and integrate faster because the new buddy feels more freedom to ask questions of someone at work who has been through the same experience, without being judged. It's a cultural twist on the standard mentorship program.

SOURCE: A. Silliker, "Pythian, Algonquin Recognized for Skilled Immigrant Retention Practices," *The Canadian HR Reporter*, April 9, 2012, p 10.

For example, an employee with experience in both China and Canada uses one to improve performance in the other, instead of simply relying on expertise in one culture at the expense of the other. Ambicultural employees therefore are a particular and cross-cultural version of the contingency approach studied in Chapter 1. According to Chen and Miller, ambicultural employees possess the following 10 characteristics:[14]

1. Recognition of the shortcomings of prevailing Western and Eastern business models to meet the challenges and complexities presented by globalization

2. Openness to new ways of thinking and ability to see the benefits of other cultural and business perspectives

3. Understanding that business must balance social, geopolitical, environmental, and human needs

4. Ability to transcend divisions around the globe

5. Dedication to integrating global awareness into everyday actions

6. Emphasis on unity and morality

7. Ability to balance social good and self-interest

8. Emphasis on trust-based and legal relationships

9. Equal appreciation for teamwork and individual stars

10. Commitment to continued learning, to sharing knowledge and experience with others, and to reaching the peak of professional achievement and humanity

Developing skilled employees and managers who move comfortably between cultures takes time. Consider, for

Jessie Inman, CEO of the Confederation Centre of the Arts in PEI, has developed valuable global management skills as a result of working overseas at various senior leadership positions for 30 years.

How Strong Is Your Potential for Ethnocentrism?

INSTRUCTIONS: If you were born and raised or have spent most of your life in *Canada*, circle one number from the following scale for each item. If you are from a different country or culture, substitute the country/language you most closely identify with for the terms *Canadian* and *English* or *French*, and then rate each item. Calculate a total score by adding up all the circled numbers. Compare your total score to the scoring key provided below.

1 = STRONGLY DISAGREE   4 = AGREE
2 = DISAGREE   5 = STRONGLY AGREE
3 = NEUTRAL

1	I was raised in a way that was [truly] Canadian.	1—2—3—4—5
2	Compared to how much I criticize other cultures, I criticize Canadian culture less.	1—2—3—4—5
3	I am proud of Canadian culture.	1—2—3—4—5
4	Canadian culture has had a positive effect on my life.	1—2—3—4—5
5	I believe that my children should read, write, and speak [only] English or French.	1—2—3—4—5
6	I go to places where people are Canadian.	1—2—3—4—5
7	I admire people who are Canadian.	1—2—3—4—5
8	I would prefer to live in a Canadian community.	1—2—3—4—5
9	At home, I eat [only] Canadian food.	1—2—3—4—5
10	Overall, I am Canadian.	1—2—3—4—5

Total score _____

Scoring

10–23 = Low potential for ethnocentrism
24–36 = Moderate potential for ethnocentrism
37–50 = High potential for ethnocentrism

SOURCE: Adapted from and survey items excerpted from J.L. Tsai, Y-W Ying, and P.A. Lee, "The Meaning of 'Being Chinese' and 'Being American': Variation among Chinese American Young Adults," *Journal of Cross-Cultural Psychology*, May 2000, pp 302–32.

example, this comment by the head of Gillette, who wants twice as many global managers on the payroll: "We could try to hire the best and the brightest, but it's the experience with Gillette that we need. About half of our [expatriates] are now on their fourth country. It takes 10 years to make the kind of Gillette manager I'm talking about."[15]

Importantly, these global skills will help employees in a culturally diverse country such as Canada do a more effective job on a day-to-day basis. An example of this is Jessie Inman, CEO of the Confederation Centre of the Arts (CCA) in Prince Edward Island. Inman started her career as an administrative assistant at the Centre 30 years ago, but in 1979 she moved away from the island to earn her MBA from The Netherlands, moving on to accept international senior management positions in

both Indonesia and Australia. She is fluent in English, French, and Indonesian. It was Inman's international leadership experience, as well as the broad insight she could bring from a programming perspective, that were major contributing factors to the search committee announcing her appointment.[16]

THE HOFSTEDE STUDY: HOW WELL DO CANADIAN MANAGEMENT THEORIES APPLY IN OTHER COUNTRIES?

LO 2

The short answer to this important question is: *not very well*. This answer derives from a landmark study conducted nearly 30 years ago by Dutch researcher Geert Hofstede. His unique cross-cultural comparison of 116,000 IBM employees from 53 countries worldwide focused on four cultural dimensions:

- **Power distance** How much inequality does someone expect in social situations?[17]

- **Individualism–collectivism** How loosely or closely is the person socially bonded?

- **Masculinity–femininity** Does the person embrace stereotypically competitive, performance-oriented masculine traits, or nurturing, relationship-oriented feminine traits?

- **Uncertainty avoidance** How strongly does the person desire highly structured situations?

Table 14.1 provides a summary of Hofstede's dimensions, based on the work of communications professors Ting-Toomey and Chung, as they relate to various situations such as family, workplace environments, school situations, relationships, and communication episodes. As students of OB, it's important to note that Hofstede's four cultural dimensions are the foundation of future cultural dimensions research and that they all appear as relevant and applicable across 62 nations (we'll speak more about the GLOBE project shortly). For now, recognize that the Canadian sample ranked at a moderate level on power distance and uncertainty avoidance, and at a high level on individualism and masculinity.[18]

The high degree of variation among cultures led Hofstede to two major conclusions:

1. Management theories and practices need to be adapted to local cultures. This is particularly true for made-in-Canada management theories, such as Mintzberg's organizational structure, and Japanese team management practices. *There is no one best way to manage across cultures.*[19]

2. Cultural arrogance is a luxury that individuals, companies, and nations can no longer afford in a global economy.

TABLE 14.1

VALUE CHARACTERISTICS WITHIN HOFSTEDE'S DIMENSIONS

SITUA-TIONS	POWER DISTANCE		CULTURE IDENTITY		GENDER ROLES		UNCERTAINTY AVOIDANCE	
	SMALL	LARGE	INDIVIDUA-LISTIC	COLLECTI-VISTIC	FEMI-NINE	MASCU-LINE	STRONG	WEAK
General	Emphasize interpersonal equality	Emphasize status-based difference	"I" identity	"We" identity	Flexible gender roles	Complementary gender roles	Uncertainty is a threat	Uncertainty is valued
Family	Children may contradict parents	Children should obey parents	Nuclear family	Extended family	Emphasize nurturance	Emphasize achievement	Reinforce family rules	Dynamic and changing
Relation-ship	Younger people are smart	Older people are wise	Privacy regulation	Relational harmony	Both take initiative	Males take initiative	Low mobility	High mobility
School	Teachers ask for feedback	Teachers lecture	Individual competition	Teamwork	Social adjustment is critical	Academic performance is critical	Routines are welcome	Challenges are welcome
Work-place	Subordinates expect consultation	Subordinates expect guidance	Personal competence	In-group emphasis	Work in order to live	Live in order to work	Encourage clear procedure	Encourage risk-taking
Com-muni-cation	Informal communication patterns	Formal communication patterns	Direct communication patterns	Indirect communication patterns	Fluid gender communication	"Masculine" toughness and "feminine" softness	Conflict is negative	Conflict can be positive

SOURCE: Adapted from S. Ting-Toomey and L. C. Chung, *Understanding Intercultural Communication*, 2nd Edition, Oxford University Press, Inc. New York, New York, (2012) pp 47–52.

LO 3 Becoming Cross-Culturally Competent

Cultural anthropologists believe we can learn interesting and valuable lessons by comparing one culture with another. Over the years, researchers have suggested many dimensions to help contrast and compare the world's rich variety of cultures. We discuss five cultural perspectives in this section that are summarized in Table 14.2. These five perspectives are especially relevant to current and aspiring global employees: (1) basic cultural dimensions and cultural intelligence, (2) individualism versus collectivism, (3) high-context and low-context cultures, (4) monochronic and polychronic time orientation, and (5) cross-cultural leadership. Separately or together, these cultural distinctions can become huge stumbling blocks when doing business across cultures. But first we need to think about cultural stereotyping and the need for *cultural intelligence*.

BASIC CULTURAL DIMENSIONS—CULTURAL INTELLIGENCE NEEDED

An important qualification needs to be made at this time. All of the cultural differences discussed in this chapter and elsewhere need to be viewed as tendencies and patterns rather than as absolutes. As soon as you fall into the trap of assuming all Italians are this, all Koreans will do that, and so on, potentially useful generalizations become mindless stereotypes.

Professors with extensive foreign work experience advise, "As teachers, researchers, and managers in cross-cultural contexts, we need to recognize that our original characterizations of other cultures are best guesses that we need to modify as we gain more experience."[20] Consequently, they argue, we will be better prepared to deal with foreseeable cultural paradoxes. By paradox, they mean there are always exceptions to the rule, i.e., individuals who do not fit the expected cultural pattern.

An excellent example of such a paradox is Stan Shih, the founder and former CEO of Acer Group, which at the time of this writing is the second-largest PC maker in the world behind HP. Shih is known as Taiwan's "godfather of IT." He is perhaps equally well-known for his untraditional Chinese management philosophies and practices. For instance, he explicitly forbade his children from working in or controlling the company, arguing that he wanted to "debunk the traditional Chinese culture of 'family ruling the kingdom.'" While he founded the company, he credits Acer's success to the efforts of many and sees himself only as a representative for them. Besides, he says, the shareholders deserve the company to be run by the very best and most qualified people. Keeping control in the family is not the way to assure this goal.[21]

Workers can expect to encounter many cultural paradoxes in large and culturally diverse nations (such as Canada) and companies. This is where the need for cultural intelligence arises.

Cultural intelligence can be defined as the ability to make a decision, enact (ratify) change, and accurately interpret ambiguous (unclear) cross-cultural situations that are

> **Cultural intelligence**
>
> The ability to make a decision, enact change, and accurately interpret ambiguous cross-cultural situations that are consistent with cultural expectations.

TABLE 14.2

FIVE CULTURAL PERSPECTIVES

FACTORS OF PERSPECTIVE	DESCRIPTION
1. Basic Cultural Dimensions and Developing Cultural Intelligence	• G. Hofstede and GLOBE Dimensions – The ability to decide, change, and interpret ambiguous cross-cultural situations
2. Individualism vs. Collectivism	• Cultures that give priority to personal freedom and choice versus those that emphasize shared goals
3. High-Context vs. Low-Context Cultures	• Those cultures that rely on non-verbal cues versus those that communicate primarily from written and spoken words
4. Monochronic vs. Polychronic Time Orientation	• Individuals who perceive time as limited, precise, and schedule-driven versus individuals who view time as flexible and multidimensional
5. Cross-cultural Leadership – Positive & Negative Attributes	• Leadership and cultural variation – Identifying culturally endorsed (positive) leadership attributes versus universally negative attributes

consistent with cultural expectations. This is an important skill in today's diverse workplaces. Two organizational behaviour (OB) scholars explain:

A person with high cultural intelligence can somehow tease out of a person's or group's behaviour those features that would be true of all people and all groups, those peculiar to this person or this group, and those that are neither universal nor idiosyncratic. The vast realm that lies between those poles is culture.[22]

Those interested in developing their cultural intelligence need to first develop their emotional intelligence (EI), discussed in Chapter 3. They then need to be exposed to and work in ambiguous cross-cultural situations.

Being culturally intelligent can lead to opportunities such as new product development, to explore new markets. That's what a few large companies did when they employed anthropologists to research how people use technology in Asia and the Pacific Rim emerging countries to learn more about values and habits. This resulted in the new smartphone targeted to Muslim consumers with unique features that appeal to their specific needs.

Nine Basic Cultural Dimensions from the GLOBE Project
Project GLOBE (Global Leadership and Organizational Behaviour Effectiveness) is a massive and ongoing attempt to "develop an empirically based theory to describe, understand, and predict the impact of specific cultural variables on leadership and organizational processes and the effectiveness of these processes."[23] You will recall our brief discussion of this research in Chapter 10. We will spend the next several pages discussing the findings of this important body of research.

These smartphones are targeted to Muslim consumers and include features such as an automatic listing and announcement of prayer times anywhere in the world, a compass showing the direction of prayer toward Mecca, and a complete transcription of the Koran in Arabic with accompanying English translation.

Since the project was launched in Calgary, Alberta, in 1994, GLOBE has evolved into a network of more than 160 scholars from 62 societies. Most of the researchers are native to the particular cultures they study, thus greatly enhancing the credibility of the results. During the first two phases of the GLOBE project, a list of nine basic cultural dimensions was developed and statistically validated. Translated questionnaires based on the nine dimensions were administered to thousands of managers in the banking, food, and telecommunications industries around the world to build a database. Results are published on a regular basis.[24] Much work and many more years are needed to attain the project's goal, as stated above. In the meantime, we have been given a comprehensive, valid, and up-to-date tool for better understanding cross-cultural similarities and differences. The nine cultural dimensions from the GLOBE project are:

1. **Power distance** How much unequal distribution of power should there be in organizations and society?

2. **Uncertainty avoidance** How much should people rely on social norms and rules to avoid uncertainty and limit unpredictability?

3. **Institutional collectivism** How much should leaders encourage and reward loyalty to the social unit, as opposed to the pursuit of individual goals?

4. **In-group collectivism** How much pride and loyalty should individuals have for their family or organization?

5. **Gender egalitarianism** How much effort should be put into minimizing gender discrimination and role inequalities?

6. **Assertiveness** How confrontational and dominant should individuals be in social relationships?

7. **Future orientation** How much should people delay gratification by planning and saving for the future?

8. **Performance orientation** How much should individuals be rewarded for improvement and excellence?

9. **Humane orientation** How much should society encourage and reward people for being kind, fair, friendly, and generous?[25]

Notice how the two forms of collectivism, along with the dimensions of power distance and uncertainty avoidance, correspond to the similarly-labelled variables in Hofstede's classic study discussed earlier. It is important to understand how Hofsteded and the GLOBE findings are related.

Where did Canada rank on these dimensions?

- **High:** performance, future orientation, and individualism

- **Moderately High:** assertiveness, uncertainty avoidance, and humane orientation
- **Moderately Low:** power distance
- **Low:** in-group collectivism and gender differentiation[26]

Remember, the GLOBE project is an attempt to try and understand, as well as predict, cultural behaviours as they exist within organizations as a whole. This is illustrated by a recent survey that compared Canadian female leadership development programs to those of other countries (see the Focus on Diversity feature box for key findings). Once again, it is important to keep in mind that the broad profile mentioned earlier regarding Canada is for its organizations—not to be confused with the characteristics and values of the many subcultures of people that live within Canada. A case in point would be the potentially contrasting values of Canadian Aboriginal people, Francophone people, and newly-landed immigrants to Canada. We explore this in more detail over the next few sections.

Bringing the GLOBE Cultural Dimensions to Life   A fun and worthwhile exercise is to reflect on your own cultural roots, family traditions, and belief system and develop a personal cultural profile, using as many of the GLOBE dimensions as possible. For example, which of the

GLOBE cultural dimensions relates to the following biographical sketch?

Courtney is a 21-year-old student who has put her 4th year of studies on hold to volunteer as a classroom teacher in an elementary school located in Inuvik, Northwest Territories. Like many her age, she has no money saved for a rainy day; in fact, she's in debt from her first three years at school. Courtney says, "I'm not sure what I want to do with my life. I've spent three years studying theory, but how is that helping me? Listen, I'm still young, so I think I'll travel for one year and see the world. I'll figure it out while I'm gone. For now I might as well enjoy travelling, see the world, and be happy. I can worry about paying off my debt later."

If you said "future orientation," you're right! Indeed, her behaviour is counter to Canadians who are notorious when it comes to saving (see Table 14.3). Courtney scores low on future orientation and thus has inadequate savings for the future.

Let's take another example, except this time we'll relate it to an organization. Which of the GLOBE cultural dimensions relate to this scenario?

Sergio is a citizen of Spain working in Canada for two years on a contract basis as a software

DOES CANADA LACK FEMALE LEADERSHIP DEVELOPMENT PROGRAMS?

The results of a recent survey showed that 82 percent of respondents across Canada—including human resources, talent management, and diversity leaders from a variety of industries—said they do not have a clear strategy or philosophy for the development of women into leadership roles. Considering the survey also covered professionals in Asia, the Middle East, the United States, and Africa, this is a concern for Canada, who ranked last for not having enough strategies in place for developing female leaders. Is this a contradiction to the GLOBE findings that state Canada has a low ranking for gender differences?

The results are certainly interesting, but as one HR expert stated, "Perhaps (Canadian employers) don't see women's leadership as a separate initiative;

they really see it as part of their overarching diversity and inclusion initiatives." Is it also possible that survey respondents equate leadership as a factor related to power distance? If this were the case, then the moderately low ranking for power distance in Canada could explain the high percentage response for employers that do not have female leadership development programs. In any event, remember this survey went to HR industry professionals whose job it is to find clear gaps in the system and ensure gender equality is in place. Clearly these survey results warrant further investigation to confirm hunches practitioners have about the findings.

SOURCE: A. Silliker, "Employers Lack Strategies to Develop Female Leaders: Survey," *Canadian HR Reporter*, April 11, 2011, p 3.

TABLE 14.3

COUNTRIES RANKING HIGHEST AND LOWEST ON THE GLOBE CULTURAL DIMENSIONS

DIMENSION	HIGHEST	LOWEST
Power distance	Morocco, Argentina, Thailand, Spain, Russia	Denmark, Netherlands, South Africa—Black sample, Israel, Costa Rica
Uncertainty avoidance	Switzerland, Sweden, German—former West, Denmark, Austria	Russia, Hungary, Bolivia, Greece, Venezuela
Institutional collectivism	Sweden, South Korea, Japan, Singapore, Denmark	Greece, Hungary, Germany—former East, Argentina, Italy
In-group collectivism	Iran, India, Morocco, China, Egypt	Denmark, Sweden, New Zealand, Netherlands, Finland
Gender egalitarianism	Hungary, Poland, Slovenia, Denmark, Sweden	South Korea, Egypt, Morocco, India, China
Assertiveness	Germany—former East, Austria, Greece, U.S., Spain	Sweden, New Zealand, Switzerland, Japan, Kuwait
Future orientation	Singapore, Switzerland, Netherlands Canada—English speaking, Denmark	Russia, Argentina, Poland, Italy, Kuwait
Performance orientation	Singapore, Hong Kong, New Zealand, Taiwan, U.S.	Russia, Argentina, Greece, Venezuela, Italy
Humane orientation	Philippines, Ireland, Malaysia, Egypt, Indonesia	Germany—former West, Spain, France, Singapore, Brazil

SOURCE: Adapted from M. Javidan and R.J. House, "Cultural Acumen for the Global Manager: Lessons from Project GLOBE," *Organizational Dynamics,* Spring 2001, pp 289–305.

engineer for ABC Inc. He is the team leader for a cross-functional self-managed team. Sergio is having difficulty with a decision that was made prior to his arrival. Currently, the office asks the team for production paperwork to be completed prior to starting a project ... but he would prefer to file the paperwork after the project is started, once the specifics of the job are known and details are assigned. Sergio hesitates to disagree with the current process. He doesn't want to take problems to his boss for fear of looking incompetent, and instead decides to not file the paperwork as requested. He begins experiencing interpersonal conflict from members of the team who believe he isn't doing his job. As a result, he is stressed. "I don't know what to do!" says Sergio.

In this case, Sergio comes from a high-power distance culture like Spain, but is working in a moderately low-power distance culture like Canada. He doesn't want to offend his boss or be perceived as violating chain of command by not following formal process, so instead he is stressed and paralyzed to act. In Spain, he would be expected to take problems to his boss and follow the chain of command of formal authority; that is what he is used to. In Canada, he has been given the position and authority of being a team member, and management expects him to be empowered and lead the cross-functional team. Sergio would benefit from a face-to-face meeting with the department manager to review the concept of shared decision making and empowerment, and re-examine the functions of being a team leader.

Country Profiles and Practical Implications How do different countries score on the GLOBE cultural dimensions? Data from 18,000 managers yielded the profiles in Table 14.3. A quick overview shows a great deal of cultural diversity around the world. But thanks to the nine GLOBE dimensions, we have a more precise understanding of *how* cultures vary. Closer study reveals telling cultural *patterns*, or cultural fingerprints, for different nations. For example, Australia's moderate scores on gender egalitarianism explain why there is still evidence of gender bias in that country, while Switzerland's high scores on uncertainty avoidance and future orientation help explain its centuries of political neutrality and world-renowned banking industry. Singapore is known as a great place to do business because it is clean and safe and its people are well-educated and hardworking. This is no surprise, considering Singapore's high scores on institutional collectivism, future orientation, and performance orientation. In contrast, Russia's low scores on future orientation and performance orientation could foreshadow a slower-than-hoped-for transition from a centrally planned economy to free enterprise capitalism. These illustrations bring us to an important practical lesson: *Knowing the cultural tendencies of foreign business partners and competitors can give you a strategic competitive advantage.*

INDIVIDUALISM VERSUS COLLECTIVISM: A CLOSER LOOK

Have you ever been torn between what you personally wanted and what a group, an organization, or society expected of you? If so, you have firsthand experience with a fundamental and important cultural distinction in both the Hofstede and GLOBE studies: individualism versus collectivism. Awareness of this distinction can spell the difference between success and failure in cross-cultural business dealings.

Individualistic and Collectivist Cultures   Characterized as "I" and "me" cultures, *individualistic cultures* give priority to individual freedom and choice. *Collectivist cultures*, oppositely called "we" and "us" cultures, rank shared goals higher than individual desires and goals. People in collectivist cultures are expected to lower their own wishes and goals to those of the relevant social unit. A worldwide survey of 30,000 managers by Trompenaars and Hampden-Turner, who prefer the term *communitarianism* to collectivism, found the highest degree of individualism in Israel, Romania, Nigeria, Canada, and the United States. Countries ranking lowest in individualism—thus qualifying as collectivist cultures—are Egypt, Nepal, Mexico, India, and Japan. Brazil, China, and France are also toward the collectivist end of the scale.[27]

Individualistic culture

Primary emphasis on personal freedom and choice.

Collectivist culture

Personal goals are less important than community goals and interests.

Dualistic Cultures   You can expect to encounter both individualists and collectivists in culturally diverse countries such as Canada. As economist Walter Block, PhD, debated in an article that appeared in the *Edmonton Journal:*

> Because of (Canadian) Aboriginals' so-called collectivist approach to governance, individuals are forbidden from owning property on reserves, most federal monies are paid to the band rather than to individuals (so the chief and council get to decide who gets paid and how much), too many women

who have married non-natives are denied their rights by their own bands, and there is little accountability among far too many leaders ... any change to federal law that weakens the collectivist mindset is helpful" (in his opinion, to create a more individualistic mindset).

Whether you agree or disagree with Dr. Block is not the point; rather, the fact that two different cultural orientations can exist within the same country illustrates the need for organizations that service the Canadian Aboriginal community to be sensitive and respectful of their collectivist values. Conversely, Dr. Block would argue that those in the Aboriginal communities need to be sensitive and respectful toward federal laws, such as the Canadian Human Rights Act.

Allegiance to Whom?   The Aboriginal example brings up an important question about collectivist cultures. Specifically, which unit of society predominates? For Canadian Aboriginals, the band is the key reference group. But, as Trompenaars and Hampden-Turner observe, important differences exist among collectivist (or communitarian) cultures:

> For each single society, it is necessary to determine the group with which individuals have the closest identification. They could be keen to identify with their trade union, their family, their corporation, their religion, their profession, their nation, or the state apparatus. The French tend to identify with la France, la famille, le cadre; the Japanese with the corporation; the former eastern bloc with the Communist Party; and Ireland with the Roman Catholic Church. Communitarian goals may be good or bad for industry depending on the community concerned, its attitude, and relevance to business development.[28]

HIGH-CONTEXT AND LOW-CONTEXT CULTURES

People from *high-context cultures* are those who look at a broader, more holistic approach to understanding each other. This means that more than words are taken into consideration; instead, things such as the strength of a relationship, time approximation, relative space allowance, and/or communication all work together to give meaning to behaviour. Figure 14.2 summarizes the characteristics of countries with high-context cultures, which include China, Korea, Japan, Vietnam, Mexico, and Arab cultures. They

High-context cultures

Primary meaning derived from various non-verbal situational cues.

FIGURE 14.2 Contrasting High-Context and Low-Context Cultures

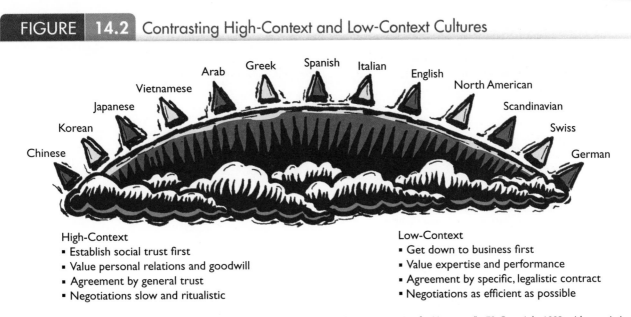

High-Context
- Establish social trust first
- Value personal relations and goodwill
- Agreement by general trust
- Negotiations slow and ritualistic

Low-Context
- Get down to business first
- Value expertise and performance
- Agreement by specific, legalistic contract
- Negotiations as efficient as possible

SOURCE: Reprinted from *Business Horizons*, vol. 36, No. 3, M. Munter, "Cross-Cultural Communication for Managers," p 72. Copyright 1993, with permission from Elsevier.

rely heavily on situational cues for meaning when interacting with others.[29] Non-verbal cues, such as official position, status, or family connections, convey messages more powerfully than do spoken words. Thus, we come to better understand the ritual of exchanging *and reading* business cards in Japan. Japanese culture is relatively high context. Business cards, listing employer and official position, convey vital silent messages about status to members of Japan's homogeneous society. Also, people from high-context cultures who are not especially talkative during a first encounter with a stranger are not necessarily being unfriendly—they are simply taking time to collect contextual information.

Reading the Fine Print in Low-Context Cultures
In *low-context cultures*, written and spoken words carry the burden of shared meanings. Again, referring to Figure 14.2, low-context cultures include those found in Canada, Germany, Switzerland, Scandinavia, the United States, and Great Britain. True to form, Germany has precise written rules for even the smallest details of daily life. In high-context cultures, agreements tend to be made on the basis of someone's word or a handshake, after a rather prolonged get-acquainted and trust-building period. Low-context Canadians, who have cultural roots in Northern Europe, see the handshake as a signal to get a signature on a detailed, lawyer-approved, iron-clad contract.

> *Low-context cultures*
>
> Primary meaning derived from written and spoken words.

Avoiding Cultural Collisions Misunderstanding and miscommunication often cause problems in international business dealings when the parties are from high-versus low-context cultures. A Mexican business professor made this instructive observation:

> *Over the years, I have noticed that across cultures there are different opinions on what is expected from a business report. (North American) managers, for instance, take a pragmatic, get-to-the-point approach, and expect reports to be concise and action-oriented. They don't have time to read long explanations—"Just the facts, ma'am." Latin American managers will usually provide long explanations that go beyond simple facts . . . I have a friend who is the Latin America representative for a (North American) firm and has been asked by his boss to provide regular reports on sales activities. His reports are long, including detailed explanations on the context in which the events he is reporting on occur and the possible interpretations that they might have. His boss regularly answers these reports with very brief messages, telling him to "cut the crap and get to the point!"[30]*

Awkward situations such as this can be avoided when those on both sides of the context divide make good-faith attempts to understand and accommodate their counterparts.

TABLE 14.4

LONGEST AND SHORTEST WORK HOURS

LONGEST WORK HOURS	AVERAGE WORK HOURS PER WEEK*	SHORTEST WORK HOURS	AVERAGE WORK HOURS PER WEEK*
1. Turkey	48.9	1. The Netherlands	30.5
2. South Korea	44.6	2. Norway	33.9
3. Mexico	43.3	3. Denmark	33.7
4. Greece	42.1	4. Ireland	34.9
5. Czech Republic	41.4	5. Switzerland	35.2

* For 2011

SOURCE: The Organisation for Economic Co-operation and Development, "Labour Force Statistics of the Average Usual Weekly Hours Worked on the Main Job," http://stats.oecd.org/ (retrieved August 15, 2012).

MONOCHRONIC AND POLYCHRONIC TIME ORIENTATION—DIFFERENT CULTURAL PERCEPTIONS

In Canadian culture, time seems to be a simple matter. It is linear, relentlessly marching forward (never backward), in standardized chunks. When working across cultures, however, time becomes a very complex matter. For example, consider this example of a Canadian company that established a joint venture partnership with a Mexican company:

The joint venture company manufactured a Canadian-designed product in Mexico, basing its production numbers on estimates from the Mexican company of how much its employees could sell in the Mexican market. The Canadian company soon noticed its Mexican partner had not made several payments for goods manufactured by the joint venture, and was surprised to find that the Mexicans had been stockpiling the product in inventory because they were not selling nearly the amount they forecasted. Instead of lowering the forecast over time to be consistent with the Mexican demand, the Mexicans continued to order the same amount each quarter so as not to disappoint the Canadians. To reduce inventory, the Canadian company was forced to flog old product in the Mexican market for two years.[31]

Notice how the time implication of the inventory depreciating and losing value was not a priority to the Mexican partner, but became an unfortunate long-term concern for the Canadian company. When it comes to regulating time, we are all affected by the norms and values of time from our own culture. Table 14.4 lists those countries whose labour-force works over 40 hours per week versus those that work less on average. The need for patience in cross-cultural business deals where perceptions of time vary can be explained in part by the distinction between *monochronic time* (Canada) and *polychronic time* (Mexico):

The former is revealed in the ordered, precise, schedule-driven use of public time that typifies and even caricatures efficient Northern Europeans and North Americans. The latter is seen in the multiple and cyclical activities and concurrent involvement with different people in Mediterranean, Latin American, and especially Arab cultures.[32]

A Matter of Degree Monochronic and polychronic are relative rather than absolute concepts. You can use Table 14.5 as a relative guide for studying purposes. Generally, the more things a person tends to do at once, the more polychronic that person is.[33] Thanks to computers and advanced telecommunications systems, highly polychronic employees can engage in multi-tasking.[34] For instance, it is possible to talk on the telephone, read and respond to email messages, print a report, check a cell phone message, and eat a stale sandwich all at the same time. Unfortunately, this extreme polychronic behaviour too often is not as efficient as hoped, and can be very stressful.[35] Monochronic people prefer to do one thing at a time. What is your attitude toward time?

Practical Implications Low-context cultures, such as that of Canada, tend to run on monochronic time, while high-context cultures, such as that of China, tend to run on polychronic time. People in polychronic cultures view time as flexible, fluid, and multidimensional, so the sequence of what task they prefer to complete first is varied. The Germans and Swiss have made an exact science of monochronic time. In fact, a radio-controlled watch made by a German company, Junghans, is "guaranteed to lose no more than one second in one million years."[36]

Monochronic time

Preference for doing one thing at a time because time is limited, precisely segmented, and schedule driven.

Polychronic time

Preference for doing more than one thing at a time because time is flexible and multidimensional.

TABLE 14.5
GENERAL CHARACTERISTICS OF MONOCHRONIC AND POLYCHRONIC TIME

MONOCHRONIC TIME SCHEDULE	POLYCHRONIC TIME SCHEDULE
Clock dependent	Time is affected by situational factors
Appointments are scheduled	Time is fluid, flexible, and elastic
Activities are arranged in timed segments, one at a time	Activities can occur simultaneously
Time pressures place more emphasis on being task-oriented	Relationship-orientation takes priority
Anticipation of what will happen if deadline is missed places focus on the future	Focus is on past and current timelines, placing less emphasis on the future
Focus is on achieving goals and tangible outcomes	Focus is on historical perspective as everything is relative

Time is more elastic in polychronic cultures. During the Islamic holy month of Ramadan in Middle Eastern nations, for example, the faithful fast during daylight hours, and the general pace of things markedly slows.[37] Employees need to reset their mental clocks when doing business across cultures, as many are polychronic.

LO 4 CROSS-CULTURAL LEADERSHIP—LESSONS FROM THE GLOBE PROJECT

Earlier in the chapter we discussed the GLOBE Project in general. In Chapter 10, we discussed how leadership prototypes are influenced by national cultural values. Here we link the research results directly to international leadership. In phase 2 of the GLOBE Project, researchers set out to discover which, if any, attributes of leadership were universally liked or disliked. They surveyed 17,000 middle managers working for 951 organizations across 62 countries. Their results, summarized in Table 14.6, have important implications for trainers and global managers today, as well as in the future. Visionary and inspirational charismatic leaders who are good team builders generally do the best. On the other hand, self-centred leaders, seen as loners or face-savers, generally receive a poor reception worldwide (see Chapter 10 for a comprehensive treatment of leadership).[38] Local and foreign managers who heed these results are still advised to use a contingency approach to leadership, using their cultural intelligence to read the local people and culture.[38] David Whitwam, the

TABLE 14.6
LEADERSHIP ATTRIBUTES UNIVERSALLY LIKED AND DISLIKED ACROSS 62 NATIONS

UNIVERSALLY POSITIVE LEADER ATTRIBUTES	UNIVERSALLY NEGATIVE LEADER ATTRIBUTES
Trustworthy	Loner
Just	Asocial
Honest	Non-cooperative
Foresight	Irritable
Plans ahead	Non-explicit
Encouraging	Egocentric
Positive	Ruthless
Dynamic	Dictatorial
Motive arouser	
Confidence builder	
Motivational	
Dependable	
Intelligent	
Decisive	
Effective bargainer	
Win–win problem solver	
Administrative skilled	
Communicative	
Informed	
Coordinator	
Team builder	
Excellence oriented	
Involvement oriented	

SOURCE: Excerpted and adapted from P.W. Dorfman, P.J. Hanges, and F.C. Brodbeck, "Leadership and Cultural Variation: The Identification of Culturally Endorsed Leadership Profiles," in *Culture, Leadership, and Organizations: The GLOBE Study of 62 Societies*, eds R.J. House, P.J. Hanges, M. Javidan, P.W. Dorfman, and V. Gupta (Thousand Oaks, CA: Sage, 2004), Tables 21.2 and 21.3, pp 677–78.

long-time CEO of appliance maker Whirlpool, recently framed the challenge this way:

Leading a company today is different from the 1980s and '90s, especially in a global company. It requires a new set of competencies. Bureaucratic structures don't work anymore. You have to take the command-and-control types out of the system. You need to allow and encourage broad-based involvement in the company. Especially in consumer kinds of companies, we need a diverse workforce with diverse leadership. You need strong regional leadership that lives in the culture. We have a North American running the North American business, and a Latin American running the Latin American business.[39]

Preparing for a Foreign Assignment

As the reach of global companies continues to grow, so too do the opportunities for living and working in foreign countries. Not only do employers want to develop employees with global-business capabilities, but in some locations, the demand for local talent with necessary skills continues to outstrip the supply. In China, for example, fast-growing businesses are hard-pressed to find enough managers with leadership and teamwork skills. Companies therefore need talented people who are willing to work in China and help to develop the leaders of the future. More generally, global players need a vibrant and growing cadre (team) of employees who are willing and able to do business across cultures.

The purpose of this final section is to help you prepare yourself and others to work successfully in foreign countries. In fact, when *Fortune* listed "Five Ways to Ignite Your Career," the number-one suggestion was this: "Go global. International operations aren't a backwater—they're a way to prove you get it."[40] The financial crisis a few years back has forced global companies, such as TD Canada Trust, EllisDon, KPMG LLP, and Siemans Canada Ltd. to get much more creative and flexible in their international assignments. As a result, they modified qualifications, duration, expectations, compensation, career stage, and repatriation.[41]

TRACKING CANADIAN FOREIGN ASSIGNMENTS

As we use the term here, *expatriate* refers to anyone living and/or working outside their home country. *Repatriate* refers to anyone who is transferred back home after a foreign assignment. Hence, they are said to be *expatriated* when transferred to another country and *repatriated* when transferred back home. Karen Adams, Senior Vice President at the Toronto office of HSBC, is the perfect example of a Canadian citizen who expatriated from the bank's Vancouver office in the mid-1990s to seek international employment opportunities with HSBC's international manager program, which offers world transfers. For over 17 years, Adams was posted to Dubai, India, Hong Kong, South Korea, China, Jordan, and England, working at various international HSBC offices that lasted two to three years each. Adams was repatriated back to her current job in Toronto for HSBC. "I know it helped my career and helped broaden my horizons. There were many more positives (than negatives) than I'd even hoped for," said Adams.[42]

> **Expatriate**
>
> Anyone living or working in a foreign country.

> **Repatriate**
>
> Anyone transferred back home after a foreign assignment.

According to a global relocation trend survey measuring employer interest in relocation initiatives, there is renewed optimism in the global marketplace (61 percent of employers surveyed expected to transfer employees). Credit is being given to pent-up demand from corporations who held back their global growth strategies until financial stability was restored throughout major world markets.[43] At the same time, a poll conducted by research company Ipsos reported that 10 percent of Canadian employees are *not* anxious to take a full-time job overseas. This compares to employees from Mexico (34 percent), Brazil (32 percent), and Russia (31 percent), who were more likely to say they would relocate internationally.[44] Why the resistance from Canadian employees?

The Canadian Employee Relocation Council conducts surveys related to corporate relocation policies and found over the years that the three major concerns about relocation are:

- Family issues (uprooting school-aged children as well as affecting the spouse's career)
- Career planning ("How long will I be gone and what will happen upon my return?")
- International security (staying away from such political hot spots such as Columbia, Syria, and the Middle East, which rank near the top).[45]

Globally, the countries most cited for relocation destinations are China, England, Ireland, Scotland, and the United States, with emerging interest being shown in Brazil and India.[46] Most employees are sent to manage foreign operations or sales forces, to expand into a new market, or to do jobs the local work force lacks the skills to perform. Men between the ages of 40 and 49 working in construction, engineering, or IT are most likely to take on a reassignment. Only 9 percent of employees 20–29 years of years go on international assignments, and just 18 percent of women. Canadian firms typically make a relocation investment in excess of $1 million to keep an employee overseas for three years.[47]

Looking at Table 14.7, it becomes easier to understand the high cost for employee relocation in certain cities around the globe. Tokyo, Geneva, and Zurich are commonly found to be the most expensive cities to live in as they appear on all three lists.

AVOIDING OB TROUBLE SPOTS IN THE FOREIGN ASSIGNMENT CYCLE

Finding the right person (often along with a supportive and adventurous family) for a foreign position is a complex, time-consuming, and costly process.[48] For our

TABLE 14.7

THE COST OF RELOCATION—MOST EXPENSIVE CITIES TO LIVE IN WORLDWIDE

RANK	MERCER INTERNATIONAL—HR AND FINANCIAL SERVICES CONSULTING FIRM	UBS—SWISS BANK	ECA INTERNATIONAL—HUMAN RESOURCE CONSULTANTS
1	Luanda, Angola	Oslo, Norway	Tokyo, Japan
2	Tokyo, Japan	Zurich, Switzerland	Oslo, Norway
3	Ndjamena, Chad	Geneva, Switzerland	Geneva, Switzerland
4	Moscow, Russia	Copenhagen, Denmark	Nagoya, Japan
5	Geneva, Switzerland	Stockholm, Sweden	Zurich, Switzerland
6	Osaka, Japan	Tokyo, Japan	Yokohama, Japan
7	Zurich, Switzerland	Sydney, Australia	Bern, Switzerland
8	Singapore	Helsinki, Findland	Stavanger, Norway
9	Hong Kong, China	Toronto, Canada	Basel, Switzerland
10	Sao Paulo, Brazil	Singapore	Kobe, Japan

SOURCE: The City Mayors Foundation, May 2012, http://www.citymayors.com/statistics/expensive-cities-intro.html

purposes, it is sufficient to narrow the focus to common OB trouble spots in the foreign assignment cycle. Referring to Figure 14.3, there are four stages in the foreign assignment cycle, each with related OB trouble spots:

1. **Selection and training** This stage takes place in the home country prior to leaving. At this point, unrealistic expectations are identified and corrected. A growing trend is for companies to assign outside mentors or consultants who specialize in preparing professionals for their foreign assignment. They can provide a complete package, including advice on housing, schools, and tax implications. According to an earlier study, Canadian companies that saw room for improvement during this phase often cited the urgency to get a position filled as a reason why employees didn't get enough preparation before starting their assignment.[49]

2. **Arrival and adjustment** This stage takes place in the foreign country, where the professional can typically experience culture shock. If possible,

candidates should be given a chance to go to the country, have a look around, and see whether this is something they want to do. For example, when Kim-Tien Huynh left her hometown of Montreal to study and work in China, she felt prepared to make the necessary adjustments for the cultural characteristics the country is infamous for: crowded places, language barriers, and fears of falling victim to China's many traffic accidents. "There's a big difference in the rhythm of work in Canada and China," Ms. Huynh said.[50]

3. **Settling in and acculturating** This stage also takes place in the foreign country, where the professional feels somewhat without corporate support. An earlier study found only 54 percent of expatriates felt their company did a good job of keeping in touch, and half of the companies surveyed reported they communicated differently with foreign workers than with employees in Canada, often relying on email and dedicated websites. The "out of sight, out of mind" syndrome can be overcome by constant communication between the head office and foreign placement using such technology as Skype, Web-Ex, MSN video calls, etc.[51]

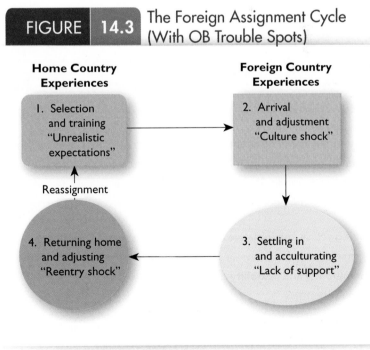

FIGURE 14.3 The Foreign Assignment Cycle (With OB Trouble Spots)

Home Country Experiences

1. Selection and training "Unrealistic expectations"

4. Returning home and adjusting "Reentry shock"

Reassignment

Foreign Country Experiences

2. Arrival and adjustment "Culture shock"

3. Settling in and acculturating "Lack of support"

4. Returning home and adjusting This stage takes place back home, where the professional experiences re-entry shock. Resistance from others and feeling that they don't fit in become the biggest concerns for repatriated professionals. The organization Toronto Homecoming is dedicated to helping expatriates readjust back into Canada. Their annual four-day Homecoming Conference is a networking event connecting potential employers with Canadians living abroad. For example, Chris Allen moved back to Toronto after living in Tokyo for eight years working for Nissan Infiniti. Admitting he "felt a bit out of the loop" when he returned with his wife and two year-old son, he says, "I didn't realize how much had changed. Family Day had become a new holiday!"[52]

Placing an employee overseas costs a firm $100,000 per employee on average, according to Stephen Cryne, president and CEO of the Canadian Employee Relocation Council.[53] That's an awful lot of money to throw away, so it's important for employers to anticipate trouble spots and neutralize the effects early on. Otherwise, the costs for another failed foreign assignment will grow.[54] In the next section we discuss strategies for each of the four stages.

STAGE 1: Avoiding Unrealistic Expectations with Cross-Cultural Training Realistic job previews (RJPs) have proven to be effective at bringing people's unrealistic expectations about a pending job assignment down to earth. RJPs provide a realistic balance of good and bad news (recall the discussion of RJPs in Chapter 11 as an anticipatory socialization tool that organizations can use before onboarding new employees). People with realistic expectations tend to quit less often and be more satisfied than those with unrealistic expectations. RJPs are a must for future expatriates. In addition, cross-cultural training is required.

Cross-cultural training is any type of structured experience designed to help departing employees adjust to a foreign culture. The trend is toward more of this type of training. Although costly, companies believe cross-cultural training is less expensive than failed foreign assignments. Programs vary widely in type and also in rigour.[55] Of course, the greater the difficulty, the greater the time and expense:

> **Cross-cultural training**
>
> Structured training experiences to help people adjust to a new culture/country.

- **Easiest** Pre-departure training is limited to informational materials, including books, lectures, films, videos, and Internet searches.

- **Moderately difficult** Experiential training is conducted through case studies, role playing, assimilators (simulated intercultural incidents), and introductory language instruction.

- **Most difficult** Departing employees are given some combination of the preceding methods, plus comprehensive language instruction and field experience in the target culture.

As a general rule of thumb, the more rigorous the cross-cultural training, the better. The nine competencies detailed in Table 14.8 should be the core of any

---

TABLE 14.8

KEY CROSS-CULTURAL COMPETENCIES

CROSS-CULTURAL COMPETENCY CLUSTER	KNOWLEDGE OR SKILL REQUIRED
Building relationships	Ability to gain access to and maintain relationships with members of the host culture
Valuing people of different cultures	Empathy for difference; sensitivity to diversity
Listening and observation	Know cultural history and reasons for certain cultural actions and customs
Coping with ambiguity	Recognize and interpret implicit behaviour, especially non-verbal cues
Translating complex information	Knowledge of local language, symbols or other forms of verbal language, and written language
Taking action and initiative	Understand intended and potentially unintended consequences of actions
Managing others	Ability to manage details of a job, including maintaining cohesion in a group
Adaptability and flexibility	Views change from multiple perspectives
Managing stress	Understand own and other's mood, emotions, and personality

SOURCE: Excerpted from Y. Yamazaki and D.C. Kayes, "An Experiential Approach to Cross-Cultural Learning: A Review and Integration of Competencies for Successful Expatriate Adaptation," *Academy of Management Learning and Education,* December 2004, Table 2, p 372.

TRAINING NEEDS TO FIT LOCAL CULTURE

Brazil

- Building personal relationships is key in Brazilian culture, so talk about yourself.

- Time is much more event-oriented in Brazil.

- In terms of personal space, program participants who approach you during class activities may stand much closer to you than you are used to.

- Power is accepted and respected. Those who have high status positions are not questioned, even when they have doubts about their stance taken.

- What may seem like fighting or arguing [during group discussions] is normal communication behaviour.*

China

- Trainees expect the trainer to lead the class as the expert. Lecture is the preferred delivery method.

- Harmony and order are valued. Trainees do not want to stand out. Make sure not to highlight the performance of any one individual. It could cause the individual and class to feel uncomfortable.

- Although China is a group-oriented culture, minimize your use of small group discussions. There is a belief that learning is more powerful when the knowledge comes from the trainer as opposed to the trainees.

- Because relationships are critical [right at the start] tell trainees about yourself and your organization.**

France

- Although English is the predominant business language in France, your credibility is dependent on your mastery of the French language, and training delivery in French is preferred. The same applies for all support material (books, evaluation forms, multimedia, etc.), Videos should be in French or contain French subtitles.

- Participants seek the intellectual stimulation of debate and exchange. Provide ample time for discussions and be flexible with your program.

- Expect to be continuously challenged. The relatively direct communication style of French audiences can be perceived as confrontational. However, note that the challenge is a positive sign as it reveals participants' passionate interest in the subject.

Reflect on the cultural dimensions discussed in this chapter that are evident in these training tips.

SOURCES: *Excerpted from N. Orkin, "Focus on Brazil," *Training*, May 2008, p 20; **Excerpted from N. Orkin, "Focus on China," *Training*, July–August 2008, p 18; and ***Excerpted from K. Blanchard-Cattarossi and S. Redrupp, "Focus on France," *Training*, January 2009, p 18.

---

comprehensive cross-cultural training program. For more cross-cultural training tips, see the International OB feature box.

STAGE 2: Avoiding Culture Shock   Have you ever been in a totally unfamiliar situation and felt disoriented and perhaps a bit frightened? If so, you already know something about *culture shock*. According to anthropologists, culture shock involves anxiety and doubt caused by an overload of unfamiliar expectations and social cues.[56] Consider your first year as a student at your current school—remember experiencing a variation of culture shock after leaving high school? An expatriate employee or family member may be thrown off-balance by an avalanche

> *Culture shock*
>
> Anxiety and doubt caused by an overload of new expectations and cues.

of strange sights, sounds, and behaviours. Among them may be unreadable road signs, strange-tasting food, an inability to use your left hand for social activities (in Islamic countries, the left hand is the toilet hand), or a failure to get a laugh with your sure-fire joke. For the expatriate employee trying to concentrate on the fine details of a business negotiation, culture shock is more than an embarrassing inconvenience—it's a disaster! Like the confused first year post-secondary student who quits and goes home, culture-shocked employees often panic and go home early.

STAGE 3: Support During the Foreign Assignment A support system needs to be in place, especially during the first six months when everything is so new to the expatriate.[57]

Host-country sponsors assigned to individual employees or families are recommended because they serve as cultural seeing-eye dogs. In a foreign country, where even the smallest errand can turn into an utterly exhausting production, sponsors can get things done quickly because they know the cultural and geographical territory. Another way to support expatriates during the transition phase of a new foreign assignment is to maintain an active dialogue with established mentors from back home. This can be accomplished via email, telephone, and, when possible, an occasional face-to-face meeting.[58]

STAGE 4: Avoiding Re-entry Shock Strange as it may seem, many otherwise successful expatriate employees encounter their first major difficulty only after their foreign assignment is over. Why? Returning to your native culture is taken for granted because it seems so routine and ordinary. But having adjusted to another country's way of doing things for an extended period of time can put your own culture and surroundings in a strange new light. Three areas for potential re-entry shock are work, social activities, and general environment (e.g., politics, climate, transportation, food).

Upon returning to Canada, a repatriated employee who lived for a number of years in Japan noticed a big difference in workplace communication. He had become more accustomed to indirect, non-verbal communication methods while in Japan. "In Toronto it's very straight and direct," he said. "You can just make a bold statement—that was an adjustment I had to make,"[59] Re-entry shock can be reduced through employee career counselling and home-country mentors and sponsors. Simply being forewarned about the problem of re-entry shock is a big step toward effectively dealing with it.[60]

Overall, the key to a successful foreign assignment is making it a well-integrated link in a career chain, rather than treating it as an isolated adventure. That is how Toronto native Farhan Thanwar looks at his time working overseas as an IT entrepreneur. Starting his IT career after graduating from the University of Waterloo, Thanwar has grown from working in diverse international locations. Through it all, he's migrated through various social and business networks that have led him to his latest job opportunity back in Canada. It's all connected in a path filled with unexpected adventure, discovery, and experiences.[61]

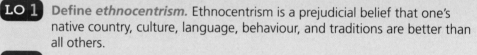

Summary of Learning Objectives

 Define *ethnocentrism.* Ethnocentrism is a prejudicial belief that one's native country, culture, language, behaviour, and traditions are better than all others.

Explain what Hofstede concluded about applying Canadian management theories in other countries. Due to the wide variations in key dimensions Hofstede found among cultures, he warned against directly applying North American-made management theories to other cultures without adapting them first. He said there is no one best way to manage across cultures.

 Differentiate between five cultural perspectives relevant to individuals becoming cross-culturally competent. (1) Individuals wishing to become more cross-culturally competent need to understand basic cultural dimensions that exist between people from different countries, as well as develop cultural intelligence about others. (2) People in individualistic cultures think primarily in terms of "I" and "me" and place a high value on freedom and personal choice. Collectivist cultures teach people to be "we" and "us" oriented and to subordinate personal wishes and goals to the interests of the relevant social unit (such as family, group, organization, or society). (3) People in high-context cultures (such as China, Japan, and Mexico) derive great meaning from a broad spectrum of situational cues, above and beyond written and spoken words. Low-context cultures (including Canada, Germany, and the United States) derive key information from precise, written, and/or spoken messages. (4) In monochronic cultures (e.g., Canada and Germany), time is precise and rigidly measured. Polychronic cultures (such as those found in Latin America and the Middle East) view time as multidimensional, fluid, and flexible. Monochronic people prefer to do one thing at a time, while polychronic people like to tackle multiple tasks at the same time. Polychronic people are not necessarily more efficient, but rather they have no particular preference for the sequence of completing tasks. (5) Developing the kinds of cross-cultural leadership traits that are universally liked can enhance success.

 Summarize what the GLOBE project has taught us about leadership. Across 62 cultures, the researchers identified leader attributes that are universally liked and universally disliked. The universally liked leader attributes, including trustworthy, dynamic, motive arouser, decisive, and intelligent, are associated with the charismatic/transformational leadership style that is widely applicable. Universally disliked leader attributes, such as non-cooperative, irritable, egocentric, and dictatorial, should be avoided in all cultures.

 Synthesize the four stages of the foreign assignment cycle by identifying an OB trouble spot for each stage. The four stages of the foreign assignment cycle (and OB trouble spots) are (1) selection and training (unrealistic expectations), (2) arrival and adjustment (culture shock), (3) settling in and acculturating (lack of support), and (4) returning home and adjusting (re-entry shock).

Discussion Questions

1. How would you describe the prevailing culture in your country to a stranger from another land in terms of the nine GLOBE project dimensions?

2. Why are people from high-context cultures such as China and Japan likely to be misunderstood by low-context Westerners?

3. How strong is your desire for a foreign assignment? Why? If it is strong, where would you like to work? Why? How prepared are you for a foreign assignment? What would you need to do to be better prepared?

4. What is your personal experience with culture shock?

5. Which of the OB trouble spots in Figure 14.3 do you believe is the greatest threat to expatriate employee success? Explain.

Integration of OB Concepts—Discussion Questions

1. See Chapter 3 – Relate emotional intelligence to cultural intelligence. How does one enable the other?

2. See Chapter 4 – Explain the role that values and attitude play in time-orientation differences between cultures.

3. See Chapter 10 – Describe how leadership prototypes influence national culture. Refer to Phase 2 of the GLOBE Project in terms of the universally liked or disliked attributes of leadership.

4. See Chapter 11 – Compare and contrast the role of realistic job previews (RJPs) in terms of being a valuable socialization tool as well as a cross-cultural training tool.

Google Searches

1. **Google Search:** "The Department of Foreign Affairs and International Trade" OR "Export Development Canada" OR "The Canadian Employee Relocation Council" Working in groups, choose one of the search sites and review what the organization/department can do for expatriates or Canadian repatriates. Report your findings to the rest of the class.

2. **Google Search:** "Citizenship and Immigration Canada" Go to the home site. Scroll down the menu listed on the left side of the page to "Media Centre." Look to the far right hand side at new menu listings and scroll down to "Success Stories." Double click on this. Work in small groups to analyze some of the latest postings. Share some of the stories with the rest of the class, relating cultural dimensions learned from this chapter to the personal stories selected.

3. **Google Search:** "International Monetary Fund – Nominal GDP by country" OR "CIA World Fact Book – Nominal GDP by country 201_" AND "Walmart Gross Global Sales Revenue" Compare Walmart's revenue to the GDP of the top 25 countries in the world. How much larger is Walmart compared to global countries? In your opinion, is Walmart a global company? How can an organization like Walmart prepare its managers and employees for overseas assignments? How can Walmart better integrate newly-landed Canadians into the workforce?

4. **Google Search:** "Report on Business_Globe Careers" AND "All Jobs That Are Globe Careers Jobs on Eluta.ca" By combining the *Globe and Mail* ROB Careers with an innovative job search engine, employers and job-seekers have access to the tools need for online recruitment. Consider the different kinds of jobs listed. Look for patterns—are there more IT jobs? Is a certain destination mentioned? What kind of timelines are referenced? Share your observations.

5. **Google Search:** "The Ethnic Theory of Plane Crashes" OR "Malcolm Gladwell Outliers Korean Air Flight 801" Review the story of the Korean Air Flight 801 that crashed August 6, 1997. Relate Geert Hofsteded's and Project GLOBE's "uncertainty avoidance" to why 228 of the 254 people on board died that day. Consider the possibility of ineffective communication skills stemming from cultural differences. Recount the events, including the specific language used by the Korean pilots vs. the air traffic controllers in Guam. What lessons did David Greenberg teach you about training and standards?

Experiential Exercise

The Globalized Classroom Exercise

PURPOSE   This exercise will show you how international your own classroom is by having you survey the cultural dimensions of all the students, including the professor. This exercise will heighten your cultural awareness. Approx. Timing: 25 minutes.

ACTIVITY ASSIGNMENT

- Work in small groups of five or six students.
- *Predict* the following: How many countries are represented by the students in your class? How many different languages are spoken? How many different religions are represented? How many international students in your class are studying on educational visas?—5 minutes

- *Write down* facts: Determine the demographic, mother-tongue languages, and cultural and religious backgrounds of the students in your small group. Summarize the results and hand it in.—5 minutes
- Collectively display all group submissions on the board.—5 minutes
- Review the collective profile of the class.—5 minutes
- Discuss the questions below.

   1. How accurate was your initial prediction of the diversity in your classroom?

   2. If you were close, try and find reasons for your cultural intelligence. How and where did you develop it?

   3. If your prediction was way off, find reasons for your lack of cultural intelligence. How and where could you further develop it?

OB In Action Case Study

It's All about Face-to-Face

Some road warriors fly commercial. Others take the corporate jet. Some pack their own bags. Others keep complete wardrobes in major cities. Some work through the entire plane ride. Others sleep. But if there is one thing these globetrotters agree on, it's that there is no substitute for face time—with the Abu Dhabi moneyman who holds the key to the future; with the underling who is AWOL on email; and with the spouse and kids who have been a little sullen and exasperated of late.

Schmoozing, humouring, hammering the table—all must be done in person. "I don't want to sound like a whirling dervish," says Paul Calello, Credit Suisse's (CS) investment banking chief. "But in a global world you have to get in front of your employees, spend time with your clients, and show commitment when it comes to joint ventures, mergers, and alliances. The key is thoughtful travel—travelling when necessary."

Yes, many predicted the end of face time due to technology. But, paradoxically, the great work movement unleashed by technology is making physical connection all the more important. As companies open more outposts in more emerging markets, the need to gather intensifies. That's why executives increasingly feel the inhuman pull of having to be in two, three, or four places at one time. The road warrior's art is all about finessing the strategic calculation of where to be when, and of what bets to make with their time. How do road warriors do this? By knowing cultures, organizations, and who has the power. Their jobs may be global, but their understanding must be local. It's not just companies' operations that have gotten bigger; so have these jobs.

Not so long ago it seemed as though technology might make business travel, if not obsolete, then a whole lot rarer. We're not talking about teleporting—just simple things like smartphones, corporate wikis, and videoconferencing. Coca-Cola's president and CEO-designate, Muhtar Kent, has been flying around the globe for Coke since the late 1970s. "I thought 10 or 15 years ago when the concept of videoconferencing first came out that it's really going to take the place of travel," he recalls. Of course that didn't happen, and he now spends about 150 days a year in the corporate jet.

OUTREACH PAYS

Kent considers travel key to meeting new people who might one day prove useful. Several years ago, he was eager to open a bottling plant in Albania, but was frustrated that Coke couldn't get the approvals it needed from the rudderless young government. A friend urged Kent to visit a doctor who was well-versed in local politics. He found the man's patients sitting on tangerine boxes because there were no chairs in the waiting room. "I'm interested in investing in your country," Kent recalls saying during the chat. Three years later, the doctor was Albania's first elected president, and 24 months after that Coke opened its first bottling plant in the country. The doctor-turned-president, Sali Berisha, cut the ribbon.

Kent has never forgotten the lesson. More recently, Coke was hoping to win the rights to the Vitaminwater brand from Glacéau, the US beverage maker known for its so-called enhanced waters. Kent knew one of the company's minority owners was Ratan Tata of Tata Group. He'd never met Tata. So during a business trip to India, Kent requested a dinner with him—no agenda, just to get to know each other, he said. Oh, and by the way, was it OK to bring along a Glacéau executive? It was. "And 72 days later, we closed the deal."

Meeting the right people is all very well, but road warriors who haven't done their homework on the local potentate can run into big problems. Few understand this better than Bill Roedy, the chief of MTV Networks International. His job requires getting often risqué programming into as many countries as he can without offending local sensibilities. A history enthusiast, Roedy is pretty good at figuring out the local scene. Yet he found himself with a rare case of butterflies in mid-September as his flight from London was set to touch down in the Saudi Arabian city of Jiddah. Roedy was in town to persuade the mayor of Mecca to give his blessing to MTV Arabia, the network's biggest global launch, which had the potential to reach 200 million Arabs across the region. "Presidents and sheiks don't normally watch MTV, so we have to help them overcome stereotypical views they have," says Roedy. "Nobody was more important than the mayor of Mecca, the religious center of Islam. We had to get it right."

Despite a hectic schedule that included trips to Budapest (to launch MTV Hungary), Prague (to attend a sales meeting), and New York (to discuss . . . budgets), Roedy carved out as much time in Saudi Arabia as he could. He attended recording sessions with the Arab rappers Jeddah Legends, where he learned that their lyrics tended to be about family and religion—themes that he would draw on during his meeting with the mayor of Mecca.

Finally the day arrived, and Roedy found himself providing assurances to a barrage of questions: Will there be opportunities to educate young people? (Yes.) Will there be a regular call to prayer? (Yes.) And, of course, there will be no skin, right, Mr. Roedy? (Correct.) To help seal the deal, Roedy attended an elaborate dinner in tents by the Red Sea. Ten days later, back at his London base, Roedy learned MTV Arabia would launch as scheduled in November. "Those meetings were crucial," he says.

Mark Sullivan, CEO of WhittmanHart Consulting, which advises clients about information management, flies up to 300,000 miles a year and knows well the strain that constant travel can put on a family. "My profession is riddled with failed marriages, broken families, and people who get swept up with the lifestyle," he says. Sullivan remains a road warrior for one reason: face time with his employees. About a year ago the firm's popular founder died. Sullivan, then president, knew voice messages, email blasts, and memos wouldn't do. So he and two board members hopped on a plane and in two weeks travelled to nine offices around the US to console bereft employees. "They needed a chance to swing away at you, to air concerns," says Sullivan. "If it's urgent, you've got to be physically there."

Questions for Discussion

1. If someone was under the impression that modern information and communication technology would significantly reduce the need for foreign business travel, how would you explain the real-life situation to them, based on what you just read?

2. Is face-to-face communication more important in high-context or low-context cultures? Explain.

3. Which of the cross-cultural competencies listed in Table 14-8 are evident in this case study? Explain.

4. Based on what you just read, are you more or less interested in getting a foreign assignment someday? Explain.

SOURCE: Excerpted from T. Lowry and F. Balfour, "It's All About the Face-to-Face," *BusinessWeek*, January 28, 2008.

The CONNECTion Zone Mc Graw Hill connect™

- The Presentation Assistant
- Ethical OB Dilemma
- Video Case

McGraw Hill connect™

Practise and learn online with Connect.

APPENDICES

A1 **OB Research**

A2 **Case Study Analysis—A Framework**

A1 OB Research

FIVE SOURCES OF OB RESEARCH INSIGHTS

OB gains its credibility as an academic discipline by being research-driven. Scientific rigour pushes aside speculation, prejudice, and untested assumptions about workplace behaviour. We systematically cite evidence from five different categories by drawing upon the following priority of research methodologies:

- **Meta-analyses**   A meta-analysis is a statistical pooling technique that permits behavioural scientists to draw general conclusions about certain variables from many different studies. It typically encompasses a vast number of subjects, often reaching the thousands. Meta-analyses are instructive (helpful) because they focus on general patterns of research evidence, not fragmented bits and pieces or isolated studies.

- **Field studies**   In OB, a field study probes individual or group processes in an organizational setting. Because field studies involve real-life situations, their results often have immediate and practical relevance for supervisors.

- **Laboratory studies**   In a laboratory study, variables are manipulated (changed) and measured in contrived (artificial) situations. College students are commonly used as subjects. The highly controlled nature of laboratory studies enhances research precision, but generalizing the results to organizational management requires caution.

- **Sample surveys**   In a sample survey, samples of people from specified populations respond to questionnaires. The researchers then draw conclusions about the relevant population. Generalizability of the results depends on the quality of the sampling and questioning techniques.

- **Case studies**   A case study is an in-depth analysis of a single individual, group, or organization. Because of their limited scope, case studies yield realistic but not very generalizable results.

A2 Case Study Analysis—A Framework

NINE STEPS TO CASE STUDY ANALYSIS

To be an effective manager or supervisor, you need to develop a variety of skill sets related to all facets of the organization, such as being able to: assess current conditions of a situation; anticipate potential problems; assess or identify the skills and abilities of direct reports; and accurately gauge on-the-job interdependence with colleagues/peers.

Some individuals are placed in jobs and are expected to "hit the ground running" with very little knowledge or training in how to manage people or systems. Case analysis puts you in the role of the person-in-charge who may or may not be directly referred to in the case; however, that is the perspective to take when analyzing a case. Cases intentionally have limited amounts of information. This encourages you to make inferences and assumptions about situations. Below is a simple model for analyzing OB cases.

STEP #1: SIZE UP   This step is sometimes referred to as the situation analysis. To begin, read the case thoroughly and identify any necessary data/information that appear key and relevant. In this step, try to identify critical issues and draw logical inferences from the data.

Most students tend to do a good job at collecting and summarizing the data; where they do poorly is in the drawing of inferences (e.g., What does such data imply? What does it mean?). Be sure to include the key aspects of the organization (e.g., name, market competitors, industry/sector, product type, key characters of the case and their title). Remember to stick to the facts mentioned in the case and identify all the problematic symptoms taking place in the case.

STEP #2: ASSUMPTIONS   What assumptions are you making as you read the case? Fill in the gaps of knowledge missing from the case. It is helpful to list your assumptions to focus your thinking, but also to assist others to understand the rationale used throughout the analysis.

STEP #3: PROBLEM STATEMENT   Keep this statement broad and simple. The subhead suggests a problem, not problems. To help this process, try writing the problem statement as a question (e.g., What should ABC Inc. do to restore productivity?). Eventually you'll have to link this step to your final recommendation. If they don't address one another, then there is a gap that needs to be addressed. Try not to solve the problem in this step by placing your solution within your problem statement. If the problem is solved, then most or all of those symptoms mentioned in the size-up should disappear.

STEP #4: ENVIRONMENTAL SCANNING (SWOT)   The purpose of this step is to identify strategic factors from an internal and external perspective. SWOT is the simplest way to conduct environmental scanning. SWOT is the acronym used to describe the particular situation's S = Strengths, W = Weaknesses, O = Opportunities, and T = Threats. Gauge the internal resources of the firm from the perspective of S and W only. Gauge the external market factors facing the industry in total using O and T only. Here is a guideline of what types of items can be considered in which areas:

- **S/W Gauge Internal Resources:** Review the organizational structure, culture, employee skills/knowledge, HR (Human Resources) training and motivational initiatives, R & D (Research and Development), IT (Information Technology), employee attitude, workplace morale, job satisfaction, ethical management practices, pricing strategy, product, place, and promotional position.

- **O/T Gauge External Market Factors:** Consider the external economic conditions that could possibly be faced that could pose a threat or an opportunity. Consider the demographic trends of the market: political pressures, global economic conditions, market shifts, legal changes, changing social trends that will help or harm, environmental restrictions, changes to the amount or type of competition, and impact from technological changes.

STEP #5: ORGANIZING A FIRM   When possible, review the current organizational structure as it could be creating the OB-related problems in the case. Create a diagram to show the reporting relationships in the case, identifying key departments and people/titles. How would you classify this structure? If this is not an issue, then you may ask your instructor to skip this step. But, if structure is a possible problem, it must be analyzed here.

STEP #6: ALTERNATIVE COURSES OF ACTION   Based on past experience, this area is the one where most students do a minimal job at best. Inevitably, they want to go from analysis to recommendations. They forget that one of their roles is to identify and present the various alternative courses of action that are available. The reason for presenting this step is that others may disagree with your final recommendation and dismiss your thinking. If you have several choices that you considered and analyzed, you'll be able to defend your final decision with more confidence. Each alternative presented should include at least three advantages and three disadvantages listed as part of the analysis. Your instructor will let you know if "do nothing" is an option worth mentioning as a viable alternative; some prefer analyzing the status quo because it gives purpose to the need for immediate change.

STEP #7: RECOMMENDATION Having presented the decision-maker with the range of options available, it is now time to move to the action stage. At this point, it is important to consider the following points:

- Develop and present decision-making criteria. Tell why you selected this alternative over the others. How will this alternative choice address the problem statement?
- No "rabbits out of magic hat," meaning you can't recommend something that was never analyzed. For example, if you want to say, "We recommend a combination of alternative #1 and #2," unless a combined solution was analyzed back in Step #6, it can not be selected as a recommendation. You can first offer it up as an alternative, analyzing it just like you would any other alternative with advantages and disadvantages. Then, once you have it included as one of your possible choices in Step #6, you can select it as your recommendation in Step #7.
- Try to prioritize your recommendations. What action needs to be taken immediately?
- Be sure to write down the actual recommendation you are selecting. Repeat the alternative here word-for-word from Step #6 before explaining why you picked it.
- Go back and double-check by reading your problem statement in Step 2. Does your recommendation solve the problem? If not, then either your problem is too narrow or too broad and needs to be rewritten OR your recommendation is addressing a different problem and needs to be rewritten with more focus.

STEP #8: IMPLEMENTATION This is a timeline of your recommendation. State the action, who is responsible for it, and when it should be implemented. You may wish to organize this step in a table or Excel spreadsheet. Three possible timelines are recommended: immediate action (0–6 months), short term (6–12 months), and long term (12 months+).

STEP #9: CONCLUDING REMARKS This final section should satisfy several important functions:

- Summarize the major issues and problems discussed in the report.
- Summarize the recommendation.
- Point out to the reader the ultimate impact of acting on the recommendation. It should end on a positive note, and, if possible, provide a compelling call to action.

Checklist Chart

	BRIEF DESCRIPTION	COMPLETED (X)
Step #1 SIZE UP	Summarize key points: name of firm, key characters/title, industry/sector, size of firm, various symptoms occurring in the case.	
Step #2 ASSUMPTIONS	Include statements that are not found in the case but which you infer (conclude) to be true.	
Step #3 PROBLEM STATEMENT	Describe the main problem causing all/most of the symptoms mentioned in the size up. If this problem is solved, then those symptoms should disappear.	
Step #4 ENVIRONMENTAL SCANNING (SWOT)	S & W—Comment on internal company resources only, referring to the firm by name. O & T—Comment on external market factors only; address all P.E.S.T.L.E. factors.	
Step #5 ORGANIZING A FIRM	If applicable, draw the organization chart for this firm as it currently exists, and then analyze its strengths/weaknesses, if applicable.	
Step #6 ALTERNATIVE COURSES OF ACTION	List possible alternative courses of action that can be taken to solve the problem statement.	
Step #7 RECOMMENDATION	Provide the final solution to resolve the main problem.	
Step #8 IMPLEMENTATION	Create a timeline to implement the recommendation using a table insert.	
Step #9 CONCLUDING REMARKS	Write summary statements that close the report nicely.	

CASE STUDIES

These cases were written by Victoria Digby solely to provide material for class discussion. The author does not intend to illustrate either effective or ineffective handling of a managerial situation. The author may have disguised certain names and other identifying information to protect confidentiality.

Wallier Specialty Items, Inc. – Unit 1 Case Study

Mark Nash's company was faced with extraordinary, rapid growth. Over the past 12 months, sales had doubled at Wallier Specialty Items Inc. in Dawson Creek, B.C., and were expected to quadruple by the start of the next fiscal year. Nash, the Vice-President of New Business Development at Wallier, was very pleased with the strategic decisions the executive management team had made over the last 18 months to boost the company into the current circumstances of increased sales and high growth.

One day he was going over the sales forecast models when it struck him that although the growth was indeed exciting, it was also unprecedented and straining current resources. It was not uncommon to hear customers complaining about the long wait times on the phone to get answers to their questions, or employees who were becoming increasingly irritable about the number of overtime hours they were mandated to work to meet the added demand. Just the other day he heard department managers negotiating with each other to fill the office gaps as a result of increased absenteeism and turn-over.

Nash took his concerns to the next executive meeting. "I want all of us in this boardroom to reflect for a moment on what we're facing at Wallier. Yes, our sales are up at a pace that we've never experienced. Indeed, we've worked well at achieving our organizational goals. But we can't ignore the perils that can sometimes come with rapid growth such as strained resources, missed deliveries and inadequate service levels. I have to ask two questions: (1) Did we prepare our workforce and our processes adequately? and (2) What price has Wallier paid for such growth?"

The boardroom fell silent. Some participants nodded their head in agreement while others sat in their seat gazing at the person across from them. Finally, Karen Trikowski, a department manager with three years' experience, spoke up. "Mark, I am so pleased to hear that someone else has finally recognized what I've been noticing for quite some time now. Sure we're growing—our sales are up and the bottom line is looking great. But I've never had such a disgruntled group of employees in all my life! If one more person calls in sick, I'll have a mutiny on my hands. I can't get orders fulfilled in time for a number of reasons … but that doesn't matter as much as my concern over my employees. I'm wondering if we may be pushing our employees too hard. I've been thinking maybe I need to hire more staff to pick up the overload."

"Karen, the reason work isn't getting done has nothing to do with a lack of employees in your department … heck, you have more than I do and mine aren't calling in sick or feeling overwhelmed. Personally, I think you need to take better control over their behaviour. Before we implemented our latest strategic action, did you inform your staff that we were anticipating an increase in demand? Have you done an analysis of how much time it should take to fulfill a telephone order or deliver inner-office mail? People in my department don't waste time. I tell them what they have to do and follow-up with them often to ensure they get things done. I think my job is to push them beyond their comfort level," said department manager Paul Grafton.

Another manager, Pat Wong, spoke up. "Paul, I think Karen is saying that even with months of advanced warning and preparation, the volume of orders we're experiencing can sometimes be so large that the staff can't keep up. When faced with natural occurrences like illness or emergencies, it can create quite a dilemma throughout the office. Now I pride myself in being an approachable and caring manager—I help out with the workload in the office as often as I can. If necessary, I stand right next to them at the front counter to either answer the phone or help with customer desk orders. Over the last several months, I too have put in many overtime hours. Karen, have you thought about stepping up and helping out the staff during such high demand times?"

Before Karen could answer, Michael Schidau, the IT manager, spoke up quickly to state his opinion on the matter. "We are facing a classic "people versus machines" question. Given our demand is up and our orders are up, that is putting greater stress on all our resources. But that doesn't mean we have to hire more people to pick up the slack. That's what machines are for. It is in the company's best interest to push our production capabilities to capacity using as many of our resources as possible. That means we acquire more capital assets, depreciate them over 25 years, and operate them 24/7. I think as an executive committee, we should be spending our time investigating what kind of IT resources we need to buy in order to help our people be more productive. Once we get the equipment, I can have my people conduct in-service training on how to use it in the workplace. The answer is getting new and improved technology, not hiring more people!"

"Perhaps if we hired better qualified people!" said Chris Martin, the operations manager.

"Come on Chris, that's not the issue. When we find them, we hire good people," argued Randall Smith, the Human Resource Manager. "Remember that it was only a few years ago that we were in one of the worst economic downturns in recent business history. We lost people. Good people. With this recent growth in our sales, however it's been difficult to quickly fill all the positions posted because people are afraid of leaving their current job to come work for a new company. They are concerned about stability and job security. I can't blame them. So it takes more effort to recruit and hire the kind of people we should be selecting for the future. I believe this is an opportunity for Wallier to diversify itself, find new people with creative talents and abilities—that takes time!"

"Well Randall, we don't have the luxury of getting more time. I'm afraid we have a problem now and before it gets worse we need to find a solution to it, and fast!" exclaimed Nash.

Mark Nash could feel the tempers in the room heating up. He didn't realize that the executive management team was so divided over how to deal with the situation. Nash began to wonder how other organizations deal with similar growing pains.

▶ Do We Stay Or Do We Go? – Unit 2 Case Study

BACKGROUND

John and Su Wang had worked hard to put their business plan together. They invested about $75,000 to start their W.O.W. Chocolatiers candy store in downtown Guelph, Ontario. They knew it would be challenging, but they weren't prepared for the enormous amount of responsibility in running a small organization, especially one that sells food items. John thought at first that it was a good idea and things would just flow easily. Su admitted she had been overwhelmed at times with the constant battle to train employees, schedule staff, deal with equipment acquisition issues and deal with food inspectors checking in unannounced ordering the new owners to make changes. Had they made the right decision? Should they stay in Guelph running this small chocolate store, or should they admit to failure and give up, move back to the big city, and return to their old jobs?

SU PHILIPS

Su Philips was in her final year at the University of Toronto—Faculty of Law School, only a few weeks away from graduation. At the age of 26, she was looking forward to getting out and begin practising law with her father and brother. Her specialty was employment and labour law. Her father always mentioned how proud he was of his children and how he looked forward to placing their names on the letterhead of the company: "Philips, Philips & Philips Law Firm has a nice ring to it, eh?" he would say to friends. Su always knew that after gradation she would eventually follow in the footsteps of her grandfather, father, and brother—all lawyers working on Bay Street. Su used to tell her friends that ever since she was a young child her mother promised to run an ad with Su's picture in the Toronto Star announcing her graduation from law school with honours. "You will do it sweetie, I just know you will and your father and I will be so proud of you," her mother would exclaim.

During her time at school, Su wasn't sure what area of law she wanted to practise. After taking a criminal law class, she decided she couldn't represent someone who she knew was guilty. She thought she wanted to practise international law, but decided it wasn't for her. After much thought, followed by intense discussion with her father, Su settled on focusing her studies on employment/labour law. So, now it was happening. Within three months, Su would be leaving the campus life and working in downtown Toronto. She realized that she would have to article for a year, but Su was prepared for the long hours and interesting life she was about to embark upon.

When Su was called to the bar in Ontario, her father agreed to mentor her in the area of employment and labour law. This meant that any time he knew of a high profile case taking place in the city, he would intervene to get Su assigned to the case. "I will make you the best lawyer in the province! When the judges see you coming, they'll know who you are by the incredible reputation you will have earned," her father would say. For the next seven years Su was involved in some of the most powerful high-profile labour cases in the province. She learned a lot and became well-versed in the art of out-of-court settlements to avoid the big media attention. Her nickname became "Shark Lady." One day she was working late and decided to take a break from her research and grab a coffee down the street at the local Starbucks. While in line, she began talking to the person in front of her, a nice person who worked in the financial markets on Bay Street. They even joked around with each other back on the street, agreeing to a potential meeting in the future at Starbucks. Little did Su know how influential this person would become in her life. Her world was about to change forever.

JOHN WANG

At the age of 20, John Wang graduated with honours with a three-year accounting diploma from George Brown College in downtown Toronto. He always knew that he was good with numbers, so it was no surprise to him or his family that he was accepted into the Schulich School of Business—York University. He wanted to pursue a double major in accounting and finance. He figured there would always be a job in one of those fields, no matter what the economy was like, so staying in school for a few more months to gain career flexibility made sense to John. He worked hard for the years it took to get the undergraduate degree in addition to the few more to earn his MBA. When it came time to meet the recruiters on campus, John decided he would give his resumé to each and every company that would take it. In the end, RBC Capital Markets was the company that John agreed to join upon graduating. Two months after his last exam, John walked out of the campus life that he had known for the last eight years and began working on the third floor of the Royal Bank Plaza located in the heart of the financial district of Toronto—Bay Street.

Within eight years of working at RBC, John was earning an annual income of $250,000 and was on the edge of moving up into the executive ranks. He had worked hard to get to the position he held in the company. Long hours, travelling, personal commitment, and sacrifice were normal behaviours in John's life. He had the nice car he always wanted, Armani suites, the corner office, the respect of his peers, and was planning the next ten years of his life when it happened—he met Su Philips at Starbucks and they became good friends.

CAREER GAME-CHANGER

After that initial meeting at Starbucks, Su and John bumped into each other again on Bay Street and eventually began spending a lot of time with each other talking about life, their careers, and the future. By now, Su was in her mid-30s and getting a bit frustrated with her job. She mentioned to John one day that there was a disconnect between the professional Su and the personal Su. "I don't feel like I'm maximizing my talents," she told John.

"I'm a creative, sensitive person but my job doesn't allow me to express that side of me. I've practised law for many years and it has been so good to me. But I want more to my life. I need more. I'm just not sure this is what I want to be doing when I'm 55 (years old)!?! I don't want to be known as Shark Lady. It has served me well up to this point, but that's not who I want to continue to be. I want to reinvent myself," she said with a grin on her face.

"Whooaaahh Su, where did this come from? You've never expressed any kind of discontentment in your job. Why now? What's up?" asked John.

"John, it's not about earning a six-figure salary anymore, nor is it about getting my name in the paper about the successful case I won for my client. The other day I was talking to my old roommate, Shelly, and she was telling me that after years of talking about it, her and her sister are finally going to open a yoga studio. Here she is, a trained lawyer, and she's going to teach yoga classes! At first I was angry at her for selling out because we always talked about practising law. But then I began thinking about what she had said. With the help of a consultant, Shelly and her sister were able to put together a business plan and get the kind of funding they needed to open their first studio. I think that is what takes me aback the most—her reaction to it all. John, while Shelley was telling me about her new career venture, you should have seen the excitement in her eyes! She was so alive and enthusiastic in what she was doing. I envied her John . . . I did, I became jealous of her!"

"What are you jealous of, Su? You have a successful career as a lawyer. You can take any trip you want, buy any clothes you see, purchase a terrific condo downtown, and drive any car you dream of. What more can you ask of yourself?" said John.

"Well, all I know is that I have never felt the way Shelly feels about her new career choice. I want to feel that excitement of waking up in the morning knowing that you are about to embark upon an exciting journey that no one else has predicted or planned for you. Explore new avenues. Try something new. Meet new people," said Su.

"Su, what are we really talking about here? Be honest with me. What do you mean by 'predicted' or 'planned' for you?"

"I mean that I want to follow MY dreams, explore MY choices, and develop that sensitive creative side that I know I have the capability of developing. I've been thinking about opening up my own restaurant, John. I think it would be so exciting to be the owner of my own business and work for myself! I can see myself greeting people as they walk in, the regulars that sit in the same booth and order their "usual" meal. I like the idea of building a relationship with my customers in a friendly manner and making their evenings pleasant."

"Seriously? I didn't realize you felt that way."

"Well, I do. So, what do you think of that? A successful Bay Street lawyer quits her professional job to open her own restaurant in some small town in southwest Ontario."

"I'd say good for you. Go for it!"

"You don't think it's a crazy idea?"

"Su, I have to admit, I too have thought about giving in to my own entrepreneurial itch!"

"You're kidding, right? I can't believe I'm hearing you talk this way. What is it that you want to do?"

"I have thought about going back to school to take a few cooking classes and maybe opening up a chocolate candy store. I figure that unless I'm prepared to sacrifice my life even more just to move into the executive wing at the bank, which I am not, I've pretty well reached the highest level at the organization that interests me. The last few months I've been meeting a lot of very aggressive entrepreneurs and they have planted the small business seed in my head. Rather than working for someone else, I have been thinking that it may be time to work for myself. Hearing you talk about switching careers is quite timely, actually."

"Oh my goodness. I can't believe we're talking this way! Who would ever have imagined that John Wang would be talking about taking a cooking class and opening a chocolate store," Su said laughing.

"Who would ever have thought Su Philips was thinking about opening up her own restaurant? I say, let's go into business together! Let's open up a store!" After a brief laugh followed by a moment of silence, John spoke up, "I'm serious. Really, I am Su. So, where do we go from here?"

"Well, I think the first step is to just think about it a bit more to ensure that we're not just over-reacting to a fleeting thought. If we bring the subject up again in a few months and we feel the same way, then we can explore it a bit more. How's that?" said Su.

"I agree totally. Let's think about what we're really saying here—leaving our jobs, our careers that we've worked so hard to achieve . . . it's a big step. If after several weeks we still feel the urge to pursue a change, then we can begin by doing some research around the kind of business that appeals to us both, consider location options, and so on. OK?"

"OK, John. That sounds good."

BREAKING AWAY

For both John and Su, the next several weeks proved to be a time of reflection and long-term consideration of what they had talked about earlier. Both were too well-trained and logical to just quit what they were doing and start all over in a totally different occupation.

At times Su found herself daydreaming, especially when she had to work long hours over a weekend to prepare for an upcoming case. "It's a done deal," she would tell her client. Trust me, I know what I'm doing." Su was confident and mentally tough.

But week after week, Su could feel her level of enthusiasm and interest becoming strained. The things that used to motivate her at her job were not having the same effect anymore.

Likewise, John found himself working late at night and thinking about how his talents were being used to help further the interests of others rather than his own. Often he would find himself thinking how differently he would have handled situations, either those that involved clients or even those that were related to internal office issues. John noticed that when he wasn't quoting the same mantra as those around him, he was being labelled as a trouble maker, a lone cowboy in the office—which made him even more mad and distant. John started to become defensive in his dealings with others in the office, wondering why asking questions and presenting alternatives was such a bad thing. His attitude became more negative at work. Slowly he started to pull away from his peers. When John did speak up in meetings, he would only ask questions that made others around him feel uncomfortable. They were direct in nature and challenged the decisions made by the executive team. John began isolating himself from his peers as others began ignoring him when he spoke.

One evening, John was working late at his desk when he was approached by his manager, Jeff Flecher.

"John, have you got a minute?" asked Jeff.

"Sure Jeff, what's up?" replied John.

"I want to talk to you about something that has me wondering—are you OK? Is there anything you want to tell me? Because there is talk in the office that you're not very happy with your job and being employed by RBC. It's just not like you. There has been a change in your behaviour over the last month or two, and frankly I can't figure out what it is!"

"Jeff, tell me. Am I getting my work done? Are the tasks assigned to me being completed on time and below budget? Are the clients satisfied with my performance?"

"Yes John, they are. But that is not what I am referring to. It's your attitude. You're being defensive, short, and blunt in meetings. It seems like there is no pleasing you. There was talk at one time of moving you into the executive ranks of this organization, but I'm not sure that is still an option open to you."

"Oh great! So threatening me is supposed to encourage me to change? You're saying that I am being a problem employee. Do I have to remind you that I've been here for almost ten years and never have I brought problems to you or any manager for that matter. I've always figured it out. I've worked hard and put in long hours. I've given this job a lot of myself. I'm just wondering if it's been worth it!?!"

"John, you are not a problem employee. You have been a good employee. We have worked together for many years. I have benefitted as a department manager having you here. May I ask what are you looking for John? What is it that you want?"

"Right now, Jeff, I want to end this conversation and get back to work. . . I have a lot to do and it's late. I don't want to be here through the night, like I have done so many times before, working alone on a deal."

"OK John, I hear you and respect your request to get back to work. I'm leaving for home now, but in the morning, if you change your mind and want to talk, let me know. We'll go have a coffee together. OK? John, do you hear what I'm saying?"

"Yeah, yeah Jeff, I hear ya. I'm fine."

"OK John. Thanks for talking. Have a good evening."

John felt bad. The conversation he had with Jeff didn't go very well. John's behaviour even surprised himself. Why was he taking his frustration out on Jeff? Jeff had been a good boss over the years. John didn't realize that others in the office were talking about him to the degree they were. He felt angry at the situation and frustrated by it at the same time. He decided to pick up the phone and call Su to discuss what just happened.

"Hey Su, got a minute?" asked John.

"Hi John. Yeah sure. What's up?" said Su on the other end of the phone.

"I've been thinking . . . I want to talk about leaving our current jobs and pursuing that entrepreneurial dream of owning a business, becoming my own boss and determining my own destination. But I can't do it alone. I want to go into business with you. Are you ready to make the leap? I now it's a big step, but I think I'm ready to go. What do you say?"

"I know, I've been thinking about it too. Ever since we had our conversation, I've been thinking about it and I can't deny that it's very tempting. Tempting to the point of saying yes."

The two friends talked for an hour more, covering such issues as what it would mean financially, socially, and emotionally. They both referred to an article they had read in *The Globe and Mail* about the number of professional people across the country quitting their jobs and switching careers to something totally different. The article seemed to comfort them, making them feel not that unusual. They agreed to spend the next weekend talking more seriously about the new adventure and plan their exit strategy from their current employers.

BUILDING THE DREAM

The first step to owning a business was to study every shopping district in the city to figure out what kind of business appealed to them both, and which neighbourhood was booming. They settled on the positive interest people were having toward chocolate. "Who doesn't like chocolate?" John kept saying out loud to Su. They decided to test some unique chocolate recipes in their own kitchen and sell them at local flea markets on the weekend to test market interest. Renting a kiosk for the summer months seemed a logical start; they could do it together and learn along the way. Throughout the next several months, John and Su experimented with all sorts of different chocolate recipes. They went on store tours throughout the city to check out the competition and made notes of their observations. Summer came and their trial experience at local flea markets wasn't all it was cranked up to be. The chocolate melted in the heat and they ended up giving most of their product away. In the end, the flea markets didn't attract the kind of demographic that demanded quality chocolate and pastries. Overall, they were disappointed to learn that the big city market was already saturated with stores offering chocolate products. They had given almost 12 months to this project and with no success. It was time to step back from the project and take a break.

The next two months went by with little to no discussion about opening a chocolate store. Both John and Su continued to work at their professional jobs and focus on their careers a bit longer. But before long, they were back at it, talking about the dream of opening their own store, the pros and cons of being an owner/operator, and what went wrong with their previous efforts.

In an attempt to regroup and try again, John and Su concluded that they had to try a different approach and maybe even consider somewhere else. They expanded their chocolate store research to the smaller communities outside of Toronto until they came upon a town called Guelph. John did a Google search and learned from the Guelph website that the city was located in one of the strongest economic regions in Canada, declaring itself as "an ideal destination for companies to access major markets and customers." With a population of just under 120,000, Guelph could offer an educated workforce, an established economic base, and a positive quality of life—just the kind of qualities that John and Su were looking for to start a business and their new lives together.

One late summer weekend, the couple went to Guelph to visit the various neighbourhoods where businesses seemed to be flourishing. After hours of searching, they soon settled on a neighbourhood with a burgeoning food culture and a kind of bohemian affluence from the university crowd that lived nearby. They contacted a local landlord for the area to book a series of meetings to begin the process of making their chocolate store a reality. They would need funding, but that wouldn't happen without a business plan. They would need clear indications that their product appealed to the Guelph market and they didn't have that indicator yet. There was so much to do, but both John and Su were filled with renewed enthusiasm for what they were about to embark upon.

In a few weeks it would be fall and the annual Oktoberfest festival was being promoted in and around the Guelph region. John and Su felt this would be a perfect time to rent a kiosk and test their recipes with festival patrons. While the couple focused on this at night and on weekends, they delegated certain tasks to others. They hired a consultant to help write a business plan and register the corporation with the province, a lawyer to work with the store landlord, an accountant to set up new books and open a bank account, and so on.

The seven-day festival proved to be an outstanding success. The patrons were enthusiastic about the chocolate candies and pastries. The local media interviewed John and Su for upcoming articles. At the end of the week, the couple came away with a small profit. They felt they had the evidence they needed—now it was time to make the tough decision. John had to give final notice to RBC and Su had to tell her partners at the Philips law firm she was leaving.

THE LONG ROAD AHEAD

The law firm was busy that day, Su was nervous as she approached her father's office to give notice of her leaving. Knocking on the door as she peeked in around the wall, Su could see her father working at his desk.

"Dad, can I speak to you for a minute?" asked Su.

"Sure dear, come on in. How are you today?" said the father.

"I'm fine. I'm good. Ahhh, I . . . ah . . . just need to tell you . . . ah . . . something that . . . ah . . ." she was stammering on her words and trying to look her father in the eye at the same time, but with great difficulty.

Eventually, Su was able to get her entire rehearsed speech out so that her father could understand what it was that she wanted to talk about. When she was done, great relief came over her. She felt exhausted but comfortable with her decision to leave the firm and what she was about to do with her career.

"Well, I can't say I'm surprised," said the father. "You and John have been working for over 18 months on this idea of a chocolate store; I could see it coming. I have to tell you that this is going to break your mother's heart, Su. But I understand this is something you feel you have to do. We're going to miss you around here. Go follow your dream knowing that you are always welcome to come back."

For John, it was no different in terms of being nervous at RBC. He bumped into his boss Jeff by the lunchroom and asked him if he could spare a moment to talk about something. "Sure John, let's go to my office and sit down. It's more comfortable there. OK?" said Jeff. It took a few minutes for John to express his feelings of discontent. John made sure that Jeff knew that it wasn't because of poor management or bad treatment over the years; instead, John was leaving to follow a dream.

"Jeff, you have been a great person to work with over the years. My interest in this field has changed. I have to explore this other side of me. It's something that I feel I just have to do!" exclaimed John.

"John, first I want to thank you for taking the time to come in and talk so candidly about your situation. I think we've all had a notion for a while that your level of satisfaction toward this job was just not the same. I have to be honest. You have changed. Your level of engagement has been decreasing over the last several quarters and it was beginning to reflect in your quality of work. I was going to talk to you about it again very soon if things didn't correct themselves."

As the meeting ended on a very positive note, John walked away from Jeff's office with feelings of relief and an internal desire of excitement. He did it. He was leaving for a new life and new start.

The next few weeks proved to be a mixture of emotions for the couple as they packed up their big city jobs and lives to move east along the 401 highway to Guelph. For months, their lives were filled with early morning meetings, late night visits to the store, and general chaos. The space John and Su ended up renting used to be a restaurant, so that really cut down on the need for permits and major renovations. They had budgeted $40,000 but spent only $25,000, mostly on equipment, ingredients, and packaging for the products. By the spring, their store, W.O.W. Chocolatiers (Wonderful-And-Oh-So-Mouth-Watering!), was opened and operating seven days a week, 10 hours per day.

It proved to be a challenge to find their niche in the chocolate-making world. John and Su hired some counter staff but insisted on making all the products themselves. The chocolate-dipped chips proved to be popular, as were the bacon dipped in peanut butter and chocolate treats. By the second year, Su planned on turning the store into a café and chocolate salon by adding pastries, home-made ice cream, and an espresso machine. John's accounting side kept him realistic as they continued to plough every penny they made back into the business, basically paying to work!

By the end of the second season, the couple had to admit that while they were following their dream, they had days when they were so exhausted they actually asked themselves why they had decided to open a store. After all, both had worked so hard to become professionals, to put themselves through school. But, they decided to give themselves an additional two-year trial period. "Even if this doesn't work John, I'll never return to law," said Su. "As a lawyer, your interactions with people aren't always happy. Now I go home every day with a sense of satisfaction and accomplishment."

"I totally agree," said John. "I don't see myself ever returning back to a large bank or accounting firm. And besides, everybody loves chocolate!"

▶ To Spy Or Not To Spy? – Unit 3 Case Study

"All things are possible with the right technology!" said Helmut Schwartz, the recently appointed CEO of Globe Alive, Inc. (GAI), an Edmonton-based software company. Speaking at a monthly management meeting of GAI executives, Schwartz continued. "With the right technology in our organization, we can facilitate efficient communication between global partners, discern in-bound supply chain elements from out-bound shipments, expedite customer orders in a timely manner, electronically transfer funds around the world, and monitor employees to ensure they are being productive. And that list is by no means exhaustive. Believe me when I say, all things are possible with the right technology. When I shared that vision with the executive interview panel a few months ago, I was being sincere. I believed it then and I believe it now. This philosophy is the driving force behind everything I do here at GAI and I strongly suggest it become your philosophy as well so that together we can build a brighter stronger future for this organization!"

Unfortunately, not every member of the management team was buying into the philosophy. After the meeting, a few members decided to go out to lunch together where some began speaking out against Schwartz and his belief that technology held the answer to many managerial issues.

"You know, technology offers a lot, but it can't do it all," said Stuart Miller, Director of the Human Resource Department. "Technology can't build a team-oriented workforce at GAI. Employees are not the same as out-bound shipments—monitoring and measuring the activities of boxes is not the same as motivating or leading people!"

"I had heard rumours that Helmut was thinking about introducing spyware into the network system. Is it possible that he has already started the ball rolling by hiring a company to work with our IT people? Has anyone else heard that?" inquired Ali Khan, Marketing Manager.

"I've been talking to my department about the value of HR metric services and the benefits they offer, especially when measuring turnover, resignation rates, sick days . . . things like that. But I have *never* heard anyone speak about introducing spyware into our organization. Where did that come from?" asked Miller.

"I think it's a big mistake Stuart. How are we to build trust between management and non-managerial staff if we use spyware to watch every move our employees make? It is counterproductive," argued Thuy Singh, Production Manager.

"I agree with Thuy and I don't appreciate Helmut forcing his philosophy on us," said Patrick Photo, Operations Manager.

Soon everyone at the table was nodding their head in agreement. Among the four executives eating lunch together, there was little support for introducing surveillance software at GAI. But what were they to do next?

HELMUT SCHWARTZ, CEO

Helmut Schwartz was a 48 year old ex-tech guy from Ottawa, Ontario. After graduating from Georgian College with a three-year IT diploma, Schwartz went on to earn his degree from Carleton University in computer science. Schwartz cut his career teeth working in Kanata, the hi-tech centre outside of Ottawa, and for the next 25 years he did everything from writing programming for such companies as Nortel and Mitel, to selling mainframes for HP. On a sales call to Smart Technologies one day, Schwartz was introduced to the idea of jumping into management, something he had always been interested in pursuing but had never had the opportunity to do. Schwartz had ideas—a lot of them—and always felt he was being held back by those around him who didn't have the same drive or passion to explore new IT territory. Eventually he made it to vice-president in charge of network systems at Smart Tech, overhauling and revitalizing the computer network system unlike anything the industry had witnessed before. It became the envy of the entire Kanata region and there was talk that Schwartz was soon going to be offered the position of president.

When the CEO position at GAI became available, Schwartz was approached by an executive head-hunting firm and invited to interview for the medium-sized software company out west. After flying to Edmonton for the initial interview, Schwartz felt that leading a firm like GAI was the opportunity he'd been looking for to take his career to a new level. When the position was finally offered, Schwartz eagerly accepted with the understanding that he would help GAI develop into a global organization with the help of the right technology. His knowledge and belief in technology was well-known across the industry and was a contributing factor for the GAI board of directors who eventually came to a consensus to hire him as CEO.

The first few months out west proved to be a frustrating time for Schwartz. There were so many differences between Kanata and Edmonton—both geographically and socially—that he knew it would take some time before he felt comfortable in his new surroundings. But the frustration was also occurring at work where he felt there was a lot of resistance to new ideas and a lack of innovative thinking at the tech firm. Based on conversations with the HR Director, Stuart Miller, Schwartz learned that he was the first senior executive to ever be hired from outside of the GAI organization; all others were from the southern Alberta region and had moved up the ranks throughout the organization, including both the previous president and CEO. In addition to that, Schwartz was only the second senior executive to lead the firm since its creation in 1997.

The principles that guided the previous executive team seemed far more limited and traditional when compared to the strategic philosophy Schwartz embraced. Within weeks of his arrival to the GAI offices, Schwartz introduced weekly strategy meetings that were mandatory for all managers, he insisted upon professional development for all employees, but especially the managers, and he scheduled off-site management meetings that were at times innovative brainstorming sessions that became part sales, operation, and HR-oriented. "I want to get these people out of their comfort zone to stop thinking locally and shifting toward a mindset of change. I represent the new philosophy of the board and I need to develop this team into a more competitive global organization," thought Schwartz.

STUART MILLER

Stuart Miller was one of the first managers hired by the GAI executive team in 1997. At the time he was recruited, Miller had held a number of HR jobs around the Edmonton area, including many years with the federal government, a few years in the banking and financial services industry as HR manager at Canadian Western Bank, and eventually head of the HR department for Briskal Systems Ltd., a growing computer software company. During his employment at Briskal, Stuart became involved in the Human Resources Institute of Alberta (HRIA), where he was able to network with other HR professionals in the Edmonton area. When the opportunity presented itself, Miller completed the courses needed to earn his CHRP designation as an HR professional. He felt this certification, together with his good reputation at Briskal, would provide the kind of knowledge, skills, abilities, and other attributes to qualify him for many HR positions in the city.

One evening, Miller was attending an HRMA meeting and overheard a member talking about a new company that was going to be opening a large office in the city called Globe Alive. The rumour on the street suggested it was going to be hiring over 250 people. Moreover, their market focus was going to be assisting in the network design and servicing for Canadian companies who were conducting business in a foreign country. When Miller heard about Globe Alive, he thought it would be a great fit for him and made a conscious decision to investigate further.

At the age of 40, Miller was looking for an executive position. More specifically, he wanted to become the HR director of an up-and-coming firm that would provide new opportunities for growth and development. He felt he was ready for a change, and believed he had the relevant experience to head up a department and the certification to oversee the recruitment and hiring of 250 people. After throwing his resumé into the pile of applicants, Miller was granted an interview and offered the position within 24 hours to become the new HR Director of Globe Alive, Inc. Over the years, Miller saw the company grow and prosper under the direction of the new management team. Although they never did grow to the intended target size of 250 employees, they nonetheless became a medium-sized firm. Working together, the management team was able to create policy, processes, and systems that would guide the organization for years to come. Miller especially enjoyed strategy meetings, as he felt great satisfaction knowing that he was contributing to the development of a structure that would serve GAI for decades. Throughout his years at GAI, Miller remained committed to the human services industry by networking through his Edmonton HRMA contacts, maintained his CHRP certification by attending workshops and monthly meetings to stay informed, and always tried to keep his sights on new and upcoming issues facing the HR industry.

Several months ago, Miller helped the GAI board of directors find an executive recruiting firm to replace the soon-to-retire CEO, Stan Ryder. After several weeks of interviewing various candidates, a new CEO was decided upon: Helmut Schwartz. Miller didn't know much about him other than hearing he was a tech guy from out east with a reputation for making significant changes to organizational systems.

STAN RYDER

Stan Ryder was one of the original founders of GAI. He had recruited his friends from various Edmonton-based businesses to join him at GAI, which was how the original executive team was created. They were friends in the boardroom and outside of the office. They trusted each other a great deal and never felt the need to question the overall direction GAI was going. Ryder scheduled management meetings on an ad hoc basis, and they were usually informal discussions held in his office rather than the GAI boardroom.

CHANGES BEGIN

The first few weeks Helmut Schwartz worked at GAI were about observation, although he did spend time meeting people, asking questions, and trying to understand process. The employees didn't know what to expect of him at first, but over a few more weeks of hearing him talk, people began to understand the kind of person Schwartz was. He was driven, arriving at his office by 7 a.m. each morning and not leaving until well past 8 p.m. most nights. He was involved, asking questions, seeking advice, and making inquiries. Whenever possible, he would stop and talk to employees to ask who they were, what they did, and what they needed to do their job better.

At the first monthly management meeting, Schwartz announced that he wanted people from the executive team to become innovative leaders for the organization. He challenged them all to find new and innovative ways to run the business and to bring ideas back to the team to share and discuss. Schwartz was known for making changes and used the first official management meeting to do just that.

Stuart Miller found the executive team challenge refreshing and welcoming, believing that other managers would feel the same. He spent the next several days reflecting on his duties as a senior manager, the processes developed within the HR area, and how changes could be implemented within his department. He was having difficulty seeing things anew, admitting to himself that perhaps he was not the best person to assess the need for change since he was so instrumental in creating past practices. On his way to the elevator one evening, Miller ran into Patrick Photo, Operations Manager, who was also leaving for the day. He and Photo were hired within two days of each other back in 1997. As colleagues, they had shared a long and respectful working relationship. Standing in the lobby waiting for the elevator to arrive, their conversation began.

"How's it going Patrick?" asked Miller.

"Not bad Stuart, and you?" responded Photo.

"I'm good, but I have to admit, I'm having trouble fulfilling Helmut's directive to find new and innovative ways to change my department. I have looked around at what we do and how we do it and I don't see one thing that needs to be changed. It all seems to be working and I certainly don't believe in change just for the sake of change. Know what I mean?"

"Stuart, I have to be honest, I haven't even started to look around for things to change. My days are so filled with fires that have to be put out that I don't have to go looking for more work, thank you. I figure this is Helmut's attempt to try to make his mark on the company. I don't need to make a mark—I already made mine years ago. If he thinks we need to change, then shouldn't he be the one to identify it and give reasons why?"

"Hmm, never thought of it that way. Maybe you're right."

"Sure I'm right. And I'll tell you one more thing. He's pushing himself around the departments, asking questions, and the other managers don't like it. They are wondering what his intentions are. Is he being nosey? Is he checking up on us? Does he think he's the big shot now around here telling others what to do? I don't know what you think, but I believe that if he keeps this up, there's going to be some problems around here."

Just then the elevator door opened and the two men joined the others already inside for the ride down. "Let's talk about this later," said Photo. "Yeah, that's a good idea," agreed Miller.

The next day Miller was away from the office attending an HRIA workshop on HR Analytic Benchmarking Services, part of his CHRP designation requirements to earn the necessary points by attending professional development activities. The workshop facilitator was from a company called HR Analytic Systems that provides a benchmark of norms for organizations to gauge whether their employee performance is stronger or weaker than the provincial and/or national averages. Miller found the day-long workshop very informative, especially as it related to gathering data on turnover. GAI was having a rash of people leaving in the last eight months, and Miller couldn't identify causes or reasons. The workshop got him thinking. Maybe this could be something to introduce back at the office as part of Helmut's initiative to find new and innovative ideas on how to improve the organization, specifically for the HR Department. Before leaving that day, Miller collected as much information as he could in anticipation of presenting the idea to the GAI management team.

Back at the office, Miller became excited about the prospect of implementing an analytical data collection program to begin tracking HR trends within the organization: sick days, attrition rates, turnover, retirements, job openings, first-year resignation rates, etc. Within a few weeks, he had shared his idea with all of his key employees within the department and collectively they agreed that GAI could easily begin introducing the data collection and tracking process before the month ended. This was good news, Miller thought. He had buy-in from his people and the process appeared to need little resources to get it started. Shirley Zimba, a long-time department employee, jumped at the opportunity to take the lead by conducting a gap analysis of what they needed, what they had, and what they wanted to achieve. In the meantime, Miller put in an agenda request to Helmut for 10 minutes at the next monthly management meeting. He would present his idea then.

HR METRICS

Originally started by the BC Human Resources Management Association (BC HRMA), the HR Metrics Service is now an inter-provincial collaboration involving four HR associations across Canada. The service provides data on more than 100 metrics, from revenue per full-time employee and 90-day voluntary turnover rates, to the cost revenue percentage of learning and development. A participating organization receives quarterly and annual reports that show its scores against a comparison range, enabling employers to track their progress and benchmark their performance.

The HR Metrics Service is the first comprehensive source of metrics that a company can benchmark against externally. Even if an organization is tracking certain metrics internally, comparing their results against those who they may compete against for talent is worthwhile knowledge.

THE MEETING

It was only the fourth executive management meeting since Schwartz was hired, and Miller was going to be the first person to make a presentation on implementing a data collection and tracking process within the HR Department. The meeting began, Schwartz introduced the agenda, and soon Miller was standing at the podium enthusiastically showing a Prezi presentation about the benefits of changing the processes within the HR Department. Members of the executive team were impressed with the information Miller brought forward, and even Schwartz complimented Miller on the creative initiative.

"I really enjoy the idea of analytics and tracking data of our employees. It is for that reason that I would like to present my own creative and innovative idea to you all today, and it builds upon the HR idea. It's called surveillance software and I'd like to tell you more about it. I've spent the last few months visiting every department of this organization and I have witnessed an awful lot of time being wasted, resources being underutilized, and a general lack of productivity in the workplace as employees spend too much time on their computers doing personal things!" said Schwartz.

Walking up to the boardroom podium, Schwartz plugged in a small memory stick and opened a file while continuing to talk. "With the assistance of our IT department, I think it would be beneficial to increase our productivity by introducing surveillance software into the network system. There are several products on the market, and I won't go into them all, but collectively they offer a broad range of applications that can benefit the workplace. For example, one can tell us what sites our employees have visited and for how long and also take screenshots that reveal exactly what our employees were doing on those sites. Managers will be able to scan through employee surfing history page by page, or receive short summaries of employee habits. I'm sure you can imagine just how beneficial this could be for your department."

Stopping for a moment to smile and take a drink of water, Schwartz went on. "Another product analyzes an entire organization's email, determines what the average employee's correspondence profile looks like, and targets those who deviate from that norm for further scrutiny. The idea here is to catch data leakers, whistleblowers, abusive employees, and sexual harassers. It can also identify those employees spreading time-wasting Web links or who might be contemplating a move to a competitor. That's it! That is my creative and innovative idea to help make this company more productive and efficient. Like I've always said, all things are possible with the right technology."

Schwartz kept talking, but moved to more general terms about the value of technology in finding solutions to management problems—but no one was listening. The management team was in shock by what they had just heard. Did the new CEO really want to begin spying on employees? Monitoring sick days was one thing, and they unanimously agreed that it was a good idea from an HR perspective. But surveillance software to watch employee Internet and email behaviour was something that the management team had never talked about nor heard concerns over. Was productivity really a problem at GAI, or was this Schwartz's way of gaining control?

SOFTWARE OPTIONS

- SpectorSoft, one of the world's largest purveyors of surveillance software, designs products used by more than 50,000 organizations. Founded in Florida in 1998, the company first described its products as "spyware" then later coined the phrase "stealth" solutions; today it is commonly referred to as monitoring software. They also have a home version, marketed to parents who want to spy on their kids. SpectorSoft promises its customers that their programs record "every exact detail" of employee Internet activity.

- Websense is another popular program. It is used by both organizations (the CBC in Canada) and governments (China and Yemen) to block websites. It has been criticized as being a tool of oppressive regimes to filter websites containing forbidden keywords, such as names of political dissenters.

- Cataphora is claimed by some to be the most sophisticated workplace spyware. Cataphora looks for possibly distressed employees who write in ALL CAPS, devious employees who give conflicting information to different people, and suspicious employees who suddenly take conversations off-line.

- IBM Algorithm software snoops on employee email to build user-friendly visualizations of complicated work relationships. By tracking the colourful, radiating spheres emanating from the new employee in sales, a manager can see that this employee is building a vast professional network within the firm. The new employee probably considers her daily chatter with friends at other companies something to hide from the boss. To her it's networking, but to the boss it is cyber slacking.

PRIVACY LAWS

The 1983 Canadian Privacy Act puts limits and obligations on over 150 federal government departments and agencies on the collection, use, and disclosure of personal information. It also gives Canadians the right to find out what personal information the federal government has about them by making a formal request under the Privacy Act.

The governments of all provinces and territories in Canada, except Newfoundland and Labrador, also have their own provincial legislation governing the collection, use, and disclosure of personal information. The legislation varies from province to province, but the general right to access and collect personal information exists in all, and each has a commissioner or ombudsman who is authorized to handle complaints.

The laws controlling privacy in the private sector fall under The Personal Information Protection and Electronic Documents Act, or PIPEDA, which regulates how private sector organizations collect, use, and disclose personal information in the course of business activities. PIPEDA establishes ten principles that organizations must follow when collecting, using, and disclosing personal information in the course of commercial activity: accountability, identifying purpose, consent, limiting collection or use, disclosure and retention, accuracy, safeguards, openness, individual access, and challenging compliance.

According to some law experts, almost every employer monitors employees. It has become a fact of corporate life not even worth discussing, some argue. Many companies ask employees to sign away every possible claim to their own data, even agreeing to be spied upon when signing their employment contract. Organizations are advised to have well-publicized and well-written policies in place prior to introducing actions that could potentially violate employee privacy rights.

THE LUNCH DISCUSSION

". . . philosophy as well so that together we can build a brighter stronger future for this organization!" Schwartz concluded.

After a few more agenda items were discussed, it was time for the management meeting to break for lunch. Four executives from the management team hurried out the door to meet in the lobby. "Who's ready for lunch?" asked Photo.

As they made their way out the door, each manager was reflecting on what they had just sat through in the morning meeting.

▶ The Right Fit – Unit 4 Case Study

It was 10 a.m. on a Friday in May and Masi Wang was walking down Yonge Street in downtown Toronto looking for the Canadian head office for Brown Dawg Enterprises. It was going to be his first job interview as an accounting clerk since graduating from college with a three-year business accounting diploma. Masi was nervous but looking forward to the opportunity to start working.

MASI WANG

When Masi accepted the offer to go to George Brown College three years ago, he was excited about living in Toronto and all that it had to offer an 18-year-old from Listowell, Ontario. The adjustment to living away from home proved to be an easy one as Masi quickly made friends in his first year business classes.

Masi was a conservative and mild-mannered student. He attended on-campus presentations from the CGA and welcomed occasions to be mentored by his professors about their younger years working in the accounting field. Masi excelled while studying at George Brown. He was an outstanding student, earning high marks in all his classes. He managed to get two semester cycles under his belt at Revenue Canada as a co-op student. By year three, Masi became president of the 68-member Business Accounting Club.

One month before the end of his graduating year, Masi was told by his academic advisor to register his availability with the placement office so that he could begin interviewing for jobs. Masi agreed that this would probably be a good idea and so one afternoon, during a spare, he walked into the placement office to speak to a liaison officer about applying for accounting jobs. During his meeting, he was told that he could expect to find jobs at Revenue Canada, KPMG, and many other organizations in the greater GTA.

"Is there any specific type of organization you are interested in Masi?" asked the liaison officer.

"Not really, I will work in pretty much any organization. As long as it's an accounting department, I'll be happy!" replied Masi.

"OK, then leave your resumé with me and once I get something that I believe will interest you, I'll let you know immediately."

And with that, Masi left. Five weeks passed before he heard back from the placement office regarding a job opening at a company called Brown Dawg Enterprises, a well-known national-brand energy drink manufacturer. The firm was looking for a junior accounting clerk to work in their accounting department. The pay was well above the average salary typically found with such jobs, and the successful candidate was expected to start as soon as possible. Masi thought this would be a wonderful job and agreed to set up an interview on his own.

The receptionist who answered the phone sounded pleasant and professional when Masi called Brown Dawg. But the music playing through his iPhone when his call was being transferred to the HR department. was loud and unconventional; it was promoting a Legends-in-the-Halo competition

taking place in a few weeks. How unusual, Masi thought to himself, before being interrupted by the other person picking up.

"Shirley 'The Crusher' Davison here, how may I help you?" said the person on the phone.

"Yes, I am calling about an accounting clerk position. My name is Masi Wang. I just graduated from college in accounting and I was told to contact you by the college placement office for an interview?" said Masi.

"Oh yeah, we need a numbers person for sure. So, ah Masi, right? That's awesome. Listen, are you free to come in this Friday morning?"

"Yes, no problem." responded Masi.

"OK, cool. I'll meet you in our lobby at 10:30 and we'll go from there. How's that?"

"That is fine. I'll bring my resumé and references with me. Thank you Shirley," said Masi.

"Hey, no problem Masi, I'm stoked to meet ya. See you then!" exclaimed Shirley.

Masi prepared for the interview just like he was taught in school. He planned on wearing a suit and crisp white button-down shirt. He rehearsed answers to incorporate as many accounting and business terms as possible. "I want to appear to be professional and knowledgeable!" he told his roommate.

THE INTERVIEW

With some difficulty, Masi eventually found the head office of Brown Dawg Enterprises that Friday morning in May, mainly because there was no sign on the building—instead it was more of a symbol in the shape of a big dog. The front entrance to the main lobby was bold and impressive with its massive chrome and glass doors. A group of art students from the Ontario College of Art were holding a lobby gallery for parents and visitors. The music playing over the PA was indie rock, the kind Masi had never heard before except on TV. Masi made his way through the crowd to what appeared to be a receptionist sitting at a most unusual desk—a big clear plastic table with a big blue exercise ball as a chair. "Hey, what's up?" asked the receptionist.

Masi introduced himself to the receptionist, "Hello, my name is Masi Wang and I have an appointment this morning at 10:30 with Ms. Davison."

"Oh yeah, Crush just called me a few minutes ago. She's expecting you and said to have a seat. She'll be out soon. Hey, let me ask you something. Do you like this song that is playing on the PA?" the receptionist said with a slight grin on his face.

"I've never heard it before," replied Masi.

"Would you buy it if you could to listen to it again?" asked the receptionist.

"Ah, I prefer to listen to top 40," Masi said.

"Oh, ok. Thanks for the feedback. Like I said, Shirley will be right out."

Masi noticed how casually the receptionist was dressed. He had a shaved head, big spacers in his ear lobes, a slight beard, and he wore a t-shirt with a big brown dog on it, jeans, and black high-end sneakers. He was also answering switchboard calls through his wireless headset and tablet computer on the desk. Masi turned to take in the sheer size and interesting style of the room. It was massive by lobby standards, approximately 30' × 30'. No chairs were evident, but there were polished chrome benches the length of a wall and clear glass tables that looked like big long footlockers next to them. The floor was brushed metal that reflected dozens of potlights above. The ceiling-to-floor columns in the hallway were massive monoliths of chrome that dominated the view to the street. It was something out of *Architectural Digest,* Masi thought. He didn't sit. He felt uncomfortable, so he stood there with a briefcase in his hand, waiting. It all seemed so unreal compared to what Masi had experienced during his co-op term at Revenue Canada.

Within a few minutes, Masi was approached by a young woman who reached out her hand to welcome.

"Hi, you must be Masi. I'm Shirley!"

"Yes, hello. Nice to meet you," replied Masi.

"Follow me, we're meeting people in the boardroom," said Shirley.

Masi followed Shirley through the lobby. He noticed how casually she was dressed as well, very urban—black tights, shoes, skirt, top. The only colour she wore was red lipstick. Her hair was shaved on one side with the rest combed to cover her eyes with a giant set of bangs. She wore huge pierced hoop earrings in both ears and lots of wristbands of twine and thread. Masi was beginning to feel a bit out of place. Brown Dawg was not your typical organization, and he could only imagine what the accounting department would be like. He began to wonder if he had made a mistake. He didn't look like these people. He didn't listen to the kind of music that they seemed to prefer. The casual nature of their conversation and attitude was not the traditional business behaviour he was expecting.

While Shirley walked Masi through the hallways of the multi-floored Brown Dawg organization, he couldn't help notice the play-like workstations along the way where employees were sitting on the floor using giant cubes or big exercise balls, all talking in small groups about their work. The lunch area had a pool table, several video-game stations, and a massive rock-climbing wall in it. Shirley mentioned that the office supplied free, daily healthy meals for the staff, and in good weather, employees were able to go to the rooftop patio to enjoy the downtown skyline.

"Here we are," said Shirley walking toward a boardroom that was completely made of glass on two of the principle walls. The table was one huge piece of clear plastic, and big pod-like chairs on wheels were pushed around the perimeter. One back wall had a 10' × 10' Smartboard screen that came down from the ceiling and the opposing front wall had all sorts of writing on it—it was one giant whiteboard. A small group of individuals sat on the table writing on the glass wall with dry-erase markers, making notes for discussion. They were talking seriously, but then broke into laugher as they noticed Shirley and Masi approaching. Masi also noticed that they too dressed casually, just like Shirley, except some of these people wore baseball caps. He walked in behind Shirley while the group greeted them both in general terms. Some shook Masi's hand while others motioned for everyone to sit because the interview was about to start.

"Masi, sometimes at this place we have to work late into the night, evenings, and sometimes holidays. Are you able to adjust your schedule to be flexible in such a way?" asked the first person sitting around the table.

"Well, since I would be working in accounting, I don't see what could possibly be so urgent that would require me to have to work such unusual hours," Masi replied.

"What is your favourite video game?" asked the next person sitting around the table.

"I've played Rollercoaster Tycoon with some friends, but I am not really into gaming that much," smiled Masi.

"The company owns a recording studio on the main floor. It's something that our president likes to do—record independent rock bands that few people know about. Josh, our receptionist, told us that you prefer Top 40 music, is that correct?"

"Ah, yes, that's correct. I'm pretty conservative in my musical taste," said Masi.

Shirley looked at Masi for a moment and then glanced over to one of the people sitting around the table. After a few seconds of staring at each other, they both put their heads down and began writing. Here they were, already ten minutes into the interview, and not one question regarding accounting or business at all. He felt like he wasn't fitting in at all. Masi began to wonder if he had made a mistake in asking for an interview with this company.

 ## Bundles For Overseas – Unit 5 Case Study

Suhail Farwa, a factory labourer, survived the last recession and felt lucky—that is, until he found himself working 12-hour days due to the surge in workload, receiving a smaller pay cheque as taxes increased, and hearing about the potential clawback on company benefits. It became too much to take and his resentment grew, leading him to consider a business idea that he had always wanted to explore but had never been motivated to do. Suhail's entrepreneurial vision involved starting an import/export business operating out of a large warehouse in an industrial neighbourhood just outside of Winnipeg, Manitoba. Originally from Morocco, Suhail still had family and other contacts in Africa. He immigrated to Canada a poor man 20 years earlier with his wife and twin

children. Now, decades later, Lameese, the daughter, was graduating with a diploma in general business administration and Shamir, the son, was graduating with his diploma in IT—both from Red River Community College. Both had expressed interest in starting a small business with their father. When Suhail first asked his daughter how she would feel about working in Morocco, Lameese thought it would be a perfect fit. Shamir was cautiously optimistic because the idea of a family business interested him, but he wondered how much technology would be assessible in northern Africa. Even with enthusiasm from the family, Suhail wondered if he was ready to take the risk by quitting his current job and becoming the owner of a global organization.

SUHAIL FARWA

When his family was young and they didn't have a lot of money, working in a factory was the only job Suhail could find in Winnipeg. The pay and benefits were rewarding enough to keep him satisfied for many years. But then it hit—the worst Canadian recession since the 1930s. People were losing their jobs. Companies were going bankrupt. Suhail's firm decided to lay off dozens of people and also cut salaries by 10 percent across the board. Few workers grumbled about the measures since it meant the company and their jobs didn't disappear like many of their benefits had. Suhail soon found himself working longer hours just to keep up. He wasn't exercising, his sleeping patterns were off, and his home life was becoming a wreck. In a word, Suhail was exhausted.

Years earlier, his brother in Morocco had discussed the possibility of starting an import/export business that would become a family-run operation with Suhail working out of North America and his brother, Mo, looking after the distribution within northern Africa. Suhail disregarded the idea as being too risky. But now, in the stressful post-recession era, he was ready to reconsider the offer, Suhail knew he had to do something to get his life back in order and maybe help his children start their careers.

THE BUSINESS

Mo Ashad knew that the number of Moroccans needing affordable clothing was increasing. They had some disposable income to purchase good used clothing, but there wasn't enough of it in his country to go around. He had an idea for a small business where his brother, Suhail, who lived in Canada, would purchase used clothing by the pound from various charity donation centres. The idea went like this: Suhail would secure enough used clothing to fill a container, sort the clothing, and bundle it for overseas shipping. Mo would take possession of it in Morocco. Once landed, Mo would find vendors in the local marketplace to sell it. The idea was to purchase huge quantities of used clothing for 15 cents (Cdn.) per pound, but to sell it to specific buyers in Africa for 20–25 cents (Cdn.) per pound.

Back in Winnipeg, Suhail started the search for a vacant warehouse in the city. One weekend he took Lameese and Shamir with him to find the right location for the business. That was the easy part, since so many businesses had gone bankrupt—there were plenty of choices to consider. Then they had to discuss the supply chain and accounting needs of the new business. Shamir had some good ideas based on some research he had done about transportation costs, custom brokerages, as well as specialized software options worth considering. It seemed to be falling into place. Suhail began feeling confident that this new company could have a chance at succeeding!

THE TWINS

Shamir and Lameese had been very close all their lives. Throughout grade school, they found common interests and similar goals in who they were and how they wanted to live their lives. Growing up in Canada offered so many opportunities that their father and mother had never experienced back in their native country of Morocco. Although their parents tried to celebrate many of their cultural traditions from the old country, Shamir and Lameese saw themselves as North American; for example, they wore jeans, played X-box, ate hamburgers, had Facebook accounts, and tweeted about music videos .

Growing up, Lameese saw herself as a business owner ever since she had seen Oprah on TV talk about women empowerment and entrepreneurship opportunities for females. Some day she wanted to have a job, make a difference in the world, and travel. When her father approached her about starting a small family business with her Uncle Mo in north Africa, she was thrilled. It offered all the things that she hoped to do with her career.

Shamir had always enjoyed spending time on techie things in high school, especially on Apple products. He spent hours on his iPod, iPad, iPhone, and iMac, hot-synching, uploading, troubleshooting—you name it, he knew how to do it. Friends and family would call him for advice when they couldn't make things work on their computer systems. Shamir seemed to have a natural interest and ability to make multi-media presentations for his classes. His ability to integrate technology from various sources was almost an instinct. Going into IT at Red River was a natural step for him. While studying in his program, Shamir took some commerce classes on the side to strengthen his knowledge of management principles, accounting, and general business disciplines.

Hearing his father make the offer of starting a small family business was something that Shamir never expected. His Uncle Mo was always trying to find a new business idea to try, but his father didn't strike him as being a risk taker and Shamir knew from his business courses that many firms fail. He recalled the Stats Can report that said 95 percent of small businesses (1–99 employees) survive for one full year, 85 percent survive for three years, and 70 percent survive for five years. If this business didn't succeed, Shamir knew his father would be devastated. On a more personal level, Shamir was cautious about the business because he wondered how much accessibility there would be in Morocco for him to use his IT skills.

GETTING READY

A few months after Lameese and Shamir graduated from Red River, their father sent them to Morocco to meet with their Uncle Mo to discuss the details of the new business venture. Suhail couldn't afford to take time off work, so he had to trust his children to complete the business trip without him. The twins had not been to Morocco since they were young children and it had been a while since they had spent time with cousins, aunts, and uncles. The trip was a graduation present from their family, so it had a personal side to it, but it was also a chance for them to investigate how the new business would operate from the other side.

Prior to the trip, the parents sat down with them to discuss the different types of experiences to be expected in Morocco. For one, the role of women in business was very different. Besides religious traditions, there would be cultural distinctions that they would have to be sensitive to—after all, they didn't want to shame the family. Comparing Canada to Morocco was like comparing apples to oranges, they were told, enjoy it for "what it is, not what it isn't."

"Lameese, you must respect the way of life our family back in Morocco is choosing to live. It is not Canada. They will not look kindly toward you if they feel you are judging them. Remember, you are the only female member of our family to have ever earned a diploma. You have opinions and ideas and that is good. But do not be surprised if you are made to feel less than they when speaking," said the mother.

"And Shamir, you will be expected to be a strong representative of this family. You may become frustrated by the lack of advancement and infrastructure within their homes and businesses. While it is easy to do something here with all of your computer knowledge, it will be at times impossible there. You must not take on a superiority attitude with your Uncle Mo. He will not tolerate your behaviour very long and I don't want to get a phone call from him telling me how disrespectful you are being to him and the family. Do you understand?" said Suhail.

"Yes, I understand. Don't worry, I won't do anything stupid," said Shamir.

"You guys are making us nervous! We know that Canada is not the same as Morocco. We're going over to investigate, right? Along the way we're going to see family and reconnect. That's all good. But Dad, let's keep our goal in mind. Shamir and I are going over there to get what we need to make this new company venture a success. I don't want to see you work so hard and be stressed out all the time. It's not healthy. I want to return in two weeks with enough information for you to make an informed decision on whether to stay at your current job or give them notice to leave," said Lameese.

Suhail felt a little better after their discussion, but deep inside he still felt uneasy about taking the risk to quit his current job to start a small import/export business. He knew that his brother Mo operated according to Moroccan business principles and he wondered if there would be cultural clashes between him and the twins. But then he remembered that he wasn't dealing with a stranger—it was his family, and that was enough to provide comfort.

VIDEO CASES

OB 4TH EDITION VIDEO SEGMENTS

(AVAILABLE ON KINICKI 4th EDITION DVD AND WITHIN CONNECT)

PLEASE GO TO ▓connect™ TO VIEW THE VIDEOS. INSTRUCTORS, PLEASE NOTE THAT THESE SEGMENTS ARE AVAILABLE ON DVD FOR CLASSROOM VIEWING. ANSWERS ARE PROVIDED WITHIN THE CONNECT INSTRUCTOR SITE.

CORRESPONDING TEXT UNIT	VIDEO TITLE/TIME/ SOURCE	VIDEO DESCRIPTION/ QUESTIONS
Unit #1 Introduction to Organizational Behaviour	***Managing Religious Diversity at Work*** 3:42 min. *McGraw-Hill Management video library*	The video describes how Ford Motor Company manages religious diversity in the workplace. It discusses the pros and cons of recognizing and allowing for religious expression in today's diverse organizations. **1.** Do you anticipate more or less demand for a meditation-type room located onsite within an organization? **2.** Why would Ford Motor Company offer a prayer room on Fridays especially?
Unit #1 Introduction to Organizational Behaviour	**Talent Management at Aviva** 4:08 min. *Canadian HR Reporter TV* www.hrreporter.com	Ramona Tobler, VP HR business partner for underwriting and finance at Aviva, talks about the company's talent management system and how it is used to create conversations about employees' futures. **1.** What is "talking talent" at Aviva? **2.** How is "talking talent" implemented on a daily basis?
Unit #1 Introduction to Organizational Behaviour	**Talent Management at The City of Brampton, Ontario** 3:36 min. *Canadian HR Reporter TV* www.hrreporter.com	Lisa Murray, skills development and education specialist at the Ontario municipality of Brampton, talks about how her organization handles talent management. **1.** How can talent management offer an organization a competitive advantage? **2.** Talent management isn't anything new because organizations have always wanted to hire the best. Why is it becoming such a big consideration today?
Unit #1 Introduction to Organizational Behaviour	**Using Metrics to Drive Business Goals** 2:27 min. *Canadian HR Reporter TV* www.hrreporter.com	Sooky Lee, vice-president of HR at ADP Canada, talks about how metrics are helping HR departments do more with less, become more proactive in problem solving, and free up time to focus on strategic goals that help drive the business. **1.** What is meant by HR metrics and how is ADP Canada using them? **2.** By having HR metrics available, how is an organization better able to anticipate problems?

(Continued)

CORRESPONDING TEXT UNIT	VIDEO TITLE/TIME/ SOURCE	VIDEO DESCRIPTION/ QUESTIONS
Unit #2 Managing Individual Behaviour	**Hiring and Individual Differences at Zappos** 6:36 min. *McGraw-Hill Management video library*	This video discusses how the organizational culture at Zappos supports individual differences. The video also highlights hiring practices and the Zappos $3000 "quit offer." 1. How do Zappos Family Core Values facilitate and support their employees to act individually when providing customer service? 2. Why is the recruitment/selection process at Zappos so lengthy and unusual?
Unit #2 Managing Individual Behaviour	**Personality, Abilities and the Building of Facebook** 10:51 min. *McGraw-Hill Management video library*	This interview with Mark Zuckerberg, the founder and CEO of Facebook, addresses questions surrounding Zuckerberg's personal life and success as it relates to Facebook. 1. What sort of things does Zuckerberg value based on what you've heard? 2. In the video, the Harvard twins present their opinion of Zuckerberg's character. Compare and contrast their opinion from those who bought Facebook stock at the IPO only to have it lose almost 50 percent of its value in six months.
Unit #2 Managing Individual Behaviour	**The Challenge of Work-Life Balance** 3:04 min. *McGraw-Hill Management video library*	This video discusses the challenge of balancing work and home roles in the current economy. Cell phones, pagers, email, and other technologies have blurred the boundaries between work and home. Many workers and their families feel stress and experience problems because of work pressures. 1. What does *work-life balance* mean? 2. In the future, do you expect more or less work-life conflict among employees? Explain your answer.
Unit #2 Managing Individual Behaviour	**Gender Differences Controversy** 8:06 min. *McGraw-Hill Management video library*	This video discusses research on the differences between the sexes and the "nature and nurture" debate about the origin of these differences. 1. What do research findings state about male versus female behaviour? 2. The video states that male and female brains differ. Provide a short list of those differences.
Unit #2 Managing Individual Behaviour	**Google: The Digital Age and Your Memory** 4:24 min. *McGraw-Hill Management video library*	Researcher Betsy Sparrow discusses the effect of communications technology on learning and memory. 1. What are some of the cognitive consequences of having information at our fingertips (e.g., conducting a Google search rather than holding something in memory)? 2. What sorts of things are being relegated to external sources versus having such knowledge within our own memory?

(Continued)

CORRESPONDING TEXT UNIT	VIDEO TITLE/TIME/ SOURCE	VIDEO DESCRIPTION/ QUESTIONS
Unit #2 Managing Individual Behaviour	**Conducting OHS Incident Investigations** 3:16 min. *Canadian HR Reporter TV* www.hrreporter.com	Jerry Traer, program and training specialist with Workplace Safety North, talks about conducting proper incident investigations and how to ensure recommendations are implemented. 1. When it comes to the investigation of an incident at work, why is the role of the supervisor in charge at the time so important? 2. What can we learn from best practices when it comes to incident investigations?
Unit #2 Managing Individual Behaviour	**Moving Entry-Level Employees Through The Ranks** 3:21 min. *Canadian HR Reporter TV* www.hrreporter.com	Maria Oboardi, vice-president of people at Softchoice, talks about how her company is bringing opportunity to employees who start in entry-level positions at its call centres. 1. How is Softchoice bringing opportunity to employees in its call centres? 2. How is Softchoice supporting employee development internally?
Unit #2 Managing Individual Behaviour	**Harnessing Baby Boomers in the Workplace** 4:42 min. *Canadian HR Reporter TV* www.hrreporter.com	Michael Adams, president of Environics, talks about what boomers want in the workplace and how employers can put their expertise to use. 1. How can the expertise of baby boomers be harnessed in the workplace? 2. When it comes to re-hiring baby boomers as contract workers, how does an organization formalize itself in terms of policies, systems, and practices around their needs?
Unit #3 Managing Group and Team Behaviour	**Decision Making Overload** 7:27 min. *McGraw-Hill Management video library*	This video focuses on decision-making overload—the sheer number of decisions people must make in everyday life. It discusses how people make decisions and how emotions impact decision-making. 1. How realistic is it to expect individuals to use the rational decision-making model when faced with choice? 2. According to the video, is it possible to make a completely 100 percent rational decision?
Unit #3 Managing Group and Team Behaviour	**Leadership at Japan Airlines** 2:04 min. *McGraw-Hill Management video library*	This video is about leadership at Japan Airlines and focuses on former CEO Haruka Nishimatsu. Nishimatsu is shown as a leader who does away with fancy executive perks and develops strong relationships with his employees. 1. What kind of leader is Nishimatsu trying to be? 2. What sort of behaviours does Nishimatsu demonstrate on the job?
Unit #3 Managing Group and Team Behaviour	**Accenture Friends Campus Recruitment (or search "Accenture")** 2:49 min. *Canadian HR Reporter TV* www.hrreporter.com	Lisa Kramer, campus recruiting lead for Accenture and winner of TalentEgg's 2012 Campus Recruiter of the Year award, talks about how Accenture uses social media for campus recruitment. Tactics include announcing on-campus events and conducting online focus groups. 1. What role is social media playing in the recruitment and selection process for Accenture? 2. Why is recruiting in "real time" so important to Accenture?

(Continued)

CORRESPONDING TEXT UNIT	VIDEO TITLE/TIME/ SOURCE	VIDEO DESCRIPTION/ QUESTIONS
Unit #4 Managing Systems That Affect Behaviour	**Organizational Culture at Zappos** 7:06 min. *McGraw-Hill Management video library*	This video describes the unique culture at Zappos and the company's focus on both employee and customer satisfaction. 1. What are some of the shared beliefs at Zappos? 2. Provide examples of Zappos's culture through artifacts, language use, etc.
Unit #4 Managing Systems That Affect Behaviour	**Huge Benefits in Getting Organizational Design Right (or search "Laura Stepp")** 4:50 min. *Canadian HR Reporter TV* www.hrreporter.com	Laura Stepp, former Director of Americas at Intel's consulting services and a senior consultant with Kates Kesler, discusses how Intel's HR department reacted to a restructuring that saw a 40 percent cut to the department. 1. Why is it so important for the HR Department to consider the role of organizational design as one of its core areas of responsibilities? 2. After cutting 40 percent of their workforce, how did the HR department at Intel change their focus?
Unit #4 Managing Systems That Affect Behaviour	**Is the Worker a Contractor or an Employee?** 5:29 min. *Canadian HR Reporter TV* www.hrreporter.com	Simon Health, a lawyer with Keyser Mason Ball LLP in Mississauga, Ontario talks about the difference between employees and contractors (both dependent and independent) and how companies can differentiate between the two for legal reasons. 1. In Ontario, what is the difference between a "true employee," a "true independent contractor," and a "dependent contractor"? 2 To an employer, why are independent contractors so appealing in terms of hiring?
Unit #5 Managing Change and Change Agents That Affect Behaviour	**Depressing Jobs** 2:33 min. *McGraw-Hill Management video library*	This video discusses on-the-job stress and depression. Certain jobs are highlighted as having higher rates of employee depression than others. 1. Why are some jobs more depressing than others? 2. Are these jobs more depressing or are people who are prone to depression more likely to do these kinds of jobs?
Unit #5 Managing Change and Change Agents That Affect Behaviour	**Appreciative Inquiry and Changing Workplace Culture** 4:32 min. *Canadian HR Reporter TV* www.hrreporter.com	Kathy Sabo, Toronto Western Hospital senior vice-president, talks with HR Reporter TV about her team's use of appreciative inquiry and how it led to the development of their Positive Learning Program. 1. What is appreciative inquiry and what benefits does it provide the organization? 2. What is the role of inspiration within appreciative inquiry?
Unit #5 Managing Change and Change Agents That Affect Behaviour	**CSA's Workplace Ergonomics Standard** 2:28 min. *Canadian HR Reporter TV* www.hrreporter.com	Norma McCormick, president of Corporate Health Works and a member of the Canadian Standards Association (CSA) workplace ergonomics standard committee, talks about reducing workplace stress and injury and CSA Z1004, the new workplace ergonomics standard. 1. When it comes to workplace health and safety, how does the new workplace ergonomics standard compare to the old office ergonomics standard? 2. What is in the new workplace ergonomics standard?

(Continued)

CORRESPONDING TEXT UNIT	VIDEO TITLE/TIME/ SOURCE	VIDEO DESCRIPTION/ QUESTIONS
Unit #5 Managing Change and Change Agents That Affect Behaviour	**HR's Role in a Business Transformation** 4:26 min. *Canadian HR Reporter TV* www.hrreporter.com	John Sicard, COO of Kinaxis in Ottawa, Ontario talks about the role HR plays when business is undergoing a major transformation, including getting employees involved and overcoming their resistance to change. **1.** Why did Kinaxis feel the need for change? **2.** How did Kinaxis merge their transformation with the current culture of the organization (learn, laugh, share, connect)?

ADDITIONAL ONLINE VIDEO RESOURCES		DESCRIPTION
Unit #2 Managing Individual Behaviour	**Any episode** *Dragons' Den—CBC TV* www.cbc.ca/dragonsden/	While viewing an episode of this TV show, consider the perception of individuals who are sitting as judges and those who are presenting. Analyze the self-concept of the entrepreneurs selling their business idea. Try to identify the values of the dragons (judges) who invest their money and whether they conflict with or complement the values of the entrepreneurs. Identify how dragon motivations differ from those of the entrepreneur.
Unit #2 Managing Individual Behaviour	**Susan Cain: The Power of Introverts** 10:34 min. *TED Conferences* www.ted.com	It can be difficult, even shameful, to be an introvert. But, as Susan Cain argues in this passionate talk, introverts bring extraordinary talents and abilities to the world and should be encouraged and celebrated.
Unit #3 Managing Group and Team Behaviour	**Mark Forsyth: What's a Snollygoster? A Short Lesson in Political Speak** 6:40 min. *TED Conferences* www.ted.com	Most politicians choose their words carefully to shape the reality they hope to create. But does it work? Mark Forsyth strolls through the English language, telling stories, making connections, and banishing hobgoblins.
Unit #3 Managing Group and Team Behaviour	**Margaret Heffernan: Dare to Disagree** 12:56 min. *TED Conferences* www.ted.com	Most people instinctively avoid conflict, but as Margaret Heffernan (the former CEO of five businesses) shows us, good disagreement is central to progress. She illustrates how the best partners aren't echo chambers, and how great research teams, relationships, and businesses allow people to deeply disagree.

ENDNOTES

CHAPTER 1

[1] *Canadian HR Reporter,* "2 Million Unfilled Ontario Jobs by 2031: Study," March 8, 2010, p 1; and *The Globe and Mail,* "Economy in Transition," February 5, 2009, p 1A.

[2] H.L. Tosi, Jr. and J.W. Slocum, Jr., "Contingency Theory: Some Suggested Directions," *Journal of Management,* Spring 1984, p 9.

[3] H. Mintzberg, "The Manager's Job: Folklore and Fact," *Harvard Business Review,* July–August 1975, p 61. Also see M.M. Clark, "NLRB General Counsel's Office Issues Liberal Criteria for Defining 'Supervisor,'" *HR Magazine,* February 2004, p 30.

[4] See T.J. Tentenbaum, "Shifting Paradigms: From Newton to Chaos," *Organizational Dynamics,* Spring 1998, pp 21–32; and R.W. Oliver, *The Shape of Things to Come* (New York: McGraw-Hill, 1999).

[5] Essential sources on reengineering are M. Hammer and J. Champy, *Reengineering the Corporation: A Manifesto for Business Revolution* (New York: HarperCollins, 1993); and J. Champy, *Reengineering Management: The Mandate for New Leadership* (New York: HarperCollins, 1995). Also see "Anything Worth Doing is Worth Doing from Scratch," *Inc.,* May 18, 1999 (20th Anniversary Issue).

[6] For thoughtful discussion, see G.G. Dess, A.M.A. Rasheed, K.J. McLaughlin, and R.L. Priem, "The New Corporate Architecture," *Academy of Management Executive,* August 1995, pp 7–20.

[7] F.W. Taylor, *The Principles of Scientific Management,* (1911); and *The Modern History Sourcebook,* Fordham University website, www.fordham.edu/halsall/mod/1911taylor.html.

[8] Ibid.

[9] Ibid.

[10] See M. Parker Follett, *Freedom and Coordination* (London: Management Publications Trust, 1949).

[11] As quoted in P. LaBarre, "The Industrialized Revolution," *Fast Company,* November 2003, pp 116, 118.

[12] See J.M. Ivancevich, T.N. Duening, and W. Lidwell, "Bridging the Manager-Organizational Scientist Collaboration Gap," *Organizational Dynamics,* no. 2, 2005, pp 103–117; E.W. Ford, W.J. Duncan, A.G. Bedeian, P.M. Ginter, M.D. Rousculp, and A.M. Adams, "Mitigating Risks, Visible Hands, Inevitable Disasters, and Soft Variables: Management Research That Matters to Managers," *Academy of Management Executive,* November 2005, pp 24–38; and J.M. Bartunek, S.L. Rynes, and R.D. Ireland, "What Makes Management Research Interesting, and Why Does It Matter?," *Academy of Management Journal,* February 2006, pp 9–15.

[13] "The Canadian Population in 2011: Population Counts and Growth," Census, 2011 Analytical Products, Statistics Canada website, www12.statcan.gc.ca/census-recensement/2011, July 2012.

[14] This discussion is based on material in R.R.Thomas, Jr., *Redefining Diversity* (New York: AMACOM, 1996), pp 4–9.

[15] This distinction is made by M. Loden, *Implementing Diversity* (Chicago: Irwin, 1996).

[16] "Canada's Best Diversity Employers in 2011," *The Globe and Mail Report on Business,* February 20, 2011, www.theglobeandmail.com.

[17] A. Tomlinson, "Concrete Ceiling Harder to Break Than Glass for Women of Colour," *Canadian HR Reporter,* December 17, 2001, pp 7, 13.

[18] A.M. Morrison, *The New Leaders: Guidelines on Leadership Diversity in America* (San Francisco: Jossey-Bass Inc., 1992).

[19] Empirical support is provided by H. Ibarra, "Race, Opportunity and Diversity of Social Circles in Managerial Networks," *Academy of Management Journal,* June 1995, pp 673–703; and P.J. Ohlott, M.N. Ruderman, and C.D. McCauley, "Gender Differences in Managers' Developmental Job Experiences," *Academy of Management Journal,* February 1994, pp 46–67.

[20] M. Campeau, "Casting A Wider Net: Hiring Internationally Trained Workers," *H.R. Professional,* January 2012, p 24.

[21] "Top 10 Crooked CEOs," *Time Magazine,* March 12, 2009, www.time.com/time/specials/packages/article/0,28804,1903155_1903156,00.html.

[22] A. Stern, "Update 1 – Ex Media Mogul Conrad Black Sent Back To Prison," *Reuters,* June 24, 2011, www.reuters.com/article/2011/06/24/idUSN1E75N1J420110624.

[23] T. Tedesco, "Drabinsky Denied Bail," *Financial Post,* October 14, 2011, www.nationalpost.com/related/topics/Drabinsky+denied+bail/5552009/story.html.

[24] M. Lewis, "Nortel Execs Head To Trial Over Lost Billions," *Toronto Star,* January 8, 2012, p 1A.

[25] *Academy of Management Review* by A.J. Dabaub, Copyright 1995 by Academy of Management (NY). Reproduced with permission of Academy of Management (NY) in the format Textbook via Copyright Clearance Centre (See 8th US edition p 22, Figure 1.4).

[26] As quoted in D. Jones, "Military a Model for Execs," *USA Today,* June 9, 2004, p 4B.

[27] For a good discussion of values, see S.D. Steiner and M.A. Watson, "The Service Learning Component in Business Education: The Values Linkage Void," *Academy of Management Learning and Education,* December 2006, pp 422–434. For more on courage, see J. McCain, "In Search of Courage," *Fast Company,* September 2004, pp 53–56; D. Lidsky, "How Do You Rate? Take the Courage Quiz," *Fast Company,* September 2004, pp 107–109; and K.K. Reardon, "Courage," *Harvard Business Review,* Special Issue: The Tests of a Leader, January 2007, pp 58–64.

[28] See S. Baker, "Wiser About the Web," *BusinessWeek,* March 27, 2006, pp 54–58; S. Levy and B. Stone, "The New Wisdom of the Web," *Newsweek,* April 3, 2006, pp 46–53; and A. Lashinsky, "The Boom Is Back," *Fortune,* May 1, 2006, pp 70–87.

[29] M.J. Mandel and R.D. Hof, "Rethinking the Internet," *BusinessWeek,* March 26, 2001, p 118. Also see G.T. Lumpkin and G.G. Dess, "E-Business Strategies and Internet Business Models: How the Internet Adds Value," *Organizational Dynamics,* no. 2, 2004, pp 161–173; and T.J. Mullaney, "E-Biz Strikes Again!" *BusinessWeek,* May 10, 2004, pp 80–82.

[30] A. Bernasek, "Buried in Tech," *Fortune,* April 16, 2001, p 52.

[31] See M.A. Tucker, "E-Learning Evolves," *HR Magazine,* October 2005, pp 74–78; S. Boehle, "Putting the 'Learning' Back in E-Learning," *Training,* January 2006, pp 30–34; B. West, "Online, It's All About Design," *Training,* March 2006, p 76; and J. Gordon, "Seven Revelations About E-Learning," *Training,* April 2006, pp 28–31.

CHAPTER 2

[1] Examples can be found in T. Lowry, "'A McKinsey of Pop Culture'?," *BusinessWeek,* March 26, 2007, pp 104–108; and "Virtual Marketing Makes a False Impression," *BizEd,* March/April 2007, pp 54, 56.

[2] Object perception is discussed by L.J. Rips, S. Blok, and G. Newman, "Tracing the Identity of Objects," *Psychological Bulletin,* January 2006, pp 1–30.

[3] S.T. Fiske and S.E. Taylor, *Social Cognition,* 2nd ed. (Reading, MA: Addison-Wesley Publishing, 1991), pp 1–2.

[4] The negative bias was examined by N. Kyle Smith, J.T. Larsen, T.L. Chartrand, J.T. Cacioppo, H.A. Katafiasz, and K.E. Moran, "Being Bad Isn't Always Good: Affective Context Moderates the Attention Bias Toward Negative Information," *Journal of Personality and Social Psychology*, February 2006, pp 210–220.

[5] E. Rosch, C.B. Mervis, W.D. Gray, D.M. Johnson, and P. BoyesBraem, "Basic Objects in Natural Categories," *Cognitive Psychology*, July 1976, p 383.

[6] For a thorough discussion about the structure and organization of memory, see L.R. Squire, B. Knowlton, and G. Musen, "The Structure and Organization of Memory," in *Annual Review of Psychology*, eds. L.W. Porter and M.R. Rosenzweig (Palo Alto, CA: Annual Reviews Inc., 1993), vol. 44, pp 453–495.

[7] Implicit cognition is discussed by Y. Dunham, A.S. Baron, and M.R. Banaji, "From American City to Japanese Village: A Cross-Cultural Investigation of Implicit Race Attitudes," *Child Development*, September 2006, pp 1268–1281; and A.G. Greenwald and M.R. Banaji, "Implicit Social Cognition: Attitudes, Self-Esteem, and Stereotypes," *Psychological Review*, January 1995, pp 4–27.

[8] Supreme Court of Canada – British Columbia (Public Service Employee Relations Commission) vs. BCGSEU (British Columbia Government Service Employees' Union) (1999), 3S.C.R.3. Commonly referred to as "The Meiorin" case.

[9] Details of this study can be found in C.K. Stevens, "Antecedents of Interview Interactions, Interviewers' Ratings, and Applicants' Reactions," *Personnel Psychology*, Spring 1998, pp 55–85.

[10] The effectiveness of rater training was supported by D.V. Day and L.M. Sulsky, "Effects of Frame-of-Reference Training and Information Configuration on Memory Organization and Rating Accuracy," *Journal of Applied Psychology*, February 1995, pp 158–167.

[11] Results can be found in J.S. Phillips and R.G. Lord, "Schematic Information Processing and Perceptions of Leadership in Problem-Solving Groups," *Journal of Applied Psychology*, August 1982, pp 486–492.

[12] Results can be found in M. Sandy Hershcovis, N. Turner, J. Barling, K.A. Arnold, K.E. Dupré, M. Inness, M.M. Le Blanc, and N. Sivanathan, "Predicting Workplace Aggression: A Meta-Analysis," *Journal of Applied Psychology*, January 2007, pp 228–238; and S. Thau, K. Aquino, and R. Wittek, "An Extension of Uncertainty Management Theory to the Self: The Relationship between Justice, Social Comparison Orientation, and Antisocial Work Behaviours," *Journal of Applied Psychology*, January 2007, pp 250–258.

[13] See S. Begley, "All In Your Head? Yes, and Scientists Are Figuring Out Why," *The Wall Street Journal*, March 17, 2006, p B1.

[14] C.M. Judd and B. Park, "Definition and Assessment of Accuracy in Social Stereotypes," *Psychological Review*, January 1993, p 110.

[15] For a thorough discussion of stereotype accuracy, see M.C. Ashton and V.M. Esses, "Stereotype Accuracy: Estimating the Academic Performance of Ethnic Groups," *Personality and Social Psychology Bulletin*, February 1999, pp 225–236.

[16] Stereotype formation and maintenance is discussed by J.V. Petrocelli, Z.L. Tormala, and D.D. Rucker, "Unpacking Attitude Certainty: Attitude Clarity and Attitude Correctness," *Journal of Personality and Social Psychology*, January 2006, pp 30–41.

[17] See S. Madon, M. Guyll, S.J. Hilbert, E. Kyriakatos, and D.L. Vogel, "Stereotyping the Stereotypic: When Individuals Match Social Stereotypes," *Journal of Applied Social Psychology*, January 2006, pp 178–205.

[18] Results are presented in E. Tahmincioglu, "Men Rule—At Least in Workplace Attitudes," *MSNBC*, www.msnbc.msn.com/id/17345308/, accessed March 6, 2007.

[19] See M.E. Heilman and T.G. Okimoto, "Why Are Women Penalized for Success at Male Tasks?: The Implied Communality Deficit," *Journal of Applied Psychology*, January 2007, pp 81–92.

[20] See J.D. Olian, D.P. Schwab, and Y. Haberfeld, "The Impact of Applicant Gender Compared to Qualifications on Hiring Recommendations: A Meta-Analysis of Experimental Studies," *Organizational Behaviour and Human Decision Processes*, April 1988, pp 180–195.

[21] Results from the meta-analyses are discussed in K.P. Carson, C.L. Sutton, and P.D. Corner, "Gender Bias in Performance Appraisals: A Meta-Analysis," paper presented at the 49th Annual Academy of Management Meeting, Washington, DC: 1989. Results from the field study can be found in T.J. Maurer and M.A. Taylor, "Is Sex by Itself Enough? An Exploration of Gender Bias Issues in Performance Appraisal," *Organizational Behaviour and Human Decision Processes*, November 1994, pp 231–251.

[22] See J. Landau, "The Relationship of Race and Gender to Managers' Ratings of Promotion Potential," *Journal of Organizational Behaviour*, July 1995, pp 391–400.

[23] Results can be found in K.S. Lyness and M.E. Heilman, "When Fit Is Fundamental: Performance Evaluations and Promotions of Upper-Level Female and Male Managers," *Journal of Applied Psychology*, July 2006, pp 777–785.

[24] For a complete review, see S.R. Rhodes, "Age-Related Differences in Work Attitudes and Behaviour: A Review and Conceptual Analysis," *Psychological Bulletin*, March 1983, pp 328–367. Also see S. DeArmond, M. Tye, P.Y. Chen, A. Krauss, D.A. Rogers, and E. Sintek, "Age and Gender Stereotypes: New Challenges in a Changing Workplace and Workforce," *Journal of Applied Social Psychology*, September 2006, pp 2184–2214.

[25] See G.M. McEvoy, "Cumulative Evidence of the Relationship between Employee Age and Job Performance," *Journal of Applied Psychology*, February 1989, pp 11–17.

[26] A thorough discussion of the relationship between age and performance is contained in D.A. Waldman and B.J. Avolio, "Aging and Work Performance in Perspective: Contextual and Developmental Considerations," in *Research in Personnel and Human Resources Management*, ed. G.R. Ferris (Greenwich, CT: JAI Press, 1993), vol. 11, pp 133–162.

[27] For details, see B.J. Avolio, D.A. Waldman, and M.A. McDaniel, "Age and Work Performance in Nonmanagerial Jobs: The Effects of Experience and Occupational Type," *Academy of Management Journal*, June 1990, pp 407–422.

[28] D.H. Powell, "Aging Baby Boomers: Stretching Your Workforce Options," *HR Magazine*, July 1998, p 83.

[29] Results can be found in R.W. Griffeth, P.W. Hom, and S. Gaertner, "A Meta-Analysis of Antecedents and Correlates of Employee Turnover: Update, Moderator Tests, and Research Implications for the Next Millennium," *Journal of Management*, 2000, pp 463–488.

[30] See J.J. Martocchio, "Age-Related Differences in Employee Absenteeism: A Meta-Analysis," *Psychology and Aging*, December 1989, pp 409–414.

[31] See J.L. Eberhardt, "Imaging Race," *American Psychologist*, February 2005, pp 181–190.

[32] Summaries of this research can be found in M. Greer, "Automatic Racial Stereotyping Appears Based on Facial Features in Addition to Race," *Monitor on Psychology*, January 2005, p 14; and L. Winerman, "Racial Stereotypes Can Speed Visual Processing," *Monitor on Psychology*, January 2005, p 15.

[33] B. Kennedy "Toronto Police Accused of Racial Profiling" *Toronto Star*, Sept. 9/2011, www.thestar.com/news/article/1051358—toronto-police-accused-of-racial-profiling.

[34] Statistics Canada – Visible Minorities and Victimization Report. Samuel Perreault, Executive Summary, www.statcan.gc.ca/pub/85f0033m/85f0033m2008015-eng.pdf.

[35] J. Stewart, "Muslim Women Settle Discrimination Suit With UPS," *The Mississauga News*, November 19, 2008.

[36] P. O'Neil, "Racism, Poverty, Aboriginal Issues cited in UN Report On Canada," *CanWest News Service*, February 5, 2009.

[37] Ibid.

[38] K. Pendakur, *Visible Minorities In Canada's Workplaces—A perspective on the 2017 Projection*, 2005, p 9, www.sfu.ca/~pendakur/

[39] These statistics were reported in C. Komp, "Unemployment, Poverty Higher for People with Disabilities," *The New Standard*, October 4, 2006, www.newstandardnews.net/content/index.cfm/items/3727

[40] The OADA reference can be found in A. Silliker, "Rising Number of Disability complaints Tops List of Discrimination Beefs: CHRC," *Canadian HR Reporter*, May 9, 2011, p 3.

[41] Kelley's model is discussed in detail in H.H. Kelley, "The Processes of Causal Attribution," *American Psychologist*, February 1973, pp 107–128.

[42] For examples, see J. Susskind, K. Maurer, V. Thakkar, D.L. Hamilton, and J.W. Sherman, "Perceiving Individuals and Groups: Expectancies, Dispositional Inferences, and Causal Attributions," *Journal of Personality and Social Psychology*, February 1999, pp 181–191; and J. McClure, "Discounting Causes of Behaviour: Are Two Reasons Better than One?," *Journal of Personality and Social Psychology*, January 1998, pp 7–20.

[43] The effect of the self-serving bias was tested and supported by P.E. De Michele, B. Gansneder, and G.B. Solomon, "Success and Failure Attributions of Wrestlers: Further Evidence of the Self-Serving Bias," *Journal of Sport Behaviour*, August 1998, pp 242–255; and C. Sedikides, W.K. Campbell, G.D. Reeder, and A.J. Elliot, "The Self-Serving Bias in Relational Context," *Journal of Personality and Social Psychology*, February 1998, pp 378–386.

[44] Details may be found in S.E. Moss and M.J. Martinko, "The Effects of Performance Attributions and Outcome Dependence on Leader Feedback Behaviour Following Poor Subordinate Performance," *Journal of Organizational Behaviour*, May 1998, pp 259–274; and E.C. Pence, W.C. Pendelton, G.H. Dobbins, and J.A. Sgro, "Effects of Causal Explanations and Sex Variables on Recommendations for Corrective Actions Following Employee Failure," *Organizational Behaviour and Human Performance*, April 1982, pp 227–240.

[45] See D. Konst, R. Vonk, and R.V.D. Vlist, "Inferences about Causes and Consequences of Behaviour of Leaders and Subordinates," *Journal of Organizational Behaviour*, March 1999, pp 261–271.

[46] See J. Silvester, F. Patterson, E. Ferguson, "Comparing Two Attributional Models of Job Performance in Retail Sales: A Field Study," *Journal of Occupational and Organizational Psychology*, March 2003, pp 115–132.

CHAPTER 3

[1] See G.A. Odums, "A New Year's Resolution: Optimize Older Workers," *Training and Development*, January 2006, pp 34–36; P. Babcock, "Detecting Hidden Bias," *HR Magazine*, February 2006, pp 50–55; J.A. Segal, "Time Is on Their Side," *HR Magazine*, February 2006, pp 129–133; A. Fisher, "The Sky's the Limit," *Fortune*, May 1, 2006, pp 124B–124H; S. Kehrli and T. Sopp, "Managing Generation Y," *HR Magazine*, May 2006, pp 113–119; and M. Orey, "White Men Can't Help It: Courts Have Been Buying the Idea That They Have Innate Biases," *BusinessWeek*, May 15, 2006, pp 54, 57.

[2] Data from "If We Could Do It Over Again," *USA Today*, February 19, 2001, p 4D.

[3] See D.S. Vogt and C.R. Colvin, "Assessment of Accurate Self-Knowledge," *Journal of Personality Assessment*, June 2005, pp 239–251; L.M. Roberts, J.E. Dutton, G.M. Spreitzer, E.D. Heaphy, and R.E. Quinn, "Composing the Reflected Best-Self Portrait: Building Pathways for Becoming Extraordinary in Work Organizations," *Academy of Management Review*, October 2005, pp 712–736;

S. Srivastava and J.S. Beer, "How Self-Evaluations Relate to Being Liked by Others: Integrating Sociometer and Attachment Perspectives," *Journal of Personality and Social Psychology*, December 2005, pp 966–977; N. Haslam, P. Bain, L. Douge, M. Lee, and B. Bastian, "More Human Than You: Attributing Humanness to Self and Others," *Journal of Personality and Social Psychology*, December 2005, pp 937–950; G.D. Bromgard, D. Trafimow, and I.K. Bromgard, "Valence of Self-Cognitions: The Positivity of Individual Self-Statements," *The Journal of Social Psychology*, no. 1, 2006, pp 85–94; and S.P. Forrest III and T.O. Peterson, "It's Called Andragogy," *Academy of Management Learning and Education*, March 2006, pp 113–122.

[4] V. Gecas, "The Self-Concept," in *Annual Review of Sociology*, eds. R.H. Turner and J.F. Short, Jr. (Palo Alto, CA: Annual Reviews Inc., 1982), vol. 8, p 3.

[5] L. Festinger, *A Theory of Cognitive Dissonance* (Stanford, CA: Stanford University Press, 1957), p 3. Also see T. Lombardo, "Thinking Ahead: The Value of Future Consciousness," *The Futurist*, January/February 2006, pp 45–50.

[6] A Canadian versus Japanese comparison of self-concept can be found in J.D. Campbell, P.D. Trapnell, S.J. Heine, I.M. Katz, L.F. Lavallee, and D.R. Lehman, "Self-Concept Clarity: Measurement, Personality Correlates, and Cultural Boundaries," *Journal of Personality and Social Psychology*, January 1996, pp 141–156. Also see R.W. Tafarodi, C. Lo, S. Yamaguchi, W.W.S. Lee, and H. Katsura, "The Inner Self in Three Countries," *Journal of Cross-Cultural Psychology*, January 2004, pp 97–117.

[7] Based in part on a definition found in V. Gecas, "The Self-Concept." Also see N. Branden, *Self-Esteem at Work: How Confident People Make Powerful Companies* (San Francisco: Jossey-Bass, 1998).

[8] H.W. Marsh, "Positive and Negative Global Self-Esteem: A Substantively Meaningful Distinction or Artifacts?" *Journal of Personality and Social Psychology*, April 1996, p 819.

[9] Ibid.

[10] See P. Borghesi, "I Was Out of a Job—And an Identity," *Newsweek*, January 30, 2006, p 13.

[11] See D.G. Gardner, L. Van Dyne, and J.L. Pierce, "The Effects of Pay Level on Organization-Based Self-Esteem and Performance: A Field Study," *Journal of Occupational and Organizational Psychology*, September 2004, pp 307–322.

[12] A.J. Fiacco, "Over 50? Keep Foot in Door," *Arizona Republic*, June 20, 2004, p D4.

[13] Ibid.

[14] E. Diener and M. Diener, "Cross-Cultural Correlates of Life Satisfaction and Self-Esteem," *Journal of Personality and Social Psychology*, April 1995, p 662. For cross-cultural evidence of a similar psychological process for self-esteem, see T.M. Singelis, M.H. Bond, W.F. Sharkey, and C.S.Y. Lai, "Unpackaging Culture's Influence on Self-Esteem and Embarrassability," *Journal of Cross-Cultural Psychology*, May 1999, pp 315–341. Also see Z. Stambor, "People Rate Their Self-Esteem High across Cultures," *Monitor on Psychology*, December 2005, p 13.

[15] See C. Kobayashi and J.D. Brown, "Self-Esteem and Self-Enhancement in Japan and America," *Journal of Cross-Cultural Psychology*, September 2003, pp 567–580.

[16] C. Huang, "Mean-Level Change in Self-Esteem from Childhood through Adulthood: Meta-Analysis of Longitudinal Studies," *Review of General Psychology*, 2010, pp 251–260.

[17] Based on data in F.L. Smoll, R.E. Smith, N.P. Barnett, and J.J. Everett, "Enhancement of Children's Self-Esteem through Social Support Training for Youth Sports Coaches," *Journal of Applied Psychology*, August 1993, pp 602–610.

[18] W.J. McGuire and C.V. McGuire, "Enhancing Self-Esteem by Directed-Thinking Tasks: Cognitive and Affective Positivity Asymmetries," *Journal of Personality and Social Psychology*, June 1996, p 1124.

[19] F. Giblin and B. Lakey, "Integrating Mentoring and Social Support Research within the Context of Stressful Medical Training," *Journal of Social and Clinical Psychology*, 2010, pp 771–796.

[20] S. Begley, "Real Self-Esteem Builds on Achievement, Not Praise for Slackers," *The Wall Street Journal*, April 18, 2003, p B1. Also see A. Dijksterhuis, "I Like Myself But I Don't Know Why: Enhancing Implicit Self-Esteem by Subliminal Evaluative Conditioning," *Journal of Personality and Social Psychology*, February 2004, pp 345–355; and J.V. Wood, S.A. Heimpel, I.R. Newby-Clark, and M. Ross, "Snatching Defeat from the Jaws of Victory: Self-Esteem Differences in the Experience and Anticipation of Success," *Journal of Personality and Social Psychology*, November 2005, pp 764–780.

[21] D.L. Ferris, H. Lian, D.J. Brown, F.X.J. Pang, and L.M. Keeping, "Self-Esteem and Job Performance," *Personnel Psychology*, 2010, pp 561–593.

[22] M.E. Gist, "Self-Efficacy: Implications for Organizational Behaviour and Human Resource Management," *Academy of Management Review*, July 1987, p 472. Also see A. Bandura, "Self-Efficacy: Toward a Unifying Theory of Behavioural Change," *Psychological Review*, March 1977, pp 191–215; M.E. Gist and T.R. Mitchell, "Self-Efficacy: A Theoretical Analysis of Its Determinants and Malleability," *Academy of Management Review*, April 1992, pp 183–211; and T.J. Maurer and K.D. Andrews, "Traditional, Likert, and Simplified Measures of Self-Efficacy," *Educational and Psychological Measurement*, December 2000, pp 965–973.

[23] F. Giblin and B. Lakey, "Integrating Mentoring and Social Support Research within the Context of Stressful Medical Training," *Journal of Social and Clinical Psychology*, 2011, pp 771–796.

[24] Based on D.H. Lindsley, D.A. Brass, and J.B. Thomas, "Efficacy-Performance Spirals: A Multilevel Perspective," *Academy of Management Review*, July 1995, pp 645–678.

[25] See, for example, V. Gecas, "The Social Psychology of Self-Efficacy," *Annual Review of Sociology*, eds. W.R. Scott and J. Blake (Palo Alto, CA: Annual Reviews, Inc., 1989), vol. 15, pp 291–316; C.K. Stevens, A.G. Bavetta, and M.E. Gist, "Gender Differences in the Acquisition of Salary Negotiation Skills: The Role of Goals, Self-Efficacy, and Perceived Control," *Journal of Applied Psychology*, October 1993, pp 723–735; and D. Eden and Y. Zuk, "Seasickness as a Self-Fulfilling Prophecy: Raising Self-Efficacy to Boost Performance at Sea," *Journal of Applied Psychology*, October 1995, pp 628–635.

[26] For more on learned helplessness, see V. Gecas, "The Social Psychology of Self-Efficacy"; M.J. Martinko and W.L. Gardner, "Learned Helplessness: An Alternative Explanation for Performance Deficits," *Academy of Management Review*, April 1982, pp 195–204; and C.R. Campbell and M.J. Martinko, "An Integrative Attributional Perspective of Empowerment and Learned Helplessness: A Multimethod Field Study," *Journal of Management*, no. 2, 1998, pp 173–200. Also see A. Dickerson and M.A. Taylor, "Self-Limiting Behaviour in Women: Self-Esteem and Self-Efficacy as Predictors," *Group and Organization Management*, June 2000, pp 191–210.

[27] For an update on Bandura, see D. Smith, "The Theory Heard 'Round the World," *Monitor on Psychology*, October 2002, pp 30–32.

[28] Research on this connection is reported in R.B. Rubin, M.M. Martin, S.S. Bruning, and D.E. Powers, "Test of a Self-Efficacy Model of Interpersonal Communication Competence," *Communication Quarterly*, Spring 1993, pp 210–220.

[29] Data from A.D. Stajkovic and F. Luthans, "Self-Efficacy and Work-Related Performance: A Meta-Analysis," *Psychological Bulletin*, September 1998, pp 240–261.

[30] Based in part on discussion in V. Gecas, "The Social Psychology of Self-Efficacy."

[31] See S.K. Parker, "Enhancing Role Breadth Self-Efficacy: The Roles of Job Enrichment and Other Organizational Interventions," *Journal of Applied Psychology*, December 1998, pp 835–852.

[32] The positive relationship between self-efficacy and readiness for retraining is documented in L.A. Hill and J. Elias, "Retraining

Mid-career Managers: Career History and Self-Efficacy Beliefs," *Human Resource Management*, Summer 1990, pp 197–217. Also see A.M. Saks, "Longitudinal Field Investigation of the Moderating and Mediating Effects of Self-Efficacy on the Relationship between Training and Newcomer Adjustment," *Journal of Applied Psychology*, April 1995, pp 211–225.

[33] See A.D. Stajkovic and F. Luthans, "Social Cognitive Theory and Self-Efficacy: Going beyond Traditional Motivational and Behavioural Approaches," *Organizational Dynamics*, Spring 1998, pp 62–74.

[34] See P.C. Earley and T.R. Lituchy, "Delineating Goal and Efficacy Effects: A Test of Three Models," *Journal of Applied Psychology*, February 1991, pp 81–98.

[35] See P. Tierney and S.M. Farmer, "Creative Self-Efficacy: Its Potential Antecedents and Relationship to Creative Performance," *Academy of Management Journal*, December 2002, pp 1137–1148.

[36] See W.S. Silver, T.R. Mitchell, and M.E. Gist, "Response to Successful and Unsuccessful Performance: The Moderating Effect of Self-Efficacy on the Relationship between Performance and Attributions," *Organizational Behaviour and Human Decision Processes*, June 1995, pp 286–299; R. Zemke, "The Corporate Coach," *Training*, December 1996, pp 24–28; and J.P. Masciarelli, "Less Lonely at the Top," *Management Review*, April 1999, pp 58–61.

[37] For a comprehensive update, see S.W. Gangestad and M. Snyder, "Self-Monitoring: Appraisal and Reappraisal," *Psychological Bulletin*, July 2000, pp 530–555.

[38] M. Snyder and S. Gangestad, "On the Nature of Self-Monitoring: Matters of Assessment, Matters of Validity," *Journal of Personality and Social Psychology*, July 1986, p 125.

[39] Data from M. Kilduff and D.V. Day, "Do Chameleons Get Ahead? The Effects of Self-Monitoring on Managerial Careers," *Academy of Management Journal*, August 1994, pp 1047–1060.

[40] Data from D.B. Turban and T.W. Dougherty, "Role of Protege Personality in Receipt of Mentoring and Career Success," *Academy of Management Journal*, June 1994, pp 688–702.

[41] See F. Luthans, "Successful vs. Effective Managers," *Academy of Management Executive*, May 1988, pp 127–132. Also see I.M. Jawahar and J. Mattsson, "Sexism and Beautyism Effects in Selection as a Function of Self-Monitoring Level of Decision Maker," *Journal of Applied Psychology*, May 2005, pp 563–573; M.R. Barrick, L. Parks, and M.K. Mount, "Self-Monitoring as a Moderator of the Relationships between Personality Traits and Performance," *Personnel Psychology*, Autumn 2005, pp 745–767; and K.G. DeMarree, S.C. Wheeler, and R.E. Petty, "Priming a New Identity: Self-Monitoring Moderates the Effects of Nonself Primes on Self-Judgments and Behaviour," *Journal of Personality and Social Psychology*, November 2005, pp 657–671.

[42] See A. Bandura, *Social Learning Theory* (Englewood Cliffs, NJ: Prentice Hall, 1977). A further refinement is reported in A.D. Stajkovic and F. Luthans, "Social Cognitive Theory and Self-Efficacy: Going Beyond Traditional Motivational and Behavioural Approaches," *Organizational Dynamics*, Spring 1998, pp 62–74. Also see M. Uhl-Bien and G.B. Graen, "Individual Self-Management: Analysis of Professionals' Self-Managing Activities in Functional and Cross-Functional Work Teams," *Academy of Management Journal*, June 1998, pp 340–350.

[43] For related research, see M. Castaneda, T.A. Kolenko, and R.J. Aldag, "Self-Management Perceptions and Practices: A Structural Equations Analysis," *Journal of Organizational Behaviour*, January 1999, pp 101–120. An alternative model is discussed in K.M. Sheldon, D.B. Turban, K.G. Brown, M.R. Barrick, and T.M. Judge, "Applying Self-Determination Theory to Organizational Research," *Research in Personnel and Human Resources Management*, vol. 22, eds. J.J. Martocchio and G.R. Ferris (New York: Elsevier, 2003), pp 357–393.

44 See L. Nash and H. Stevenson, "Success That Lasts," *Harvard Business Review,* February 2004, pp 102–109.

45 C. Duhigg, "The Power of Habit: Why We Do What We Do in Life and Business," Random House, February 28, 2012.

46 For excellent tips on self-management, see C.P. Neck, "Managing Your Mind," *Internal Auditor,* June 1996, pp 60–63.

47 C. Zastrow, *Talk to Yourself: Using the Power of Self-Talk* (Englewood Cliffs, NJ: Prentice Hall, 1979), p 60. Also see C.C. Manz and C.P. Neck, "Inner Leadership: Creating Productive Thought Patterns," *Academy of Management Executive,* August 1991, pp 87–95; C.P. Neck and R.F. Ashcraft, "Inner Leadership: Mental Strategies for Nonprofit Staff Members," *Nonprofit World,* May–June 2000, pp 27–30; and T.C. Brown, "The Effect of Verbal Self-Guidance Training on Collective Efficacy and Team Performance," *Personnel Psychology,* Winter 2003, pp 935–964.

48 R. Kreitner and F. Luthans, "A Social Learning Approach to Behavioural Management: Radical Behaviourists 'Mellowing Out,'" *Organizational Dynamics,* Autumn 1984, p 63.

49 See K. Painter, "We Are Who We Are, or Are We?," *USA Today,* October 3, 2002, p 9; S. Begley, "In the Brave Guppy and Hyper Octopus, Clues to Personality," *The Wall Street Journal,* October 10, 2003, p B1; and S. Kuchinskas, "A Match Made in Hormones," *Business 2.0,* January/February 2006, p 24.

50 For more on personality measurement and assessment, see C.H. Van Iddekinge, P.H. Raymark, and P.L. Roth, "Assessing Personality with a Structured Employment Interview: Construct-Related Validity and Susceptibility to Response Inflation," *Journal of Applied Psychology,* May 2005, pp 536–552; P. Barrett, "What If There Were No Psychometrics? Constructs, Complexity, and Measurement," *Journal of Personality Assessment,* October 2005, pp 134–140; E.D. Heggestad, M. Morrison, C.L. Reeve, and R.A. McCloy, "Forced-Choice Assessments of Personality for Selection: Evaluating Issues of Normative Assessment and Faking Resistance," *Journal of Applied Psychology,* January 2006, pp 9–24; S. Stark, O.S. Chernyshenko, F. Drasgow, and B.A. Williams, "Examining Assumptions about Item Responding in Personality Assessment: Should Ideal Point Methods Be Considered for Scale Development and Scoring?" *Journal of Applied Psychology,* January 2006, pp 25–39; and J.R. Matthews and L.H. Matthews, "Personality Assessment Training: View from a Licensing Board," *Journal of Personality Assessment,* February 2006, pp 46–50.

51 Data from S.V. Paunonen et al., "The Structure of Personality in Six Cultures," *Journal of Cross-Cultural Psychology,* May 1996, pp 339–353. Also see C. Ward, C. Leong, and M. Low, "Personality and Sojourner Adjustment: An Exploration of the Big Five and the Cultural Fit Proposition," *Journal of Cross-Cultural Psychology,* March 2004, pp 137–151.

52 See M.R. Barrick and M.K. Mount, "The Big Five Personality Dimensions and Job Performance: A Meta-Analysis," *Personnel Psychology,* Spring 1991, pp 1–26. Also see R.P. Tett, D.N. Jackson, and M. Rothstein, "Personality Measures as Predictors of Job Performance: A Meta-Analytic Review," *Personnel Psychology,* Winter 1991, pp 703–742; and S.E. Seibert and M.L. Kraimer, "The Five-Factor Model of Personality and Career Success," *Journal of Vocational Behaviour,* February 2001, pp 1–21.

53 Barrick and Mount, "The Big Five Personality Dimensions and Job Performance: A Meta-Analysis," p 18. Also see J.E. Kurtz and S.B. Tiegreen, "Matters of Conscience and Conscientiousness: The Place of Ego Development in the Five-Factor Model," *Journal of Personality Assessment,* December 2005, pp 312–317; and N.M. Dudley, K.A. Orvis, J.E. Lebiecki, and J.M. Cortina, "A Meta-Analytic Investigation of Conscientiousness in the Prediction of Job Performance: Examining the Intercorrelations and the Incremental Validity of Narrow Traits" *Journal of Applied Psychology,* January 2006, pp 40–57.

54 See H. Zhao and S.E. Seibert, "The Big Five Personality Dimensions and Entrepreneurial Status: A Meta-Analytical Review," *Journal of Applied Psychology,* March 2006, pp. 259–271.

55 Based on S.E. Seibert and M.L. Kraimer, "The Five-Factor Model of Personality and Career Success," *Journal of Vocational Behavior,* February 2001, pp 1–21. For more insights on extraversion, see D.S. DeRue, J.R. Hollenbeck, M.D. Johnson, D.R. Ilgen, and D.K. Jundt, "How Different Team Downsizing Approaches Influence Team-Level Adaptation and Performance," *Academy of Management Journal,* February 2008, pp 182–196; and J. Welch and S. Welch, "Release Your Inner Extrovert," *BusinessWeek,* December 8, 2008, p 92.

56 Barrick and Mount, "The Big Five Personality Dimensions and Job Performance: A Meta-Analysis," p 21. Also see D.M. Tokar, A.R. Fischer, and L.M. Subich, "Personality and Vocational Behaviour: A Selective Review of the Literature, 1993–1997," *Journal of Vocational Behaviour,* October 1998, pp 115–153; and K.C. Wooten, T.A. Timmerman, and R. Folger, "The Use of Personality and the Five-Factor Model to Predict New Business Ventures: From Outplacement to Start-up," *Journal of Vocational Behaviour,* February 1999, pp 82–101.

57 For details, see L.A. Witt and G.R. Ferris, "Social Skill as Moderator of the Conscientiousness-Performance Relationship: Convergent Results across Four Studies," *Journal of Applied Psychology,* October 2003, pp 809–820. Also see H. Liao and A. Chuang, "A Multilevel Investigation of Factors Influencing Employee Service Performance and Customer Outcomes," *Academy of Management Journal,* February 2004, pp 41–58.

58 Lead researcher W. Fleeson, as quoted in M. Dittmann, "Acting Extraverted Spurs Positive Feelings, Study Finds," *Monitor on Psychology,* April 2003, p 17. Also see L.D. Smillie, G.B. Yeo, A.F. Furnham, and C.J. Jackson, "Benefits of All Work and No Play: The Relationship between Neuroticism and Performance as a Function of Resource Allocation," *Journal of Applied Psychology,* January 2006, pp 139–155.

59 J.M. Crant, "Proactive Behaviour in Organizations," *Journal of Management,* no. 3, 2000, p 439.

60 Ibid., pp 439–441. Also see J.A. Thompson, "Proactive Personality and Job Performance: A Social Capital Perspective," *Journal of Applied Psychology,* September 2005, pp 1011–1017; and B. Erdogan and T.N. Bauer, "Enhancing Career Benefits of Employee Proactive Personality: The Role of Fit with Jobs and Organizations," *Personnel Psychology,* Winter 2005, pp 859–891.

61 For inspiration, see P. Burrows, "HP's Ultimate Team Player," *BusinessWeek,* January 30, 2006, pp 76–78; B. Hagenbaugh and S. Kirchhoff, "From BET to Hotels to Banking, Johnson Keeps Moving Forward," *USA Today,* April 12, 2006, pp 1B–2B; and P.B. Gray, "Business Class," *Fortune,* April 17, 2006, pp 336B–336H.

62 As quoted in C. Salter, "Matt Glotzbach," *Fast Company,* March 2008, p 78.

63 See S.B. Gustafson and M.D. Mumford, "Personal Style and Person-Environment Fit: A Pattern Approach," *Journal of Vocational Behaviour,* April 1995, pp 163–188; and T.M. Glomb and E.T. Walsh, "Can Opposites Attract? Personality Heterogeneity in Supervisor-Subordinate Dyads as a Predictor of Subordinate Outcomes," *Journal of Applied Psychology,* July 2005, pp 749–757.

64 For an instructive update, see J.B. Rotter, "Internal versus External Control of Reinforcement: A Case History of a Variable," *American Psychologist,* April 1990, pp 489–493. A critical review of locus of control and a call for a meta-analysis can be found in R.W. Renn and R.J. Vandenberg, "Differences in Employee Attitudes and Behaviours." Based on Rotter's (1966), "Internal-External Locus of Control: Are They All Valid?," *Human Relations,* November 1991, pp 1161–1177.

65 B.K. Fuller, M.C. Spears, and D.F. Parker, "Entrepreneurial Tendencies: Evidence from China and India," *International Journal of Management and Marketing Research,* 2010, pp 39–52.

66 For an overall review of research on locus of control, see P.E. Spector, "Behaviour in Organizations as a Function of Employee's Locus of Control," *Psychological Bulletin*, May 1982, pp 482–497; the relationship between locus of control and performance and satisfaction is examined in D.R. Norris and R.E. Niebuhr, "Attributional Influences on the Job Performance–Job Satisfaction Relationship," *Academy of Management Journal*, June 1984, pp 424–431; and salary differences between internals and externals are examined by P.C. Nystrom, "Managers' Salaries and Their Beliefs about Reinforcement Control," *Journal of Social Psychology*, August 1983, pp 291–292. Also see S.S.K. Lam and J. Schaubroeck, "The Role of Locus of Control in Reactions to Being Promoted and to Being Passed Over: A Quasi Experiment," *Academy of Management Journal*, February 2000, pp 66–78.

67 R. Solomon, as quoted in D. Vera and A. Rodriguez-Lopez, "Strategic Virtues: Humility as a Source of Competitive Advantage," *Organizational Dynamics*, no. 4, 2004, pp 394–395.

68 Ibid., p 395.

69 For interesting reading on intelligence, see J.R. Flynn, "Searching for Justice: The Discovery of IQ Gains over Time," *American Psychologist*, January 1999, pp 5–20; and E. Benson, "Intelligent Intelligence Testing," *Monitor on Psychology*, February 2003, pp 48–54.

70 For an excellent update on intelligence, including definitional distinctions and a historical perspective of the IQ controversy, see R.A. Weinberg, "Intelligence and IQ," *American Psychologist*, February 1989, pp 98–104. Genetics and intelligence are discussed in R. Plomin and F.M. Spinath, "Intelligence: Genetics, Genes, and Genomics," *Journal of Personality and Social Psychology*, January 2004, pp 112–129.

71 Ibid. Also see M. Elias, "Mom's IQ, Not Family Size, Key to Kids' Smarts," *USA Today*, June 12, 2000, p 1D; and R. Sapolsky, "Score One for Nature—or Is It Nurture?" *USA Today*, June 21, 2000, p 17A.

72 S.L. Wilk, L. Burris Desmarais, and P.R. Sackett, "Gravitation to Jobs Commensurate with Ability: Longitudinal and Cross-Sectional Tests," *Journal of Applied Psychology*, February 1995, p 79. Also see J. Menkes, "Hiring for Smarts," *Harvard Business Review*, November 2005, pp 100–109.

73 B. Azar, "People Are Becoming Smarter—Why?" *APA Monitor*, June 1996, p 20. Also see "'Average' Intelligence Higher than It Used to Be," *USA Today*, February 18, 1997, p 6D.

74 See D. Lubinski, "Introduction to the Special Section on Cognitive Abilities: 100 Years after Spearman's (1904) 'General Intelligence,' Objectively Determined and Measured," *Journal of Personality and Social Psychology*, January 2004, pp 96–111.

75 See H. Gardner, *Frames of Mind: The Theory of Multiple Intelligences*, 10th Anniversary Edition (New York: Basic Books, 1993); and H. Gardner, *Intelligence Reframed: Multiple Intelligences for the 21st Century* (New York: Basic Books, 2000).

76 For a good overview of Gardner's life and work, see M.K. Smith, "Howard Gardner and Multiple Intelligences," *Encyclopedia of Informal Education*, 2002, www.infed.org/thinkers/gardner.htm. Also see B. Fryer, "The Ethical Mind: A Conversation with Psychologist Howard Gardner," *Harvard Business Review*, March 2007, pp 51–56.

77 See K. Albrecht, "Social Intelligence: Beyond IQ," *Training*, December 2004, pp 26–31; and A.A. Loort, "Multiple Intelligences: A Comparative Study Between the Preferences of Males and Females," *Social Behavior and Personality*, 2005, 33(1).

78 S. Hamm, "Bill's Co-Pilot," *BusinessWeek*, September 14, 1998, pp 85, 87.

79 B. Ortutay, "Jobs Often Moved To Tears While Opening Up For Biography," Associated Press, MSN Today Books,, Oct. 26/11, www.today.msnbc.msn.com/id/45052948/ns/today-books/t/jobs-often-moved-tears-while-opening-biography/.

80 R.S. Lazarus, *Emotion and Adaptation* (New York: Oxford University Press, 1991), p 6. Also see J.A. Russell and L.F. Barrett, "Core Affect, Prototypical Emotional Episodes, and Other Things Called Emotion: Dissecting the Elephant," *Journal of Personality and Social Psychology*, May 1999, pp 805–819; S. Fineman, *Understanding Emotion at Work* (Thousand Oaks, CA: Sage, 2003); D. DeSteno, R.E. Petty, D.D. Rucker, D.T. Wegener, and J. Braverman, "Discrete Emotions and Persuasion: The Role of Emotion-Induced Expectancies," *Journal of Personality and Social Psychology*, January 2004, pp 43–56; L.A. King, J.A. Hicks, J.L. Krull, and A.K. Del Gaiso, "Positive Affect and the Experience of Meaning in Life," *Journal of Personality and Social Psychology*, January 2006, pp 179–196; and G. Morse, "Decisions and Desire," *Harvard Business Review*, January 2006, pp 42–51.

81 Based on discussion in R.D. Arvey, G.L. Renz, and T.W. Watson, "Emotionality and Job Performance: Implications for Personnel Selection," *Research in Personnel and Human Resources Management*, vol. 16, ed. G.R. Ferris (Stamford, CT: JAI Press, 1998), pp 103–147. Also see L.A. King, "Ambivalence over Emotional Expression and Reading Emotions," *Journal of Personality and Social Psychology*, March 1998, pp 753–762; and J.L. Tsai and Y. Chentsova-Dutton, "Variation among European Americans in Emotional Facial Expression," *Journal of Cross-Cultural Psychology*, November 2003, pp 650–657.

82 Data from S.D. Pugh, "Service with a Smile: Emotional Contagion in the Service Encounter," *Academy of Management Journal*, October 2001, pp 1018–1027.

83 Drawn from P. Totterdell, S. Kellett, K. Teuchmann, and R.B. Briner, "Evidence of Mood Linkage in Work Groups," *Journal of Personality and Social Psychology*, June 1998, pp 1504–1515. Also see C.D. Fisher, "Mood and Emotions while Working: Missing Pieces of Job Satisfaction," *Journal of Organizational Behaviour*, March 2000, pp 185–202; K.M. Lewis, "When Leaders Display Emotion: How Followers Respond to Negative Emotional Expression of Male and Female Leaders," *Journal of Organizational Behaviour*, March 2000, pp 221–234; and A. Singh-Manoux and C. Finkenauer, "Cultural Variations in Social Sharing of Emotions: An Intercultural Perspective," *Journal of Cross-Cultural Psychology*, November 2001, pp 647–661.

84 As quoted in D. Jones, "Music Director Works to Blend Strengths," *USA Today*, October 27, 2003, p 6B.

85 A.R. Hochschild, , *The Managed Heart—Commercialization of Human Feeling* (Berkley, CA: University of California Press, 1983).

86 N.M. Ashkanasy and C.S. Daus, "Emotion in the Workplace: The New Challenge for Managers," *Academy of Management Executive*, February 2002, p 79. Also see A.A. Grandey, "When 'The Show Must Go On': Surface Acting and Deep Acting as Determinants of Emotional Exhaustion and Peer-Rated Service Delivery," *Academy of Management Journal*, February 2003, pp 86–96; C.M. Brotheridge and R.T. Lee, "Development and Validation of the Emotional Labour Scale," *Journal of Occupational and Organizational Psychology*, September 2003, pp 365–379; Y. Guerrier and A. Adib, "Work at Leisure and Leisure at Work: A Study of the Emotional Labour of Tour Reps," *Human Relations*, November 2003, pp 1399–1417; A.A. Grandey, G.M. Fisk, and D.D. Steiner, "Must 'Service With a Smile' Be Stressful? The Moderating Role of Personal Control for American and French Employees," *Journal of Applied Psychology*, September 2005, pp 893–904; R.H. Gosserand and J.M. Diefendorff, "Emotional Display Rules and Emotional Labor: The Moderating Role of Commitment," *Journal of Applied Psychology*, November 2005, pp 1256–1264; S. Burling, "Stress Study Shows Ills of Call-Center Workers," *The Arizona Republic*, December 10, 2005, p D3; and P. O'Connell, "Taking the Measure of Mood," *Harvard Business Review*, March 2006, pp 25–26.

87 Data from A.M. Kring and A.H. Gordon, "Sex Differences in Emotions: Expression, Experience, and Physiology," *Journal of Personality and Social Psychology*, March 1998, pp 686–703.

[88] "Is There Multiple Intelligence? EQ vs. IQ," York University, Psychology Department., www.psych.yorku.ca/peterp/3090/.../EQ%20Presentation.ppt.

[89] Ibid.

[90] D. Goleman, "What Makes A Leader?" *Harvard Business Review*, January 2004, www.hbr.org/2004/01/what-makes-a-leader/ar/pr.

[91] D. Goleman, *Emotional Intelligence* (New York: Bantam Books, 1995), p 34. For more, see M. Dittmann, "How 'Emotional Intelligence' Emerged," *Monitor on Psychology*, October 2003, p 64; M.M. Tugade and B.L. Fredrickson, "Resilient Individuals Use Positive Emotions to Bounce Back from Negative Emotional Experiences," *Journal of Personality and Social Psychology*, February 2004, pp 320–333; I. Goldenberg, K. Matheson, and J. Mantler, "The Assessment of Emotional Intelligence: A Comparison of Performance-Based and Self-Report Methodologies," *Journal of Personality Assessment*, February 2006, pp 33–45; and J.E. Barbuto Jr. and M.E. Burbach, "The Emotional Intelligence of Transformational Leaders: A Field Study of Elected Officials," *The Journal of Social Psychology*, February 2006, pp 51–64.

[92] See the box titled "Get Happy Carefully" on page 49 of D. Goleman, R. Boyatzis, and A. McKee, "Primal Leadership: The Hidden Driver of Great Performance," *Harvard Business Review, Special Issue: Breakthrough Leadership*, December 2001, pp 43–51.

[93] J.S. Lublin, "Surviving the Pressure with a Ready Plan or, Literally, a Script," *The Wall Street Journal*, March 2, 2004, p B1.

[94] M.N. Martinez, "The Smarts That Count," *HR Magazine*, November 1997, pp 72–78.

[95] "What's Your EQ at Work?" *Fortune*, October 26, 1998, p 298.

[96] Based on M. Davies, L. Stankov, and R.D. Roberts, "Emotional Intelligence: In Search of an Elusive Construct," *Journal of Personality and Social Psychology*, October 1998, pp 989–1015; and K.A. Barchard, "Does Emotional Intelligence Assist in the Prediction of Academic Success?" *Educational and Psychological Measurement*, October 2003, pp 840–858. Also see B.P. Chapman and B. Hayslip, Jr., "Incremental Validity of a Measure of Emotional Intelligence," *Journal of Personality Assessment*, October 2005, pp 154–169.

[97] A. Fisher, "Success Secret: A High Emotional IQ," *Fortune*, October 26, 1998, p 294. Also see D. Goleman, "Never Stop Learning," *Harvard Business Review, Special Issue: Inside the Mind of the Leader*, January 2004, pp 28–29.

CHAPTER 4

[1] Schwartz's theory is discussed in S.H. Schwartz, "Universals in the Content and Structure of Values: Theoretical Advances and Empirical Tests in 20 Countries," *Advances in Experimental Social Psychology*, ed. M. Zanna (New York: Academic Press, 1992), pp 1–65.

[2] A. Bardi and S.H. Schwartz, "Values and Behavior: Strength and Structure of Relations," *Personality and Social Psychology Bulletin*, October 2003, p 1208.

[3] Ibid., pp 1207–1220; and A. Bardi, R.M. Calogero, and B. Mullen, "A New Archival Approach to the Study of Values and Value-Behavior Relations: Validation of the Value Lexicon," *Journal of Applied Psychology*, May 2008, pp 483–497.

[4] See E. Davidov, P. Schmidt, and S.H. Schwartz, "Bringing Value Back in the Adequacy of the European Social Survey to Measure Values in 20 Countries," *Public Opinion Quarterly*, Fall 2008, pp 420–445.

[5] See A. Bardi and S.H. Schwartz, "Values and Behavior: Strength and Structure of Relations."

[6] P.B. Brown, "What I Know Now," *Fast Company*, February 2005, p 96.

[7] This example was derived from D. Lieberman, "L.A. Times' Publisher Forced Out Over Refusal to Cut Staff," *USA Today*, October 6, 2006, p 1B.

[8] For a thorough discussion of person-culture fit, see A.L. Kristof-Brown, R.D. Zimmerman, and E.C. Johnson, "Consequences of Individuals' Fit at Work: A Meta-Analysis of Person-Job, Person-Organization, Person-Group, and Person-Supervisor Fit," *Personnel Psychology*, Summer 2005, pp 281–342.

[9] Supportive results can be found in H.A. Elfenbein and C.A. O'Reilly III, "Fitting In: The Effects of Relational Demography and Person-Culture Fit on Group Process and Performance," *Group and Organization Management*, February 2007, pp 109–142; and C. Ostroff, Y. Shin, and A. Kinicki, "Multiple Perspectives of Congruence: Relationships between Value Congruence and Employee Attitudes," *Journal of Organizational Behaviour*, September 2005, pp 591–624.

[10] See P. Sellers, "A Kinder, Gentler Lehman Brothers," *Fortune*, January 22, 2007, pp 36–38; K. Gurchiek, "Give Us Your Sick," *HR Magazine*, January 2007, pp 91–93; and M.J. Frase, "International Commuters," *HR Magazine*, March 2007, pp 91–95.

[11] L. Duxbury speaks on workplace health and wellness for Convention Connection Speakers Bureau, June 1, 2010, www.conventionconnection.net/speakers/linda-duxbury.

[12] P.L. Perrewé and W.A. Hochwarter, "Can We Really Have It All? The Attainment of Work and Family Values," *Current Directions in Psychological Science*, February 2001, p 31.

[13] Results can be found in A.H. Eagly and L.L. Carli, *Through the Labyrinth* (Boston: Harvard Business School Press, 2007).

[14] W. Bairos Rozeluk interview, *Global Communications and Public Affairs*, Google Canada, 10 Dundas Street East, 6th floor, Toronto, Ontario April 1, 2009.

[15] Examples can be found in S. Shellenbarger, "Employers Step Up Efforts to Lure Stay-at-Home Mothers Back to Work," *The Wall Street Journal*, February 9, 2006, p D1.

[16] V. Galt "Work-Life Balance: The Impossible Dream," *The Globe and Mail*, October 7, 2011, www.theglobeandmail.com/report-on-business/careers/top-employers/top-employers-2012/work-life.

[17] Results can be found in M.T. Ford, B.A. Heinen, and K.L. Langkamer, "Work and Family Satisfaction and Conflict: A Meta-Analysis of Cross-Domain Relations," *Journal of Applied Psychology*, January 2007, pp 57–80; and W.J. Casper, L.T. Eby, C. Cordeaux, A. Lockwood, and D. Lambert, "A Review of Research Methods in IO/OB Work-Family Research," *Journal of Applied Psychology*, January 2007, pp 28–43.

[18] V. Galt, "Work-Life Balance: The Impossible Dream," *The Globe and Mail*, October 7, 2011, www.theglobeandmail.com/report-on-business/careers/top-employers/top-employers-2012/work-life.

[19] Ibid.

[20] T.R. Nielson, D.S. Carlson, and M.J. Lankau, "The Supportive Mentor as a Means of Reducing Work-Family Conflict," *Journal of Vocational Behaviour*, December 2001, pp 374–375.

[21] Based on S. Parasuraman and C.A. Simmers, "Type of Employment, Work-Family Conflict and Well-Being: A Comparative Study," *Journal of Organizational Behaviour*, August 2001, pp 551–568.

[22] Fanshawe College, 2nd Floor of Student Centre Building—London, Ont., and the University of Western Ontario, University College Bulding 2nd Floor location—London, Ontario.

[23] These results are discussed in L. Winerman, "A Healthy Mind, a Longer Life," *Monitor on Psychology*, November 2006, pp 42–44.

[24] See D.A. Harrison, D.A. Newman, and P.L. Roth, "How Important Are Job Attitudes? Meta-Analytic Comparisons of Integrative Behavioural Outcomes and Time Sequences," *Academy of Management Journal*, April 2006, pp 305–325.

[25] M. Fishbein and I. Ajzen, *Belief, Attitude, Intention and Behaviour: An Introduction to Theory and Research* (Reading, MA: Addison-Wesley Publishing, 1975), p 6.

[26] The components or structure of attitudes are thoroughly discussed in A.P. Brief, *Attitudes in and around Organizations* (Thousand Oaks, CA: Sage, 1998), pp 49–84.

[27] For details about this theory, see L. Festinger, *A Theory of Cognitive Dissonance* (Stanford, CA: Stanford University Press, 1957). Also see J.V. Petrocelli, Z.L. Tormala, and D.D. Rucker, "Unpacking Attitude Certainty: Attitude Clarity and Attitude Correctness," *Journal of Personality and Social Psychology,* January 2007, pp 30–41; and S.C. Wheeler, P. Brinol and A.D. Hermann, "Resistance to Persuasion As Self-Regulation: Ego-depletion and Its Effects on Attitude Change Processes," *Journal of Experimental Social Psychology,* January 2007, pp 150–156.

[28] See B.M. Staw and J. Ross, "Stability in the Midst of Change: A Dispositional Approach to Job Attitudes," *Journal of Applied Psychology,* August 1985, pp 469–480. Also see J. Schaubroeck, D.C. Ganster, and B. Kemmerer, "Does Trait Affect Promote Job Attitude Stability?" *Journal of Organizational Behaviour,* March 1996, pp 191–196.

[29] Data from P.S. Visser and J.A. Krosnick, "Development of Attitude Strength over the Life Cycle: Surge and Decline," *Journal of Personality and Social Psychology,* December 1998, pp 389–410.

[30] I. Ajzen, "The Theory of Planned Behaviour," *Organizational Behaviour and Human Decision Processes,* vol. 50, 1991, p 188.

[31] See R.P. Steel and N.K. Ovalle II, "A Review and Meta-Analysis of Research on the Relationship between Behavioural Intentions and Employee Turnover," *Journal of Applied Psychology,* November 1984, pp 673–686.

[32] Results can be found in M.R. Barrick and R.D. Zimmerman, "Reducing Voluntary Turnover through Selection," *Journal of Applied Psychology,* January 2005, pp 159–166.

[33] Drawn from I. Ajzen and M. Fishbein, *Understanding Attitudes and Predicting Social Behaviour* (Englewood Cliffs, NJ: Prentice Hall, 1980); and C.S. Lu, K.H. Lai, and T.C.E. Cheng, "Application of Structural Equation Modeling to Evaluate the Intention of Shippers to Use Internet Services in Liner Shipping," *European Journal of Operational Research,* July 2007, pp 845–867; A. McKinlay and S. Cowan, "'If You're Frail You've Had It': A Theory of Planned Behaviour Study of Nurses' Attitudes Towards Working with Older Patients," *Journal of Applied Social Psychology,* April 2006, pp 900–917; J.G. Pesek, R.D. Raehsler, and R.S. Balough, "Future Professionals and Managers: Their Attitudes Toward Unions, Organizational Beliefs, and Work Ethic," *Journal of Applied Social Psychology,* June 2006, pp 1569–1594; D. Albarracín, B.T. Johnson, M. Fishbein, and P.A. Muellerleile, "Theories of Reasoned Action and Planned Behaviour as Models of Condom Use: A Meta Analysis," *Psychological Bulletin,* January 2001, pp 142–161; and P.W. Hom and C.L. Hulin, "A Competitive Test of the Prediction of Reenlistment by Several Models," *Journal of Applied Psychology,* February 1981, pp 23–39.

[34] Supportive research is presented in T.L. Webb and P. Sheeran, "Does Changing Behavioural Intentions Engender Behaviour Change: A Meta-Analysis of the Experimental Evidence," *Psychological Bulletin,* March 2006, pp 249–268.

[35] Results can be found in M.L. Kraimer, S.J. Wayne, R.C. Liden, and R.T. Sparrowe, "The Role of Job Security in Understanding the Relationship between Employees' Perceptions of Temporary Workers and Employees' Performance," *Journal of Applied Psychology,* March 2005, pp 389–398.

[36] The concept of commitment and its relationship to motivated behaviour is thoroughly discussed by J.P. Meyer, T.E. Becker, and C. Vandenberghe, "Employee Commitment and Motivation: A Conceptual Analysis and Integrative Model," *Journal of Applied Psychology,* December 2004, pp 991–1007.

[37] J.P. Meyer and L. Herscovitch, "Commitment in the Workplace: Toward a General Model," *Human Resource Management Review,* Autumn 2001, p 301.

[38] J.P. Meyer and N.J. Allen, "A Three-Component Conceptualization of Organizational Commitment," *Human Resource Management Review,* Spring 1991, p 67.

[39] See R.E. Johnson and C.H. Chang, "'I' Is to Continuance as 'We' Is to Affective: The Relevance of the Self-Concept For Organizational Commitment," *Journal of Organizational Behaviour,* August 2006, pp 549–570; and J.P. Meyer, T.E. Becker, and R. Van Dick, "Social Identities and Commitments at Work: Toward an Integrative Model," *Journal of Organizational Behaviour,* August 2006, pp 665–683.

[40] This definition was provided by D.M. Rousseau, "Psychological and Implied Contracts in Organizations," *Employee Responsibilities and Rights Journal,* June 1989, 121–139.

[41] See T. Dulac, J.A.M. Coyle-Shariro, D. Henderson, and S.J. Wayne, "Not All Responses to Breach Are the Same: The Interconnection of Social Exchange and Psychological Contract Processes in Organizations," *Academy of Management Journal,* December 2008, pp 1079–1098; K.A. Orvis, N.M. Dudley, and J.M. Cortina, "Conscientiousness and Reactions to Psychology Contract Breach: A Longitudinal Field Study," *Journal of Applied Psychology,* September 2008, pp 1183–1193; and Z.X. Chen, A.S. Tsui, and L. Zhong, "Reactions to Psychological Contract Breach: A Dual Perspective," *Journal of Organizational Behavior,* July 2008, pp 527–548.

[42] Results can be found in N.P. Podsakoff, J.A. LePine, M.A. LePine, "Differential Challenge Stressor-Hindrance Stressor Relationships with Job Attitudes, Turnover Intentions, Turnover, and Withdrawal Behaviour: A Meta-Analysis," *Journal of Applied Psychology,* March 2007, pp 438–454.

[43] Results can be found in M. Riketta, "Attitudinal Organizational Commitment and Job Performance: A Meta-Analysis," *Journal of Organizational Behaviour,* March 2002, pp 257–266.

[44] Results can be found in R.W. Griffeth, P.W. Hom, and S. Gaertner, "A Meta-Analysis of Antecedents and Correlates of Employee Turnover: Update, Moderator Tests, and Research Implications for the Next Millennium," *Journal of Management,* 2000, pp 463–488. Also see P.F. McKay, D.R. Avery, S. Tonidandel, M.A. Morris, M. Hernandez, and M.R. Hebl, "Racial Differences in Employee Retention: Are Diversity Climate Perceptions the Key?" *Personnel Psychology,* Spring 2007, pp 35–62.

[45] These examples were discussed in R. Levering and M. Moskowitz, "The 100 Best Companies to Work For," *Fortune,* January 22, 2007, p 94.

[46] D. Jermyn, "Deeley Harley-Davidson Gives Staff A Free Ride," *The Globe and Mail,* October 7, 2011, www.theglobeandmail.com/report-on-business/careers/top-employers/top-employers-2012/work-life.

[47] *The Globe and Mail,* "Telus Corporation," October 7, 2011, www.theglobeandmail.com/report-on-business/careers/top-employers/top-employers-2012/work-life.

[48] *The Globe and Mail,* "Ceridian Canada," October 7, 2011, www.theglobeandmail.com/report-on-business/careers/top-employers/top-employers-2012/work-life.

[49] I.M. Paullay, G.M. Alliger, and E.F. Stone-Romero, "Construct Validation of Two Instruments Designed to Measure Job Involvement and Work Centrality," *Journal of Applied Psychology,* April 1994, p 224.

[50] Testimonials, www.skibanff.com.

[51] Results can be found in S.P. Brown, "A Meta-Analysis and Review of Organizational Research on Job Involvement," *Psychological Bulletin,* September 1996, pp 235–255.

[52] Results can be found in J.M. Diefendorff, D.J. Brown, A.M. Kamin, and R.G. Lord, "Examining the Roles of Job Involvement and Work Centrality in Predicting Organizational Citizenship Behaviours and Job Performance," *Journal of Organizational Behaviour,* February 2002, pp 93–108.

[53] Results can be found in N.A. Bowling, T.A. Beehr, and L.R. Lepisto, "Beyond Job Satisfaction: A Five-Year Prospective Analysis of the Dispositional Approach to Work Attitudes," *Journal of Vocational Behaviour,* October 2006, pp 315–330.

[54] See S. Sonnentag and U. Kruel, "Psychological Detachment from Work During Off-Job Time: The Role of Job Stressor, Job Involvement, and Recovery-Related Self-Efficacy," *European Journal of Work and Organizational Pscyhology,* June 2006, pp 197–217.

[55] See J. Wegge, K.H. Schmidt, C. Parkes, and R. van Dick, "Taking a Sickie: Job Satisfaction and Job Involvement as Interactive Predictors of Absenteeism in a Public Organization," *Journal of Occupational and Organizational Psychology,* March 2007, pp 77–90.

[56] Results can be found in R.R. Hastings, "Silent Generation Speaks Up about Work, *HR Magazine,* September 2008, p 30.

[57] Supportive results can be found in "Job Satisfaction Palls Quickly for Most Workers," *HR Magazine,* March 2007, p 16; S. Miller, "Satisfaction with Pay, Benefits Falling," *HR Magazine,* January 2007, pp 38–39; and "Middle Managers Unhappy," *HR Magazine,* July 2006, p 16.

[58] For a review of these models, see A. Brief, *Attitudes in and around Organizations,* (Sage Publications, 1998).

[59] The survey was conducted by Hewitt and Associates and results are presented in J. Saranow, "Anybody Want to Take a Nap?," *The Wall Street Journal,* January 24, 2005, p R5.

[60] For a review of need satisfaction models, see E.F. Stone, "A Critical Analysis of Social Information Processing Models of Job Perceptions and Job Attitudes," *Job Satisfaction: How People Feel about Their Jobs and How It Affects Their Performance,* eds. C.J. Cranny, P. Cain Smith, and E.F. Stone (New York: Lexington Books, 1992), pp 21–52.

[61] See J.P. Wanous, T.D. Poland, S.L. Premack, and K.S. Davis, "The Effects of Met Expectations on Newcomer Attitudes and Behaviours: A Review and Meta-Analysis," *Journal of Applied Psychology,* June 1992, pp 288–297.

[62] A complete description of this model is provided by E.A. Locke, "Job Satisfaction," *Social Psychology and Organizational Behaviour,* eds. M. Gruneberg and T. Wall (New York: John Wiley & Sons, 1984).

[63] G. Johnson, "Wanted: Workers with a Healthy Sense of Adventure," *The Globe and Mail,* October 7, 2011, www.theglobeand-mail.com/report-on-business/careers/top-employers/top-employers-2012/work-life.

[64] Results can be found in J. Cohen-Charash and P.E. Spector, "The Role of Justice in Organizations: A Meta-Analysis," *Organizational Behaviour and Human Decision Processes,* November 2001, pp 278–321.

[65] A thorough discussion of this model is provided by C.L. Hulin and T.A. Judge, "Job Attitudes," *Handbook of Psychology,* vol. 12, eds. W.C. Borman, D.R. Ilgen, and R.J. Klimoski (Hoboken, NJ: John Wiley & Sons, Inc., 2003), pp 255–276.

[66] A summary and interpretation of this research is provided by B.M. Staw and Y. Choen-Charash, "The Dispositional Approach to Job Satisfaction: More than a Mirage, but Not Yet an Oasis," *Journal of Organizational Behaviour,* February 2005, pp 59–78.

[67] See R.D. Arvey, T.J. Bouchard Jr., N.L. Segal, and L.M. Abraham, "Job Satisfaction: Environmental and Genetic Components," *Journal of Applied Psychology,* April 1989, pp 187–192. Also see S.E. Hammpson, L.R. Goldberg, T.M. Vogt, and J.P. Dubanoski, "Mechanisms by Which Childhood Personality Traits Influence Adult Health Status: Educational Attainment and Healthy Behaviours," *Health Psychology,* January 2007, pp 121–125.

[68] See C. Dormann and D. Zapf, "Job Satisfaction: A Meta-Analysis of Stabilities," *Journal of Organizational Behaviour,* August 2001, pp 483–504.

[69] P. Wakeman, "The Good Life and How to Get It," *Inc.,* February 2001, p 50.

[70] See A.J. Kinicki, F.M. McKee-Ryan, C.A. Schriesheim, and K.P. Carson, "Assessing the Construct Validity of the Job Descriptive Index: A Review and Meta-Analysis," *Journal of Applied Psychology,* February 2002, pp 14–32.

[71] See S.P. Brown, "A Meta-Analysis and Review of Organizational Research on Job Involvement," *Psychological Bulletin, 120*(2), 1996, 235–255.

[72] D.W. Organ, "The Motivational Basis of Organizational Citizenship Behaviour," *Research in Organizational Behaviour,* eds. B.M. Staw and L.L. Cummings (Greenwich, CT: JAI Press, 1990), p 46.

[73] Results can be found in B.J. Hoffman, C.A. Blair, J.P. Meriac, and D.J. Woehr, "Expanding the Criterion Domain? A Quantitative Review of the OCB Literature," *Journal of Applied Psychology,* March 2007, pp 555–566.

[74] Supportive results can be found in D. Kamdar, D.J. McAllister, and D.B. Turban, "'All in a Day's Work': How Follower Individual Differences and Justice Perceptions Predict OCB Role Definitions and Behaviour," *Journal of Applied Psychology,* July 2006, pp 841–855; and B.J. Tepper, M.K. Duffy, J. Hoobler, and M.D. Ensley, "Moderators of the Relationship between Coworkers' Organizational Citizenship Behaviour and Fellow Employees' Attitudes," *Journal of Applied Psychology,* June 2004, pp 455–465.

[75] Supportive findings are presented in T.D. Allen, "Rewarding Good Citizens: The Relationship Between Citizenship Behaviour, Gender, and Organizational Rewards," *Journal of Applied Social Psychology,* January 2006, pp 120–143; and T.W. Lee, T.R. Mitchell, C.J. Sablynski, J.P. Burton, and B.C. Holtom, "The Effects of Job Embeddedness on Organizational Citizenship, Job Performance, Volitional Absences, and Voluntary Turnover," *Academy of Management Journal,* October 2004, pp 711–722.

[76] These results can be found in K. Gurchiek, "'I Can't Make It to Work Today, Boss. . .Gotta Round Up My Ostriches'," *HR Magazine,* March 2005, p 30 .

[77] These cost estimates are provided in E. Robertson Demby, "Do Your Family-Friendly Programs Make Cents?" *HR Magazine,* January 2004, pp 74–78.

[78] See R.D. Hackett, "Work Attitudes and Employee Absenteeism: A Synthesis of the Literature," *Journal of Occupational Psychology,* 1989, pp 235–248.

[79] A thorough review of the cognitive process associated with quitting is provided in C.P. Maertz Jr. and M.A. Campion, "Profiles in Quitting: Integrating Process and Content Turnover Theory," *Academy of Management Journal,* August 2004, pp 566–582.

[80] Results can be found in P.W. Hom and A.J. Kinicki, "Toward a Greater Understanding of How Dissatisfaction Drives Employee Turnover," *Academy of Management Journal,* October 2001, pp 975–987.

[81] Statistics are presented in A. Fisher, "Playing For Keeps," *Fortune,* January 22, 2007, p 85; and "CFO: All Pain, No Gain," *Fortune,* February 5, 2007, p 18.

[82] Y. Lermusiaux, "Calculating the High Cost of Employee Turnover," accessed April 15, 2005, p 1, www.ilogos.com/en/expertviews/articles/strategic/200331007_YL.html. The various costs of employee turnover are also discussed by W.G. Bliss, "Cost of Employee Turnover," accessed April 15, 2005, www.isquare.com/turnover.cfm.

[83] See Y. Lermusiaux, "Calculating the High Cost of Employee Turnover." An automated program for calculating the cost of turnover can be found at "Calculate Your Turnover Costs," accessed April 15, 2005, www.keepemployees.com/turnovercalc.htm.

[84] Techniques for reducing employee turnover are discussed by K. Gurchiek, "Execs Take Exit Interview Seriously," *HR Magazine,* January 2007, p 34; and J. Brandon, "Rethinking the Time Clock," *Business 2.0,* March 2007, p 24.

[85] Results can be found in R. Griffeth, P. Hom, and S. Gaertner, "A Meta-Analysis of Antecedents and Correlates of Employee Turnover," *Journal of Management,* 2000, *26*(3), 463–488.

[86] Results can be found in N.P. Podsakoff, J.A. LePine, and M.A. LePine, "Differential Challenge Stressor-Hindrance Stressor Relationships with Job Attitudes, Turnover Intentions, Turnover, and

Withdrawal Behaviour: A Meta-Analysis," *Journal of Applied Psychology,* 2007, *92*(2), 438–454.

[87] The various models are discussed in T.A. Judge, C.J. Thoresen, J.E. Bono, and G.K. Patton, "The Job Satisfaction–Job Performance Relationship: A Qualitative and Quantitative Review," *Psychological Bulletin,* May 2001, pp 376–407.

[88] Ibid.

[89] One example is provided by D.J. Schleicher, J.D. Watt, and G.J. Greguras, "Reexamining the Job Satisfaction–Performance Relationship: The Complexity of Attitudes," *Journal of Applied Psychology,* February 2004, pp 165–177.

[90] Results can be found in J.K. Harter, F.L. Schmidt, and T.L. Hayes, "Business-Unit-Level Relationship between Employee Satisfaction, Employee Engagement, and Business Outcomes: A Meta-Analysis," *Journal of Applied Psychology,* April 2002, pp 268–279.

CHAPTER 5

[1] T.R. Mitchell, "Motivation: New Direction for Theory, Research, and Practice," *Academy of Management Review,* January 1982, p 81.

[2] A review of content and process theories of motivation is provided by R.M. Steers, R.T. Mowday, and D.L. Shapiro, "The Future of Work Motivation Theory," *Academy of Management Review,* July 2004, pp 379–387.

[3] For a complete description of Maslow's theory, see A.H. Maslow, "A Theory of Human Motivation," *Psychological Review,* July 1943, pp 370–396.

[4] See W.B. Swann Jr., C. Chang-Schneider, and K.L. McClarty, "Do People's Self-Views Matter?" *American Pscyhologist,* February–March 2007, pp 84–94.

[5] See "Comp and Hiring Landscape: Still Rocky in 2007," *HR Magazine,* February 2007, p 14; R. Wiles, "Tips Aimed to Help Debt-Ridden Workers, Boost Productivity," *The Arizona Republic,* March 3, 2007, p D1; and A. Johnson, "4 Generations Can Challenge Management," *The Arizona Republic,* September 21, 2006, pp D1, D5.

[6] A sample is provided by L. Bassi and D. McMurrer, "Maximizing Your Return on People," *Harvard Business Review,* March 2007, pp 115–124.

[7] For a complete review of ERG theory, see C.P. Alderfer, *Existence, Relatedness, and Growth: Human Needs in Organizational Settings* (New York: Free Press, 1972).

[8] Ibid. Also see J.P. Wanous and A. Zwany, "A Cross-Sectional Test of Need Hierarchy Theory," *Organizational Behaviour and Human Performance,* February 1977, pp 78–97.

[9] L. Buchanan, "Managing One-to-One," *Inc.,* October 2001, p 87.

[10] H.A. Murray, *Explorations in Personality* (New York: John Wiley & Sons, 1938), p 164.

[11] See the discussion in "Can't We All Just Get Along?" *HR Magazine,* April 2005, p 16.

[12] See G.D. Parsons and R.T. Pascale, "Crisis at the Summit," *Harvard Business Review,* March 2007, pp 80–89; D.K. McNeese-Smith, "The Relationship between Managerial Motivation, Leadership, Nurse Outcomes and Patient Satisfaction," *Journal of Organizational Behaviour,* March 1999, pp 243–259; and A.M. Harrell and M.J. Stahl, "A Behavioural Decision Theory Approach for Measuring McClelland's Trichotomy of Needs," *Journal of Applied Psychology,* April 1981, pp 242–247.

[13] Evidence for the validity of motivation training can be found in H. Heckhausen and S. Krug, "Motive Modification," *Motivation and Society,* ed. A.J. Stewart (San Francisco: Jossey-Bass, 1982).

[14] Results can be found in D.B. Turban and T.L. Keon, "Organizational Attractiveness: An Interactionist Perspective," *Journal of Applied Psychology,* April 1993, pp 184–193.

[15] See T.W.H. Ng, K.L. Sorensen, and D.C. Feldman, "Dimensions, Antecedents, and Consequences of Workaholism: A Conceptual

Integration and Extension," *Journal of Organizational Behaviour,* January 2007, pp 111–136.

[16] See F. Herzberg, B. Mausner, and B.B. Snyderman, *The Motivation to Work* (New York: John Wiley & Sons, 1959).

[17] F. Herzberg, "One More Time: How Do You Motivate Employees?" *Harvard Business Review,* January–February 1968, p 56.

[18] For a thorough review of research on Herzberg's theory, see C.C. Pinder, *Work Motivation: Theory, Issues, and Applications* (Glenview, IL: Scott, Foresman, 1984).

[19] Supportive results can be found in N.R. Lockwood, "Leveraging Employee Engagement for Competitive Advantage," *2007 SHRM Quarterly,* 2007, pp 1–11; and "Respect: Find Out What It Means to Employees," *Training,* June 2006, p 12.

[20] The generalizability of the equity norm was investigated by T.M. Begley, C. Lee, and C. Hui, "Organizational Level as a Moderator of the Relationship between Justice Perceptions and Work-Related Reactions," *Journal of Organizational Behaviour,* September 2006, pp 705–721; and R. Loi, N. Hang-Yue, and S. Foley, "Linking Employees' Justice Perceptions to Organizational Commitment and Intention to Leave: The Mediating Role of Perceived Organizational Support," *Journal of Occupational and Organizational Psychology,* March 2006, pp 101–120.

[21] H. Mackenzie, *Canada's CEO Elite 100 – The 0.01%,* Canadian Centre for Policy Alternatives, January 2012, p 3. Also see D. Flavelle, "Highest paid Canadian CEOs got 27 per cent pay hike," *Toronto Star,* January 2, 2012.

[22] Ibid.

[23] M.N. Bing and S.M. Burroughs, "The Predictive and Interactive Effects of Equity Sensitivity in Teamwork-Oriented Organizations," *Journal of Organizational Behaviour,* May 2001, p 271.

[24] Ibid., pp 271–290; and K.S. Sauley and A.G. Bedeian, "Equity Sensitivity: Construction of a Measure and Examination of Its Psychometric Properties," *Journal of Management,* 2000, pp 885–910.

[25] See V.H. Vroom, *Work and Motivation* (New York: John Wiley & Sons, 1964).

[26] For a complete discussion of Vroom's theory, see V.H. Vroom, *Work and Motivation* (New York: John Wiley & Sons, 1964). Also see E.E. Lawher III, *Motivation in Work Organizations,* (Belmont, California: Wadsworth, 1973), p 45.

[27] Results can be found in W. van Eerde and H. Thierry, "Vroom's Expectancy Models and Work-Related Criteria: A Meta-Analysis," *Journal of Applied Psychology,* October 1996, pp 575–586.

[28] See J.P. Wanous, T.L. Keon, and J.C. Latack, "Expectancy Theory and Occupational/Organizational Choices: A Review and Test," *Organizational Behaviour and Human Performance,* August 1983, pp 66–86.

[29] See the discussion in T.R. Mitchell and D. Daniels, "Motivation," *Handbook of Psychology,* vol. 12, eds. W.C. Borman, D.R. Ilgen, and R.J. Klimoski (Hoboken, NJ: John Wiley & Sons, Inc., 2003), pp 225–254.

[30] See "Insights on Maximizing the Value of Employee Awards," *The Power of Incentives,* 2006, pp 103–110; J. Useem, "What's That Spell? Teamwork," *Fortune,* June 12, 2006, pp 65–66; and S.J. Dubner, "The Freaky Side of Business," *Training,* February 2006, pp 8–10.

[31] E.A. Locke, K.N. Shaw, L.M. Saari, and G.P. Latham, "Goal Setting and Task Performance: 1969–1980," *Psychological Bulletin,* July 1981, p 126.

[32] Thorough discussions of MBO are provided by P.F. Drucker, *The Practice of Management* (New York: Harper, 1954); and P.F. Drucker, "What Results Should You Expect? A User's Guide to MBO," *Public Administration Review,* January–February 1976, pp 12–19.

[33] As quoted in M. Kimes, "How Do I Groom and Keep Talented Employees?" *Fortune,* November 10, 2008, p 26.

[34] See "Great Quotes of Rory McIlroy" at www.allgreatquotes.com. Also see "Jack Nicklaus—Following Rory McIlroy's Record Setting Victory in the US Open and at the Age of 22", www.nicklaus.com/nicklaus_news/rory-mcilroy-2.php.

[35] Results can be found in P.M. Wright, "Operationalization of Goal Difficulty as a Moderator of the Goal Difficulty–Performance Relationship," *Journal of Applied Psychology*, June 1990, pp 227–234.

[36] See A.P. Tolli and A.M. Schmidt, "The Role of Feedback, Causal Attributions, and Self-Efficacy in Goal Revision," *Journal of Applied Psychology*, May 2008, pp 692–701.

[37] See G.P. Latham and E.A. Locke, "Enhancing the Benefits and Overcoming the Pitfalls of Goal Setting," *Organizational Dynamics*, November 2006, pp 332–340.

[38] See M.J. Ferguson, "On Becoming Ready to Pursue a Goal You Don't Know You Have: Effects of Nonconscious Goals on Evaluative Readiness," *Journal of Personality and Social Psychology*, December 2008, pp 1268–1294. Action planning in a sales context is discussed by P. Keegan, "Sales Slip-Ups," *Fortune*, September 29, 2008, p 108.

[39] Supportive results can be found in S.E. Humphrey, J.D. Nahrgang, and F.P. Morgeson, "Integrating Motivational, Social, and Contextual Work Design Features: A Meta-Analytic Summary and Theoretical Extension of the Work Design Literature," *Journal of Applied Psychology*, September 2007, pp 1332–1356.

[40] See J.J. Donovan and D.J. Radosevich, "The Moderating Role of Goal Commitment on the Goal Difficulty-Performance Relationship: A Meta-Analytic Review and Critical Reanalysis," *Journal of Applied Psychology*, April 1998, pp 308–315.

[41] See G.P. Latham and E.A. Locke, "Enhancing the Benefits and Overcoming the Pitfalls of Goal Setting," *Organizational Dynamics*, 2006, pp 332–338.

[42] J.L. Bowditch and A.F. Buono, *A Primer on Organizational Behaviour* (New York: John Wiley & Sons, 1985), p 210.

[43] This framework was proposed by M.A. Campion and P.W. Thayer, "Development and Field Evaluation of an Interdisciplinary Measure of Job Design," *Journal of Applied Psychology*, February 1985, pp 29–43.

[44] See the related discussion in S. Wagner-Tsukamoto, "An Institutional Economic Reconstruction of Scientific Management: On the Lost Theoretical Logic of Taylorism," *Academy of Management Review*, January 2007, pp 105–117.

[45] K. Dunker, "On Problem-Solving," *Psychological monographs: General and Applied (Goskin Lectures at Harvard University)*,vol. 58, issue 270 (Greenwood Press, 1972).

[46] D. Pink, "Ted Lectures," August 23, 2009, www.ted.com/talks/dan_pink_on_motivation.html.

[47] This type of program was developed and tested by M.A. Campion and C.L. McClelland, "Follow-Up and Extension of the Interdisciplinary Costs and Benefits of Enlarged Jobs," *Journal of Applied Psychology*, June 1993, pp 339–351.

[48] T.R. Shea, "Quick-Decision Hiring," *HR Magazine*, September 2006, pp 123–124.

[49] J.R. Hackman, G.R. Oldham, R. Janson, and K. Purdy, "A New Strategy for Job Enrichment," *California Management Review*, Summer 1975, p 58.

[50] Definitions of the job characteristics were adapted from J.R. Hackman and G.R. Oldham, "Motivation through the Design of Work: Test of a Theory," *Organizational Behaviour and Human Performance*, August 1976, pp 250–279.

[51] See F.P. Morgeson and S.E. Humphrey, "The Work Design Questionnaire (WDQ): Developing and Validating a Comprehensive Measure for Assessing Job Design and the Nature of Work," *Journal of Applied Psychology*, November 2006, pp 1321–1339.

[52] These examples were taken from R. Levering and M. Moskowitz, "The 100 Best Companies to Work for 2007," *Fortune*, January 22, 2007, p 94; and R. Levering and M. Moskowitz, "The 100 Best Companies to Work For," *Fortune*, January 24, 2005, p 76.

[53] Supportive results were found by S.K. Parker, H.M. Williams, and N. Turner, "Modeling the Antecedents of Proactive Behaviour at Work," *Journal of Applied Psychology*, May 2006, pp 636–652; and J.B. Fuller, L.E. Marler, and K. Hester, "Promoting Felt Responsibility for Constructive Change and Proactive Behaviour: Exploring Aspects of an Elaborated Model of Work Design," *Journal of Organizational Behaviour*, December 2006, pp 1089–1120.

[54] See R.F. Piccolo and J.A. Colquitt, "Transformational Leadership and Job Behaviours: The Mediating Role of Core Job Characteristics," *Academy of Management Journal*, April 2006, pp 327–340; and S. Ohly, S. Sonnentag, and F. Pluntke, "Routinization, Work Characteristics and Their Relationship with Creative and Proactive Behaviours," *Journal of Organizational Behaviour*, May 2006, pp 257–279.

[55] The turnover meta-analysis was conducted by R.W. Griffeth, P.W. Hom, and S. Gaertner, "A Meta-Analysis of Antecedents and Correlates of Employee Turnover: Update, Moderator Tests, and Research Implications for the Next Millennium," *Journal of Management*, 2000, pp 463–488. Absenteeism results are discussed in Y. Fried and G.R. Ferris, "The Validity of the Job Characteristics Model: A Review and Meta-Analysis," *Personnel Psychology*, Summer 1987, pp 287–322.

[56] Results can be found in M.R. Kelley, "New Process Technology, Job Design, and Work Organization: A Contingency Model," *American Sociological Review*, April 1990, pp 191–208.

[57] Productivity studies are reviewed in R.E. Kopelman, *Managing Productivity in Organizations* (New York: McGraw-Hill, 1986).

[58] See A. Athavaley, "The Ball's in Your Cubicle," *The Wall Street Journal*, February 27, 2007, pp D1, D3.

[59] See R. Malkin, S.D. Hudock, C. Hayden, T.J. Lentz, J. Topmiller, and R.W. Niemeier, "An Assessment of Occupational Safety and Health in Selected Small Business Manufacturing Wood Pallets—Part 1. Noise and Physical Hazards," *Journal of Occupational and Environmental Hygiene*, April 2005, pp D18–D21.

[60] M. Maynard, "At Toyota, a Global Giant Reaches for Agility," *New York Times*, February 22, 2008, www.nytimes.com. Also see N. Woodward, "Easing Back Pain," *HR Magazine*, April 2008, pp 57–60.

[61] "NINDA Repetitive Motor Disorders Information Page," last updated March 30, 2005, www.ninds.nih.gov/disorders/repetitive_motion/repetitive_motion.htm.

[62] M. Mancini, "MSD injury still big issue for organizations," *Canadian HR Reporter*, April 25, 2011, p D9.

[63] *Macleans Magazine*, "Canada's Best Employers," October 20, 2011, www2.macleans.ca.

[64] B. Baltes, T.E. Briggs, J.W. Huff, J.A. Wright and G.A. Newman, "Flexible and compressed workweek schedules; A meta-analysis of their effects on work-related criteria," *Journal of Applied Psychology*, vol. 84, 1999, pp 496–513.

[65] *Macleans Magazine*, "Canada's Best Employers," October 20, 2011, www2.macleans.ca.

[66] R.S. Gajendran and D.A. Harrison, "The good the bad and the unknown about telecommuting: Meta-analysis of psychological mediators and individual consequences," *Journal of Applied Psychology*, vol. 92, 2007, pp 1524–1541.

[67] S. Klie, "Mistrust 'number one barrier' to telework," *Canadian HR Reporter, 21*(11), June 2, 2008 pp 13, 19; and L. Grensing-Pophal, *Finding, Hiring, and Keeping the Right People* (1997).

[68] *Macleans Magazine*, "Canada's Best Employers," October 20, 2011, www2.macleans.ca.

[69] B. Baltes, T.E. Briggs, J.W. Huff, J.A. Wright, and G.A. Newman, "Flexible and compressed workweek schedules; A meta-analysis of their effects on work-related criteria," *Journal of Applied Psychology*, vol. 84, 1999, pp 496–513.

[70] G. Johns and A. Saks, *Organizational Behaviour*, 8th ed. (Pearson, 2011), pp 204–305.

CHAPTER 6

1 See R. Mirchandani, "Postmodernism and Sociology: From the Epistemological to the Empirical," *Sociological Theory*, March 2005, pp 86–115.

2 This definition is based in part on one found in D. Horton Smith, "A Parsimonious Definition of 'Group': Toward Conceptual Clarity and Scientific Utility," *Sociological Inquiry*, Spring 1967, pp 141–167. Also see W.B. Swann, Jr., J.T. Polzer, D.C. Seyle, and S.J. Ko, "Finding Value in Diversity: Verification of Personal and Social Self-Views in Diverse Groups," *Academy of Management Review*, January 2004, pp 9–27.

3 E.H. Schein, *Organizational Psychology*, 3rd ed. (Englewood Cliffs, NJ: Prentice Hall, 1980), p 145. For more, see L.R. Weingart, "How Did They Do That? The Ways and Means of Studying Group Process," *Research in Organizational Behaviour*, vol. 19, eds. L.L. Cummings and B.M. Staw (Greenwich, CT: JAI Press, 1997), pp 189–239.

4 See R. Cross, N. Nohria, and A. Parker, "Six Myths about Informal Networks—and How to Overcome Them," *MIT Sloan Management Review*, Spring 2002, pp 67–75; C. Shirky, "Watching the Patterns Emerge," *Harvard Business Review*, February 2004, pp 34–35; P. Chattopadhyay, M. Tluchowska, and E. George, "Identifying the Ingroup: A Closer Look at the Influence of Demographic Dissimilarity on Employee Social Identity," *Academy of Management Review*, April 2004, pp 180–202; S. Allen, "Water Cooler Wisdom," *Training*, August 2005, pp 30–34; and E. Watters, "The Organization Woman," *Business 2.0*, April 2006, pp 106–110.

5 For an instructive overview of five different theories of group development, see J.P. Wanous, A.E. Reichers, and S.D. Malik, "Organizational Socialization and Group Development: Toward an Integrative Perspective," *Academy of Management Review*, October 1984, pp 670–683. Also see L.R. Offermann and R.K. Spiros, "The Science and Practice of Team Development: Improving the Link," *Academy of Management Journal*, April 2001, pp 376–392; and A. Chang, P. Bordia, and J. Duck, "Punctuated Equilibrium and Linear Progression: Toward a New Understanding of Group Development," *Academy of Management Journal*, February 2003, pp 106–117.

6 See B.W. Tuckman, "Developmental Sequence in Small Groups," *Psychological Bulletin*, June 1965, pp 384–399; and B.W. Tuckman and M.A.C. Jensen, "Stages of Small-Group Development Revisited," *Group and Organization Studies*, December 1977, pp 419–427. An instructive adaption of the Tuckman model can be found in L. Holpp, "If Empowerment Is So Good, Why Does It Hurt?" *Training*, March 1995, p 56.

7 See T. Postmes, R. Spears, A.T. Lee, and R.J. Novak, "Individuality and Social Influence in Groups: Inductive and Deductive Routes to Group Identity," *Journal of Personality and Social Psychology*, November 2005, pp 747–763.

8 A useful resource book is T. Ursiny, *The Coward's Guide to Conflict: Empowering Solutions for Those Who Would Rather Run than Fight* (Naperville, IL: Sourcebooks, 2003). Also see J. Li and D.C. Hambrick, "Factional Groups: A New Vantage on Demographic Faultlines, Conflict, and Disintegration in Work Teams," *Academy of Management Journal*, October 2005, pp 794–813; and M.D. Johnson, J.R. Hollenbeck, S.E. Humphrey, D.R. Ilgen, D.Jundt, and C.J. Meyer, "Cutthroat Cooperation: Asymmetrical Adaptation to Changes in Team Reward Structures," *Academy of Management Journal*, February 2006, pp 103–119.

9 For related research, see M. Van Vugt and C.M. Hart, "Social Identity as Social Glue: The Origins of Group Loyalty," *Journal of Personality and Social Psychology*, April 2004, pp 585–598.

10 See C.M. Mason and M.A. Griffin, "Group Task Satisfaction: The Group's Shared Attitude to Its Task and Work Environment," *Group and Organization Management*, December 2005, pp 625–652.

11 C. Gersick, "Times and Transition in Work Teams: Toward A New Model of Group Development," *Academy of Management Journal*, vol. 31, no 1, March 1988, pp 9–41.

12 G. Graen, "Role-Making Processes within Complex Organizations," *Handbook of Industrial and Organizational Psychology*, ed. M.D. Dunnette (Chicago: Rand McNally, 1976), p 1201. Also see S.D. Dobrev and W.P. Barnett, "Organizational Roles and Transition to Entrepreneurship," *Academy of Management Journal*, June 2005, pp 433–449; M.A. Eys, A.V. Carron, M.R. Beauchamp, and S.R. Brays, "Athletes' Perceptions of the Sources of Role Ambiguity," *Small Group Research*, August 2005, pp 383–403; and T. Schellens, H. Van Keer, and M. Valcke, "The Impact of Role Assignment on Knowledge Construction in Asynchronous Discussion Groups: A Multilevel Analysis," *Small Group Research*, December 2005, pp 704–745.

13 See K.D. Benne and P. Sheats, "Functional Roles of Group Members," *Journal of Social Issues*, Spring 1948, pp 41–49.

14 See H.J. Klein and P.W. Mulvey, "Two Investigations of the Relationships among Group Goals, Goal Commitment, Cohesion, and Performance," *Organizational Behaviour and Human Decision Processes*, January 1995, pp 44–53; D.F. Crown and J.G. Rosse, "Yours, Mine, and Ours: Facilitating Group Productivity through the Integration of Individual and Group Goals," *Organizational Behaviour and Human Decision Processes*, November 1995, pp 138–150; and D. Knight, C.C. Durham, and E.A. Locke, "The Relationship of Team Goals, Incentives, and Efficacy to Strategic Risk, Tactical Implementation, and Performance," *Academy of Management Journal*, April 2001, pp 326–338.

15 A. Zander, "The Value of Belonging to a Group in Japan," *Small Group Behaviour*, February 1983, pp 7–8. Also see E. Gundling, *Working GlobeSmart: 12 People Skills for Doing Business across Borders* (Palo Alto, CA: Davies-Black Publishing, 2003).

16 R.R. Blake and J. Srygley Mouton, "Don't Let Group Norms Stifle Creativity," *Personnel*, August 1985, p 28.

17 See D. Kahneman, "Reference Points, Anchors, Norms, and Mixed Feelings," *Organizational Behavior and Human Decision Processes*, March 1992, pp 296–312; and J.M. Marques, D. Abrams, D. Paez, and C. Martinez-Taboada, "The Role of Categorization and In-Group Norms in Judgments of Groups and Their Members," *Journal of Personality and Social Psychology*, October 1998, pp 976–988.

18 *The Globe and Mail Report on Business*, "Canada's Top 100 Employers 2012," November 2011, www.theglobeandmail.com/report-on-business/careers/top-employers/the-list-canadas-top-100-employers-for-2012/article639713/.

19 See J. Pfeffer, "Bring Back Shame," *Business 2.0*, September 2003, p 80.

20 D.C. Feldman, "The Development and Enforcement of Group Norms," *Academy of Management Review*, January 1984, pp 50–52.

21 Ibid.

22 J.R. Katzenbach and D.K. Smith, *The Wisdom of Teams: Creating the High-Performance Organization* (New York: Harper Business, 1999), p 45; J.E. Mathieu, L.L. Gibson, and T.M. Ruddy, "Empowerment and Team Effectiveness: An Empirical Test of an Integrated Model," *Journal of Applied Psychology*, January 2006, pp 97–108; P. Balkundi and W.A. Harrison, "Ties, Leaders, and Time in Teams: Strong Inference about Network Structure's Effects on Team Viability and Performance," *Academy of Management Journal*, February 2006, pp 49–68; and J.M. Howell and C.M. Shea, "Effects of Champion Behaviour, Team Potency, and External Communication Activities on Predicting Team Performance," *Group and Organization Management*, April 2006, pp 180–211.

23 J.R. Hackman, "Why Teams Don't Work," *Theory and Research on Small Groups*, vol. 4, 1998, pp 245–267.

24 Condensed and adapted from J.R. Katzenbach and D.K. Smith, *The Wisdom of Teams: Creating the High Performance Organization* (New York: HarperBusiness, 1999), p 214. Also see B. Beersma, J.R. Hollenbeck, S.E. Humphrey, H. Moon, D. Conlon, and D.R. Ilgen, "Cooperation, Competition, and Team Performance: Toward

a Contingency Approach," *Academy of Management Journal,* October 2003, pp 572–590; L.L. Gilson, J.E. Mathieu, C.E. Shalley, and T.M. Ruddy, "Creativity and Standardization: Complementary or Conflicting Drivers of Team Effectiveness?" *Academy of Management Journal,* June 2005, pp 521–531; B. Fischer and A. Boynton, "Virtuoso Teams," *Harvard Business Review,* July/August 2005, pp 116–123; R.D. Hof, "Teamwork Supercharged," *BusinessWeek,* November 21, 2005, pp 90–94; J.E. Mathieu, L.L. Gibson, and T.M. Ruddy, "Empowerment and Team Effectiveness: An Empirical Test of an Integrated Model," *Journal of Applied Psychology,* January 2006, pp 97–108; P. Balkundi and W.A. Harrison, "Ties, Leaders, and Time in Teams: Strong Inference about Network Structure's Effects on Team Viability and Performance," *Academy of Management Journal,* February 2006, pp 49–68; and J.M. Howell and C.M. Shea, "Effects of Champion Behaviour, Team Potency, and External Communication Activities on Predicting Team Performance," *Group and Organization Management,* April 2006, pp 180–211.

[25] See M.P. Hillmann, P. Dongier, R.P. Murgallis, M. Khosh, E.K. Allen, and R. Evernham, "When Failure Isn't an Option," *Harvard Business Review,* July/August 2005, pp 41–50.

[26] J.R. Katzenbach and D.K. Smith, "The Discipline of Teams," *Harvard Business Review,* March/April 1993, p 112.

[27] "A Team's-Eye View of Teams," *Training,* November 1995, p 16.

[28] J. Welch and S. Welch, "Company Man or Free Agent," *BusinessWeek,* February 12, 2007, p 106. Also see M. de Rond, "Lessons from the Oxford and Cambridge Boat Race," *Harvard Business Review,* September 2008, p 28; and E. Catmull, "How Pixar Fosters Collective Creativity," *Harvard Business Review,* September 2008, pp 64–72.

[29] Data from "Workforce Readiness and the New Essential Skills," *SHRM Workplace Visions,* no. 2, 2008, Table 3, p 5.

[30] As quoted in A. Fisher, "How to Get Hired by a 'Best' Company," *Fortune,* February 4, 2008, p 96.

[31] G. Chen, L.M. Donahue, and R.I. Klimoski, "Training Undergraduates to Work in Organizational Teams," *Academy of Management Learning and Education,* March 2004, Appendix A, p 40. (See Kreitner, 3rd US Edition, p 233.)

[32] Data from C. Joinson, "Teams at Work," *HR Magazine,* May 1999, pp 30–36.

[33] B. Dumaine, "Who Needs a Boss?" *Fortune,* May 7, 1990, p 52. Also see D. Vredenburgh and I.Y. He, "Leadership Lessons from a Conductorless Orchestra," *Business Horizons,* September/October 2003, pp 19–24; and C.A. O'Reilly III and M.L. Tushman, "The Ambidextrous Organization," *Harvard Business Review,* April 2004, pp 74–81.

[34] Adapted from Table 1 in V.U. Druskat and J.V. Wheeler, "Managing from the Boundary: The Effective Leadership of Self-Managing Work Teams," *Academy of Management Journal,* August 2003, pp 435–457.

[35] L.A. Hill, "Becoming the Boss," *Harvard Business Review,* January 2007, p 54. Also see the second Q&A in J. Welch and S. Welch, "It's Business-Bashing Time," *BusinessWeek,* March 10, 2008, p 92; and D. Coutu, "Why Teams Don't Work," *Harvard Business Review,* May 2009, pp 99–105.

[36] See A.E. Randal and K.S. Jaussi, "Functional Background Identity, Diversity, and Individual Performance in Cross-Functional Teams," *Academy of Management Journal,* December 2003, pp 763–774; and G.S. Van Der Vegt and J.S. Bunderson, "Learning and Performance in Multidisciplinary Teams: The Importance of Collective Team Identification," *Academy of Management Journal,* June 2005, pp 532–547.

[37] Excerpted from "Fast Talk," *Fast Company,* February 2004, p 50. For cross-functional teams in action, see B. Nussbaum, "How to Build Innovative Companies: Get Creative!" *BusinessWeek,* August 1, 2005, pp 61–68; C. Edwards, "Inside Intel," *BusinessWeek,* January 9, 2006, pp 46–54; "How to Break Out of Commodity Hell," *BusinessWeek,* March 27, 2006, p 76; and B. Finn, "Outside-In R&D," *Business 2.0,* April 2006, p 85.

[38] For example, see J. Merritt, "How to Rebuild a B-School," *BusinessWeek,* March 29, 2004, pp 90–91.

[39] See *Training,* "1996 Industry Report: What Self-Managing Teams Manage," October 1996, p 69.

[40] See L.L. Thompson, *Making the Team: A Guide for Managers* (Upper Saddle River, NJ: Prentice Hall, 2000).

[41] See P.S. Goodman, R. Devadas, and T.L. Griffith Hughson, "Groups and Productivity: Analyzing the Effectiveness of Self-Managing Teams," *Productivity in Organizations,* eds. J.P. Campbell, R.J. Campbell and Associates (San Francisco: Jossey-Bass, 1988), pp 295–327. Also see R.C. Liden, S.J. Wayne, and M.L. Kraimer "Managing Individual Performance in Work Groups," *Human Resource Management,* Spring 2001, pp 63–72; R. Batt, "Who Benefits from Teams? Comparing Workers, Supervisors, and Managers," *Industrial Relations,* January 2004, pp 183–209; F.P. Morgeson, "The External Leadership of Self-Managing Teams: Intervening in the Context of Novel and Disruptive Events," *Journal of Applied Psychology,* May 2005, pp 497–508; and S. Kauffeld, "Self-Directed Work Groups and Team Competence," *Journal of Occupational and Organizational Psychology,* March 2006, pp 1–21.

[42] For more, see W.F. Cascio, "Managing a Virtual Workplace," *Academy of Management Executive,* August 2000, pp 81–90; and the collection of articles on E-leadership and virtual teams in *Organizational Dynamics,* no 4, 2003.

[43] See A.M. Townsend, S.M. DeMarie, and A.R. Hendrickson, "Virtual Teams: Technology and the Workplace of the Future," *Academy of Management Executive,* August 1998, pp 17–29.

[44] See C. Saunders, C. Van Slyke, and D.R. Vogel, "My Time or Yours? Managing Time Visions in Global Virtual Teams," *Academy of Management Executive,* February 2004, pp 19–31.

[45] Based on P. Bordia, N. DiFonzo, and A. Chang, "Rumor as Group Problem Solving: Development Patterns in Informal Computer-Mediated Groups," *Small Group Research,* February 1999, pp 8–28.

[46] See K.A. Graetz, E.S. Boyle, C.E. Kimble, P. Thompson, and J.L. Garloch, "Information Sharing in Face-to-Face, Teleconferencing, and Electronic Chat Groups," *Small Group Research,* December 1998, pp 714–743.

[47] Based on F. Niederman and R.J. Volkema, "The Effects of Facilitator Characteristics on Meeting Preparation, Set Up, and Implementation," *Small Group Research,* June 1999, pp 330–360.

[48] Based on J.J. Sosik, B.J. Avolio, and S.S. Kahai, "Inspiring Group Creativity: Comparing Anonymous and Identified Electronic Brainstorming," *Small Group Research,* February 1998, pp 3–31. For practical advice on brainstorming, see C. Caggiano, "The Right Way to Brainstorm," *Inc.,* July 1999, p 94. Also see A.M. Hardin, M.A. Fuller, and J.S. Valacich, "Measuring Group Efficacy in Virtual Teams: New Questions in an Old Debate," *Small Group Research,* February 2006, pp 65–85.

[49] Based on M.M. Montoya-Weiss, A.P. Massey, and M. Song, "Getting It Together: Temporal Coordination and Conflict Management in Global Virtual Teams," *Academy of Management Journal,* December 2001, pp 1251–1262.

[50] J. Hyatt, "A Surprising Truth about Geographically Dispersed Teams," *MIT Sloan Management Review,* Summer 2008, pp 5–6.

[51] See B.L. Kirkman, B. Rosen, C.B. Gibson, P.E. Tesluk, and S.O. McPherson, "Five Challenges to Virtual Team Success: Lessons from Sabre, Inc.," *Academy of Management Executive,* August 2002, pp 67–79; P.J. Hinds and D.E. Bailey, "Out of Sight, Out of Sync: Understanding Conflict in Distributed Teams," *Organization Science,* November–December 2003, pp 615–632; and Y. Shin, "Conflict Resolution in Virtual Teams," *Organizational Dynamics,* November 2005, pp 331–345.

[52] See E. Kelley, "Keys to Effective Virtual Global Teams," *Academy of Management Executive,* May 2001, pp 132–133.

[53] Practical perspectives are offered in "Virtual Teams that Work," *HR Magazine,* July 2003, p 121; D.D. Davis, "The Tao of Leadership in Virtual Teams," *Organizational Dynamics,* no. 1, 2004, pp 47–62;

A. Majchrzak, A. Malhotra, J. Stamps, and J. Lipnack, "Can Absence Make a Team Grow Stronger?" *Harvard Business Review,* May 2004, pp 131–137; and J. Gordon, "Do Your Virtual Teams Deliver Only Virtual Performance?" *Training,* June 2005, pp 20–26.

[54] See, for example, P. Suciu, "Listen Up, Soldiers," *Newsweek,* July 11, 2005, p 70; J. Alsever, "Hello Muddah, Hello Faddah . . . What Executives Learn at Summer Camp," *Fast Company,* September 2005, p 30; and S. Datta, "Cooking Up a Better Team," *Business 2.0,* May 2006, p 143.

[55] Canadian Outback Adventures and Events, www.canadianoutback .com.

[56] As quoted in C. Tkaczyk, "Keeping Creatives Happy," *Fortune,* March 16, 2009, p 40.

[57] See J. Brett, K. Behfar, and M.C. Kern, "Managing Multicultural Teams," *Harvard Business Review,* November 2006, pp 83–91.

[58] See D. McDonald, "Why We All Hate Offsites," *Business 2.0,* May 2006, pp 79–80.

[59] G. Lowe, "Best Workplaces 2006: Trust is tops—building a better workplace culture," *Canadian Business,* April 10–23, 2006, www.canadianbusiness.com/shared/print.jsp?Content=20060410_ 76260_76260&adzone=managing/.

[60] Ibid.

[61] See D.M. Rousseau, S.B. Sitkin, R.S. Burt, and C. Camerer, "Not So Different After All: A Cross-Discipline View of Trust," *Academy of Management Review,* July 1998, pp 393–404; and A.C. Wicks, S.L. Berman, and T.M. Jones, "The Structure of Optimal Trust: Moral and Strategic Implications," *Academy of Management Review,* January 1999, pp 99–116.

[62] J.D. Lewis and A. Weigert, "Trust as a Social Reality," *Social Forces,* June 1985, p 971. Trust is examined as an indirect factor in K.T. Dirks, "The Effects of Interpersonal Trust on Work Group Performance," *Journal of Applied Psychology,* June 1999, pp 445–455. Also see J.B. Cunningham and J. MacGregor, "Trust and the Design of Work: Complementary Constructs in Satisfaction and Performance," *Human Relations,* December 2000, pp 1575–1588.

[63] P. Lencioni, *The Five Dysfunctions of a Team—A Field Guide* (San Francisco CA: Jossey-Bass, 2005).

[64] See R. Zemke, "Little Lies," *Training,* February 2004, p 8.

[65] For support, see G.M. Spreitzer and A.K. Mishra, "Giving Up Control without Losing Control: Trust and Its Substitutes' Effects on Managers' Involving Employees in Decision Making," *Group and Organization Management,* June 1999, pp 155–187. Also see G. Johnson, "11 Keys to Leadership," *Training,* January 2004, p 18.

[66] Adapted from F. Bartolomé, "Nobody Trusts the Boss Completely—Now What?" *Harvard Business Review,* March/April 1989, pp 135–142. For more on building trust, see R. Galford and A.S. Drapeau, "The Enemies of Trust," *Harvard Business Review,* February 2003, pp 88–95; L.C. Abrams, R. Cross, E. Lesser, and D.Z. Levin, "Nurturing Interpersonal Trust in Knowledge-Sharing Networks," *Academy of Management Executive,* November 2003, pp 64–77; C. Huxham and S. Vangen, "Doing Things Collaboratively: Realizing the Advantage or Succumbing to Inertia?" *Organizational Dynamics,* no. 2, 2004, pp 190–201; S.A. Joni, "The Geography of Trust," *Harvard Business Review,* March 2004, pp 82–88; P. Evans and B. Wolf, "Collaboration Rules," *Harvard Business Review,* July/August 2005, pp 96–104; and R. Goffee and G. Jones, "Managing Authenticity: The Paradox of Great Leadership," *Harvard Business Review,* December 2005, pp 86–94.

[67] I.L. Janis, *Groupthink,* 2nd ed. (Boston: Houghton Mifflin, 1982), p 9. Alternative models are discussed in K. Granstrom and D. Stiwne, "A Bipolar Model of Groupthink: An Expansion of Janis's Concept," *Small Group Research,* February 1998, pp 32–56; A. R. Flippen, "Understanding Groupthink from a Self-Regulatory Perspective," *Small Group Research,* April 1999, pp 139–165; and M. Harvey, M.M. Novicevic, M.R. Buckley, and J.R.B. Halbesleben, "The Abilene

Paradox after Thirty Years: A Global Perspective," *Organizational Dynamics,* no. 2, 2004, pp 215–226.

[68] Ibid. For an alternative model, see R.J. Aldag and S. Riggs Fuller, "Beyond Fiasco: A Reappraisal of the Groupthink Phenomenon and a New Model of Group Decision Processes," *Psychological Bulletin,* May 1993, pp 533–552. Also see A.A. Mohamed and F.A. Wiebe, "Toward a Process Theory of Groupthink," *Small Group Research,* August 1996, pp 416–430.

[69] Adapted from Janis, *Groupthink,* pp 174175. Also see J.M. Wellen and M. Neale, "Deviance, Self-Typicality, and Group Cohesion: The Corrosive Effects of the Bad Apples on the Barrel," *Small Group Research,* April 2006, pp 165–186.

[70] D.D. Henningsen, M.L.M. Henningsen, J. Eden, and M.G. Cruz, "Examining the Symptoms of Groupthink and Retrospective Sensemaking," *Small Group Research,* February 2006, pp 36–64.

[71] Based on discussion in B. Latane, K. Williams, and S. Harkins, "Many Hands Make Light the Work: The Causes and Consequences of Social Loafing," *Journal of Personality and Social Psychology,* June 1979, pp 822–832; and D.A. Kravitz and B. Martin, "Ringelmann Rediscovered: The Original Article," *Journal of Personality and Social Psychology,* May 1986, pp 936–941.

[72] See S.J. Karau and K.D. Williams, "Social Loafing: Meta-Analytic Review and Theoretical Integration," *Journal of Personality and Social Psychology,* October 1993, pp 681–706; and L. Thompson, "Improving the Creativity of Organizational Work Groups," *Academy of Management Executive,* February 2003, pp 96–109.

[73] See S.J. Zaccaro, "Social Loafing: The Role of Task Attractiveness," *Personality and Social Psychology Bulletin,* March 1984, pp 99–106; J.M. Jackson and K.D. Williams, "Social Loafing on Difficult Tasks: Working Collectively Can Improve Performance," *Journal of Personality and Social Psychology,* October 1985, pp 937–942; and J.M. George, "Extrinsic and Intrinsic Origins of Perceived Social Loafing in Organizations," *Academy of Management Journal,* March 1992, pp 191–202.

[74] For complete details, see K. Williams, S. Harkins, and B. Latane, "Identifiability as a Deterrent to Social Loafing: Two Cheering Experiments," *Journal of Personality and Social Psychology,* February 1981, pp 303–311.

[75] See J.M. Jackson and S.G. Harkins, "Equity in Effort: An Explanation of the Social Loafing Effect," *Journal of Personality and Social Psychology,* November 1985, pp 1199–1206.

[76] Both studies are reported in S.G. Harkins and K. Szymanski, "Social Loafing and Group Evaluation," *Journal of Personality and Social Psychology,* June 1989, pp 934–941. Also see R. Hoigaard, R. Safvenbom, and F.E. Tonnessen, "The Relationship between Group Cohesion, Group Norms, and Perceived Social Loafing in Soccer Teams," *Small Group Research,* June 2006, pp 217–232.

[77] Data from J.A. Wagner III, "Studies of Individualism-Collectivism: Effects on Cooperation in Groups," *Academy of Management Journal,* February 1995, pp 152–172. Also see P.W. Mulvey and H.J. Klein, "The Impact of Perceived Loafing and Collective Efficacy on Group Goal Processes and Group Performance," *Organizational Behaviour and Human Decision Processes,* April 1998, pp 62–87; P.W. Mulvey, L. Bowes-Sperry, and H.J. Klein, "The Effects of Perceived Loafing and Defensive Impression Management on Group Effectiveness," *Small Group Research,* June 1998, pp 394–415; and H. Goren, R. Kurzban, and A. Rapoport, "Social Loafing vs. Social Enhancement: Public Goods Provisioning in Real-Time with Irrevocable Commitments," *Organizational Behaviour and Human Decision Processes,* March 2003, pp 277–290.

[78] See S.G. Scott and W.O. Einstein, "Strategic Performance Appraisal in Team-Based Organizations: One Size Does Not Fit All," *Academy of Management Executive,* May 2001, pp 107–116.

CHAPTER 7

[1] Excerpted from J. McGregor, "Job Review in 140 Keystrokes," *BusinessWeek*, March 23–30, 2009, p 58.

[2] See D.G. Kolb, P.D. Collins, and E.A. Lind, "Requisite Connectivity: Finding Flow in a Not-So-Flat World," *Organizational Dynamics*, April–June 2008, pp 181–189; and N.R. Lockwood, "Effective Organizational Communication: A Competitive Advantage," *SHRM Research Quarterly, HR Magazine*, December 2008, pp 1–9.

[3] Data from G. Naik, "A Hospital Races to Learn Lessons of Ferrari Pit Stop," *The Wall Street Journal*, November 14, 2006, pp A1, A10.

[4] Based on "Why Am I Here," *Training*, April 2006, p 13. For a similar interpretation, see D. Robb, "From the Top," *HR Magazine*, February 2009, pp 61–63.

[5] J.L. Bowditch and A.F. Buono, *A Primer on Organizational Behaviour*, 4th ed. (New York: John Wiley & Sons, 1997), p 120.

[6] For a detailed discussion about selecting an appropriate medium, see B. Barry and I. Smithey-Fulmer, "The Medium and the Message: The Adaptive Use of Communication Media in Dyadic Influence," *Academy of Management Review*, April 2004, pp 272–292.

[7] G.A. Fowler, "In China's Offices, Foreign Colleagues Might Get an Earful," *The Wall Street Journal*, February 13, 2007, p B1.

[8] Communication noise is discussed by J. Sandberg, "Office Minstrels Drive the Rest of Us Nuts but Are Hard to Silence," *The Wall Street Journal*, February 14, 2006, p B1.

[9] Ideas for improving personal communication skills are discussed in J.S. Lublin, "Improv Troupe Teaches Managers How to Give Better Presentations," *The Wall Street Journal*, February 6, 2007, p B1; and R. Tucker, "Four Key Skills to Master Now," *Fortune*, October 30, 2006, p 123.

[10] See "Interpersonal Effectiveness Training: Beyond the Water Cooler," *Training*, April 2006, p 10.

[11] For a thorough discussion of these barriers, see C.R. Rogers and F.J. Roethlisberger, "Barriers and Gateways to Communication," *Harvard Business Review*, July–August 1952, pp 46–52.

[12] Ibid., p 47.

[13] The use of jargon and acronyms is discussed by C. Hymowitz, "Mind Your Language: To Do Business Today, Consider Delayering," *The Wall Street Journal*, March 27, 2006, p B1.

[14] O. Ross, "OMG, xprts r all 'cybr tok is koo,'" *Toronto Star*, July 3, 2011, p IN3.

[15] Excerpted from J. Sandberg, "It Says 'Press Any Key.' Where's the Any Key?," *The Wall Street Journal*, February 20, 2007, p B1.

[16] R.L. Daft and R.H. Lengel, "Information Richness: A New Approach to Managerial Behaviour and Organizational Design," *Research in Organizational Behaviour*, eds. B.M. Staw and L.L. Cummings (Greenwich, CT: JAI Press, 1984), p 196.

[17] Details of this example are provided in L. Grensing-Pophal, "Spread the Word—Correctly," *HR Magazine*, March 2005, pp 83–88.

[18] See E. Binney, "Is E-Mail the New Pink Slip?," *HR Magazine*, November 2006, pp 32, 38; and D.M. Cable and K.Y.T. Yu, "Managing Job Seekers' Organizational Image Beliefs: The Role of Media Richness and Media Credibility," *Journal of Applied Psychology*, July 2006, pp 828–840.

[19] See B. Barry and I.S. Fulmer, "The Medium and the Message: The Adaptive Use of Communication Media in Dyadic Influence," *Academy of Management Review*, April 2004, pp 272–292; and A.F. Simon, "Computer-Mediated Communication: Task Performance and Satisfaction," *The Journal of Social Psychology*, June 2006, pp 349–379.

[20] See R.E. Rice and D.E. Shook, "Relationships of Job Categories and Organizational Levels to Use of Communication Channels, Including Electronic Mail: A Meta-Analysis and Extension," *Journal of Management Studies*, March 1990, pp 195–229.

[21] Results can be found in J.D. Johnson, W.A. Donohue, C.K. Atkin, and S. Johnson, "Communication, Involvement, and Perceived Innovativeness," *Group and Organization Management*, March 2001, pp 24–52; and B. Davenport Sypher and T.E. Zorn Jr., "Communication-Related Abilities and Upward Mobility: A Longitudinal Investigation," *Human Communication Research*, Spring 1986, pp 420–431.

[22] J.A. Waters, "Managerial Assertiveness," *Business Horizons*, September/October 1982, p 25.

[23] See F. Timmins and C. McCabe, "How Assertive Are Nurses in the Workplace? A Preliminary Pilot Study," *Journal of Nursing Management*, January 2005, pp 61–67.

[24] J. Swartz, "Yahoo's New CEO Finds Plenty on Her Plate," *USA Today*, January 15, 2009, p 3B. For more, see J. Swartz, "Yahoo to Lay Off Up to 700 Staffers after Profit Drops," *USA Today*, April 22, 2009, p 3B.

[25] J.A. Waters, "Managerial Assertiveness," *Business Horizons*, September/October 1982, p 27.

[26] This statistic was provided by A. Fisher, "How Can I Survive a Phone Interview?" *Fortune*, April 19, 2004, p 54.

[27] Problems with body language analysis are discussed in A. Pihulyk, "Communicate with Clarity: The Key to Understanding and Influencing Others," *The Canadian Manager*, Summer 2003, pp 12–13.

[28] Related research is summarized by J.A. Hall, "Male and Female Nonverbal Behaviour," *Multichannel Integrations of Nonverbal Behaviour*, eds. A.W. Siegman and S. Feldstein (Hillsdale, NJ: Lawrence Erlbaum, 1985), pp 195–226.

[29] See R.E. Axtell, *Gestures: The Do's and Taboos of Body Language around the World* (New York: John Wiley & Sons, 1991).

[30] See J.A. Russell, "Facial Expressions of Emotion: What Lies Beyond Minimal Universality?," *Psychological Bulletin*, November 1995, pp 379–391.

[31] Norms for cross-cultural eye contact are discussed by C. Engholm, *When Business East Meets Business West: The Guide to Practice and Protocol in the Pacific Rim* (New York: John Wiley & Sons, 1991).

[32] See R.D. Ramsey, "Ten Things That Never Change for Supervisors," *SuperVision*, April 2007, pp 16–18; "CEOs Emphasize Listening to Employees," *HR Magazine*, January 2007, p 14; and M. Marchetti, "Listen to Me!" *Sales and Marketing Management*, April 2007, p 12.

[33] See D. Knight, "Perks Keeping Workers out of Revolving Door," *The Wall Street Journal*, April 30, 2005, p D3; and G. Rooper, "Managing Employee Relations," *HR Magazine*, May 2005, pp 101–104.

[34] The discussion of listening styles is based on "5 Listening Styles," June 19, 2004, www.crossroadsinstitute.org/listyle.html; and "Listening and Thinking: What's Your Style,", last modified August 10, 2002, www.pediatricservices.com/prof/prof-10.htm.

[35] See the related discussion in J. Condrill, "What Is Your Listening Style?" *Authors' Den*, July 7, 2005, www.authorsden.com/visit/viewarticle.asp?id=18707; and D.A. Nadler, "Confessions of a Trusted Counselor," *Harvard Business Review*, September 2005, pp 68–77.

[36] These recommendations were excerpted from J. Jay, "On Communicating Well," *HR Magazine*, January 2005, pp 87–88.

[37] D. Tannen, "The Power of Talk: Who Gets Heard and Why," *Harvard Business Review*, September–October 1995, p 139.

[38] For a thorough review of the evolutionary explanation of sex differences in communication, see A.H. Eagly and W. Wood, "The Origins of Sex Differences in Human Behavior," *American Psychologist*, June 1999, pp 408–423.

[39] See D. Tannen, "The Power of Talk: Who Gets Heard and Why," *Negotiation: Readings, Exercises, and Cases*, 3rd ed., eds. R.J. Lewicki and D.M. Saunders (Boston, MA: Irwin/McGraw-Hill, 1999),

pp 160–173; also see J. Ewers, "Ladies, Cool It if You Want Cash," *U.S. News and World Report*, September 24, 2007, p 57.

[40] This definition was taken from J.C. Tingley, *Genderflex: Men and Women Speaking Each Other's Language at Work* (New York: American Management Association, 1994), p 16.

[41] D. Tannen, "The Power of Talk," pp 147–148.

[42] H.B. Vickery III, "Tapping into the Employee Grapevine," *Association Management*, January 1984, pp 59–60.

[43] The most recent research is discussed by S.M. Crampton, J.W. Hodge, and J.M. Mishra, "The Informal Communication Network: Factors Influencing Grapevine Activity," *Public Personnel Management*, Winter 1998, pp 569–584; "Pruning the Company Grapevine," *Supervision*, September 1986, p 11; and R. Half, "Managing Your Career: 'How Can I Stop the Gossip?'" *Management Accounting*, September 1987, p 27. These statistics were obtained from "Kids' Lives 'Saturated' by Media, Study Says," *Arizona Republic*, March 10, 2005, p A7.

[44] For more, see A. Lashinsky, "The True Meaning of Twitter," *Fortune*, August 18, 2008, pp 39–42; D. Kadlec, "How Not to Act Your Age at Work," *Money*, December 2008, pp 44, 46; S.H. Wildstrom, "What to Entrust to the Cloud," *BusinessWeek*, April 6, 2009, pp 89–90; and C. Edwards, "Soon TVs and PCs May Work Like the Wii," *BusinessWeek*, April 13, 2009, p 52.

[45] A. Fisher, "E-Mail Is for Liars," *Fortune*, November 24, 2008, p 57.

[46] A. Pentland, "How Social Networks Network Best," *Harvard Business Review*, February 2009, p 37. Also see G. Morse, "Conversation: Wikipedia Founder Jimmy Wales on Making the Most of Company Wikis," *Harvard Business Review*, April 2008, p 26; E.M. Lira, P. Ripoll, J.M. Peiro, and A.M. Zornoza, "The Role of Information and Communication Technologies in the Relationship between Group Effectiveness and Group Potency," *Small Group Research*, December 2008, pp 728–745; and G. Dutton, "Tech Check," *Training*, January 2009, pp 24–26.

[47] *Canadian HR Reporter*, "Many Young Employees Ignore IT Policies: Survey," December 14, 2011, www.hrreporter.com.

[48] "Most wired generation prepares to take the reigns," CTV, March 24, 2008, http://ottawa.ctvnews.ca/most-wired-generation-prepares-to-take-the-reigns-1.284619

[49] D. Tapscott, *Grown Up Digital: How the Net Generation Is Changing Your World* (New York: McGraw-Hill, 2009), p 36. Also see the table "How Does Your Generation Communicate?" in "Generation Gap," *Executive Travel*, November–December 2008, pp 60–61.

[50] J.L. Yang, "How to Get a Job," *Fortune*, April 13, 2009, p 51. Also see J. Graham, "Cake Decorator Finds Twitter a Tweet Recipe for Success," *USA Today*, April 1, 2009, p 5B; and S. Jayson, "For Teens, a Friend Online Usually a Friend Offline, Too," *USA Today*, April 2, 2009, p 7D.

[51] See E. Agnvall, "Meetings Go Virtual," *HR Magazine*, January 2009, pp 74–77; J. Mullich, "How to Pick Your Mobile Lifestyle," *The Wall Street Journal*, April 1, 2009, pp A11–A12; and L. Cauley, "FCC Pursues Goal of Nationwide Affordable, Fast Internet," *USA Today*, April 8, 2009, p 5B.

[52] J.A. Pearce II, "Successful Corporate Telecommuting with Technology Considerations for Late Adopters," *Organizational Dynamics*, January–March 2009, p 17.

[53] M. Conlin, "Telecommuting: Out of Sight, Yes. Out of Mind, No," *BusinessWeek*, February 18, 2008, p 60.

[54] Results are reported in K. Gurchiek, "Telecommuting Could Hold Back Careers," *HR Magazine*, March 2007, p 34.

[55] T.D. Golden, J.F. Veiga, and R.N. Dino, "The Impact of Professional Isolation on Teleworker Job Performance and Turnover Intentions: Does Time Spent Teleworking, Interacting Face-to-Face, or Having Access to Communication-Enhancing Technology Matter?" *Journal of Applied Psychology*, November 2008, p 1412.

CHAPTER 8

[1] D. Tjosvold, *Learning to Manage Conflict: Getting People to Work Together Productively* (New York: Lexington Books, 1993), p xi.

[2] Ibid., pp xi–xii. High-tech change is discussed in B. Stone, "Big Bucks, Big Thinker," *Newsweek*, May 22, 2006, p 46.

[3] See M. Conlin, "Good Divorce, Good Business," *BusinessWeek*, October 31, 2005, pp 90–91.

[4] J.A. Wall Jr. and R. Robert Callister, "Conflict and Its Management," *Journal of Management*, no. 3, 1995, p 517.

[5] Ibid., p 544.

[6] D. Stead, "The Big Picture," *BusinessWeek*, January 8, 2007, p 11.

[7] See M.A. von Glinow, D.L. Shapiro, and J.M. Brett, "Can We Talk, and Should We? Managing Emotional Conflict in Multicultural Teams," *Academy of Management Review*, October 2004, pp 578–592; C. Palmeri, "Hair-Pulling in the Dollhouse," *BusinessWeek*, May 2, 2005, pp 76–77; and G. Colvin, "CEO Knockdown," *Fortune*, April 4, 2005, pp 19–20.

[8] K. Cloke and J. Goldsmith, *Resolving Conflicts at Work: A Complete Guide for Everyone on the Job* (San Francisco: Jossey-Bass, 2000), pp 25, 27, 29.

[9] D. Brady, "It's All Donald, All the Time," *BusinessWeek*, January 22, 2007, p 51.

[10] See P.J. Sauer, "Are You Ready for Some Football Clichés?," *Inc.*, October 2003, pp 97–100; and V.P. Rindova, M. Becerra, and I. Contardo, "Enacting Competitive Wars: Competitive Activity, Language Games, and Market Consequences," *Academy of Management Review*, October 2004, pp 670–686.

[11] Cloke and Goldsmith, *Resolving Conflicts at Work*, pp 31–32. Also see K. Fackelmann, "Arguing Hurts the Heart in More Ways Than One," *USA Today*, March 6, 2006, p 10D; D. Meyer, "The Saltshaker Theory," *Inc.*, October 2006, pp 69–70; J. Welch and S. Welch, "The Blame Game—Forget It," *BusinessWeek*, March 5, 2007, p 92; and J. Welch and S. Welch, "The Right Way to Say Goodbye," *BusinessWeek*, March 26, 2006, p 144.

[12] See M.J. Martinko, S.C. Douglas, and P. Harvey, "Understanding and Managing Workplace Aggression," *Organizational Dynamics*, no. 2, 2006, pp 117–130; Z. Stambor, "Bullying Stems From Fear, Apathy," *Monitor on Psychology*, July–August 2006, pp 72–78; T.J. Brown and K.E. Sumner, "Perceptions and Punishments of Workplace Aggression: The Role of Aggression Content, Context, and Perceiver Variables," *Journal of Applied Social Psychology*, October 2006, pp 2509–2531; and J. Deschenaux, "Bills Prohibit Employer Bans on Firearms," *HR Magazine*, February 2007, pp 34, 39.

[13] See S. Alper, D. Tjosvold, and K.S. Law, "Interdependence and Controversy in Group Decision Making: Antecedents to Effective Self-Managing Teams," *Organizational Behaviour and Human Decision Processes*, April 1998, pp 33–52; and T. Simons and R.S. Peterson, "When to Let Them Duke It Out," *Harvard Business Review*, June 2006, pp 23–24.

[14] S.P. Robbins, "'Conflict Management' and 'Conflict Resolution' Are Not Synonymous Terms," *California Management Review*, Winter 1978, p 70. For examples of functional and dysfunctional conflict, see D. Dahl, "Case Study: Michael Kalinsky Was Sick of Fighting with his Vice President, who Was Also his Ex-Brother-in-Law. Was Firing him too Drastic?" *Inc.*, October 2006, pp 51–54; J.S. Lublin and E. White, "Drama in the Boardroom," *The Wall Street Journal*, October 2, 2006, pp B1, B3; and S. Clifford, "The Worst Case Scenario," *Inc.*, November 2006, p 111.

[15] Cooperative conflict is discussed in Tjosvold, *Learning to Manage Conflict: Getting People to Work Together Productively*. Also see A.C. Amason, "Distinguishing the Effects of Functional and Dysfunctional Conflict on Strategic Decision Making: Resolving a Paradox for Top

Management Teams," *Academy of Management Journal,* February 1996, pp 123–148.

[16] Excerpted from K Sulkowicz, "Analyze This," *BusinessWeek,* September 29, 2008, p 19.

[17] Adapted in part from discussion in A.C. Filley, *Interpersonal Conflict Resolution* (Glenview, IL: Scot, Foresman, 1975), pp 9-12; and B. Fortado, "The Accumulation of Grievance Conflict," *Journal of Management Inquiry,* December 1992, pp 288–303.

[18] Adapted from discussion in Tjosvold, *Learning to Manage Conflict,* pp 12–13. A. Bizman and Y. Yinon, "Intergroup Conflict Management Strategies as Related to Perceptions of Dual Identity and Separate Groups," *Journal of Social Psychology,* April 2004, pp 115–126; and R.J. Crisp and J.K. Nicel, "Disconfirming Intergroup Evaluations: Asymmetric Effects for In-Groups and Out-Groups," *Journal of Social Psychology,* June 2004, pp 247–271.

[19] L. Gardenswartz and A. Rowe, *Diverse Teams at Work: Capitalizing on the Power of Diversity* (New York: McGraw-Hill, 1994), p 32.

[20] C.M. Pearson and C.L. Porath, "On the Nature, Consequences, and Remedies of Workplace Incivility: No Time for 'nice'? Think Again," *Academy of Management Executive,* February 2005, p 7. Also see L.M. Cortina, "Unseen Injustice: Incivility as Modern Discrimination in Organizations," *Academy of Management Review,* January 2008, pp 55–75; and S. Lim, L.M. Cortina, and V.J. Magaley, "Personal and Workgroup Incivility: Impact on Work and Health Outcomes," *Journal of Applied Psychology,* January 2008, pp 95–107.

[21] IAPA Resources–Resource Articles, March 2011, "New Legislation Tackles Workplace Violence and Harassment—Just How Widespread is Workplace Violence?"

[22] R.T. Lee, *Dealing With Workplace Harassment and Bullying: Some Recommendations for Employment Standards of Manitoba* (Winnipeg, MB: University of Manitoba, December 12, 2005), p 2.

[23] Ibid., p 3.

[24] S. Dobson, "Incivility Common Workplace Issue, Finds Survey," *Canadian HR Reporter,* October 10, 2011, p 1.

[25] See D.L. Coutu, "In Praise of Boundaries: A Conversation with Miss Manners," *Harvard Business Review,* December 2003, p 41–45; R. Kurtz, "Is Etiquette A Core Value?" *Inc.,* May 2004, p 22; and K. Gurchiek, "Office Etiquette Breaches: Dial It Down," *HR Magazine,* May 2006, p 36.

[26] P. Falcone, "Days of Contemplation," *HR Magazine,* February 2007, p 107.

[27] For practical advice, see N. Nicholson, "How to Motivate Your Problem People," *Harvard Business Review, Special Issue: Motivating People,* January 2003, pp 56–65; and M. Archer, "How to Work With Annoying People," *USA Today,* March 20, 2006, p 4B.

[28] Based on discussion in G. Labianca, D.J. Brass, and B. Gray, "Social Networks and Perceptions of Intergroup Conflict: The Role of Negative Relationships and Third Parties," *Academy of Management Journal,* February 1998, pp 55–67. Also see A. Bizman and Y. Yinon, "Intergroup Conflict Management Strategies as Related to Perceptions of Dual Identity and Separate Groups," *Journal of Social Psychology,* April 2004, pp 115–126; and R.J. Crisp and J.K. Nicel, "Disconfirming Intergroup Evaluations: Asymmetric Effects for In-Groups and Out-Groups," *Journal of Social Psychology,* June 2004, pp 247–271.

[29] See L.A. Rudman and S.A. Goodwin, "Gender Differences in Automatic In-Group Bias: Why Do Women Like Women More than Men Like Men?" *Journal of Personality and Social Psychology,* October 2004, pp 494–509; G. Cowan, "Interracial Interactions at Racially Diverse University Campuses," *Journal of Social Psychology,* February 2005, pp 49–63; and G.B. Cunningham, "The Influence of

Group Diversity on Intergroup Bias Following Recategorization," *The Journal of Social Psychology,* October 2006, pp 533–547.

[30] See C.D. Batson, M.P. Polycarpou, E. Harmon-Jones, H.J. Imhoff, E.C. Mitchener, L.L. Bednar, T.R. Klein, and L. Highberger, "Empathy and Attitudes: Can Feeling for a Member of a Stigmatized Group Improve Feelings toward the Group?" *Journal of Personality and Social Psychology,* January 1997, pp 105–118.

[31] For more, see N.J. Adler, *International Dimensions of Organizational Behavior,* 4th ed. (Cincinnati, OH: South-Western, 2002); P. Engardio, "The Future of Outsourcing," *BusinessWeek,* January 30, 2006, pp 50–58; F. Balfour, "One Foot in China," *BusinessWeek,* May 1, 2006, pp 44–45; E. Iwata, "Immigrants Courted as Good Customers," *USA Today,* May 11, 2006, p 3B; L. Buchanan, "The Thinking Man's Outsourcing," *Inc.,* May 2006, pp 31–33; B. Helm, "Life on the Web's Factory Floor," *BusinessWeek,* May 22, 2006, pp 70–71; B. Einhorn, "The Hunt for Chinese Talent," *BusinessWeek,* May 22, 2006, p 104; and R. Buderi, "The Talent Magnet," *Fast Company,* June 2006, pp 80–84.

[32] Reprinted from A. Rosenbaum, "Testing Cultural Waters," *Management Review,* July/August 1999, p 43, copyright 1999, American Management Association. Reproduced with permission of American Management Association via Copyright Clearance Center.

[33] See H.M. Guttman, "Conflict Management as a Core Leadership Competency," *Training,* November 2005, pp 34–39.

[34] A statistical validation for this model can be found in M.A. Rahim and N.R. Magner, "Confirmatory Factor Analysis of the Styles of Handling Interpersonal Conflict: First-Order Factor Model and its Invariance across Groups," *Journal of Applied Psychology,* February 1995, pp 122–132. Also see M.A. Rahim, "Managing Conflict in Organizations," *Transaction Publishers* (New Brunswick, New Jersey: 2011); and M.A. Rahim, "Toward a Theory of Managing Organizational Conflict," *The International Journal of Conflict Management,* 2002, vol. 13, no. 3, pp 206–235.

[35] M.A. Rahim, "A Strategy for Managing Conflict in Complex Organizations," *Human Relations,* January 1985, p 84.

[36] See R. Rubin, "Study: Bullies and Their Victims Tend to Be More Violent," *USA Today,* April 15, 2003, p 9D; D. Salin, "Ways of Explaining Workplace Bullying: A Review of Enabling, Motivating and Precipitating Structures and Processes in the Work Environment," *Human Relations,* October 2003, pp 1213–1232; K. Gurchiek, "Bullying: It's Not Just on the Playground," *HR Magazine,* June 2005, p 40; L.W. Andrews, "When It's Time For Anger Management," *HR Magazine,* June 2005, pp 131–135; and K. Hannon, "You Can Take That Bully Down, Gently," *USA Today,* July 5, 2005, p 4B.

[37] For more on managing conflict, see G. Roper, "Managing Employee Relations," *HR Magazine,* May 2005, pp 101–104; Y. Shin, "Conflict Resolution in Virtual Teams," *Organizational Dynamics,* no. 4, 2005, pp 331–345; and M. DuPraw, "Cut the Conflict with Consensus Building," *Training,* May 2006, p 8.

[38] See J. Rasley, "The Revolution You Won't See on TV," *Newsweek,* November 25, 2002, p 13; and C. Bendersky, "Organizational Dispute Resolution Systems: A Complementarities Model," *Academy of Management Review,* October 2003, pp 643–656.

[39] B. Morrow and L.M. Bernardi, "Resolving Workplace Disputes," *Canadian Manager,* Spring 1999, p 17.

[40] Adapted from discussion in K.O. Wilburn, "Employment Disputes: Solving Them Out of Court," *Management Review,* March 1998, pp 17–21; and Morrow and Bernardi, "Resolving Workplace Disputes," pp 17–19, 27. Also see L. Ioannou, "Can't We Get Along?" *Fortune,* December 7, 1998, p 244[E]; and D. Weimer and S.A. Forest, "Forced into Arbitration? Not Any More," *BusinessWeek,* March 16, 1998, pp 66–68.

[41] For more, see M.M. Clark, "A Jury of Their Peers," *HR Magazine*, January 2004, pp 54–59.

[42] Wilburn, "Employment Disputes: Solving Them Out of Court," p 19.

[43] See R.E. Jones and B.H. Melcher, "Personality and the Preference for Modes of Conflict Resolution," *Human Relations*, August 1982, pp 649–658.

[44] See R.A. Baron, "Reducing Organizational Conflict: An Incompatible Response Approach," *Journal of Applied Psychology*, May 1984, pp 272–279.

[45] See G.A. Youngs Jr., "Patterns of Threat and Punishment Reciprocity in a Conflict Setting," *Journal of Personality and Social Psychology*, September 1986, pp 541–546.

[46] For more details, see V.D. Wall Jr. and L.L. Nolan, "Small Group Conflict: A Look at Equity, Satisfaction, and Styles of Conflict Management," *Small Group Behaviour*, May 1987, pp 188–211. Also see S.M. Farmer and J. Roth, "Conflict-Handling Behaviour in Work Groups: Effects of Group Structure, Decision Processes, and Time," *Small Group Research*, December 1998, pp 669–713.

[47] Based on B. Richey, H.J. Bernardin, C.L. Tyler, and N. McKinney, "The Effects of Arbitration Program Characteristics on Applicants' Intentions toward Potential Employers," *Journal of Applied Psychology*, October 2001, pp 1006–1013.

[48] See M.E. Schnake and D.S. Cochran, "Effect of Two Goal-Setting Dimensions on Perceived Intraorganizational Conflict," *Group and Organization Studies*, June 1985, pp 168–183. Also see O. Janssen, E. Van De Vliert, and C. Veenstra, "How Task and Person Conflict Shape the Role of Positive Interdependence in Management Teams," *Journal of Management*, no. 2, 1999, pp 117–142.

[49] See K.K. Smith, "The Movement of Conflict in Organizations: The Joint Dynamics of Splitting and Triangulation," *Administrative Science Quarterly*, March 1989, pp 1–20. Also see J.B. Olson-Buchanan, F. Drasgow, P.J. Moberg, A.D. Mead, P.A. Keenan, and M.A. Donovan, "Interactive Video Assessment of Conflict Resolution Skills," *Personnel Psychology*, Spring 1998, pp 1–24; and D.E. Conlon and D.P. Sullivan, "Examining the Actions of Organizations in Conflict: Evidence from the Delaware Court of Chancery," *Academy of Management Journal*, June 1999, pp 319–329.

[50] Based on C. Tinsley, "Models of Conflict Resolution in Japanese, German, and American Cultures," *Journal of Applied Psychology*, April 1998, pp 316–323; and S.M. Adams, "Settling Cross-Cultural Disagreements Begins with 'Where' Not 'How,'" *Academy of Management Executive*, February 1999, pp 109–110. Also see K. Ohbuchi, O. Fukushima, and J.T. Tedeschi, "Cultural Values in Conflict Management: Goal Orientation, Goal Attainment, and Tactical Decision," *Journal of Cross-Cultural Psychology*, January 1999, pp 51–71; and R. Cropanzano, H. Aguinis, M. Schminke, and D.L. Denham, "Disputant Reactions to Managerial Conflict Resolution Tactics: A Comparison among Argentina, the Dominican Republic, Mexico, and the United States," *Group and Organization Management*, June 1999, pp 124–154.

[51] Based on a definition in M.A. Neale and M.H. Bazerman, "Negotiating Rationally: The Power and Impact of the Negotiator's Frame," *Academy of Management Executive*, August 1992, pp 42–51.

[52] See K. Tyler, "Good-Faith Bargaining," *HR Magazine*, January 2005, pp 48–53; S. Clifford, "Something for Nothing," *Inc.*, May 2005, pp 54, 56; L. Stern, "Getting Your Slice," *Newsweek*, October 9, 2006, pp 66–67; P. Bathurst, "Once Offered the Job, it Can Pay to Negotiate," *The Arizona Republic*, December 10, 2006, p EC 1; and E. Pooley, "Get a Killer Raise in 2007," *Canadian Business*, January 14, 2007, pp 61–62.

[53] Data and quote from J. Yang and K. Carter, "USA Today Snapshots," *USA Today*, March 9, 2009, p 1B.

[54] M.H. Bazerman and M.A. Neale, *Negotiating Rationally* (New York: Free Press, 1992), p 16. Also see G. Cullinan, J. Le Roux, and R. Weddigen, "When to Walk Away from a Deal," *Harvard Business Review*, April 2004, pp 96–104; P.B. Stark and J. Flaherty, "How to Negotiate," *Training and Development*, June 2004, pp 52–54; K. Tyler, "The Art of Give-and-Take," *HR Magazine*, November 2004, pp 107–116; D. Ertel, "Getting Past Yes: Negotiating as if Implementation Mattered," *Harvard Business Review*, November 2004, pp 60–68; and M. Kaplan, "How to Negotiate Anything," *Money*, May 2005, pp 117–119.

[55] Good win–win negotiation strategies can be found in R.R. Reck and B.G. Long, *The Win–Win Negotiator: How to Negotiate Favorable Agreements That Last* (New York: Pocket Books, 1987); R. Fisher and W. Ury, *Getting to YES: Negotiating Agreement without Giving In* (Boston: Houghton Mifflin, 1981); and R. Fisher and D. Ertel, *Getting Ready to Negotiate: The Getting to YES Workbook* (New York: Penguin Books, 1995). Also see B. Spector, "An Interview with Roger Fisher and William Ury," *Academy of Management Executive*, August 2004, pp 101–108; B. Booth and M. McCredie, "Taking Steps toward 'Getting to Yes' at Blue Cross and Blue Shield of Florida," *Academy of Management Executive*, August 2004, pp 109–112; C. Woodyard, "Working Hand-in-Hand," *USA Today*, February 6, 2007, pp 1B–2B; E.A. Grant, "Playing Hard to Get," *Inc.*, March 2007, pp 104–109; and N. Brodsky, "The Paranoia Moment. Are They Stalling? Is This Deal About to Fall Apart?" *Inc.*, April 2007, pp 67–68.

[56] See L.R. Weingart, E.B. Hyder, and M.J. Prietula, "Knowledge Matters: The Effect of Tactical Descriptions on Negotiation Behaviour and Outcome," *Journal of Personality and Social Psychology*, June 1996, pp 1205–1217.

[57] For more, see A. Valenzuela, J. Srivastava, and S. Lee, "The Role of Cultural Orientation in Bargaining under Incomplete Information: Differences in Causal Attributions," *Organizational Behaviour and Human Decision Processes*, January 2005, pp 72–88; K. Lee, G. Yang, and J.L. Graham, "Tension and Trust in International Business Negotiations: American Executives Negotiating with Chinese Executives," *Journal of International Business Studies*, September 2006, pp 623–641; and L.E. Metcalf, A. Bird, M. Shankarmahesh, Z. Aycan, J. Larimo, and D.D. Valdelamar, "Cultural Tendencies in Negotiation: A Comparison of Finland, India, Mexico, Turkey, and the United States," *Journal of World Business*, December 2006, pp 382–394.

[58] Adapted from M.H. Bazerman, "The Mythical Fixed Pie," *Negotiation*, November 2003. (Program on Negotiation at Harvard Law School.)

[59] "Why Your Selling Price May Be Too High," by the Editors (reproduced in its entirety), *Negotiation*, October 2007. (Program on Negotiation at Harvard Law School.)

[60] "Why Your Next Negotiation Power Trip Could Backfire," by the Editors (reproduced in its entirety), *Negotiation*, December 2007. (Program on Negotiation at Harvard Law School.)

[61] "Are You Sure That's What You Want?" by the Editors, *Negotiation*, July 2008. (Program on Negotiation at Harvard Law School.)

[62] Adapted from "Are You Overly Committed to the Deal?" by the Editors, *Negotiation*, April 2008. (Program on Negotiation at Harvard Law School.)

[63] For supporting evidence, see J.K. Butler Jr., "Trust Expectations, Information Sharing, Climate of Trust, and Negotiation Effectiveness and Efficiency," *Group and Organization Management*, June 1999, pp 217–238.

[64] See H.J. Reitz, J.A. Wall Jr., and M.S. Love, "Ethics in Negotiation: Oil and Water or Good Lubrication?" *Business Horizons*, May–June 1998, pp 5–14; M.E. Schweitzer and J.L. Kerr, "Bargaining under the Influence: The Role of Alcohol in Negotiations," *Academy of Management Executive*, May 2000, pp 47–57; and A.M. Burr, "Ethics

in Negotiation: Does Getting to Yes Require Candor?," *Dispute Resolution Journal*, May–July 2001, pp 8–15.

[65] For related research, see A.E. Tenbrunsel, "Misrepresentation and Expectations of Misrepresentation in an Ethical Dilemma: The Role of Incentives and Temptation," *Academy of Management Journal*, June 1998, pp 330–339.

[66] Based on R.L. Pinkley, T.L. Griffith, and G.B. Northcraft, "'Fixed Pie' a la Mode: Information Availability, Information Processing, and the Negotiation of Suboptimal Agreements," *Organizational Behaviour and Human Decision Processes*, April 1995, pp 101–112.

[67] Based on B. Barry and R. A. Friedman, "Bargainer Characteristics in Distributive and Integrative Negotiation," *Journal of Personality and Social Psychology*, February 1998, pp 345–359. Also see K.J. Sulkowicz, "The Psychology of the Deal," *BusinessWeek*, April 9, 2007, p 14.

[68] For more, see J.P. Forgas, "On Feeling Good and Getting Your Way: Mood Effects on Negotiator Cognition and Bargaining Strategies," *Journal of Personality and Social Psychology*, March 1998, pp 565–577. Also see G.A. van Kleef, C.K.W. De Dreu, and A.S.R. Manstead, "The Interpersonal Effects of Anger and Happiness in Negotiations," *Journal of Personality and Social Psychology*, January 2004, pp 57–76; and G.A. van Kleef, C.K.W. De Dreu, and A.S.R. Manstead, "The Interpersonal Effects of Emotions in Negotiations: A Motivated Information Processing Approach," *Journal of Personality and Social Psychology*, October 2004, pp 510–528.

[69] Data from B. Campbell and M.M. Marx, "Toward More Effective Stakeholder Dialogue: Applying Theories of Negotiation to Policy and Program Evaluation," *Journal of Applied Social Psychology*, December 2006, pp 2834–2863.

[70] Drawn from L.H. Chusmir and J. Mills, "Gender Differences in Conflict Resolution Styles of Managers: At Work and at Home," *Sex Roles*, February 1989, pp 149–163.

[71] Based on A.E. Walters, A.F. Stuhlmacher, and L.L. Meyer, "Gender and Negotiator Competitiveness: A Meta-Analysis," *Organizational Behaviour and Human Decision Processes*, October 1998, pp 1–29.

[72] "New Car Negotiations: Are Women Better than Men?" PON–Harvard University–Online in Business Negotiations, *Negotiations Daily*, February 3, 2012.

[73] L. Babcock, S. Laschever, M. Gelfand, and D. Small, "Nice Girls Don't Ask," *Harvard Business Review*, October 2003, p 14. Also see L.A. Barron, "Ask and You Shall Receive? Gender Differences in Negotiators' Beliefs about Requests for a Higher Salary," *Human Relations*, June 2003, pp 635–662; L.D. Tyson, "New Clues to the Pay and Leadership Gap," *BusinessWeek*, October 27, 2003, p 36; D. Kersten, "Women Need to Learn the Art of the Deal," *USA Today*, November 17, 2003, p 7B; A. Fels, "Do Women Lack Ambition?" *Harvard Business Review*, April 2004, pp 50–60; B. Brophy, "Bargaining for Bigger Bucks: A Step-by-Step Guide to Negotiating Your Salary," *Business 2.0*, May 2004, p 107; and H.R. Bowles, L. Babcock, and K.L. McGinn, "Constraints and Triggers: Situational Mechanics of Gender in Negotiation," *Journal of Personality and Social Psychology*, December 2005, pp 951–965.

CHAPTER 9

[1] L.H. Chusmir, "Personalized versus Socialized Power Needs among Working Women and Men," *Human Relations*, February 1986, p 149.

[2] R.I. Sutton, "Are You Being A Jerk Again?," *BusinessWeek*, August 25–September 1, 2008, p 52.

[3] As quoted in L. Buchanan, "That's Quite a Story: How I Did It," *INC.*, November 2006, p 113.

[4] Based on D.W. Cantor and T. Bernay, *Women in Power, The Secrets of Leadership* (Boston: Houghton Mifflin, 1992). Also see S. Jayson, "At Home, Women Hold the Power," *USA Today*, September 25, 2008,

p 8D; and J. Shambora and B. Kowitt, "50 Most Powerful Women," *Fortune*, October 13, 2008, pp 165–178.

[5] S. Sandberg, "Changing the World, One Job At A Time," *Newsweek*, October 13, 2008, p 68.

[6] See J.R.P. French and B. Raven, "The Bases of Social Power," *Studies in Social Power*, ed. D. Cartwright (Ann Arbor: University of Michigan Press, 1959), pp 150–167. Also see S.M. Farmer and H. Aguinis, "Accounting for Subordinate Perceptions of Supervisor Power: An Identity-Dependence Model," *Journal of Applied Psychology*, November 2005, pp 1069–1083.

[7] G. Edmondson, "Power Play at VW," *BusinessWeek*, December 4, 2006, p 45. Also see M. Weinstein, "Alpha Male on Your Hands: Here's How to Deal," *Training*, October 2006, p 16.

[8] See M. Maccoby, "Why People Follow the Leader: The Power of Transference," *Harvard Business Review*, September 2004, pp 76–85; and G.R. Weaver, L.K. Trevino, and B. Agle, "'Somebody I Look Up To:' Ethical Role Models in Organizations," *Organizational Dynamics*, no. 4, 2005, pp 313–330.

[9] See D. Kipnis, S.M. Schmidt, and I. Wilkinson, "Intraorganizational Influence Tactics: Explorations in Getting One's Way," *Journal of Applied Psychology*, August 1980, pp 440–452. Also see C.A. Schriesheim and T.R. Hinkin, "Influence Tactics Used by Subordinates: A Theoretical and Empirical Analysis and Refinement of the Kipnis, Schmidt, and Wilkinson Subscales," *Journal of Applied Psychology*, June 1990, pp 246–257; G. Yukl and C.M. Falbe, "Influence Tactics and Objectives in Upward, Downward, and Lateral Influence Attempts," *Journal of Applied Psychology*, April 1990, pp 132–140; and G. Yukl and B. Tracey, "Consequences of Influence Tactics Used with Subordinates, Peers, and the Boss," in *Organizational Influence Processes*, eds. L.W. Porter, H.L. Angle, and R.W. Allen (Armonk, NY: M E Sharpe, 2003), 2nd ed., pp 96–116.

[10] Based on Table 1 in G. Yukl, C.M. Falbe, and J.Y. Youn, "Patterns of Influence Behaviour for Managers," *Group and Organization Management*, March 1993, pp 5–28. An additional influence tactic is presented in B.P. Davis and E.S. Knowles, "A Disrupt-then-Reframe Technique of Social Influence," *Journal of Personality and Social Psychology*, February 1999, pp 192–199. For more on ingratiation, see D.B. Yoffie and M.Kwak, "With Friends Like These: The Art of Managing Complementors," *Harvard Business Review*, September 2006, pp 88–98.

[11] For comprehensive coverage, see L.W. Porter, H.L. Angle, and R.W. Allen, eds., *Organizational Influence Processes*, 2nd ed. (Armonk, NY: ME Sharpe, 2003); and The Society for Human Resource Management and Harvard Business School Press, *The Essentials of Power, Influence and Persuasion* (Boston: Harvard Business School Press, 2006).

[12] Based on discussion in G. Yukl, H. Kim, and C.M. Falbe, "Antecedents of Influence Outcomes," *Journal of Applied Psychology*, June 1996, pp 309–317.

[13] C.F. Seifert and G. Yukl, "Effects of Repeated Multi-Source Feedback on the Influence Behavior and Effectiveness of Managers: A Field Experiment," *The Leadership Quarterly*, 2010, pp 856–866.

[14] Supportive results can be found in S. Hysong, "The Role of Technical Skill in Perceptions of Managerial Performance," *The Journal of Management Development*, 2008, pp 275–290; and R.W. Kolodinsky, D.C.F. Treadway, and G.R. Ferris, "Political Skill and Influence Effectiveness: Testing Portions of an Expanded Ferris and Judge (1991) Model," *Human Relations*, December 2007, pp 1747–1778. Also see T.R. Clark, "Engaging the Disengaged," *HR Magazine*, April 2008, pp 109–112.

[15] Data from G. Yukl, H. Kim, and C.M. Falbe, "Antecedents of Influence Outcomes," pp 309–317.

[16] Based on C. Pornpitakpan, "The Persuasiveness of Source Credibility: A Critical Review of Five Decades' Evidence," *Journal of Applied Social Psychology*, February 2004, pp 243–281.

[17] S.A. Furst and D.M. Cable, "Employee Resistance to Organizational Change: Managerial Influence Tactics and Leader–Member Exchange," *Journal of Applied Psychology*, March 2008, pp 453–462.

[18] S. Chakrabarty, G. Brown, and R.E. Widing, "Closed Influence Tactics: Do Smugglers Win in the Long Run?" *Journal of Personal Selling and Sales Management*, Winter 2010, pp 23–32.

[19] I. Stern and J.D. Westphal, "Stealthy Footsteps to the Boardroom: Executive's Backgrounds, Sophisticated Interpersonal Influence Behavior, and Board Appointments," *Administrative Science Quarterly*, 2010, pp 278–319.

[20] C.F. Seifert and G. Yukl, "Effects of Repeated Multi-Source Feedback on the Influence Behavior and Effectiveness of Managers," pp 856–866.

[21] See C.L. Pearce and C.C. Manz, "The New Silver Bullets of Leadership: The Importance of Self- and Shared Leadership in Knowledge Work," *Organizational Dynamics*, no. 2, 2005, pp 130–40.

[22] W.A. Randolph and M. Sashkin, "Can Organizational Empowerment Work in Multinational Settings?" *Academy of Management Executive*, February 2002, p 104. Also see N.R. Lockwood, "Leveraging Employee Engagement for Competitive Advantage: HR's Strategic Role," *HR Magazine*, 2007 SHRM Research Quarterly, March 2007, pp 1–12. Also see R.C. Liden and S. Arad, "A Power Perspective of Empowerment and Work Groups: Implications for Human Resources Management Research," *Research in Personnel and Human Resources Management*, vol. 14, ed. G.R. Ferris (Greenwich, CT: JAI Press, 1996), pp 205–251.

[23] K. Greasley, A. Bryman, A. Dainty, and A. Price, et al., "Understanding Empowerment from an Employee Perspective; What Does It Mean and Do They Want It?" *Team Performance Management*, 2008, pp 39–55; see also G.M. Spreitzer, "Social Structural Characteristics of Psychological Empowerment," *Academy of Management Journal*, April 1996, pp 483–504.

[24] H. Liao, K. Toya, D.P. Lepak, and Y. Hong, "Do They See Eye to Eye? Management and Employee Perspectives of High-Performance Work Systems and Influence Processes on Service Quality," *Journal of Applied Psychology*, 2009, pp 371–391.

[25] As quoted in M. Bartiromo, "What to Expect at Davos," *Business Week*, January 29, 2007, p 100. Also see G. Mangurian, "Responsibility Junkie," *Harvard Business Review*, October 2006, p 30.

[26] R.M. Hodgetts, "A Conversation with Steve Kerr," *Organizational Dynamics*, Spring 1996, p 71. For example, see B. De Lollis, "Hotels Train Employees to Think Fast," *USA Today*, November 29, 2006, pp 1B–2B.

[27] L. Shaper Walters, "A Leader Redefines Management," *Christian Science Monitor*, September 22, 1992, p 14. Also see B. George, P. Sims, A.N. McLean, and D. Mayer, "Discovering Your Authentic Leadership," *Harvard Business Review*, February 2007, pp 129–138.

[28] For a 15-item empowerment scale, see Table 1 on page 103 of B.P. Niehoff, R.H. Moorman, G. Blakely, and J. Fuller, "The Influence of Empowerment and Job Enrichment on Employee Loyalty in a Downsizing Environment," *Group and Organization Management*, March 2001, pp 93–113.

[29] F. Vogelstein, "Star Power: Greg Brown, Motorola," *Fortune*, February 6, 2006, p 57.

[30] Quotes and data from J. Yang and V. Salazar, "USA Today Snapshots," *USA Today*, February 10, 2009, p 1B. Also see A.L. Kalleberg, "The Mismatched Worker: When People Don't Fit Their Jobs," *Academy of Management Perspectives*, February 2008, pp 24–40; and L. Petrecca, "Many Satisfied With Job Despite Tough Times," *USA Today*, March 13, 2009, p 3B.

[31] H. Malcolm and C. Sokoloff, "Values, Human Relations, and Organization Development," *The Emerging Practice of Organizational Development*, eds. W. Sikes, A. Drexler, and J. Gant (San Diego: University Associates, 1989), p 64.

[32] R.W. Allen, D.L. Madison, L.W. Porter, P.A. Renwick, and B.T. Mayes, "Organizational Politics: Tactics and Characteristics of Its Actors,"

California Management Review, Fall 1979, p 77. A comprehensive update can be found in K.M. Kacmar and R.A. Baron, "Organizational Politics: The State of the Field, Links to Related Processes, and an Agenda for Future Research," *Research in Personnel and Human Resources Management*, vol. 17, ed. G.R. Ferris (Stanford, CT: JAI Press, 1999), pp 1–39. Also see K.A. Ahearn, G.R. Ferris, W.A. Hochwarter, C. Douglas, and A.P. Ammeter, "Leader Political Skill and Team Performance," *Journal of Management*, no. 3, 2004, pp 309–327; P.L. Perrewé and D.L. Nelson, "Gender and Career Success: The Facilitative Role of Political Skill," *Organizational Dynamics*, no. 4, 2004, pp 366–378; G.R. Ferris, D.C. Treadway, R.W. Kolodinsky, W.A. Hochwarter, C.J. Kacmar, C. Douglas, and D.D. Frink, "Development and Validation of the Political Skill Inventory," *Journal of Management*, no. 1, 2005, pp 126–152; and T.B. Lawrence, M.K. Mauws, B. Dyck, and R.F. Kleysen, "The Politics of Organizational Learning: Integrating Power into the 4I Framework," *Academy of Management Review*, January 2005, pp 180–191.

[33] See P.M. Fandt and G.R. Ferris, "The Management of Information and Impressions: When Employees Behave Opportunistically," *Organizational Behaviour and Human Decision Processes*, February 1990, pp 140–158.

[34] D.J. Burrough, "Office Politics Mirror Popular TV Program," *Arizona Republic*, February 4, 2001, p EC1.

[35] L.B. MacGregor Serven, *The End of Office Politics as Usual* (New York: American Management Association, 2002), p 5. Also see K.J. McGregor, "Sweet Revenge: The Power of Retribution, Spite, and Loathing in the World of Business," *BusinessWeek*, January 22, 2007, pp 64–70; D.A. Kaplan, "Suspicions and Spies in Silicon Valley," *Newsweek*, September 18, 2006, pp 40–47; J. Fox, "Board Games," *Fortune*, October 2, 2006, pp 23–24, 26; G. Anders and A. Murray, "Behind H-P Chairman's Fall, Clash With a Powerful Director," *The Wall Street Journal*, October 9, 2006, pp A1, A14; and P. Burrows, "Controlling the Damage at HP," *BusinessWeek*, October 9, 2006, pp 36–44.

[36] Quotes and data from J. Yang and K. Simmons, "USA Today Snapshots," *USA Today*, November 17, 2008, p 1B.

[37] For a wide range of perspectives, see www.business.com/magazine/content/08_34/b4097030713566.htm?chan=magazine+channel_special+report, accessed March 24, 2009. For practical tips, see C. Hawley, *100+ Tactics for Office Politics*, 2nd ed. (Hauppauge, NY: Barron's Educational Series, 2008).

[38] R. Bhasin, "On Playing Corporate Politics," *Pulp and Paper*, October 1985, p 175. Also see G.R. Ferris, P.L. Perrewé, W.P. Anthony, and D.C. Gilmore, "Political Skill at Work," *Organizational Dynamics*, Spring 2000, pp 25–37; R.M. Kramer, "When Paranoia Makes Sense," *Harvard Business Review*, July 2002, pp 62–69; J. Barbian, "Office Politics: Swinging with the Sharks," *Training*, July 2002, p 16; L.P. Frankel, *Nice Girls Don't Get the Corner Office: Unconscious Mistakes Women Make That Sabotage Their Career* (New York: Warner, 2004); T. Estep, "Winning the Rat Race," *Training and Development*, January 2005, pp 71–72; and S.B. Bacharach, "Politically Proactive," *Fast Company*, May 2005, p 93; and R.M. Kramer, "The Great Intimidators," *Harvard Business Review*, February 2006, pp 88–96.

[39] Data from M. Weinstein, "Training Today: Q&A," *Training*, January–February 2007, p 7. Also see A. Pomeroy, "Politics 101 for Women," *HR Magazine*, June 2006, pp 24, 26; and C. Wilbert, "You Schmooze, You Win," *Fast Company*, July–August 2006, p 109.

[40] First four based on discussion in D.R. Beeman and T.W. Sharkey, "The Use and Abuse of Corporate Politics," *Business Horizons*, March–April 1987, pp 26–30. For supportive evidence, see C.C. Rosen, P.E. Levy, and R.J. Hall, "Placing Perceptions of Politics in the Context of the Feedback Environment, Employee Attitudes, and Job Performance," *Journal of Applied Psychology*, January 2006, pp 211–220.

41 A. Raia, "Power, Politics, and the Human Resource Professional," *Human Resource Planning*, no. 4, 1985, p 203.

42 A.J. DuBrin, "Career Maturity, Organizational Rank, and Political Behavioural Tendencies: A Correlational Analysis of Organizational Politics and Career Experience," *Psychological Reports,* October 1988, p 535.

43 This three-level distinction comes from A.T. Cobb, "Political Diagnosis: Applications in Organizational Development," *Academy of Management Review,* July 1986, pp 482–496.

44 An excellent historical and theoretical perspective of coalitions can be found in W.B. Stevenson, J.L. Pearce, and L.W. Porter, "The Concept of 'Coalition' in Organization Theory and Research," *Academy of Management Review,* April 1985, pp 256–268.

45 See H. Ibarra and M. Hunter, "How Leaders Create and Use Networks," *Harvard Business Review,* January 2007, pp 40–47; and N. Anand and J.A. Conger, "Capabilities of the Consummate Networker," *Organizational Dynamics,* no. 1, 2007, pp 13–27.

46 Allen et al., "Organizational Politics," p 77. Also see D.C. Treadway, W.A. Hochwarter, C.J. Kacmar, and G.R. Ferris, "Political Will, Political Skill, and Political Behaviour," *Journal of Organizational Behaviour,* May 2005, pp 229–245.

47 See the second Q&A in J. Welch and S. Welch, "Avoiding Strikes—and Unions," *BusinessWeek,* January 15, 2007, p 92; S. Berfield, "Mentoring Can Be Messy," *BusinessWeek,* January 29, 2007, pp 80–81; and the second Q&A in J. Welch and S. Welch, "The Succession Opportunity," *BusinessWeek,* February 5, 2007, p 106.

48 For a review of research on rational decision making, see K.E. Stanovich, *Who Is Rational?* (Mahwah, NJ: Lawrence Erlbaum, 1999), pp 1–31.

49 Strengths and weaknesses of the rational model are discussed by M.H. Bazerman, *Judgment in Managerial Decision Making* (Hoboken, NJ: John Wiley & Sons, Inc., 2006).

50 Results can be found in J.P. Bymes, D.C. Miller, and W.D. Schafer, "Gender Differences in Risk Taking: A MetaAnalysis," *Psychological Bulletin,* May 1999, pp 367–383.

51 H.A. Simon, "Rational Decision Making in Business Organizations," *American Economic Review,* September 1979, p 510.

52 For a complete discussion of bounded rationality, see H.A. Simon, *Administrative Behaviour,* 2nd ed. (New York: Free Press, 1957).

53 Biases associated with using shortcuts in decision making are discussed by A. Tversky and D. Kahneman, "Judgment under Uncertainty: Heuristics and Biases," *Science,* September 1974, pp 1124–1131.

54 For a study of the availability heuristic, see L.A. Vaughn, "Effects of Uncertainty on Use of the Availability of Heuristic for Self-Efficacy Judgments," *European Journal of Social Psychology,* March/May 1999, pp 407–410.

55 The discussion of styles was based on A.J. Rowe and R.O. Mason, *Managing with Style: A Guide to Understanding, Assessing, and Improving Decision Making* (San Francisco: Jossey-Bass, 1987).

56 Ibid. Also see M.J. Dollinger and W. Danis, "Preferred Decision-Making Styles: A Cross-Cultural Comparison," *Psychological Reports,* 1998, pp 755–761.

57 E. Sadler-Smith and E. Shefy, "The Intuitive Executive: Understanding and Applying 'Gut Feel' in Decision-Making," *Academy of Management Executive,* November 2004, p 77.

58 Based in part on E. Sadler-Smith and E. Shefy, "The Intuitive Executive: Understanding and Applying 'Gut Feel' in Decision Making," *Academy of Management Executive,* November 2004, pp 76–91; and C.C. Miller and R.D. Ireland, "Intuition in Strategic Decision Making: Friend or Foe in the Fast-Paced 21st Century," *Academy of Management Executive,* Februrary 2005, pp 19–30.

59 See E. Dane and M.G. Pratt, "Exploring Intuition and Its Role in Managerial Decision Making," *Academy of Management Review,* January 2007, pp 33–54.

60 See D. Begley, "You Might Help a Teen Avoid Dumb Behaviour by Nurturing Intuition," *The Wall Street Journal,* November 3, 2006, p B1.

61 Results were reported in "The Ethical Mind," *Harvard Business Review,* March 2007, pp 51–56.

62 The decision tree and resulting discussion is based on C.E. Bagley, "The Ethical Leader's Decision Tree," *Harvard Business Review,* February 2003, pp 18–19.

63 The details of this case are discussed in J. Ross and B.M. Staw, "Organizational Escalation and Exit: Lessons from the Shoreham Nuclear Power Plant," *Academy of Management Journal,* August 1993, pp 701–732.

64 Supportive results can be found in H. Moon, "Looking Forward and Looking Back: Integrating Completion and Sunk-Cost Effects within an Escalation-of-Commitment Progress Decision," *Journal of Applied Psychology,* February 2001, pp 104–113.

65 Definition is based on R.J. Sternberg, "What Is the Common Thread of Creativity?," *American Psychologist,* April 2001, pp 360–362.

66 P. Magnusson, "Small Biz vs. the Terrorists," *Business Week,* March 4, 2002, p 68.

67 P. Wells, "Freedom To Fail Is What Made Steve Jobs," *Macleans Magazine,* October 24, 2011, p 12.

68 See the related discussion in T.M. Amabile, "How to Kill Creativity," *Harvard Business Review,* September/October 1998, pp 77–87.

69 G.W. Hill, "Group versus Individual Performance: Are N + 1 Heads Better Than One?" *Psychological Bulletin,* May 1982, p 535.

70 These guidelines were derived from G.P. Huber, *Managerial Decision Making* (Glenview, IL: Scott, Foresman, 1980), p 149.

71 I.L. Janis, *Groupthink,* 2nd ed. (Boston: Houghton Mifflin, 1982). For an alternative model, see R.J. Aldag and S. Riggs Fuller, "Beyond Fiasco: A Reappraisal of the Groupthink Phenomenon and a New Model of Group Decision Processes," *Psychological Bulletin,* May 1993, pp 533–552. Also see A.A. Mohamed and F.A. Wiebe, "Toward a Process Theory of Groupthink," *Small Group Research,* August 1996, pp 416–430.

72 These recommendations were obtained from G. Parker, *Team Players and Teamwork: The New Competitive Business Strategy,* (Jossey-Bass Publishers, 1990).

73 These recommendations and descriptions were derived from B. Nussbaum, "The Power of Design," *BusinessWeek,* May 17, 2004, p 86–94.

74 See J. Baruah and P.B. Paulus, "Effects of Training on Idea Generation in Groups," *Small Group Research,* October 2008, pp 523–541.

75 See J.G. Lloyd, S. Fowell, and J.G. Bligh, "The Use of the Nominal Group Technique as an Evaluative Tool in Medical Undergraduate Education," *Medical Education,* January 1999, pp 8–13; and A.L. Delbecq, A.H. Van de Ven, and D.H. Gustafson, *Group Techniques for Program Planning: A Guide to Nominal Group and Delphi Processes* (Glenview, IL: Scott, Foresman, 1975).

76 See N.C. Dalkey, D.L. Rourke, R. Lewis, and D. Snyder, *Studies in the Quality of Life: Delphi and Decision Making* (Lexington, MA: Lexington Books: DC Heath and Co., 1972).

77 An application of the Delphi technique can be found in A. Graefe and J.S. Armstrong, "Comparing Face-to-Face Meetings, Nominal Groups, Delphi and Prediction Markets on an Estimating Task," *International Journal of Forecasting,* January–March 2011, pp 183–195.

78 See P. Dvorak, "Best Buy Taps 'Prediction Market'; Imaginary Stocks Let Workers Forecast Whether Retailer's Plans Will Meet Goals," *The Wall Street Journal,* September 16, 2008, p B1.

79 See K. Maher, "Wal-Mart Seeks New Flexibility in Worker Shifts," *The Wall Street Journal,* January 3, 2007, pp A1, A11.

[80] See Z. Guo, J. D'Ambra, T. Turner, and H. Zhang, "Improving the Effectiveness of Virtual Teams: A Comparison of Video-Conferencing and Face-to-Face Communication in China," *IEEE Transactions on Professional Communication,* March 2009, p 1–16; and K. McNamara, A.R. Dennis, and T.A. Carte, "It's the Thought that Counts: The Mediating Effects of Information Processing in Virtual Team Decision Making," *Information Systems Management,* Winter 2008, p 20–32.

[81] M. Weinstein, "So Happy Together," *Training,* May 2006, p 38.

[82] See D. Tapscott, *Grown Up Digital* (New York: McGraw-Hill, 2009).

CHAPTER 10

[1] See S. Lieberson and J.F. O'Connor, "Leadership and Organizational Performance: A Study of Large Corporations," *American Sociological Review,* April 1972, pp 117–130.

[2] Results can be found in K.T. Dirks, "Trust in Leadership and Team Performance: Evidence from NCAA Basketball," *Journal of Applied Psychology,* December 2000, pp 1004–1012; and D. Jacobs and L. Singell, "Leadership and Organizational Performance: Isolating Links between Managers and Collective Success," *Social Science Research,* June 1993, pp 165–189.

[3] The multiple levels of leadership are discussed by F.J. Yammarino, F. Dansereau, and C.J. Kennedy, "A Multiple-Level Multidimensional Approach to Leadership: Viewing Leadership through an Elephant's Eye," *Organizational Dynamics,* 2001, pp 149–163.

[4] The four commonalities were identified by P.G. Northouse, *Leadership: Theory and Practice,* 4th ed. (Thousand Oaks, CA: Sage Publications, 2007), p 3.

[5] Ibid.

[6] B. Kellerman, "Leadership: Warts and All," *Harvard Business Review,* January 2004, p 45.

[7] B.M. Bass, *Bass and Stogdill's Handbook of Leadership: Theory, Research, and Managerial Applications,* 3rd ed. (New York: Free Press, 1990), p 383.

[8] For a discussion about the differences between leading and managing, see B. Bass and R. Bass, *The Bass Handbook of Leadership,* (Free Press, 2008), pp 651–681.

[9] Ellis Don Corporate website: See 'careers', www.ellisdon.com.

[10] Ibid.

[11] For a summary, see B. Bass and R. Bass, *The Bass Handbook of Leadership,* pp 103–135.

[12] Implicit leadership theory is discussed by B. Bass and R. Bass, *The Bass Handbook of Leadership,* pp 46–78; and J.S. Mueller, J.A. Goncalo, and D. Kamdar, "Recognizing Creative Leadership: Can Creative Idea Expression Negatively Relate to Perceptions of Leadership Potential?," *Journal of Experimental Social Psychology,* in press.

[13] Results can be found in R.G. Lord, C.L. De Vader, and G.M. Alliger, "A Meta-Analysis of the Relation between Personality Traits and Leadership Perceptions: An Application of Validity Generalization Procedures," *Journal of Applied Psychology,* August 1986, pp 402–410.

[14] See M.W. Dickson, C.J. Resick, and P.J. Hanges, "Systematic Variation in Organizationally-Shared Cognitive Prototypes of Effective Leadership Based on Organizational Form," *The Leadership Quarterly,* October 2006, pp 487–505; and F.C. Brodbeck et al., "Cultural Variation of Leadership Prototypes across 22 European Countries," *Journal of Occupational and Organizational Psychology,* March 2000, pp 1–29.

[15] For related reading, see E. Van de Vliert, "Autocratic Leadership around the World," *Journal of Cross-Cultural Psychology,* January 2006, pp 42–59; M. Javidan, P.W. Dorfman, M. Sully de Luque, and R.J. House, "In the Eye of the Beholder: Cross Cultural Lessons in Leadership from Project GLOBE," *Academy of Management Perspectives,* February 2006, pp 67–90; G.B. Graen, "In the Eye of the Beholder: Cross-Cultural Lesson in Leadership from Project GLOBE: A Response Viewed from the Third Culture Bonding (TCB) Model of Cross-Cultural Leadership," *Academy of Management Perspectives,* November 2006, pp 95–101; R.J. House, M. Javidan, P.W. Dorfman, and M. Sully de Luque, "A Failure of Scholarship: Response to George Graen's Critique of GLOBE," *Academy of Management Perspectives,* November 2006, pp 102–114; and P. Caligiuri and I. Tarique, "Predicting Effectiveness in Global Leadership Activities," *Journal of World Business,* in press, 2009.

[16] J. Guyon, "David Whitwam," *Fortune,* July 26, 2004, p 174.

[17] Results can be found in J.M. Kouzes and B.Z. Posner, *The Leadership Challenge* (San Francisco, CA: Jossey-Bass, 1995). Also see R. Birchfield, "Leaders Must Restore Trust," *New Zealand Management,* March 2009, pp 32–33.

[18] See J. Antonakis, N.M. Ashkanasy, and M.T. Dasborough, "Does Leadership Need Emotional Intelligence?" *The Leadership Quarterly,* April 2009, pp 247–261; and M.P. McEnrue, K.S. Groves, and W. Shen, "Emotional Intelligence Development: Leveraging Individual Characteristics," *Journal of Management Development,* 2009, pp 150–174.

[19] Results can be found in T.A. Judge, J.E. Bono, R. Ilies, and M.W. Gerhardt, "Personality and Leadership: A Qualitative and Quantitative Review," *Journal of Applied Psychology,* August 2002, pp 765–780.

[20] See T.A. Judge, A.E. Colbert, and R. Ilies, "Intelligence and Leadership: A Quantitative Review and Test of Theoretical Propositions," *Journal of Applied Psychology,* June 2004, pp 542–552.

[21] Kellerman's research can be found in B. Kellerman, *Bad Leadership* (Boston: Harvard Business School Press, 2004).

[22] K. Willyerd, "Ten Clues It's Time To Replace Your Head of HR," *Harvard Business Review, HBR Blog Network,* September, 27, 2011.

[23] L. Sandler, "Lehman Cash Flows May Reach $40.5 Billion, Firm Says," *Bloomberg,* July 26, 2012, www.bloomberg.com/news/print.

[24] "Former Citigroup VP Sentenced to 8 Years in prison after pleading guilty to embezzlement in NY," *Canadian Business,* June 29, 2012, www.canadianbusiness.com/print/89536.

[25] M. O'Toole, "Former CEO Chris Mazza Tells Gruelling Hearing Into Ornge Scandal He Is Just A Scapegoat," *National Post,* July 18, 2012, www.news.nationalpost.com/2012/07/18/former-ceo-chris-mazza-tells-gruelling-hearing-into-ornge-scandal-he-is-just-a-scape-goat/.

[26] "Ebbers Sentenced to 25 Years In Prison," *Associated Press,* July 13, 2005, www.msnbc.msn.com.

[27] Y. Q. Mui, "Circuit City Cuts 3,400 'Overpaid Workers,'" *Washington Post,* March 29, 2007, www.washingtonpost.com/wp-dyn/content/article/2007/03/28/AR2007032802185.html; and J. Krames "Who You Fire Shapes The Team," *Jeffrey Krames Blog,* October 26, 2009, www.jeffreykrames.com/2009/10/26/who-you-fire-shapes-the-team-part-of-a-series-on-firing/.

[28] Ibid., trait definitions, pp 40–46. Some of the personal examples were taken from "The Worst Managers," *BusinessWeek,* January 19, 2009, p 42.

[29] Gender and the emergence of leaders was examined by A.H. Eagly and S.J. Karau, "Gender and the Emergence of Leaders: A Meta-Analysis," *Journal of Personality and Social Psychology,* May 1991, pp 685–710; and R.K. Shelly and P.T. Munroe, "Do Women Engage in Less Task Behavior than Men?" *Sociological Perspectives,* Spring 1999, pp 49–67.

[30] See A.H. Eagly, S.J. Karau, and B.T. Johnson, "Gender and Leadership Style among School Principals: A Meta-Analysis," *Educational Administration Quarterly,* February 1992, pp 76–102.

[31] Supportive findings are contained in J.M. Twenge, "Changes in Women's Assertiveness in Response to Status and Roles: A Cross-Temporal Meta-Analysis, 1931–1993," *Journal of Personality and Social Psychology,* July 2001, pp 133–145.

[32] For a summary of this research, see R. Sharpe, "As Leaders, Women Rule," *BusinessWeek*, November 20, 2000, pp 74–84. Also see C. Casaburi, "Avon, the New, and Glass Ceilings," *BusinessWeek*, February 6, 2006, p 104.

[33] The process of preparing a development plan is discussed by L. Morgan, G. Spreitzer, J. Dutton, R. Quinn, E. Heaphy, and B. Barker, "How to Play to Your Strengths," *Harvard Business Review*, January 2005, pp 75–80.

[34] See N. Doss, "Fast Food: East Meets West at Hamburger University," *BusinessWeek*, January 31–February 6, 2011, pp 22–23; and H. Dolezalek, "Talent Scout," *Training*, February 2010, pp 52–56.

[35] See B. Reeves, T.W. Malone, and T. O'Driscoll, "Leadership's Online Labs," *Harvard Business Review*, May 2008, pp 59–66.

[36] Results can be found in T.A. Judge, R.F. Piccolo, and R. Ilies, "The Forgotten Ones? The Validity of Consideration and Initiating Structure in Leadership Research," *Journal of Applied Psychology*, February 2004, pp 36–51.

[37] See V.H. Vroom, "Leadership," *Handbook of Industrial and Organizational Psychology*, ed. M.D. Dunnette (Chicago: Rand McNally, 1976).

[38] For corporate examples of leadership development see J. Sandberg, "Trying to Tease Out My Leadership Talent in One Easy Seminar," *The Wall Street Journal*, March 28, 2006, p B1; J. Sandberg, "The Sensitive Me Won't Be Leading Corporate America," *The Wall Street Journal*, April 11, 2006, p B1; and S. Max, "Seagate's Morale-athon," *BusinessWeek*, April 3, 2006, p 110–112.

[39] See B.M. Bass, *Bass and Stogdill's Handbook of Leadership: Theory, Research, and Managerial Applications*, 3rd ed. (New York: The Free Press, 1990), chapters 20–25.

[40] The relationships between the frequency and mastery of leader behavior and various outcomes were investigated by F. Shipper and C.S. White, "Mastery, Frequency, and Interaction of Managerial Behaviors Relative to Subunit Effectiveness," *Human Relations*, January 1999, pp 49–66.

[41] M. Liedtke, "Marissa Mayer's Top 3 Challenges As Yahoo CEO," *Canadian Business*, July 18, 2012, www.canadianbusiness.com/print/91453.

[42] F.E. Fiedler, "Job Engineering for Effective Leadership: A New Approach," *Management Review*, September 1977, p 29.

[43] For more on this theory, see F.E. Fiedler, "A Contingency Model of Leadership Effectiveness," *Advances in Experimental Social Psychology*, vol. 1, ed. L. Berkowitz (New York: Academic Press, 1964); and F.E. Fiedler, *A Theory of Leadership Effectiveness* (New York: McGraw-Hill, 1967).

[44] See L.H. Peters, D.D. Hartke, and J.T. Pohlmann, "Fiedler's Contingency Theory of Leadership: An Application of the Meta-Analyses Procedures of Schmidt and Hunter," *Psychological Bulletin*, March 1985, pp 274–285; and C.A. Schriesheim, B.J. Tepper, and L.A. Tetrault, "Least Preferred Co-Worker Score, Situational Control, and Leadership Effectiveness: A Meta-Analysis of Contingency Model Performance Predictions," *Journal of Applied Psychology*, August 1994, pp 561–573.

[45] C. Levy, "Is Lazardis/Balsillie Exit Enough To Save RIM?" *Yahoo Canada Finance*, January 23, 2012, www.ca.finance.yahoo.com.

[46] For more detail on this theory, see R.J. House, "A Path–Goal Theory of Leader Effectiveness," *Administrative Science Quarterly*, September 1971, pp 321–338.

[47] This research is summarized by R.J. House, "Path–Goal Theory of Leadership: Lessons, Legacy, and a Reformulated Theory," *Leadership Quarterly*, Autumn 1996, pp 323–352.

[48] Ibid.

[49] Examples can be found in K. Brokker, "The Pepsi Machine," *Fortune*, February 6, 2006, pp 68–72; B. Morris, "Star Power: Ursula Burns," *Fortune*, February 6, 2006, p 57; and P. Burrows, "HP's Ultimate Team Player," *BusinessWeek*, January 30, 2006, pp 76–78.

[50] R.J. House and R.N. Aditya, "The Social Scientific Study of Leadership: Quo Vadis?" *Journal of Management*, 1997, p 457.

[51] A thorough discussion of shared leadership is provided by C.L. Pearce, "The Future of Leadership: Combining Vertical and Shared Leadership to Transform Knowledge Work," *Academy of Management Executive*, February 2004, pp 47–57.

[52] M. Levy, "Coaching Success Boils Down to Three Traits," *USA Today*, November 2, 2005, p 6C. This research is summarized in B.J. Avolio, J.J. Soskik, D.I. Jung, and Y. Berson, "Leadership Models, Methods, and Applications," *Handbook of Psychology*, eds. W.C. Borman, D.R. Ilgen, R.J. Klimoski (Hobohen, NJ: John Wiley & Sons, 2003), vol. 12, pp 277–307.

[53] This research is summarized in B.J. Avolio, J.J. Soskik, D.I. Jung, and Y. Berson, "Leadership Models, Methods, and Applications," *Handbook of Psychology*, eds. W.C. Borman, D.R. Ilgen, R.J. Klimoski (Hoboken, NJ: John Wiley & Sons, 2003), vol. 12, pp 277–307.

[54] See R. Siklos, "Bob Iger Rocks Disney," *Fortune*, January 19, 2009, pp 80–86.

[55] Results can be found in P.M. Podsakoff, S.B. MacKenzie, M. Ahearne, and W.H. Bommer, "Searching for a Needle in a Haystack: Trying to Identify the Illusive Moderators of Leadership Behaviors," *Journal of Management*, 1995, pp 422–470. Also see S. Yun, S. Faraj, and H.P. Sims Jr., "Contingent Leadership and Effectiveness of Trauma Resuscitation Teams," *Journal of Applied Psychology*, November 2005, pp 1288–1296.

[56] For a complete description of this theory, see B.J. Avolio and B.M. Bass, *A Manual for Full-Range Leadership Development* (Binghamton, NY: Center for Leadership Studies, 1991). The manual is now published by www.mindgarden.com.

[57] Examples can be found in J. Sandberg, "Too-Nice Boss?" *The Arizona Republic*, March 2, 2008, p EC1; and K. Kelly, "Cayne to Step Down as Bear Stearns CEO," *The Wall Street Journal*, January 8, 2008, pp A1, A18.

[58] Results can be found in A.H. Eagly, M.C. Johannesen-Schmidt, and M.L. van Engen, "Transformational, Transactional, and Laissez-Faire Leadership Styles: A Meta-Analysis Comparing Women and Men," *Psychological Bulletin*, June 2003, pp 569–591.

[59] A definition and description of transactional leadership is provided by J. Antonakis and R.J. House, "The Full-Range Leadership Theory: The Way Forward," *Transformational and Charismatic Leadership: The Road Ahead*, eds. B.J. Avolio and F.J. Yammarino (New York: JAI Press, 2002), pp 3–34.

[60] Excerpted from P. Dvorak, "Outsider CEO Translates A New Message in Japan," *The Wall Street Journal*, March 10, 2008, p B4.

[61] U.R. Dumdum, K.B. Lowe, and B.J. Avolio, "A Meta-Analysis of Transformational and Transactional Leadership Correlates of Effectiveness and Satisfaction: An Update and Extension," *Transformational and Charismatic Leadership: The Road Ahead*, eds. B.J. Avolio and F.J. Yammarino (New York: JAI Press, 2002), p 38.

[62] Supportive research is summarized by Bass and Bass, *The Bass Handbook of Leadership*, pp 618–648.

[63] P. Dvorak, "Outsider CEO Translates a New Message in Japan," *The Wall Street Journal*, March 3, 2008.

[64] Supportive results can be found in T.M. Hautala, "The Relationship between Personality and Transformational Leadership," *Journal of Management Development*, 2006, pp 777–794; and J.E. Bono and T.A. Judge, "Personality and Transformational and Transactional Leadership: A Meta-Analysis," *Journal of Applied Psychology*, October 2004, pp 901–910.

[65] See A.H. Eagly, M.C. Johannesen-Schmidt, and M.L. van Engen, "Transformational, Transactional, and Laissez-Faire Leadership Styles," *Psychological Bulletin*, July 2003, pp 569–591.

[66] See B.J. Avolio, R.J. Reichard, S.T. Hannah, F.O. Walumbwa, and A. Chan, "A Meta-Analytic Review of Leadership Impact Research: Experimental and Quasi-Experimental Studies," *The Leadership Quarterly*, 2009, pp 764–784.

[67] These definitions are derived from R. Kark, B. Shamir, and C. Chen, "The Two Faces of Transformational Leadership: Empowerment and Dependency," *Journal of Applied Psychology*, April 2003, pp 246–255. Also see A.E. Rafferty and M.A. Griffin, "Refining Individualized Consideration: Distinguishing Developmental Leadership and Supportive Leadership," *Journal of Occupational and Organizational Psychology*, March 2006, pp 37–61.

[68] B. Nanus, *Visionary Leadership* (San Francisco: Jossey-Bass, 1992), p 8.

[69] T. Bisoux, "Making Connections," *BizEd*, January–February 2009, p 22. Also see "Carl-Henric Svanberg," *The New York Times*, March 16, 2011, www.topics.nytimes.com/top/reference/timestopics/people/s/carlhenric_svanberg/index.html?8qa&scp=1-spot&sq=carl+henric+svanberg&st=nyt.

[70] J. Reingold, "Meet Your New Leader," *Fortune*, November 24, 2008, p 146.

[71] R. Martin, "How Successful Leaders Think," *Harvard Business Review*, June 2007, pp 60–67.

[72] See R. Kark, B. Shamir, and G. Chen, "The Two Faces of Transformational Leadership," *Journal of Applied Psychology*, April 2003, pp 246–255.

[73] Supportive results can be found in W.H. Bommer, G.A. Rich, and R.S. Rubin, "Changing Attitudes about Change: Longitudinal Effects of Transformational Leader Behavior on Employee Cynicism about Organizational Change," *Journal of Organizational Behavior*, November 2005, pp 733–753; B.M. Bass, B.J. Avolio, D.I. Jung, and Y. Berson, "Predicting Unit Performance by Assessing Transformational and Transactional Leadership," *Journal of Applied Psychology*, April 2003, pp 207–218; and J.E. Bono and T.A. Judge, "Self-Concordance at Work: Toward Understanding the Motivational Effects of Transformational Leaders," *Academy of Management Journal*, October 2003, pp 554–571.

[74] Results can be found in U.R. Dumdum, K.B. Lowe, and B.J. Avolio, "A Meta-Analysis of Transformational and Transactional Leadership Correlates of Effectiveness and Satisfaction: An Update and Extension." Also see R.T. Keller, "Transformational Leadership, Initiating Structure, and Substitutes for Leadership: A Longitudinal Study of Research and Development Project Team Performance," *Journal of Applied Psychology*, January 2006, pp 202–210.

[75] See K.B. Lowe, K.G. Kroeck, and N. Sivasubramaniam, "Effectiveness Correlates of Transformational and Transactional Leadership: A Meta-Analytic Review of the MLQ Literature," *Leadership Quarterly*, 1996, pp 385–425. Also see B.R. Agle, N.J. Nagarajan, J.A. Sonnenfeld, and D. Srinivasan, "Does CEO Charisma Matter? An Empirical Analysis of the Relationship among Organizational Performance, Environmental Uncertainty, and Top Management Team Perceptions of CEO Charisma," *Academy of Management Journal*, February 2006, pp 161–174.

[76] See A.J. Towler, "Effects of Charismatic Influence Training on Attitudes, Behavior, and Performance," *Personnel Psychology*, Summer 2003, pp 363–381; and L.A. DeChurch and M.A. Marks, "Leadership in Multi-team Systems," *Journal of Applied Psychology*, March 2006, pp 311–329.

[77] These recommendations were derived from J.M. Howell and B.J. Avolio, "The Ethics of Charismatic Leadership: Submission or Liberation," *The Executive*, May 1992, pp 43–54.

[78] An overall summary of servant-leadership is provided by L.C. Spears, *Reflections on Leadership: How Robert K Greenleaf's Theory of Servant-Leadership Influenced Today's Top Management Thinkers* (New York: John Wiley & Sons, 1995).

[79] D. MacMillan, "Survivor: CEO Edition," *BusinessWeek*, March 1, 2010, p 35.

[80] J. Stuart, *Fast Company*, September 1999, p 114.

[81] "The Best Advice I Ever Got," *Fortune*, May 12, 2008, p 74.

[82] Supportive results can be found in F.O. Walumbwa, C.A. Hartnell, and A. Oke, "Servant Leadership, Procedural Justice Climate, Service Climate, Employee Attitudes, and Organizational Citizenship Behavior: A Cross-Level Investigation," *Journal of Applied Psychology*, May 2010, pp 517–529; and R.C. Liden, S.J. Wayne, H. Zhao, and D. Henderson, "Servant Leadership: Development of a Multidimensional Measure and Multi-Level Assessment," *The Leadership Quarterly*, April 2008, pp 161–177.

[83] The role of followers is discussed by D.S. DeRue and S.J. Ashford, "Who Will Lead and Who Will Follow? A Social Process of Leadership Identity Construction in Organizations," *Academy of Management Review*, October 2010.

[84] B. Bass and R. Bass, *The Bass Handbook of Leadership*, p 408.

[85] See L. Bossidy, "What Your Leader Expects of You and What You Should Expect in Return," *Harvard Business Review*, April 2007, pp 58–65.

[86] See R. Goffee and G. Jones, "Followership: It's Personal, Too," *Harvard Business Review*, December 2001, p 148.

[87] This checklist was proposed by J.J. Gabarro and J.P. Kotter, "Managing Your Boss," *Harvard Business Review*, January 2005, pp 92–99.

[88] These ideas were partially based on B. Dattner, "Forewarned Is Forearmed," *BusinessWeek*, September 1, 2008, p 50; and P. Drucker, "Managing Oneself," *Harvard Business Review*, January 2005, pp 2–11.

[89] The following suggestions were discussed by Gabarro and Kotter, "Managing Your Boss." Also see J. Banks and D. Coutu, "How to Protect Your Job in a Recession," *Harvard Business Review*, September 2008, pp 113–116.

CHAPTER 11

[1] E.H. Schein, "Culture: The Missing Concept in Organization Studies," *Administrative Science Quarterly*, June 1996, p 236.

[2] M. Heuser, "A Walk With Henry Mintzberg–A Reflection Paper," Summer 2009, p 3, www.peoplexpert.eu/download/heuser_2009_a_walk_with_henry_mintzberg.pdf.

[3] *Canadian HR Reporter*, "CEO's Talk–Jack Lohman, CEO, Royal BC Museum," May 27, 2012, p 11.

[4] See the related discussion in L. Buchanan, "The Office," *Inc.*, February 2007, p 120; and R. Berner, "My Year at Wal-Mart," *BusinessWeek*, February 12, 2007, pp 70–74.

[5] To see all the lists that have named Bombardier, see D. Jermyn, "The List: Canada's Top 100 Employers in 2012," *The Globe and Mail*, October 17, 2011, www.theglobeandmail.com. Also see D. Jermyn, "The List: Canada's Best Diversity Employers for 2012," February 22, 2012; "Financial Post's Top Best Companies To Work For–2012," *Financial Post*, February 1, 2012, www.canadastop100.com/fplo; D. Jermyn, "Canada's Top Employers For New Canadians–2012," *The Globe and Mail*, March 14, 2012, www.theglobeandmail.com; and *The Montreal Gazette*, "Montreal's Top Employers," February 1, 2012, www.canadastop100.com/montreal/.

[6] *Canadian HR Reporter*, "CEO's Talk–Keith Dewar, CEO, Health PEI," May 27, 2012 p 11.

[7] T. Hormby, *A History of Apples Lisa, 1979-1986, Low End Mac*, posted October 6, 2005, retrieved on March 2, 2007.

[8] Lululemon corporate website, About Us Tab, Company History Link, "Naming The Company," www.lululemon.com/about/history, accessed on August 3, 2012.

[9] R. Gupta, "HTML5 Tipped Not To Be The Future Of Apps," *Daily Deal Media* on Yahoo Blog, posted July 29, 2012, www.dailydealmedia.com/789html5-tipped-not-to-be-the-future-of-apps.

[10] "Top Employers or Canadians Over 40 For 2012," www.eluta.ca/top-emloyer-ellisdon.

[11] Press Release, Tim Horton's Inc., "Tim Horton's Rolls Out New Look," November 2001, www.timhortons.com/ca/pdf/careerwear.pdf.

[12] *Architectural Record* – Montreal 115 Studios for Cirque du Soleil, accessed on Aug 3, 2012, www.archrecord.construction.com/projects/bts/archives/multifamhousing/04_cirque/overview.asp.

[13] S.H. Schwartz, "Universals in the Content and Structure of Values: Theoretical Advances and Empirical Tests in 20 Countries," *Advances in Experimental Social Psychology*, ed. M.P. Zanna (New York: Academic Press, 1992), p 4.

[14] T. Taylor, "CEO of the Year: Christine Day," *The Globe and Mail*, November 24, 2011, www.theglobeandmail.com.

[15] Lululemon corporate website, Community Tab, Responsibility Link, "Creating Community Legacies," Stories, accessed on August 3, 2012, www.lululemon.com.

[16] Ibid. Community Tab, Ambassadors Link, "Our Ambassadors," Stories.

[17] P. Babcock, "Is Your Company Two-Faced?" *HR Magazine*, January 2004, p 43.

[18] "CEO's Talk–Jim Nowakowski, president and founder, JNE Welding," *Canadian HR Reporter*, May 21, 2012.

[19] WestJet Website, "Basic Info–Awards," www.facebook.com/westjet/info.

[20] Ibid. "President's Message."

[21] Ibid. "About Westjet," "Community Investment" tab.

[22] Ibid. "WestJet Great Jobs."

[23] Ivey School of Business–UWO, "WestJet Leaders Focus On The Power of People," April 14, 2011.

[24] *Canadian Business*, "*WestJet Tops List of Canadian's 10 Most Admired Corporate Cultures*,"January 16, 2008, www.canadianbusiness.com.

[25] See C. Ostroff, A. Kinicki, and M. Tamkins, "Organizational Culture and Climate," *Handbook of Psychology*, vol. 12, eds. W.C. Borman, D.R. Ilgen, and R.J. Klimoski (New York: Wiley and Sons, 2003), pp 565–593.

[26] See the related discussion in S. Ten Have, W. Ten Have, A.F. Stevens, M. Vander Elst, and F. Pol-Coyne, *Key Management Models: The Management Tools and Practices that will Improve Your Business* (San Francisco: Jossey-Bass, 2003); and P. Kwan and A. Walker, "Validating the Competing Values Model as a Representation of Organizational Culture Through Inter-Institutional Comparisons," *Organizational Analysis*, 2004, pp 21–37.

[27] A thorough description of the CVF is provided in K.S. Cameron, R.E. Quinn, J. Degraff, and A.V. Thakor, *Creating Values Leadership* (Northampton, MA: Edward Elgar, 2006); and K.S. Cameron and R.E. Quinn, *Diagnosing and Changing Organizational Culture* (New York: Addison-Wesley, 1999).

[28] "Reuters–Timeline: Key Dates In The History of Nortel," January 14, 2009, www.reuters.com/assets/print?aid=USTRE50D3N120090115.

[29] Results can be found in C. Hartnell, Y. Ou, and A. Kinicki, "Organizational Culture and Organizational Effectiveness: A Meta-Analytic Investigation of the Competing Values Framework's Theoretical Suppositions," *Journal of Applied Psychology*, in press. Also see S.A. Sackman, "Culture and Performance," *The Handbook of Organizational Culture and Climate* 2nd ed., ed. N.M. Ashkanasy, C.P.M. Wilderom, and M.F. Peterson (Los Angeles: Sage, 2011), pp 188–224.

[30] Mergers are discussed by L. Tepedino and M. Watkins, "Be a Master of Mergers and Acquisitions," *HR Magazine*, June 2010, pp 53–56.

[31] See the related discussion in V. Sathe and E.J. Davidson, "Toward a New Conceptualization of Culture Change," *Handbook of Organizational Culture and Climate*, eds. N.M. Ashkanasay, C.P.M. Wilderom, and M.F. Peterson (Thousand Oaks, CA: Sage Publications, 2000), pp 279–296; and M. Nunno, "The Effects of the ARC Organizational Intervention on Caseworker Turnover, Climate, and Culture in Children's Services Systems," *Child Abuse and Neglect*, August 2006, pp 849–854.

[32] *Canadian HR Reporter*, "CEO's Talk–Kathy Bardswick, President and CEO, the Co-operators Group," May 21, 2012.

[33] D.A. Durbin, "Ford Cuts Part of Culture Shift," *The Arizona Republic*, January 24, 2006, p D3.

[34] The mechanisms were based on material contained in E.H. Schein, "The Role of the Founder in Creating Organizational Culture," *Organizational Dynamics*, Summer 1983, pp 13–28.

[35] Comeco website, "About Comeco," "Comeco's Vision and Values," www.cameco.com/about/vision.

[36] Architectural Record–Montreal, "115 Studios for Cirque du Soleil," accessed on August 3, 2012, www.archrecord.construction.com/projects/bts/archives/multifamhousing/04_cirque/overview.asp.

[37] Real Canadian Superstore website, "FAQ," www.realcanadianspuerstore.ca/LCLOnline/faqStoreServices.

[38] Skate Canada website, "Get Involved–Become A Coach or Official," "Coachings Training," www.skatecanada.ca/GetInvolved/BecomeaCoachorOfficial/CoachesTraining/CoachingVisionandKeyMessages.

[39] S. Holmes, "Cleaning Up Boeing," *BusinessWeek*, March 13, 2006, p 66.

[40] G. Pitts, "Mogen Smed: Some Chaos, A Little Bit of Anarchy, No Meetings," *The Globe and Mail*, March 9, 2009.

[41] A. Sharp, "Balsillie Sought Major Strategy Shift Before he Quit RIM," *Toronto Star*, April 14, 2012, p B6.

[42] Practical examples can be found in P. Dvorak, "A Firm's Culture Can Get Lost in Translation," *The Wall Street Journal*, April 3, 2006, pp B1, B3; and B.E. Litzky, K.A. Eddleston, and D.L. Kidder, "The Good, the Bad, and the Misguided: How Managers Inadvertently Encourage Deviant Behaviors," *Academy of Management Perspectives*, February 2006, pp 91–102.

[43] P. Gallant, "Cisco's Flexible, Transparency Keep Employees Happy," *Toronto Star*, November 23, 2011, www.thestar.com/printarticle/1091471.

[44] L. Gerstner, Jr., "Who Says Elephants Can't Dance," May 15, 2003,

[45] Wal-mart corporate website, "Get To Know Us," Our Story, Culture, www.walmart.com.

[46] J. Van Maanen, "Breaking In: Socialization to Work," *Handbook of Work, Organization, and Society*, ed. R. Dubin (Chicago: Rand-McNally, 1976), p 67.

[47] Adapted from material in D.C. Feldman, "The Multiple Socialization of Organization Members," *Academy of Management Review*, April 1981, pp 309–318. Reprinted by permission of The Academy of Management via The Copyright Clearance Center.

[48] Supportive evidence is provided by R.W. Griffeth and P.W. Hom, *Retaining Valued Employees* (Thousand Oaks, CA: Sage Publications, 2001), pp 46–65.

[49] See J.M. Phillips, "Effects of Realistic Job Previews on Multiple Organizational Outcomes: A Meta-Analysis," *Academy of Management Journal*, December 1998, pp 673–690.

[50] A. Silliker, "Structured Onboarding Makes For Happier, More Confident Employee's: Survey," *Canadian HR Reporter*, August 15, 2011, p 6N.

[51] Ibid.

[52] Onboarding programs are discussed by J. McGregor, "How to Take the Reins at Top Speed," *BusinessWeek*, February 5, 2007, pp 55–56; and J.M. Brodie, "Getting Managers On Board," *HR Magazine*, November 2006, pp 105–108.

[53] These results are presented in "Outsider Longer," *Training*, March 2007, p 6.

[54] See J.P. Slattery, T.T. Selvarajan, and J.E. Anderson, "Influences of New Employee Development Practices on Temporary Employee Work-Related Attitudes," *Human Resource Development Quarterly*, 2006, pp 279–303.

[55] See E.H. Offstein and R.L. Dufresne, "Building Strong Ethics and Promoting Positive Character Development: The Influence of HRM at the United States Military Academy at West Point," *Human Resource Management*, Spring 2007, pp 95–114.

[56] See D. Cable and C. Parsons, "Socialization Tactics and Person-Organization Fit," *Personnel Psychology*, Spring 2001, pp 1–23.

[57] R. Levering and M. Moskowitz, "The 100 Best Companies to Work For: And the Winners Are . . ." *Fortune*, January 23, 2006, p 94.

[58] A review of stage model research can be found in B.E. Ashforth, *Role Transitions in Organizational Life: An Identity-Based Perspective* (Mahwah, NJ: Lawrence Erlbaum Associates, 2001).

[59] See J.A. Gruman, A.M. Saks, and D.I. Zweig, "Organizational Socialization Tactics and Newcomer Proactive Behaviours: An Integrative Study," *Journal of Vocational Behaviour*, August 2006, pp 90–104; and H.D. Cooper-Thomas and N. Anderson, "Organizational Socialization," *Journal of Managerial Psychology*, 2006, pp 492–516.

[60] For a thorough review of research on the socialization of diverse employees with disabilities, see A. Colella, "Organizational Socialization of Newcomers with Disabilities: A Framework for Future Research," *Research in Personnel and Human Resources Management*, ed. G.R. Ferris (Greenwich, CT: JAI Press, 1996), pp 351–417.

[61] This definition is based on the network perspective of mentoring proposed by M. Higgins and K. Kram, "Reconceptualizing Mentoring at Work: A Developmental Network Perspective," *Academy of Management Review*, April 2001, pp 264–288.

[62] Results can be found in T.D. Allen, L.T. Eby, M.L. Poteet, and E. Lentz, "Career Benefits Associated with Mentoring for Protégés: A Meta-Analysis," *Journal of Applied Psychology*, February 2004, pp 127–136; and T.D. Allen, L.T. Eby, and E. Lentz, "Mentorship Behaviours and Mentorship Quality Associated with Formal Mentoring Programs: Closing the Gap Between Research and Practice," *Journal of Applied Psychology*, May 2006, pp 567–578.

[63] See the University of Waterloo website, "Communication, Leadership and Social Innovation." Under the "Leading to Leadership" section is a description of Peggy Sum, accessed on August 3, 2012, www.clsi.uwaterloo.ca/121peggysum.html. Also see the description of Vivek and Peggy by going to the GetStock photo library and review image 2083205330 for picture description.

[64] Career functions are discussed in detail in K. Kram, *Mentoring of Work: Developmental Relationships in Organizational Life* (Glenview, IL: Scott, Foresman, 1985).

[65] This discussion is based on M. Higgins and K. Kram, "Reconceptualizing Mentoring at Work."

[66] Ibid.

[67] Supportive results can be found in T. Allen, M. Poteet, and J. Russell, "Protégé Selection by Mentors: What Makes the Difference?" *Journal of Organizational Behaviour*, May 2000, pp 271–282.

[68] Recommendations for improving your networking skills can be found in S. Berfield, "Mentoring Can Be Messy," *BusinessWeek*, January 29, 2007, pp 80-81.

[69] A. Silliker "HRIA's Virtual Mentorship Program Eliminates Geographical Boundaries," *Canadian HR Reporter*, April 25, 2011, p 7N.

[70] Results can be found in "Leadership Needs Development," *Training*, February 2006, p 7.

[71] See S. Tonidandel, D.R. Avery, and M.G. Phillips, "Maximizing Returns on Mentoring: Factors Affecting Subsequent Protégé Performance," *Journal of Organizational Behaviour*, January 2007, pp 89–110.

[72] This recommendation was derived from J. Welch and S. Welch, "Ideas the WelchWay: Avoiding Strikes—and Unions," *BusinessWeek*, January 15, 2007, p 92.

CHAPTER 12

[1] C.I. Barnard, *The Functions of the Executive* (Cambridge, MA: Harvard University Press, 1938), p 73.

[2] Drawn from E.H. Schein, *Organizational Psychology*, 3rd ed. (Englewood Cliffs, NJ: Prentice Hall, 1980), pp 12–15.

[3] For related reading, see N. Bennett and S.A. Miles, "Second in Command: The Misunderstood Role of the Chief Operating Officer," *Harvard Business Review*, May 2006, pp 71–78.

[4] H. Mintzberg, "Organization Design: fashion or fit?" *Harvard Business Review*, January 1, 1981.

[5] Ibid.

[6] For an interesting historical perspective of hierarchy, see P. Miller and T. O'Leary, "Hierarchies and American Ideals, 1900–1940," *Academy of Management Review*, April 1989, pp 250–265. Also see H.J. Leavitt, "Why Hierarchies Thrive," *Harvard Business Review*, March 2003, pp 96–102.

[7] For an excellent overview of the span of control concept, see D.D. Van Fleet and A.G. Bedeian, "A History of the Span of Management," *Academy of Management Review*, July 1977, pp 356–372. Also see E.E. Lawler III and J.R. Galbraith, "New Roles for the Staff: Strategic Support and Service," *Organizing for the Future: The New Logic for Managing Complex Organizations*, eds. J.R. Galbraith, E.E. Lawler III, and Associates (San Francisco: Jossey-Bass, 1993), pp 65–83.

[8] See G. Anders, "Overseeing More Employees–With Fewer Managers," *The Wall Street Journal*, March 24, 2008, p B6.

[9] T. Hindle, "Idea: Span of Control," *The Economist*, Nov. 9, 2009, www.economist.com/node/14301444/print.

[10] For a comparison of functional and product departmentation, see J. McCann and J. Galbraith, "Interdepartmental Relations," in *Handbook of Organizational Design*, (Oxford: Oxford University Press), 1981; and A.H. Walker and J.W. Lorsch, "Organizational choice: Product vs. Function," *Harvard Business Review*, November–December 1968, pp 129–138.

[11] See Bayer Health Care-Corporate Profile Website, www.bayerhealthcare.com, referenced May 2012. Also see D. Mote, "Management and Structure," 2012, www.enotes.com/matrix.

[12] Treatment of these forms of departmentation can be found in R.L. Daft, *Organization Theory and Design* 9th ed. (Cincinnati, OH: Thompson South-Western; Robey, D., 1991); and *Designing Organizations* 3rd ed. (Homewood, IL: Irwin.)

[13] Ibid.

[14] Ibid.

[15] R.H. Waterman, Jr. (1987). *The Renewal Factor* (New York: Bantam Books; McElroy, J. 1985); and "Ford's new way to build cars," *Road and Track*, p 156–158.

[16] From R.E. Miles and C.C. Snow, "Causes of Failure in Network Organizations," *California Management Review*, ivol. 34, no. 4.

[17] Refer to the Industry Canada website, www.ic.gc.ca, "Telecommunications Service In Canada: An Industry Overview. Section 5: Company Financial Profiles. Subsection 5.2-1," Telus Corporation Organizational Chart.

[18] C. Capos, "Nearly Modular Structure Offers The Best of Both Worlds," *Michigan In The News.*, February 26, 2008, www.bus.umich.edu/newsroom.

[19] R. Slater, *The G.E. Way Fieldbook* (New York: McGraw-Hill, 2000) pg 73-74.

[20] For an illustrative management-related metaphor, see J.E. Beatty, "Grades as Money and the Role of the Market Metaphor in Management Education," *Academy of Management Learning and Education*, June 2004, pp 187–196. Also see C. Oswick and P. Jones, "Beyond Correspondence? Metaphor in Organization Theory," *Academy of Management Review*, April 2006, pp 483–485; and J. Cornelissen, "Metaphor in Organization Theory: Progress and the Past," *Academy of Management Review*, April 2006, pp 485–488.

[21] See W.R. Scott, "The Mandate Is Still Being Honored: In Defense of Weber's Disciples," *Administrative Science Quarterly*, March 1996, pp 163–171. Also see D. Jones, "Military a Model for Execs," *USA Today*, June 9, 2004, p 4B.

[22] Based on M. Weber, *The Theory of Social and Economic Organization*, trans. A.M. Henderson and T. Parsons (New York: Oxford University Press, 1947). An instructive analysis of the mistranslation of Weber's work is found in R.M. Weiss, "Weber

on Bureaucracy: Management Consultant or Political Theorist?," *Academy of Management Review*, April 1983, pp 242–248.

[23] For a critical appraisal of bureaucracy, see R.P. Hummel, *The Bureaucratic Experience*, 3rd ed. (New York: St. Martin's Press, 1987). The positive side of bureaucracy is presented in C.T. Goodsell, *The Case for Bureaucracy: A Public Administration Polemic* (Chatham, NJ: Chatham House Publishers, 1983).

[24] P. Keat and P. Young, *Managerial Economics*, 4th ed. (Upper Saddle River, NJ Pearson Education Inc., 2003) pp 384–395. See reference to evaluate the efficiency of the alternative methods of allocating scare resources.

[25] See G. Pinchot and E. Pinchot, "Beyond Bureaucracy," *Business Ethics*, March–April 1994, pp 26–29; and O. Harari, "Let the Computers Be the Bureaucrats," *Management Review*, September 1996, pp 57–60.

[26] For examples of what managers are doing to counteract bureaucratic tendencies, see B. Dumaine, "The Bureaucracy Busters," *Fortune*, June 17, 1991, pp 36–50; and C.J. Cantoni, "Eliminating Bureaucracy-Roots and All," *Management Review*, December 1993, pp 30–33.

[27] J.D. Thompson, *Organizations in Action* (New York: McGraw-Hill, 1967), pp 6–7. Also see A.C. Bluedorn, "The Thompson Interdependence Demonstration," *Journal of Management Education*, November 1993, pp 505–509.

[28] For interesting updates on the biological systems metaphor, see A.M. Webber, "How Business Is a Lot Like Life," *Fast Company*, April 2001, pp 130–136; E. Bonabeau and C. Meyer, "Swarm Intelligence: A Whole New Way to Think about Business," *Harvard Business Review*, May 2001, pp 106–114; and R. Adner, "Match Your Innovation Strategy to Your Innovation Ecosystem," *Harvard Business Review*, April 2006, pp 98–107.

[29] R.L. Daft and K.E. Weick, "Toward a Model of Organizations as Interpretation Systems," *Academy of Management Review*, April 1984, p 293. Also see J. Reingold, "My (Long) Day at the Top," *Fast Company*, June 2006, pp 64–66.

[30] See M. Crossan, "Altering Theories of Learning and Action: An Interview with Chris Argyris," *Academy of Management Executive*, May 2003, pp 40–46; D. Gray, "Wanted: Chief Ignorance Officer," *Harvard Business Review*, November 2003, pp 22, 24; and G.T.M. Hult, D.J. Ketchen, Jr., and S.F. Slater, "Information Processing, Knowledge Development, and Strategic Supply Chain Performance," *Academy of Management Journal*, April 2004, pp 241–253.

[31] Maple Leaf Foods website, "'We Take Care' Maple Leaf's Vertical Coordination Strategy: A Key to Enhanced Safety," www.mapleleaf.com. Also see *Report on Business Magazine*, "Top Forty Under 40," May 2002, p 73.

[32] R. Kaplan and D. Norton, "The Balanced Scorecard—Measures That Drive Performance," *Harvard Business Review*, January–February 1992.

[33] K. Cameron, "Critical Questions in Assessing Organizational Effectiveness," *Organizational Dynamics*, Autumn 1980, p 70. Also see T.D. Wall, J. Michie, M. Patterson, S.J. Wood, M. Sheehan, C.W. Clegg, and M. West, "On the Validity of Subjective Measures of Company Performance," *Personnel Psychology*, Spring 2004, pp 95–118; W.F. Joyce, "What Really Works: Building the 4+2 Organization," *Organizational Dynamics*, no. 2, 2005, pp 118–129; and J. Kirby, "Toward a Theory of High Performance," *Harvard Business Review*, July–August 2005, pp 30–39.

[34] See G.H. Seijts, G.P. Latham, K. Tasa, and B.W. Latham, "Goal Setting and Goal Orientation: An Integration of Two Different Yet Related Literatures," *Academy of Management Journal*, April 2004, pp 227–239.

[35] For discussion of a very goal-oriented company, see "What Makes GE Great?" *Fortune*, March 6, 2006, pp 90–96.

[36] See the Mountain Equipment Co-op Corporate website, "Sustainability/accountability Report," accessed May 2012 www.meca.ca.

[37] "Interview: M. Scott Peck," *Business Ethics*, March/April 1994, p 17. Also see C.B. Gibson and J. Birkinshaw, "The Antecedents, Consequences, and Mediating Role of Organizational Ambidexterity," *Academy of Management Journal*, April 2004, pp 209–226.

[38] See P. Puranam, H. Singh, and M. Zollo, "Organizing for Innovation: Managing the Coordination-Autonomy Dilemma in Technology Acquisitions," *Academy of Management Journal*, April 2006, pp 263–280; R.E. Herzlinger, "Why Innovation in Health Care Is So Hard," *Harvard Business Review*, May 2006, pp 58–66; and D.L. Laurie, Y.L. Doz, and C.P. Sheer, "Creating New Growth Platforms," *Harvard Business Review*, May 2006, pp 80–90.

[39] Cameron, "Critical Questions in Assessing Organizational Effectiveness," p 67. Also see W. Buxton, "Growth from Top to Bottom," *Management Review*, July/August 1999, p 11.

[40] See R.K. Mitchell, B.R. Agle, and D.J. Wood, "Toward a Theory of Stakeholder Identification and Salience: Defining the Principle of Who and What Really Counts," *Academy of Management Review*, October 1997, pp 853–896; T.J. Rowley and M. Moldoveanu, "When Will Stakeholder Groups Act? An Interest-and Identity-Based Model of Stakeholder Group Mobilization," *Academy of Management Review*, April 2003, pp 204–219; G. Kassinis and N. Vafeas, "Stakeholder Pressures and Environmental Performance," *Academy of Management Journal*, February 2006, pp 145–159; and N.A. Gardberg and C.J. Fombrun, "Corporate Citizenship: Creating Intangible Assets across Institutional Environments," *Academy of Management Review*, April 2006, pp 329–346.

[41] Human Rights First—Press Release, "Human Rights First Welcomes Facebook as Observer to the Global Network Initiative," May 3, 2012, www.humanrightsfirst.org.

[42] See J. Welch and S. Welch, "How Healthy Is Your Company?" *BusinessWeek*, May 8, 2006, p 126.

[43] For updates, see M. Goold and A. Campbell, "Do You Have a Well-Designed Organization?" *Harvard Business Review*, March 2002, pp 117–124; and J.A.A. Sillince, "A Contingency Theory of Rhetorical Congruence," *Academy of Management Review*, July 2005, pp 608–621.

[44] B. Elgin, "Running the Tightest Ships on the Net," *BusinessWeek*, January 29, 2001, p 126.

[45] See D.A. Morand, "The Role of Behavioural Formality and Informality in the Enactment of Bureaucratic versus Organic Organizations," *Academy of Management Review*, October 1995, pp 831–872.

[46] "Canada's Top 100 Employers: National Competition – 2012," accessed May 2012, www.Canadastop100.com/national/.

[47] See G.P. Huber, C.C. Miller, and W.H. Glick, "Developing More Encompassing Theories about Organizations: The Centralization-Effectiveness Relationship as an Example," *Organization Science*, no. 1, 1990, pp 11–40; and C. Handy, "Balancing Corporate Power: A New Federalist Paper," *Harvard Business Review*, November/December 1992, pp 59–72. Also see A. Slywotzky and D. Nadler, "The Strategy Is the Structure," *Harvard Business Review*, February 2004, p 16; and N. Gull, "Managing on the Front Lines," *Inc.*, May 2004, p 24.

[48] P. Kaestle, "A New Rationale for Organizational Structure," *Planning Review*, July/August 1990, p 22. For examples, see N. McKinstry, "Changing Direction," *Fortune*, November 14, 2005, p 153; A.A. King, M.J. Lenox, and A. Terlaak, "The Strategic Use of Decentralized Institutions: Exploring Certification with the ISO 14001 Management Standard," *Academy of Management Journal*, December 2005, pp 1091–1106; and A. Barrett, "J&J: Reinventing How It Invents," *BusinessWeek*, April 17, 2006, pp 60–61.

[49] Details of this study can be found in T. Burns and G.M. Stalker, *The Management of Innovation* (London: Tavistock, 1961). Also see W.D. Sine, H. Mitsuhashi, and D.A. Kirsch, "Revisiting Burns and Stalker: Formal Structure and New Venture Performance in Emerging Economic Sectors," *Academy of Management Journal*, February 2006, pp 121–132; and N. Nohria, "Survival of the Adaptive," *Harvard Business Review*, May 2006, p 23.

[50] D.J. Gillen and S.J. Carroll, "Relationship of Managerial Ability to Unit Effectiveness in More Organic versus More Mechanistic Departments," *Journal of Management Studies*, November 1985, pp 674–675.

[51] J.D. Sherman and H.L. Smith, "The Influence of Organizational Structure on Intrinsic versus Extrinsic Motivation," *Academy of Management Journal*, December 1984, p 883.

[52] See J.A. Courtright, G.T. Fairhurst, and L.E. Rogers, "Interaction Patterns in Organic and Mechanistic Systems," *Academy of Management Journal*, December 1989, pp 773–802.

[53] See J.R. Galbraith and E.E. Lawler III, "Effective Organizations: Using the New Logic of Organizing," J.R. Galbraith, E.E. Lawler III, and Associates, eds., *Organizing for the Future: The New Logic for Managing Complex Organizations* (San Francisco: Jossey-Bass, 1993), pp 285–299.

CHAPTER 13

[1] A. Silliker, "M&A's Increase Risk of Anxiety," *Canadian HR Reporter*, March 26, 2012, p 1.

[2] Ibid, p 9.

[3] Forces for change are thoroughly discussed by L.R. Beach, *Leadership and the Art of Change* (Thousand Oaks, CA: Sage, 2006).

[4] B. Fenlon, "Canada's Visible Minorities Top Five Million." *The Globe and Mail*, April 8, 2008.

[5] *Media Corp Canada,* "SportsDirect Inc.–Atlantic Canada's Top Employers and Nova Scotia's Top Employers for 2012," www.eluta.ca/top-employer-sportsdirect.

[6] PriceWaterhouse Cooper Report on workforce performance, "With a Multi-generational workforce, is Gen X getting the squeeze?" *Canadian Newswire Group*, March 15, 2012, www.newservice.ca.

[7] M.L. Alch, "Get Ready for the Net Generation," *Training and Development*, February 2000, pp 32, 34.

[8] "SportsDirect Inc–Atlantic Canada's Top Employers and Nova Scotia's Top Employers for 2012," Media Corp Canada, www.eluta.ca/top-employer-sportsdirect.

[9] S. Covey, *The 8th Habit from Effectiveness to Greatness,* Franklin Covey Co, Simon and Schuster, 2004.

[10] Ibid.

[11] M. Brownlow, "Smartphone Statistics and Market Share," *Email Marketing Report Online,* September 2012, www.email-marketing-reports.com/wireless-mobile/smartphone-statistics.htm.

[12] Ibid.

[13] Ibid.

[14] I. Hardy, "Ipsos: Apple Leads in Canadian Smartphone and Tablet Market Share, RIM is Second," *Mobile Syrup Mobile News and Reviews for Canadians,* September 17, 2012, http://mobilesyrup.com/2012/09/17/ipsos-reid-apple-leads-in-Canadian-smartphone-and-tablet-market-share-rim-is-second/.

[15] B. Tuttle, "Real Winners with Apples' New iPad: Kids who Will Inherit their Parents Old iPads," *Time Magazine,* March 7, 2012, www.moneyland.time.com.

[16] M. Hartley, "Canadians Still Wary of Online Shopping," *Financial Post,* March 19, 2012, www2.canada.com/technology/canadians+still+wary+online+shopping/6323976/story.html?id=6323976.

[17] Ibid.

[18] Productivity in the service industry is discussed by S. Hamm, S.E. Ante, A. Reinhardt, and M. Kripalani, "Services," *BusinessWeek,* June 21, 2004, pp 82–83.

[19] Examples are provided by G. Edmondson, "The Race to Build Really Cheap Cars," *BusinessWeek,* April 23, 2007, pp 44–48; and D. Welch, "Why Toyota Is Afraid of Being Number One," *BusinessWeek,* March 5, 2007, pp 42–50.

[20] See the related discussion in J.W. Upson, D.J. Ketchen, Jr., and R.D. Ireland, "Managing Employee Stress: A Key to the Effectiveness of Strategic Supply Chain Management," *Organizational Dynamics,* 2007, pp 78–92.

[21] "44 Percent of Employers Expect to Pursue M & A's in Next Year: Survey," *Canadian HR Reporter,* October 25, 2012, www.hrreporter.com.

[22] "One-Half of Canadian Exec's Pursuing M & A's this Year: Survey," *Canadian HR Reporter,* May 9, 2012, www.hrreporter.com.

[23] Examples are provided in J. Lublin and P. Dvorak, "How Five New Players Aid Movement to Limit CEO Pay," *The Wall Street Journal,* March 13, 2007, pp A1, A20; and A. Tomisawa, "Matsushita Aims to Boost Quality, Guard Image with Suppliers Rules," *The Wall Street Journal,* March 30, 2007, p A12.

[24] "TransCanada reapplies for Keystone XL permit," *CBC News,* May 4, 2012, www.cbc.ca/news/business/story.

[25] S. Dobson, "Expats Flee Middle East Chaos," *Canadian HR Reporter,* March 28, 2012, p 1.

[26] Deloitte Report, "Gaining Ground In The Sands 2012," *Canadian HR Reporter,* April 23, 2012, www.hrreporter.com.

[27] J. Berkow, "As Shares Fall, RIM Welcomes Rival Devices," *Vancouver Sun,* April 4, 2012, www.vancouversun.com.

[28] "Canadian Tourism Commissions Corporate Plan 2012–2016," p 6, www.en-corporate.canada.travel/.

[29] "Malfunctioning Technology Top Office Complaint," *Canadian HR Reporter,* May 9, 2012, www.hrreporter.com.

[30] For a thorough discussion of the model, see K. Lewin, *Field Theory in Social Science* (New York: Harper & Row, 1951).

[31] "The Ornge Scandal," *Ottawa Citizen,* March 22, 2012, www.ottawacitizen.com.

[32] T. Talaga, "Documents Reveal ORNGE's Deficit," *Toronto Star,* May 25, 2012, p A8.

[33] Ibid.

[34] See T.A. Stewart, "Architects of Change," *Harvard Business Review,* April 2006, p 10.

[35] Languages Canada, "Vision Statement," www.languagescanada.ca.

[36] A thorough discussion of the target elements of change can be found in M. Beer and B. Spector, "Organizational Diagnosis: Its Role in Organizational Learning," *Journal of Counseling and Development,* July–August 1993, pp 642–650; and M. Hammer, "The Process Audit," *Harvard Business Review,* April 2007, pp 111–123.

[37] These errors are discussed in J.P. Kotter, "Leading Change: When Transformation Efforts Fail," *Harvard Business Review,* January 2007, pp 96–103.

[38] See F. Ostroff, "Change Management in Government," *Harvard Business Review,* May 2006, pp 141–147.

[39] Different stage-based models of OD are discussed by R.A. Gallagher, "What Is OD?" accessed May 12, 2005, www.orgdct.com/what_is_od.htm.

[40] Over 60 different OD techniques are discussed by P. Holman, T. Devane, and S. Cady, *The Change Handbook,* 2nd ed. (San Francisco: Berrett-Kohler, 2007).

[41] W.W. Burke, *Organization Development: A Normative View* (Reading, MA: Addison-Wesley Publishing, 1987), p 9.

[42] S. Terlep, "GM's Latest Change Agent Tackles Designs, Red Tape," *The Wall Street Journal,* June 15, 2011, www.online.wsj.com.

[43] See R. Gulati, "Silo Busting: How to Execute on the Promise of Customer Focus," *Harvard Business Review,* May 2007, pp 98–108.

44 G. Bushe and A. Kassam, "When Is Appreciative Inquiry Transformational?" *The Journal of Applied Behavioral Science,* vol. 41, no. 2, June 2005, p 164.

45 A. Kinicki and B. Williams, *Management: A Practical Introduction,* 2nd ed. (Burr Ridge: IL: McGraw-Hill/Irwin, 2006), p 329.

46 See R. Rodgers, J.E. Hunter, and D.L. Rogers, "Influence of Top Management Commitment on Management Program Success," *Journal of Applied Psychology,* February 1993, pp 151–155.

47 Results can be found in P.J. Robertson, D.R. Roberts, and J.I. Porras, "Dynamics of Planned Organizational Change: Assessing Empirical Support for a Theoretical Model," *Academy of Management Journal,* June 1993, pp 619–634. Also see J.M. Hiatt, *ADKAR: A Model for Change in Business, Government and Our Community* (Loveland, CO: Prosci Learning Center Publications, 2006).

48 Results from the meta-analysis can be found in G.A. Neuman, J.E. Edwards, and N.S. Raju, "Organizational Development Interventions: A Meta-Analysis of Their Effects on Satisfaction and Other Attitudes," *Personnel Psychology,* Autumn 1989, pp 461–490.

49 Results can be found in C.M. Lau and H.Y. Ngo, "Organization Development and Firm Performance: A Comparison of Multinational and Local Firms," *Journal of International Business Studies,* First Quarter 2001, pp 95–114.

50 Adapted from R.J. Marshak, *Covert Processes at Work* (San Francisco: Berrett-Koehler Publishers, 2006); and A.S. Judson, *Changing Behaviour in Organizations: Minimizing Resistance to Change* (Cambridge, MA: Blackwell, Inc., 1991).

51 An individual's predisposition to change was investigated by C.R. Wanberg and J.T. Banas, "Predictors and Outcomes of Openness to Changes in a Reorganizing Workplace," *Journal of Applied Psychology,* February 2000, pp 132–142.

52 T. Godfrey, "Ruling Expected Soon On Radiation Mail Scans," *The London Free Press,* April 11, 2011, p 9.

53 S. Laudurantaye and P. Waldie, "Zellers Era Drawing To A Close," *The Globe and Mail,* May 10, 2011, www.theglobeandmail.com/report-on-business.

54 See L. Coch and J.R.P. French Jr., "Overcoming Resistance to Change," *Human Relations,* 1948, pp 512–532.

55 L. Herscovitch and J.P. Meyer, "Commitment to Organizational Change: Extension of a Three-Component Model," *Journal of Applied Psychology,* June 2002, p 475.

56 Ibid., pp 474–487.

57 Research regarding resilience is discussed by K. Kersting, "Resilience: The Mental Muscle Everyone Has," *Monitor on Psychology,* April 2005, pp 32–33; and G.E. Mangurian, "Realizing What You're Made Of," *Harvard Business Review,* March 2007, pp 125–130.

58 Results from this study can be found in T.A. Judge, C.J. Thoresen, V. Pucik, and T.W. Welbourne, "Managerial Coping with Organizational Change: A Dispositional Perspective," *Journal of Applied Psychology,* February 1999, pp 107–122.

59 See C.R. Wanberg and J.T. Banas, "Predictors and Outcomes of Openness to Changes in a Reorganizing Workplace," *Journal of Applied Psychology,* 2000, 85(1), pp 132–142.

60 See the related discussion in E.B. Dent and S.G. Goldberg, "Challenging 'Resistance to Change,'" *Journal of Applied Behavioural Science,* March 1999, pp 25–41.

61 J.P. Kotter, "Leading Change: Why Transformation Efforts Fail," *Harvard Business Review,* 1995, p 64.

62 Communicating about organizational change is discussed in Z. Ruimin, "Raising Haier," *Harvard Business Review,* February 2007, pp 141–146; and C.M. Christensen, M. Marx, and H.H. Stevenson, "The Tools of Cooperation and Change," *Harvard Business Review,* October 2006, pp 73–81.

63 Reprinted by permission of Harvard Business School Press. Exhibit from J P Kotter and L A Schlesinger, "Choosing Strategies for Change," March/April 1979. Copyright ©1979 by the Harvard Business School of Publishing Corporation; all rights reserved.

64 J.M. Ivancevich and M.T. Matteson, *Stress and Work: A Managerial Perspective* (Glenview, IL: Scott, Foresman, 1980), pp 8–9.

65 See H. Selye, *Stress without Distress* (HarperCollins, 1974).

66 See C. Liu, P.E. Spector, and L. Shi, "Cross-National Job Stress: A Quantitative and Qualitative Study," *Journal of Organizational Behaviour,* January 2007, pp 209–239; T. Deangelis, "American: A Toxic Lifestyle?" *Monitor on Psychology,* April 2007, pp 50–52; and C. Hymowitz, "Executive Adopts Motto for Job Stress: Work Hard, Be Nice," *The Wall Street Journal,* April 16, 2007, p B1.

67 S. Jayson, "Bad Bosses Can Be Bad For Your Health," *USA Today,* August 5, 2012, www.usatoday.com/news/health/story/2012-08-05/apa-mean-bosses/56813062/1.

68 Supportive results can be found in F.M. McKee-Ryan, Z. Song, C.R. Wanberg, and A.J. Kinicki, "Psychological and Physical Well-Being during Unemployment: A Meta-Analytic Study," *Journal of Applied Psychology,* January 2005, pp 53–76.

69 Sleep deprivation is discussed by C.A. Czeisler, "Sleep Deficit: The Performance Killer," *Harvard Business Review,* October 2006, pp 53–59.

70 Results are reported in N.A. Bowling and T.A. Beehr, "Workplace Harassment from the Victim's Perspective: A Theoretical Model and Meta-Analysis," *Journal of Applied Psychology,* September 2006, pp 998–1012.

71 The discussion of appraisal is based on R.S. Lazarus and S. Folkman, *Stress, Appraisal, and Coping* (New York: Springer Publishing, 1984).

72 Results are presented in J.A. Penley, J. Tomaka, and J.S. Wiebe, "The Association of Coping to Physical and Psychological Health Outcomes: A Meta-Analytic Review," *Journal of Behavioural Medicine,* December 2002, pp 551–609. Also see M. Fugate, A. Kinicki, and G. Prussia, "Employee Coping with Organizational Change: An Examination of Alternative Theoretical Perspectives and Models," 2007, manuscript under review.

73 The impact of vacations are discussed by E. White, "For Young Workers, Taking Time Off Can be Stressful," *The Wall Street Journal,* March 27, 2007, p B10; and C. Fritz and S. Sonnentag, "Recovery, Well-Being, and Performance-Related Outcomes: The Role of Workload and Vacation Experiences," *Journal of Applied Psychology,* July 2006, pp 936–945.

74 Supportive results can be found in J.R.B. Halbesleben and W.M. Bowler, "Emotional Exhaustion and Job Performance: The Mediating Role of Motivation," *Journal of Applied Psychology,* January 2007, pp 93–106; and J.D. Jonge and C. Dormann, "Stressors, Resources, and Strain at Work: A Longitudinal Test of the Triple-Match Principle," *Journal of Applied Psychology,* November 2006, pp 1359–1374.

75 Supportive results can be found in G.E. Miller, E. Chen, and E.S. Zhou, "If It Goes Up, Must It Come Down? Chronic Stress and the Hypothalamic-Pituitary-Adrenocortical Axis in Humans," *Psychological Bulletin,* January 2007, pp 25–45; and L. Meyers, "Building a Stronger Heart," *Monitor on Psychology,* January 2007, pp 52–53.

76 R.A. Clay, "One Heart–Many Threats," *Monitor on Psychology,* January 2007, pp 46–54; J.P. Neveu, "Jailed Resources: Conservation of Resources Theory as Applied to Burnout Among Prison Guards," *Journal of Organizational Behaviour,* January 2007, pp 21–42; and J.R.B. Halbesleben, "Sources of Social Support and Burnout: A Meta-Analytic Test of the Conservation of Resources Model," *Journal of Applied Psychology,* September 2006, pp 1134–1145.

77 This pioneering research is presented in S.C. Kobasa, "Stressful Life Events, Personality, and Health: An Inquiry into Hardiness," *Journal of Personality and Social Psychology,* January 1979, pp 1–11.

78 M. Friedman and R.H. Rosenman, *Type A Behaviour and Your Heart* (Greenwich, CT: Fawcett Publications, 1974), p 84.

[79] Adapted from M. Friedman and R.H. Rosenman, *Type A Behaviour and Your Heart* (Greenwich, CT: Fawcett Publications, 1974), pp 100–102.

[80] See C. Lee, L.F. Jamieson, and P.C. Earley, "Beliefs and Fears and Type A Behaviour: Implications for Academic Performance and Psychiatric Health Disorder Symptoms," *Journal of Organizational Behaviour*, March 1996, pp 151–177; S.D. Bluen, J. Barling, and W. Burns, "Predicting Sales Performance, Job Satisfaction, and Depression by Using the Achievement Strivings and Impatience-Irritability Dimensions of Type A Behaviour," *Journal of Applied Psychology*, April 1990, pp 212–216; and M.S. Taylor, E.A. Locke, C. Lee and M.E. Gist, "Type A Behaviour and Faculty Research Productivity: What Are the Mechanisms?" *Organizational Behaviour and Human Performance*, December 1984, pp 402–418.

[81] Results from the meta-analysis are contained in S.A. Lyness, "Predictors of Differences between Type A and B Individuals in Heart Rate and Blood Pressure Reactivity," *Psychological Bulletin*, September 1993, pp 266–295.

[82] See T.Q. Miller, T.W. Smith, C.W. Turner, M.L. Guijarro, A.J. Hallet, "A Meta-Analytic Review of Research on Hostility and Physical Health," *Psychological Bulletin*, March 1996, pp 322–348; and N. Geipert, "Don't Be Mad," *Monitor on Psychology*, January 2007, pp 50–51.

[83] P. Chisholm, "Redesigning Work," *Macleans*, March 5, 2001, p 36.

[84] A. Silliker, "Employers in Best Position to Fight Depression," *Canadian HR Reporter*, January 30, 2012, p 3.

[85] D. Matwichuk, "HRIS an Early Warning System for Employee Burnout," *Canadian HR Reporter*, April 25, 2011, p 12.

[86] An evaluation of stress-reduction programs is conducted by P.A. Landsbergis and E. Vivona-Vaughan, "Evaluation of an Occupational Stress Intervention in a Public Agency," *Journal of Organizational Behaviour*, January 1996, pp 29–48; and D.C. Ganster, B.T. Mayes, W.E. Sime, and G.D. Tharp, "Managing Organizational Stress: A Field Experiment," *Journal of Applied Psychology*, October 1982, pp 533–542.

[87] "Hans Selye's General Adaptation Syndrome, Classic Stages of Chronic Stress," www.essenceofstressrelief.com.

[88] R. Kreitner, "Personal Wellness: It's Just Good Business," *Business Horizons*, May–June 1982, p 28.

[89] A. Silliker, "Workers More Likely To Call In Sick After Stressful Day," *Canadian HR Reporter*, May 9, 2011, p 1.

[90] See T. Parker-Pope, "Doctor's Orders: Ways to Work Exercise Into a Busy Day," *The Wall Street Journal*, January 9, 2007, p D1; and M.P. McQueen, "Wellness Plans Reach Out to the Healthy," *The Wall Street Journal*, March 28, 2007, pp D1, D3.

CHAPTER 14

[1] Opportunities Overseas Expo, "2012 Schedule," www.expo-Canada.com; and "Canadian Companies Actively Recruiting Overseas," August 6, 2008, www.canadavisa.com.

[2] Also see D. Nilsen, B. Kowske, and K. Anthony, "Managing Globally," *HR Magazine*, August 2005, pp 111–115; and A. Taylor III, "How I Work," *Fortune*, March 20, 2006, pp 66, 68.

[3] Excerpted and adapted from M. Javidan, M. Teagarden and D. Bowen, "Making It Overseas," *Harvard Business Review*, April 2010.

[4] F. Trompenaars and C. Hampden-Turner, *Riding the Waves of Culture: Understanding Cultural Diversity in Global Business*, 2nd ed. (New York: McGraw-Hill, 1998), pp 6–7.

[5] See M. Mendenhall, "A Painless Approach to Integrating 'International' into OB, HRM, and Management Courses," *Organizational Behavior Teaching Review*, no. 3, 1988-89, pp 23–27.

[6] Adapted from D.R. Fuqua and D.J. Kurpius, "Conceptual Models in Organizational Consultation," *Journal of Counselling and Development*, July/August 1993, pp 602–618; and D.A. Nadler and M.L. Tushman, "Organizational Frame Bending: Principles for Managing Reorientation," *Academy of Management Executive*, August 1989, pp 194–203.

[7] See C.L. Sharma, "Ethnicity, National Integration, and Education in the Union of Soviet Socialist Republics," *The Journal of East and West Studies*, October 1989, pp 75–93; and R. Brady and P. Galuszka, "Shattered Dreams," *BusinessWeek*, February 11, 1991, pp 38–42.

[8] Proctor and Gamble company website, "Diversity and Inclusion," www.pg.com.

[9] R. Kreitner, A. Kinicki, N. Cole, and V. Digby, *OB*, 3rd Cdn ed. (Whitby, ON: McGraw-Hill,2009), p 320.

[10] See G.A. Sumner, *Folkways* (New York: Ginn, 1906). Also see J.G. Weber, "The Nature of Ethnocentric Attribution Bias: Ingroup Protection or Enhancement?" *Journal of Experimental Social Psychology*, September 1994, pp 482–504.

[11] D.A. Heenan and H.V. Perlmutter, *Multinational Organization Development* (Reading, MA: Addison-Wesley, 1979), p 17.

[12] Data from R. Kopp, "International Human Resource Policies and Practices in Japanese, European, and United States Multinationals," *Human Resource Management*, Winter 1994, pp 581–599.

[13] See D. Doke, "Shipping Diversity Abroad," *HR Magazine*, November 2003, pp 58–64; M.B. Marklein, "Foreign Student Enrollment on the Decline, Study Finds," *USA Today*, November 14, 2005, p 7D; M.B. Marklein, "USA Losing Its Advantage Drawing Foreign Students," *USA Today*, January 6, 2006, p 10A; and "Foreigners Returning to U.S. Grad Schools," *USA Today*, March 23, 2006, p 6D.

[14] Excerpted and adapted from M. Chen and D. Miller, "West Meets East: Toward an Ambicultural Approach to Management," *Academy of Management Prospectives*, November 2010, pp 17–24.

[15] C.M. Farkas and P. De Backer, "There Are Only Five Ways to Lead," *Fortune*, January 15, 1996, p 111.

[16] Confederation Centre of the Arts, "Message from CEO," www.confederationcentre.com.

[17] For related research, see G.S. Van Der Vegt, E. Van De Vliert, and X. Huang, "Location-Level Links Between Diversity and Innovative Climate Depend on National Power Distance," *Academy of Management Journal*, December 2005, pp 1171–1182.

[18] Adapted from G. Hofstede, "Cultural Constraints in Management Theories," *Academy of Management Executive*, February 1993, p 91; G. Hofstede, "The Cultural Relativity of Organizational Practices and Theories," *Journal of International Business Studies*, no. 14, 1983, pp 75–89.

[19] A similar conclusion is presented in the following replication of Hofstede's work: A. Merritt, "Culture in the Cockpit: Do Hofstede's Dimensions Replicate?" *Journal of Cross-Cultural Psychology*, May 2000, pp 283–301. Another extension of Hofstede's work can be found in S.M. Lee and S.J. Peterson, "Culture, Entrepreneurial Orientation, and Global Competitiveness," *Journal of World Business*, Winter 2000, pp 401–416.

[20] J.S. Osland and A. Bird, "Beyond Sophisticated Stereotyping: Cultural Sensemaking in Context," *Academy of Management Executive*, February 2000, p 67.

[21] H.C. Lin and S.T. Hou, "Managerial Lessons from the East: An Interview with Acer's Stan Shih," *Academy of Management Perspectives*, November 2010, pp 6–16.

[22] P.C. Earley and E. Mosakowski, "Cultural Intelligence," *Harvard Business Review*, October 2004, p 140; and I. Alon and J.M. Higgins, "Global Leadership Success Through Emotional and Cultural Intelligences," *Business Horizons*, November–December 2005, pp 501–512.

[23] R. House, M. Javidan, P. Hanges, and P. Dorfman, "Understanding Cultures and Implicit Leadership Theories across the Globe: An Introduction to Project GLOBE," *Journal of World Business*, Spring 2002, p 4.

[24] See J.C. Kennedy, "Leadership in Malaysia: Traditional Values, International Outlook," *Academy of Management Executive*, August 2002, pp 15–26; M. Javidan and A. Dastmalchian, "Culture and Leadership in Iran: The Land of Individual Achievers, Strong Family Ties, and Powerful Elite," *Academy of Management Executive*, November 2003, pp 127–142; and M. Javidan, G. K. Stahl, F. Brodbeck, and C.P.M. Wilderom, "Cross-Border Transfer of Knowledge: Cultural Lessons from Project GLOBE," *Academy of Management Executive*, May 2005, pp 59–76.

[25] Adapted from the list in R.J. House, M. Javidan, P.J. Hanges, and P.W. Dorfman, "Understanding Cultures and Implicit Leadership Theories across the Globe," pp 5–6.

[26] R.J. House, P.J. Hanges, M. Javidan, P.W. Dorfman, and V. Gupta, *Culture, Leadership and Organizations* (Thousand Oaks, CA: Sage Publications, 2004).

[27] Data from F. Trompenaars and C. Hampden-Turner, *Riding the Waves of Culture: Understanding Cultural Diversity in Global Business*, chapter 5. For relevant research evidence, see J. Allik and A. Realo, "Individualism Collectivism and Social Capital," *Journal of Cross-Cultural Psychology*, January 2004, pp 29–49; A.K. Lalwani, S. Shavitt, and T. Johnson, "What Is the Relation Between Cultural Orientation and Socially Desirable Responding?" *Journal of Personality and Social Psychology*, January 2006, pp 165–178; C. Robert, W.C. Lee, and K. Chan, "An Empirical Analysis of Measurement Equivalence with the INDCOL Measure of Individualism and Collectivism: Implications for Valid Cross-Cultural Inference," *Personnel Psychology*, Spring 2006, pp 65–99; and W. McEwen, X. Fang, C. Zhang, and R. Burkholder, "Inside the Mind of the Chinese Consumer," *Harvard Business Review*, March 2006, pp 68–76.

[28] F. Trompenaars and C. Hampden-Turner, *Riding the Waves of Culture: Understanding Cultural Diversity in Global Business*, p 56. The importance of relationships in Eastern and Western cultures is explored in S.H. Ang, "The Power of Money: A Cross-Cultural Analysis of Business-Related Beliefs," *Journal of World Business*, Spring 2000, pp 43–60.

[29] See M. Munter, "Cross-Cultural Communication for Managers," *Business Horizons*, May–June 1993, pp 69–78.

[30] I. Adler, "Between the Lines," *Business Mexico*, October 2000, p 24.

[31] Millan, Kras, Jacques, et al., "Doing Business in Mexico: The Human Resource Challenges," *Business Quarterly*, September 22, 1995.

[32] R.W. Moore, "Time, Culture, and Comparative Management: A Review and Future Direction," *Advances in International Comparative Management*, vol. 5, ed. S.B. Prasad (Greenwich, CT: JAI Press, 1990), pp 7–8.

[33] See A.C. Bluedorn, C.F. Kaufman, and P.M. Lane, "How Many Things Do You Like to Do at Once? An Introduction to Monochronic and Polychronic Time," *Academy of Management Executive*, November 1992, pp 17–26.

[34] "Multitasking" term drawn from S. McCartney, "The Breaking Point: Multitasking Technology Can Raise Stress and Cripple Productivity," *The Arizona Republic*, May 21, 1995, p D10.

[35] See M. Archer, "Too Busy to Read this Book? Then you Really Need to," *USA Today*, April 17, 2006, p 10B.

[36] O. Port, "You May Have to Reset this Watch–In a Million Years," *BusinessWeek*, August 30, 1993, p 65.

[37] See M. Toda and K. Morimoto, "Ramadan Fasting–Effect on Healthy Muslims," *Social Behavior and Personality*, no. 1, 2004, pp 13–18.

[38] See T. Scandura and P. Dorfman, "Leadership Research in an International and Cross-Cultural Context," *The Leadership Quarterly*, April 2004, pp 277–307; M. Javidan and N. Lynton, "The Changing Face of the Chinese Leadership," *Harvard Business Review*, December 2005, pp 28, 30; and M. Javidan, P.W. Dorfman, M.S. de Luque, and R.J. House, "In the Eye of the Beholder: Cross Cultural Lessons in Leadership from Project GLOBE," *Academy of Management Perspectives*, February 2006, pp 67–90.

[39] J. Guyon, "David Whitwam," *Fortune*, July 26, 2004, p 174.

[40] A. Fisher, "Five Ways to Ignite Your Career," *Fortune*, February 6, 2006, p 50.

[41] C. Geissler and L. Kuhn, "Developing Your Global Know-How," *Harvard Business Review*, March 2011, pp 71–75.

[42] W. Immen, "Have Job, Will Travel?," *The Globe and Mail*, February 8, 2012, www.theglobeandmail.com.

[43] "2011 Global Relocation Trends Survey by Brookfield Global Relocation Services–'Relocation numbers Moving Back Up,'" *Canadian HR Reporter*, August 15, 2011, p 1.

[44] "Global Mobility Survey Finds Canadian Employees Are Less Likely To Take A Full Time Job Overseas," *Canadian Newswire Services*, February 9, 2012, www.newswire.ca.

[45] S. Cryne, "Foreign Assignments Increasing, Along with Employee Resistance," *Canadian HR Reporter*, September 27, 2004, www.canadianhrreporter.com/ArticleView.aspx?l=1&articleid=3416.

[46] "2011 Global Relocation Trends Survey by Brookfield Global Relocation Services–'Relocation numbers Moving Back Up,'" *Canadian HR Reporter*, August 15, 2011, p 1.

[47] W. Immen, "Ready To Work Abroad?" *The Globe and Mail*, November 12, 2003, www.theglobeandmail.com.

[48] An excellent reference book on this topic is J.S. Black, H.B. Gregersen, and M.E. Mendenhall, *Global Assignments: Successfully Expatriating and Repatriating International Managers* (San Francisco: Jossey-Bass, 1992). Also see M.B. Hess and P. Linderman, *The Expert Expatriate: Your Guide to Successful Relocation Abroad* (Yarmouth, Maine: Intercultural Press, 2002); and E. Gundling, *Working GlobeSmart: 12 People Skills for Doing Business across Borders* (Palo Alto, CA: Davies-Black Publishing, 2003).

[49] R. Kreitner, A. Kinicki, N. Cole, and V. Digby, *OB*, 3rd Cdn. Ed. (Whitby, ON: McGraw-Hill, 2009), p 332.

[50] A. Fong, "A Bit Out of the Loop," *Financial Post*, May 5, 2012, www.business.financialpost.com.

[51] W. Immen, "Ready To Work Abroad?" *The Globe and Mail*, November 12, 2003, www.theglobeandmail.com; and "Cigna International Expatriate Benefits," Mercer Human Resource Consulting and International SOS of Canada.

[52] Ibid.

[53] "2011 Global Relocation Trends Survey by Brookfield Global Relocation Services–'Relocation numbers Moving Back Up,'" *Canadian HR Reporter*, August 15, 2011, p 1.

[54] See J. Carter, "Globe Trotters," *Training*, August 2005, pp 22–28; M.A. Shaffer, D.A. Harrison, H. Gregersen, J.S. Black, and L.A. Ferzandi, "You Can Take It With You: Individual Differences and Expatriate Effectiveness," *Journal of Applied Psychology*, January 2006, pp 109–125; and Y. Gong and J. Fan, "Longitudinal Examination of the Role of Goal Orientation in Cross-Cultural Adjustment," *Journal of Applied Psychology*, January 2006, pp 176–184.

[55] See K. Roberts, E.E. Kossek, and C. Ozeki, "Managing the Global Workforce: Challenges and Strategies," *Academy of Management Executive*, November 1998, pp 93–106.

[56] See D. Stamps, "Welcome to America: Watch Out for Culture Shock," *Training*, November 1996, pp 22–30; L. Glanz, R. Williams, and L. Hoeksema, "Sensemaking in Expatriation–A Theoretical Basis," *Thunderbird International Business Review*, January–February 2001, pp 101–19; E. Marx, *Breaking Through Culture Shock: What You Need to Succeed in International Business* (London: Nicholas Brealey Publishing, 2001); G.K. Stahl and P. Caligiuri,

"The Effectiveness of Expatriate Coping Strategies: The Moderating Role of Cultural Distance, Position Level, and Time on the International Assignment," *Journal of Applied Psychology,* July 2005, pp 603–615; and R. Takeuchi, M. Wang, and S.V. Marinova, "Antecedents and Consequences of Psychological Workplace Strain During Expatriation: A Cross-Sectional and Longitudinal Investigation," *Personnel Psychology,* Winter 2005, pp 925–948.

[57] See H.H. Nguyen, L.A. Messe, and G.E. Stollak, "Toward a More Complex Understanding of Acculturation and Adjustment," *Journal of Cross-Cultural Psychology,* January 1999, pp 5–31.

[58] For more, see S. Overman, "Mentors Without Borders," *HR Magazine,* March 2004, pp 83–86; and E. Krell, "Budding Relationships," *HR Magazine,* June 2005, pp 114–118.

[59] A. Fong, "A Bit Out of the Loop," *Financial Post,* May 5, 2012, www.business.financialpost.com.

[60] See L.K. Stroh, H.B. Gregersen, and J.S. Black, "Closing the Gap: Expectations versus Reality among Repatriates," *Journal of World Business,* Summer 1998, pp 111–124; and K. Tyler, "Retaining Repatriates," *HR Magazine,* March 2006, pp 97–102.

[61] 2011 participant Farhan Thanwar profile, Toronto Homecoming, www.torontohomecoming.ca.

GLOSSARY

Photo Credits

CHAPTER 1

p. 1 ©DreamPictures/Shannon Faulk/Blend Images/Corbis
p. 12 Photo by Jennifer Roberts for Postmedia News

CHAPTER 2

p. 21 © Hill Street Studios/Getty Images
p. 25 Porsche Cars North America
p. 27 © Ryan McVay/Getty Images
p. 33 Toronto Star/getstock.com

CHAPTER 3

p. 42 © Image Source/Getty Images
p. 45 *New Yorker* Cartoon
p. 51 © Graham Hughes/The Canadian Press
p. 58 © The McGraw-Hill Companies, Inc./ Jill Braaten, photographer

CHAPTER 4

p. 67 Pashapixel/Dreamstime.com/getstock .com
p. 71 © Cartoon Resource
p. 73 REUTERS/Vincent Kessler
p. 74 Used by permission of Fahad Meer
p. 84 Ian Shipley/IND/GetStock.com

CHAPTER 5

p. 95 Szefei/Dreamstime.com/getstock.com
p. 108 © Cartoon Resource
p. 109 © Chris O'Meara/The Canadian Press
p. 111 Simon Hayter/Getstock.com
p. 114 Chris Gascoigne/GetStock.com

CHAPTER 6

p. 121 Arne9001/Dreamstime.com/getstock .com
p. 129 © Ryan McVay/Getty Images
p. 130 Andrew Wallace/GetStock.com
p. 131 Riccardo S. Savi/Getty Images
p. 135 © Javier Pierini/Getty Images
p. 136 FARCUS® is reprinted with permission from LaughingStock Licensing Inc., Ottawa, Canada. All rights reserved.

CHAPTER 7

p. 145 Rtimages/GetStock.com
p. 150 David R. Frazier Photolibrary, Inc./ getstock.com
p. 158 (top) Dragon_fang/Dreamstime.com/ GetStock.com; (bottom left) Justmeyo/ Dreamstime.com/GetStock.com; (bottom right) © Christopher Bernard/istockphoto.ca
p. 163 © Jon Feingersh/Getty Images
p. 168 Chris Ryan/OJO Images/Getty Images

CHAPTER 8

p. 174 © Jetta Productions/Getty Images
p. 178 Creatista/Dreamstime.com/getstock .com
p. 182 © Jlhope/Dreamstime.com/getstock .com
p. 186 Terry Vine/Getty Images

CHAPTER 9

p. 197 © Robert Churchill/Getty Images
p. 202 © Joachim E. Röttgers/getstock.com
p. 208 © 2002 Ted Goff. Used by permission.

p. 212 © Roy Hsu /Getty Images
p. 218 Simon Potter/Getty Images

CHAPTER 10

p. 227 Wavebreakmediamicro/Dreamstime .com/getstock.com
p. 237 © Gabriela Hasbun/getstock.com
p. 239 (left) © Nathan Denette/The Canadian Press; (right) © J.P. Moczulski/ The Canadian Press Images
p. 245 Courtesy of Fuji Fire and Marine Insurance Co., Ltd.

CHAPTER 11

p. 257 Jon Feingersh/Getty Images
p. 261 © Bloomber via Getty Images
p. 276 Bernard Weil/GetStock.com

CHAPTER 12

p. 285 © Lane Oatey/Getty Images
p. 295 Vince Talotta/GetStock.com
p. 299 © Don Denton/The Canadian Press

CHAPTER 13

p. 312 © Jon Feingersh/Blend Images LLC
p. 315 © Stephen Simpson/Getty Images
p. 335 © Veer

CHAPTER 14

p. 342 © Devonyu/Dreamstime.com/ getstock.com
p. 347 Jim Day/Charlottetown Guardian
p. 351 © Tengku Bahar/AFP/Getty Images

NAME INDEX

SUBJECT INDEX

A

abilities, and performance, 56–58
Aboriginal peoples, 304, 335, 354
absenteeism, and job satisfaction,
86–87, 86f
abuse of power, 204
accessibility, workplace, 33
accountability, in teams, 143
accountability practices, and
diversity, 11, 12t
achievement, need for, 102, 103
acquisitions, 313
action plans, in goal-setting, 109–110
active listening, 159–161
Adams equity model, 97t, 104–106
adaptive change, 317, 318f
added-value. See integrative negotiation
adhocracy culture, 265, 266f
adjourning, 126, 126f
administrative impersonality, 295, 295f
affective commitment, 79, 79f, 80, 81
affective component of attitudes, 75
affiliation, need for, 102, 103
age, and needs, 100
age stereotypes, 31
aggression, 27
aggressive style of communication,
154, 156t
agreeableness, 52t
Alderfer's ERG theory, 97t, 100–101, 101f
alternate work schedules, 97t, 115–116
alternative dispute resolution
(ADR), 185–186, 191
ambiculturalism, 346–347
analytical style of decision making, 213f
anticipatory socialization, 272–273
antisocial behaviour, 27
applicant tracking systems, 56
appreciative listeners, 159
arbitration, 186
assertive style of communication,
154, 156t
assumptions, in organizational
culture, 262–263
attention, 24
attibutional tendencies, 35–36
attitudes
behaviour and intentions, 76–78
cognitive dissonance, 76
components, 75
definition, 75
job involvement, 81–82
job satisfaction, 82–89, 93–94
nature of, 75–76
organizational commitment, 78–81
stability, 76

vs. values, 75
work, 78–89
attributions. See causal attributions
automated experience, 213f, 214
autonomy, 114
availability heuristic, 211
avoiding, 185, 185t

B

balanced scorecard, 297
bankruptcy, 309
barriers to communication, 149–152,
149t, 151f
behaviour
attitudes and, 75–78
worldwide, 343–344
behavioural component of attitudes, 75
behavioural style of decision
making, 213f
behavioural styles theory of leadership,
231t, 236–237
benchmarking standards, 19–20
best practices. See skills & best practices
bias, 28, 35–36, 56
biological open system, 296
bodily-kinesthetic intelligence, 57
body ideals, 28
body movements and gestures, 157, 158f
bonuses and merit pay, 244
boundaryless organization, 293
bounded rationality models, 211
brainstorming, 218
buddy systems, 347
bullying, 27
bureaucracy, 294–296, 295f

C

case studies. See also OB in action case
studies
checklist, 370
company growth and staff
resources, 371–372
definition, 368
fitting in a new company, 380–381
import/export businesses of
immigrants, 381–383
quitting a job to start a new
enterprise, 372–376
steps, 368–370
surveillance of staff, 376–379
causal attributions, 33–36
definition, 33–34
dimensions of behaviour, 34f, 35
managerial implications, 36
central tendency, 26t

centralized decision making, 301
change
agents, 322
conflict and, 175
external, 313–316, 314f, 339
forces of, 313–317
internal, 314f, 316–317, 340
Kotter's eight steps, 321, 321t
Lewin's model, 317–319, 318f
occupational stress, 328–335
overview, 313
personal characteristics and, 325–326
planned, 317–323
resilience to, 326
resistance to, 324–326
restructuring and, 339–341
systems model, 319–321, 320f
target elements, 319–320
through organization development,
321–323
types, 317, 318f
change and acquisition phase, 274
charisma, 200
charts, in organizations, 287, 288f
clan culture, 265, 266f
closed system, 296
coalition level of political action,
207, 207f
coercive power, 200
cognitions, 43
cognitive component of attitudes, 75
cognitive dissonance, 76
cognitive open system, 296–297
collective commitment, 264, 264f
collectivism, 354
collectivist culture, 354
commitment, 78, 216
to change, 325
organizational, 78–81, 79f
common goal, 286
communication
active listening, 159–161
barriers, 149–152, 149t, 151f
basic dimensions, 147–154
definition, 147
digital age, 164–168
effectiveness, 153, 153f, 159–161, 161t,
167–168
employee productivity, 164
face-to-face, 153, 153f, 365–366
formal and informal channels, 163–164
gender differences, 161–163
grapevine, 163–164
internet generation, 165–166, 167t
interpersonal, 154–164
media and, 152–154, 153f

emotional stability, 52t
emotions, 59–62
    positive and negative, 59, 60f
empathetic listeners, 159
employee assistance programs
    (EAPs), 333
employee productivity, 164
employment
    diversity and, 32, 33
    equity, 11
    self-esteem, 44
employment rights, for minorities, 346
empowerment, 202–204
enacted values, 262
encoding, 148, 149t
environmental factors, 35
equal opportunities, 346
equity, 82
    employment, 11
    job satisfaction and, 85
    motivation and, 104–106
    relationships, 104, 105f
equity sensitivity, 105–106
equity theory, 104–106
ERG theory, 97t, 100–101, 101f
escalation of commitment, 216
escape strategy, 329
espoused values, 261–262
ethics. See also law and ethics at work
    in business and corporations, 214–215
    challenge of, 13–14
    decision tree, 215–216, 215f
    in negotiation, 189–190, 190t
    power, 204–205
ethnocentrism, 345–346
eustress, 328
evaluative listeners, 159
event memory, 25
expatriates, 183, 358
expectancy, 106
expectancy theory, 106–108, 107t
expectations, and discrepancies, 82f, 84
expert power, 200
expertise, as source of intuition, 213f, 214
external attributions, 35
external forces for change, 313–316,
    314f, 339
external locus of control, 55
extraversion, 52t, 54
eye contact, 158f, 159

F

face-to-face communication, 153, 153f,
    365–366
facial expressions, 157, 158f
facilitation, 186
fairness. See equity
family life vs. work conflict, 71–75, 72f
feedback, 109, 114, 149, 149t
feelings, as source of intuition, 213f, 214
field studies, 368

flextime, 115
focus on diversity
    age of workers, 13
    applicant tracking systems, 56
    counselling, 335
    differences in teams, 133
    female CEOs, 235
    female leadership development, 352
    gender and communication, 162
    gender and conflict, 191
    generational differences, 83
    mentoring and generations, 279
    needs and desires by age of
        employees, 100
    Parks Canada management plan, 304
    prison guards, 32
    women and socialized power, 199
followers, of leadership, 245–246,
    248–249
foreign assignments
    Canadians, 358
    cost, 359t
    cycle, 359f
    face-to-face communication, 365–366
    OB trouble spots, 358–362, 359f
    stages, 359–362, 359f
foreign workers and population, 8–10, 15
formal and informal channels of commu-
    nication, 163–164
formal groups, 122–124, 125
forming, 125, 126f
framework of rules, 295, 295f
frustration-regression in need theory, 101
full-range model of leadership, 243–249
functional conflict, 177–178
functional departmentation, 288–289, 289f
fundamental attribution bias, 35

G

Gen Y, 165–166, 167t, 279
gender
    communication differences, 161–163
    conflict handling, 191
    emotional labour, 60
    leadership, 235, 352
    self-esteem, 44
    socialized power, 199
    stereotyping, 30–31
general adaptation syndrome, 334
general life values, 72
generational differences
    job satisfaction, 82, 83
    mentoring, 279
    needs and desires, 100
generic effectiveness, 297–299
geographic departmentation, 290
gestures and body movements, 157, 158f
glass ceiling, 11
global boards, as formal groups, 125
global economy, 343–344
global mind-set development

Canadian management theories
    abroad, 348–349
competencies, 344
cultural influences on OB, 345f
ethnocentrism, 345–346
global work experience, 346–348
Hofstede's dimensions, 348–349, 349t
societal and organizational cultures,
    344–345, 345f
globalization, 14–16, 343–344
goal accomplishment, 297, 298f
goal commitment, 110
goal specificity, 109
goals, definition, 108
goal-setting theory, 97t, 108–110
gossips, 163–164
grapevine, 163–164
Great Recession, 5
group behaviour, 2, 4f. See also work
    group
    formal and informal groups, 122–124
    fundamentals, 122–129
    member roles, 127
    norms, 128–129
    pattern establishment, 126–127
    social networking, 124
    Tuckman's five-stage theory, 124–126
group cohesiveness, 126
group effectiveness, 136–137
group problem solving, 58
groups
    conflict within, 181–182, 182f
    decision making, 217–219, 217t
    definition, 122
    functional roles, 128t
    informal, 122–124
    in organizations, 2–3, 4f
    problem-solving techniques, 218–219
    sociological criteria, 124f
groupthink, 136, 218

H

habits, 51
halo, 26t
hand gestures, 157, 158f
hardiness, 330
Herzberg motivator-hygiene theory, 97t,
    103–104, 103f
hierachy of authority, 287, 294–295, 295f
hierarchical culture, 266f, 266
high self-monitor, 48–49, 50
high-context cultures, 354–355, 355f
hiring. See recruitment
holistic hunch, 213f, 214
holistic wellness approach, 335
honesty, in leadership, 233–234
horizontal loading, 111
human capital, investment in, 5
human relations, benchmarking
    data, 19–20
human relations movement, 6f, 7

McGraw-Hill
Ryerson
Connect. Learn. Succeed.

Get Connected.

Stay Connected.

McGraw-Hill Connect™

Q: STUDENTS...

Want to get **better grades**? *(Who doesn't?)*

Prefer to do your **homework online**? *(After all, you're online anyway...)*

Need **a better way** to **study** before the big test? *(A little peace of mind is a good thing...)*

A: With **McGraw-Hill's *Connect*,**™

STUDENTS GET:

- **Easy online access** to homework, tests, and quizzes assigned by your instructor.

- **Immediate feedback** on how you're doing. (No more wishing you could call your instructor at 1 a.m.)

- **Quick access** to lectures, practice materials, eBook, and more. (All the material you need to be successful is right at your fingertips.)

- A Self-Quiz and Study tool that **assesses your knowledge** and **recommends** specific readings, supplemental study materials, and additional practice work.

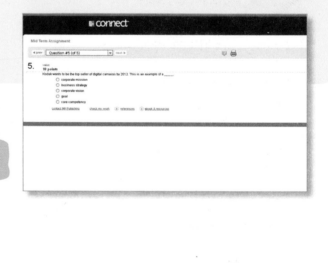